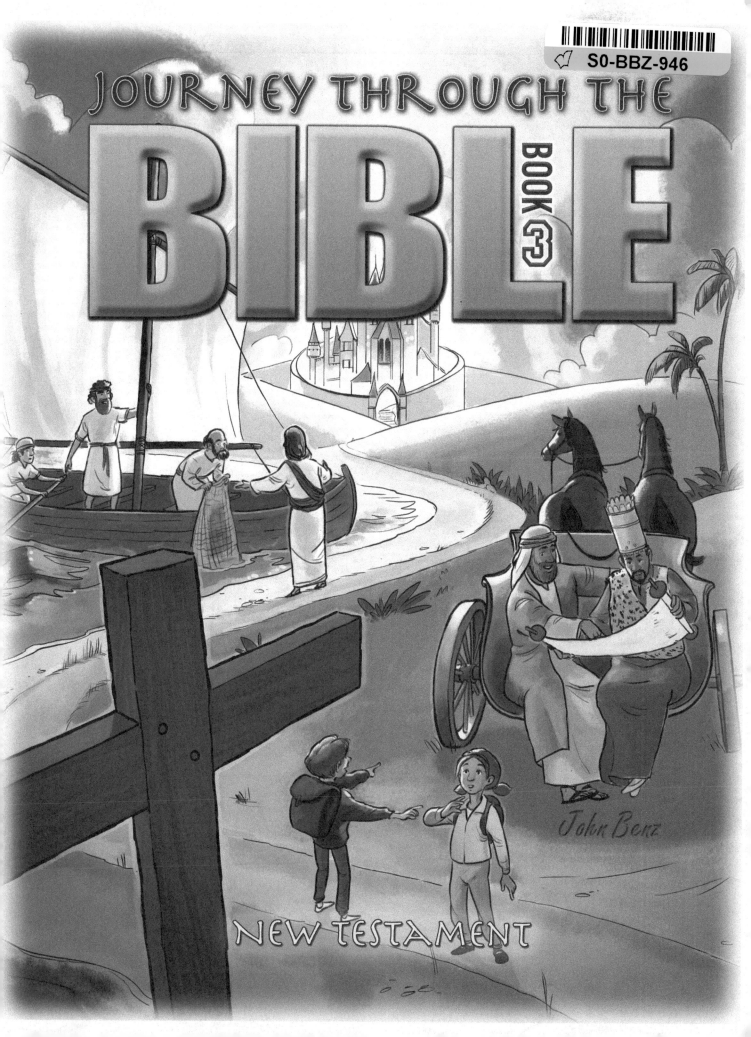

A publication of
Christian Liberty Press
502 West Euclid Avenue
Arlington Heights, Illinois 60004
www.christianlibertypress.com
www.shopchristianliberty.com

Written by John Benz
Layout and editing by Edward J. Shewan
Copyediting by Diane C. Olson
Cover design by Bob Fine
Cover image and unit title images by David Miles,
        copyright © 2015 Christian Liberty Press
Text images and charts copyright © 2008 Crossway,
        used with permission

ISBN 978-1-935796-27-5 (print)
ISBN 978-1-629820-27-9 (eBook PDF)

Contents

Introduction vii

Note to Parents ix

UNIT 1   Introduction, Matthew, and Mark 1

LESSON 1	Old Testament Overview 1
LESSON 2	Intertestamental History 2
LESSON 3	Key Groups in the New Testament 3
LESSON 4	Setting of the New Testament 4
LESSON 5	Introduction to the Gospels 5
LESSON 6	Introduction to Matthew 6
LESSON 7	The Birth and Childhood of Jesus: Matthew 1–2 8
LESSON 8	John the Baptist and Jesus' Ministries: Matthew 3–4 8
LESSON 9	The Sermon on the Mount, Part 1: Matthew 5 10
LESSON 10	The Sermon on the Mount, Part 2: Matthew 6–7 11
LESSON 11	Miracles: Matthew 8–9 12
LESSON 12	The Calling and Commission of the Twelve: Matthew 10 13
LESSON 13	Doubt and Opposition: Matthew 11–12 14
LESSON 14	Kingdom Parables: Matthew 13 15
LESSON 15	Lost Friends, Miracles, and Opposition: Matthew 14–15 16
LESSON 16	Peter's Confession and the Transfiguration: Matthew 16:1–17:13 17
LESSON 17	Faith, Humility, and Reconciliation: Matthew 17:14–18:35 19
LESSON 18	The Last Will Be First: Matthew 19–20 20
LESSON 19	The Triumphal Entry: Matthew 21:1–27 22
LESSON 20	A Battle of Wits: Matthew 21:28–23:39 24
LESSON 21	The Olivet Discourse: Matthew 24 26
LESSON 22	Parables for Preparation: Matthew 25 28
LESSON 23	Preparation for the True Passover: Matthew 26 28
LESSON 24	The Passion of the Christ: Matthew 27 30
LESSON 25	The Resurrection and the Great Commission: Matthew 28 31
LESSON 26	Introduction to Mark 32
LESSON 27	The Beginning of Jesus' Ministry: Mark 1 33
LESSON 28	Miracles, Opposition, and Disciples: Mark 2–3 34
LESSON 29	Jesus' Parables: Mark 4:1–34 35
LESSON 30	The Incredible Power and Authority of Jesus: Mark 4:35–5:43 36
LESSON 31	Mission and Tragedy: Mark 6 37
LESSON 32	True Defilement and True Faith: Mark 7:1–8:9 38
LESSON 33	Peter's Confession and the Transfiguration: Mark 8:10–9:13 40
LESSON 34	Preparations for the Cross: Mark 9:14–50 41
LESSON 35	Back to Judea: Mark 10 41
LESSON 36	Into Jerusalem: Mark 11:1–26 43
LESSON 37	Jesus, the Expert Debater: Mark 11:27–12:44 44
LESSON 38	The Sermon on the Mount of Olives: Mark 13 46

LESSON 39   *The Last Night with the Disciples: Mark 14:1–52*...48

LESSON 40   *The Trial, Crucifixion, and Resurrection: Mark 14:53–16:20*...........................49

UNIT 2   Luke and John 53

LESSON 41   *Introduction to Luke*...53

LESSON 42   *The Birth Narrative: Luke 1–2*...53

LESSON 43   *Jesus' Baptism, Genealogy, and Temptation: Luke 3:1–4:13*.......................54

LESSON 44   *Jesus' First Ministry in Galilee: Luke 4:14–44*...55

LESSON 45   *Ministry Foundations and Opposition: Luke 5:1–6:16*..............................56

LESSON 46   *The Sermon on the Plain: Luke 6:17–49*...57

LESSON 47   *Jesus the Prophet: Luke 7*...58

LESSON 48   *More Teachings and Healings: Luke 8*..59

LESSON 49   *Jesus the Messiah: Luke 9:1–50*...60

LESSON 50   *Preparations for Jesus' Departure: Luke 9:51–10:24*.................................60

LESSON 51   *The Final Teaching Circuit, Part 1: Luke 10:25–11:34*..............................61

LESSON 52   *The Final Teaching Circuit, Part 2: Luke 12–13*.......................................62

LESSON 53   *The Final Teaching Circuit, Dinner and Discipleship: Luke 14*.................63

LESSON 54   *The Final Teaching Circuit, Lessons for Pharisees: Luke 15–16*................64

LESSON 55   *The Final Teaching Circuit, The Kingdom of God: Luke 17:1–18:14*.........65

LESSON 56   *The Final Teaching Circuit, The End of the Journey: Luke 18:15–19:46*.....66

LESSON 57   *The Battle with the Religious Leaders: Luke 19:47–21:4*............................67

LESSON 58   *The Olivet Discourse: Luke 21:5–38*...68

LESSON 59   *The Lord's Supper and the Arrest and Trial: Luke 22*...............................69

LESSON 60   *The Trial Under Pilate and the Crucifixion: Luke 23*...............................70

LESSON 61   *He Is Risen!: Luke 24*...72

LESSON 62   *Introduction to John*..73

LESSON 63   *John's Prologue: John 1:1–18*..74

LESSON 64   *The Baptist, the First Sign, and the Temple Cleansing: John 1:19–2:25*.......76

LESSON 65   *Nicodemus: John 3*...77

LESSON 66   *The Samaritan Woman: John 4*...79

LESSON 67   *Healing and Opposition: John 5*...80

LESSON 68   *The Bread of Life: John 6*..81

LESSON 69   *The Feast of Tabernacles: John 7*..83

LESSON 70   *False Belief: John 8*...84

LESSON 71   *The Healing of the Blind Man: John 9*...86

LESSON 72   *The Good Shepherd and Lazarus: John 10–11*..87

LESSON 73   *The Anointing and the Triumphal Entry: John 12*....................................89

LESSON 74   *The Last Supper: John 13–14*...90

LESSON 75   *The Vine and the Branches: John 15*...91

LESSON 76   *Final Warnings: John 16*...93

LESSON 77   *Jesus' High Priestly Prayer: John 17*..94

LESSON 78   *The Trial and Crucifixion of Jesus: John 18–19*.......................................95

LESSON 79   *The Resurrection: John 20*...96

LESSON 80   *Peter's Redemption: John 21*...97

UNIT 3 Acts, Romans, and 1 & 2 Corinthians.. **101**

LESSON 81   *Introduction to Acts*..*101*

LESSON 82   *The Ascension and the Replacement of Judas: Acts 1*.....................*102*

LESSON 83   *Pentecost: Acts 2*...*103*

LESSON 84   *The Gospel Spreads: Acts 3–4*..*104*

LESSON 85   *Discipline and Deacons: Acts 5–6*...*106*

LESSON 86   *Stephen's Sermon: Acts 7*...*107*

LESSON 87   *To Judea and Samaria: Acts 8*..*108*

LESSON 88   *The Conversion of Saul: Acts 9*...*109*

LESSON 89   *Cornelius and the Gentile Church: Acts 10–11*.............................*111*

LESSON 90   *The First Missionary Journey: Acts 12–14*...................................*112*

LESSON 91   *The Jerusalem Council: Acts 15:1–35*..*114*

LESSON 92   *The Second Missionary Journey: Acts 15:36–18:22*.......................*115*

LESSON 93   *The Third Missionary Journey: Acts 18:23–21:14*.........................*117*

LESSON 94   *Paul in Jerusalem: Acts 21:15–23:22*...*119*

LESSON 95   *Before Gentiles and Kings: Acts 23:23–26:32*...............................*120*

LESSON 96   *To Rome: Acts 27–28*...*121*

LESSON 97   *Introduction to the Epistles*...*122*

LESSON 98   *Introduction to Paul's Epistles*...*124*

LESSON 99   *Introduction to Romans: Romans 1*..*125*

LESSON 100 *Do Not Judge: Romans 2*...*126*

LESSON 101 *The Gospel: Romans 3*..*127*

LESSON 102 *Abraham and Adam: Romans 4–5*...*129*

LESSON 103 *The Battle Against Sin: Romans 6–7*...*130*

LESSON 104 *Slaves or Children?: Romans 8*...*132*

LESSON 105 *What about Israel?: Romans 9–11*...*133*

LESSON 106 *How Then Shall We Live?: Romans 12*...*135*

LESSON 107 *Government and Conscience: Romans 13–14*................................*136*

LESSON 108 *Concluding Words: Romans 15–16*..*138*

LESSON 109 *Introduction to 1 Corinthians: 1 Corinthians 1–2*.......................*139*

LESSON 110 *Spiritual Architects and Being a Good Father: 1 Corinthians 3–4*....*140*

LESSON 111 *Sexual Immorality and Marriage: 1 Corinthians 5–7*....................*141*

LESSON 112 *Idolatry, Hair, and the Lord's Supper: 1 Corinthians 8–11*.............*143*

LESSON 113 *Spiritual Gifts and Love: 1 Corinthians 12–14*.............................*144*

LESSON 114 *The Resurrection and Final Greetings: 1 Corinthians 15–16*...........*147*

LESSON 115 *Introduction to 2 Corinthians: 2 Corinthians 1–2*.......................*148*

LESSON 116 *The New Covenant and Paul's Ministry: 2 Corinthians 3–4*...........*149*

LESSON 117 *Paul's Ministry Résumé: 2 Corinthians 5–6*.................................*150*

LESSON 118 *Godly Sorrow and Generous Giving: 2 Corinthians 7–8*.................*151*

LESSON 119 *Cheerful Giving and Paul's Further Defense: 2 Corinthians 9–10*.....*153*

LESSON 120 *Strength in Weakness: 2 Corinthians 11–13*.................................*154*

UNIT 4   The Epistles and Revelation 157

LESSON 121   *Introduction to Galatians: Galatians 1–2* 157

LESSON 122   *Faith vs. Works: Galatians 3–4* 158

LESSON 123   *Freedom in the Spirit: Galatians 5–6* 159

LESSON 124   *Introduction to Ephesians: Ephesians 1–2* 161

LESSON 125   *The Mystery of the Gospel and the Body of Christ: Ephesians 3–4* 162

LESSON 126   *Christian Living and Spiritual Warfare: Ephesians 5–6* 163

LESSON 127   *Introduction to Philippians: Philippians 1–2* 165

LESSON 128   *Joy, Peace, and Contentment in Christ: Philippians 3–4* 166

LESSON 129   *Introduction to Colossians, Supremacy of Christ: Colossians 1–2* 168

LESSON 130   *The New Life and Freedom: Colossians 3–4 & Philemon* 170

LESSON 131   *Holy Living and Christ's Return: 1 Thessalonians 1–5* 172

LESSON 132   *Clarification about Jesus' Return: 2 Thessalonians 1–3* 173

LESSON 133   *Right Doctrine and Right Leaders: 1 Timothy 1–3* 174

LESSON 134   *Godliness with Contentment: 1 Timothy 4–6* 176

LESSON 135   *Preserve the Gospel: 2 Timothy 1–2* 178

LESSON 136   *Final Words: 2 Timothy 3–4* 179

LESSON 137   *Order and Good Works: Titus 1–3* 180

LESSON 138   *Jesus Is Better Than the Prophets: Hebrews 1–2* 182

LESSON 139   *Heavenly Rest: Hebrews 3–4* 183

LESSON 140   *Jesus, the Great High Priest: Hebrews 5–6* 185

LESSON 141   *A New Priest, a New Covenant, and a New Law: Hebrews 7–9* 186

LESSON 142   *Endurance and Faith: Hebrews 10–11* 187

LESSON 143   *Finish the Race: Hebrews 12–13* 189

LESSON 144   *The Proverbs of the New Testament: James 1–2* 191

LESSON 145   *The Tongue, Heavenly Wisdom, and Prayer: James 3–5* 193

LESSON 146   *Graceful Suffering: 1 Peter 1–2* 195

LESSON 147   *Marriage, Witness, and Warfare: 1 Peter 3–5* 196

LESSON 148   *False Teachers in the Last Days: 2 Peter 1–3, Jude* 198

LESSON 149   *A Beautiful Symphony: 1 John 1–3* 201

LESSON 150   *Marks of a True Christian: 1 John 4–5* 203

LESSON 151   *Wise Hospitality: 2 John & 3 John* 204

LESSON 152   *Introduction to Revelation* 205

LESSON 153   *The Glorious Son of Man and the Seven Churches: Revelation 1–3* 209

LESSON 154   *Heavenly Worship: Revelation 4–5* 212

LESSON 155   *The Seals Are Opened: Revelation 6–7* 214

LESSON 156   *The Trumpet Judgments: Revelation 8–11* 216

LESSON 157   *The Unholy Trinity: Revelation 12–14* 219

LESSON 158   *The Bowl Judgments: Revelation 15–16* 221

LESSON 159   *The Fall of Babylon and the Great Feasts: Revelation 17–19* 223

LESSON 160   *The End of the Story: Revelation 20–22* 225

              Index 229

Introduction

The *Journey Through the Bible* curricula is designed to encourage students to encounter the biblical text firsthand. Many students grow up hearing Bible stories in Sunday school or from their parents or even from similar home-schooling curricula. The work that these people and programs do for students is very valuable for their growth and maturity. The goal of this curricula, however, is to go beyond the stories of the Bible and to have students read the Bible itself. In fact, this ninth grade curriculum, along with the seventh and eighth grade curricula in the *Journey Through the Bible* series, will take students through the entire Bible. Within these three years, students will have read the entire Bible.

For this year, we will look at the New Testament. The translation that we are going to use for this curriculum is the New King James Version (NKJV). Since the King James Version of the Bible is the most widely used translation out there, we chose the the NKJV version because it is a little easier for students to read. While it is possible to complete this curriculum using other translations of the Bible, the questions in the workbook use the language and phrases of the NKJV. As a result, it may be difficult at times to find the answers to these questions without using an NKJV.

There are three components to this curriculum. The *first component* is the **workbook**. The workbook is divided into four units of forty days of reading per unit. On the top right-hand corner of each workbook page is the Bible reading that the student should do for that day. As he or she reads, there are ten questions from the Bible reading that the student is to answer in the workbook. The vast majority of the questions in the workbook can be answered just using the biblical text itself, but there are a few questions that require using outside sources such as a dictionary. Many of these questions are designed to bring out some of the important points in the text. On average, the student will read about two chapters of the Bible per day. Also included on each workbook page is a set of three questions that come from the lesson book.

The *second component* to this curriculum is the **lesson book**. The lessons in this book are designed to help students understand what they are reading. This is not designed to be a theology book that teaches a particular view of theology; rather, it is a survey of the New Testament, which is designed to bring clarity to the reading that the students are doing. On theological issues for which there is debate, the approach of this book is to examine the various options and allow students to decide for themselves which view is most plausible. As students read their daily lesson, they will need to answer three questions from the lesson book; these questions appear at the bottom of the corresponding page in the workbook. These questions are designed to hold students accountable to read through the lesson book. It is recommended that students read through the daily lesson before doing the Bible reading and answering the questions in the workbook.

There are two features within the lesson book that are worth noting. *First*, periodically there will be some **vocabulary words** that are typed in bold print. These are words that may be significant or may just be words that are not commonly used in everyday speech. Often these words will appear in the questions from the lesson in the workbook. *Second*, it is worth noting the **thought questions** at the end of many of the lessons. These questions are designed to help the student think about the reading in a more critical manner. Some of these questions are designed to bring out the theology of the passage, some are designed to prompt the student to think more deeply about what is actually happening in the passage, and some are designed to help the student think about applying the passage to his or her life.

The *third component* to this curriculum are the **tests**. Each quarter the student will take tests based on the questions in the workbook. There will be one test for every twenty days in the student's workbook, though the tests can be divided in half to cover only ten days at a time.

John Benz

Note to Parents:

In Deuteronomy 6:5–7, it says: "You shall love the LORD your God with all your heart, with all your soul, and with all your strength. And these words which I command you today shall be in your heart. You shall teach them diligently to your children, and shall talk of them when you sit in your house, when you walk by the way, when you lie down, and when you rise up."

Scripture makes it clear that the primary responsibility for teaching children lies with the parents, particularly the fathers. This curriculum will be most effective if parents discuss the reading and lesson with the students after they do the work. The thought questions at the end of most lessons provide an excellent opportunity for discussion between parents and their students. In addition, parents are encouraged to use the daily readings for family devotionals. Although these questions are not included with the curriculum, here are some questions that can be asked after every lesson:

1. What is something that this passage teaches you about God?

2. What is something you can pray for as a result of this passage?

3. What is one question you have from this passage?

When you discuss the passage with your students, they will be far more likely to think about the passage and how to apply it to their lives.

UNIT 1: *Introduction, Matthew, and Mark*

Old Testament Overview

Lesson 1

While this course is designed to cover the New Testament, it is impossible to fully understand the New Testament without at least a basic understanding of the Old Testament first. Since there are thirty-nine books in the Old Testament, we obviously cannot go into any depth of detail about the history of the Old Testament. Nevertheless, a basic understanding of that history is important, so we will cover that in this lesson. There are many different ways that we can break down the Old Testament, but for the sake of this lesson we will break it down into five sections: Creation–Tower of Babel, the Patriarchs (Abraham–Joseph), the Exodus, Joshua–Solomon, and the Divided Kingdom–Post Exile.

God's story begins where most stories begin, at the beginning. In this *first section*, we see in Genesis 1 that God creates everything in six days and rests on the seventh day. On days 1–3, God separates things, thus creating light, the skies and seas, and the dry land. On days 4–6, God fills what He creates on the first three days by creating the "lights" (sun, moon, and stars), the birds and fish, and the animals. The only creation that is made in the image of God is humanity. After each day of creation, God sees that what He created is good. In Genesis 2, we learn that humanity is placed in paradise, the garden of Eden. The only thing that is not good is that the first human, Adam, is alone and has no helper. So God creates a woman, and the first man and woman are married. Everything is perfect, but this only lasts for a short while until sin enters the world. God gives the man and woman one command, namely that they could not eat of the Tree of the Knowledge of Good and Evil. However, in chapter 3, an enemy enters creation. The serpent, which John will later identify as "the great dragon … that serpent of old" (Revelation 12:9), tempts the woman to eat from that tree.

When the woman and her husband eat of the tree, sin enters the world and the consequences are tragic. Men will have to work hard to procure their food, and childbirth will be painful for women. Humanity is kicked out of paradise, and death and decay enter the world. Humanity loses its innocence; and every human is born with a disposition towards sin, known as the sinful nature. And God also predicts that there will be a cosmic struggle between the seed of the serpent (Satan) and the Seed of the woman (whom we find out later in the New Testament is Jesus Christ), which will eventually result

in the Seed of the woman defeating Satan. Throughout the entire Old Testament, we are left searching for that Seed of the woman who will defeat Satan.

Yet before things get better, they get much worse. Sin begins to permeate humanity; and within one generation it progresses to murder when Cain kills Abel. It gets so bad by the time of Noah that it is said that humanity is only evil all the time. Noah is the only righteous person left on the earth. So God destroys the earth with a flood, preserving humanity through Noah and his family. However, even after the flood, sin begins to permeate humanity once again as the people of the earth build the Tower of Babel. This tower stands as a symbol of rebellion as humanity basically tells God that they do not need Him. So God slows down the progression of sin by confusing humanity's languages and by spreading people throughout the earth.

The *second section* of God's story begins with a man by the name of Abram. God calls Abram while he is tending his flocks and tells him to go to the land that He will show him. Abram trusts God and believes Him and goes to the land of Canaan. God promises Abram (whose name He changes to Abraham) that He will give the land of Canaan to his descendants. The only problem is that Abraham has no descendants. Yet when Abraham is 100 years old, he has a child, Isaac. God promises to be with Abraham and his family; and as a sign of this covenant, all of Abraham's descendants are to be circumcised. Isaac eventually becomes a father to two sons, Jacob and Esau. God chooses Jacob to be the child of promise and eventually changes Jacob's name to Israel. Israel has twelve sons who will become the ancestors of the twelve tribes of Israel. One of Israel's sons, Joseph, is sold into slavery in Egypt by his brothers because they are jealous of him. However, God works with Joseph and places him in a position of power and authority in Egypt. Because of a famine in the land of Canaan, Joseph arranges for his father Israel and his family to settle down in the land of Goshen in Egypt. There the descendants of Israel remain for centuries.

The *third section* of God's story takes place centuries later. The Israelites have grown from about seventy people to about two million. Because of the large numbers of the Israelites, the Egyptians are afraid and enslave the Israelites. God eventually raises up Moses and calls him to speak to Pharaoh so that he will let the Israelites go. When Pharaoh refuses to let the people go, God sends plagues upon the Egyptians. God sends ten plagues to devastate the nation of Egypt. For the final plague, God prepares to send His angel of death to kill the firstborn sons of all of the Egyptians. In order for the Israelites to survive this plague, God has each household slaughter a lamb and smear its blood on their doorposts. When the angel of death sees this blood covering the people, he passes over that house. This becomes the foundation of the Passover Festival. After the final plague, the Israelites are allowed to leave Egypt; and when the Egyptian army pursues them, Moses parts the Red Sea and the Israelites escape on dry ground. While in the wilderness, God gives the Israelites the Law and establishes the tabernacle and worship for the people of Israel. Sadly, the Israelites rebel in the wilderness; and because of their refusal to listen to God, that generation is cursed to wander in the wilderness.

The *fourth section* of God's story picks up with the next generation of the Israelites. After Moses and the rest of his generation die, Joshua becomes the next leader of Israel. He leads Israel through a series of battles in the Promised Land, and the Israelites are able to establish themselves in the land of Canaan. Yet after the land of Canaan is divided among the twelve tribes of Israel, it is the responsibility of each of the tribes to drive out the inhabitants of the land from their inheritance. Sadly, each of the tribes fails at this, and the people become a snare to the Israelites. The Israelites fall into idolatry. When the Israelites rebel, God strengthens their enemies, and the Israelites are enslaved once again. However, when they cry out to God for help, God raises up a number of judge-heroes who rescue the Israelites from their enemies. The last of these judges is a man named Samuel. Samuel is not only a judge; he is also a priest and a prophet. Yet because Samuel's sons are wicked, the people demand that Samuel give them a king. So, reluctantly, Samuel appoints Saul as the first king of Israel. Saul starts off well and wins some great victories for the Israelites; but he disobeys God on a number of occasions, and God rejects him as king. In his place, God chooses David to be the next king. David establishes Jerusalem as the capital city of Israel and brings the ark of the covenant to Jerusalem. He also establishes the Levites as worship leaders in Israel. David also defeats all of Israel's major enemies. David desires to build the temple for God; however, God promises David that his descendants will always be kings in Israel. So rather than David building the temple, David's son Solomon builds it instead. Solomon is known for his wisdom, but even he is disobedient to God, which leads to the last section of Israel's history.

The *fifth section* of God's story begins after Solomon's reign when the nation of Israel is split into two kingdoms. For 200 years, Israel is divided into the Northern Kingdom, called Israel or Ephraim, and the Southern Kingdom of Judah. At one point, under the reign of Ahab and Jezebel, the worship of God almost disappears in Israel. However, Elijah helps to restore the worship of God. Yet, in the year 723 B.C., the Northern Kingdom is destroyed by the Assyrians. Judah survives for a time; but in the year 586 B.C., Judah is conquered by the Babylonians because of the people's disobedience. It is hard to overstate the significance of this event. Israel is reduced to only a few thousand people, the king is removed from power, Jerusalem is demolished, and the temple is destroyed. Yet God still preserves the Israelites, even while in Babylon; and in the year 539 B.C., Cyrus the Great issues a decree allowing the Israelites to return to their land. Over the next few hundred years, the Israelites begin to reestablish themselves as a nation. In the year 516 B.C., because of the prophecies of Haggai and Zechariah, and the generosity of the king of Persia, the temple is rebuilt. About fifty years later, Nehemiah leads a group of Israelites to Jerusalem in order to rebuild the walls of Jerusalem. It takes fifty-two days to rebuild the walls, and Jerusalem is also rebuilt. By the end of the Old Testament, the Israelites are living in the Persian Empire. They have a temple, and Jerusalem is rebuilt; but the Israelites are poor and have no king. The very last words of the Old Testament prophesy that a King will come from the line of David who will rescue Israel; but before He comes, God will send a prophet in the spirit and power of Elijah.

When our story picks up in the New Testament, the Israelites are waiting for the "Elijah" that is to come. They long for the Messiah, the King from the line of David who will rescue them from their enemies. Unfortunately, for many of the people of Israel, the Messiah that they expect is not the Messiah that they will get. Jesus will come to conquer a different enemy, but we will see this in due time.

Intertestamental History
Lesson 2

Between the pages of the Old and New Testaments, there are over 400 years of history that take place. When the Old Testament ends, the Israelites are living in the Persian Empire. Jerusalem has been rebuilt; but in a time of poverty, the temple is rebuilt but is a shell of what it once was. Yet in the opening pages of the New Testament, we learn that the Israelites are living in the Roman Empire, and Jerusalem is a thriving city with a beautiful temple. For this lesson, we are going to examine the events that bridge this 400-year gap.

The Persian Empire will stand as the dominant power in the Middle East for 200 years. However, with the rise of Philip of Macedon in Greece and the conquests of his son, Alexander the Great, the Persian Empire is conquered and replaced with the Greek Empire. Because of advanced military techniques and the leadership of Alexander the Great, the Greek Empire spreads farther than any kingdom before it. In fact, the Greek Empire not only spreads into northern Africa, but even as far east as India. If not for Alexander the Great's early death at the age of thirty-three, the Greek Empire could have expanded even farther.

When Alexander the Great dies, the Greek Empire is divided between his four generals, thus forming four smaller kingdoms. For the sake of this study, we will look at two of these four kingdoms, the Seleucid Empire and the Ptolemaic Empire. The reason that these two empires are relevant to the nation of Israel is that Israel is situated in between these empires; and over the next 150 years, these kingdoms will fight over control of Palestine (present day Israel).

Particularly relevant to this study is the reign of one of the Seleucid kings, Antiochus IV Epiphanes. Antiochus IV Epiphanes is known for his strong disdain and hatred for the Jewish people. He does a number of things that are extremely offensive to the Jewish people. Not only does he try to **Hellenize** the Jewish people by forcing them to take on Greek names, participate in Greek games, and wear Greek clothing, but he also directly attacks Jewish worship. He desecrates the temple by sacrificing a pig (an unclean animal) to Zeus (the head of the Greek gods) and makes it illegal to make sacrifices in the temple.

The offenses of Antiochus IV Epiphanes eventually lead to a rebellion by the Jewish people. This rebellion begins when an elderly priest, Mattathias ben Johanan, is told to make a pagan sacrifice. When he refuses, a younger Jewish priest agrees to make the sacrifice instead. However, rather than allowing him to make that sacrifice, Mattathias kills the young priest and the Greek official who commands this sacrifice; and he and his family flee into the mountains of Israel. Under the leadership of Mattathias' son, Judas Maccabeus (nicknamed the "Hammer," possibly derived from the Aramaic term *maqqaba*), this army engages in a form of guerilla warfare against the Seleucid army. Eventually, this Jewish army attacks Jerusalem and reconquers it for Israel. The Festival of Lights, known as "Hanukkah," is celebrated today, which commemorates the rededication of the temple after Jerusalem is reconquered. Through political involvement, the Jewish state gains its independence

from the Seleucid Empire for over 100 years. This period of time is known as the Hasmonean Dynasty.

This political strength, however, does not last forever in Israel. As the Roman Empire begins to grow in power, the Roman ruler Pompey conquers Jerusalem for Rome in the year 63 B.C. Because of Israel's political instability, this victory is fairly easy for the Roman army. Shortly before the New Testament, power was consolidated in Rome; and the Roman Empire entered into the *Pax Romana*, a period of Roman peace. This provides the context for the New Testament.

> **Hellenize:** the spreading of Greek culture and language

> *Pax Romana:* a period of Roman peace beginning in 27 B.C. with the reign of Augustus

Key Groups in the New Testament
Lesson 3

As you read through the New Testament, there are a number of people groups who do not appear in the Old Testament. Jesus interacts with members from each of these groups, and it is worthwhile to examine their origins and particular beliefs. For this lesson, we will focus on these groups.

The group with which Jesus interacts the most is the **Pharisees**. This group is established during the period of the Hasmonean Dynasty. After the temple is reconsecrated and the worship of God is restored in Israel, many of the Israelites take seriously the call to obey and honor the Law of Moses. The Pharisees are famous for their strong emphasis on personal holiness and strict adherence to the Law. In fact, the Pharisees also hold to something called in the New Testament "the tradition of the elders." Because it is such a grave violation to the Pharisees to break the Law, they develop a whole set of laws designed to protect people from breaking the Law. For example, in the Law it says not to work on the Sabbath, but "work" is not completely defined in the Law. So the Pharisees develop a set of laws to govern more precisely what would be considered work. Because the Law is so important for the Pharisees, many of the Pharisees memorize the entire Old Testament. The Pharisees prove to be Jesus' most consistent opponents throughout His public ministry. Jesus will condemn the Pharisees for neglecting the heart of the Law and for their overemphasis on the letter of the Law.

The next group with which Jesus interacts also develops during the Hasmonean Dynasty—the **Sadducees**. The Sadducees are a particular class of priests who hold most of the power in the temple. While not every priest is a Sadducee, most of the priesthood is controlled by the Sadducees. Unlike the Pharisees, who are mostly hostile to Rome, the Sadducees work together with the Romans. Because of this, many of the Sadducees hold much political power and personal wealth. In addition, the Sadducees also control the **Sanhedrin**, a group of religious leaders who serve as judges regarding religious matters. The Sadducees are also famous for rejecting the notion of an afterlife or the resurrection. Jesus will clash with the Sadducees over the resurrection, and the Sadducees will play a big role in Jesus' trial and crucifixion.

The next group in the New Testament is the **Herodians**. These are Jewish people who support the Herodian Dynasty in Israel. Most of the Jews are not very fond of this dynasty because Herod and his family are Edomites rather than Israelites. Yet those who do support this king call themselves Herodians. Conversely, another group of Jewish people with which Jesus interacts in Israel are called the **Zealots**. The Zealots are revolutionaries who oppose Rome and seek to gain Israel's independence. One of the twelve disciples, Simon, is a Zealot. This must have made for some interesting conversations between him and Matthew, a tax collector for Rome.

The final group that we will observe is the **Essenes**. While Jesus does not directly interact with the Essenes, this group produces the Dead Sea Scrolls, which are some of the earliest biblical manuscripts we have found. This group splits off from the rest of Israel and forms their own community in order to purify themselves in hope of bringing in the Messiah.

> **Pharisees:** a Jewish sect known for their strict adherence to the Law of Moses
>
> **Sadducees:** a Jewish sect that controls the priesthood and Sanhedrin; rejects the idea of the afterlife
>
> **Sanhedrin:** a religious governing body that judges religious cases in Israel
>
> **Herodians:** Jewish supporters of the Herodian Dynasty in Israel
>
> **Zealots:** Jewish revolutionaries who oppose Rome and seek Israel's independence
>
> **Essenes:** a Jewish sect that seeks purification by forming their own community

Setting of the New Testament
Lesson 4

There are several different factors that we can examine when thinking about the setting of the New Testament. However, for the sake of time and space, we are going to look at three types of context: religious, philosophical, and cultural.

There are a number of religious groups that we will encounter in the New Testament. *First*, we will look at the religions within the Roman Empire. The dominant religion throughout the Roman Empire is **polytheism**, the belief in many gods. Within this set of beliefs, there are specific gods for specific parts of life. For example, there is a god of war and a god of wine. It is common within Roman polytheism that humans are able to defeat the gods. In the book of Acts, Paul encounters followers of this belief on at least three separate occasions. In Lystra, the people believe that Paul and Barnabas are gods after a lame man is healed. The people even try to sacrifice to them. The city of Ephesus, where Paul spends much time, is famous for its temple to Artemis. When Paul goes to Athens, he sees the altars to all of the various gods and uses a specific altar to an unknown god as a door to share the gospel with the people there.

Second, another religion develops during the time of the New Testament known as **Gnosticism**. Gnostics believe that there are two forces in the universe that wage war against each other. One of these forces is good, and the other is evil. Gnostics believe that the material world is evil, while the spiritual world is good. In order to achieve salvation, Gnostics argue that one needs to have special knowledge. While this belief is not fully developed until after the New Testament, there are some early forms of this that may have influenced certain books of the New Testament such as Colossians and 1 John.

Third, the various cults that exist in the Roman Empire are also relevant to the New Testament. First, there is the **cult of the emperor**. As with Pharaoh of Egypt, many people believe that the Roman emperors are actually gods, and these cults are devoted to the emperors. The early emperors are not seen as gods until they die, but later emperors demand and receive worship as gods while they are still alive. There are also **mystery cults** throughout the Roman Empire. These cults are similar to the Gnostics in that they offer salvation through initiation into their cults. Often there are secret passwords or codes that a person must know to get into these cults.

The religion of the Jews is expressed in two main forms. Central to Jewish worship is the temple and the sacrificial system. According to the Law, Jewish men are required to go to Jerusalem three times a year: for the Passover Feast, the Feast of Pentecost, and the Feast of Tabernacles. One of the ways that scholars have figured out that Jesus ministers for over three years is the number of Passover Festivals that we see Him going to Jerusalem to celebrate. In addition to these festivals, there are regular Sabbath services every week. For those Jews who do not live near the city of Jerusalem, they regularly meet in **synagogues** ("assemblies"). Synagogues, which emphasize worship and studying the Law, are similar to assemblies of Christians; in fact, the church structure was derived from synagogue worship. When Paul begins to spread the gospel to the Gentile world, he goes first to the Jewish synagogues until he is kicked out; then he turns his attention to the Gentiles.

One of the things for which the Greeks are famous is the development of philosophy. The works that began under the Greek Empire continue on into the Roman Empire. While the scope of this lesson cannot cover all of the various works of philosophy that develop over this time, there are two types of philosophies that appear in the New Testament. **Stoicism** is a philosophy that focuses on how to avoid pain. The phrase that describes Stoicism is "this is not my cup." In order to protect oneself from pain, there is a detachment from the things and people of this world. To this day, to be stoic means to be aloof or cold or unemotional. **Epicureanism**, or hedonism, is practically the opposite of Stoicism. Epicureanism teaches that pleasure is the chief goal in life. This does not mean that people should always pursue immediate pleasure, which satisfies in the moment, because withholding temporary pleasure can mean greater pleasure in the future. Paul will encounter Stoic and Epicurean philosophers in his journeys.

There are also a number of things worth noting about the cultural setting of the New Testament. Because of the Hellenization done by Alexander the Great and the Greek Empire, by the time of the New Testament everyone in the Roman Empire is able to speak Greek. This proves to be incredibly beneficial for the spreading of the gospel. Also, because the Roman Empire is enjoying a time of peace, the Romans are able to draw attention inward and to improve the living conditions of the people. This involves making a number of roads to connect the various parts of the Roman Empire. These will be the very roads that Paul and other Christians will travel upon as they spread the gospel. Also because of this peace, there is less fear of bandits and raiders while traveling on these roads. The Romans also make travel by sea easier, as well.

> **polytheism:** the belief in many gods

> **Gnosticism:** a belief that there are two cosmic forces at war (good and evil) and that salvation is acquired through special knowledge

> **cult of the emperor:** devoted followers of the emperors, who worship the emperor as a god

> **mystery cults:** groups of people who offer salvation through initiation into the group

> **synagogues:** centers of worship for Jews throughout the Roman Empire

> **Stoicism:** a philosophy that focuses on avoiding pain by detaching oneself from everything

> **Epicureanism:** a philosophy that teaches that pleasure is the chief goal in life

Introduction to the Gospels
Lesson 5

According to Jewish law, in order for something to be accepted in a court of law, it must be confirmed to by the testimony of two witnesses (Deuteronomy 19:15). Because the life, death, and resurrection of Jesus is the most important event in history, God chose to give us four witnesses to attest to the historical reliability of Jesus' life. The first four books of the New Testament are called the **gospels** because all four of them tell us the "good news" that comes through Jesus Christ. While we will examine the specific themes and goals of each gospel in their individual introductions, the overall goal of each gospel is to convert the reader to faith in Jesus Christ.

The first three gospels—Matthew, Mark, and Luke—are known as the **synoptic** gospels. The word *synoptic* means "with similar or same eyes." They are called this because the material in these three gospels is very similar. In fact, there are sections of these gospels that are identical in words and in order of events. As we go through the various lessons on the life of Christ through the gospels, we will see many of the same events mentioned in each gospel, although each author will add his own emphasis and organization of these events.

Because of the nature of the Greek language, it is incredibly unlikely that long sections of the gospels would be identical. Yet there are portions of Matthew, Mark, and Luke that are word-for-word identical. This has led scholars to believe that the gospel authors had access to the other gospels and used them as sources for their material. Only two of the authors of the gospels were disciples of Jesus during His earthly ministry (Matthew and John), so we know that at least two of the authors had to get their information from sources. In light of this, there are two main theories as to which authors use the others as sources. The first theory is that Matthew was the first gospel written and that Mark and Luke use his writings as a source. In favor of this is the fact that Matthew appears first in the Bible. But this theory has a difficult time explaining why Mark would leave out so much material from Matthew's gospel if he had access to it. The second theory is called the *Q Theory*. This theory states that Mark must have been the first gospel written and that Matthew and Luke use it as a source. This could explain why Mark has so much less material. However, there is a lot of material that both Matthew and Luke have in common that Mark does not have. For this material, it is suggested that there was another source, called **Q**, that has the material in common between Matthew and Luke. Q was probably a collection of Jesus' sayings. If this theory is correct, Mark would have written his gospel first, and both Matthew and Luke would have used Mark, Q, and their individual sources.

One of the benefits of assuming that the gospel writers had access to the other gospels is that it can reveal the emphasis of that particular author. For example, in the almost identical passages in Matthew 7:7–11 and Luke 11:9–13 about prayer, Matthew finishes by saying that God will give "good things" to those who ask Him; yet Luke says that God will give "the Holy Spirit" to those who ask Him. This gives us a clue as to one of Luke's themes, the role of the Holy Spirit. Luke identifies one of the "good things" that Matthew mentions as the "Holy Spirit." This type of comparative study is called **redaction criticism**.

The gospel of John is very unique compared to the other three gospels. We will examine this gospel in more detail in the lesson on the introduction to John.

> **gospel:** "good news," a theological history of the life of Jesus

> **synoptic:** "with similar eyes," the title given to the first three gospels

> **Q:** a possible document used by Matthew and Luke that contains Jesus' sayings

> **redaction criticism:** a comparative study of similar passages from different books

Introduction to Matthew

Lesson 6

The first book of the New Testament, and the first gospel that we will cover in this class, is the gospel of Matthew. For this lesson, and with all introductory lessons for New Testament books, we will examine the author, the audience, and the major themes in the book.

It is important to note from the beginning that none of the gospel writers identifies who he is within the book that he writes. The only reason we attribute the first gospel to Matthew, the second to Mark, and so forth is because church tradition tells us that these are the authors. However, there is some internal evidence to back up each of these authors as the actual authors of these books. The first piece of evidence that supports Matthew as the author of the first gospel is his relative insignificance as a disciple. If someone were going to choose a disciple to author one of the gospels, he would choose Peter or one of the more popular disciples. The fact that it has been attributed to Matthew, who does not play a prominent role after his initial conversion, suggests that it is authentic. In addition, when referring to Matthew's calling to be a disciple, Mark and Luke refer to him as *Levi*, whereas the first gospel calls him *Matthew*. Matthew undoubtedly went by both names, but the best explanation for why the first gospel calls him by a different name could be that Matthew preferred to call himself by that name.

For the sake of this class, we will assume that Matthew is the author of the first gospel. We do not know much about Matthew, but we do know a few things about him. *First,* we know that he was originally a tax collector. When Jesus encounters Matthew, He calls him to follow Him; Matthew leaves everything to follow Jesus. Immediately, Matthew throws a party in his home and invites Jesus and His disciples. He also agrees to give back money to anyone that he might have cheated. In those days, tax collectors were despised by the Jews as traitors because they work for the Roman government. In addition, many of the tax collectors would charge people extra money and keep it for themselves. *Second,* we know that Jesus chooses Matthew as one of the twelve disciples.

While we do not know a lot about Matthew's audience, we can infer from internal evidence that he writes to a Jewish audience. Unlike Mark and Luke, Jesus does not explain Hebrew sayings. Matthew also uses the more technical phrase "kingdom of heaven" rather than the phrase "kingdom of God" that Mark and Luke use. Jews

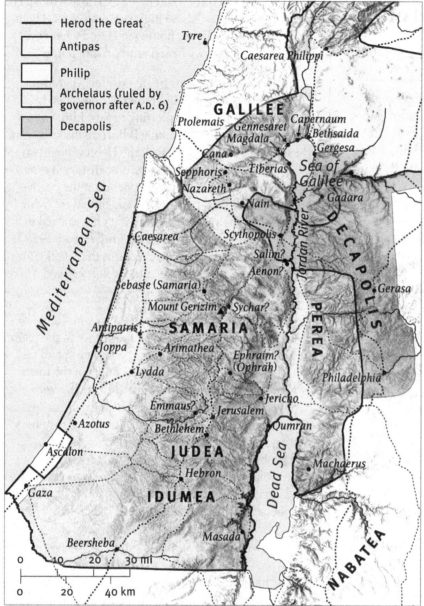

The Setting of Matthew

The events in the book of Matthew take place almost entirely within the vicinity of Palestine, an area extending roughly from Caesarea Philippi in the north to Beersheba in the south. During this time it was ruled by the Roman Empire. The opening chapters describe events surrounding Jesus' birth in Judea, where Herod had been appointed king by the Romans. The closing chapters end with Jesus' death, resurrection, and ascension during the rule of Pontius Pilate and the tetrarchs Antipas and Philip.

would understand the phrase "kingdom of heaven" as a reference to the Messianic Kingdom of the Old Testament. Matthew's genealogy goes back to Abraham, the ancestor of the Jews. Matthew also draws attention to King David in his genealogy of Jesus Christ and refers to Jesus as the "Son of David." Also, Matthew consistently points out Jesus as the Messiah promised in the Old Testament.

This leads us to examine the major themes in the gospel of Matthew. *First*, Matthew, more than any other gospel writer, draws attention to how Jesus fulfills the prophecies in the Old Testament. Regularly Matthew uses the phrase "this took place to fulfill what was written through the prophet…." *Second*, Matthew places a much bigger emphasis on the kingdom of heaven

than the other gospel writers. Matthew 13 is filled with parables, all designed to explain the nature of the kingdom of heaven. *Third*, the Sermon on the Mount, from Matthew 5–7, depicts Jesus as the new Moses who fulfills and expands on the Old Testament Law. *Fourth*, Matthew draws attention to Jesus' focus on Israel as His mission ground. In fact, it is not until the Great Commission at the end of Matthew's gospel that Jesus explicitly sends out His disciples to bring the gospel to all the nations. As one reads this book, it is important to remember that Jesus is Jewish and came to offer salvation to His people first.

The Birth and Childhood of Jesus: Matthew 1–2

Lesson 7

Matthew's gospel begins with Jesus' genealogy. There are a number of things worth pointing out from Matthew's genealogy. *First,* Matthew organizes Jesus' genealogy into three groups of fourteen generations, from Abraham to David, from David to captivity in Babylon, and from that captivity until Jesus is born. It is not clear why Matthew emphasizes the number 14. Some have suggested that the name "David" when turned into numbers has the value of 14. It is also possible that it is a reference to completion, as the number 7 is in 14 (14 = 7 x 2). *Second,* Matthew's genealogy goes back only to Abraham. As mentioned in the introduction, this is to show that Jesus is the true Israelite. *Third,* Matthew draws attention to four women in Jesus' genealogy— Tamar, Rahab, Ruth, and Bathsheba. Three of these four women are Gentiles, and three of them were involved with sexual immorality. Perhaps Matthew mentions this to show that Jesus offers salvation and redemption to all kinds of people, even the social outcasts.

After the genealogy, Matthew picks up the story of Jesus shortly after Mary conceives. Though Mary is a virgin, because of the power of the Holy Spirit she conceives. When Joseph discovers that she is pregnant, he plans to divorce her quietly. If a woman was found to be pregnant out of wedlock, she could be killed; so Joseph's desire to divorce her quietly is a way of protecting her. Even though they were not married in Jewish culture, betrothal is considered to be a binding promise, like marriage. However, the angel Gabriel comes to Joseph in a dream and tells him to take Mary as his wife. Joseph listens to the angel; and in the course of time, Mary gives birth to Jesus while in Bethlehem. The child is named *Jesus,* which means "God saves."

The next event in Matthew's account of the life of Christ comes about two years later. Some "wise men" come from the East to see Jesus. These wise men are probably nobles from the land of Persia, but it is possible that they come from even farther east. They are able to find the child because a star guides them, similarly to how the cloud and pillar of fire had guided the Israelites during the Exodus. Contrary to popular portrayals, there is nothing in the text that tells us that there are three wise men. The reason people assume there are three wise men is because there are three types of gifts that they give Jesus. These gifts will prove to be very practical, as they most likely provide the money

necessary for the travels and living expenses that Mary, Joseph, and Jesus will have in the years to come. Having been warned in a dream not to tell Herod where the child is staying, the wise men return a different way.

King Herod is famous for being extremely paranoid. He was even willing to kill his own family when he suspected that they were plotting against him. So in response to hearing that a king is born in his kingdom, Herod issues a decree to kill all the Hebrew boys two years old or younger in his kingdom. History is repeating itself, for this same thing happened at the beginning of Israel's history while the Israelites were living in Egypt. Nevertheless, Joseph and Mary are warned in a dream to flee, so they go to Egypt until Herod dies. One of the things we will see about Jesus is that He is going to relive the history of Israel, but He will succeed where the Israelites had failed.

Finally, when Herod dies, Joseph, Mary, and Jesus return to Israel; but to stay safe, they move to the region of Galilee to the very north. Jesus will then spend the rest of His childhood and early adult life in the town of Nazareth in Galilee, working as a carpenter with His earthly father. Matthew does something curious in this part of the story. He says that this fulfills the prophecy that says that "He shall be called a Nazarene" (2:23). The problem is that there is no prophecy saying that the Messiah will come from Nazareth. The solution to this is that the Hebrew word for "branch" is *nezer*. It is prophesied that the Messiah will be called the "branch." So the fact that Jesus is from Nazareth may be a reference to this prophecy of the branch.

Thought Question:

> Read the context of Isaiah 7 and 8 (which contains the prophecy about the virgin birth). Who originally fulfills this prophecy in Isaiah's time?

John the Baptist and Jesus' Ministries: Matthew 3–4

Lesson 8

If you remember from the first lesson on the overview of the Old Testament, the very last words of the Old Testament speak of the prophet Elijah, who will come to prepare the way for the Messiah. In Matthew 3, we see the fulfillment of this prophecy. John the Baptist is the one who comes in the spirit of Elijah and prepares the way for Jesus. In fact, John the Baptist is characterized as a man who wears camel's hair and a leather belt around his waist; this is almost the exact same description of Elijah from 2 Kings 1:8. So how does John the Baptist prepare the way for Jesus? John calls the people to repent of their sins so that when the Messiah comes, they will be ready to receive Him. People come from all over the nation of Israel to the Jordan River to be baptized by John. John baptizes people with water for repentance, but he knows that the Messiah will baptize the people with the Holy Spirit and with fire.

One of the ways that John prepares the way for Jesus is through his interactions with the Sadducees and the Pharisees. We see in Matthew 3 that John reserves some of his harshest words for the religious leaders of the day. In fact, he calls them a "Brood of vipers" (3:7). Like a viper, they wait around and strike people when they are not suspecting. John argues that these religious leaders are hurting the very people they are supposed to be leading. We will learn more through the life of Jesus precisely how these religious leaders are hurting the people. This interaction between John and the religious leaders foreshadows some of the very same interactions that Jesus will have with the religious leaders.

From John's message, we can deduce some of his expectations for the Messiah. John pictures the Messiah with two tools in His hand, both having to do with judgment. *First*, he says that the ax is laid at the root of the tree. Throughout the Old Testament, Israel has been characterized as a tree that would be cut down. Here, John predicts that the Messiah is going to bring judgment and destruction upon those in Israel who do not repent. *Second*, John mentions the winnowing fork. The winnowing fork is used in farming to separate the wheat from the chaff. When the wheat is harvested, so also is the useless chaff. One way that the harvesters separate the wheat from the chaff is to throw them both up in the air with the winnowing fork. Because the chaff has no substance, the chaff blows away while the wheat falls back down. The chaff is then gathered and burned as fuel for fire. Here, John believes that the Messiah is going to separate the righteous (wheat) from the unrighteous (chaff). He is going to gather the wheat into the barn (salvation) but burn the chaff with fire (hell fire).

Some time later, John the Baptist will send his disciples to Jesus to see if He really is the Messiah. How could John be so sure now that Jesus is the Messiah but doubt it later? Most likely it is because John expects Jesus to bring judgment to the wicked and to separate the righteous from the wicked. However, this does not happen at Jesus' first coming. This will only happen when Jesus comes again.

When Jesus comes out to the Jordan to be baptized by John, John refuses at first. After all, John should be baptized by Jesus. Yet Jesus insists and says that this is necessary to fulfill all righteousness. However, if John's baptism is a baptism of repentance, for what does Jesus need to repent? This comes back to Jesus' reenactment and fulfillment of Israel's history. Here Jesus repents on behalf of the nation of Israel. When Jesus comes out of the water, two things happen. *First*, the Holy Spirit descends on Jesus like a dove. Jesus' public ministry, which will follow this event, will be done in the power of the Holy Spirit. *Second*, God affirms Jesus' place and relationship as God's Son with a voice from heaven. This affirmation will be crucial for the temptations that Jesus is about to face.

The very first thing that the Holy Spirit does after filling Jesus is send Him away into the wilderness to be tempted. Just as the Israelites begin their history by wandering for forty years in the wilderness, Jesus begins His ministry by wandering in the wilderness for forty days. Unlike Israel, however, Jesus does not give in to temptation but remains faithful. After fasting for forty days, Matthew informs us that Jesus is hungry. This seems like an unnecessary detail after Jesus not eating for forty days, but it reminds us of His humanity. It is when Jesus is at His weakest that Satan chooses to tempt Him.

Satan tempts Jesus three different times. The first time Satan tempts Jesus to use His power to turn rocks into bread. This temptation is twofold: *first*, Satan is tempting Jesus to provide for His physical needs; and *second*, Satan is tempting Jesus to prove that He is the Son of God. This is why God's voice from heaven is so crucial at this point in His ministry. God has already affirmed to Jesus that He is God's Son and that God loves Him. So Jesus has nothing to prove here and resists, saying that "Man shall not live by bread alone, but by every word that proceeds from the mouth of God" (4:4). Even though Jesus has not eaten for forty days, He has feasted on Scripture by meditating on it. The second temptation is similar to the first in that Satan tempts Jesus to prove that He is the Son of God and to use His power for personal gain. Quoting Psalm 91, Satan tempts Jesus to throw Himself down from the temple so that God will save Him. Perhaps Satan tries to defeat Jesus at His own game of quoting Scripture. Conveniently, Satan stops the quote right before it says "the young lion and the serpent you shall trample underfoot" (Psalm 91:13). This is a reference to Genesis 3 where God prophesies that the Seed of the woman will crush the head of the seed of the serpent. Jesus is the Seed of the woman, and Satan is the seed of the serpent. Once again, Jesus quotes Scripture saying it is not good to test the Lord. Finally, Satan goes for it all and tempts Jesus a third time. Here Satan offers Jesus glory without the cross. Jesus knows that He will receive all authority and power after He dies, but this is a temptation to bypass the cross. All Jesus has to do is worship Satan, and all the kingdoms of the world will be His. Yet Jesus quotes Scripture a third time saying we are to worship God alone.

There are a couple of lessons we can learn from how Jesus responds to temptation. *First*, Jesus resists Satan by quoting Scripture. In Ephesians 6, the only offensive weapon in the armor of God is the sword of the Spirit, the Word of God. Jesus skillfully uses Scripture to counter each temptation. Contrast this with the first temptation in the garden of Eden. When Eve is tempted, she does not even remember the name of the tree from which they cannot eat. The reason Jesus is able to resist temptation and Adam and Eve fail is largely due to their knowledge of God's word. *Second*, all of Jesus' quotes are from Deuteronomy, the book written to the Israelites wandering in the wilderness. It is likely that He had been meditating on this book over the forty days in the wilderness. Jesus prepares Himself with the right Scripture for the right context.

Shortly after Jesus is baptized, John the Baptist is put in prison and Jesus picks up where John leaves off. In fact, Jesus' message about the kingdom is the exact same as John's: "Repent, for the kingdom of heaven is at hand" (3:2, 4:17). And many of the people who had originally followed John begin to come to Jesus. One of the crucial elements of Jesus' ministry is choosing His disciples. We see early on that Jesus calls Andrew, Peter, James, and John to follow Him; and they leave everything to follow Him. He then begins His public ministry by preaching about the kingdom and healing the sick. Because of this, His fame begins to spread, and more and more people begin to follow Him.

Thought Questions:

1. If John the Baptist's main job is to prepare the way for Jesus and our mission is to prepare people for Jesus, what principles can we learn from John to complete our mission?

2. In light of the lesson and this passage, what are some practical steps that you can take to help overcome temptations in the future?

The Sermon on the Mount, Part 1: Matthew 5

Lesson 9

In Matthew 5–7, we have the most famous sermon ever given, the Sermon on the Mount. This whole sermon is a commentary on the Ten Commandments and principles that we can learn from them. Because this sermon has so much to apply, we will look at this sermon over the course of two lessons. Matthew 5 can be divided into three sections: the beatitudes, salt and light, and fulfillment of the Law.

First, Jesus begins this sermon by turning our expectations upside down. He begins with a series of beatitudes, or blessings, that we would not expect. According to Jesus, in His kingdom the poor, the mourners, the meek, the hungry, the merciful, the pure, the peacemakers, and the persecuted are blessed. This is the exact opposite of the world in which we live. In this world, the rich, the happy, the powerful, the satisfied, the cut-throats, the impure, the conflict-makers, and the persecutors are considered "blessed." Jesus turns this on its head. Jesus' kingdom is not for the "haves" but for the "have-nots." Later, Jesus will say that He did not come to the healthy, but for the sick. It is only those who realize that they are blind and sick who can receive Jesus. Salvation is not given to those who do not feel that they need to be saved.

Second, Jesus follows up this shake-up of expectations by calling His disciples to make a difference in this world. He uses two metaphors to describe the role that we are supposed to play in this world. First, He says that we are to be the "salt of the earth." The role of salt is both to preserve food and also to add flavor to food. As the "salt of the earth," we are to be purposeful in making an impact on this world for the kingdom of God. Related to this, Jesus calls us the "light of the world." We have a responsibility to bring "light" or truth to this world. Both of these metaphors bring out the responsibility we have as Jesus' disciples to impact this world and make it a better place. More precisely, we have been given the "light" of salvation and the Word of God, and it is our responsibility to bring this to a world that is lost and in the dark.

Third, following this introduction to His sermon, Jesus draws His attention to the Law. He makes it clear that He has not come to abolish the Law but to fulfill it. For those who say that the Old Testament simply does not apply to us, Jesus Himself says that He did not come to abolish the Law. The question we must ask when reading the Old Testament is not, "Does this apply to me?"

but rather, "How does Jesus fulfill this passage?" Jesus goes even further to say that anyone who relaxes even the least of the commandments will be called least in the kingdom of heaven. To those who argue that we do not have to live a righteous life because of what Jesus did on the cross, He says that our righteousness must surpass even that of the Pharisees, who go so far as to even tithe on their spices.

So how does Jesus fulfill the cornerstone of the Law, the Ten Commandments? First, He fully obeys every one of them. Yet, in the Sermon on the Mount, He does something else with them: He expands them. Jesus expands the prohibition of murder to make it an issue of the heart. If we harbor anger and hatred in our hearts, we commit murder in our hearts. He expands the prohibition of adultery to include lust. If we lust after someone, we commit adultery in our hearts. He then addresses the issue of divorce in the Law. While it is true that Moses allows divorce, Jesus clarifies that it should only be in issues of sexual immorality that divorce is allowed. Regarding oaths, rather than creating a calculus of what oaths are valuable, He says to just speak the truth and there is no need for oaths. Regarding justice in the Law, rather than "eye for an eye," Jesus says to love your enemies and pray for those who persecute you. Rather than focusing on revenge, we should focus on showing love even to our enemies. Rather than lowering the standard, Jesus finishes chapter 5 by telling us to "be perfect" (5:48).

Thought Questions:

1. Explain how it can be a blessing to mourn, as Jesus says in the beatitudes.

2. If Jesus did not come to abolish the Law, why do you think that we don't observe the Old Testament food laws (such as not eating pork) or the sacrificial laws anymore?

3. Since we are told to turn the other cheek when someone strikes us, does this mean that we should just take abuse? If not, how can we respond to abuse in a manner consistent with Jesus' commands here?

The Sermon on the Mount, Part 2: Matthew 6–7

Lesson 10

After speaking about issues of the heart in Matthew 5, Jesus talks about the outward expression of the heart in chapter 6. Especially in light of the call to be salt and light from chapter 5, it is impossible to have faith without an outward expression of religious activities. Yet many people do these religious activities with wrong motives and in the wrong manner.

For much of chapter 6, Jesus suggests doing religious deeds not to be seen by others, but to do them in secret so that we could please God with them. First, Jesus addresses giving money to the poor. Apparently, the Pharisees and the religious leaders of Jesus' day would make a public spectacle of their giving so that everyone could see what they were doing. Jesus suggests doing just the opposite, to give in such a way that nobody can see you. If we do our good deeds so that others can see them and think that we are very religious, Jesus argues that the praise of others is our reward. However, if we do our charitable deeds in such a way that only God can see them, then God will reward us. This same thing applies to public prayers. Jesus says not to pray in such a manner that people think you are very religious. Rather, pray in secret so that God will reward you. Once again, it appears that the religious leaders of the day prayed in such a manner that everyone would think they are very religious.

In light of this, Jesus offers a simple model of prayer. While it is beneficial to examine this prayer in detail, it is important to notice first and foremost that it is a simple, quick prayer. Long prayers do not have more power than short prayers; in fact, it may be tempting to give long prayers rather than short ones so that others will praise us and think we are religious. Nevertheless, there are some observations to be made about the "Lord's Prayer." This prayer can be broken down into two sections. This prayer begins by seeking the things that please God (praising His name, and praying for His will to be done and for His kingdom to come). It is only after praying for the things that please God that the prayer turns personal. Here Jesus says to pray that God will take care of our physical needs (daily bread), to confess sins, and to ask for help to overcome temptation.

Following another example of religious activities to be done in private (fasting), Jesus speaks about money and trusting God to provide. Jesus warns us not to love money or focus our lives on earning more money, but rather we should spend our lives investing in things that have eternal value. The treasures that we should store up should be those treasures that will benefit us in heaven. In light of this, Jesus finishes chapter 6 by telling us not to worry about the things that money gives us, such as food or clothes. If we focus on the things of eternal value, i.e. the kingdom of heaven, we can trust that God will provide everything we need.

Jesus finishes the Sermon on the Mount in chapter 7 with a number of different topics. First, He tells us not to judge others but to examine ourselves before pointing out flaws in other people. Related to this, He warns us to be careful about the things that are valuable to us that we do not entrust them to those who cannot respect them. This involves being careful to whom we give our secrets. Next, Jesus invites us to have an honest prayer life. It is okay to ask God for things. He is our heavenly Father and will not fault us for asking. In fact, we miss out on things because we do not ask for them. Jesus then summarizes the Law with the Golden Rule, "whatever you want men to do to you, do also to them" (7:12). Following this, Jesus warns us about false teaching. There are a lot of paths that lead to destruction, but only one narrow path that leads to life. There are many false teachers (prophets) who will try to lead us astray. Yet Jesus tells us to examine their lives and the fruit that they bear, for even some who perform miracles will not enter heaven. Finally, Jesus finishes the Sermon on the Mount with a charge to do more than just listen to Him but to put the things that He says into practice.

Thought Questions:

1. Jesus says that God will not forgive our sins if we do not forgive others. Does this mean that we can lose our salvation if we hold onto grudges and refuse to forgive people? Why or why not?

2. Why do you think it is that Jesus will say, "I never knew you," to some people who perform miracles in His name? What does this warning mean for us today?

Miracles: Matthew 8–9
Lesson 11

Jesus is not only a great Teacher, but He is a powerful miracle worker. As one could imagine, as word gets out about the many miracles and healings that Jesus performs, wherever He goes large crowds amass to see Him and to be healed by Him. At times, the crowds get so large and they push with so much force that Jesus and His disciples have to retreat to the seas just so that they will not get crushed. Yet Jesus never seems to see these crowds as burdens or as a nuisance; rather, He usually takes His time and meets the needs of each individual in the group. In chapters 8–9, we see many of these miracles that Jesus performs.

After Jesus comes down from the mountain where He preaches the Sermon on the Mount, He is met by a leper. This leper believes that Jesus can heal him; and through his faith, Jesus heals him. However, Jesus does something else that must have been just as incredible to the man; Jesus also touches him. It is possible that this leper had not been touched in years, yet Jesus is willing to touch him and restore him. The next miracle that Matthew mentions is the healing of a centurion's servant. There are a couple of things worth noting about this miracle. First, the centurion has enough faith in Jesus that he does not even ask Jesus to go in person to heal the servant but to merely say the word. As a man of authority, the centurion understands that Jesus has authority to do this miracle with simply a word. Jesus says that this Gentile centurion has more faith than anyone in Israel. He turns this into a warning for the Israelites that if they do not have faith, the kingdom will be given to the Gentiles.

Following this event, Jesus and His disciples go to Peter's house. Jesus heals Peter's mother-in-law, and she serves them. That night, large crowds gather around that house, and Jesus heals many and casts out demons. Yet, when the crowds get too large, Jesus tells His disciples to get a boat ready so that they can travel to the other side. On His way to the boat, Jesus encounters two people who offer to follow Him but are not willing to go right away. Jesus warns them about the cost of following Him, and they do not follow.

While on the boat, a great storm arises and shakes the boat so that it looks like the boat will sink. However, while the disciples are panicking, Jesus is quietly sleeping down below in the boat. When the disciples wake up Jesus, He rebukes the storm and the storm immediately stops, showing that Jesus has authority even over nature. Upon arriving on the other side of the sea, Jesus encounters two demon-possessed men. These men are so strong and terrifying that nobody would pass through that direction. Yet, when these demons see Jesus, they beg Him for mercy. Jesus gives them permission to leave the men and go into a herd of pigs, and they lead the pigs into the water where they all die.

Jesus then returns back to His home in Nazareth. Here, a paralytic is brought to Jesus to be healed. Rather than simply healing the man, Jesus tells the man that his sins are forgiven. It is one thing to have the authority to heal someone, but to have the authority to forgive sins is something else. The religious leaders who are there understand what Jesus is doing and accuse Him of blasphemy. Yet Jesus knows their hearts and heals the man, showing that He has authority even to forgive sins. Jesus then travels from there and meets Matthew, a tax collector, and tells him to follow Him. Matthew leaves everything and follows Jesus. When the Pharisees see Jesus eating with tax collectors, they sneer; but Jesus informs them that He came for the sick, not the healthy. Chapter 9 finishes with more miracles. Jesus heals a bleeding woman, raises a girl from the dead, gives sight to the blind, and casts out demons. However, the Pharisees resist Him; this will be a bigger problem in days to come.

Thought Question:

Why do you think that Jesus allows the demons to go into the herd of pigs?

The Calling and Commission of the Twelve: Matthew 10

Lesson 12

During the course of Jesus' ministry, He accomplishes many things. He heals the sick, casts out demons, and teaches about the kingdom of God. Of course, the most significant thing that Jesus accomplishes is giving His life so that we could be forgiven. Yet another incredibly significant aspect of Jesus' mission is the development of His disciples. Jesus knows that His time on earth is short and that He will return to the Father. When He leaves, He will need to entrust His work and message of the kingdom to others who will spread the word. This is why Jesus spends so much time focusing on the twelve.

In Matthew 10, Jesus chooses the twelve disciples from the midst of all His followers. It is clear from the other gospels, particularly John, that the twelve are not the only disciples who follow Jesus. So Jesus separates the twelve from the rest of the disciples and chooses them to be His close disciples. Jesus will spend the better part of three years with these twelve disciples, living with them and teaching them many things.

We know more about some of the twelve than we do about the others. Peter is the most famous of the twelve and the one who seems to be the leader of the

The Twelve Apostles*

Matthew 10:2–4	Mark 3:16–19	Luke 6:14–16	John (various verses)	Acts 1:13
1. Simon, who is called Peter	1. Simon (to whom he gave the name Peter)	1. Simon, whom he named Peter	Simon Peter (1:40–42)	1. Peter
2. Andrew his [Simon Peter's] brother	4. Andrew	2. Andrew his [Simon Peter's] brother	Andrew, Simon Peter's brother (1:40)	4. Andrew
3. James the son of Zebedee	2. James the son of Zebedee	3. James	unnamed son of Zebedee (21:2)	3. James
4. John his [James's] brother	3. John the brother of James	4. John	unnamed son of Zebedee (21:2)	2. John
5. Philip	5. Philip	5. Philip	Philip of Bethsaida (1:43–44)	5. Philip
6. Bartholomew	6. Bartholomew	6. Bartholomew	Nathanael of Cana (1:45–49; 21:2)**	7. Bartholomew
7. Thomas	8. Thomas	8. Thomas	Thomas called the Twin (11:16)	6. Thomas
8. Matthew the tax collector	7. Matthew (Levi, son of Alphaeus, a tax collector, 2:14)	7. Matthew (Levi, tax collector, 5:27)		8. Matthew
9. James the son of Alphaeus	9. James the son of Alphaeus	9. James the son of Alphaeus		9. James the son of Alphaeus
10. Thaddaeus	10. Thaddaeus	11. Judas the son of James	Judas (not Iscariot) (14:22)	11. Judas the son of James
11. Simon the Zealot	11. Simon the Zealot	10. Simon who was called the Zealot		10. Simon the Zealot
12. Judas Iscariot	12. Judas Iscariot	12. Judas Iscariot	Judas the son of Simon Iscariot (6:71)	12. Matthias replaces Judas [who had died] (Acts 1:26)

Others in the NT are regarded as apostles besides the Twelve, notably James the brother of Jesus (Acts 15:12–21; 1 Cor. 15:7; Gal. 1:19), Paul (Acts 14:4, 14; 1 Cor. 9:1; 15:8–9), and Barnabas (Acts 14:4, 14).

**Nathanael is probably Bartholomew, since he is closely associated with Philip. He is certainly not Levi/Matthew, who already has two names and who was from Capernaum. It is possible but unlikely that he is Thaddeus/Judas or Simon the Zealot.*

group. He consistently is prone to act first and think later. He will be the one who confesses that Jesus is the Christ first, and he will be foundational for the building of the Church after Jesus ascends to heaven. Peter and his brother Andrew, another member of the twelve, work as fishermen before following Jesus. Their fishing partners, James and John, are the next two most famous disciples of the twelve. During the life of Christ, James and John ask on multiple occasions for Jesus to give them special power and authority in His kingdom. Later, John, the author of the fourth gospel, identifies himself merely as "the disciple whom Jesus loved." Peter, James, and John are given special privileges within the twelve; they are the ones whom Jesus requests to be with Him in the garden of Gethsemane before He is betrayed. We do not know much about Philip other than that he is from the same city as Peter, Andrew, James, and John. Thomas will be famous for doubting that Jesus is resurrected, but he also has one of the best confessions of faith in the gospels. Church tradition states that Thomas may have been the first person to bring the gospel to India. We know that Matthew is a tax collector before Jesus calls him to follow Him, and Matthew is the author of this gospel. Also, Judas Iscariot is infamous as the one who betrays Jesus. Simon the Canaanite is also called Simon the Zealot in the other gospels. As we learned from the introductory lessons, Zealots were revolutionaries who opposed Rome and fought for Israel's independence. There must have been interesting conversations between Simon the Zealot and Matthew the tax collector. We know almost nothing about Bartholomew, James, and Lebbaeus (or Judas Thaddaeus).

Jesus does not simply call these disciples so that they can learn. These disciples are immediately put to work. Jesus sends them out as an extension of His own ministry. Just as Jesus heals the sick, casts out demons, and proclaims the kingdom of heaven, so also do His disciples. Jesus spends the rest of chapter 10 preparing the twelve for the mission that they are about to do. This is not going to be an easy mission. They are to bring practically nothing with them on this journey, but they are to depend on the generosity of others. They should expect to be persecuted and hated just as Jesus is persecuted and hated. However, God will be with them, and the Holy Spirit will give them the words to say. Following Jesus is very costly, and Jesus warns them that they will be rejected even by their own families. They will be rewarded, but suffering will come first. Jesus sends them out only among the cities of Israel. It is not yet time for the message to go to the Samaritans or Gentiles; that will come later.

Thought Question:

Why do you think that Jesus tells His disciples to bring practically nothing with them as they preach in the cities of Israel?

Doubt and Opposition: Matthew 11–12

Lesson 13

Chapter 11 begins with a question from the disciples of John the Baptist. As mentioned in the lesson on chapter 3, John the Baptist had certain expectations of the Messiah. He pictures the Messiah as a man with an ax in His hand, ready to cut down the tree of all who refuse to repent. He also pictures the Messiah with a winnowing fork, ready to separate the righteous from the unrighteous. After a year of Jesus ministering, this separation and judgment has not yet occurred. It would appear by the question of John's disciples that he is confused about Jesus and may be starting to doubt if Jesus is the Messiah that he expected. Yet Jesus responds to the inquiry of John's disciples by drawing attention to His miracles and making a reference to a passage in Isaiah that speaks of the Messiah performing miracles.

Following this question, Jesus begins to speak about John the Baptist. Jesus confirms that John the Baptist is indeed the fulfillment of the passage from Malachi that speaks of the return of Elijah the prophet to prepare the way for the Lord. This implies that Jesus is the Messiah Himself, considering that John directed people to Jesus. Though John's mission is to call the people to repentance, we see Jesus condemning a number of cities because they refuse to repent when He performed miracles there. While many are prepared to receive the Messiah, it appears that most are not ready to receive Jesus. Thus, as John the Baptist had expected, Jesus does call down judgment upon those who refuse to repent; but contrary to John's expectations, this judgment does not occur right away. In light of this call of judgment by Jesus upon the cities that refuse to repent, there is also an offering of salvation. Jesus calls upon all who hear Him to come to Him, and He offers to give them rest. Once again, Jesus offers salvation to those who are sick, not to those who are well.

The opposition by the religious leaders takes center stage in chapter 12. It is clear that the Pharisees are searching for things of which to accuse Jesus. As He and His disciples pass through the fields on the Sabbath, His disciples grab some grain and eat it. According to the tradition of the elders, this is work; so the Pharisees accuse Jesus and His disciples of desecrating the Sabbath. However, these rules are in addition to the Law of Moses, and Jesus does not need to submit to them. Besides, Jesus Himself has authority over the Sabbath. Jesus then heals a man with a withered hand on the Sabbath, and the Pharisees once again seek to accuse Him of breaking the Sabbath. Yet Jesus argues that it is right to do good and heal on the Sabbath. Because Jesus directly challenges the Pharisees in the synagogue, presumably in front of the people, the Pharisees begin to plot how they can destroy Jesus.

A little later, Jesus casts out a demon from a man who is blind and mute, and the man is healed. However, when the crowds start to believe that Jesus might be the Messiah, the Pharisees accuse Him of being demon-possessed. They believe that He is able to cast out demons because He is possessed by Beelzebub (Satan). Yet Jesus argues that their logic is ridiculous. In fact, He goes further to argue that their persistent refusal to believe in Him, even to the point of believing that Satan is fighting against himself, will lead to their damnation. The "unforgivable sin" of blasphemy against the Holy Spirit is a persistent refusal to accept the works of the Holy Spirit through Jesus Christ. Because of their careless words, they will be judged; for words reflect the nature of our hearts. The words of the Pharisees reveal their stubborn refusal to accept and believe in Jesus. The Pharisees respond by asking Jesus to give them a sign to prove His authority. The only sign that Jesus offers is the sign of Jonah, who was in the earth for three days but was "resurrected" at the end. Jesus' death and resurrection is the only sign needed for faith. Once again, Jesus speaks judgment upon that generation for their refusal to believe.

Thought Question:

Based on the lesson and this passage, explain in your own words what the unforgivable sin of blasphemy against the Holy Spirit is.

Kingdom Parables: Matthew 13

Lesson 14

God sent Jesus to earth in order to establish His kingdom. As mentioned earlier, the Jews of Jesus' day have a number of expectations concerning the kingdom of God. *First*, they expect that kingdom to come suddenly when the Messiah appears. *Second*, they expect there to be a separation on that day between the righteous and the wicked, with the wicked being destroyed. *Third*, they expect the kingdom to be an earthly kingdom

established in Israel with all of the other nations submitting to Israel, including Rome. However, the kingdom that Jesus establishes is going to look very different from the one that the Jews expect. Jesus' teachings from the parables in Matthew 13 are going to challenge the Jewish expectations of the kingdom.

The first parable that Matthew records is the parable of the sower. This parable is actually going to be the key for understanding all of Jesus' parables. In this parable, a sower sows seeds in various places on his farm. Some of the seeds fall along the path, others fall among the rocks, others grow among the thorns, but still others grow in the good soil. Jesus gives this parable to the crowds but does not explain what it means, so His disciples ask Him in private to explain further. They first ask Jesus why He chooses to teach in parables rather than speaking plainly. Jesus quotes Isaiah's commission in Isaiah 6 to explain why He speaks in parables. Rather than telling these stories simply to illustrate a point, He actually tells these stories in order to hide the point from those who are not willing to listen. Jesus knows that people come to Him with different motives. He speaks in parables in order to further harden the hearts of those who are not sincere. In fact, this is actually what the message of the parable of the sower is all about. God is the Sower, and the seed is the Word of God. The pathway represents those who do not receive His word at all because Satan snatches it before it can bear fruit. The rocky soil represents those who accept the word but do not let it sink in; when tough times come, they fall away because they have no roots. The thorny soil represents those who do accept the word, but they do not bear fruit because they are distracted by the things of this world. Finally, the good soil represents those who come with ears ready to hear, and these people yield incredible fruit from God's word.

In the parable of the weeds, Jesus speaks about another farmer who plants good seed in his field, but an enemy comes and plants useless weeds in that same field. When the servants see the weeds growing along with the wheat, they ask if they should pluck up the weeds. The master, however, tells them to let them grow together lest some of the wheat be harmed by plucking up the weeds. The message of this parable is that both the wicked and the righteous will coexist for a time in the kingdom of God. Rather than the immediate separation that the Jews expect, they will grow together.

In the next two parables, Jesus speaks about the slow-growing nature of the kingdom. Remember that the Jews expected the Messiah to bring the kingdom all at once. Yet Jesus compares the kingdom of heaven to a mustard seed that starts extremely small but grows to become a big tree. In addition, Jesus compares the kingdom of heaven to yeast that slowly works its way through the bread until the whole loaf rises. In both of these parables, we see that the kingdom is going to start small, but eventually grow to become huge. Historically, this is exactly what happens: the kingdom starts with Jesus, then the twelve disciples, then thousands on the day of Pentecost, and eventually is spread throughout the whole world.

After explaining the parable of the weeds to the disciples, Jesus offers two more parables that relate to one another. The kingdom is compared to both a treasure found in a field and a pearl of great price. In both of these parables, a person finds something so valuable that he gladly sells all that he has in order to get that valuable thing. This tells us that the kingdom of God is a treasure, and we need to be willing to pay whatever we can to get that kingdom.

Jesus finishes this section of teaching with two final parables. In the parable of the net, Jesus speaks once again about the coming separation of the righteous from the wicked. We have already learned that both will coexist in the kingdom for some time, but here we see once again that there will eventually be that separation at the end of the age. To conclude this section about the kingdom, Jesus says that the person who understands the kingdom is like the master of a house who brings out both new and old. Here Jesus is talking about the old treasures as teachings from the Old Testament, and the new treasures are the new insights that Jesus offers. These new insights do not contradict the old, but rather draw out the meanings of the old even more.

Sadly, this chapter ends on a regrettable note. Jesus returns home and begins to preach in the synagogue there. However, rather than the people being overjoyed that one of their own people is the Messiah, they refuse to believe in Him. They cannot see past that person who had grown up in that city, and very few people there believe in Jesus. In fact, it is so deplorable there that Jesus is unable to perform many miracles because of their unbelief.

Thought Questions:

1. How might Jesus' teachings about the coexistence of the wicked and the righteous in the kingdom help explain some of the scandals in churches in America?

2. Why do you think Jesus tries to further harden the hearts of those who are not ready to listen?

3. Why do you think it is so difficult for people in Jesus' hometown to believe in Him?

Lost Friends, Miracles, and Opposition: Matthew 14–15

Lesson 15

John the Baptist is one of the greatest prophets in the Bible. He is given the incredible privilege of being the one who would prepare the people for the coming of the Messiah. John also does an incredible job with the responsibilities that God gives him. For a while, John the Baptist and Jesus both minister to the people at the same time. Yet from the moment John baptizes Jesus in the Jordan, he knows that he must fall more into the background so that Jesus could be front and center. Sadly, in Matthew 14, we learn that the ministry of John the Baptist comes to an end when he is unjustly put to death.

Because John had spoken out against Herod's relationship with his brother's wife, Herod has John put in prison. However, because of John's popularity with the people and because Herod enjoys listening to John, he keeps him in prison rather than killing him. Yet, one day, Herod throws a party for his birthday, and the daughter of the woman whom John condemns Herod for marrying dances for Herod. She pleases Herod so much by her dance that he offers to give her whatever she wants. When she asks her mother, she tells her to ask for the head of John the Baptist on a platter. Because this takes place publicly, Herod reluctantly agrees, and John the Baptist is put to death.

When Jesus finds out about this, He goes off to a solitary place, presumably to think and pray. John had been an important ally of Jesus, and likely the two were friends; so Jesus wants to mourn and think about what will come next. However, the crowds see Jesus go off by Himself and follow Him. When Jesus sees them, rather than sending them away, He has compassion on them and teaches them and heals them. Yet, when it gets late, Jesus sees that they need food. So Jesus tells His disciples to give food to the crowd. However, the cost of food for such a crowd would be huge, so His disciples question Him. Jesus then performs a miracle and feeds the entire crowd with only a few fish and a few loaves of bread. Like Moses, Jesus provides a form of manna to the people. Everyone is amazed by this miracle, as over 5,000 men are there, and likely as many women and children are there, as well.

Having ministered to the crowds, Jesus finally gets the alone time that He wanted before, so He sends away

His disciples on the nearby lake. However, after Jesus is done praying, He comes to join the disciples; the problem is that He is on land and they are in a boat, so Jesus walks on water to come to them. As one could imagine, the disciples are terrified when they see Jesus walking on water. Yet Jesus comforts them by letting them know that it is He and that they do not have to be afraid. Peter, being the kind of person who acts first and thinks later, asks Jesus to let him walk on water, as well, and Jesus agrees. Peter walks on water for a short distance but then gets scared by the wind and begins to sink; but Jesus saves him. Of course, the disciples are amazed and worship Jesus. Then, when they arrive at the other side of the lake, Jesus performs more miracles and heals many there.

Contrasted with the faith of the crowds is the stubborn rejection of Jesus by the religious leaders. Once again, the religious leaders confront Jesus because He and His disciples do not follow their traditions. In this case, they condemn Jesus because His disciples do not wash their hands before they eat. Rather than trying to justify Himself, Jesus points out the hypocrisy of their traditions. According to their traditions, it is perfectly acceptable to take money that children can use to provide for their parents and give it to the synagogue or temple instead. Jesus points out by this that their traditions go against the commandment to honor your parents. Jesus then quotes Isaiah, who had earlier rebuked the people because their religion was only a matter of outward actions rather than coming from the heart.

Privately, Jesus talks to His disciples about the religious leaders. Apparently, these religious leaders are offended by Jesus' words. When the disciples tell Jesus about this, He dismisses it and compares the religious leaders to blind people who are trying to lead other blind people. However, Jesus goes on to address the original issue with which the religious leaders have a problem. Jesus says that these people are so concerned with outward washings that they are ignoring their dirty hearts. It is far more important to work on the heart than to just focus on the outward actions.

Following this confrontation with the faithless religious leaders, Jesus goes into the thoroughly Gentile area of Tyre and Sidon. There He is met by a Canaanite woman who begs Jesus to cast out a demon from her daughter, but Jesus ignores her. She is so persistent that Jesus finally replies to her that it is wrong to give the children's food to the dogs. This would be very insulting. So why does Jesus say this? Jesus is teaching everyone a lesson: He had come to first save the lost people of Israel. God had made a covenant with Israel, and He is keeping His promise by offering salvation to Israel first. Yet this woman has incredible faith; and in the midst of an insult, she replies to Jesus reminding Him that even the dogs get some scraps from the table. Jesus is so impressed by her faith that He heals her daughter.

Jesus travels from there back to the Sea of Galilee and again heals and teaches the crowds. When it grows late, Jesus tells His disciples to feed the crowds. Sadly, the disciples do not seem to have a great memory because they once again question this command. However, Jesus again takes a few fish and some loaves of bread and feeds this crowd, as well. This crowd has 4,000 men, as well as women and children.

Thought Questions:

1. Even though Jesus needs to mourn the loss of John the Baptist, He still ministers to the crowds. What lessons can we learn from this?

2. Why is it not a sin for Jesus to compare the Canaanite woman to a dog?

Peter's Confession and the Transfiguration: Matthew 16:1–17:13

Lesson 16

As we have already seen, Jesus' greatest source of opposition during the days of His ministry comes from the very people who should be the most eager to accept Him, the religious leaders. In chapter 16, the religious leaders decide to confront Jesus again, this time asking Him to give them a sign from heaven to prove that He is from God. This request reveals the stubborn and rebellious nature of their hearts. Jesus has given an incredible number of signs to the people that had been well known to everyone. These religious leaders do not ask this because they want to believe; they ask this so that they could test Jesus.

Jesus, however, knows the hearts of these men and refuses to give them a sign. Rather, Jesus tells them that the only sign that they will receive is the sign of Jonah. Yet, what is the sign of Jonah? Elsewhere, Jesus clarifies that the sign of Jonah is the coming crucifixion and resurrection of the Messiah. Just as Jonah had spent three days and nights in the midst of the earth when he was swallowed by the fish, so also will Jesus be in the earth but raised on the third day.

In light of this interaction with the religious leaders, Jesus seizes on the opportunity and warns His disciples privately to be careful about the leaven of the religious leaders. As often is the case with people, when Jesus speaks in metaphor, the disciples take Him literally. They assume that Jesus is talking about actual leaven and bread and think that Jesus is rebuking them for forgetting their bread. It appears that the disciples are not that much brighter than the religious leaders, for if Jesus were concerned about physical bread, after the two miracles of feeding the crowds that Jesus had recently performed, the disciples should surely know it would be no problem for Jesus to make bread. Jesus clarifies that the leaven that He is warning them about is metaphorical for the teachings of the religious leaders. Jesus warns the disciples to be careful about the teaching of the religious leaders, lest it corrupt them just as leaven works its way throughout a whole loaf of bread.

Following this warning about the religious leaders, a major turning point occurs in the ministry of Jesus. Jesus decides to test the disciples to see what they believe about Him. First, Jesus asks them about His reputation, what the people are saying about Him. They reply that some people think He is John the Baptist, while others think He is Elijah or Jeremiah or one of the other prophets. Then Jesus makes it personal and asks the disciples who they think He is. Peter, who never seems to be afraid to speak his mind, speaks for the disciples and declares that Jesus is the Christ, or Messiah. This is probably the smartest thing that Peter has ever said up until this point. Jesus blesses Peter for this confession and commends him for listening to the Father who had revealed that to him.

Jesus' blessing of Peter has led to much debate over the years within Christianity. Jesus tells Peter that He will build the Church upon the rock that is Peter. The name *Peter* literally means "rock" or "stone." Jesus says that He is going to give Peter the keys to the kingdom of heaven and that God will support the decisions that Peter makes. If Peter looses something on earth (forgives it), God will loose it in heaven; and if Peter binds something on earth (condemns), God will also bind it in heaven. In other words, Jesus is giving Peter the authority to oversee church discipline. However, the question remains as to who precisely is given this authority. The Roman Catholic Church believes that this blessing is given first to Peter and then passed down every generation to the next bishop of Rome, known as the *pope* (which means "papa"). They believe this because Peter ultimately died as a leader of the church in Rome. Other Christians argue that this authority is only given to Peter for the critical role that he will play in the development of the early church. This authority, therefore, is never intended to be passed down from generation to generation.

Sadly for Peter, his moment of glory quickly comes to an end. After blessing Peter, Jesus begins to plainly tell the disciples that He has to go to Jerusalem, and there He will be put to death but will be raised on the third day. In fact, from the moment of this confession, Jesus draws all of His focus towards Jerusalem for the upcoming crucifixion. Yet the idea of a Suffering Servant Messiah rather than a Conquering King Messiah does not sit well with Peter, so Peter rebukes Jesus. Jesus does not allow this kind of talk to continue, however; He immediately rebukes Peter, calling him Satan because he is not thinking about the things of God. Jesus' greatest temptation during His life is the temptation to avoid the suffering of the cross. When Peter suggests that the cross should not happen, he is being used by Satan to tempt Jesus. The disciples still do not fully understand what it means to be disciples of the Messiah, so Jesus tells them what awaits them. As His disciples, they also must be willing to deny themselves and take up their crosses to die with Him. Following Jesus will not bring free glory; rather, it will cost them their lives. Yet, when they are willing to give up their lives for the gospel, they will gain far more in return.

Jesus finishes this teaching by telling the disciples that some of them will still be alive and will see Jesus as the Son of Man coming in His kingdom. The reference to the kingdom of the Son of Man comes from Daniel 7 and refers to when the Father gives the kingdom to the Son. Although there is certainly room for interpretation of this prophecy, the very next story is likely the fulfillment of this prophecy. Six days after Peter's confession, Jesus takes Peter, James, and John with Him up on a mountain and reveals His glory to them. This event is called the Transfiguration; in it Jesus is transformed, and His face shines brightly and His clothes become a bright light. Moses and Elijah also appear and talk to Jesus about His coming death and resurrection (see Luke 9:31). There is a lot of speculation as to why precisely it is Moses and Elijah. Moses represents the Law, and Elijah represents the Prophets. So when Peter sees these two men meeting with Jesus, he offers to make them some tents, not understanding fully what is happening. However, before Peter can start to pitch tents, the Father speaks to the disciples, confirming that Jesus is His beloved Son and telling them to listen to Him. This whole incident is very similar to Jesus' baptism, and God's words are basically the same in both places. In both of these situations, God confirms His love for Jesus just before He enters into a great temptation.

After Jesus returns to normal, He and the disciples return down the mountain. Jesus commands them to keep this incident a secret until He is raised from the dead. This provides an opportunity for the disciples to get some clarification on something concerning Jesus. The disciples know the prophecy from Malachi that says that Elijah must come before the Messiah will come. Since Jesus is indeed the Messiah, the disciples wonder who Elijah was. Jesus confirms to them that John the Baptist was in fact the Elijah who was to come.

Thought Questions:

1. Why do you think that the Pharisees and Saddu-cees ask Jesus for a sign?

2. Why do you think that Jesus is transfigured before the disciples?

Faith, Humility, and Reconciliation: Matthew 17:14–18:35

Lesson 17

Now that Jesus' disciples know that He is in fact the Christ, Jesus has some final lessons to teach His disciples before He faces the cross. It has been clear from the moment that Peter confessed that Jesus is the Christ that the disciples still have much to learn about the nature of the kingdom that Jesus has come to bring. Peter himself followed his great confession with a sinful rebuke of Jesus when Jesus had begun to speak about His coming suffering. Therefore, in the days leading up to Jesus' death, He draws His attention towards His disciples.

After Jesus, Peter, James, and John return from the mountain where Jesus had been transfigured, they are immediately met by a man who begs Jesus to heal his son. His son has been afflicted by a demon, and this demon has caused the child much harm. This man had previously brought his son to the rest of the disciples, but they were unable to cast the demon out of the boy. Yet, when they bring the boy to Jesus, He rebukes the demon, and the demon leaves the boy. When the disciples ask Jesus why they were unable to cast out this demon, Jesus reveals that this kind of demon could only be cast out by faith, through prayer and fasting. This reveals something to us about the nature of demons. Not all demons are the same, and some demons are more difficult to deal with than others. Nevertheless, Jesus uses this as an opportunity to teach His disciples about faith. Even though this kind

of demon cannot be cast out without faith, it does not take much faith to do this. Faith is the decision that we make to actively trust in the character and promises of God. Jesus also tells us that with even a little faith we will be able to move mountains.

It is important to Jesus that the disciples understand that He must die, so once again as they come to Galilee He tells them plainly that He will be betrayed and killed and will be raised up on the third day. This still is very difficult for the disciples, so they are filled with sorrow. When Jesus and His disciples arrive in Caper-naum, Peter is confronted by the people who receive the temple tax. It was required of every person to pay the temple tax, yet Jesus had not yet paid the tax. When Peter comes to Jesus about this, Jesus sees this as another teachable moment for His disciples. In one sense, it is absurd for Jesus to pay the temple tax since the money from that tax is supposed to go to God; and since Jesus is God, He would be paying Himself. He mentions this to Peter in order to teach him that Jesus is in fact the Son of God. To prove this, Jesus tells Peter to go fishing and the first fish that he catches will have the perfect amount of money in its mouth to pay the temple tax. Peter does this, and the fish does in fact have the money in its mouth.

At the time when the disciples should be preparing for Jesus' death, instead the disciples are worried about who is going to be the greatest in the kingdom of heaven. The disciples are still concerned about personal glory rather than God's divine plan of salvation. So Jesus once again takes this opportunity to teach His disciples some valuable lessons. The disciples are worried about who is the greatest in the kingdom, yet they need to be focused first on simply how to get into the kingdom. So Jesus calls a child to Himself and tells the disciples that they need to become like a little child if they want to be in the kingdom of heaven. In fact, to answer their question, Jesus tells them that the person who humbles himself like a little child will be greatest in the kingdom. Little children are not concerned about greatness or compar-ing themselves to others; they want to enjoy life, and they are content knowing that they are safe and loved by their parents. Like little children, the disciples need to abandon their ambition for self-glory and simply find joy and comfort that they are loved by God.

Jesus takes this object lesson from the little child fur-ther. Jesus tells the disciples that for anyone who causes a little child to sin, it would be better for that person to be put to death. In fact, whatever causes anyone to sin should be severed, whether it be their hand, their foot, or even their own eyes. The focus and intentions of the disciples are in the wrong place. They are concerned with glory and greatness when they should be worried about their own sins and their need for righteousness. Jesus returns to His original illustration and says that they should not despise the little children, for their angels are in the presence of God Himself. This statement about these angels has led many to believe that there are guardian angels for children. This is certainly possible. Nevertheless, through the illustration of this child, Jesus is telling the disciples that greatness in the kingdom comes through humility, not ambition. Again, Jesus illustrates the importance of humility with the parable of the lost sheep. Just as a shepherd rejoices over a lost sheep that returns more than he rejoices over ninety-nine that are not lost, so also God rejoices more over a sinner who repents than those who do not need to repent. The disciples should be overjoyed that they simply get to be in the kingdom; they should not worry about being the greatest in that kingdom.

Next, Jesus takes this opportunity to teach His disciples about forgiveness and reconciliation. Jesus details a four-step process for dealing with sins and offenses. The *first step* in dealing with an offense is to confront the person one-to-one. Far too often people skip this step, and it has disastrous effects. When we complain to others first, we do not solve the problem at all, and we sin against that person by slandering his or her name. When we bring others with us at first, it puts the other person on the defense because he or she will feel outnumbered. If the person does not repent when we confront him or her directly, we move on to the next step. The *second step* in dealing with an offense is to bring two or three other witnesses to confront the person. By bringing it up this next level, hopefully the other person will see how serious the sin is and repent. If he or she does not repent with the second step, we are to move on to the third step. In the *third step*, we are to bring the matter before the church and have the church confront the person. If the person is still stubborn and does not repent, Jesus says to treat that person like a heathen and a tax collector; this is the *fourth step*. There is much debate as to what precisely Jesus means by this last statement. Some suggest that this means the person is to be kicked out of the community of believers, just as a heathen was not allowed into the temple. Yet others point to how Jesus interacts with heathens and tax collectors, and they suggest that Jesus is telling us to treat the person like a nonbeliever by sharing the gospel with that person. Whichever is the more appropriate application, Jesus goes on to tell the disciples that God is going to support the decisions that the church makes when it disciplines one of its members.

Peter recognizes that the goal of this whole process is forgiveness. However, it is possible for a person to take advantage of this process, so he asks Jesus how many times we are supposed to keep forgiving a person when he or she sins against us. When Peter suggests seven times, Jesus raises it exponentially by telling him seventy times seven. To illustrate this point, Jesus tells the parable of the unmerciful servant. In this parable, a servant owes his master a massive debt. Yet, mercifully, the master completely forgives that debt. However, when that man sees a fellow servant who owes him a little money, he forces the man to pay him back. Jesus points out that the master who had originally forgiven that servant will require every penny to be restored when he finds out about this servant's unforgiving attitude. The lesson here is simple: because we have been forgiven so much by God, we have no excuse not to forgive another person.

Thought Questions:

1. Do you think that the story of the temple tax reveals Jesus' supernatural knowledge (knowing that the fish has the money), or reveals Jesus' power over nature (Jesus makes it so that the fish has the money)? Why?

2. What are some practical lessons you can learn about the nature of faith from little children?

3. If we are commanded to forgive people over and over again, does this mean we should let people hurt us over and over again? Is there a way to forgive someone but still protect ourselves?

The Last Will Be First: Matthew 19–20

Lesson 18

From the moment of Peter's confession, Jesus and His disciples begin their journey towards Jerusalem. In chapter 19, they arrive in the region of Judea near to the city of Jerusalem. As the end of Jesus' life draws closer and closer, He continues to teach His disciples more and more about the nature of the kingdom and how they should live their lives.

In His famous Sermon on the Mount, Jesus teaches us that divorce is not acceptable, except for the case of adultery or sexual immorality. In light of this teaching, the Pharisees in Judea try to trap Jesus. They bait Jesus into this trap by asking Him if it is okay to divorce a wife for any reason. They know that Jesus will say that it is not acceptable except in the case of sexual immorality.

Jesus knows their hearts, and so He appeals to creation and the first marriage between Adam and Eve to support His answer. This is precisely what the Pharisees expect Jesus to say, so they ask Him why Moses allows for divorce in the Law. It would appear that Jesus' teachings contradict the teachings of Moses, so the Pharisees feel that they have Him trapped. However, Jesus explains that God allowed Moses to give this permission because of the hardness of the people's hearts, not because this is what God ultimately wants. Moses understood that there are some situations that would result in torture for those in marriage, so he provided a way out to protect from the hardness of heart. Yet Jesus goes back before the Law was ever given to show that God's intention for marriage was that it would be permanent. Jesus reiterates that the only acceptable occasion for divorce is when the covenant has already been broken by sexual immorality. Realizing the permanent nature of marriage, His disciples conclude that it is better not to get married. They understand just how serious this covenant is. There is practically no way out of this commitment. However, Jesus tells them that only some people are able to truly embrace singleness. Eunuchs are unable to get married, and not many people can make that kind of commitment. There are some people, though, who can make that commitment and should.

Regrettably, the fact that the disciples are fairly slow to understand Jesus' teachings becomes evident in the next section of Matthew. Jesus had just used a small child as an example of how the disciples are supposed to view the kingdom. He has just warned them about how serious it would be to cause one of the little children to sin. Yet, when people bring little children to Jesus to have Him bless them, the disciples rebuke these people. Yet Jesus is a patient and good Teacher; He tells the disciples once again that the kingdom of heaven belongs to these children and that they should not hinder the little children from coming to Him.

Jesus is then met by a rich young man. This man asks Jesus the question that many of us would love to hear from someone. He asks Jesus what he must do in order to have eternal life. Jesus does not tell this man to give a simple prayer and then he would be saved; instead, Jesus begins to quote from the Law. Jesus quotes many of the Ten Commandments and adds that we are to love our neighbor as ourselves. Interestingly, Jesus leaves out the commandment not to covet. This man says that he has indeed followed these commandments since he was young, but he recognizes that he is still lacking something. Then Jesus tells the man to do the one thing that this man cannot do. He tells the man to sell all of his possessions, give them to the poor, and

then come and follow Jesus. This man is unwilling to give up so much for Jesus, so he walks away sadly.

This incident becomes yet another great teaching tool for Jesus. This rich young man would appear to be the ideal candidate for the kingdom of God. He has clearly been blessed by God, and he has worked hard to follow the Law. Yet this man is not able to even enter the kingdom because he is not willing to give up his money. Jesus seizes on this opportunity and tells the disciples that it is nearly impossible for a rich man to enter the kingdom. The disciples are astonished by this and ask, "Who then can be saved?" Jesus humbles the disciples by telling them that no man can save himself, but with God all things are possible. It is possible that this teaching makes the disciples nervous, so Peter speaks up and reminds Jesus that the disciples had given up everything to follow Jesus. Jesus tells Peter that their sacrifice will be rewarded and that someday they will rule over the twelve tribes of Israel. However, they are not the only ones who will be rewarded for their sacrifices, for everyone who has experienced loss for the kingdom will receive a hundredfold and eternal life. At this point the disciples must be feeling pretty good. Yet Jesus reminds them that the first will be last and the last first in the kingdom of God.

Rather than being greatest in the kingdom, Jesus reminds them once again that they should be overjoyed just to be in the kingdom at all. He illustrates this point with His next parable. In this parable, Jesus speaks about a landowner who had hired a number of people to work in his field for a denarius. Throughout the day he hired more and more people, offering each of them a denarius. At the end of the day, every person received the same wage, even though some worked more than others. When the people complain, the landowner reminds them that it is his prerogative to give whatever wage he wants and that they should be grateful for the work. So also is the kingdom of God a reward that God can choose to give to whomever He wants. Once again, Jesus reminds them that the last will be first, and the first last in the kingdom.

Again, Jesus speaks to His disciples about the suffering that awaits Him in Jerusalem. He tells them that He will be handed over to the Gentiles and He will be beaten and crucified, but He will be raised on the third day. With the number of times that Jesus has warned the disciples, it is fairly astonishing just how surprised they will be when these things take place. Sadly, still the disciples miss the point and start asking about their own glory. This time, the mother of James and John comes to Jesus and requests that her two sons could sit on His right and left side when He gets His kingdom. Jesus has already told the disciples that they would be given thrones to judge the twelve tribes; now they want even more glory. To sit on the right and the left of the true King would bring incredible glory. However, rather than offering this glory, Jesus draws attention to the suffering that they must endure with Him. When Jesus speaks about His baptism and His cup, He is speaking about the suffering that He is about to endure. He tells them that they will indeed suffer as He will, but He cannot give them their request.

It is a dangerous thing to leave power in the hands of those who want glory. When Jesus leaves, He will leave the kingdom of God into the hands of the disciples. If they continue to seek glory, they will become tyrants. So Jesus tells them not to be like the Gentiles, who use their positions of power to control and use those below them. Rather than seeking power for power's sake, Jesus tells them that they need to serve one another. The best leaders in Christ's kingdom and in the Church today are not the powerful pastors, but the humble servants who sacrifice themselves to provide for those in their care. Sadly, there are some powerful pastors today who use the power of their positions to control and abuse the people in their churches. Jesus Himself is the greatest example of servant-leadership. He could have demanded that people serve Him, but instead He set an example for us by humbly serving others.

Chapter 20 ends with yet another healing, this time of two blind men. As the disciples had done with those who brought children, they try to quiet these men. Yet, as Jesus had done with the children, He goes to these blind men. They ask Jesus to open their eyes. So Jesus has compassion on them and heals them, as well.

Thought Questions:

1. Why do you think the disciples conclude that it is better not to get married after hearing Jesus' teachings about divorce? What does this tell you about marriage?

2. Think about the leaders in your life. Do they use their authority to lord over others, or are they humble servants?

The Triumphal Entry: Matthew 21:1–27

Lesson 19

It has been said that the gospels are really stories about the death and resurrection of Jesus with very long introductions. While Jesus does a lot with the life and ministry that He has on earth, the primary task that He has been given by the Father is to pay the penalty for our sins. Ever since Peter's confession, Jesus has been very straightforward with His disciples, telling them plainly that He is going to die and be raised from the dead when He gets to Jerusalem. And now, in chapter 21, Jesus and His disciples finally arrive in Jerusalem.

In the Law of Moses, it is required that every Jewish man comes to the city of Jerusalem at least three times a year to celebrate the yearly festivals (Deuteronomy 16:16). One of these festivals is the Feast of Unleavened Bread, or the Feast of Passover. During this festival, the population of Jerusalem would swell up to ten times its normal size. Because of the influx of such a large number of people, it was common for people to arrive in the city a week early just to be able to find a place to lodge. With the Passover taking place on Friday night, Jesus and His disciples arrive on the previous Sunday. The event of the Triumphal Entry on Sunday marks the beginning of what has become known as the Holy Week.

Jesus does not merely walk into Jerusalem for this event, however. He tells His disciples to go into one of the local villages and to get a donkey and a colt for Him. It is possible that Jesus had previously arranged this deal, or this could be an example of divine foreknowledge that the Holy Spirit gives Jesus. When the disciples get into the village, they find a donkey and a colt just as Jesus had told them. This decision by Jesus to come into Jerusalem on a donkey is not an arbitrary decision but a purposeful decision. Jesus is well familiar with the prophecy in Zechariah 9:9 that says that when the Messiah comes into Jerusalem, He will not come on a war horse as a conquering king, but humbly on a donkey. By entering into Jerusalem on a donkey, Jesus is making two very clear statements: He is the Messiah, and He is a humble King.

It is not only Jesus who is familiar with this prophecy, for when the crowds see Him entering on a donkey a massive crowd develops around Him. There is an incredible celebration as people place palm branches and cloaks on the ground to pave the way for Jesus. This is why the Triumphal Entry is also called Palm

Sunday. As the crowds accompany Jesus into Jerusalem, the people begin to quote Psalm 118, as they shout, "Hosanna to the Son of David! Blessed is He who comes in the name of the Lord!" (verse 9; Psalm 118:26).

The way that this scene is developing, the natural next step would be for Jesus to be crowned King. After all, He is identifying Himself as the promised Messiah, and the crowds are praising Him as the Messiah. We know from the other gospels that Jesus arrives late that night and that He goes to the temple the next day; however, Matthew mentions it here to highlight the contrast of what

Harmony of the Events of Holy Week

Day	Event	Matthew	Mark	Luke	John
Friday/Saturday	Jesus arrives in Bethany				12:1
	Mary anoints Jesus				12:2–8
	Crowd comes to see Jesus				12:9–11
Sunday	Triumphal entry into Jerusalem	21:1–11	11:1–10	19:28–44	12:12–18
	Some Greeks seek Jesus				12:20–36
	Enters temple		11:11		
	Returns to Bethany	21:17	11:11		
Monday	Jesus curses the fig tree	21:18–19	11:12–14		
	Clears the temple	21:12–13	11:15–17	19:45–46	
	Returns to Bethany with the Twelve		11:19		
Tuesday	Disciples see the withered fig tree on the return to Jerusalem	21:20–22	11:20–21		
	Temple controversies in Jerusalem	21:23–23:39	11:27–12:44	20:1–21:4	
	Olivet Discourse on the return to Bethany	24:1–25:46	13:1–37	21:5–36	
Wednesday	Jesus continues daily teaching in the temple			21:37–38	
	Sanhedrin plots to kill Jesus	26:3–5	14:1–2	22:1–2	
Wednesday/Thursday	Preparations for the Passover	26:17–19	14:12–16	22:7–13	
Thursday	Passover meal/Last Supper	26:20–35	14:17–26	22:14–30	
	Upper Room Discourse				13:1–17:26
	Jesus prays in Gethsemane	26:36–46	14:32–42	22:39–46	
Friday	Betrayal and arrest (*after midnight?*)	26:47–56	14:43–52	22:47–53	18:2–12
	Jewish trial:				
	—before Annas				18:13–24
	—before Caiaphas and part of the Sanhedrin	26:57–75	14:53–72	22:54–65	18:19–24
	—before full Sanhedrin (*after sunrise?*)	27:1–2	15:1	22:66–71	
	Roman trials:				
	—before Pilate	27:2–14	15:2–5	23:1–5	
	—before Herod			23:6–12	
	—before Pilate	27:15–26	15:6–15	23:13–25	18:28–19:16
	Crucifixion (*approx. 9:00 A.M. to 3:00 P.M.*)	27:27–54	15:16–39	23:26–49	19:16–37
	Burial (*evening*)	27:57–61	15:42–47	23:50–54	19:38–42
Sunday	Empty-tomb witnesses	28:1–8	16:1–8	24:1–12	
	Resurrection appearances	28:9–20	16:9–20	24:13–53	20:1–21:25

Jesus sees in the temple with the excitement and joy that accompanies Jesus into the city. When Jesus goes into the temple, the priests and religious leaders should recognize this and anoint Him as their King. Instead, when Jesus enters the temple, He finds that it is corrupt. The Court of the Gentiles, the one part of the temple where Gentiles were allowed, and which was supposed to be devoted to prayer, is a marketplace. So Jesus cleanses the temple by driving out all of the money changers and business people from the temple. Rather than being "a house of prayer," the temple has become "a den of thieves" (verse 13). Even worse, when the religious leaders see the people praising Jesus and shouting, they demand that He silence the crowds. Yet Jesus refuses, telling them that God has ordained this praise.

Later, Jesus and His disciples are traveling to Jerusalem, and Jesus sees a fig tree that has no figs on it. Jesus curses the fig tree; and immediately, it begins to wither. We know from the other gospels that there is a gap in time between when Jesus curses the fig tree and when it is fully withered. However, when the disciples ask Jesus how this fig tree could wither so soon, Jesus reminds them once again about the incredible power of faith. While this fig tree serves as a lesson to the disciples about the power of faith, it also is a metaphor for Israel. Like the fig tree, Israel should be producing the fruit of righteousness; but when it fails to produce righteousness, it will be destroyed.

As Jesus enters the temple again, He begins a series of interactions with the religious leaders that will ultimately make these religious leaders look incredibly foolish. The chief priests and elders come to Jesus and confront Him about where He gets the authority to do and say the things that He does. Jesus has already told them on many occasions that His authority comes from God Himself, but He knows that they have already made up their minds about Him. So Jesus masterfully answers their question with another question. Jesus asks them what they think about John the Baptist and the works that he did. He asks them if they think that John's baptism was from heaven (God) or from man. It had been well known that John the Baptist had directed people to Jesus and supported Him, so if they say that John was from God, they would have to acknowledge that Jesus is from God. However, if they deny John the Baptist and say that he was not from God, the crowds would turn on them since everyone respects John the Baptist. So they simply say that they do not know. So Jesus refuses to answer their question, as well.

Thought Question:

If Jesus cleanses the temple because they buy and sell things there, is it wrong to buy and sell things in church?

A Battle of Wits: Matthew 21:28–23:39

Lesson 20

For a long time, Jesus has known that persecution and death await Him in Jerusalem. Now that He has arrived, it is time for there to be a confrontation between Jesus and the religious leaders. Between chapters 21 and 23, Jesus engages in a number of discussions or discourses about and with the various religious groups in Jerusalem; and at every step, Jesus proves Himself to be the far superior person.

We saw in the last lesson that it is the religious leaders who initiate this series of conflicts between Jesus and them. Jesus now responds with a series of parables, all directed at the religious leaders. In the first parable, Jesus speaks about two sons of a vineyard owner. The first son says he will go and work in the vineyard but does not end up going, and the second son says he will not go but ends up going. When He asks the Pharisees which son has done better, they agree that the one who actually goes and works is the better son. Jesus then hits them with the point of this parable: they are the son who is all words, who says he will go but does not. The tax collectors and harlots are the ones who are actually doing the work, and as such are better.

In the next parable, Jesus compares the religious leaders to the tenants of a vineyard. In this parable, the vineyard owner lends out his vineyard to some tenants, but when he sends his servants to collect the fruit of the vineyard, the tenants beat and kill the servants. Finally, the owner of the vineyard sends his own son, thinking that they would not possibly mistreat his son; but they kill the son, hoping to take his inheritance for themselves. When Jesus asks the religious leaders what the vineyard owner will do to the tenants, they acknowledge that he will kill all of those tenants and lease out the vineyard to those who will produce fruit. After citing Psalm 118, which speaks of the stone that the builders rejected becoming the chief cornerstone, Jesus tells the religious leaders that they are the wicked tenants and that the kingdom of God will be taken away from them and given to another nation. That other nation refers to the Gentiles, who will receive the kingdom after the Jews reject it. The religious leaders perceive that Jesus is talking about them, but they cannot do anything because of the crowds.

In a third parable, Jesus speaks of a great wedding feast. The king arranges this wedding for his son. Yet, when he invites the guests to come to this wedding, they refuse. Like the tenants in the previous parable, the guests of this wedding seize and kill the servants of the king. When the king discovers this, he has the guests put to death. Since the king still needs guests for his son's wedding, he opens the invitation to all who would come. Many come to this wedding, but one is found at the wedding who is not prepared with the appropriate clothes. This guest is thrown out from the wedding because he is not prepared. In this parable, the religious leaders (which represent Israel in general) are the original guests who refuse the invitation and are put to death. The new guests are the Gentiles and "sinners." And the one who is kicked out from the wedding is the person who does not have faith in Jesus Christ and as such is not clothed with His righteousness. With all three of these parables, Jesus makes it clear that judgment is coming upon the Jews in general and the religious leaders in particular because of their rejection of Himself. Nevertheless, because of their rejection, the kingdom will be given to Gentiles and sinners.

After Jesus gives these parables, the religious leaders fire back at Jesus with a series of questions designed to trap Jesus. The first of these groups to confront Jesus is the Herodians, the supporters of King Herod. They attempt to trap Jesus by asking Him whether or not the people should pay taxes to Caesar. If Jesus says "yes," He will lose popularity with the people; but if Jesus says "no," this would be seen as an act of treason that would get Jesus arrested and possibly killed. Yet Jesus sees their trap and tells them that they are to give Caesar what is Caesar's and give God what is God's. By saying this, Jesus affirms the validity of governments while still calling people to obey and honor God.

The next trap is set by the Sadducees. The Sadducees are a religious and political group that has power in the Sanhedrin, the governing body that oversees the synagogues in that area. These people do not believe in the resurrection or anything supernatural, and they only follow the first five books of Moses as Scripture. They attempt to trap Jesus with an apparent contradiction in the Law. They bring up a hypothetical situation wherein a woman marries seven brothers because each one dies. At the resurrection, they ask, whose wife will she be? However, Jesus simply shrugs off this trap and fires back, telling them that they know neither the Scriptures nor the power of God. In the resurrection,

she will be nobody's wife but will be single like the angels. This tells us that marriage is only for this life and not the next. As proof that this life is not all that there is and that there will be a resurrection someday, Jesus quotes the Scriptures that speak about God as the God of Abraham, Isaac, and Jacob, even though they are dead. Yet God says this in the present tense, implying that these men still exist, thus proving that there is life after death.

Following this, Jesus faces a question from an expert in the Law. This expert in the Law asks Jesus what the greatest commandment is in all of the Law. Jesus' first answer is one that would not have surprised the people, for it had been widely accepted as the greatest commandment in the Law. Jesus quotes the **Shema** from Deuteronomy 6, which says that we are to love God with everything we have. However, Jesus gives a second command that this expert in the Law is not expecting, the command to love our neighbors as ourselves. To Jesus, these two commandments are linked together, for we cannot love God if we do not love one another. In fact, Jesus argues that these two commandments summarize the entire Law.

Now it is Jesus' turn to trap the religious leaders. When the Pharisees are gathered together, Jesus asks them a question concerning the Christ. He asks them whose descendant the Christ is supposed to be. They answer that the Christ is supposed to be a descendant of David. However, Jesus then quotes Psalm 110, which states, "The LORD said to my Lord…" (22:44). It is clear that this passage speaks about the Christ, but if David was the most powerful person in Israel and the first LORD is God, then who is the second "Lord" in this verse? Jesus quotes this to show that the second "Lord" has to be someone greater than David for him to call the person "Lord." Jesus indicates that this other Lord is the Christ but is also God Himself. The Pharisees have no answer to Jesus' question, so they remain silent. In addition, they see that they cannot trap Jesus, so they stop asking Him questions.

With the religious leaders silent and defeated, Jesus goes on the offensive against these leaders. Jesus speaks to the crowds, warning them about the damaging hypocrisy of the religious leaders. Out of respect and submission to their positions of authority, Jesus says that the people are to obey the leaders, but they are not to imitate their way of life. The religious leaders do all of their religious deeds in order to gain praise and admiration from others. They put burdens on people but refuse to help them. They love to be called "teacher" or "Rabbi," but only God is our true Teacher and Rabbi. These people strive to be the greatest, yet in Jesus' kingdom, the one who is the greatest is the one who is the best servant and the one who humbles himself, unlike these religious leaders.

Jesus then sends a series of woes against the religious leaders. For a prophet to send a woe is tantamount to condemning that person or nation to destruction. Rather than going into detail about each of the woes that Jesus sends, there are some common themes that can be identified in all of them. Jesus condemns these leaders because they are hypocrites. They go to incredible lengths to appear to be holy and righteous, yet they ruin people's lives with their teachings and their actions. They make up ridiculous rules or laws and use their authority to condemn people just because they do not follow their made up rules. They go to ridiculous lengths to obey even the minutest detail of their rules and laws, yet they neglect the far greater matters of justice and mercy and faith. They are so concerned with appearance that they completely neglect the far more important matters of the heart and of character. These leaders are vipers, poisoning and killing the people around them. They are just like the leaders from Israel's past who regularly killed God's servants, the prophets. Like those previous leaders, these religious leaders are planning to kill the greatest Prophet Israel will ever have, Jesus Himself.

After confronting the religious leaders, Jesus offers a lament over Jerusalem, just as the prophet Jeremiah had done centuries before. Jesus identifies Jerusalem as the one who kills the prophets and laments the fact that He longs to give salvation to the people, yet they are not willing. As a result, their house is going to be desolate. When Jesus says that Jerusalem's house is desolate, He speaks about not only the lack of salvation of the people but also the coming destruction of the temple. In fact, in the very next chapter, Jesus is going to speak directly about the destruction of the temple. Then Jesus finishes this discourse saying that He will not be coming back to Jerusalem until the people there are ready to praise Him as the Messiah by quoting Psalm 118, as the crowds did when Jesus first entered Jerusalem.

> **Shema:** Deuteronomy 6:4–6, called the Shema because, in these verses, the first word in Hebrew is *shema*

Thought Questions:

1. How do you feel you would fare if you engaged in a battle of the wits as Jesus does here? What are some ways you could better prepare yourself for this kind of battle?

2. When Jesus speaks these woes upon the Pharisees in chapter 23, what emotion do you think He is conveying? Are there any situations today where we should respond the way that Jesus does here? What are those situations?

The Olivet Discourse: Matthew 24

Lesson 21

We have seen during the Holy Week that this should have been the week that Jesus is crowned king by the Israelites. He enters Jerusalem as the prophesied King from Zechariah by riding in on a donkey. He even goes into the temple where a king would normally be crowned. Yet when Jesus gets there, He sees corruption and experiences rejection from the religious leaders. At the end of chapter 23, Jesus laments over Jerusalem and speaks of its coming destruction. This theme is what permeates the Olivet Discourse in chapter 24.

There are some passages in Scripture that are more controversial and open to interpretation than others. When it comes to prophecies about the future, there is much room for debate. For the sake of this class, multiple interpretations will be offered, but it is up to the student to discern for himself or herself which interpretation best fits the text.

This discourse begins in the temple as the disciples are admiring the building. As they are admiring the temple, Jesus tells them plainly that the temple is going to be destroyed. It is important to remember this prophecy as we examine the rest of the discourse. After Jesus and His disciples leave the temple, they head to the Mount of Olives; there the disciples ask Jesus two questions: "When will these things be?" and "What will be the sign of Your coming, and of the end of the age?" (verse 3). The disciples appear to connect the destruction of the temple with Jesus' coming and the end of the age. The rest of Jesus' discourse is His answer to these two questions.

Jesus begins His answer by telling the disciples that things are going to get really messy before these things come to be. There are going to be wars and rumors of wars. There are going to be cataclysmic destructive events such as earthquakes, famines, and pestilence. False teachers will arise and attempt to deceive people, claiming to be the Christ. And after these things, the disciples will be persecuted and put to death and hated by people because of Jesus. In addition, there will be lawlessness, and the love of many will grow cold. Finally, the gospel will be preached to all the nations before the end comes. There are two primary interpretations as to when these things will take place. The first interpretation is that these events have to take place in the lifetime of the disciples and refer to the chaotic years leading up to the destruction of the temple in A.D. 70. The second option is that these events refer to the Great Tribulation near the end of the world. There are plenty of parallels between the kinds of things that Jesus predicts will happen here and the events described in the book of Revelation.

In verse 15, Jesus gives a clear sign that the end is coming soon. When the "abomination of desolation" is found standing in the holy place of the temple, then it will be time to flee. This abomination of desolation is the person prophesied by Daniel in chapters 9 and 11. In the context of Daniel, this man enters and shuts down the temple. This abomination of desolation is also called the Antichrist elsewhere in Scripture. Here in Matthew 24, Jesus warns the disciples that the clear sign to get out of Jerusalem is when they see this man in the temple. Jesus warns them to get out of the city and flee to the mountains. Because destruction is going to follow so quickly, they are not to look back but simply to flee, just as Lot and his family were to flee Sodom and not look back. Jesus warns the disciples again to be on guard from false messiahs. Jesus makes it clear that when He returns, it will not be in secret but everyone will know that He has returned. There have been people since this time that have claimed to be the return of Jesus; but Jesus makes it clear that we will know for sure when He returns. Once again, as with the previous prophecy, some believe that this will be fulfilled with the destruction of the temple in A.D. 70, but others believe it will be fulfilled near the end of the world.

Jesus next quotes Isaiah 13 and speaks about the darkening of the sun and the moon and the falling of the stars from the sky. These events are supposed to take place immediately after the previous events. As this is taking place, Jesus will return on the clouds of heaven with His angels. All of the tribes of the earth will see this sign and will mourn as they see judgment coming. With a trumpet call, Jesus will gather together all of the elect (Christians). There are three popular interpretations of this prophecy. *First*, people believe that this is referring to Jesus' second coming at the end of the Great Tribulation near the end of the world. *Second*, others believe that this event refers to the **rapture**, a time either before or in the middle of the Great Tribulation when Jesus will take away Christians from the earth in order to spare us from the destruction that is coming. *Third*, some believe that this refers to the destruction of the temple in A.D. 70. According to this third view, the sun and moon being darkened and the stars falling are symbols representing the destruction of a nation. In the case of Isaiah, whom Jesus quotes here, these signs were mentioned with reference to the destruction of Babylon. There are times in Scripture when the sun, moon, and stars represent the leaders of nations. One such example is Joseph's dream, in which the twelve tribes are represented by twelve stars. Under this view, the gathering of the elect does not refer to Christians being taken away from the earth, but the spread of the gospel to the entire world.

Just as it is difficult to explain the gathering of the elect by those who believe that this was fulfilled with the destruction of the temple, the next passage is difficult to explain for those who believe that these events are in the future. After using a fig tree to encourage His disciples to read the signs of the times, Jesus says in verse 34 that "this generation will by no means pass away till all these things take place." It would appear based on this statement that all of the things that Jesus has just prophesied would have to take place within one generation. If a generation is approximately forty years, the destruction of the temple fits that requirement. For those who believe in a future fulfillment of this passage, it has been argued that "generation" could mean race; thus this would mean that these events would happen before humanity is done on this earth.

Jesus compares these events with the situation of the people during Noah's day. The people in that day continued to live their normal lives, not realizing that destruction is coming suddenly. Also, when these prophecies are fulfilled, they will come suddenly while people are living their normal lives. Jesus gives a couple of scenarios in which one person will be taken and one person will be left behind when these things happen. As with the rest of these prophecies, there are at least two main interpretations of this passage. The *first interpretation* is the possibility that this is a reference to the rapture, when one person will be taken while others are left behind. Viewing this as a reference to the destruction of the temple, the *second interpretation* is the explanation that the Roman army will take some captive when they conquer Jerusalem while leaving others behind.

Even though there is much room for disagreement concerning the specifics of this prophecy, the message of this prophecy is clear. More important than when Jesus returns is how we are to live as we wait for that day. If we are found to be lazy and rebellious as we wait for Jesus, we will be punished like the hypocrites. We need to live each day as if Jesus could return.

rapture: an event either at the beginning or the middle of the Great Tribulation when Jesus will take away the Christians from the earth

Thought Question:

How might you live your life differently if you knew that Jesus would return today?

Parables for Preparation: Matthew 25

Lesson 22

We learned in the last lesson that some incredible things are in store for the disciples and the world in the future. While it is interesting to debate the specifics as to what is going to happen and when it is going to happen, Jesus is far more concerned with how we live our lives as we wait for Him. Jesus knows that He is going to die soon, and eventually He will go to be with the Father. While He is gone, Jesus is concerned with how His people live their lives. In chapter 25, Jesus gives two parables and a straightforward teaching, all of which make the same point: we need to live our lives as though Jesus could return any moment.

The first parable that Jesus gives in chapter 25 is about a wedding. In this parable, the bridegroom goes on a journey. While he is gone, there are ten virgins who are supposed to attend the wedding when the bridegroom arrives. Five of these virgins are wise and keep extra oil for their lamps, but five are foolish and do not bring reserves. Because the bridegroom is delayed in his return, the five foolish virgins run out of oil and have to go out to get more oil. However, while these foolish virgins are gone, the bridegroom arrives and the wedding takes place. Because these foolish virgins are not ready, they are not allowed to join in with the wedding. The message of this parable is simple: we need to be ready because we do not know when Jesus will return.

The second parable also carries the theme of living well while the master is gone. In the parable of the talents, there is a master who gives money to his servants while he travels on a journey. To one of his servants he gives five talents, to another two talents, and to the third he gives one talent. Both the servant who receives five talents and the one who receives two talents wisely invest that money so that they double the return. The person who receives only one talent, however, buries it in the ground because he is afraid. While both of the first two servants are rewarded by the master, the one who does nothing with the money is cast away, and the talent is

taken away from him. The message of this parable is that we have to make the most of the time that we have while Jesus is away. When Jesus returns, we will have to give an account of what we did with our lives. If we are lazy and do nothing with our lives while He is gone, that meeting will not be pleasant. Yet, if we are faithful, we will be rewarded.

After making these two parables, Jesus gives a straightforward teaching. Jesus is going to leave; however, there is a day when He will return with His angels and take His throne. On that day, all of the nations will be gathered together, and there will be a great separation. Scholars call this separation the judgment of the sheep and the goats. On the right, the King will reward and bless the sheep because of what they did while He was away. While the King was away, these people took care of the poor and the needy and, in doing so, truly served the King. Yet, on the left, the King will condemn the goats, for they refused to help out the poor and the needy and, in doing so, neglected the King Himself. The message of this teaching is the same as the last parable: while Jesus is gone, we need to continue to serve others and do good works, for when we serve others we are really serving Jesus. Yet, if we are lazy and rebellious while He is gone and neglect those in need, only judgment and condemnation await us when Jesus returns.

Thought Question:

How faithful do you think you have been with the talents and resources God has given you? What might be some ways you can be more faithful?

Preparation for the True Passover: Matthew 26

Lesson 23

Jesus has spent a lot of time and energy preparing His disciples for His upcoming crucifixion and resurrection. In chapter 26, the time draws close for all that Jesus has prepared His disciples to encounter.

The first story we encounter in Matthew 26 actually takes place before Jesus ever enters Jerusalem during the Holy Week. We learn that the religious leaders have had enough of Jesus and conspire together to try to trick and arrest Jesus. Then we are told the story of Jesus' anointing with oil while He was at Bethany. We know from the other gospel accounts that this event takes place on the Saturday before the Holy Week, but Matthew includes it here because it connects with Jesus' betrayal. While Jesus is eating, a woman comes into the room and pours a very expensive flask of perfume on Jesus' head. His disciples rebuke this woman because she could have sold that perfume to give the money to the poor. Yet Jesus rebukes the disciples, telling them that she is doing a very good thing and that they will always have the poor, but they will not have Jesus for long. In fact, Jesus sees this anointing as preparation for His upcoming burial. Because of this event, Judas goes to the religious leaders and agrees to betray Jesus for thirty pieces of silver.

On Thursday night, Jesus and His disciples gather together to partake of the Passover meal. It was customary for people to celebrate the Passover on Friday; but Jesus knows that He is going to be crucified on that day, so they eat the meal on Thursday. It is more than a mere coincidence that Jesus will be betrayed during this particular festival. The Passover Festival commemorates the last plague on Egypt, the death of the firstborn. It is called the Passover because the angel of the Lord passed over any house that had the blood of a pure, spotless lamb over the doorpost. God has the Israelites go through the ritual of killing a pure, spotless lamb and covering their doorposts with its blood because that is going to be a picture of what Jesus will come to do. Jesus is going to be the ultimate Passover Lamb whose blood will save His people from ultimate death.

As they are eating the meal, Jesus tells the disciples that one of the twelve is going to betray Him that very night. Each of the disciples denies that he will betray Him, but Jesus cryptically shows that Judas is going to be the one. Then Jesus gives what has become known as the Lord's Supper. Here Jesus transforms some of the symbolism for the traditional elements of the Passover meal. Jesus takes the bread, breaks it, and gives it to the disciples. He tells them that this bread now represents His body, which is going to be broken for them. He also takes the wine and tells them that the wine represents His blood, which will be shed for the forgiveness of sins. By doing this, Jesus establishes this meal as a practice that the Church will follow for centuries. To this day, Christians still observe this practice in order to remember and preach Jesus' death on our behalf.

After the meal, Jesus brings His disciples to the Mount of Olives and to the garden of Gethsemane. Along the way, Jesus tells the disciples that they will all stumble that very night. Yet Peter, as always, speaks up and tells Jesus that he will never stumble. Jesus tells Peter that he will not only stumble, but he will deny Jesus three times before the rooster crows. When they get to the garden of Gethsemane, Jesus brings His three closest disciples—Peter, James, and John—to be with Him. Jesus wants these disciples to wait and pray while He

spends some time in prayer. Jesus' prayer is very powerful. Jesus knows that He is not only about to face the wrath of man, but also the wrath of God. His humanity really shows in this prayer as He asks God to take away the cup of His wrath that Jesus will have to take. Jesus does not want to suffer, but His greater desire is to obey His Father. So even more than His own will, Jesus prays for the Father's will to be done. Sadly, on three separate occasions Jesus returns to His disciples and finds them asleep. In the moments when Jesus needs His friends the most, they cannot stay awake with Him.

As Jesus meets His sleeping disciples for the third time, He tells them to get up, for He is about to be betrayed. Because it is night and it would be hard to identify people in the dark, Judas tells the religious leaders that the person he kisses is the One they are to arrest. When Judas meets Jesus, he brings with him a multitude with weapons to arrest Him. When Jesus is arrested, one of His disciples, who is identified as Peter in John 18:10, cuts off the ear of the servant of the high priest. However, Jesus rebukes this disciple and tells him to put his sword away. If Jesus wanted to fight this moment, He could call upon legions of angels, but He has to go through this. When His disciples see Him peaceably surrender to the crowds, they all flee.

Jesus is then brought to the house of Caiaphas, the high priest. The trial that Jesus goes through is completely illegal. According to the laws of the Jews, if a person is to stand trial it needs to be in the open, not in secret like this trial. Even though false witnesses make their accusations against Jesus, their testimonies contradict one another; and they say nothing that would merit death. Finally, one witness misquotes a statement that Jesus makes about the temple. Jesus actually had said for them to destroy the temple and He would raise it in three days, referring to His body (John 2:19). However, they accuse Jesus of saying that He was going to destroy the temple. Yet, even with this false accusation, Jesus remains silent. Finally, the high priest makes Jesus take an oath and asks Him plainly if He is the Christ. Jesus affirms that He is indeed the Christ and that He is going to be sitting at the right hand of the Father and He will come on the clouds of heaven (Daniel 7:13–14). When Jesus says this, He quotes Daniel's prophecy, which speaks of the Christ receiving a kingdom from God as He comes on the clouds. It is this statement that leads the high priest to condemn Jesus. Then the guards spit in Jesus' face and strike Him and mock Him.

Meanwhile, we learn that Peter has followed Jesus to His mock trial. On three separate occasions, people accuse Peter of being one of Jesus' disciples. Each time, presumably out of fear, Peter denies that he knows Jesus. After the third denial, Peter hears the rooster crow. Realizing that he had done precisely what Jesus had predicted and that he had just betrayed Jesus, Peter leaves and weeps bitterly.

Thought Question:

Why do you think the disciples abandon Jesus when He is arrested rather than going with Him?

The Passion of the Christ: Matthew 27

Lesson 24

When it comes to the trial and crucifixion of Christ, the gospel writers make it abundantly clear that Jesus is completely innocent and that the trials He endures are completely unjust. We learned in the last lesson that the trial under Caiaphas is completely illegal and that, even with false witnesses coming forward, Jesus is completely innocent. However, after Jesus admits that He is the Christ, the religious leaders now have their "evidence" to put Jesus to death.

Even though the religious leaders have declared that Jesus is worthy of death, they do not have the authority to put Jesus to death; so they bring Him to Pilate. Pontius Pilate, the Roman governor of that region, does have the authority to execute criminals; so Jesus stands trial before him, as well. However, before we learn the details of this trial, we see what happens to Judas, who had betrayed Jesus. Because of the incredible guilt of his betrayal, Judas gives the money back to the chief priests and then hangs himself. With that money, the priests buy a potter's field in which to bury strangers. Matthew makes reference to two prophets. Zechariah earned thirty pieces of silver, which he threw into the temple to the potter who worked there (Zechariah 11:12–13); and Jeremiah, the "prophet of woe," bought a field according to God's instruction (Jeremiah 32:9).

As with His trial before Caiaphas, when accusations are made against Jesus before Pilate, Jesus remains silent. Yet, also as with the trial before Caiaphas, when asked a direct question about who He is, Jesus affirms that He is the King of the Jews. The innocence of Jesus is proven once again by the response of Pilate. Pilate tells the crowd that he sees nothing wrong in Jesus that would merit death. In order to bring back some sanity to the crowds, Pilate gives them a choice of whom they would like to have released to them. It was customary during the Passover Feast for the governor to release one pris-

oner to the people. Pilate gives the crowd the choice to release Jesus or a murderer named Barabbas or Jesus to the people. Ironically, the name *Barabbas* means "Son of the father." The people would rather have a murderer released in their midst than to have the true "Son of the Father" released. This also highlights how incredibly unjust and wicked this whole situation is. The religious leaders are so desperate to get rid of Jesus that they would let a dangerous criminal free in their midst. In addition, in the midst of all of this, Pilate's wife warns him not to do anything to Jesus because He is innocent.

Rather than releasing Jesus, the crowds begin to riot, shouting that they want Jesus to be crucified. So Pilate has Jesus scourged before He would be crucified. The scourging in itself would be enough to almost kill a man, as it would have destroyed His back. Yet the injustice continues as Jesus is brought before the Roman soldiers and mocked. They put a scarlet robe and a crown of thorns on Jesus and beat Him. When they take off that robe after the scourging, it would reopen all of the wounds that had been caused. Finally, they send Jesus to be crucified.

Because of the destruction of Jesus' body by all of the beatings and the scourging, the guards force Simon of Cyrene to carry Jesus' cross for Him. When Jesus arrives at Golgotha, just outside the city of Jerusalem, they take His clothes and divide them among the soldiers and cast lots for them in order to fulfill yet another prophecy. When Jesus is crucified, they mockingly put up a sign over Him saying that He is the King of the Jews. Even on the cross Jesus is mocked by all who pass by and even by the two thieves who are crucified with Him.

From about the sixth hour (noon), until the ninth hour (3 p.m.), there is darkness over the land while Jesus is on the cross. It is only fitting that darkness would fill the land as the people try to get rid of the Light of the World. Finally, at the ninth hour, Jesus cries out, "Eli, Eli, lama sabachthani," which means, "My God, My God, why have You forsaken Me?" When Jesus says this, He is quoting Psalm 22, known as a Messianic Psalm. Of all the things that Jesus has to endure, the worst is that Jesus is facing the wrath of God as He bears our sins on the cross. Finally, rather than slowly slipping off into death, Jesus lets out a loud noise and then gives up His spirit.

At that moment, the veil of the temple that separates the Holy Place from the Most Holy Place is torn in two from top to bottom. That veil represents the barrier between God and humanity. With Jesus dying, there is no longer that wall of separation between God and man. Also, there is an earthquake and many people are raised from the dead and are seen walking around Jerusalem. Even the centurion and the soldiers with him acknowledge that Jesus is the Son of God. Rather than allowing Jesus to be buried with criminals, one of His followers, Joseph of Arimathea, asks for permission to bury Jesus in a new tomb that he had just made. So Jesus is buried in the tomb of a rich man, fulfilling yet another prophecy about the Christ.

Interestingly, even though the disciples do not seem to remember all of the times when Jesus had informed them about His death and resurrection, the religious leaders do remember what Jesus had said. Because Jesus had spoken about a resurrection, the chief priests and the Pharisees ask for guards to be sent to watch over the tomb. If the disciples were to steal the body, they could argue that Jesus had been resurrected and the leaders' "problem" would never end. So soldiers are dispatched to watch over the tomb. This provides even more proof for the reliability of the resurrection. Because of these soldiers, it is clear that neither the disciples, nor anyone else, could have stolen the body of Jesus. The only explanation for the empty tomb has to be a supernatural one. However, we will examine that in the next chapter.

Thought Questions:

1. Why do you think the crowds are so vehement to have Jesus killed?

2. Why do you think Jesus remains silent when all of the accusations are made against Him?

The Resurrection and Great Commission: Matthew 28

Lesson 25

In Genesis 3, when God curses the serpent, He says that He will place enmity between the Seed of the woman and the seed of the serpent; the serpent's seed will strike the heel of the woman's Seed, but the Seed of the woman will crush its head. While this does speak to the kind of relationship that humans have with snakes, most scholars believe this ultimately to be a prophecy about the battle between Jesus and Satan. With the cross, it would appear at first sight that Satan has had a great victory; however, we will see in chapter 28 that Satan merely struck Jesus' heel, and Jesus is about to crush his head.

Early on Sunday morning, some of the women who had followed Jesus go to the tomb to try to prepare His body further. Yet, when they get to the tomb, they find that the stone that sealed the tomb had been rolled

back and Jesus was not in the tomb. To their shock, they meet an angel at the tomb who tells them that Jesus has risen from the dead. They are to go and tell the disciples to go to Galilee to meet Jesus. Filled with fear and joy, the women go to tell the disciples the good news. On the way to meet the disciples, however, the women are met by Jesus Himself. Jesus Himself also tells the women to tell the disciples to meet Him in Galilee.

We learned in chapter 27 that the Jews had hired some guards to watch over the tomb to make sure that nobody could steal the body. In chapter 28, we learn that these guards go back to the religious leaders to tell them what had happened with the empty tomb. The religious leaders know that if the word of the empty tomb spreads, the popularity of Jesus will not be able to be contained. So they pay a large sum of money to the guards to get them to tell people that the disciples stole the body. Even to this very day, some people try to explain away the resurrection by saying that the disciples stole the body. As a side note, it is absurd to believe that the disciples actually stole the body. Later, every one of the disciples, with the exception of John, will die for his belief in the resurrection. It is hard to believe that one person would die for something he knows is a lie, let alone ten.

The disciples listen to Jesus and go to Galilee to meet Him. When they see Jesus there, they worship Him, but some of the disciples doubt what they are seeing. However, Jesus uses this meeting to commission His disciples for the work that they are to do while He is gone. Because of His faithfulness to the Father even unto death, Jesus has been given all authority in heaven and on earth. The cross was not Jesus' defeat, but His ultimate source of victory. It is with the authority that Jesus has received that He now sends His disciples.

During Jesus' earthly ministry, He had been very careful to focus His mission primarily on the Israelites. Yet now Jesus commissions His disciples to bring the gospel to all the nations, not just Israel. The main verb in this commission is to *make disciples* (μαθητευω). Just as Jesus had invested so much time and energy into the disciples, they are to do the same thing for others. There are three ways that we are to make disciples of all the nations. *First*, we are to do this as we go. This does not mean that we all need to go overseas in order to make disciples; rather, it means we are to take advantage of any opportunity daily to make disciples. *Second*, as we go, we are to baptize others in the name of the Trinity. When a person is baptized, he or she publicly identifies with Christ and proclaims to the world that he or she is a Christian. *Third*, along with baptism, we are to teach others to obey everything that Jesus had commanded. The Great Commission is not simply about sharing the gospel; it is about taking that gospel and teaching people how to be mature disciples of Jesus. In addition, even though Jesus is about to leave and go back to the Father, He reminds the disciples that He will always be with them. When Jesus leaves, the Father will send the Holy Spirit to be with the disciples so that Jesus will be able to be with them always.

Thought Question:

Why do you think it is not until after the resurrection that Jesus explicitly sends out His disciples to the nations outside of Israel?

Introduction to Mark
Lesson 26

As mentioned in the introductory lesson to the gospels, even though Mark appears as the second gospel in the New Testament, some scholars believe that it was actually the first gospel written. Mark is the simplest of all of the gospels. Compared to the other synoptic gospels, Mark omits a large portion of the teachings of Jesus. Though, rather than omitting these teachings of Christ, some scholars conclude that Mark did not have access to them. But since there are so many sections of Matthew, Mark, and Luke that are exactly the same, it is likely that two of these authors use the third one as a source. It is more likely that Matthew and Luke used Mark as their source than that Mark simply omits large sections of Matthew or Luke.

Mark's full name is John Mark. From Acts we learn that John Mark was one of the Apostle Paul's early travel companions. During Paul's first missionary journey, Mark abandoned Paul and Barnabas (Acts 13:13). Because of this, when Barnabas wants to take Mark with them on their second missionary journey, Paul disagrees so strongly that Paul and Barnabas part ways (Acts 15:37–39). Yet it appears that Paul and Mark had been reconciled, for in 2 Timothy 4:11 Paul specifically asks for Mark to be sent to him. Because Mark was not one of Jesus' disciples during His earthly ministry, Mark had to receive the information for his gospel from one of the disciples. Church tradition tells us that Peter is the primary person from whom Mark receives the information for his gospel. Moreover, Peter calls Mark "my son" in 1 Peter 5:13, and he probably knew Mark early on because the church met in the home of Mark's mother (Acts 12:12). This tells us a lot about the humility that Peter develops over the years, for

Peter and the disciples do not look very good in Mark's gospel. One of the themes that runs throughout Mark's gospel is the failure of the disciples. Even though Mark was not around during the earthly ministry of Jesus, it is possible that he does make an appearance in his own gospel. In Mark's account of Jesus' arrest, he includes a superfluous detail about a young man who was there who runs away naked when the soldiers grab him (Mark 14:51–52). Mark's gospel is the only gospel that mentions this story, and it is possible that the young man is Mark himself.

Unlike the gospel of Matthew, which is directed towards a Jewish audience, Mark's gospel is directed towards a Gentile audience. In Matthew's gospel, the kingdom is called the kingdom of heaven; but in Mark's gospel, it has the more generic term "the kingdom of God." Mark also makes references to the Latin names of certain things, which makes sense if his audience is in Rome, where Latin was spoken. Whereas Matthew places a large focus on the fulfillment of Old Testament Scriptures, Mark focuses on Jesus as the heroic Man of action. The word "immediately" is used often throughout Mark's gospel, showing Jesus always working. Jesus as the heroic Man of action would appeal to the Gentiles in Rome whose culture is filled with stories of heroes.

The dating of Mark is dependent upon whether or not Matthew used Mark as a source for his gospel or if Mark used Matthew as the source of his gospel. If this was the first gospel written, it could have been written as early as the late 50s A.D. If the audience of this letter is indeed Roman Christians, it was likely written in the early to mid-60s A.D. before Emperor Nero began to severely persecute Christians in Rome. If Mark was written after Matthew, it would obviously place this letter later, closer to the mid-60s A.D.

As mentioned earlier, one of the themes that permeates the gospel of Mark is the failure of the disciples. Mark seems to highlight their failure more than any other gospel. Another theme that runs throughout Mark's gospel is Jesus' power over demons. It makes sense that Mark would emphasize Jesus' authority over demons since Mark portrays Jesus as a hero.

There is one textual issue that merits discussion here. As scholars have discovered more and more manuscripts of Mark's gospel, it has become increasingly difficult to believe that the end of Mark's gospel (Mark 16:9–20) was included in the original gospel. All of the earliest manuscripts of Mark's gospel do not contain these verses. This does not mean that these verses could not be considered as part of Scripture, for it is possible that this section had simply been lost in some of the places where these early manuscripts have been found. However, if this section of Mark was not originally included in Mark's gospel, it leaves us with a difficult question: Do we read and preach this section in the same way we would read the rest of the Bible? Upon examining the content of this section, almost everything that is contained there is also found in the other gospels. The only unique material in this section is the part in which Jesus says that Christians could pick up snakes and drink poison without getting hurt. We do see Paul being bitten by a snake later in Acts 28:3 without getting hurt. Yet common sense would tell us not to drink poison or pick up dangerous snakes anyway. It is recommended to simply connect the teachings in this section with the other parts of Scripture that say the same thing. For example, Mark contains an abbreviated form of the Great Commission found in Matthew's gospel. When reading and meditating on this section of Mark's gospel, it would be prudent to then read the Great Commission from Matthew's gospel.

The Beginning of Jesus' Ministry: Mark 1

Lesson 27

In the introduction to the gospels, we learned that the gospels of Matthew, Mark, and Luke are known as the synoptic gospels. They are called this because these gospels look at the life of Christ through similar eyes. There are going to be large sections of these gospels that are either exactly the same, or largely the same. As a result, the lessons that we cover in Mark and Luke will cover much of the same material as Matthew. Yet each author also does add a different perspective to these stories.

From the beginning of Mark, we see a glaring difference between his gospel and Matthew's: Mark completely omits the birth narrative of Jesus. Matthew's gospel begins with the birth and early life of Jesus and how His early life fulfills prophecies from Scripture. Mark's gospel, however, picks up with the beginning of Jesus' public ministry as an adult. If Mark's gospel had been written first, it is possible that he simply did not have access to the birth narrative of Jesus. Yet it also fits the focus of Mark for this gospel to begin with action. Throughout his gospel Mark emphasizes Jesus as a heroic Man of action; so it only makes sense to begin the story with the beginning of Jesus' mission.

The event that marks the beginning of Jesus' ministry is the baptism by John the Baptist. Mark quotes a combination of Isaiah and Malachi's prophecies that speak of a messenger who will come before the Messiah to prepare the way for Him. John the Baptist is that messenger who prepared the way for Jesus by calling people to repent of their sins and be baptized. John the Baptist makes it abundantly clear that he is not the Messiah, but One is coming after him who will be the promised Messiah.

It is clear from the very beginning of Mark's gospel that Mark wants to get straight to the point. Rather than giving all of the background that Matthew gives about the baptism, Mark simply says that Jesus is baptized and that the Father affirms Jesus as His beloved Son. Like Matthew, Mark mentions the temptation in the wilderness, which immediately follows the baptism; however, Mark simply says that Jesus was tempted for forty days, without mentioning the specifics of those temptations. Mark also simplifies the calling of the first disciples. We learn that Jesus walks by the Sea of Galilee and calls Simon and Andrew, and later James and John, to leave their boats and follow Him. Of course, Mark highlights that the disciples leave everything and immediately follow Jesus.

Mark next highlights some of the various aspects of Jesus' work and ministry. As a minister of the gospel, Jesus publicly and boldly preaches the gospel in the synagogues. The people are amazed by the way that Jesus teaches, for unlike the other teachers, Jesus speaks with authority. Moreover, that authority is seen not only in the way that Jesus teaches, but also in the way that He interacts with demons. While in the synagogue, Jesus encounters a demon-possessed person and sternly rebukes the demon, and it submits to Him and leaves the person. As with Jesus' preaching, the people are amazed by the authority with which Jesus speaks, and His fame begins to spread around the region of Galilee.

Another major aspect of Jesus' ministry is the miracles that Jesus performs. After leaving the synagogue, Jesus heals Peter's mother-in-law of a sickness. As soon as she is healed of her sickness, she begins to provide for Jesus and His disciples; and Peter's house becomes the center of Jesus' mission in that town. People from all over that town bring their sick to Jesus and He heals them. More demon-possessed people are brought to Jesus, and He casts the demons out, sternly charging them to remain silent.

Even though Jesus is an incredible hero, He is human and realizes His need to recover. After a long day of ministry, Jesus gets up early and goes off to a solitary place to spend time in prayer and to seek out more direction from His Father. His disciples seek Him out and eventually find Him and let Him know that, once again, the whole town had come together to be healed by Him. Yet, to their surprise, Jesus does not go back to that town, but rather to the other towns in the area. Jesus has a message to spread, and He does not want to get bogged down in one area until that message spreads throughout Israel. As Jesus had done in the first town in Galilee, He goes throughout all of the towns, preaching in the synagogues and casting out demons.

The first chapter ends with yet another healing, this time of a leper. This leper has great faith and believes fully that Jesus can heal him; the issue is whether or not Jesus would be willing to heal him. As a leper, this person would have been used to being an outcast, seen as a sinner by the religious elite. If Jesus is a teacher like the other teachers, He would not be seen with a leper. However, Jesus is not like the other teachers, and He touches the leper and heals him. According to the Law of Moses, if a person touches a leper, he or she would be ceremonially unclean; so it is possible that this person had not experienced physical touch in years. Jesus has compassion on this man and touches him and heals him. As Jesus had done with the demons before in this chapter, He tells this man to remain silent about what Jesus has done for him. Yet the leper does not listen and tells everyone who would listen about what Jesus had done for him. As a result, Jesus no longer has the freedom to go into the cities because of the crowds. Yet, even in the more isolated places, people come out to Jesus to be healed.

Thought Question:

Why do you think Jesus tells the leper not to tell anyone about the healing?

Miracles, Opposition, and Disciples: Mark 2–3

Lesson 28

As one would expect, because of the incredible miracles of Jesus and the authority with which He speaks, He becomes quite popular wherever He goes. In chapters 2 and 3 of Mark, we see Jesus' ministry grow as He brings the gospel to even more areas. In addition, we also see in these chapters two other critical aspects of Jesus' ministry, His opposition and the choosing of the twelve disciples.

The first story we encounter in chapter 2 is the healing of the paralytic. Because of the incredible popularity that Jesus develops, very large crowds amass around Jesus. These crowds become so dense that the friends of this paralytic have to go up on the roof and dig a hole to lower the paralytic to Jesus. Rather than simply healing the paralytic, Jesus uses this as an opportunity to reveal more about Himself and His authority. So He says to the paralytic, "Son, your sins are forgiven you." When Jesus says this, the scribes and religious leaders present are appalled. The only person who could offer forgiveness is God Himself, the One who had been sinned against. For Jesus to forgive sins would be equivalent to us deciding to let one of our friends off the hook for stealing from another friend. The only person who has the authority to forgive is the one who is sinned against. By offering forgiveness, Jesus is making a very real claim to be God. To prove that Jesus has this authority, He heals the paralytic so that he is able to get up and walk out of that place.

From there, Jesus goes out to the sea in order to teach the crowds. Along the way, He meets a tax collector called Levi. This Levi is also called Matthew, the writer of the first gospel. When Jesus calls Levi to come and follow Him, he leaves everything and goes with Jesus. Levi then throws a party in his house and invites many of his friends. However, when the religious leaders see Jesus eating with these "sinners," they judge Jesus. Yet Jesus knows what these men are thinking and explains to them that these "sinners" are the very reason why Jesus came, for it is not the healthy who need a doctor but the sick.

This theme of opposition and judging continues over the next stories. Apparently, it was customary in Jesus' day for religious leaders and their followers to regularly fast. However, Jesus and His disciples do not engage in the ritual of fasting. When Jesus is confronted about this lack of fasting, He speaks to them in a parable. He tells them that it is inappropriate to fast when the bridegroom is around because that is a time of feasting. However, when the bridegroom leaves, that will be the time for fasting. By saying this, Jesus is foreshadowing His coming death and resurrection. Jesus then gives two analogies to illustrate His point. Both the examples of unshrunk cloth on an old garment and new wine in old wineskins teach the lesson that something new belongs with a new system. Jesus is not following the customs of the old system because He is bringing something completely new.

Once again, Jesus faces opposition from the Pharisees when His disciples grab some heads of grain on the Sabbath. Because the Pharisees were strict proponents of the Law and the tradition of the elders, they confront Jesus on this Sabbath violation. The Pharisees are so interested in the letter of the Law that they overlook common sense. Jesus' disciples are not eating an entire meal or doing any work, but they are snacking on some grain. Jesus reminds the Pharisees that even David had violated the strict letter of the Law when he ate the consecrated bread, which was reserved for only the priests. In the Pharisees' efforts to follow the strict letter of the Law, they had forgotten what the true purpose of the Sabbath is, to give rest. However, the Pharisees are hard-hearted and stubborn and will not receive what Jesus is teaching them. This is made evident when the Pharisees spy on Jesus to see if He will heal a man on the Sabbath. When a man with a shriveled hand comes to Jesus to be healed, the Pharisees watch intently in order to accuse Jesus. Nevertheless, Jesus confronts them and asks them if it is lawful on the Sabbath to do good or evil, to save life or to kill. The Pharisees know that they are being ridiculous, but because of their hardened hearts they refuse to answer Jesus. Jesus is grieved by their hardness of heart, so He heals the man in front of them. As a result of this, the Pharisees begin to conspire against Jesus to put Him to death.

After healing more people and casting out more demons, Jesus goes up on a mountain and chooses the twelve disciples. As mentioned before, these disciples play a vital role in Jesus' mission. Jesus knows that He is going to die and return to the Father, so while Jesus is gone, He is going to have to entrust His mission to others. So Jesus chooses the twelve disciples to give power over sicknesses and demons and to share the message of the kingdom.

From there, Jesus brings the twelve with Him into a house, and once again a huge crowd gathers around Him. There is so much ministry to do that Jesus does not even eat. His family and friends try to help and force Him to get some rest, but they do not understand what He is doing. In addition, the scribes come down from Jerusalem and begin to accuse Him of being demon-possessed. Yet Jesus quickly confronts them with their accusations and rebukes them for this serious accusation. Jesus shows them how ridiculous their ideas are, for if Satan is using Jesus to cast out his own demons, he would be fighting himself. It does not make sense for Satan to attack himself. Rather, Jesus argues, the fact that Jesus is casting out demons is proof that Jesus has overpowered Satan. It is impossible to plunder a strong man's house unless you first subdue the strong man. The scribes should see these demon exorcisms as proof that Jesus is conquering Satan, not that Satan is controlling Jesus. Nevertheless, these accusations are very serious, and Jesus tells the scribes that this kind of blasphemy against the Holy Spirit is unforgiveable. If a person is so stubborn that he refuses to see the clear

evidence that Jesus is conquering Satan by casting out demons, he cannot be forgiven.

After Jesus rebukes these scribes, His family, which had been trying to get Him to rest, comes and asks Him to come to them. However, rather than going out to His mother and brothers who had been calling for Him, Jesus uses this as an opportunity to teach the people. Jesus looks around at His disciples and says that they are His true family. Jesus is not disrespecting His genetic family by saying this. Rather, Jesus is revealing to the disciples how important they are to Him.

Thought Questions:

1. Have you ever met someone as stubborn and hard-hearted as the Pharisees here? How do you think you should respond to such people?

2. What might be some ways that you have seen people focus on the strict letter of the law when they should rather be focused on the heart of the law?

Jesus' Parables: Mark 4:1–34
Lesson 29

There are large portions of Jesus' teachings that Mark does not include in his gospel, but he does include for us some of Jesus' parables. As we have already seen earlier in Matthew's gospel, parables are stories that are designed to teach a lesson. Though Jesus employs a number of methods for teaching, it appears that parables are His preferred method of teaching. It is possibly because of the popularity of these parables that Mark includes these in his gospel.

The first parable that Mark includes is the parable of the sower. As we learned in Matthew's gospel, this parable is actually a parable about parables. In this parable, Jesus describes four different kinds of people who hear His words. The *first soil*, the path, represents those people who hear Jesus speak, but before the word can take any root in them, Satan snatches it away. The *second soil* is rocky, which represents those who receive Jesus' teachings with excitement, but because the word does not get rooted deeply in them, when trials or persecutions come, these people fall away. The *third soil* is thorny, which represents those who hear and receive Jesus' teachings, but because of the distractions of this life, that word does not bear much fruit. The *fourth soil* is good, which represents those who have prepared their hearts to receive Jesus' teachings; as a result, these people grow in leaps and bounds.

Jesus explains to His disciples privately why He speaks to the crowds in parables. The parables are an ingenious way to express truth to those who are prepared to listen while hiding the truth from those who do not really want to listen. As Jesus explains this to His disciples, He quotes Isaiah 6, wherein Isaiah receives his commission from God. Rather than being commissioned to soften people's hearts, Isaiah is commissioned by God to reveal to the people just how hard their hearts truly are. In the same way, Jesus' parables serve to distinguish between those with hard hearts and those who truly want to learn from Him.

Mark also connects this parable with some other teachings that Jesus gives. Just as a lamp is designed to provide light to people, Jesus has come to shine the light of His word to people. Yet Jesus warns the people that they have a responsibility when listening to Jesus' teachings. The more that a person hears, the greater responsibility he has to apply that message. However, if a person refuses to put into practice the things that Jesus says, he or she will be in danger of losing that message altogether. It is not enough merely to listen to Jesus' teachings; we must play an active role in seeking to apply that word.

The final parables all have to do with the notion of something gradually growing. From Matthew's gospel, we learned that the kingdom of God (or heaven) is one that will not come suddenly but will grow over time. Mark adds a new element to this gradually growing kingdom by the way that he organizes these parables. It is not only the kingdom that grows gradually, but the word itself grows gradually in those who hear it. God causes His word to grow in the hearts and minds of those who are ready to hear it so that it continues to transform each person. In essence, the kingdom grows in that person as the Word of God transforms him or her.

Thought Question:

Can you think of a time when you would be described as the "good soil"? Can you think of a time when the word of God really bore fruit in your life?

The Incredible Power and Authority of Jesus: Mark 4:35–5:43

Lesson 30

Throughout Jesus' early ministry, He amazes people with His incredible authority and power. Unlike the

other teachers, Jesus does not merely quote other teachers but speaks with the authority that only the Author of Scripture could have. Jesus also demonstrates His power and authority and deity through the incredible miracles that He performs. So far in Mark's gospel, we have already encountered some of Jesus' power and authority as He casts out demons and heals the sick; but in chapters 4 and 5, Jesus will show an even greater presentation of His power and authority.

After Jesus is done teaching the crowds, He and His disciples get into some boats in order to cross over the sea. Yet, that night, while Jesus is sleeping in the stern of the boat, a great storm arises and begins to sink the boat. We know that this must be a severe storm, considering that many of Jesus' disciples are fishermen and would know how to handle a small storm. However, as the disciples are panicking from this great storm, Jesus continues to sleep peacefully down below. So the disciples wake Him and accuse Him of not caring about their plight. Nevertheless, Jesus gets up and rebukes the wind, and the storm instantly ceases. Jesus then turns to His disciples and asks them why they are afraid and have no faith. If the disciples truly know who Jesus is and what He is capable of doing, they would not panic; but rather, they would be calm, knowing that Jesus could take care of this. Yet the disciples have never seen anything like this before, for no normal man has power over nature itself. By calming the storm, Jesus shows His disciples that He has authority over far more than just sickness; even nature itself submits to Him.

As Jesus and His disciples arrive on the other side of the sea, they are met immediately by a demon-possessed man. Now Jesus has already cast out quite a few demons, but this demon-possessed man is particularly interesting. The demon in this man has given this man superhuman strength so that this man could not be controlled or shackled by the people in the nearby towns. This man has left the nearby towns and has settled near the mountains and the tombs. One could only imagine how terrified the people of the surrounding villages would be as they hear the cries of this demon-possessed man by the tombs. Yet, when this man sees Jesus, he instantly bows down before Jesus and is terrified by Him. This demon knows that Jesus is the Son of God and has power and authority over him, so he begs Jesus not to torment him. When Jesus asks this demon his name, the demon says that he is Legion, for there are many demons in that man. This man is not afflicted by one demon, but by a legion of demons. It is possible that there are over 2,000 demons afflicting this man, for when Jesus allows these demons to go into the pigs, over 2,000 pigs rush into the water and drown. When the people of that town come out to see what has happened, they are amazed that the demon-possessed man is in his right mind, but they do not know how to handle Jesus so they ask Him to leave. Interestingly, even though Jesus does not allow this man to come with Him, He encourages this man to tell his family and friends about what Jesus had done for him. Consistently to this point, Jesus had been telling people to remain silent about what He had done, but He gives this man permission to tell others.

Following this incident, Mark highlights two more great healings that are intertwined. After Jesus leaves the region where He had healed the demon-possessed man, He is met by one of the rulers of the local synagogue, called Jairus, on the other side of the sea. This man has a very sick daughter who is dying, and he comes to Jesus to heal his daughter. Jairus has faith in Jesus and knows that Jesus can heal his daughter. So Jesus goes with the man. However, as Jesus goes on His way to Jairus' house, a large crowd amasses around Jesus. One woman, who had been afflicted by bleeding for twelve years, touches Jesus' garment and is healed from her affliction. This woman is completely desperate when she comes to Jesus. According to the Law of Moses, when a woman bleeds, she is considered ceremonially unclean until she stops, and anyone who touches her could be considered unclean, as well. The implication of this for the woman is that she had basically been a social outcast for twelve years. She had already spent all of her money on physicians to try to get healed, but nothing had worked. Now that she touches Jesus, she is healed. Once again, this highlights the power and authority of Jesus, for He does not even have to do anything for this healing to take place. Jesus does not even know at first who had been healed, but He does know that power had gone out from Him. When Jesus finds out who had touched Him, He encourages her and tells her that her faith had made her well.

As Jesus and the crowd draw near to the house of Jairus, they are met with bad news; Jairus' daughter has died. Those who give the message to Jairus encourage him to send Jesus away, but Jesus tells the ruler of the synagogue to believe in Him. Jesus then takes His three closest disciples—Peter, James, and John—and they enter into Jairus' house. As they enter, Jesus tells the people not to weep, for the girl is only asleep, but the people ridicule Jesus and do not believe Him. Then Jesus goes into the girl's room and says to the girl, *Talitha, cumi*, which means, "Little girl, I say to you, arise" (5:41). Immediately, the girl gets up and walks around. Jesus has raised a dead girl to life! Not only does Jesus have power over demons and sickness and

nature, but He has power over death itself. Yet once again, Jesus tells them not to tell anyone what had happened. Perhaps Jesus knows that if word of this got out, the religious leaders would put Him to death before the appointed time.

Thought Question:

Why do you think Jesus tells the healed demon-possessed man to tell others about Him?

Mission and Tragedy: Mark 6
Lesson 31

Wherever Jesus goes, it appears that His ministry is always accompanied by amazing miracles and demonstrations of His power. We have just recently seen Jesus exercise authority and control over sicknesses, over demons, over nature, and even over life and death. Yet there is one place where Jesus is going to be unable to perform many signs and miracles—His hometown.

When Jesus returns to His hometown, He teaches in the synagogue, as is His pattern in all of the cities in Israel. As is the pattern with the rest of Israel, the people are amazed when they hear Jesus speak. Yet, in His hometown, that astonishment is not simply because of the authority and power of His words but because they remember Him as the carpenter's son, not as a great teacher. This gives us some insight into Jesus' life before His ministry. It is very likely that Jesus lives a normal carpenter's life before He is baptized by John and begins His public ministry. Because the people in His hometown cannot see past their history with Jesus, they do not place much faith in Jesus, and Jesus is unable to perform many miracles. Even though Jesus has power and authority in Himself, God refuses to do miracles for people who refuse to put their faith and trust in Him.

Even though Jesus is an incredible miracle worker, He knows that His main mission is to bring the gospel to the cities in Israel. Practically speaking, this would take a very long time if Jesus does this by Himself. So Jesus takes this opportunity to give His disciples practical ministry experience, and He sends them out in pairs to preach the gospel to the surrounding cities. Any decent teacher knows that there is no better way to learn than through experience, and Jesus gives His disciples that practical experience here. However, part of their lesson is to learn faith and dependence on God. Up until this point, even though His disciples have chosen to follow Jesus and learn from Him, they have not exhibited very much faith. So Jesus tells the disciples not to bring any provisions with them on their journey but to trust in God and the hospitality of the cities in which they preach. Jesus also equips His disciples for the potential rejection that they may face. Interestingly, Jesus gives His disciples permission to withhold the gospel from the cities that refuse to welcome them. There is a lesson for us in this story that requires wisdom: there may be times when it is wise and acceptable to withhold the gospel from those who are hostile towards God.

As the disciples are engaging in this ministry, something tragic happens. John the Baptist had previously been arrested by King Herod because of the words that he had spoken against Herod's unlawful relationship with Herodias. Because the people respect John the Baptist and because Herod himself respects John the Baptist, Herod refuses to put John to death. In fact, Herod often goes to John in order to listen to the things that he says. Yet, one day, Herod makes a foolish vow that he will grow to regret. When Herodias' daughter dances for him during one of his parties, he tells her that he will give her whatever she asks. After consulting with her mother, she asks for the head of John the Baptist on a platter. Because of the vow that Herod had made in front of the people, he reluctantly agrees and John is put to death.

It is not entirely clear from Mark's gospel if Jesus and His disciples hear about the death of John the Baptist, but Matthew's gospel makes it clear that Jesus hears about John's death while the disciples are doing their mission. Because of that information and because Jesus wants to discuss with His disciples their mission, He makes plans to go to a deserted place with them. Yet, when the people see Jesus and His disciples, a large crowd develops around Jesus. Even though Jesus and His disciples are weary from their ministry and from the news of John's death, Jesus still has compassion on the crowd and teaches them. When it gets late, Jesus tells His disciples to provide some food for the crowds. The cost of such a meal would be huge, and the disciples question Jesus' command; of course, Jesus is testing His disciples. Jesus then takes a few loaves of bread and some fish; and just as God had provided manna for the Israelites in the wilderness and oil and flour for the widow in Elijah's day (1 Kings 17), He causes the limited food to regenerate. As a result of this, the entire crowd of over 5,000 men (with probably as many women and children) is fed. By the end of this meal, there is far more food left over than what was originally distributed.

After this incredible miracle, Jesus finally gets His opportunity to get alone. So He sends out His disciples to the other side of the lake, and He withdraws by

Himself to spend some time in prayer. In the middle of the night, Jesus decides to join His disciples, but He does so in an incredible manner. Rather than going out in another boat, Jesus decides to abandon the laws of physics and to walk on the water to the disciples. As one could imagine, the disciples are absolutely frightened by this experience and assume that Jesus is a ghost or a spirit. Jesus, however, reveals Himself to the disciples and tells them not to be afraid. Interestingly, Mark leaves out the story of Peter walking on the water with Jesus. If Peter was indeed Mark's source for much of his gospel, it is possible that Peter leaves that story out as an act of humility. Once again, the disciples are amazed by this event; but we are told that their hearts are still hardened, and they still did not understand what happened with the feeding of the 5,000.

When Jesus and His disciples arrive on the other side of the lake, once again large crowds amass before Jesus. Many people come to Him in order to be healed from their sicknesses. Jesus' popularity continues to grow among the people; but as we will see in the next chapters, as Jesus grows more popular with the people, He becomes an even greater threat to the religious leaders. It is only a matter of time before their plots to get rid of Jesus will come to fruition.

Thought Questions:

1. What do you think it would have been like to grow up with Jesus and then suddenly see Him as this miracle-working Teacher? Imagine that this were one of your friends; do you think you would have a hard time believing in Him like the people in His hometown do?

2. What might be a situation today in which we are to shake off the dust of our feet like the disciples are to do for the cities that reject them?

True Defilement and True Faith: Mark 7:1–8:9

Lesson 32

All of the incredible things that Jesus does increases His popularity and His name among the people of Israel. Word about Jesus spreads throughout the entire nation. While the crowds flock to Jesus by the hundreds and thousands in order to be healed and to hear His teaching, the religious leaders also come to Him in order to discredit Him. Before Jesus had come, the religious leaders had a lot of power in Israel; but with Jesus' ever-increasing popularity, the power and influence of the religious leaders has declined. So in Mark 7, we see once again that the religious leaders come to Jesus in order to challenge Him and discredit His authority.

It is pretty clear that these Pharisees and scribes come to Jesus in order to find something with which they can accuse Jesus. Jesus has been ministering in upper Israel in the region of Galilee, so when the Pharisees and the scribes come and visit Jesus, it is a purposeful journey. It does not take long for these religious leaders to find something about which to accuse Jesus. According to Jewish tradition, whenever a Jewish person comes from the marketplace, because of the possibility of touching something that is unclean, he is supposed to go through a very specific ritual of hand washing. Yet Jesus and His disciples do not engage in this ritual, so the religious leaders confront Jesus about this.

Jesus immediately responds by confronting the Pharisees. Jesus quotes Isaiah, who had rebuked the Israelites centuries before for acting like hypocrites. For the Israelites in Isaiah's day, as it is in Jesus' day, the religious life of the leaders had become mere ritual. These people go through the motions and follow a number of rules, but their hearts are not engaged with what they do. Rather than loving God with all of their hearts, these religious leaders are only focused on behavior and outward ritual. Jesus then reveals the hypocrisy of the Pharisees. These people are so focused on their own traditions that they neglect the direct commandments in Scripture. Apparently, according to the tradition of the elders, it is perfectly acceptable for a person to take money that he should use to provide for his parents and instead give it to the synagogue as an offering (called Corban). But the fifth commandment says that we are to honor our parents. So the very tradition to which the Pharisees hold people goes against the explicit commands in Scripture.

Jesus then gathers a crowd around Him and uses this encounter as an opportunity to teach something to the crowds. While the religious leaders are so focused on maintaining outward appearance and avoiding uncleanness, Jesus argues that the thing about which people ought to be worried is their hearts. It is not food or outward things that defile a man, but it is the sinful desires within a man that defile him. As always, Jesus expands on the outward commands in Scripture and brings them to a matter of the heart. God is far more concerned with the heart of a man than He is with outward rituals or appearances.

The story of the healing of the Syro-Phoenician woman's daughter is related to this teaching about defilement. According to the tradition of the elders, if a Jewish man or woman touches a Gentile, he or she would become unclean. So when Jesus goes to the region of Tyre and Sidon, He would be considered unclean according to the traditions of the Jews. When Jesus gets to these cities, He intends to remain hidden; but His reputation precedes Him and a woman begs Him for a healing. This woman wants Jesus to cast out a demon from her daughter. Jesus' response may seem harsh at first, but it is important to remember Jesus' mission. Jesus had been sent to the lost sheep of Israel to offer them salvation. When Jesus says that it is wrong to take the food from the children and give it to the dogs, He is telling her that His mission is to bring salvation to Israel. But this woman is persistent and argues that even the dogs will eat crumbs from the table. This woman does not want much; she would be happy with even a little bit from Jesus. Jesus is impressed with this woman's faith and agrees to heal her daughter.

From there, Jesus continues to minister in the region of the Gentiles known as the Decapolis. Here He is brought a man who is deaf and has a speech impediment. Unlike many of Jesus' healings, Jesus does not heal this man with mere words. It is possible that Jesus does not use mere words because this man could not hear the words. So Jesus puts His fingers in the man's ears and then spits and touches the man's tongue, and the man is healed. Of course, when Jesus tells the people not to mention this miracle, they tell everyone.

After this, Jesus and His disciples find themselves in a familiar situation. Massive crowds have developed around Jesus, and after three days Jesus commands His disciples to give the crowds some food. The disciples apparently had not learned from the feeding of the 5,000 because once again they tell Jesus that this would be much too expensive for them. So Jesus performs yet another miracle of food and uses just a few fish and a few loaves of bread to feed the entire crowd. This time there are 4,000 men, in addition to the women and the children. The disciples clearly have a lot to learn about faith.

Thought Questions:

1. What do you think it would look like today to honor God with our lips but to have our hearts far from God?

2. When Jesus tells His disciples to feed the crowds the second time, why do you think they question Jesus again?

Peter's Confession and the Transfiguration: Mark 8:10–9:13

Lesson 33

Even though Jesus had refuted the Pharisees who had confronted Him about washing His hands, the Pharisees are far from done with their confrontations with Jesus. In chapter 8, the Pharisees once again come to the region where Jesus is teaching in order to confront and discredit Him. This time, rather than accusing Jesus of wrongdoing, they demand that Jesus give them a sign to prove that He has the authority to do and say the things that He has been doing and saying. Jesus knows that these people have no faith and no desire to follow Him but are looking for another reason to accuse Him, so He refuses to give them a sign. After all, Jesus has performed hundreds of signs already; if they will not believe the signs that they have already seen and heard, Jesus is not going to perform for them.

We have already seen that one of the themes of Mark's gospel is the failure of the disciples; this is highlighted in the next few stories. After Jesus leaves the Pharisees without giving them a sign, He warns His disciples to beware of the leaven of the Pharisees. As the disciples often do, rather than understanding the figurative language of Jesus, they take Him literally. Because they had forgotten to bring bread with them for their journey, they assume He is rebuking them for forgetting to bring the bread. The disciples amaze Jesus here, but for a negative reason. They do not grasp the things that Jesus has said and done before them. Jesus clarifies and tells them that the leaven of the Pharisees is their teaching. Just as a little bit of leaven will take over the whole loaf of bread, a little bit of Pharisaical teaching can ruin the whole person. Jesus is warning His disciples to not be like the Pharisees.

Following this teaching, Jesus performs yet another strange healing. Some people bring a blind man to Jesus in order to have Jesus give him his sight back. Once again, just as Jesus had previously done with the deaf man, Jesus uses His hands and spit to heal this man. Jesus spits on this man's eyes and puts His hands on him. However, rather than an immediately perfect healing, this man can see, but his sight is not clear. The blind man sees people, but they are as big as trees. So Jesus puts His hands on him again, and the man is given full sight. There has been much speculation as to why this two-stage healing rather than just healing him fully at once. Perhaps the best explanation is that this

is a form of foreshadowing Peter's confession. Peter is about to have a moment in which he can see clearly, but sadly he will follow this moment of clarity with another moment of blindness.

One of the key turning points in Jesus' ministry occurs with Peter's confession. From the point of Peter's confession, Jesus will then draw His focus to Jerusalem, where He will face the cross. After asking His disciples about His reputation, Jesus asks His disciples plainly who they think He is. Peter, always prone to speak first, confesses that Jesus is the Christ. Unlike Matthew's gospel, Mark does not mention Jesus' encouraging words to Peter. Rather, Mark highlights how quickly Jesus begins to tell His disciples about His upcoming death and resurrection in Jerusalem. Peter then rebukes Jesus for talking about these things. Peter can conceive of Jesus as the Conquering King, but he cannot conceive of a Suffering Servant. So Jesus rebukes Peter because he is now only thinking about the things of man rather than the things of God. In light of Jesus' own suffering that He is about to endure, Jesus speaks openly to His disciples about the suffering and persecutions that they are also going to have to endure. It is going to be costly to follow Jesus, but they will gain their whole life if they are faithful to Jesus and the gospel.

Now that the disciples know that Jesus is the Messiah, He reveals His true nature to His disciples in Mark 8. Jesus brings His closest disciples—Peter, James, and John—with Him onto a high mountain. There Jesus reveals His glory to them by being transfigured. Jesus' clothes become exceedingly white, and Jesus Himself shines before them. Also, both Moses and Elijah appear before Jesus. Yet Peter still does not understand clearly what is happening, so he offers to pitch a tent for Jesus, Moses, and Elijah. Just as with Jesus' baptism, God speaks from heaven and affirms that Jesus is His beloved Son. Yet, here, God adds that they need to listen to Jesus. On the way down from the mountain, Jesus warns His disciples not to tell anyone about this meeting until He is raised from the dead. Jesus also affirms that John the Baptist had indeed been the fulfillment of the prophecy concerning Elijah. John the Baptist was the one who had come in the spirit of Elijah in order to prepare the world for the coming of the Messiah, Jesus. And now with His glory revealed and His identity discovered, Jesus begins His journey to Jerusalem.

Thought Question:

Why do you think Mark does not mention the positive things that Jesus says to Peter after his confession?

Preparations for the Cross: Mark 9:14–50

Lesson 34

When Jesus and His three disciples come down from the mountain, He finds the rest of the disciples in the middle of a dispute. While Jesus was gone, a man brought his demon-possessed son to the disciples in order to have them cast out the demon. The disciples, however, had been unsuccessful in their attempts to cast out the demon. Jesus asks the man how long this demon had afflicted this boy, and the father informs Him that it afflicted the boy since he was very young. After the man asks Jesus if He can do anything, Jesus seizes on the moment and uses it to teach the man about faith. Jesus tells the man that he can do anything if he believes in Jesus. The man's response is a powerful response. He says in verse 24, "Lord I believe; help my unbelief!" This man wants to believe fully in Jesus but asks for help in his doubt. So Jesus turns to the boy and commands the demon to leave the boy. The demon leaves violently, and it appears that the boy is dead; but Jesus picks up the boy, and the boy is fine. When Jesus' disciples ask Him privately why they could not cast out the demon, He informs them that this kind of demon can only come out through fasting and prayer.

In the early days of Jesus' ministry, His main focus was to bring the gospel to all the cities of Israel. However, now that He has been revealed to His disciples, Jesus draws His attention primarily to the preparation of His disciples for His coming death and resurrection. So Jesus takes His disciples away to a private place where He can tell them more about what is about to happen. Sadly, even though Jesus talks plainly to His disciples, they still do not understand what He is saying to them, but they are afraid to ask Him.

There is a lot for Jesus' disciples to learn before Jesus goes to the cross. Rather than meditating on the things that Jesus had told them about His upcoming death and resurrection, the disciples dispute among themselves who will be the greatest among them in Jesus' kingdom. Jesus knows what they are thinking, so He begins to teach them about the importance of humility in His kingdom. Rather than fighting over who should be first in Jesus' kingdom, they should instead focus on being servants to everyone else. To illustrate the importance of humility in His kingdom, Jesus takes a child in His arms and encourages His disciples to receive these young children. Children do not bring a person social prestige

or power, yet these are the ones on which Jesus wants His disciples to focus.

It is almost as though the disciples ignore what Jesus is saying about children, based on John's response. John does not address the children at all, but instead mentions to Jesus that they had rebuked a man for casting out a demon in Jesus' name. Because that person was not one of the disciples, they assumed that it is wrong for that person to do anything in Jesus' name. This reveals the pride that seems to govern the disciples. Like people who have been given access to a secret club, they feel that only they are supposed to be the privileged ones. So Jesus tells the disciples not to hinder such a person, for those who seek to do good in Jesus' name are on His side. Jesus reminds the disciples that the kingdom is not about them, but about Jesus; and it is open to more than just the disciples.

Jesus then returns to His illustration of the child. He warns the disciples not to do anything that might cause one of these little ones to stumble. In their struggle for power and authority in Jesus' kingdom, it is likely that they would not value children. Yet, as servants, it will be their job to protect the little ones. Rather than worrying about who is going to be the greatest in Jesus' kingdom, the disciples need to be worried about getting into the kingdom in the first place. Just because they have been given the privilege of being Jesus' disciples that does not make it safe for them to do whatever they please. They still need to be diligent to fight against sin. If their hand or their eye or their foot causes them to sin, it is better to remove these parts than to allow that sin to doom them to hell.

Thought Questions:

1. What might we learn about demons from Jesus' interaction with the demon-possessed boy and His explanation to His disciples afterwards?

2. What might be some things that you need to give up in order to fight against sin?

Back to Judea: Mark 10

Lesson 35

Jesus is a Man who has incredible patience with His disciples. For years He has been teaching and preparing His disciples for His coming death and resurrection and for their future ministry when He returns to the Father. Time and time again, however, the disciples prove that they have not understood the things that Jesus says. Nevertheless, in these final days as Jesus makes His journey to Jerusalem, He continues to patiently teach and exhort His disciples, in spite of their lack of understanding.

In chapter 10, we see that Jesus and His disciples have arrived in the region of Judea on the east side of the Jordan River. It is likely that He and His disciples are not very far from where John the Baptist had done much of His ministry. Just as large crowds had amassed around John the Baptist, large crowds amass to see Jesus. As was His custom, Jesus begins to teach the crowd. Yet, as He is teaching, some Pharisees come and try to discredit Jesus again by asking a tough question. In His famous Sermon on the Mount, Jesus had previously told the crowds that the only acceptable reason for divorce is sexual immorality. The Pharisees confront Jesus about this teaching by asking Him if it is lawful for a man to divorce his wife. They expect Jesus to give His normal teaching on this subject, but Jesus responds with a question for them. Jesus asks them what the Law says about divorce. They clearly already know and tell Jesus that Moses does allow for a husband to divorce his wife and to give her a certificate of divorce in order to protect her from any false accusations of abandonment or adultery. They think that they have Jesus in a contradiction, but Jesus reveals God's heart on the matter here. God did indeed allow for divorce because of the hardness of people's hearts, but divorce was never the intention. Marriage was always designed to be for life because God has joined the two together. When the disciples ask Jesus privately about the same matter, Jesus gives them His common teaching on the subject that anyone who divorces his or her spouse and marries another commits adultery.

The disciples prove once again just how poorly they have been paying attention to Jesus when people bring children to Jesus. Jesus had just told the disciples in the previous chapter that they are to be like children in their faith and that they are to protect little children and not do anything that might cause them to stumble. Yet, in this chapter, when people bring small children to Jesus to be blessed by Him, the disciples rebuke the people. We are told that this greatly displeases Jesus, and Jesus reiterates His teaching about children. He tells His disciples not to hinder these children, but rather they should learn from these children.

Jesus is next met by a rich young man who asks Him the question that many of us would want people to ask us, "What shall I do that I may inherit eternal life?" (verse 17).This is a man who had been trying really hard to obey the Law, as evidenced by his response when Jesus brings up the Ten Commandments. As

Jesus begins to recite the Ten Commandments, the man tells Jesus that he had kept these laws since he was a child. Mark adds something to this story that Matthew had not told us, namely that Jesus loves this man. Jesus then gives this man one command that he is not willing to follow. He is to sell all that he has and give it to the poor; then he can come and follow Jesus. This man had worked hard throughout his life, but the one thing that he needs is Jesus, not his riches or his good works. Sadly, this man is not willing to depart from all his money, and he is sad and leaves.

Jesus then turns to His disciples and tells them that it is extremely difficult for rich people to enter the kingdom of God. As long as a person believes that his or her riches will protect and save him, he has no need for a Savior. To illustrate just how difficult it is for a rich person to enter the kingdom of God, Jesus says that it is easier to fit a camel through the eye of a needle than for a rich person to enter the kingdom of God. Peter responds to this by mentioning that he and the other disciples did what the rich man would not do—they gave up everything to follow Jesus. Jesus acknowledges what the disciples have done and also teaches them that anyone who makes great sacrifices for Jesus and the kingdom will be rewarded both in this world and in the age to come. However, rather than sounding like the prosperity gospel, which states that Jesus will make us healthy and wealthy, Jesus makes sure to mention that persecutions are a part of the "rewards" we will receive for our sacrifices. In addition, as Jesus has been telling His disciples (though they do not appear to grasp it at this point), in His kingdom the last will be first and the first last.

As Jesus had just done in the previous chapter, He directly speaks about the events that are awaiting them in Jerusalem. As the disciples had just done in the previous chapter, rather than praying or asking questions about Jesus' upcoming death and resurrection, they instead fight over who will be given more authority and honor in Jesus' kingdom. In this instance, it is James and John who ask Jesus for a favor. They ask Jesus if they may have the privilege of sitting on His right and left side when He gets His kingdom. Patiently, Jesus answers their question. Jesus tells them that He cannot grant their request, but He also uses this request as an opportunity to teach them something. If they want to sit with Jesus in His kingdom, they are going to have to go through the same suffering and sacrifice that Jesus is about to endure. Rather than fighting to have the positions of honor in Jesus' kingdom, they should focus on following in Jesus' footsteps. This leads Jesus to teach the disciples more about what kind of leaders they are going to have to be in His kingdom. Jesus is not going to give them authority so that they can lord that authority over others. For Jesus, authority is merely greater opportunity to serve. Unlike this world, which uses authority as power and control, Jesus says that the greatest leader is the one who turns out to be the greatest servant. Even Jesus Himself did not come to be served but rather to serve others, so we have no excuse.

The final event mentioned in chapter ten is the healing of blind Bartimaeus. As this man hears Jesus and His disciples walking along the road, he calls out for Jesus to have mercy on him. The people around Jesus warn this man to be quiet, but this makes Bartimaeus even more determined. So Jesus calls the man to Himself and asks the man what he wants. The man asks to receive his sight. Even though it is pretty obvious what this man desires, Jesus still gives this man the opportunity to ask Jesus. Jesus heals the man and tells him that his faith has made him well. Of course, this man is immediately healed, and he begins to follow Jesus along with the crowds.

Thought Questions:

1. According to the standards of most people around the world, if a family has two cars and a working television, they would be considered rich. What implications might this have for Jesus' teachings about the difficulty of rich people getting into heaven?

2. Why do you think Jesus makes Bartimaeus ask to be healed, even though it is obvious what this man desires from Jesus? What implications might this have for your prayer life?

Into Jerusalem: Mark 11:1–26

Lesson 36

In Luke's account of the gospel, in Luke 9:51, we learn that shortly after Peter's confession Jesus sets His face towards Jerusalem. In other words, Jesus has a firm resolve to head to Jerusalem, where He knows that torture and death await Him. Along the way on this journey, Jesus has been purposely teaching and preparing His disciples for the events that are about to unfold and for what life will be like when He is gone. The disciples have a mission to do; and in many ways, their real mission will begin shortly after Jesus faces the cross.

It is required in the Law of Moses that Jewish men from around the world are to gather together to the temple in order to celebrate three annual feasts (Deuteronomy 16:16). The festival that Jesus and His disciples are

going to Jerusalem to follow is the Feast of the Passover, also known as the Feast of Unleavened Bread. Because so many people travel to Jerusalem to this feast, many people come to the city early in order to get a place to stay for the week. Jesus and His disciples arrive a week early in Jerusalem, and the events that will follow over the next week will change the world.

As Jesus and the disciples get close to Jerusalem, Jesus sends out two of His disciples into a nearby village in order to retrieve a donkey's colt for Jesus. It is unclear whether or not this is a divine foreknowledge by Jesus or if He had prearranged this event. However, when the disciples get to the village, they find the colt exactly where Jesus had told them; and when the people nearby question them for taking the colt, the two disciples tell them that Jesus has need of it and will send it back quickly. So the people let the disciples take the colt to Jesus. We have already learned through Matthew's gospel that Jesus decides to enter Jerusalem on this colt in order to fulfill the prophecy from Zechariah 9:9 that states that the Messiah will enter Jerusalem humbly, on a colt. This is going to be Jesus' huge revelation to the Jewish nation; sadly, the ones who should be the most excited to see the Messiah are the very ones who oppose Jesus the most.

Considering the incredible miracles that Jesus has performed and the reputation that Jesus had developed, it is reasonable to assume that many people had begun to suspect that Jesus is the Messiah. When the crowds see Jesus enter Jerusalem in the manner that the Messiah was to enter, many people become more confident that Jesus is the Messiah. We will learn from John's gospel that there was already a large crowd walking with Jesus before He gets the colt, but now the crowd gets even larger. The people give Jesus a king's welcome by laying down their coats and palm branches on the road before Jesus as He enters the city. In addition, the people begin to shout Scripture from Psalm 118, which speaks about the coming Messiah. Everything is building for what should be the coronation ceremony of the true King of Israel. However, there is not a king's welcome awaiting Jesus when He arrives in Jerusalem.

From Matthew's gospel alone, it would appear that Jesus cleanses the temple on that very day; but Mark's gospel makes it clear that Jesus does not cleanse the temple until the next day. When Jesus arrives in Jerusalem, He does enter the temple, but because it is already late, He returns to the town of Bethany for the night. The next day, as Jesus and His disciples are returning to Jerusalem, Jesus curses a fig tree. This fig tree has green leaves, but because it is not the season for figs, it has no fruit. Jesus does not curse the fig tree out of anger, but as an illustration for Israel. Jesus has already told His disciples that any tree that does not bear fruit will be cut down, and Israel is supposed to be that tree that bears fruit. Because Israel is not bearing the appropriate fruit for God, the nation is in danger of being destroyed like this fig tree.

It is on Monday when Jesus cleanses the area of the temple called the Court of the Gentiles, which was set aside for Gentiles to pray. Rather than being a place where prayer could be offered for the nations, this part of the temple was turned into a marketplace for people to buy and sell animals. It is not wrong in itself for people to buy and sell animals near the temple, for people come from a long distance and will need these animals for sacrifices. The issue here is that the Jews used this part of the temple, which was designed specifically as a place for the Gentiles to pray, for their own selfish gain. Filled with zeal, Jesus begins to drive out all of the money changers and shuts down the marketplace. He rebukes the people for turning God's house, which was to be for prayer, into a den of robbers. Naturally, this kind of public event draws a lot of people's attention, including the chief priests and the scribes. They had already been looking for a way to destroy Jesus, but this event makes them all the more desperate to get rid of Jesus.

The next day, on Tuesday, as Jesus and the disciples travel to Jerusalem once again, they see that the tree that Jesus had cursed had withered. Peter points this out to Jesus; and as Jesus often does, He turns this into a teachable moment. Jesus tells the disciples that it is not Jesus' power that makes these things happen, but it is His faith in God. If we have even a little faith, we can make mountains move. By saying this, Jesus is encouraging us to be bold in our prayers. God rewards our trust in Him, and He will grant our requests when we make them by faith. Of course, this does not mean that we will get everything for which we pray, especially when those things ultimately do not benefit us eternally. Jesus also reminds the disciples to include forgiveness as a regular part of their prayers. If we do not forgive others, Jesus says, God will not forgive us. Considering the incredible mercy of God towards us when He forgives us, we have no excuse to hold a grudge against anyone else, but rather we should forgive.

Thought Questions:

1. How much faith would you say you have when you pray? What are some things that might prevent you from praying with faith?

2. If the temple was supposed to be a place of prayer for all nations and we are now the new temple of God, what implications should this have for our prayer lives? How often do you pray for the nations?

Jesus, the Expert Debater: Mark 11:27–12:44

Lesson 37

By this point in Mark's gospel, we know that the religious leaders in Jerusalem have been trying to find a way to silence Jesus for quite some time. Jesus poses a threat to their popularity and their position as leaders in Israel. With every miracle and public appearance that Jesus makes, these religious leaders become all the more desperate to get rid of Jesus. Before resorting to extreme measures to get rid of Jesus, these religious leaders attempt to publicly disgrace and discredit Jesus while He is in Jerusalem. Of course, it will be these leaders who are disgraced and discredited, and the people will be even more amazed with Jesus.

In the middle of the week, the chief priests, the scribes, and the elders of the land come to Jesus and ask Him where He gets the authority to do the things that He has done. Remember that He had just cleansed the temple a day or two before and practically shut down the temple in the process. These leaders do not ask Jesus this question because they want to follow Him, but because they want to trap Him. However, Jesus wisely answers their question with another question. Since they are so interested in where Jesus gets His authority, He asks them about their opinion on John the Baptist, whether his baptism was from heaven or from men. If they answer that John's baptism was from heaven, they would acknowledge that Jesus' authority is also from heaven, since John pointed people to Jesus. However, if they say that John's baptism was from man, they would be discredited by the crowds, since John is held in such high regard. Knowing that there is no answer that works out to their benefit, they refuse to answer Jesus. So Jesus in turn refuses to directly answer their question.

Now that the confrontation has begun, Jesus reacts by telling the crowd and the religious leaders a parable. Instantly, the religious leaders know that Jesus is talking about them, considering the nature of the parable. Jesus speaks about a vineyard owner who leases out his land to vinedressers and goes away. When the time for the harvest comes, the owner sends servants to the vinedressers in order to receive some of the fruit. The vinedressers, however, beat these servants and give them no fruit. When the owner of the vineyard sends his own son, expecting some decency out of the vinedressers, they kill the son. Jesus makes it clear that the religious leaders are the vinedressers in this story, and He hints to them that He knows they are planning to kill Him. Yet, through this parable, Jesus also warns the religious leaders that judgment is coming upon them for what they are about to do.

Earlier, when Jesus had entered Jerusalem, the crowds shout from Psalm 118, which speaks about the Messiah. Jesus quotes this same Psalm again after He tells this parable. In this case, Jesus quotes this passage to show that the people are going to reject the Messiah (the chief cornerstone). They will reject Jesus, but He will rise to become the chief cornerstone upon which God will build His kingdom. Mark tells us that the religious leaders clearly perceive that He has been talking about them. However, because the religious leaders are afraid of the crowd, they do not lay hands on Jesus right there.

Even though the chief priests and the elders leave Jesus, they send some other people to try to trap Jesus. The first group of challengers is one that is unexpected, some Pharisees and Herodians. Normally, the Herodians and the Pharisees would never be seen together, but their desire to get rid of Jesus unites them. This group tries to trap Jesus with a question about taxes. They ask Jesus whether it is lawful or not to pay taxes to Caesar. If Jesus simply says, "No," they could have Him arrested for treason. Yet, if Jesus simply says, "Yes," then He would lose popularity with the crowds. Wisely, Jesus finds the hidden third option and tells them to pay Caesar what belongs to Caesar, and to pay God what belongs to God. In essence, Jesus says to pay the tax, but He does so in a way that shows why one should pay taxes.

Next, a group of Sadducees come to Jesus with another hard question in order to trap Him. Historically, the Sadducees controled much of the priesthood of Israel, but ironically they did not believe in many supernatural things such as angels, demons, or even the afterlife. In addition, the Sadducees only accepted the first five books of Moses as Scripture, not the rest of the Old Testament. These people try to trap Jesus with a question about the resurrection on the last day. They give Jesus a scenario where a woman marries seven brothers within the same family because the first six brothers die. They then ask Jesus whose wife she will be in the resurrection. Jesus responds by going straight to the heart of the matter. He rebukes them for not knowing the Scriptures and the power of God. This woman will be nobody's wife because there is no marriage in heaven. Jesus then directly challenges their rejection of the resurrection by quoting Exodus when God identifies Himself as the God of Abraham, Isaac, and Jacob to show that these three men still exist. God does not say that He *was* the God of these three men, but rather He *is* the God of these men; therefore, these men still exist.

The next group to question Jesus is the scribes or experts in the Law. One from among the scribes asks Jesus to tell him what the first and greatest commandment is in the Law. Jesus quotes the Shema from Deuteronomy 6, which tells us that there is only one God and that we should love Him with all that we have. Jesus, however, expands on His answer and gives the second greatest commandment, which is to love our neighbors as ourselves. Unlike the other people who question Jesus, it appears that this man has some sincerity; and Jesus commends him and tells him that he is not far from the kingdom of God.

With His opponents silenced, Jesus now proceeds to teach the crowds. Jesus teaches the crowds that the Messiah is more than a mere descendant of David. In Psalm 110, which David writes, he says that "the LORD said to my Lord…." Yet if David is the most powerful person in the nation of Israel at this time and the first "LORD" is God Himself, who is the second "Lord"? Jesus tells us that the second "Lord" is the Messiah Himself and that this Messiah must be greater than David. He cannot be a mere king, therefore, but must be someone even greater.

Jesus then warns the people to watch out for the religious leaders. These people do not use their position in order to help out the people, but so that they could receive praise from the people. They love to have positions of honor. They make long prayers not because they are sincere but that others would praise their piety. Moreover, because of their rules, they are even hurting the poor and the widows. To illustrate this, as Jesus is sitting in the temple, He points out to His disciples a poor widow who puts two mites into the treasury. This would be equivalent to a few dollars in today's society. The religious leaders would not look highly upon this woman since she gave so very little money. Yet Jesus points out that she makes a far larger sacrifice than the rest of the gifts that wealthier people give.

Thought questions:

1. What lessons can you learn from the generosity of the poor widow in this story?

2. What principles can you learn from Jesus' method of argumentation with these religious leaders for potential arguments today?

The Sermon on the Mount of Olives: Mark 13

Lesson 38

One of the days when Jesus and His disciples leave the temple, the disciples take time to admire the architecture of the temple. King Herod had spent decades rebuilding and beautifying the temple so that the structure that the disciples see is incredibly beautiful. Some scholars have even suggested that Herod's temple could have rivalled the beauty and glory of Solomon's temple. In light of the beauty of this temple, it must be all the more shocking when Jesus informs His disciples that the temple is going to be destroyed.

We have already examined Jesus' Olivet Discourse when we looked at Matthew 24. When examining Jesus' teachings in Mark 13, it is important to remember that there is more than one way to interpret the prophecies that Jesus gives in this discourse. Jesus is clearly speaking about events that are future to Him and His disciples; but it is a matter of debate as to how far in the future these events will take place. Because of the context, it is clear that at least part of what Jesus says pertains to the destruction of the temple in A.D. 70. Some scholars would argue that the entire Olivet discourse pertains to the destruction of the temple. But because of the exaggerated language that Jesus uses with this prophecy, many Christians believe that a large portion of this prophecy will be fulfilled during the end times. It is worth noting that the language of Mark's gospel, more so than Matthew's, supports the fulfillment of this prophecy to be the destruction of the temple and Jerusalem.

In both Matthew and Mark's gospel, the disciples respond to Jesus' initial statement about the destruction of the temple with two questions. In Matthew, they ask, "When will these things be? And what will be the

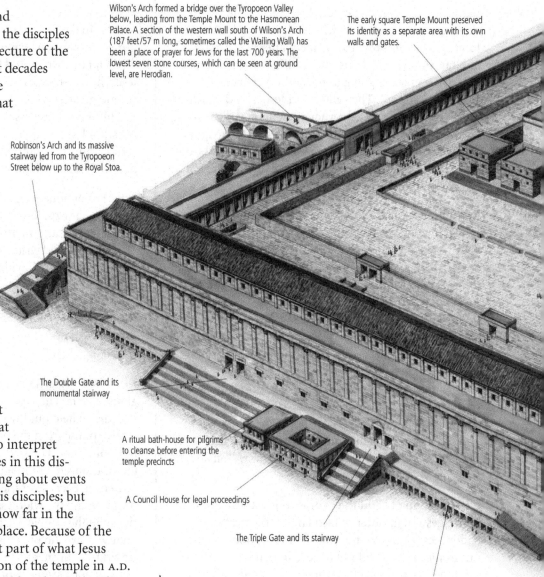

THE TEMPLE MOUNT IN THE TIME OF JESUS

Herod's Temple Mount was the focal point of Jerusalem during the time of Jesus. Sitting atop Jerusalem's northeastern ridge, it occupied one-sixth of the city's area. Under Herod the Great, the Temple Mount's foundation was expanded to encompass approximately 1.5 million square feet (140,000 square meters). Its foundational walls were constructed using gigantic stones, the largest found being 45 feet long, 11.5 feet high, and 12 feet thick (13.7 m by 3.5 m by 3.7 m).

Wilson's Arch formed a bridge over the Tyropoeon Valley below, leading from the Temple Mount to the Hasmonean Palace. A section of the western wall south of Wilson's Arch (187 feet/57 m long, sometimes called the Wailing Wall) has been a place of prayer for Jews for the last 700 years. The lowest seven stone courses, which can be seen at ground level, are Herodian.

The early square Temple Mount preserved its identity as a separate area with its own walls and gates.

Robinson's Arch and its massive stairway led from the Tyropoeon Street below up to the Royal Stoa.

The Double Gate and its monumental stairway

A ritual bath-house for pilgrims to cleanse before entering the temple precincts

A Council House for legal proceedings

The Triple Gate and its stairway

Small shops, which had a narrow street built above them, were built along the southern wall of the Temple Mount.

sign of Your coming, and of the end of the age?" (Matthew 24:3). However, here in Mark, they ask, "When will these things be? And what will be the sign when all these things will be fulfilled?" (verse 4). It would appear that Matthew interprets this prophecy to be referring to the end of the age, whereas Mark interprets this prophecy to be referring to the destruction of the temple.

Jesus begins His response by warning His disciples about the things they are going to face in their lifetime.

The Antonia Fortress was where Herod (and later the Romans) commanded the garrison in order to protect the temple and to suppress religiously motivated rebellion.

Herod's Temple

The Court of the Women was the farthest point of the inner temple complex that women could enter.

The Pool of Israel was probably used to wash sacrificial animals before they were led to the Temple Mount.

The Golden Gate, then known as the Shushan Gate

Stairs descended from the Muster Gate into the Kidron Valley and eventually went up to the Mount of Olives.

The eastern city wall of Jerusalem

Solomon's Porch, the portico built along the eastern wall, was a place of congregation (cf. John 10:23; Acts 3:11).

The soreg (a low, latticed screen or railing) prohibited Gentiles or non-purified Jews from entering the temple courts.

The Court of the Gentiles was the area between the soreg and the outer walls of the early square Temple Mount.

The Royal Stoa was a 912-foot-long (278 m) portico, containing four rows of 40 columns. The Sanhedrin met in the central apse after c. A.D. 30. This may have been where Jesus cleansed the temple. The southeast corner overlooking the Kidron Valley created a drop of 140 feet (43 m) to the street below, and 300 feet (91 m) to the valley below. This may be the "pinnacle of the temple" mentioned in Matt. 4:5 and Luke 4:9.

Temple Mount Architectural Plan

N

0   250   500 ft
0   50   100   150 m

be aware that persecutions are coming their way. The disciples are going to be arrested and brought before government officials; even their own family members will be willing to betray believers in the days to come. Yet they should not worry about what they will say in that day, for the Holy Spirit will give them the words.

In verse 14, Jesus answers the disciples' questions more directly. All of the other signs and cataclysmic events are not to concern the disciples, but when the abomination of desolation appears where he ought not, then it will be time for action. We know from Matthew's gospel that the place where the abomination of desolation appears is the temple. From Mark's gospel, we learn that this abomination that causes desolation will shut down the temple when he arrives. Typically, this person is believed to be the Antichrist, who will come to power and oppose Christians and the gospel. Jesus warns His disciples that the time to flee from Judea and Jerusalem will be when this man appears in the temple. There are two primary ways of interpreting who this abomination of desolation might be. For those who interpret this prophecy to be only referring to the end times, this abomination of desolation would be the future Antichrist who will come during a seven year period of time known as the Great Tribulation. For those who believe that this was fulfilled during the destruction of the temple, the abomination of desolation would be the Emperor Titus, who went into the temple as the Romans destroyed Jerusalem in A.D. 70.

Many scholars believe that verse 24 is the turning point in this prophecy, where Jesus begins to talk about

There will be many false teachers who will arise in order to deceive people. Many people will claim to be Jesus, but Jesus warns the disciples not to believe them. Things are going to get really difficult. There will be wars and rumors of even more wars, and there will be cataclysmic natural disasters such as famines and earthquakes. Yet Jesus tells the disciples that these major events are not indicators of the end. Rather than focusing on these cataclysmic events, the disciples should events that will take place during the end times. Jesus says that after the days of the abomination of desolation, the sun and moon will be darkened and the stars will fall from the heavens. If this is to be taken literally, one would expect there to be some mention of it by historians, but there is not. Moreover, as these cataclysmic events are taking place, the Son of Man will come on the clouds and gather the elect together. This is understood to be a future time when Jesus will gather all of the Christians together as He gloriously returns to establish His kingdom. The other possibility for this passage is that this prophecy is not to be taken literally but figuratively. The darkening of the sun, moon, and stars can symbolize the darkening of a nation as Jerusalem and Israel are conquered. The coming of the Son of Man would be a coming of judgment upon Jerusalem rather than His second coming. Both of these interpretations have their difficulties. The literal interpretation can neglect the context of the temple and the statement in verse 30 that all of these things would have to happen in that generation; whereas the figurative interpretation can fail to explain the gathering of the elect.

While there is room for different interpretations as to the specific fulfillment of this prophecy, the overall point of this prophecy is very clear. Jesus uses a fig tree to illustrate His main point in this prophecy. When the branches of the fig tree grow tender and put forth leaves, this is an indicator that summer is near. So also, Jesus tells the disciples that all of these signs will tell them that Jesus is near. Jesus Himself does not know when He is going to return. However, the disciples need to always be ready, because Jesus could return at any moment. This is a good lesson for us, as well. We may not know exactly how things are going to develop, but we must be ready at any time for Jesus to return.

Thought question:

Do you believe that Jesus is talking primarily about the end times, the destruction of the temple, or both in this prophecy? If both, in which verse do you believe that He changes from the destruction of the temple to the end times?

The Last Night with the Disciples: Mark 14:1–52

Lesson 39

After Jesus utterly humiliates the religious leaders in front of all the people in Jerusalem, the religious leaders finally decide to resort to trickery in order to have Jesus put to death. If they were to publicly arrest Jesus

during the feast, the crowds would only side with Jesus more. They wonder how they can get Jesus without the crowds noticing. Then their opportunity comes when Judas Iscariot, one of Jesus' own disciples, comes to the religious leaders in order to betray Jesus.

Chapter 14 begins with the story of Jesus' anointing at Bethany. When we covered this story in Matthew's gospel, we learned that this event actually takes place before the Triumphal Entry. This story is mentioned at this point in Matthew and Mark's gospels because it gives us the back story as to why Jesus is betrayed by Judas. While Jesus and His disciples are reclining at the house of Simon the leper, who had presumably been healed by Jesus, a woman comes to them, breaks a flask of expensive perfume, and anoints Jesus' head with it. Some who are there are furious at this woman for wasting such an expensive flask of perfume. They reason that she would have better served God by selling the perfume and giving the money to the poor. From John's gospel we learn that Judas has a problem with this because he had been stealing money from Jesus all along and wanted the donation to be made so that he could have some money for himself (John 12:4–6). When Jesus corrects the disciples and tells them that this woman is doing a better thing by anointing Him rather than giving the money to the poor, this pushes Judas over the edge; consequently, he goes to the religious leaders in order to betray Jesus.

Unlike Matthew's gospel, Mark seems to imply some divine knowledge with regards to the finding of the upper room by the disciples. When the disciples ask Jesus where He would like to celebrate the Passover meal, He tells the disciples that they will find a person with a pitcher of water, and he will show them a room. If Jesus had prearranged this meeting, it would not explain how He would know that the man would have a pitcher of water when the disciples find him. Nevertheless, they go to the upper room and prepare the Passover meal. While eating the Passover meal, Jesus informs the disciples that one of them will betray Him. Even though all of them deny that it is them, Jesus warns them that severe consequences will await the one who betrays Him. Then Jesus takes the elements of the Passover meal and transforms the symbolism to now refer to His death. The bread is now to represent Jesus' broken body, and the wine is now to represent Jesus' blood, which will be shed to bring about a new covenant.

Then Jesus and His disciples leave the upper room in order to go to the Mount of Olives. On the way, Jesus informs the disciples that they are going to abandon Him that very night in order to fulfill a prophecy from Zechariah 13:7 about the sheep scattering when the

Shepherd is struck. Of course, Peter speaks up and boasts that he will never stumble. Mark's gospel differs from Matthew's gospel in that Jesus predicts in Mark's gospel that the rooster will crow twice before Peter denies Jesus three times, whereas Matthew's gospel mentions only one crow of the rooster. After this, Jesus takes Peter, James, and John with Him to a solitary place in order to pray. Jesus asks His disciples to pray as He goes off alone to spend time with the Father. The prayer that Jesus offers is incredibly powerful, and we can learn much from it. Jesus knows what awaits Him and asks for God to take the cup of suffering away from Him. Even though Jesus makes His request known to the Father, He still agrees to submit to the will of the Father. Sadly, in these last moments that Jesus gets to have with His disciples, rather than them being faithful to pray with Him, they fall asleep. Jesus warns them about the power of the flesh and tells them to watch and pray so that they will not fall into temptation. Finally, after the third time that Jesus finds His disciples asleep, He tells them to get up because He is about to be betrayed.

The plan of the religious leaders is to find a way to arrest Jesus away from the crowds so that there would not be a riot. The best time to do this is late at night so that nobody would see. However, late at night it would be easy for Jesus to slip away and avoid arrest. So the plan is for Judas to lead the guards to Jesus and kiss Jesus so that they will know that it is in fact Jesus. As Jesus and His disciples get up from prayer, Judas does exactly that. When Judas kisses Jesus, the guards immediately seize Jesus. Perhaps believing that the time to conquer Rome and establish Jesus' kingdom has come, one of the disciples—which is Peter (cf. John 18:10)—takes out a sword and cuts off the ear of the high priest's servant. Mark does not mention that Jesus heals this servant's ear, but rather that Jesus confronts the guards for their unlawful arrest.

Mark adds a very strange detail at this point in his gospel. Apparently, when Jesus is arrested, there is a young man who decides to follow Jesus. When the guards grab this young man, he takes off the linen cloth that he is wearing and runs away naked. This is a curious story that does not add anything to the narrative of the arrest, and it is only found in Mark's gospel. The likely explanation is that this young man is Mark himself.

Thought Questions:

1. Can you think of a time when you really did not want to do something that God wanted you to do, but like Jesus you chose to pursue God's will over your own?

2. What do you think it is about the anointing that bothers Judas to the point that he betrays Jesus?

3. Can you think of an example in your own life when the spirit in you wanted to do something but your flesh was weak?

The Trial, Crucifixion, and Resurrection: Mark 14:53–16:20

Lesson 40

Throughout Mark's gospel, we have seen Jesus as the divine hero. Jesus has proven to conquer sickness, nature, demons, and even death itself. But Jesus' ultimate victory will not come by killing His enemies; rather, Jesus conquers His enemies by sacrificing Himself and submitting to death. Also in Mark's gospel, even through the incredibly unjust trial and cruelty that Jesus faces, He maintains His resolve and completes the mission that the Father had sent Him to accomplish.

As with Matthew's gospel, Mark's gospel highlights the complete lack of justice in Jesus' trial. The mere fact that this trial takes place in secret and at night already shows that this is not a legitimate trial. Moreover, as the high priest seeks to find witnesses to accuse Jesus, there is no accusation made that is worthy of the death penalty. On top of that, the false witnesses that testify against Jesus contradict one another and prove to be unreliable witnesses. In Matthew's gospel, we saw that the accusation that the high priest finally holds on to is that Jesus said that He would destroy the temple and raise it in three days. However, Mark adds that even in this false accusation the witnesses contradict one another. Finally, the high priest asks Jesus directly if He is the Christ. Jesus affirms that He is indeed the Christ and that He is going to be given the authority of the Father when He comes to Him on the clouds of heaven. The high priest sees this confession by Jesus as an act of blasphemy and condemns Jesus to death. This once again shows the lack of justice in this trial; rather than allowing for the possibility that Jesus is indeed the Christ, the high priest condemns Jesus for claiming to be the Christ.

Because the Jews do not have the authority to execute one of their criminals, the religious leaders bring Jesus to the Roman governor, Pontius Pilate. Meanwhile, we learn that Peter had followed Jesus into the courtyard of the high priest. As Jesus had predicted, on three separate occasions Peter is asked if he is one of Jesus' disciples. After the first time that Peter denies knowing Jesus, the rooster crows; after the third time, the rooster crows again. Peter then remembers Jesus' prediction that he would deny Jesus, and he goes away and weeps.

Mark's account of Jesus' trial before Pilate is briefer than Matthew's, yet the injustice of this trial is still at the center of Mark's gospel. When Pilate asks Jesus if He is the King of the Jews, Jesus affirms that it is so. Yet, when all of the other accusations are fired against Him, Jesus remains silent. Jesus' innocence is once again seen as even Pilate himself is amazed by how Jesus handles Himself in the midst of such accusations. Pilate recognizes that this accusation against Jesus is made because the religious leaders are jealous of Jesus. Rather than declaring Jesus innocent, as Pilate knows He is, Pilate attempts to appease the crowd that is gathering by offering to set free one of his prisoners. Pilate gives the crowd the option to set free a murderer named Barabbas or to set free Jesus. This option seems like a no-brainer: either set free a murderer or a person who claims to be a king. Yet the chief priests rile up the crowds to ask for the murderer Barabbas to be released. When Pilate asks what they want him to do with Jesus, they yell out that they want Him crucified.

Pilate is afraid of the crowd, so he orders Jesus to be scourged and crucified. We learn in Romans 13 that the government officials get their authority from God in order to protect the innocent and punish the guilty. Pilate fails in his duties out of fear of the crowds and he condemns the innocent while setting free the guilty. Not only is Jesus scourged, but afterwards He is brought before the Roman soldiers, and they mock Him and beat Him some more. Finally, Jesus is brought to Golgotha where He is crucified. Yet the mocking does not stop with the Roman soldiers. Even on the cross, Jesus is mocked by the thieves on the nearby crosses and by the chief priests and people who walk by Him. Around the sixth hour of the day, darkness covers the land until the ninth hour. Then Jesus cries out, "Eloi, Eloi, lama sabachthani" (15:34), which is a quote from Psalm 22, asking God why He has forsaken Jesus. For the first time in history, Jesus is not experiencing unity and intimacy with the Father, as He bears the sins of the world on the cross. Finally, after being offered some sour wine, Jesus cries out with a loud voice and breathes His last.

When Jesus dies, the veil of the temple that separates the Holy Place from the Most Holy Place is torn in two from top to bottom. And when the Roman centurion who is nearby sees this, even he acknowledges that Jesus is the Son of God. After Jesus dies, Joseph of Arimathea gets permission to take down Jesus' body and put Him in his tomb. Then Jesus is prepared and placed in the tomb, and the tomb is sealed with a large boulder. Mark

also points out that some of the women who had been following Jesus see where Jesus is buried. This apparently insignificant detail is very important for those who argue that the women go to the wrong tomb. These women know exactly where the tomb is, since they see Him buried.

Before examining the last chapter of Mark's gospel, there is a textual issue that needs to be addressed here. Over the centuries, archaeologists have found thousands of manuscripts of the Bible. One of the amazing things about the Bible, and an excellent reason why we can trust the Bible, is that overwhelmingly these manuscripts are almost identical. However, there are a few passages in the Bible where the ancient manuscripts do not match. One of these passages is Mark 16:9–20. As scholars have dated the various manuscripts that have been found, Mark 16:9–20 is not found in the earliest manuscripts. This casts some doubt as to whether or not this section of Scripture was included in the original gospel that Mark wrote. If this gospel does end after verse 8, it ends on a cliffhanger; the women find the empty tomb and are told that Jesus has risen, but they leave the empty tomb amazed and afraid and say nothing to anyone. This does fit the theme of discipleship failure that has been present throughout Mark's gospel. If verses 9–20 were part of the original gospel, somehow the ending would have had to be cut off from all of the earliest manuscripts. Even if this section was not included in the original gospel, just about all of the material in these last verses can be found and supported elsewhere in the Bible. So for the sake of this class, we will examine this section as we would the rest of the New Testament.

Very early on Sunday morning, on the third day after Jesus had died, some of the women who had been following Jesus go to the empty tomb in order to anoint Jesus' body. There are some differences between Matthew's and Mark's accounts of the resurrection, but all of them can be reconciled. For example, Matthew only mentions Mary Magdalene and another Mary, whereas Mark also mentions a third woman, Salome. Matthew does not say that Mary Magdalene and the other Mary are the only two women; these are just the only two that Matthew mentions. Matthew mentions that the women see an angel on the now rolled away stone, whereas Mark adds that they meet this angel after they had entered the tomb. In both gospels, the angel tells the women that Jesus has risen and tells them to go get the disciples and tell them to go to Galilee where they will meet Jesus.

Jesus' first resurrection appearance is to Mary Magdalene on Sunday morning. Mark adds that Jesus had previously cast out seven demons from this woman. She tells the disciples about Jesus' appearance, but the disciples refuse to believe. Mark also mentions that Jesus had met two disciples on their way into the country; these are likely the two disciples that Luke 24 mentions on the road to Emmaus. Once again, they tell the disciples, and still they do not believe. Finally, Jesus appears to the eleven and rebukes them for their unbelief. Jesus then gives the disciples the Great Commission. Mark summarizes the Great Commission that Matthew had mentioned, but he adds some details about the commission. Mark adds that there will be great signs that will accompany the gospel. The disciples will cast out demons, speak in tongues, handle snakes safely, drink poison and still live, and they will heal the sick. After commissioning the disciples, Jesus ascends into heaven. Then the disciples go and spread the gospel throughout the Roman world; but we will examine that in far more detail when we get to the book of Acts.

Thought Questions:

1. Would you treat Mark 16:9–20 as Scripture? Why or why not?

2. What do you think is the guards' motivation for beating and mocking Jesus?

3. What do you think it is that causes even the Roman centurion to acknowledge that Jesus is the Son of God after He dies?

UNIT 2: *Luke and John*

Introduction to Luke

Lesson 41

The author of the third gospel is the physician Luke. While Luke does not identify himself as the author, there is much evidence to suggest it was he. First, church history has always identified Luke as the author, from as early as 100 years after the death of Jesus. Second, Luke is the only traveling companion of Paul's who could have been there for all of the "we" sections in the book of Acts. The author of Acts is the same author of Luke, considering they are both written to the same person and that Acts mentions an earlier book written by the author (Acts 1:1). One of the interesting features of the book of Acts is that suddenly the author switches the narrative from third person "he" to first person "we" (see Acts 20:5 ff). This means that the author was only there for the portions of Scripture where he mentions "we." Luke is the only traveling companion of Paul's who could have been there for all of these sections. In addition, there is internal evidence to suggest that Luke is the author of the third gospel. Whereas other gospel writers give generic descriptions of diseases, Luke mentions specific names of diseases (Luke 14:2 mentions the disease "dropsy"). This makes sense if the author was a physician. Also, the Greek used in the gospel of Luke is a very proper form of Greek, consistent with an educated Gentile like Luke.

Both Luke and Acts are written to a person called "Theophilus." We do not know much about this Theophilus person. Based on the name, we can deduce that he is a Gentile. The name *Theophilus* means "lover of God"; because of this, some have suggested that this is not written to a specific man, but to anyone who loves God. Because we do not know much about Theophilus, all we can do is speculate exactly who the audience is.

Luke makes known his purpose for writing his gospel right from the very beginning. Because Jesus was so popular and the growth and movement of Christianity was so large, a number of stories began to circulate about Jesus. Some of these stories were true, but some were false. So Luke sets out to provide an orderly historical account of the life, death, and resurrection of Jesus. Luke's goal is to set straight any misconceptions or false rumors that have circulated about Jesus. Since Luke was not one of Jesus' disciples during His time on earth, Luke gets his material by interviewing others who had been with Jesus. We can deduce that one of the people that he interviewed was Mary, the mother of Jesus. Luke's birth narrative mentions the thought life of Mary on a couple of occasions; this most likely comes from Mary herself. Luke also likely interviews Peter, as well.

As one of the synoptic gospels, much of the material in Luke's gospel is exactly the same or very similar to Mark and Matthew's accounts. However, a large chunk of Luke's gospel is unique, specifically Jesus' last journey to Jerusalem, recorded in Luke 9–18. In this section, there are a number of unique parables and teachings, most notably the parable of the prodigal son. Luke also adds different details to the Passion Week and the resurrection and post-resurrection appearances of Jesus.

There are a number of themes that Luke mentions in his gospel. The first theme is that of **universality**. Luke emphasizes the universal mission of Jesus. Matthew focuses on Jesus as the Jewish Messiah, but Luke emphasizes Jesus as the Savior of the world. Matthew's genealogy goes back to Abraham, the father of the Jews; Luke's genealogy goes back to Adam and God Himself. Another theme is the importance of the Holy Spirit. This makes sense considering the role of the Holy Spirit in Acts. When Matthew says that God will give "good things" to those who ask, Luke says God will give "the Holy Spirit" to those who ask. Luke also emphasizes the importance of social outcasts for Jesus' mission. Women are given a prominent role, as well as "sinners" and other outcasts.

> **universality:** refers to the universal mission of Jesus, to the Gentiles as well as the Jews

The Birth Narrative: Luke 1–2

Lesson 42

As mentioned in the last lesson, Luke writes his gospel in order to provide an orderly account of the events in the life, death, and resurrection of Jesus. Through this, Luke wants to provide historical confidence in the events about which Theophilus had heard so much.

Luke's gospel begins with the birth of John the Baptist. Luke informs us that John is the child of an elderly priestly couple named Zacharias and Elizabeth. While Zacharias is in the temple, performing his priestly duties, he is met by the angel Gabriel. Gabriel informs him that his wife is going to get pregnant. Because Zacharias does not believe at first, he is made a mute until the child is born. When he returns home, his wife Elizabeth gets pregnant. In the interim, while Elizabeth is pregnant, the angel Gabriel also comes to Mary to inform her that she will conceive and give birth to the Savior, Jesus, even though she is a virgin. Unlike Zacharias, Mary does believe and ponders these things in her heart.

When Mary discovers that she is indeed pregnant, she goes to visit her relative Elizabeth. As soon as Elizabeth hears Mary, the baby inside her leaps in the womb, and Elizabeth is filled with the Holy Spirit. Elizabeth then begins to prophesy and proclaim the significance of Mary's Son. Mary replies with a prophecy of her own, known traditionally as the Magnificat. The main theme here is the exaltation of the humble and the humiliation of the proud. Mary is not someone special in the eyes of the world, yet God chose her to bear His Son. When Elizabeth finally gives birth to her son, their relatives want to name him after his father, but Zacharias writes down on a piece of paper that his name is John. As soon as he does this, he regains his ability to speak. He then gives the Benedictus, a prophecy about John and Jesus. First he speaks of the salvation that will come to Israel through Jesus. Then he speaks directly about his son, that he will be a prophet who will call people to repent of their sins and who will proclaim the coming forgiveness of sins and mercy of God. When John grows up, he leaves and goes out into the wilderness of Judea until the time that the **manifestation** of the Messiah would come.

Jesus is born in Bethlehem. Even though Mary and Joseph do not live in Bethlehem, they are required to go to the place of their ancestors because of a census by Caesar Augustus. When they arrive, there is no room in the inn, so they stay where the animals were kept; here, Jesus is born and placed in a manger. This is hardly the place where one would expect the King of the world to be born, but this shows the humility of God. Continuing the theme of the exaltation of the humble, the very first people to see Jesus are shepherds. Shepherds were social outcasts in Israel and did not get much respect. However, God exalts them by coming to them first and giving them the privilege of being the first witnesses of Jesus. On a side note, the fact that these shepherds are out at night is evidence that Jesus was born in the spring or summer, not in December.

When Jesus is eight days old, according to the Law of Moses, Mary and Joseph bring Him to the temple to be circumcised. When they are there, they are met by two more witnesses. The first is Simeon, who had been told when he was young that he would see the Messiah before he dies. He gives the *Nunc dimitis*, a prayer thanking God for His faithfulness (verses 29–32). Simeon does warn Mary that Jesus will be a source of division and contention and will cause grief even

to Mary (referring to His death). The other witness is Anna, a widow of eighty-four years. When she sees Jesus, she tells everyone about Him.

When Jesus is twelve, His parents take Him to Jerusalem. When they leave, Jesus stays behind, talking with the rabbis and amazing them with His understanding. When His parents find Him, He tells them that He must be in His Father's house. Then He submits to them and increases "in wisdom and stature, and in favor with God and men" (verse 52); Jesus grows up.

> **manifestation:** a sign that shows something clearly; here, the coming of the Messiah

> *Nunc dimitis:* Latin for "Now you dismiss," the first words of the Song of Simeon (Luke 2:29–32); a prayer thanking God for His faithfulness

Thought Questions:

1. Why is it not a sin for Jesus to stay behind in Jerusalem when His parents lose track of Him?

2. If Jesus is able to sit and have theological conversations with the religious leaders of His day, what implications might this have for young people today?

Jesus' Baptism, Genealogy, and Temptation: Luke 3:1–4:13
Lesson 43

Having introduced John the Baptist and Jesus, Luke now ties the two together in chapter three. John's role for Israel is to prepare people for the coming of Jesus. So, out in the wilderness of Judea, near the very spot where Elijah was taken into heaven alive, John the Baptist begins to baptize people in the Jordan. John's message is very simple—repent, because the Messiah is coming and He will judge the people of the world for their sins. John is identified as the voice who cries out in the wilderness from Isaiah 40. This repentance is more than mere confession and acknowledgement of guilt; John gives people very practical commands for how to repent. For the tax collectors, they are not to take more than they ought. For the soldiers, they are not to take advantage of the people. For everyone else, he says to be generous to others in need. John makes it very clear to the people that he is not the Messiah, but when the Messiah comes He will baptize them with fire and the Holy Spirit. As mentioned in the lesson from Matthew, John the Baptist expects Jesus to bring judgment when He reveals Himself. John eventually baptizes Jesus, and it is at this point that the Holy Spirit publicly descends upon Jesus. Jesus' ministry is done through the power of the Holy Spirit.

After Jesus' baptism, and before Jesus begins His public ministry, Luke includes a genealogy of Jesus. There are a couple of points worthy of note about Luke's genealogy of Jesus. The *first issue* is that, rather than stopping with Abraham as Matthew does, Luke traces Jesus' genealogy all the way back to Adam and then God Himself. This is consistent with Luke's theme of the universal mission of Jesus. Jesus is not just the Jewish Messiah; He is the Savior of all whom God has chosen before the foundation of the world (Ephesians 1:4). The *second issue* with Jesus' genealogy is the differences in names between Matthew and Luke's accounts. While both of these genealogies agree between Abraham and David, they differ greatly between David and Joseph. Luke identifies Joseph's father as Heli, whereas Matthew identifies Joseph's father as Jacob. Matthew traces Jesus' genealogy through Solomon, whereas Luke traces it through Nathan. There are a number of proposed solutions to this problem. The most common is that Luke's account actually traces Mary's lineage because Joseph is not Jesus' real father, whereas Matthew traces it through Joseph as Jesus' legal father. If this is the case, both Mary and Joseph are descended from David.

The first thing that the Holy Spirit does after descending upon Jesus is to send Him into the wilderness to be tempted for forty days. As mentioned in the lesson from Matthew's account, the forty days in the wilderness alludes to the forty years of wandering in the wilderness for Israel. Yet, unlike the Israelites, who were well fed and provided for in the wilderness, Jesus fasts during His forty day stay. At the end of the forty days, when Jesus is quite hungry and weak from the lack of food, this is when Satan decides to tempt Him. The *first temptation* is a practical one—Jesus is hungry, and Satan tempts Him to make food out of rocks. However, this temptation is also an attack on Jesus' relationship with His Father. Satan basically says, "If you are the Son of God, as you say you are, prove it!" Nevertheless, Jesus quotes Deuteronomy and says that "Man shall not live by bread alone, but by every word of God" (Luke 4:4; cf. Deuteronomy 8:3). The *second temptation* is the temptation for glory without the cross. Satan offers to give Jesus all authority on earth if He would simply worship him. Whether or not Satan has that authority is debatable, but he offers it to Jesus, nonetheless. Once again, Jesus quotes Deuteronomy, saying that we are to worship God alone (verse 8; cf. Deuteronomy 6:13). Finally, with respect to the *third temptation,* Satan tempts Jesus to abuse His powers as the Son of God

again. Satan tempts Jesus to throw Himself down from the temple so that God would save Him. Yet once again, Jesus quotes Deuteronomy, saying that we are not to test God in this way (verse 12; cf. Deuteronomy 6:16). When Satan sees that he is defeated, he retreats for another opportune time.

Thought Question:

Look up the passage that Satan quotes in Luke 4:10–11 (from Psalm 91:11–12). Why do you think Satan stops the quote where he does rather than reading the next verse?

Jesus' First Ministry in Galilee: Luke 4:14–44

Lesson 44

Following Jesus' baptism and the temptation in the wilderness, Jesus returns home to His hometown of Nazareth in Galilee. What better place to reveal Himself publicly than in the synagogue at His hometown? As was custom at the time, any competent man could read from the Scriptures and preach in a Jewish synagogue. So Jesus stands up and reads from Isaiah 61:1–3 and then sits down. In this passage, Isaiah speaks of a man who will heal the sick, cure the blind, proclaim freedom to those who are enslaved, and preach the gospel to the poor. Luke builds up the tension by mentioning that everyone's eyes are fixed on Jesus as He sits down. It is likely that news of Jesus' baptism and the voice from heaven and John's testimony about Jesus has reached the town of Nazareth. In addition, the passage that Jesus reads is traditionally understood as a passage about the Messiah. So when Jesus reads this passage, the people wait eagerly to see if Jesus admits that He is the Messiah.

However, when Jesus says that this passage is fulfilled today in their hearing, He receives a mixed response. The people marvel at His words, yet they wonder how He could be the Messiah, since they know where He comes from as Joseph's son. While this sounds like a reasonable cause for doubt, Jesus knows that most of them are stubborn and will not believe in Him. So He tells them that "no prophet is accepted in his own country" (verse 24). He knows that the people want Him to perform the very miracles that He has just said that He fulfills, but He refuses to give them these miracles. Instead, Jesus makes a reference to two miracles by Elijah and Elisha. During the time of the famine, God sends Elijah to a widow in Zarephath, a Gentile region (1 Kings 17). God also has Elisha heal Naaman the Syrian, even though there were plenty of lepers in Israel (2 Kings 5).

Though Jesus does not say this directly, He implies that they are not going to see His miracles, but instead the Gentiles will see His miracles.

Based on the response of the people from Nazareth, it is clear that they understand what He is implying. The thought of the Messiah going to the Gentiles and not the Jews only would have been repulsive to them. In addition, the fact that they will not see these miracles at all is even more offensive. So the people drive Him out of the synagogue and bring Him to the edge of a cliff to throw Him off. This is more than simple offense; these people with whom Jesus grew up want to kill Him. This is truly a sad scene. Once again, the tension builds, as it would appear that Jesus would die. Yet Jesus simply walks through the crowds and goes on His way. We are not told how He does this, but Jesus survives this attack.

After revealing Himself at Nazareth, Jesus goes through the other towns in Galilee, particularly to Capernaum. Jesus gets quite a different response in Capernaum. The people are amazed at His teachings because He speaks with authority. Rather than simply talking about what other Bible scholars have said, Jesus speaks as though He is the author of the Bible itself. Moreover, while Jesus is teaching in the synagogue, a man with a demon begins to interrupt Him, crying out with a loud voice. Yet Jesus rebukes the demon and tells it to be quiet and come out of the man. The demon listens to Jesus, and the people are even more amazed. News of this exorcism spreads throughout the region, and people begin to gather around to see Him.

Jesus then leaves the synagogue and goes to Simon Peter's house. Simon Peter's mother-in-law has a fever and cannot show hospitality; so Jesus heals her, and she begins to take care of them. That entire night, Jesus heals many and casts out demons from the large crowd that gathers at this house. So the following day Jesus leaves and goes off by Himself to pray and recover. The crowds, however, find Him and beg Him to come back. Yet Jesus tells them that He needs to preach in other cities, as well; consequently, He goes to the surrounding towns and preaches the gospel to them.

Thought Question:

Why do you think Jesus rebukes the demon and casts him out of the man if what the demon is saying about Jesus is true?

Ministry Foundations and Opposition: Luke 5:1–6:16
Lesson 45

From Matthew's account, we learn that Jesus calls Peter and Andrew to follow Him while they are casting out their nets at sea. Luke gives us more detail about Peter's calling. Before calling Peter to follow Him, Jesus teaches the crowds by the sea. Because the crowds have grown so large, Jesus asks Peter to let Him use his boat so that Jesus can teach from the water. After Jesus is done teaching the crowds, He tells Peter to set out to sea to go fishing. Even though Peter knows that fish do not normally come out during the day, he listens when Jesus tells him to let down his nets. The catch of fish is so great that Peter cannot pull all the fish in by himself; so he calls for his fishing partners, James and John, to come and help. Realizing that he is in the presence of a holy Man, Peter is deeply convicted of his sin and tells Jesus to go away. However, Jesus tells Peter that this miraculous catch of fish is a foreshadowing of his later ministry, for Peter will become a fisher of men. So Peter, Andrew, James, and John all leave their boats and follow Jesus.

Jesus stands at a crossroads in history. He is bringing about a new order of things and putting an end to the old order. Part of the glory of the new covenant that Jesus brings is that it comes with power. Jesus' miracles reveal this power and the greatness of this new covenant. Luke next records the story of Jesus healing a leper. This man has faith in Jesus but asks if He is willing to make him clean. For a leper, his sickness is more than just a physical ailment. Because of the ceremonial laws of the old covenant, a leper would be ceremonially unclean and cut off from the community of the people and from the temple. So by healing the leper, Jesus also restores his dignity, social status, and community. However, after this miracle, the news about Jesus spreads so far that Jesus has to regularly withdraw from the crowds.

The next miracle that Luke records is the healing of the paralytic. Because the crowds are so large, this man needs his friends to dig a hole in the roof of the house where Jesus is in order to lower their paralytic friend into the house. When Jesus sees the man, He uses this healing as an opportunity to show His authority. In this case, rather than simply healing the man, He forgives his sins. The Pharisees and teachers of the Law are furious at this, asking where Jesus gets His authority to forgive sins. This illustrates the consistent opposition that Jesus will receive from the religious leaders. By healing the paralytic, Jesus shows that He does have the authority to forgive sins. The opposition of the religious leaders is once again evident in the calling of Levi. After Jesus calls Levi (also called Matthew) to follow Him, Levi throws a party in his home and invites Jesus. When the religious leaders see Jesus eating and drinking with Levi's tax collector friends, they judge Jesus. Yet Jesus, knowing their thoughts, reminds them that it is the sick who need doctors, not the healthy. Jesus did not come to the healthy, but to the sick. In light of this opposition, Jesus speaks about putting new wine into new wineskins. If a person were to put new wine into the old wineskins, the old wineskins would crack and the new wine would leak. This teaching is an indirect challenge to the religious leaders. Jesus is bringing in the new covenant, and the old way of doing things cannot handle it. With a new covenant comes a new leader, Jesus, and the old leaders will have to accept it.

Sadly, most of the time the old religious leaders will not accept Jesus, as evidenced again in chapter 6. On two occasions, the religious leaders confront Jesus for "**desecrating**" the Sabbath by picking grain and healing. Jesus confronts the religious leaders on both occasions, showing them the heart of the Law. One of the most important elements of Jesus' earthly ministry is His disciples. So Luke tells us that Jesus prays all night before He chooses the Twelve. As we already know, the Twelve will be foundational for building Jesus' kingdom.

> **desecrating:** treating a holy place, object, practice, or day irreverently or with disrespect

Thought Questions:

1. Why do you think Peter tells Jesus to go away after the miraculous catch of fish?

2. When Jesus says to put new wine into new wineskins, what do you think the new wine and the new wineskins represent?

The Sermon on the Plain: Luke 6:17–49

Lesson 46

After Jesus chooses the twelve disciples, He and His disciples meet the crowds while on a "level place" or plain. Jesus heals many and casts out demons from many. Jesus then begins to teach the crowds. What follows is traditionally called the Sermon on the Plain.

It is clear from a basic reading of this sermon that it is an abbreviated form of the Sermon on the Mount. Some people believe that Luke merely simplifies the longer Sermon on the Mount and summarizes it with this sermon. However, we are told explicitly that the Sermon on the Mount is on a mountain while this sermon is on level ground. Since the Sermon on the Mount is a sermon based on the core of the Law, the Ten Commandments, it is plausible and likely that Jesus spoke this sermon on multiple occasions. Thus, it is likely that this sermon, while very similar to the Sermon on the Mount, is a different sermon given at a different time.

Like the Sermon on the Mount, this sermon begins with a set of beatitudes, though Luke's version is truncated. In this sermon, however, after giving the beatitudes, Jesus follows with a set of woes. Each of these woes is the antithesis of the blessings that Jesus gives with the beatitudes. While the poor are blessed in His kingdom, the rich are cursed. While the hungry are blessed, those who are full are cursed. Those who weep and are slandered will be blessed, but those who laugh and are praised will be cursed. Behind all of these antitheses is the understanding that blessings here on earth do not translate to blessings in heaven, whereas the humiliation of trials here on earth translate to blessings in heaven.

Jesus then draws His attention towards what is sometimes called the "law of love." Rather than hating our enemies and getting revenge, Jesus says that we are to love our enemies and bless those who curse us. When someone does harm to us, rather than reciprocating in like manner, we are to reciprocate with greater kindness and love. Included in this law of love is the Golden Rule, "just as you want men to do to you, you also do to them likewise" (verse 31). If we treat people the way that we want to be treated, it will be much easier to show them love. Many people only think about things from their own perspectives, but Jesus says to put yourself in the other person's shoes and treat them as you would like to be treated.

So why should we respond in love when people treat us poorly? Jesus gives three basic reasons. *First*, it is easy to be kind to people who are kind to us and to love people who love us. Nearly everyone loves the people who love him. Those in the kingdom of God are called to be different from the world, so we are to respond better than the world. *Second*, we will be rewarded in heaven for responding with love. We may not get any earthly benefits for these actions, but God will reward us. *Third*, God Himself gives mercy and grace to those who hate Him, so we are also to give mercy and grace to others.

We also need to stay humble. We are not to judge or condemn others, but rather we need to examine ourselves to see if we have done the same things. We also need to remember that we are all students of Jesus Christ Himself. Apart from Him, we are blind. It is ridiculous for a blind man to give directions to another blind man. So also it is ridiculous to try to navigate life without the influence of Jesus. Even though Jesus tells us to remain humble and to not judge or condemn others, He does warn us to pay attention to the fruits that others bear. The things that we do are a reflection of the condition of our hearts. If a person has a good heart, he will bear good fruit; if a person has a bad heart, he will bear bad fruit.

Like the Sermon on the Mount, Jesus finishes this sermon by comparing the person who follows His teaching to a person who built his house on the rock. If we put this teaching into practice, we will stand strong; but if we do not, we will fall like a house without a foundation.

Thought Questions:

1. If Jesus sends down woes upon the rich, is it a bad thing to be rich? Why or why not?

2. In your own words, what does it mean to judge others? Is it ever okay to make judgment calls about people based on their appearance? Why or why not?

Jesus the Prophet: Luke 7

Lesson 47

Even though we know that John the Baptist is the one who comes in the spirit of Elijah, Jesus' ministry looks very similar to the ministry of Elijah. Elijah and Elisha are unique as prophets in that they perform many healing miracles, and often the one healed is a Gentile. The first two miracles in Luke 7 should remind us of Elijah. The first person whom Jesus encounters is a centurion. This Gentile has a servant who is sick. Recognizing that Jesus has the authority and power to heal his servant, the centurion does not even want to bother Jesus to come to the servant but to say the word and heal from a distance. Jesus points out this man as a model of faith, a faith greater than any seen in Israel. From there, Jesus encounters a funeral for the son of a widow. Like Elijah, who raised a widow's son from the dead (1 Kings 17), Jesus raises this man from the dead. When Jesus resurrects this man, the news spreads that Jesus is a Prophet.

In light of the similarities between the ministries of Elijah/Elisha and Jesus, it is fitting that the next person we hear about is John the Baptist. When John the Baptist hears about the miracles that Jesus is perform-

ing, he sends messengers to Jesus to see if He is indeed the Messiah. Pointing out the miracles that He has performed, Jesus quotes two Messianic passages from Isaiah, from chapters 35 and 61. Jesus is doing the very things that the Messiah is supposed to do when He heals the sick and preaches the gospel. Jesus seizes this opportunity to speak well of John the Baptist. Yet Jesus also reminds the people that what He is bringing is even greater than what John the Baptist had brought. In fact, anyone who gets to be in the kingdom that Jesus is bringing will be greater than John the Baptist.

John the Baptist's role was to prepare the way for Jesus. This is evident by the way that people respond to Jesus. Those who had been baptized by John respond favorably to Jesus and glorify God because of Him. However, the religious leaders, who had refused to repent and be baptized by John, also refuse to believe in Jesus. In fact, these religious leaders accuse John the Baptist of having a demon, and they declare Jesus a glutton and a drunkard.

Because of their own self-righteousness, these religious leaders judge and condemn Jesus for the company that He keeps. In fact, when one of the Pharisees invites Jesus to his house for a meal, they are greeted by a "sinner" who anoints Jesus' feet. This woman takes a very expensive flask of fragrant oil, or perfume, pours it on Jesus' feet, and then wipes His feet with her tears and with her hair. Rather than seeing this as an incredible act of love, the Pharisee judges the woman and Jesus. The Pharisee concludes that Jesus cannot be a prophet because a prophet would not associate with a sinner.

Jesus responds to this Pharisee's attitude with a parable. There are two people who get their debts forgiven from their creditor. One of them has 50 denarii forgiven, and the other has 500 denarii forgiven. Jesus then asks the Pharisee which debtor will love the creditor more. Clearly, the one who was forgiven more will love more. Rather than judging this woman for her great sin, Jesus says that her great sin has resulted in this incredible act of love because she has been forgiven so much. On the other hand, because this Pharisee thinks that he has not done much sin, he is not capable of love. In fact, Jesus shows the Pharisee that this woman has actually served Him much better than the Pharisee, even though the Pharisee invited Him over. The Pharisee has not shown great hospitality. He had not given Jesus water for His feet, yet the woman has wiped His feet with her tears. He had not given Jesus a customary kiss of greeting, yet this woman has not stopped kissing His feet. He has not anointed Jesus' head, yet the woman has anointed Him with fragrant oil. This woman becomes the truly righteous one here because she loves Jesus so much more than the self-righteous Pharisee. Jesus then finishes this meal by forgiving her sins.

Thought Question:

Based on the parable that Jesus gives the Pharisee here, why is it a good thing for us to understand the depths of our own sins? Based on this parable, what is one way to grow in your love for Jesus?

More Teachings and Healings: Luke 8

Lesson 48

One of the themes that Luke emphasizes in his gospel is the role of social outcasts in the ministry of Jesus. We learn from the beginning of Luke 8 that it is not only the twelve who follow Jesus around, but there are also a number of women. These women not only follow Jesus, but play a major role in His ministry by providing for His and His disciples' needs. One of these women, Joanna, is married to one of the stewards for King Herod. Jesus' ministry has already impacted the house of the king.

Luke next records the parable of the sower. Since we have already encountered this parable in the gospel of Matthew and in the gospel of Mark, we are only going to summarize this parable here. This parable is a parable about parables. Jesus knows that not everyone will respond to His teachings in the same manner. Some people will not be impacted at all by His teaching because Satan will snatch it before it takes root. Others respond immediately, but when it gets difficult to follow His teaching they will fall away. Still others respond to His teaching and it takes root, but they do not put it into practice because they are distracted with the things of life. However, for those who hear His teaching and diligently put it into practice, they will grow and mature in massive ways.

Luke connects this teaching with Jesus' teaching about letting light shine. In Matthew's account, when Jesus mentions putting a light under a vessel, it is in the context of Christians being lights to the world. Here, it is not Christians who are the light, but Jesus' teaching that is the light. Jesus is providing people with the light (His teachings), and they have the responsibility to walk by that light and to learn from it. Yet there is a warning here, for to those who have been given the light of Jesus' teaching, if they do not heed it they can lose it. Jesus demands that people respond and put His teaching into practice. Even when Jesus' mother and brothers come to see Him, He says that those who put His words into practice are His true mother and brothers.

Following this teaching, Jesus and His disciples leave by boat to travel to other places. While they are sailing, however, a violent storm arises and almost capsizes the boat. When the disciples come to Jesus, they find Him asleep below deck. So Jesus wakes up and rebukes the storm, and it becomes calm. He also rebukes His disciples for their lack of faith. Upon arriving at the other side of the lake, Jesus is met by a demon-possessed man. Because of the demon, this man has superhuman strength and is forced to live in the tombs. When Jesus questions this man, it is revealed that it is actually a legion of 2,000 demons that live in this man. Jesus gives the demons permission to go into a herd of pigs, and they all run into the lake and drown. Yet this great work makes the people of that region very afraid, and they ask Jesus to leave.

When Jesus arrives back on the other side of the lake, He is met by yet another large crowd. One of the members of this crowd, a ruler of the synagogue named Jairus, asks Jesus to heal his dying daughter. Jesus agrees to heal his daughter and goes to meet the girl. On the way, however, Jesus is met by a woman who had a bleeding disorder. By simply touching the edge of His robe, she is healed of her disease. Even though Jesus does not do anything to heal this woman, He feels the power go out from Him and seeks out the woman. He tells her that it is her faith that has made her well. Yet, as He speaks to her, word arrives that Jairus' daughter has died. Even though the messenger says not to bother Jesus, He goes anyway to raise the girl from the dead. For this miracle, Jesus only allows Peter, James, and John to go in with Him. Jesus then tells the girl to get up, and she does. However, because it is not yet time for Jesus to reveal Himself fully, He tells the parents not to tell anyone what has happened.

Thought Questions:

1. What lessons can we learn about faith and life from the calming of the storm?

2. Why do you think that Jesus only allows three of His disciples to see Him raise the girl from the dead?

Jesus the Messiah: Luke 9:1–50

Lesson 49

Jesus does not merely choose the twelve disciples so that they could stay with Him and learn from Him. He also sends them out as an extension of His own ministry. Just as Jesus heals and preaches the gospel of the kingdom, so also will the twelve disciples. They are sent out throughout the towns in Israel and told not to bring much with them; they are to rely on the people of the towns for their provisions.

While the disciples are out fulfilling the mission that Jesus gives them, Luke draws our attention to King Herod. News about Jesus has spread far and wide, and even King Herod wants to know more about Him. In fact, the responses that Herod gets when he inquires about Jesus are very similar to the responses that Peter will offer when Jesus asks him who He is. Some people believe that Jesus is John the Baptist, raised from the dead; while others believe he is Elijah or one of the old prophets raised from the dead. Because of all that Herod hears concerning Jesus, he wants to meet Jesus face-to-face.

Now according to Matthew and Mark's accounts, we know that it is right around this time that Jesus receives word concerning John the Baptist's death and that He decides to go off to a deserted place to pray about it. Yet Luke does not mention this. Luke focuses on the mission of the twelve and how Jesus brings them to a deserted place to debrief their mission. However, when Jesus and His disciples arrive at a deserted place, it is not deserted. A crowd has gathered together and meets them when they get to the deserted place. Rather than being annoyed at the crowds for ruining His time with His disciples, Jesus has compassion on the crowds and teaches and heals them. When it gets late, the disciples tell Jesus to dismiss the crowds so that they can go home and eat. Instead, Jesus tells the disciples to feed the crowds. This, of course, is when Jesus miraculously feeds the 5,000. Luke's account differs from Matthew and Mark's accounts in that Peter's confession immediately follows the feeding of the 5,000 in Luke's account. Yet, in Matthew and Mark's accounts, the next event is Jesus walking on water. Luke places Peter's confession here because it is parallel to the responses to Herod's inquiry about Jesus.

Luke also adds to Peter's confession that it comes after Jesus is in prayer. While Jesus is praying, His disciples come to Him; and Jesus asks them who people say that He is. We are not told explicitly what Jesus prays for, but it would only make sense that He was praying about when to reveal that He is the Messiah. So when Jesus asks Peter who he says that Jesus is, Peter confesses that He is the Christ. Interestingly, Luke does not record Peter's rebuke. Instead, Luke focuses on Jesus' teaching about His coming death and resurrection. From the moment that Jesus acknowledges that He is the Mes-

siah to His disciples, His main focus is on His coming death and resurrection. In order for the disciples to be prepared for what is about to come, He warns them that they too must be willing to suffer.

Jesus also prepares for His coming death and resurrection through the Transfiguration. Not only is Jesus refreshed by Moses and Elijah at this time, but His disciples get to see His glory while He is on the mountain. Luke informs us that Peter, James, and John do not mention the Transfiguration to the other disciples until later. Just as with Jesus' baptism, out of the glory cloud God affirms His love for Jesus as His Son, but here God adds, "Hear Him!" (verse 35).

When Jesus and His disciples descend from the mountain, Jesus encounters a man whose son was demon-possessed. The other disciples could not cast out this demon, but Jesus casts it out. Once again, He draws their attention to His coming death. Sadly, the disciples do not get it and quarrel about who will be the greatest in the kingdom. However, Jesus reminds them to be humble and even uses a little child as the model of greatness in His kingdom.

Thought Questions:

1. Even though Jesus and His disciples need to take time to debrief after their mission, Jesus still has compassion on the crowds. What can we learn from Jesus' attitude here?

2. Why is it important for Jesus to be transfigured before the three disciples at this point in Jesus' ministry?

Preparations for Jesus' Departure: Luke 9:51–10:24

Lesson 50

Most of the material that we have encountered in Luke so far is also present in Matthew and Mark. However, starting in Luke 9:51, most of the material in the next chapters (through chapter 18) is unique to Luke.

We learn from verse 51 that, following the confession by Peter and the Transfiguration, Jesus "steadfastly set His face to go to Jerusalem." In other words, Jesus knows that He is about to die and be resurrected, so He makes up His mind to head to Jerusalem. Because He knows that He is about to die, Jesus works diligently to prepare His disciples for His departure. In order to save time, and in order to bear more fruit, Jesus sends out His disciples into the villages to prepare them for

His arrival. The Samaritans from the first village reject them, however. The explicit reason given for why they reject Jesus is because He is on His way to Jerusalem. One of the major points of dispute between the Samaritans and Jews is the importance of the temple in Jerusalem. Jews say that one must worship in Jerusalem, but the Samaritans worship God in their own region. This cultural conflict seems to be the cause of this rejection by the Samaritans.

James and John have the reputation of being the "Sons of Thunder," and their response to the rejection of the Samaritans shows us why they have this reputation. Always interested in power and authority, these two disciples ask Jesus for permission to call down fire from heaven to destroy the Samaritans, just as Elijah had done to his enemies centuries before (2 Kings 1). Yet Jesus reminds them that He did not come for judgment, but to save people.

As Jesus travels on the way through Samaria, He is met by three different people. Jesus' responses to these people reveal another theme that is prevalent in the gospel of Luke, the cost of discipleship. The first man approaches Jesus and tells Him that he will follow Him wherever He will go. This man has great intentions but does not understand to what he is committing. Following Jesus is not a walk in the park; it will involve suffering and sacrifice. Jesus approaches the second man and tells him to follow Him. However, this man is not ready to leave all and follow Jesus. This man says that he needs to first bury his father. This could mean that his father has just died, but more likely it means that his father is old and that he wants to wait until his father dies to follow Jesus. Jesus basically tells this man that He needs to be more important than even family. The third person approaches Jesus and offers to follow Him, but asks for permission to say goodbye to his family. However, Jesus says that, to follow Him, a person cannot go back to his old life. All three of these encounters highlight the cost and commitment of following Jesus. If a person is to follow Jesus, he needs to be "all in."

Just as Jesus had sent out a few of His disciples to prepare the Samaritan villages for His arrival, He then sends out seventy-two more disciples into the villages to preach the gospel and prepare them for Him. This is where Jesus gives the famous phrase, "The harvest truly is great, but the laborers are few" (verse 2). The instructions that Jesus gives the seventy-two are essentially the same instructions that Jesus had given the Twelve when He sent them out earlier to preach. They are to basically carry nothing for their journey and are to be dependent on the people from the villages to provide. If the vil-

lages reject them, they are to simply move on, knowing that God will judge those villages in the future. When the seventy-two arrive back, they are excited that they are even able to cast out demons in Jesus' name. Jesus, however, tells them not to be excited about their power and authority; rather, they are to be excited that their names are written in heaven. Following Jesus is not primarily about power and authority; it is about salvation. Nevertheless, Jesus does pull the disciples aside privately and tell them that they are blessed to see the things that they have seen, for even the prophets longed to see the things that they see.

Thought Question:

Do you think that the harvest is still plentiful but the workers are few? If so, what implications does this have for us today?

The Final Teaching Circuit, Part 1: Luke 10:25–11:54

Lesson 51

Jesus is next met on His journey by an expert in the Law. At first, this lawyer appears to understand what Jesus has been teaching all along. When this man asks Jesus what he must do to be saved, Jesus throws the question back at him. Because this man is an expert in the Law, Jesus asks him what he has concluded from his reading of the Law. This man's answer matches what we know is the heart of the Law, to love God and to love others. In fact, whereas Jesus recognizes these as two different commandments, this lawyer combines the commandment to love God and the commandment to love your neighbor into one command. Jesus commends this man and tells him to follow what he has suggested. It is here where we see this man acting like a lawyer, for he asks who his neighbor is. If we are to love our neighbor, it would be important to know who specifically we are supposed to love.

This question leads Jesus to tell the parable of the good Samaritan. In this story, a man is beaten, robbed, and left on the side of the road. Two men (a priest and a Levite), who are supposed to be religious leaders and examples for others, see this man on the side of the road and ignore him. However, the hero of this story is unexpected, a Samaritan. As we have already seen, the Jews despise Samaritans. So when it is the Samaritan who shows love to this stranger, this is designed to humble the lawyer. This story illustrates that the lawyer is asking the wrong question. The question should not be, "Who is my neighbor?", but rather, "How can I be a neighbor to people?"

Luke next mentions an interaction that Jesus has with His two friends Mary and Martha. These are the same people that Jesus stays with during the Passion Week, along with their brother Lazarus, whom Jesus raises from the dead. Here, Martha complains to Jesus that Mary is not helping out with serving Jesus. While Martha has been serving, Mary has been talking with Jesus and enjoying His company. Jesus tells Martha that there are some things that are more important than serving. Mary has chosen to spend time with Jesus, and this is more important.

Following this, Luke includes a number of Jesus' teachings on prayer. When asked how to pray, Jesus gives the Lord's Prayer. Because of the treatment that was given to the Lord's Prayer in Matthew's account, we will not examine it in detail now. However, in Luke's account, Jesus follows His teaching on the Lord's Prayer with an illustration about the importance of persistence in prayer. Just as a friend would provide bread for a friend in need even though it is inconvenient because of the persistence of the one requesting, God also wants us to be persistent when we pray. We are encouraged to ask and to seek God. Luke, however, finishes the teaching on asking and seeking with an interesting twist. According to Matthew's account of this teaching, Jesus says that God will give "good things" to those who ask of Him. Yet Luke says that God will give "the Holy Spirit" to those who ask. This makes sense in light of the fact that Luke also writes Acts. In the book of Acts, the Holy Spirit empowers the early church to spread the gospel and perform miracles. Luke simply defines one of these "good things" as "the Holy Spirit."

Next, Luke draws our attention to another event in the life of Jesus. This next interaction Jesus has is spurred on by the casting out of a mute demon. When the crowds see this, they marvel. Yet some people refuse to believe in Jesus and accuse Him of being demon-possessed, while others seek a sign from Him. Jesus, however, tells them that it is ridiculous to cast out demons through the power of a demon. Moreover, for those who ask for a sign, Jesus only offers them the sign of Jonah, who was able to get the wicked Nineveh to repent. Yet these people are worse because they refuse to repent. The light from this generation is sadly blocked out as many reject Jesus.

Thought Questions:

1. Jesus commends Mary because she does a better thing than Martha by spending time with Jesus.

Do you find that you are more prone to be like Martha, who focuses on working for Jesus, or Mary, who focuses on spending time with Jesus? How can you balance these two ideas?

2. Is there something that you can be more persistent about in your prayer life?

The Final Teaching Circuit, Part 2: Luke 12–13
Lesson 52

As Jesus draws closer to Jerusalem on His final journey, He continues to prepare the people for His departure. In chapter 12, Jesus offers a number of warnings to the crowds and to His disciples. First, Jesus warns the people not to fear men but to fear God. After all, the worst thing that man can do is kill the body, but God has power to kill the soul, as well. Because we are to fear God, we have to watch what we say and avoid hypocrisy. So we need to do what is right, even if men kill us, because it is far worse to offend God. Yet, even in that fear, we must remember that God knows us and loves us. Jesus Himself will be our Advocate before the Father, defending us in the presence of the Father; that is, if we confess Jesus before others. In addition, we have this promise that the Holy Spirit will give us the words to say when we speak of Him before others.

Next, Jesus warns the crowds about covetousness and the love of money. When a man asks Jesus to tell his brother to divide his inheritance with him, Jesus warns him about covetousness. This issue is so petty in comparison to what Jesus is offering the people. To illustrate the folly and danger of covetousness, Jesus gives a parable. In this parable, a rich farmer puts all of his hope and focus on his own wealth. In fact, he spends all of his energy and time trying to build up enough wealth so that he could live an easy life. However, as soon as he finally gets enough money to relax, he dies. This man's entire life is focused on building up something that he will not be able to enjoy. Rather than building up earthly wealth, we need to be rich towards God with good deeds so that we could get "money" that cannot be destroyed in heaven. Rather than worrying about money, therefore, we should focus on building the kingdom of God and know that God will provide for what we need. If He takes care of even the animals, we can trust that He will take care of us, who are much more valuable.

In light of this, Jesus warns the crowds to remain faithful with their lives now because they never know when

Jesus is going to come back and require them to give an account of what they have done with their lives. He gives two parables that deal with being prepared for the day of accountability. In both parables, the servants are either rewarded for being prepared for the return of their master, or reprimanded for not being prepared. We, therefore, must live in such a way that when Jesus returns, we will be ready. Moreover, with Jesus going away, there is not going to be peace, but division. In this perilous time, we need to work hard for reconciliation.

Jesus then uses some disasters as an opportunity to warn the people about judgment. Some people believe that natural disasters or calamities come only to terrible sinners. However, Jesus warns them that if they do not repent of their own wickedness, even worse things will happen to them. He then gives the parable of the fig tree to warn the people that, even though God is patient with us, we must bear the fruit of good works or we will be destroyed.

Some time later, Jesus heals another woman on the Sabbath. As has commonly been the case, the religious leaders accuse Jesus of breaking the Sabbath. Jesus, however, points out this man's hypocrisy in that he would save his own animal on the Sabbath but not a human. Jesus then gives two more parables. In the parable of the mustard seed and the parable of the leaven, He focuses on the slow but steady growth of the kingdom over time.

As Jesus draws even closer to Jerusalem, He is asked if only few are saved. Jesus responds that only those who do things the right way, who enter by the narrow gate, will be saved. There are many who will long to be saved, but do it their own way, and as a result will face judgment. Finally, after being warned that Herod wants to kill Him, He laments over the destruction that is coming to Jerusalem because of what they are about to do to Him.

Thought Questions:

1. If we deny Jesus before men, He will deny us before the angels in heaven. Does this mean that we lose our salvation if we fail to acknowledge Jesus before others? Why or why not?

2. Is it wrong to store up money? If not, how can we avoid the fate of the man from the parable in this section?

The Final Teaching Circuit, Dinner and Discipleship: Luke 14

Lesson 53

Jesus' relationship with the religious leaders is interesting. In chapter 14, Jesus is invited to eat at the house of one of the rulers of the Pharisees, even though the Pharisees want Him dead. While Jesus is eating at this man's house, a man with dropsy comes to Jesus to be healed. Considering that the Pharisees and other religious leaders have criticized Jesus on multiple occasions for healing on the Sabbath, everyone's eyes are undoubtedly on Jesus here to see if He will heal the man. Knowing what everyone is thinking, Jesus asks them directly if it is lawful to heal on the Sabbath. When they do not answer, He heals the man. To show them the ridiculous nature of their laws, Jesus points out again that these very same people would be willing to save their own animals on the Sabbath. If it is okay to do this, certainly it is okay to heal a man.

Now in a society like the one in Jesus' day, there is a high emphasis placed on social status. People were regularly concerned with how other people viewed them. As a result, when people invited others over to their houses, the seats were usually arranged in order of social standing. Jesus uses this during this meal as a chance to teach the people there about the value of humility. Rather than fighting over who gets the seat of honor, Jesus suggests sitting down at the lowest place of honor. This way, when the master of the house sees this person in the lowest seat, he can honor him by moving him to the place of honor. Yet, if they fight over the place of honor and someone higher comes along, they would have to face the embarrassment of having to move for that person. This illustrates the value of humility. Rather than fighting over who is the best, we are to humble ourselves and allow God to exalt us.

Jesus goes further with this teaching, however. Jesus knows that this Pharisee invited Him and the others over to his house because of the social and political benefits that it would offer. If this man invites men of high ranking over to his house, these men would be more likely to do a favor for him or to invite him over to their houses. Instead of this, Jesus suggests inviting people over who have nothing to offer in return. Instead of friends and family and rich people, we should host feasts for the poor and the maimed, the lame and the blind. These men offer no social status or earthly rewards, but God will reward us for this sacrifice.

Jesus also uses this dinner as an opportunity to speak of the gospel and the kingdom of God. Regularly, Jesus compares the kingdom of God to a supper that the master throws. The master is God, and the supper represents salvation. In this case, the master throws a supper and invites the normal guests. These guests, however, make up excuses for why they cannot come, just as people offer many excuses for why they reject the salvation that is offered to them. Because the regular guests refuse to come, the master invites the poor, the maimed, the lame, and the blind instead; and they enjoy the feast. Implied in this parable is a judgment upon the religious leaders. The religious leaders should be the first to accept Jesus, but because they reject Him, the poor, the sick, the lame, and the blind are receiving salvation instead.

Later, Jesus offers another teaching about the cost of discipleship. In order to illustrate the radical nature of the commitment that we are to have to Christ, Jesus tells the people that they need to hate their families and take up their cross in order to follow Him. Jesus is not suggesting that we break the commandment to honor our parents; He is saying that our devotion to Him is to be priority over even devotion to our families. Jesus then gives two illustrations that make the same point. A builder of a house counts the cost before building and an army commander gauges if he could win the battle before fighting. Both of these illustrate the importance of counting the cost of following Jesus before committing to it. Jesus demands total devotion, and people must be willing to give it to be His disciples.

Thought Question:

When you were told the gospel, were you informed about what the gospel would cost you? What is the cost of discipleship? When you share the gospel with others, do you inform them about the cost of following Jesus?

The Final Teaching Circuit, Lessons for Pharisees: Luke 15–16

Lesson 54

In the previous lesson, we saw how Jesus had dined with the Pharisees and used that experience as an opportunity to teach them more about the kingdom. In chapter 15, we see Jesus spending time with tax collectors and "sinners." Even this becomes an opportunity to teach the Pharisees and the scribes. When these men see Jesus talking with sinners, they complain about

Him. So Jesus gives them three parables, all of which illustrate the value of seeking the lost.

The *first parable* is the parable of the lost sheep. In this parable, Jesus illustrates how a good shepherd cares for his sheep so much that he would be willing to leave ninety-nine sheep behind to go after the one that is lost. When that shepherd finds that one lost sheep, he is filled with more joy than with the ninety-nine that he left behind. In the same manner, there is more joy in heaven over one sinner who repents than over ninety-nine who do not need to repent. The *second parable* is the parable of the lost coin. This illustrates the same point. When a person loses a coin, even though she may have nine others, she will search the house to find that one lost coin. When she finds it, she will be filled with joy.

Even though the *third parable* illustrates the same basic point as the first two, that God is more excited over one lost sinner who repents than many who do not need to repent, the parable of the **prodigal** son has many layers. In this story, a son abandons his family and demands his inheritance so that he could waste it on frivolous living. For a son to demand his inheritance is basically equal to telling his father that he wishes he were dead. This prodigal son then goes off to a far country and squanders all of that money on sinful living. Things get so bad for this son that he ends up as a farmhand, taking care of pigs. This is as low as it could get for a Jewish person, considering that pigs are the most unclean of animals. This son decides to go back home and beg his father to let him at least be a servant. When the son is far off, however, the father sees his son and runs to him, an act that is seen as undignified for an old man in this culture. The father receives back his son, not as a servant, but as a son, and throws a feast for him.

First, this illustrates God's incredible forgiveness. God is willing to take back people who have spit in His face and have rejected Him. In this story, the father is the one who acts strangely, accepting back his son. However, the response of the older brother in this parable is directed to the religious leaders who are judging Jesus for spending time with sinners. The older son complains that their father throws this party for the rebel son and refuses to enjoy the festivities for him. The father reminds the older son that he has a reward as well, but that he should rejoice with the father. So also, the Pharisees should rejoice with Jesus that the lost are being saved.

Jesus next uses an unexpected illustration to challenge His disciples. In the parable of the unjust steward, a man is told that he is going to be fired for doing a poor job with his work. In an effort to gain favor, he lessens the debts of the master's debtors so that they would perhaps give him some help. Jesus does not commend lying or deceit in this passage, but He commends the creativity and shrewdness of this man. If dishonest and unjust people are willing to put up so much effort to protect themselves and make money, how much more should we who are noble try hard to get eternal rewards? We cannot serve both God and money.

Jesus connects His statements on money with His challenges to the Pharisees. The Pharisees love money and the Law. In the parable of the rich man and Lazarus, it is the rich man who is suffering in Hades, whereas the poor man is in heaven. When the rich man begs Abraham to send Lazarus to warn his family about the torment that he is in, he is told that his family has Moses and the prophets to warn them; they need nothing more. Implied in this is that the Pharisees also are destined for suffering if they do not heed the Law that speaks about Jesus.

> **prodigal:** spending money or resources freely and recklessly; wastefully extravagant

Thought Questions:

1. Some people have relabeled the parable of the prodigal son as the parable of the prodigal father. What is "prodigal" about the father in this story?

2. With whom do you identify more in the parable of the prodigal son, the prodigal son or the older brother? How can you guard yourself from the attitude of the older brother?

3. Do you think it is appropriate to develop your theology of the afterlife from the parable of the rich man and Lazarus? Why or why not?

The Final Teaching Circuit, The Kingdom of God: Luke 17:1–18:14

Lesson 55

There are a number of topics that Jesus addresses as He comes close to Jerusalem in Luke 17:1–18:14. The first of these topics is forgiveness and reconciliation. Even though Jesus came to forgive us of our sins, He still warns us not to "cause offense" to others. The word here means to "cause to stumble or fall." In other words, Jesus warns us not to do anything that will lead others

into sin. On the other hand, when someone sins against us, Jesus tells us to confront that person, and when he repents we are to forgive him or her. In fact, even if this happens multiple times in a day, we are to forgive him or her every time.

Perhaps as a response to this difficult preaching, Jesus' disciples ask Him to increase their faith. However, rather than increasing their faith, Jesus suggests that it does not take much faith to do the things that God requires of us. Jesus' second response to their question reveals that the disciples may be seeking more faith for their own glory. They may want greater faith, not so that they can serve God more effectively, but so that they can do greater miracles. He argues that they need to think as servants, who simply do their work because it needs to be done. Servants are not praised for doing the work that is required of them; so also must we not seek praise for the work that God has required of us.

As Jesus continues on His journey, He is met by a group of lepers. Because they are unclean, they call out to Jesus from a distance for Him to heal them. According to the Law, a leper is unclean and exiled from the community until he or she is declared clean by the priest. Even though they are not yet healed, they listen when Jesus tells them to go to the priest. This shows that they have some real faith in Jesus. However, of the ten lepers who are healed on the way, only one returns and glorifies God and thanks Jesus. Moreover, the one that glorifies God is not even an Israelite, but a Samaritan. The lesson from this is that we need to respond to the works that God does with gratitude and praise.

The next topic that Jesus addresses in Luke's gospel is the coming kingdom of God. Some Pharisees ask Jesus when the kingdom of God will come. By asking this, the Pharisees want to know when the Messiah will come and defeat Israel's enemies and restore Israel to its former glory. Jesus' response, however, reveals that the kingdom of God is radically different from what the Pharisees expect, for it is within us. The kingdom of God is not bound to physical boundaries, but consists of the reign of Christ in the lives of believers. This is called the "already and not yet" nature of the kingdom. The kingdom is already here, yet it is also going to come in the future with glory. For the rest of chapter 17, Jesus speaks of His return. The basic message of this section is that when Jesus comes, many will not expect it, but it will be sudden. There are three main interpretations of this text. The *first interpretation* is that this coming is a coming of judgment that happens in A.D. 70. In support of this is the mention of Noah and Sodom where God's judgment is prevalent. The *second interpretation* is that this is the rapture, a time when God will take away Christians from the suffering on earth. The *third interpretation* is that this is the second coming of Christ when He will establish His kingdom on earth and destroy God's enemies.

Jesus then gives a couple of parables. In the first parable, Jesus highlights the importance of persistence in prayer. The widow in this story is given justice by the judge because of her persistence. How much more will God, who is a good Judge, give justice to His people who call out to Him? In the second parable, Jesus illustrates the importance of humility and warns against self-righteousness. The first person in this parable spends his whole prayer talking about how good he is and how he is better than the tax collector. Yet the tax collector is the one who is justified and forgiven because he simply calls upon God for mercy. The Pharisee in this story has nothing to gain from God because rather than seeking anything from God, he simply boasts of his own greatness. The gospel is about God's mercy and grace, not about our righteousness or good deeds.

Thought Questions:

1. If someone repeatedly sins against us but repents every time, we are told to forgive him or her. Does this mean that we should continue to let him or her hurt us in this way? Why or why not?

2. With whom do you identify more in the parable of the Pharisee and the tax collector? How can you develop the attitude of the tax collector more?

The Final Teaching Circuit, The End of the Journey: Luke 18:15–19:46

Lesson 56

Jesus knows what awaits Him in Jerusalem. He knows that He will be rejected and ultimately put to death and that His time with the disciples is coming to an end. Therefore, He spends much of the little remaining time teaching His disciples about the kingdom of God and preparing them for His departure.

Even though the disciples have spent over three years with Jesus at this point, there is much that they still have to learn. When people bring infants to Jesus, the disciples rebuke them because they see these infants as hindrances to Jesus' mission. Yet Jesus has a very different attitude towards these children. He points out these children as examples of how the disciples are to receive

the kingdom of God. Infants are great examples to us of faith and trust. They are completely dependent on others and have faith in their parents to take care of them. We also should have such a faith in God that we rely on Him to take care of us. In addition, infants are not concerned with pride or appearance; they are humble.

Next, Jesus is met by a rich young ruler. He gives Jesus the question that most Christians would love to hear, "What shall I do to inherit eternal life?" Yet Jesus' response, as always, goes right to the heart. He knows that this man thinks that he is good enough to get into the kingdom of God because of his own good deeds. So first, Jesus humbles the man by reminding him that only God is good. Then Jesus brings up the Law. This rich young ruler says that he has been faithful to obey all of the Law. However, Jesus conveniently leaves out the commandments not to covet and to have no other gods before God. So when this man says that he has been faithful to the Law, Jesus gives him one more challenge: sell everything he has and give it to the poor and then follow Jesus. This man goes away very sad because this sacrifice is much greater than he is willing to make. This becomes a teachable moment for the disciples. Jesus warns them that it is very difficult for a rich man to enter the kingdom of God. We must give up everything to gain the kingdom, and for a rich person that is a lot to give up. Peter, however, reminds Jesus of the sacrifice that the disciples had made to follow Him. Jesus acknowledges this sacrifice and tells them that they will be rewarded for their sacrifice. Related to this, Jesus then pulls His disciples aside and informs them once again that He is going to be killed in Jerusalem but that He is going to rise again. Yet the disciples do not understand what He is saying to them.

As Jesus nears Jericho, a city near Jerusalem in the region of Judea, He is met by a blind man on the road. When Jesus asks this man what he desires from Jesus, he asks to receive his sight. So Jesus restores the man's sight and he follows Jesus, praising God. All of those around who see this also praise God. When Jesus arrives in Jericho, He is met by another man, a rich tax collector named Zacchaeus. Being a short man, Zacchaeus climbs a tree so that he could see Jesus when He walks by. Jesus sees him and invites Himself to Zacchaeus' house for dinner. Zacchaeus is so grateful that he not only gladly receives Jesus, but he gives over half of his money to the poor and agrees to make right any financial wrongs that he had committed against the people. Unlike the rich young ruler who had walked away sad because he did not want to give up his wealth, Zacchaeus is filled with joy and willingly gives up much of his wealth. Tax collectors, however, were despised in those days and seen as unclean because of their connection with the Romans. So the people of the crowd pass judgment on Jesus for eating with the man.

Jesus then attempts to clarify some misunderstandings about the kingdom. The people of Israel are expecting the Messiah to destroy the Romans and bring the kingdom suddenly. This is not Jesus' plan, however. So He gives a modified version of His parable of the talents. Rather than simply receiving the kingdom, the king in this story must go away for a while in order to receive the kingdom. In the meanwhile, he gives his servants some responsibility with his money while he is gone. Some of the citizens of this king do not like him, however, and reject him as king; these people would be the religious leaders of the day. When the king returns, he demands an account of how his servants used that money entrusted to them. Those who are faithful in his absence are greatly rewarded. However, the one who does nothing while the king is gone loses everything. Also, those citizens who refused the king face judgment when he returns. Obviously, Jesus is the King who is going away to heaven to receive His kingdom. When He returns, He will require an account of us concerning how we use what He gives us. Yet, those who reject Jesus will die when He returns.

Jesus' journey finally comes to an end at the end of Luke 19. Here He finally enters Jerusalem during the Triumphal Entry. As He enters the city, a large crowd accompanies Him, praising God and Jesus as the coming King. The people recognize that Jesus coming on a donkey fulfills the prophecy from Zechariah 9:9 that the Messiah will come to Jerusalem on a donkey. This large crowd makes a large ruckus so that the Pharisees tell Jesus to hush the crowd. However, Jesus tells them that, even if the people are silent, nature itself will praise God in this moment. Luke adds that Jesus laments over Jerusalem around this time because of the destruction that will come because of their coming rejection of Him. Jesus is the King that the Jews have been eagerly expecting for centuries, and though they praise Him now, they will be shouting, "Crucify Him, crucify Him!" (Luke 23:21) in less than a week. This should be a glorious occasion, but instead it is a time to mourn. Even the temple is corrupt, as shown by the cleansing of the temple by Jesus. Tragically, the Israelites get everything for which they have been waiting, but they are not ready and reject their King.

Thought Questions:

1. What do you think it would look like to have the faith of a child in your relationship with Christ?

2. How do you think you would respond if Jesus told you to give everything you have to the poor and follow Him? What would be difficult for you to give up for Jesus?

3. Why do you think Zacchaeus is so willing to give up his wealth but the rich young ruler is not? What is the difference between these two men?

The Battle with the Religious Leaders: Luke 19:47–21:4

Lesson 57

For over a year, the religious leaders have been seeking to arrest and kill Jesus. Now that He has entered Jerusalem in such a majestic manner, the religious leaders are desperate to find some way to get rid of Him. Thus begins the series of debates between Jesus and the various leaders.

Their first approach is the direct approach. Jesus has been clearly speaking and acting with authority, so the leaders of the people ask Jesus from where He gets His authority. If Jesus testifies about where He gets His authority, they can argue with Him; but instead Jesus draws their attention to John the Baptist. John the Baptist had been quite popular with the people, and even though John has died, the people still believe that he was a prophet. John the Baptist had testified on multiple occasions that Jesus is the Christ. So Jesus asks the religious leaders where they believe John got his authority. If they say that John got his authority from God, then they would be admitting that John was also right about Jesus being the Christ. However, if they say that John did not get his authority from God, the people would be furious because of their admiration for John. So they remain silent. Jesus responds in like manner by not answering their question.

Jesus then responds by speaking a parable about the religious leaders. It is appropriate that Jesus compares Israel to a vineyard in this parable because God compares Israel to a vineyard in Isaiah 5. In this parable, God is the owner of the vineyard, and the vinedressers are the religious leaders. When the owner sends servants to receive the fruit from the vineyard, the vinedressers beat the servants and send them away empty handed. Finally, the owner of the vineyard sends his son; but the vinedressers kill his son, hoping to receive his inheritance. As one would expect, those vinedressers are going to be killed for their actions. The religious leaders understand that Jesus is speaking against them. Jesus then quotes Psalm 118 regarding the stone that the builders rejected, which becomes the chief **corner-stone** (verse 22). Jesus is the Stone that the religious leaders are rejecting, but He will soon become the Stone upon which everything is built.

Since the direct approach does not work, the religious leaders try to trick Jesus in His words. First, they send some men who ask Jesus whether or not it is lawful to pay taxes to Caesar. This is a trap question, for if He says "yes" the people will hate Him; but if He says not to pay taxes to Caesar, this would be an act of treason. Jesus masterfully sidesteps this question by saying to give to God what is God's and to give to Caesar what is Caesar's. Since the Roman coin has Caesar's inscription, it ultimately belongs to him; but since the temple coin does not have that inscription, it belongs to God.

Next, the Sadducees, the leaders of the Sanhedrin, come to Jesus to test Him. Because they do not believe in the concept of the resurrection or the afterlife, they give Jesus an apparently impossible situation. A woman marries seven brothers, each of whom dies; when they are raised from the dead, whose wife will she be? Jesus has already taught openly that God intends for marriage to be between one man and one woman, so will this woman have multiple husbands in heaven? Once again, Jesus masterfully trumps the question by pointing out that she will not have any husbands in heaven, since marriage is only for this earth.

Having silenced the religious leaders, Jesus asks them a question: If the Christ is a descendant of David, how can David call this person "Lord" in Psalm 110? If David is the highest authority on earth at his time, who is the "Lord" to David's "Lord"? The first Lord obviously refers to God the Father, but who is the second "Lord?" Jesus quotes this to show them that He is God the Son, but of course they do not understand this. Finally, Jesus warns the people directly about the religious leaders and their desire for honor and fame. These leaders are willing to force even the widows to give all that they have while they seek honor for themselves. As with the parable of the vineyard, Jesus says that these leaders will be condemned.

The next story is often misunderstood. Jesus looks and observes people as they give their tithes into the temple treasury. He sees the rich giving large sums of money. However, He draws His attention to a poor widow who only puts in two **mites**. Jesus points out the incredible sacrifice that this woman makes by putting in those two coins, and He commends her for this sacrifice. Traditionally, this passage is used by preachers to talk about the value of sacrificing for God's kingdom. While

this is certainly a lesson we can learn from this text, this woman also stands as an illustration of something else. At the end of chapter 20, Jesus warns the people to watch out for the religious leaders, for they "devour widows' houses" (verse 47). This woman not only stands as an example of generous giving, but also as a sign of condemnation for the religious leaders. The religious leaders are so focused on their own glory and honor that they do not lend a hand to help out the poor and needy. This woman was giving only a small amount, but her sacrifice is much greater than the large sums of money that the rich give from their excess.

> **cornerstone:** the foundation stone; the first stone set in the construction of a stone building by which all other stones are set in relation to it
>
> **mite:** a small, Jewish coin made of copper, worth a laborer's wage for a day; in Greek a *lepton*

Thought Questions:

1. What can you learn from Jesus' style of argumentation with the religious leaders?

2. What lessons can we learn about giving from the poor widow here?

The Olivet Discourse: Luke 21:5–38

Lesson 58

As we have gone through the gospels, we have already encountered the Olivet Discourse twice before. Because Matthew's gospel is directed towards a Jewish audience, the language in Matthew speaks more about the kingdom of heaven (or God) than the other gospels. Both Mark and Luke are directed towards a Gentile audience. Luke's account of the Olivet Discourse speaks more clearly about the destruction of the temple and Jerusalem than the other two synoptic gospels.

As with the other gospels, Luke informs us that the context for this teaching is the destruction of the temple. As the disciples are speaking about the beauty of the temple, Jesus shocks them by mentioning that the temple will be destroyed. As with Mark's account, Luke mentions the two questions of the disciples: "When will these things be? And what sign will there be when these things are about to take place?" (verse 7). Jesus' response will answer both of these questions as He speaks of when the destruction of the temple will come, and what the signs will be of this destruction.

Jesus first warns them not to be deceived by false messiahs or false prophets. Many will come, claiming to be Jesus, but they will not be. There will be wars, chaos, and cataclysmic events such as earthquakes. However, before these signs occur, the disciples will have to face persecutions from the people of their day. They will be brought before rulers and kings and will bear witness to the works of Jesus. Jesus encourages His disciples here, telling them not to worry beforehand what they will say, for the Holy Spirit will give them the words at the appropriate time. These persecutions will not only come from the nations; even their own families will betray them, and many will hate them because they follow Jesus.

Perhaps the most glaring difference between Matthew's account and Luke's account of the Olivet Discourse comes in verse 20. In Matthew's account, at this point Jesus warns the people about the "abomination of desolation," spoken by the prophet Daniel, standing in the temple (Daniel 12:11). Mark's account also mentions this man, traditionally understood as the Antichrist. For this reason, many people believe that it is at this point in the Olivet Discourse when Jesus begins to speak about the future tribulation. Luke, however, does not speak about the abomination of desolation at all; rather, in this account, Jesus warns the people that "when you see Jerusalem surrounded by armies, then know that its desolation is near" (verse 20). This is a clear reference to the destruction of Jerusalem and the temple. In Luke's account, Jesus is not warning the disciples about the end of the world, but about the destruction of Jerusalem. He tells His disciples to flee when the Roman army surrounds Jerusalem because Rome will destroy the city. Even more clear is when Luke says, "And Jerusalem will be trampled by Gentiles until the times of the Gentiles are fulfilled" (verse 24b).

Once Jerusalem is surrounded by this army, the signs in the heavens will take place before the coming of the Son of Man. As mentioned earlier in this book, rather than this "coming" being the rapture or the end of the world, in Luke's account it is a coming with judgment on Jerusalem. This is why He says, "Now when these things begin to happen, look up and lift up your heads, because your redemption draws near" (verse 28). Since the crucifixion and resurrection will bring **redemption** from sins, this redemption has to be something different. Jesus has already warned the disciples that they will be persecuted and hated because of their faith; this redemption is the destruction of their enemies when Jerusalem is destroyed. Because the Jews will reject and kill the disciples, their redemption is the destruction of Jerusalem.

Jesus returns to the original question with the parable of the fig tree. Just as a person can tell that summer is near by the budding of the figs from a fig tree, Jesus says that these signs should inform the disciples that the kingdom of God is near. To clarify precisely how near the kingdom of God is, Jesus tells them that these things will take place within one generation. Once the temple is destroyed and Jerusalem is destroyed, the old age will be over and the new age will begin. But Jesus does warn the disciples not to be found in sin when these things take place. The lesson from this teaching is that we must be ready for Christ to return. Like parents who warn their children not to misbehave while they are gone, Jesus warns the disciples that He will return, and so they must remain obedient.

> **redemption:** forgiveness for sins and protection from eternal damnation through sacrifice, namely through Christ's death on the cross

Thought Questions:

1. Why do you think that scholars make such a big deal out of the destruction of the temple? Why is this event significant?

2. Do you think the fear of Christ's return is an effective motivation to fight sin? Why or why not?

The Lord's Supper and the Arrest and Trial: Luke 22
Lesson 59

According to the Law, all Jewish men are to come to Jerusalem to celebrate three of the major festivals (Deuteronomy 16:16). The Passover Festival, also known as the Feast of Unleavened Bread, is one of the most important Jewish festivals. In this festival, the Jews remember God's miraculous deliverance from the Egyptians through the last plague, the death of the firstborn. In order to be spared from the death of the firstborn, the Jews had to slaughter a spotless lamb and display its blood over their doorposts so that the angel of death would pass over that house. The culmination of the Holy Week for Jesus and His disciples is the Passover meal, which they eat on Thursday night. However, Jesus not only eats this meal with His disciples, He transforms the meal and becomes the true spotless Lamb of God whose blood saves all those who are covered by Him.

Going into Thursday evening, Jesus has His disciples prepare a place to eat the Passover meal together. Jesus has been longing to eat this final meal together with His disciples for quite some time. He knows that He is going to be the real sacrifice this Passover, so He wants to enjoy this last meal. Yet Jesus transforms the elements of this meal. When He breaks bread, He tells His disciples that this bread now represents His body, which also will be broken for them. Moreover, when He takes the wine, He transforms the symbolism of the wine and says that the wine now represents His blood, which will be shed for them. The Passover will no longer be about Israel's deliverance from Egypt; it will be about our deliverance from sin and the consequences of sin.

Jesus knows that He is going to be betrayed, and while Luke's account does not draw out this knowledge as much as the other gospels, Jesus does mention here that He knows He will be betrayed. As with John's account of this event, Luke highlights the humility of Jesus with the Lord's Supper. The disciples, however, begin to argue who the greatest is among them, an argument that they have had many times before. Jesus tells them not to be like the rulers of the Gentiles, who use their authority and power for personal gain. Rather, Jesus says that they are to humble themselves and serve one another. Jesus does acknowledge that they will be given authority and a kingdom and that they will judge the twelve tribes of Israel, but they must be servants first of all.

Jesus then prepares the disciples for the events that are about to happen. First, He tells Peter to strengthen the rest of the disciples after Peter returns to Jesus. Peter is confused, and Jesus informs him that he is going to deny Jesus three times that very night before the rooster crows. Jesus also tells the disciples that the time of peace is over. Jesus has been able to protect His disciples and provide for them, but now it is time to be prepared. In fact, Jesus even has them bring two swords with them. People have come up with many theories as to why Jesus has them grab two swords. We cannot know for sure why they take two, but the swords themselves stand as symbols that the time of peace is over.

Luke gives us some unique information regarding the garden of Gethsemane. We learn that while Jesus prays for God to take away the cup of suffering from Him, God sends angels to strengthen Him. We also learn that Jesus prays so earnestly that He begins to sweat blood. Doctors have discovered a condition wherein intense amounts of stress can cause a person to bleed through the sweat glands. It makes sense that it would be Luke who points out this information, considering that he was a physician. We also learn from Luke's account that the reason the disciples are asleep is not entirely out of being tired but from sorrow. We know from Matthew and Mark's accounts of the arrest that one of Jesus'

disciples cuts off the ear of one of the servants; but Luke informs us that Jesus heals this man. When Jesus agrees to go with the crowd, His disciples scatter.

As Jesus had already predicted, Peter denies Jesus three times over the course of that evening. Having followed the crowds, Peter goes to the house of the high priest, where Jesus was held. Three times the people there accuse him of being a disciple of Jesus, but Peter denies it. We learn from Luke's account that after the rooster crows, Jesus turns and looks directly at Peter. Out of sorrow, Peter runs away.

Meanwhile, the men who had captured Jesus beat Him and mock Him while He is in the house of the high priest. Because it is illegal to have a trial before dawn, as soon as it is light, Jesus is brought before the Sanhedrin. The chief priests and the scribes ask Jesus directly if He is the Christ. However, Jesus knows that they would not believe Him, even if He admits to it, and so He does not answer directly. Nevertheless, Jesus does inform them that they will see the Son of Man sitting at the right hand of God. Jesus has regularly referred to Himself as the Son of Man; and by saying that the Son of Man will sit at the right hand of God, Jesus is admitting that He is the Messiah from Daniel 7. In this passage, Daniel sees a vision of heaven and "One like the Son of Man" who goes to the Father and receives His kingdom (Daniel 7:13–14). The religious leaders pick up on this and ask Him directly if He is the Son of God. Jesus answers by saying, "You rightly say that I am" (verse 70). Basically, Jesus says to them, "You just said it yourself." They take this as blasphemy and agree to condemn Him.

Thought Questions:

1. Why do you think Peter denies Jesus, even after Jesus tells him that he will?

2. Why do you think that Jesus tells them to bring swords, but when they use one He heals the man?

The Trial Under Pilate and the Crucifixion: Luke 23
Lesson 60

As has been mentioned before, the part of Jesus' story where there is the most unique material in each of the gospels is the story of the trial, crucifixion, and resurrection of Jesus. Each author gives us a little more information, so that we can understand more of exactly what happens. Luke adds a lot of unique material to this story.

This is only fitting, considering that Luke interviewed a lot of people to put together the material in his gospel.

Chapter 23 picks up the story with Jesus standing trial before Pontius Pilate, the Roman governor. As has been the case throughout His trial, Jesus is falsely accused. Here He is accused of forbidding people to pay taxes and for claiming to be the Christ. Jesus had done quite the opposite regarding the taxes, and He never directly admits to being the Christ while on trial. He merely says, "You rightly say that I am" (Luke 22:70). When Pilate asks Him plainly if He is the King of the Jews, once again Jesus replies by saying, "It is as you say" (Luke 23:3). Pilate cannot find anything for which to condemn Jesus; so when he finds out that Jesus is from Galilee, Pilate sees his way out. Galilee is under the jurisdiction of King Herod, and Herod happens to be in town, so Pilate sends Jesus to Herod.

Luke's gospel is the only one that mentions this interaction with Herod. Herod does not care about this trial or about Jesus. However, he had heard that Jesus is a miracle worker, and he wants Jesus to perform for him. Jesus, however, refuses to say anything to him. So Herod's soldiers mock Jesus and don Him in a gorgeous robe as a fake king. From this event, ironically, Pontius Pilate and Herod become good friends. Even through His trial, Jesus brings reconciliation, though this is not a good reconciliation. Realizing that he is not going to get his show, Herod sends Jesus back to Pilate.

When Pilate addresses the crowd, he tells them that he finds nothing wrong with Jesus. Yet the crowds shout, "Crucify Him, crucify Him!" To further illustrate the incredible injustice of this event, the people demand that Pilate release Barabbas, a known murderer, rather than releasing Jesus. Even in the midst of this, Pilate tries once again to free Jesus, stating that he finds nothing wrong with Him. By this point, however, the crowds are beginning to riot, still shouting, "Crucify Him, crucify Him!" So finally, Pilate gives in to the demands of the people and orders that Jesus be crucified.

After the long evening and extremely rough morning that Jesus has had, He is unable to bear the weight of the cross for long; so Simon of Cyrene is forced to carry the cross for Jesus. Luke next records an event that is unique to his gospel. On the road to Calvary, a large crowd follows Jesus, including a group of women who weep for Jesus. Yet Jesus turns to these women and warns them that they should be weeping for themselves rather than Him. As we have already seen with Luke's account of the Olivet Discourse, the coming destruction of Jerusalem in A.D. 70 plays a prominent role in Luke's gospel. This warning by Jesus once again highlights the coming destruction. Because the Jews have rejected their Messiah and chosen to walk in darkness rather than light, destruction will come.

As Jesus is being crucified, He says something incredible: He asks the Father to forgive those who have put Him on the cross. Even when He is undergoing incredible suffering and rejection, He is still filled with compassion and mercy. If Jesus could forgive the very people who have caused this incredible suffering to Him, we can certainly forgive others when they hurt us. While He is on the cross, He is mocked by those who stand nearby, including the rulers. Just as Satan had questioned Jesus' position as the Son of God in the wilderness when he tempted Him, the people question Jesus' position as the King of the Jews and challenge Him to prove who He is and save Himself.

Luke also includes another unique interaction, this time with the criminals on the cross. Along with the crowds, one of the criminals next to Him also mocks Him. However, the other criminal defends Jesus. He admits that both of the criminals are guilty, but Jesus had done nothing wrong to deserve this fate. Even more, this criminal exercises great faith as he asks Jesus to remember him as He receives His kingdom. This criminal had clearly heard the teachings of Jesus and, even while dying for his own sins, he turns to Jesus to save him. Thus salvation is what he receives, for Jesus tells him that he will be with Him that very day in Paradise. Throughout the book of Luke, we see Jesus bringing salvation to the outcasts and the broken; this criminal is another of these outcasts who are saved by Jesus. This poses a theological problem for those who believe that Jesus descended into hell between His death and resurrection, for if the criminal would be with Jesus that very day in Paradise, this would imply that Jesus would be in Paradise that very day.

Just as Jesus had predicted in the Olivet Discourse, the sun is darkened from the sixth hour (noon) until the ninth hour (3 p.m.). Later, in the gospel of John, Jesus is identified as the Light of the World whom the darkness cannot overcome. For a short time on the cross, it would appear that darkness has its moment of victory. As we know, however, Jesus will not stay dead for long. Whereas both Matthew and Mark record Jesus' last words as, "My God, my God, why have You forsaken Me?" (Matthew 27:46 and Mark 15:34), Luke records Jesus' last words as, "Father, 'into Your hands I commit My spirit'" (verse 46). No one can take Jesus' life from Him; He lays it down of His own accord. It is not the people who kill Jesus; it is Jesus who willingly gives His life. Unlike Matthew and Mark's accounts of the centurion's response, here the centurion refers to Jesus as a "righteous Man" rather than the "Son of God." Most likely, Luke is interpreting the phrase "Son of God" to a Gentile audience to help them understand that Jesus "was a righteous Man" (verse 47). The phrase "Son of God" has a strong Old Testament background that the Gentile audience may not have understood.

After Jesus dies, Joseph of Arimathea, "a good and just man" (verse 50), asks for the body of Jesus and places Him in a new tomb that he had purchased. Jesus' body is prepared for His burial, and some of the women who had been following Jesus observe this process and where Jesus is laid. This will prove to be quite important for those who would argue that the disciples went to the wrong tomb. There are a number of witnesses who see precisely where Jesus is laid; it is highly unlikely that all of them would pick the wrong tomb.

Fittingly, the account of Jesus' death ends with a Sabbath rest. Little do the disciples and the women know, but Jesus is about to bring a true Sabbath rest to the world.

Thought Questions:

1. Based on Pilate's response to Jesus, do you think it is fair for people to criticize and condemn Pontius Pilate for ordering Jesus' execution? Why or why not?

2. Why do you think the crowds would rather have a murderer released among them instead of Jesus?

He Is Risen!: Luke 24

Lesson 61

Because Jesus had died so soon before the Sabbath, Joseph of Arimathea did not have time to fully prepare the body. So as soon as they can come, some of the women who ministered to Jesus come to the tomb to prepare His body with spices. From Luke's account, we learn that the women who come to the tomb are "Mary Magdalene, Joanna, Mary the mother of James, and the other women with them" (verse 10). Luke offers a few unique details about the encounter at the tomb. *First*, while Luke does not mention how precisely the stone is rolled away, he does clarify that the women speak to two angels, not one. Even though Matthew and Mark only mention one angel, this does not mean that there could not have been more than one. *Second*, as with Matthew and Mark's accounts, the angels tell the women that Jesus is not here because He has been

raised from the dead. Luke adds that the angels tell the women to remember that Jesus had prophesied that He would be delivered into the hands of sinful men. However, when the women tell the disciples, the disciples do not believe them at first. Nevertheless, Peter comes and sees the empty tomb, marveling about what has happened.

The story of the disciples on the road to Emmaus is also unique to Luke, though Mark makes a reference to it in the questionable portion of Mark 16. While these disciples are traveling to Emmaus, Jesus meets them along the way. Yet these disciples do not know that it is Jesus. Considering that their hope had just died on the cross, these men are sad. However, they have also heard the account from the disciples and the women about the empty tomb. So Jesus tells them that they have misunderstood the events that have happened. He tells them that it was necessary for the Christ to suffer, according to the Scriptures. Jesus then engages in a discussion of which every theologian would love to be a part; He explains to them what all of the Old Testament Scriptures have to say about Him.

As they come close to the village of Emmaus, Jesus indicates that He is planning on continuing His journey, but the two disciples insist that He come and stay with them for the night. Jesus agrees and breaks bread with the men. As He blesses the bread, the eyes of the disciples are opened, and they recognize Jesus. Yet, as soon as they recognize Him, Jesus disappears.

When these disciples return to the other disciples, Jesus Himself appears in their midst. The disciples, however, are frightened and assume that He is a spirit. So Jesus shows them His hands and His feet so that they can see that He is very much alive. He even eats a fish and some honey in front of them. Subsequently, as He had done with the two disciples on the road to Emmaus, He opens up their understanding so that they could also comprehend what the Scriptures had said about Him. He then explains to them once again that it was necessary for Him to suffer and die and rise from the dead. It is also necessary for the disciples to preach to people from all the nations that they must repent so that they can be forgiven.

As we have already said, the gospel of Luke and the book of Acts are designed to be a companion series. Acts picks up right from where the gospel of Luke leaves off. Luke finishes with Jesus telling the disciples to remain in Jerusalem until they receive "power from on high" (verse 49). They will be His witnesses, starting in Jerusalem and then going to all the nations. Unlike the other gospels, Luke's gospel also includes the ascension, when Jesus goes into heaven. The end of Luke's gospel is simply the beginning of another story, the story of the Church. Yet we will have to wait until the book of Acts to read that story.

Thought Question:

The disciples cannot understand the cross and the resurrection until Jesus opens their understanding. What implications, if any, might this have for evangelism today?

Introduction to John

Lesson 62

The gospel of John is the most unique among the four gospels. Much of the material and structure of Matthew, Mark, and Luke is very similar. However, the material and structure of John's gospel are almost entirely unique. Because John's gospel is the most theologically developed of the gospels, most scholars believe that it is the last gospel to be written. Many scholars date this gospel after the destruction of the temple in A.D. 70, but it is also possible that John wrote this in the mid to late A.D. 60s.

The author of the gospel of John identifies himself throughout his gospel as the "disciple whom Jesus loved" (John 13:23; 19:26; 20:2; 21:7, 20). Church tradition and internal evidence suggest that this disciple is John, the brother of James and son of Zebedee. John is a fisherman by trade, and he is one of the very first disciples whom Jesus calls to follow Him. Among the twelve disciples, Peter, James, and John are given special privileges. These three are the only ones allowed in when Jesus raises the little girl to life, and these are the three who get to see Jesus on the Mount of Transfiguration. On multiple occasions, James and John ask Jesus for power and authority in His kingdom but are told to be humble and to serve. John apparently eventually gets the message to be humble, for he does not even identify himself by name throughout his gospel, only as the "disciple whom Jesus loved." John is not only the author of the fourth gospel, but he is also the author of 1 John, 2 John, 3 John, and Revelation. There are many common themes and ideas that flow throughout all of these books.

Because of John's later association with the church in Ephesus, it has been suggested that John writes his gospel to the Jewish Christians in Ephesus. As evidence for this, John devotes a lot of his gospel to emphasizing that John the Baptist is not the Messiah. We know from the book of Acts that there was a large group of followers of John the Baptist in Ephesus, even years after John the Baptist's death (Acts 19). Part of the goal of John's gospel is to show that John's purpose in ministry is to point others to Jesus Christ as the coming Messiah.

John makes the purpose of this gospel clear in chapter 20 and verse 31, "but these are written that you may believe that Jesus is the Christ, the Son of God, and that believing you may have life in His name." John does not write this gospel to simply provide a history of the events that happened with Christ; this book is designed to be evangelistic. John would not be content with people reading this book and getting information if they do not respond to that information by placing their faith and belief in Jesus Christ. This is why many Christians recommend that people begin reading the Bible with this gospel. Not only is it easy to understand, but the thrust of this entire book is to motivate the reader to come to faith in Christ.

As was said earlier in this lesson, the structure of John's gospel is different from the structure of the other gospels. John never uses the word "miracle" to refer to the wonders and healings that Jesus does; rather, he uses the word "sign" or "signs." This fits with the structure of this book, for John often connects Jesus' major teachings with some of His healing or supernatural wonders. For example, John mentions the feeding of the 5,000 and immediately follows it up with Jesus' teaching about eating His flesh and drinking His blood. John also follows the healing of the blind man with Jesus' teaching about being the Light of the World. The "signs" are designed to draw attention to the message, not just to put on a show. John also contains a number of the "I am" statements of Jesus. Some examples of the "I am" statements are: "I am the light of the world" (John 8:12, 9:5), "I am the good shepherd" (John 10:11, 14), and "I am the door of the sheep" (John 10:7). Together, these "I am" statements give us a more complete picture of what Jesus came to do. John also has an extended section on the upper room discourse between John 13 and John 17. In this section, Jesus prepares His disciples for His coming departure.

Even though John's gospel is organized thematically, it is from John's gospel that a lot of scholars develop a timeline of Jesus' life. We know that Jesus ministers for just over three years because John's gospel mentions four different Passover feasts during the time Jesus ministers on the earth. The other gospels only mention one of these feasts. Also, unlike the synoptic gospels, which focus on Jesus' ministry in Galilee primarily, John focuses heavily on Jesus' ministry in Judea.

There are a number of themes that John masterfully weaves throughout his gospel. Because the intention of this book is to inspire belief in Christ, John distinguishes *genuine faith* from false faith. Many people appear to have faith in Christ, but later we see that this faith does not endure or is based on a desire to see signs (or miracles) more than a desire to follow Christ. At one point, a large number of disciples walks away from Jesus; but when He turns to the twelve to ask if they want to leave too, they say that Jesus has the words of eternal life. Another theme that runs throughout John's gospel is *light versus darkness*. Jesus comes to provide light, but many of the people love darkness and hate the light. Those who love the light will come to Jesus, but those who hate the light will reject Him. Another theme is *truth versus falsehood*. When Jesus stands trial before Pilate, He says that He speaks on behalf of the truth; but Pilate asks, "What is truth?" (18:38). A fourth theme is that *Jesus is the Word of God*. The Word of God is God's revelation of Himself to the world; Jesus is the complete revelation of God and the complete fulfillment of His Word. A fifth theme is the theme of *witness*. To some extent, in the gospel of John the Jews are placing Jesus on trial. They want Jesus to prove that He is the Messiah, so they ask Him on multiple occasions to provide testimony and witnesses to back up His claims. John organizes his gospel to stand as a series of evidences to show that Jesus is the Messiah. There are many other themes throughout this book, but we will highlight these as we go through the book.

It has been said that the Bible is so simple that even a little child could understand it, yet so complex that even the greatest scholar could spend a lifetime discovering and learning about it. The gospel of John is a **microcosm** of this concept. It is so simple that even a child could understand it; but as we study it, we will see that there is a lot to unpack in this book.

> **microcosm:** a small group or entity that is a brief or miniature form of a larger group or entity

John's Prologue: John 1:1–18

Lesson 63

As with most stories, John's gospel starts at the beginning. Yet the beginning with which John starts is not the beginning of Jesus' life; it is the beginning of creation itself. Just as the book of Genesis begins with the phrase "In the beginning," so also does John's gospel. Jesus' ministry does not begin with the **incarnation**; it begins with the creation of the world. Here we see Jesus identified as the *logos*, or "Word," of God.

Jesus Is God: Specific Examples Where Greek *Theos* ("God") Is Applied to Jesus

John 1:1	In the beginning was the Word, and the Word was with God, and the Word was *God*.
John 1:18	No one has ever seen God; the only *God*, who is at the Father's side, he has made him known.
John 20:28	Thomas answered him, "My Lord and my *God!*"
Rom. 9:5	To them belong the patriarchs, and from their race, according to the flesh, is the Christ who is *God* over all, blessed forever. Amen.
Titus 2:13	. . . waiting for our blessed hope, the appearing of the glory of our great *God* and Savior Jesus Christ . . .
Heb. 1:8	But of the Son he says, "Your throne, O *God*, is forever and ever, the scepter of uprightness is the scepter of your kingdom."
2 Pet. 1:1	To those who have obtained a faith of equal standing with ours by the righteousness of our *God* and Savior Jesus Christ . . .

In Genesis 1, we see that God creates everything by speaking it into existence. It is through God's *logos*, or "Word," that everything comes into being. Also, the "Word of God" is associated with God's revelation to the prophets. One of the most common phrases in the prophets is "the word of the LORD came to me." What John reveals here is that Jesus is not only involved in creation itself, but it is He who has been revealing God to the prophets throughout history.

From the very first words of John's gospel, the deity of Jesus is highlighted. In fact, some of the clearest teachings about the deity of Jesus come from John's works. Along with the deity of Jesus, the Trinity is also highlighted in the first sentence. We learn that the *logos* is not only with God, but the *logos* is God. However, how can God be with God? This is where the Trinity comes in. There is one God, but three distinct Persons in the godhead. Jesus, the *logos*, is God and is with God the Father (John 1:1). At this point, it is worth mentioning one of the arguments given against the Trinity here. Some people argue from these verses that Jesus is not equal to God but is a sort of **demigod**. This is the view of Mormons and Jehovah's Witnesses. It is argued that because the definite article "the" is not before "God" at the end of this verse, that it should be translated "and the word was a God," rather than "the Word was God." This is a misunderstanding of language, however. Just as in English, the proper noun is definite enough itself that it does not require the definite article. For example, if a person's name is John, he will not go around identifying himself as "the John" to others. The very name shows that this is a particular person. The fact that there is no definite article before God does not imply that Jesus is "a" God; He is God Himself.

As the *logos*, or "Word," of God, Jesus is God's Agent of creation. Everything was made through Jesus and by Jesus. When God creates the earth, the "Father" gives the order, Jesus enacts the order, and the Spirit oversees the order. To make it abundantly clear that Jesus made everything, John says it twice, once in the positive and once in the negative. Jesus does more than simply create everything. According to John 1:4, we see that Jesus is the One who breathes life into everything. Moreover, just as Jesus is the One who gives physical life to everything, we will see later that Jesus will be the One who gives spiritual life, as well.

Jesus is also identified as the "light of men" (verse 4). Just as light allows people to see so that they can know where they are going, Jesus opens people's eyes so that they can see the truth. In verse 5, there is a double meaning that does not come out in English. It says here that the darkness cannot "comprehend" the light. This implies that those in darkness cannot understand Jesus. However, "comprehend" can also be translated "seize." The darkness cannot *understand* Jesus, but it also cannot *control* or prevent Him from doing His work. Even though Satan is able to have Jesus killed on the cross, even death cannot stop Jesus.

In the introduction, it was suggested that part of John's intention with this gospel is to show that John the Baptist is not the Messiah. In verses 6–9, John makes it abundantly clear that John the Baptist's role is to serve as a witness for Jesus. His job is to prepare people for Jesus and to serve as a witness that He is the Messiah.

Regrettably, even though Jesus created everything and everyone, when He finally reveals Himself to the world, the very people who should be embracing Him reject Him. This refers to the Jews, to whom Jesus was sent. Moreover, even though a number of Jewish people do believe in Jesus and follow Him, most people end up rejecting Him. Still, even though the Jews reject Jesus, to those who receive Him and believe in Him, He gives the right to become children of God. Once the Jews reject Jesus, the message is spread to the Gentiles so that they can become part of God's family. It is here that John introduces another theme that will be clarified in chapter 3, the theme of *being born of God*. When a person receives Jesus and believes in Him, he is given a new birth by God into His family. This birth is not genetic or based on man's decision, but based on God.

Up until this point in John's gospel, he has not identified who the Word of God is. Yet in verse 14 we are told who it is. This eternal Word of God, who created all things, puts on flesh and becomes a man, which refers to His incarnation. The term ("dwelt") used in verse fourteen could better be translated "tabernacled." In the Old Testament, the tabernacle (and later temple) is the place where God *dwells* among His people. Here in John's gospel, we see that Jesus is the ultimate tabernacle where God dwells with man. Jesus is God's presence in the world. John then testifies in verse 14 that he beheld Jesus' glory. Just as God's glory fills the old tabernacle and temple, God's glory is clearly seen through Jesus' life. It is also possible that John is making a reference here to the Transfiguration, when John gets to see Jesus in all of His glory.

Another theme that will be picked up in chapter 3 is the idea of Jesus being God's *only begotten*. There is a long history of debate as to what this means. However, the early church concluded that "only begotten" does not mean "created" but means "only one of its kind." Jesus is eternal but is *begotten* of the Father. There is a mystery here, for Jesus comes from the Father but is not a creation, and He is still eternal. Moreover, as God, Jesus is the only One who has seen God and has revealed Him to us.

The final concept that appears in the prologue to John's gospel is the idea of *grace and truth*. While there is clearly a lot of grace in the Old Testament and covenant, Jesus reveals the priority of **grace** through the cross. Moses brought the Law, revealing God's character and expectations for humanity. Yet Jesus gives the grace that enables us to fully obey and honor that Law. Much has been made over the centuries of the connection between grace and truth. Grace, at its core, is "unmerited favor." It is possible to give grace while abandoning the truth. Those who choose to tolerate sin are showing favor that is undeserved, but they are not speaking the truth with others. On the other hand, it is possible to speak the truth without showing grace. Those who always speak their mind and do not do so in love are speaking truth but neglecting grace. Jesus perfectly brings both. He speaks the truth but also offers grace.

> **incarnation:** "putting on flesh," referring to when Jesus as God is born as a human
>
> **demigod:** a divine or supernatural being that is a minor deity, a "half-god," an angel
>
> **grace:** unmerited favor; a gift given without being earned

Thought Questions:

1. In what way does Jesus serve as a light for you?

2. Are you good at balancing both grace and truth? Which one of these comes easier for you? How can you get a better balance between the two?

The Baptist, the First Sign, and the Temple Cleansing: John 1:19–2:25

Lesson 64

We have learned from the other gospels that John the Baptist's main role is to prepare the way for Jesus. In John's gospel, he will do this in more than one way. First, John makes it well known to the religious leaders that he himself is merely a messenger, sent to prepare the way for the coming Messiah. When the religious leaders ask him if he is the Christ, or Elijah, or the Prophet (Deuteronomy 18:15–19), he denies them all. For over 400 years, the Jews have been waiting to hear the Word of the Lord, and now John comes as a prophet. The very last book of the Old Testament prophesies that Elijah will return before the Messiah comes (Malachi 4:5), so this is why they ask if he is Elijah. Later, Jesus will clarify that John is in fact the Elijah that was to come. So why does John deny this? It is possible that John does not know that he is the Elijah that is to come, but he was undoubtedly aware of the prophecy in Malachi. Perhaps John's motive is to simply draw attention away from himself so that it can be on the Messiah when He comes. Rather than identifying with Elijah, John identifies with a simple voice about which Isaiah prophesies (Isaiah 40:3). John tries to draw their attention to his message, not to him.

When John sees Jesus, he immediately knows that Jesus is the Messiah who is to come. John instantly humbles himself in order to draw attention to Jesus. Whereas the other gospel writers do not identify who it is who tells them about Jesus' baptism, the gospel of John attributes this story to John the Baptist. John the Baptist testifies that he had been told that the Person whom he sees receive the Holy Spirit will be the One who will give that Holy Spirit to others. So when he sees Jesus receive the Holy Spirit, he testifies that Jesus is the One.

However, John the Baptist does not only testify about Jesus, he is also the one who gives Jesus His first disciples. John the Baptist had disciples of his own; and when he sees Jesus walking by, he directs some of his disciples to go and follow Jesus. One of these two disciples is Andrew, Simon Peter's brother. When Andrew follows Jesus, he goes and tells his brother that he has found the Messiah. When Jesus meets Simon,

He immediately changes his name to *Cephas*, which is translated *Peter*, or "stone." In Scripture, it is common for people's names to be changed after they have an encounter with God. God changes Abram's name to Abraham and Jacob's name to Israel. Peter will be the rock upon which Jesus will build His Church.

The next day, Jesus encounters Philip and tells him to follow Him. Philip agrees and tells Nathanael about Jesus, as well. Yet when Nathanael hears that Jesus is from Nazareth, he has a hard time believing that He is the Messiah. Not only is Nazareth in Galilee, a region that is largely Gentile, but it is a small, insignificant town. Nevertheless, when Jesus meets Nathanael, He knows that Nathanael doubts Him. So Jesus provides Nathanael with some proof that He is the Messiah. He tells Nathanael that He had seen him by the tree when Philip met with him. Jesus could not have seen him, considering that Philip had to go away to go get Nathanael. When Jesus reveals this, Nathanael believes and confesses that Jesus is the Messiah. However, Jesus responds with a theme that runs throughout this book. He points out that Nathanael only believes because Jesus showed him a sign or miracle. Yet He is gracious and basically says to Nathanael, "You have not seen anything yet."

It is interesting that the wedding at Cana is said to be on the third day. Considering the theological focus of John's gospel, the reference to the third day is likely an allusion to the coming resurrection on the third day. At this wedding, Jesus will revive the party that is about to die down for lack of wine. Not only are Jesus and His disciples at this wedding, but His mother is there, as well.

To understand this sign by Jesus, it is important to understand Jewish culture at this time. Unlike modern weddings in America, Jewish weddings would last days during the time of Jesus. Hospitality was also highly valued in Jewish culture. So for a couple to run out of wine in the middle of the party would be incredibly embarrassing. When this couple runs out of wine, the very celebration is in danger. So Jesus' mother, Mary, decides to jump into action. She knows who Jesus is, and so she comes to Jesus to solve this problem. Jesus' response to Mary is not as offensive as it sounds in English. If a person were to respond to his mother by calling her "woman" today, this would be rude. However, this is a term of endearment in Jesus' time. Jesus also tells Mary that His hour has not come. Jesus has a lot of teaching and preparation to do before He is ready to reveal that He is the Messiah to the people. Therefore, Jesus performs this sign privately so that only a few know about it.

It is interesting that the water that is used for this sign is the Jewish purification water. This water would be used to bathe in order to be cleansed so that one could enter the temple. Because of the importance of being clean, most Jewish people were very zealous about washing regularly. Yet Jesus transforms this water for outward cleansing into the very best wine, which will later represent His blood, which cleanses one inwardly. This wine is so good that the people are confused. It was common to bring out the best wine first, while people are still sober and can appreciate it. Once the people have had too much to drink, the cheaper wine would normally be brought out. However, this wine is the very best and is brought out later in the party. As a result of this sign, His disciples believe in Him.

The next event in the gospel of John poses a problem for interpreters. In the synoptic gospels, all three of the gospels place the cleansing of the temple during the Passion Week at the end of Jesus' ministry. Yet John puts the cleansing of the temple at the beginning of Jesus' ministry. There are a few solutions to this problem. First, it is possible that Jesus cleansed the temple twice, once at the beginning of His ministry and once at the end. Second, it is possible that the synoptic gospel writers move it right after the Triumphal Entry in order to show how unprepared the Jews are for Jesus. The last solution is that John moves it to the beginning to set the tone for the coming rejection of Jesus by the Jews. Any of these solutions can work.

When Jesus enters the temple, He is furious at what He sees. Because people travel for such long distances to make their sacrifices, the temple had turned into a marketplace where people could buy animals for the sacrifice. It is not unlawful for this to happen, but whenever money is involved, corruption is often right behind. Therefore, by the time that Jesus enters the temple, the temple feels more like a marketplace than a holy place. So Jesus makes a whip of cords and begins to drive out all of the money changers from the temple. As one could imagine, this would create quite the scene. So when Jesus is confronted about this, the Jews ask Him to prove that He has the authority to do this. They ask Jesus for a sign. However, the sign that Jesus offers them makes no sense to them. He tells them to destroy the temple so that He will raise it up in three days. This has two meanings. He is talking about His body first of all as the true Temple that would be destroyed but raised in three days. Yet, by destroying Jesus, the Jews would seal their own fate, as the temple will be

destroyed just forty years after Jesus dies. Ironically, it is this very quote that will eventually serve as evidence against Jesus when He later stands trial under the high priest, though He will be misquoted.

Thought Question:

Which of the three solutions for the chronological problem with the cleansing of the temple do you favor, and why?

Nicodemus: John 3

Lesson 65

By far the most famous verse in the Bible today is John 3:16. Whether seen at sporting events or memorized in Sunday school, most people in America have encountered this verse. Yet many people do not know the context of this verse. It all starts with a late night meeting between Jesus and a religious leader.

As we know from the synoptic gospels, Jesus is not very popular with the religious leaders of His day. As Jesus' popularity grows, so also does His opposition from the religious leaders, particularly the Pharisees. So it only makes sense that Nicodemus, a member of the Pharisees—and likely a Sadducee, as well—comes to Jesus by night. If his fellow Pharisees and Sadducees were to see him speaking to Jesus privately, it would be political suicide. As a Pharisee, Nicodemus is an expert in the Law and probably expects to have an intellectual conversation with Jesus about the Law of Moses.

Jesus, however, is an expert at getting straight to the heart. Nicodemus comes to Jesus as a fellow teacher, but his statement to Jesus and the fact that he comes alone suggests that he believes that Jesus is from God. Jesus does not even respond directly to what Nicodemus says to Him, but He goes straight to the point. Biblical knowledge is not sufficient for salvation. If a person wants to experience the kingdom of God, he or she must be born again. The phrase "born again" (ανωθεν) can also be translated "born from above" or "born anew." This has instantly derailed Nicodemus' conversation, so he asks how a person could be born twice. Jesus is clearly speaking **metaphorically**, but Nicodemus takes Him literally.

Jesus clarifies that the birth that He is talking about is a spiritual birth. When He says that a person must be born of the water and of the Spirit, He is referring to natural birth (water) and spiritual birth (Spirit). However, as is the case often with John's gospel, there can be another meaning to water, as well. John the Baptist baptized with water for repentance, but Jesus baptizes with the Spirit for salvation. This may be a subtle reference to the need for repentance and salvation. Jesus then goes on to explain the nature of the Holy Spirit. We cannot see the Holy Spirit, just as we cannot see the wind. All we can do is see the effects of each to know that they are there. Nicodemus may know, understand, and obey the Law very well; but if he is not born of the Holy Spirit, he cannot be saved. Nicodemus may have come prepared to learn from a teacher, but Jesus shows him his complete helplessness and dependence on Him for salvation. Knowledge and understanding are not enough; Nicodemus needs the Holy Spirit, and only Jesus can give it to him.

However, Nicodemus still does not understand, even with all of his teaching. So Jesus asks him how he is supposed to understand heavenly things if he cannot understand the earthly examples that He gives. By now, Nicodemus has been thoroughly humbled. Jesus is not just another good teacher; He is the Son of God who has been in the presence of God Himself. Nicodemus needs Jesus and has a lot to learn.

One of the other unique themes that John has in his gospel is the manner in which he speaks of Jesus' death. In John's gospel, Jesus does not speak of dying; rather, He speaks of being "lifted up." The cross is not about humiliation and defeat; it is about exaltation and being lifted up. So Jesus mentions the bronze serpent from the time of Moses (Numbers 21). Because the Israelites had been grumbling and complaining, God sends fiery serpents that bite and begin to kill the Israelites. In order to save the Israelites, God has Moses make a bronze serpent and place it high in the air. Every time an Israelite is bitten by a snake, he can look to the bronze serpent and be cured. So also, anyone who is dying of his or her sins can look to Jesus, who will be lifted up on the cross, and he or she will be saved.

It is after this that the famous John 3:16 comes. This verse has been characterized as "the gospel in a verse," and rightfully so. Here we learn that God loves the world so much that He gave His only Son, Jesus, to the world. The gospel is simple: whoever believes in Jesus will have eternal life. Jesus did not come in order to bring judgment and condemnation; He came to bring salvation. The world was already condemned; Jesus came to save as many as would believe. Verse 18 changes the very essence of morality. Salvation and eternity are not based on our own good deeds or bad deeds; it comes down to a simple question: "Do you believe in Jesus?" There is no condemnation for the one who believes, but the one who refuses to believe is condemned simply because he or she does not believe.

This is where the theme of light vs. darkness is highlighted. Jesus is the Light of the World. As the Light of the World, Jesus not only shows people how to live and what to do, but He reveals our true character to ourselves. Like a police officer in an interrogation room who shines a bright light on the person, Jesus reveals everything about us. We cannot hide our sins in the presence of Jesus. This is why people respond so strongly to Jesus, either by hating or loving Him. For those who do not want their deeds to be exposed, they want to stay in darkness and hate when the light is on them. However, for those who want to be cleansed, they are willing to let the light shine on them and confess their sins. According to John, people reject Jesus because they do not want to deal with their sins; they would rather hide.

Chapter 3 ends with more testimony by John the Baptist. Now that Jesus is growing in popularity, the religious leaders ask John the Baptist what he thinks about Jesus. John the Baptist identifies himself as a friend of the bridegroom who rejoices with the bridegroom. John is okay with the popularity that Jesus has because his entire purpose of ministry is to prepare people for Jesus. In fact, John says very humbly, "He must increase, but I must decrease" (John 3:30). He admits that Jesus is from heaven; and as such, He is far greater than John could ever be. Because of Jesus' heavenly origin, His words carry authority in themselves, but people are not listening to Him. John the Baptist recognizes the teachings of John 3, for he also testifies that Jesus is the Son of God and that the Father loves Him. John the Baptist also testifies, along with Jesus, that the key to everlasting life is belief in Jesus. If a person believes in Jesus, he or she will have everlasting life. However, if a person does not believe, he or she will not have everlasting life, but rather the wrath of God.

> **metaphorically:** not literally; by means of a *metaphor*, a figure of speech in which a word or phrase designates one kind of object or idea in place of another

Thought Questions:

1. Have you seen any examples of people loving darkness rather than the light? Why do you think these people prefer darkness over light?

2. How do you typically respond to God when you know you have sinned? Do you hide from God? Do you usually confess right away?

The Samaritan Woman: John 4

Lesson 66

One of the beautiful things about the gospel is that it puts every person on an even playing ground. Whether a person is an A+ student or struggles with school, whether a person is popular or a social outcast, whether a person is well-respected or hated and mocked, all people need Jesus and salvation. Jesus also gives the same offer of salvation to all people, regardless of their reputation. Jesus does not reserve the message of salvation simply for those who are privileged or perform well, but He offers it freely to all. Jesus' encounter with the Samaritan woman in John 4 illustrates this truth.

The contrast between the Samaritan woman and Nicodemus is worthy to note. Nicodemus was a well-respected teacher of the Law. In order to be a Pharisee, he would have to be very intelligent. Because of the importance that the Pharisees place on the Law and obedience to the Law, Nicodemus would have been blameless. Socially, Nicodemus was at the top of the ladder. The Samaritan woman, however, is exactly the opposite. The mere fact that she is a woman carries with it a lower status in that society. In addition, the Jews despised the Samaritans in that day and viewed them as unclean. However, the problems with this Samaritan woman go even further. This encounter takes place at the "sixth hour" of the day, which is noon. Because the people of Jesus' day did not have faucets with running water, every morning the women would go out to the well to get the water for the day. Because it was so hot in the middle of the day, the women would always go in the morning. Yet this woman is there alone at noon; why? The conversation with Jesus reveals that she had had five husbands before and was living with a man out of wedlock. This woman comes at noon because all the other women would have mocked and judged her for her sexual immorality. She is a complete social outcast. Yet, after their encounters with Jesus, both Nicodemus and the Samaritan woman are given the same salvation and redemption.

Even the responses of both the Samaritan woman and Nicodemus are similar. Jesus uses metaphors to convey the salvation message to both. To Nicodemus, He describes salvation as being *born again*; to the Samaritan woman, He describes salvation as *living water*. Both Nicodemus and the Samaritan woman take the metaphor literally instead of figuratively.

The very fact that Jesus goes through Samaria is interesting. It says that Jesus "needed to go through Samaria" (verse 4) as He traveled from Judea to Galilee. At first glance, this makes sense. Judea is in the southern portion of Palestine, and Galilee is in the northern portion of Palestine with Samaria in between the two. However, because of the hostility and hatred between the Jews and the Samaritans, most Jews would take the much longer journey over mountains and across the Jordan River, and they would travel north or south to the east of the Jordan River rather than going through Samaria. Not only is it not necessary for Jesus to travel through Samaria, it is strange for Him to do so. So when John says that Jesus "needed to go through Samaria," it is because the Holy Spirit is leading Him to do so.

Jesus meets this woman after His disciples have gone away into the city to get some food. Because He is tired, He asks the woman to give Him a drink from the water that she had just brought up from the well. This is incredibly countercultural, and the woman knows it; so she asks Him why He is even talking to her. As with Nicodemus, who was expecting a friendly discussion, this woman expects a debate; but, as with Nicodemus, Jesus makes a statement that confuses her. He offers to give her living water. Now Jesus is speaking about Himself as the Water of Life who brings satisfaction to us, but living water can also mean flowing water. So she assumes that He is talking about physical water.

The woman's next statement reveals a cultural barrier between Jews and Samaritans. Because the Samaritans are the descendants of the Northern Kingdom, which had broken off from Judah, and because the Samaritans had intermixed with the non-Jews, the Jews saw the Samaritans as half-breeds and illegitimate people. The Samaritans, however, saw themselves as legitimate Israelites. By mentioning Jacob's well, the Samaritan woman is preparing to argue that she is a legitimate Israelite. Moreover, when Jesus offers to give her other "water," she assumes that He is just another Jew claiming to be better than her people. So Jesus clarifies, as He had previously done with Nicodemus, that the water about which He is speaking is not physical but spiritual. She, however, still takes him literally and asks for this water so that she will not have to go to the well anymore.

This is when Jesus goes straight to the heart. He asks her to bring her husband with her. This woman, however, does not currently have a husband and tells Him so. So He tells her information that He should have no possible way of knowing, that she has already had five husbands and is currently living with a man out of wedlock. The woman's response to this is almost humorous, "Sir, I perceive that You are a prophet." But just as Nicodemus had an intellectual and religious barrier that Jesus had to break through, this woman still has a cultural and religious barrier to break through. One of the other debates between the Jews and the Samaritans is about where people are supposed to worship. The Jews claimed that people had to worship at the temple in Jerusalem, but the Samaritans worshiped in Samaria. When the woman brings this up to Jesus, He destroys this barrier by claiming that the time is coming soon when location will not matter because God is more concerned about worshiping in spirit and truth. God is far more concerned with the heart than the location of worship. This may be a subtle prophecy about the destruction of the temple in A.D. 70.

Jesus then gives this woman a privilege that He does not give to very many people; He reveals to her that He is the Messiah. For most people, Jesus hides this fact so that they could discover it on their own. However, He freely gives this information to the woman. So when she leaves, she goes and tells her entire village, and they all come to meet Jesus.

In the meantime, while the woman is gone, Jesus' disciples return. They try to offer Him food, but Jesus is so satisfied and filled from this conversation that He does not need food. In fact, He tells His disciples that doing the will of His Father is food for Him. He also tells the disciples His famous line about the harvest. There is a ripe harvest out there, as evidenced by the large group of Samaritans that were on their way to meet them at that very moment. These Samaritans are noble people who see Jesus for themselves, and they believe in Him.

Chapter 4 ends with another sign at Cana in Galilee. This time Jesus heals an official's son. However, following the theme of *true faith versus weak faith*, Jesus laments that "unless you people see signs and wonders, you will by no means believe" (verse 48). Jesus heals the official's son not only because He has compassion on the man and his son, but also because He wants people to believe in Him without needing signs and miracles.

Thought Questions:

1. What might be some social or cultural barriers that you may need to break through in order to share the gospel with others?

2. Another barrier for this woman is the perceived superiority of the Jewish people in their own minds. How do you think other people perceive Christians? What barriers might this create?

Healing and Opposition: John 5
Lesson 67

In the prologue to the gospel of John, we learn that Jesus came to His own, but His own did not receive Him (John 1:11). When Jesus speaks to the Samaritan woman, He tells her that salvation comes from the Jews. In chapter 5, rather than rejoicing at the salvation that Jesus offers people, the Jews reject Jesus and begin to plot His death. After four chapters of growth and fruitfulness, chapter 5 begins a new section of John's gospel filled with opposition and rejection.

This chapter begins on a positive note. As Jesus is in the temple, He encounters a group of crippled and disabled people trying to get into a pool. It was believed that every day an angel would begin to stir the water so that the first person who enters the water once it is stirred would be healed. When Jesus arrives here, He talks to a crippled man who had been unable to walk for thirty-eight years. It is interesting that this man has been unable to walk for thirty-eight years; this is the exact same number of years that the Israelites wander in the wilderness after they leave Egypt. It has been suggested that this man is symbolic of Israel itself, helpless and in need of healing. When Jesus heals this man, He tells him to pick up his mat and walk.

Rather than rejoicing at this great sign and healing, the religious leaders at the temple rebuke this man. According to the traditions of the elders, it is considered work for a person to carry his or her mat on the Sabbath. Therefore, because this man is carrying his mat on the Sabbath, the leaders rebuke him. Yet he responds by telling them that he is simply doing what the Man who healed him told him to do.

Jesus later meets this man and warns him not to go back to sin and make his condition worse. Even though this man has been healed from his infirmity, there is a far more important healing that he needs—healing from his sins. Even though this man has been healed from his condition, if he goes back to a life of sin it will have done him no good. This is why Jesus is not interested in simply performing signs or wonders. He is far more concerned about the spiritual condition of a person, not just the physical. While we are not entirely sure if this man listens to Jesus or not, his immediate response suggests that he does not listen. Knowing that the religious leaders were going to persecute Jesus, this man tells the leaders that it was Jesus who healed him.

What follows from this looks a lot like a trial. For the rest of chapter 5, Jesus defends Himself and seeks to prove to the religious leaders that He does His works with the authority of God. Because Jesus has broken the Sabbath (according to their traditions), the religious leaders begin to persecute Him. Much of Jesus' response centers on the relationship that He has with the Father. Moreover, by identifying Himself with the Father, the religious leaders rightfully discern that Jesus is putting Himself on par with God Himself.

Simply put, Jesus argues that everything that He does has been directed by the Father. By "working" on the Sabbath, Jesus is following in the footsteps of the Father, who has been "working" on the Sabbath from the beginning of time by sustaining the universe. Jesus only does what the Father has shown Him to do. The Father also loves Jesus and is preparing incredible signs and wonders to do through Him. In addition, Jesus says that the Father has entrusted the role of Judge to Him. In fact, Jesus argues in verse 23 that the people are rejecting the Father by rejecting Him as the Son because the Father has sent Him. As Judge, Jesus holds the power over eternal life; and when the resurrection of the dead occurs, it will be Jesus who gets to determine who will receive eternal life and who will be condemned. Of course, even though Jesus is the Judge, He only makes these decisions as the Father directs Him. Jesus is also a *just* Judge because He does not seek His own will but to do the will of the Father.

As in a court of law, Jesus calls forth three witnesses. The *first witness* is John the Baptist. John the Baptist was incredibly popular with the people, not only during his life but even after his death. John made it abundantly clear that his job was to point the way for the coming Messiah, and John identifies Jesus as that Messiah. The *second witness* that Jesus calls forth is the signs and works that He has performed. The basic argument here is that the myriad of miracles that Jesus has performed provide clear evidence that the Father has put His stamp of approval on Jesus' ministry. Finally, the *third witness* that Jesus calls forth is the Scriptures. These religious leaders diligently study the Scriptures because they want to discern who the Messiah would be. Yet, when the Messiah has come to them, they refuse to humble themselves and come to Him. These religious leaders, who love the Law of Moses, refuse to believe Moses' testimony about Him. In fact, Jesus does not even threaten to judge these hypocritical religious leaders; He argues that the Law itself, which they love so much, will condemn them.

Sadly, this is not the last time that Jesus will have to justify the ministry entrusted to Him by the Father. This "trial" will continue for the next few chapters of John.

Thought Question:

Imagine that you were Jesus' defense attorney in a court of law. What would be your defense for Him?

The Bread of Life: John 6

Lesson 68

One of the ways that John structures his gospel is to connect the signs that Jesus performs with His teachings on that subject. In chapter 6, we are told the story of the feeding of the 5,000. We have already encountered this miracle before in the synoptic gospels. Here, a large crowd gathers to hear Jesus "because they saw His signs which He performed on those who were diseased" (verse 2). These people are attracted to Jesus because of the incredible signs that He performs. Jesus does not fail to impress here, and He is able to take a few fish and loaves of bread and use them to feed this huge crowd of over 5,000 people. Once the people eat their fill of this food, they attempt to make Jesus king by force because they perceive that He is the Prophet, which Moses had prophesied about in Deuteronomy 18. In the previous chapter, we see that the religious leaders refused to listen to Moses' testimony about Jesus, yet this crowd of ordinary people can recognize that Jesus is the fulfillment of this prophecy.

Because Jesus knows that it is not yet His time to complete His work, He withdraws by Himself to avoid the crowds. He gives His disciples orders to cross the sea that is by them and to go to Capernaum by themselves. That night, after they had traveled three or four miles, they see Jesus coming to them, walking on water! As one would expect, they are afraid; but Jesus calms them and enters their boat. After they arrive on the other side, the crowds that Jesus had just fed the day before come over to Capernaum and find Him.

This begins the next big dialogue in John, which finishes the rest of chapter 6. Jesus discerns that the people in this crowd do not have sincere hearts but are there to see another sign. So He calls them out and challenges them to set their sights higher than a single meal. They want more food from Jesus, but Jesus tells them to pursue the food that endures to everlasting life. As with the Samaritan woman in chapter 4, Jesus masterfully uses the immediate context to share the gospel. With the Samaritan woman, Jesus offers to give her *living water* that will permanently satisfy her soul, and now here He offers *eternal bread* that can satisfy their souls. Like the Samaritan woman at the well and like Nicodemus before, the crowd completely misses the metaphor that Jesus is using to explain the gospel.

Rather than asking how they could receive this bread, the crowd asks what they must do to "work the works of God" (verse 28). Jesus once again brings up a theme that is present throughout John's gospel; namely, that the only work that God requires is to believe in Jesus. In John 3, Jesus said that He did not come into the world to condemn it but to save it. The only cause for condemnation is rejection of Jesus Christ. Amazingly, even after the miraculous feeding of the 5,000, the people ask Jesus to give them another sign to prove that what He is saying is true. These people do not have a genuine desire to follow Jesus; they just want to experience His signs and wonders.

Appropriately, the crowd connects the miracle that Jesus had performed by feeding the 5,000 with the giving of manna in the wilderness in the days of Moses. They bring this up because they want to see another sign by Jesus, but Jesus uses this as an opportunity to teach them more about Himself. While the Father did give the Israelites bread from heaven while they were in the wilderness, Jesus says that He Himself is the true Bread from heaven. Just as the Samaritan woman asks Jesus to give her the *living water* that He had spoken about, this crowd asks for the *true bread*.

Jesus responds with the first of His famous "I am" sayings in the gospel of John. Jesus identifies Himself as the Bread of Life. These people want the bread from heaven, but they refuse to believe in Jesus. Jesus is the true Bread that soothes our spiritual hunger and thirst. Jesus knows that not everyone will receive Him or believe in Him, and He says that only the people whom

the Father has given to Him will actually come to Him. This is another theme that runs throughout the gospel of John, the sovereignty of God in choosing who will be able to find salvation in Jesus. Jesus is not confused or surprised by the amount of rejection that He receives because He knows that God will lead all of the right people to Him, and those people will believe. In fact, Jesus will protect and save every person whom God the Father gives Him. So when the crowd starts to murmur and complain about the things that Jesus is saying, He says again that only those whom the Father draws will be able to come to Him.

Jesus next connects this bread metaphor with what will later become Communion. He reiterates that He is the Bread of Life and that everyone who eats of this Bread will have everlasting life. In other words, whoever believes in Him will have everlasting life. Yet then He says that the bread that He gives them is His flesh. We understand that Jesus is speaking about the crucifixion and the breaking of His body on the cross. However, as has been the pattern throughout John, the people take this literally and quarrel among themselves about this saying.

For both Nicodemus and the Samaritan woman, Jesus clarifies the metaphors that He had been using; but because Jesus knows that the crowd is not sincere, He draws out the metaphor even more. Because these people are taking Jesus literally, He tells them that only those who eat His flesh and drink His blood will be saved. This is why many Christian traditions believe that, somehow, when we take Communion we are literally taking in Jesus' flesh and blood. Jesus, however, is speaking about putting faith in His coming sacrifice on the cross.

Jesus knows that saying these things will greatly offend the crowd, but He uses this to weed out those who are not genuine in their desire to follow Him. In fact, this is precisely what happens. In verse 60, the crowd says, "This is a hard saying; who can understand it?" Jesus acknowledges once again that the only people who will be able to come to Jesus are those whom the Father has granted. So we learn in verse 66 that many of the people who had been following Jesus, but who were not genuine, turn away and stop following Jesus. When things get tough, the crowds fall away.

Then Jesus turns to the twelve and asks them if they will turn away, as well. Peter's response reveals the attitude of the kind of people whom God has drawn to Jesus. He says, "Lord, to whom shall we go? You have the words of eternal life" (verse 68). It is not clear whether or not Peter and the disciples understand what

Jesus' "I Am" Statements

Absolute "I am" statements	6:20; 8:24, 28, 58; 18:5

Metaphorical "I am" statements	
1. I am the bread of life	6:35, 48, 51
2. I am the light of the world	8:12; 9:5
3. I am the door of the sheep	10:7, 9
4. I am the good shepherd	10:11, 14
5. I am the resurrection and the life	11:25
6. I am the way, the truth, and the life	14:6
7. I am the true vine	15:1

Jesus has been saying, but Peter knows that Jesus is the One who can offer eternal life; and he clings to Jesus, even when others walk away. Jesus follows this confession with a warning that one of them will betray Him.

Later in this gospel, John will make it known that the purpose of this book is to challenge the reader to come to genuine faith in Jesus Christ and to gain eternal life. The reader should examine himself or herself to see with whom he or she identifies more: the crowd that walks away when following Jesus gets tough or the twelve disciples who cling to Jesus, even though they may not understand everything that Jesus is saying. Jesus demands genuine faith.

Thought Questions:

1. What have you been taught about the purpose of the Lord's Supper? Do you believe that you are actually eating Jesus' flesh and drinking His blood? Why or why not?

2. Jesus says that the only people who can come to Him are those whom the Father draws or gathers to Him. What implications does this have regarding evangelism and salvation?

The Feast of Tabernacles: John 7

Lesson 69

The trial that Jesus has been on throughout the book of John continues in chapter 7. The events in chapter 7 take place during the Feast of Tabernacles. This feast is one of the three great feasts that all the Jews throughout the empire are supposed to celebrate. During this feast, the people are supposed to make booths, or tents (tabernacles), and stay in them for the whole week. This feast was instituted by God in order to help the Israelites remember the forty years when they wandered in the wilderness because of their lack of faith and rebellion before they conquered the Promised Land (Leviticus 23).

We learn in the beginning of this chapter that Jesus has withdrawn to the region of Galilee in order to avoid Judea. Jesus is well aware that the religious leaders in Jerusalem have made up their minds to arrest Him in order to get Him out of the way. Jesus also knows that He still has work to do before He is to go to His death. So when His brothers suggest that Jesus make a grand public appearance in Jerusalem, Jesus refuses. Even His own brothers do not understand who Jesus is and what He came to do. Prior to the ministry of Jesus, there had been a number of other people who claimed to

be the Messiah, who had also gathered disciples. Jesus' brothers want Jesus to grow in popularity and to make Himself known so that He could gain more disciples and also political power. Not only do the religious leaders oppose Jesus and many of the Jews misunderstand Him, but even His own family does not understand Him. Nevertheless, after His family leaves for Jerusalem, Jesus goes to the city privately.

Once Jesus gets to Jerusalem, the trial continues among the Jews. Jesus is the talk of the town, and many people search for Jesus; and like His family, they expect a grand entrance. As the people murmur about Jesus, it becomes clear that there is not a consensus among the crowds about Jesus. Some believe that Jesus is a good teacher, while others follow the views of the religious leaders and accuse Him of deception. Yet none of the people speak about Jesus "openly … for fear of the Jews" (verse 13). Considering that the Jews are the ones talking, when it mentions the fear of the Jews, it really means the fear of the Jewish religious leaders.

After remaining incognito for part of the feast, in the middle of the week, Jesus finally speaks publicly in order to defend His teaching and ministry. The first issue that Jesus defends is an issue of credibility. When Jesus speaks, He speaks with authority; and He claims to speak for God. In those days, in order for a person to have authority as a teacher of the Law, he would have to study under a rabbi for quite some time. To put it in today's terms, the credibility of a person today is largely determined by the school that he or she attended. Jesus, however, never learned under a rabbi. When Jesus speaks, He speaks as though His word is simply the truth. Jesus recognizes that it can be hard to accept someone's authority if he speaks for himself, as his teaching can be corrupted by self-interest. Yet Jesus defends the way that He speaks by pointing out that He has never sought His own glory but has consistently sought to glorify the Father; His motives are not self-interest, but rather the glory of God.

Next, Jesus defends the healing that He had performed on the Sabbath. It is this act of healing that has angered the religious leaders and has led to this persecution and debate. To defend this act of healing, Jesus goes back to the source of their complaint. The religious leaders argue that healing is a type of work, and as such is a violation of the Sabbath law that Moses had given. So Jesus reminds them that Moses himself had not only allowed but also had commanded circumcision to be done on the eighth day, which is a Sabbath day. If it is okay to perform this work of circumcision on the Sabbath, how much more acceptable should it be to heal the whole person?

After Jesus says these things, the debate among the Jews continues. Jesus is speaking boldly and publicly, yet none of the religious leaders are willing to stand up to Him. The people perceive the lack of response by the religious leaders as evidence to support that Jesus is from God. Yet still there is a misunderstanding among the people. Even though the Old Testament Scriptures are clear that the Messiah will come from Bethlehem, the people take the almost **mythological** view that no one will know from where the Messiah will come. However, Jesus bites on this debate and uses it as an opportunity to teach the people more about His authority. Jesus acknowledges that the people do indeed know from where He comes; but He argues that He has truly come from God, not some city. God is the One who has sent Him to do His work.

Finally, now that the religious leaders have been backed into a corner, they send officers to Jesus to have Him come with them, but He refuses. He tells them that He is only going to be around for a short time, but then He must go to a place that they cannot follow. Jesus, of course, is speaking about His death and ascension when He goes to heaven; and because of their unbelief, they will not be able to follow Him there. Yet, as always, they do not understand what Jesus is saying and assume He is talking about the Dispersion. Some years before Jesus had come, because of persecution, many of the Jews had dispersed throughout the Roman Empire; and the Jews think that Jesus intends to go among the Greeks. Because the Jews hate the Greeks so much and consider them unclean, they would not go among them.

What begins as a debate becomes a call to salvation on the last day of the feast. Jesus stands up among the crowds and says that anyone who believes in Him will have rivers of living water flowing out of him. As John clarifies, Jesus is speaking about the Holy Spirit, who is to come on the day of Pentecost; but, of course, the people do not understand what Jesus is saying. This stirs up the debates among the crowds again as some perceive that Jesus is the Prophet about whom Moses spoke in Deuteronomy, and others begin to believe that He is the Christ. Interestingly, the crowd earlier believed that the origin of the Christ should be unknown, but this crowd is more knowledgeable and knows that the Christ will come from Bethlehem. Even though Jesus was born in Bethlehem, the crowds only know of Him growing up in Nazareth in Galilee.

Chapter 7 ends with the arrogance and hard-heartedness of the religious leaders. When the officers who were supposed to bring Jesus come back, the religious leaders ask them why they did not take Jesus by force. However, the officers are so amazed by the teachings of Jesus that they refuse to take Him by force. As "evidence" against Jesus, the religious leaders argue that none of the Pharisees believe in Jesus so He must not be from God. Since the Pharisees are supposed to be the ultimate standard of religiosity, Jesus could not possibly be from God. Not only is this arrogant, but it is factually wrong. Nicodemus, whom we encountered in chapter 3, does believe in Jesus and tries to defend Him here. Nicodemus rebukes the religious leaders for condemning Jesus without a trial. Moreover, like many hard-hearted people, when this man opposes them, they turn on Nicodemus.

> **mythological:** lacking a historical basis; of or relating to an allegorical narrative

Thought Question:

> Why do you think the religious leaders have such stubborn hearts here? What should you do when talking about Jesus if you encounter someone with a hard heart like the Pharisees here?

False Belief: John 8
Lesson 70

Chapter 8 begins on a controversial note. As scholars have continued to discover more ancient manuscripts of the Bible, the earliest manuscripts do not have John 8:1–11. Naturally, this poses a problem for us. Should we allow this new information to lead us to reject this section as Scripture, or should we hold to the tradition we have held for hundreds of years? It is out of the scope of this course to go into great detail on this issue, but here are a few thoughts: Within the text, verse 12 picks up right where chapter seven leaves off. Either way, verses 1–11 appear to be a parenthesis in the ongoing debate in chapters seven and eight. This would add evidence to suggest that these verses were not originally included in the manuscripts. However, the material in this story lines up perfectly with how Jesus regularly responds in these situations in which the Jewish leaders try to "trap" Him; moreover, there is nothing in this story that contradicts any other Scriptures. If this was not originally in the Bible, it does not mean that it did not happen. This story could have been circulating among the churches for some time before it was included in Scripture. For the sake of this course, we are going to examine this section as if it is Scripture.

As Jesus is teaching in the temple, the scribes and Pharisees bring to Him a woman caught in the act of adultery. In front of the crowds, they ask Jesus what should happen to her. This is designed to be a trap. Jesus has already developed a reputation of being someone who offers salvation and forgiveness to sinners, but the Law states that this woman should be put to death for her adultery, not to mention the man who also committed adultery in this case (Leviticus 20:10). First, this shows the hypocrisy of the religious leaders, who only accuse the woman and not the man. Second, this reveals their lack of care for the woman by using her only to trap Jesus. Now, if Jesus says to forgive this woman, He would be going against the Law and could be arrested; if He says to kill her, He would lose popularity with the people and would be viewed as a hypocrite. So, as Jesus often does, He takes a third approach—He ignores them. However, they persist; and Jesus gives a brilliant response. The common form of capital punishment in the Bible is to kill someone by throwing stones at him. The community would all throw stones so that no one person would stand out as the one who kills the person. When Jesus suggests that the one who is sinless ought to be the one who casts the first stone, He accomplishes two things: *first*, He removes the anonymity of the ones who cast the stones; and *second*, He reminds them that they too are sinners. The people walk away, one at a time, starting with the oldest, who recognize the extent of their own sin. When only Jesus and the woman remain, He pardons her but tells her to stop sinning. There is an important lesson about the gospel here: even though we are completely forgiven of our sins, we have to repent (turn away) from them.

Picking up from the previous debate, Jesus offers another one of His famous "I am" statements in verse 12. Here Jesus says that He is the Light of the World. We have already seen the theme of light vs. darkness multiple times in the gospel of John. Light is associated with truth and righteousness, and darkness is associated with sin and the state of being lost. By offering Himself as the Light of the World, Jesus is offering guidance and truth to the people.

Yet the Pharisees immediately respond with an old objection to Jesus, which we have already seen. They attack Jesus' credibility because He is speaking on His own behalf. Jesus does not have any other source to validate His claims, according to the Pharisees. To this, Jesus responds in two ways. *First*, Jesus argues that just because He speaks on His own behalf does not mean

that the things that He says are not true. *Second*, Jesus argues that the Father Himself is His other witness, testifying that the things that He is saying are the truth. In the Law, it is required that there be two witnesses in a court of law in order to substantiate a claim (Deuteronomy 19:15). Jesus and the Father are the two witnesses here. Of course, the Jews misunderstand Jesus and fail to recognize that the Father that Jesus is talking about is God Himself.

As in the previous chapter, Jesus again speaks about His coming departure to the Jews, and again they fail to understand what He means. He tells them that He is going to go away and they will not be able to find Him; and, sadly, they will die in their sins. In verse 24, Jesus clarifies that it is because of their stubborn refusal to believe in Him that they will be unable to be forgiven of their sins. This is quite the claim for Jesus. Jesus states here that salvation and forgiveness do not come from observing the Law, but through belief in Him alone. The Jews respond by asking Him who He is in order to make such powerful claims. However, Jesus knows that their hearts are hard and says that they will only be able to truly know who He is once He is "lifted up" or crucified. Only after Jesus dies will they understand who He is. As a result of this teaching, many of those who were listening begin to believe in Him.

It would appear as if this is a great moment in Jesus' ministry. Jesus has just convinced many people to believe in Him. Yet what comes next is surprising. Jesus directly challenges and rebukes those who believe in Him. These people have the beginning stages of faith, but Jesus pushes them in order to reveal that their faith is still too weak. Now that many claim to believe in Him, Jesus tells them what they need to do next; they need to abide in His word. To abide in His word not only means to continue to believe in what He says, but also means to follow and obey what He says. If a person abides in Christ's word, he or she will be set free. Naturally, we must ask from what we need to be set free. To what are the people in bondage? Because Jesus has just identified Himself as the Light of the World, the people have been in bondage to sin and darkness. They are slaves to depraved minds that cannot see the truth, and Jesus has come to set them free from that darkness.

However, the response of the crowd reveals that their earlier belief is not complete. They argue that they are descendants of Abraham and are not slaves to anything. In order to have a legitimate faith in Jesus, we must realize our need for Him; yet these people do not see their need for Jesus. So Jesus clarifies that they are indeed slaves to sin, and the mere fact that they are seeking to kill Jesus is evidence that their faith is not genuine. This is where Jesus certainly deeply offends the people. He says that He is merely doing and saying what the Father wants Him to do and say, but the people cannot receive His word because they are following their father, the devil. They claim that Abraham is their father, but Jesus argues that their real father is the devil. The people cannot receive the truth of Jesus' claims because they have been ensnared by the lies of Satan. Jesus admittedly uses a circular form of reasoning, even though it is true. Jesus says that the real evidence that they are following God is if they believe in Him. If the people do not follow God, then Jesus argues that they will not accept Jesus' words. This has implications for today. It says in Proverbs that "the fear of the LORD is the beginning of wisdom" (Proverbs 9:10). If a person has no desire to obey God, he certainly cannot accept Jesus' salvation. If the people do believe in Jesus, Jesus says that they will never die. This does not mean that their bodies will not die, as we know they all did, but this refers to the second death in the lake of fire after Judgment Day (Revelation 20).

Yet, just as the previous crowd would not let go of Moses, this crowd still continues to place faith in Abraham. They believe that simply because they are descendants of Abraham that God will save them. So Jesus makes a final claim that pushes the crowd over the edge. Jesus says that Abraham himself longed to see the day of Jesus. In fact, Jesus existed before Abraham even existed. This goes even deeper, however. For if Jesus merely wanted to say that He is older than Abraham, He would have said, "before Abraham was, I was"; instead, Jesus says, "before Abraham was, I AM" (verse 58). This is an explicit claim to the name of *Yahweh*, which means "I am." Jesus clearly is equating Himself with God. The response of the Jews confirms this as the crowd, which previously believed in Jesus, picks up stones to kill Him. This is the punishment for blasphemy (Leviticus 24:16). Yet, because it is not yet Jesus' time, He is able to walk through the crowds and escape.

Thought Questions:

1. The crowds here clearly have an incomplete belief. What might it look like today for a person to have an incomplete faith, or belief, in Jesus?

2. Jesus is able to wisely push the crowds in order to reveal their lack of faith. What might be a way to test the faith of someone who claims to believe in Jesus but does not?

The Healing of the Blind Man: John 9

Lesson 71

For a while now in the gospel of John, Jesus has been identifying Himself as the Light of the World who brings light and truth to darkness. In chapter 9, Jesus fulfills this literally as He heals a man born blind. The question that the disciples ask of Jesus reveals the predominant belief at this time regarding physical ailments. The disciples assume that this man is blind because of some sin. Because he was born blind, the disciples wonder if this blindness is because of some sin in him or because of the sins of his parents. Jesus tells them that their assumption is wrong and that this ailment has nothing to do with sin. Rather, God has made this person blind for this very moment so that God may be glorified through this healing.

The method of healing that Jesus uses for this man is different from His typical form of healing. Usually, Jesus heals people with a mere word, or even just by them touching His robe. Here, however, Jesus spits on the ground and makes clay out of the mud and puts it on the man's eyes. While we are not explicitly told why Jesus does this, it has been suggested that this man may have been born without eyes, and that when Jesus puts the clay on the man's eyes, He is literally making eyes for the man. Just as the original man, Adam, was made from the dust of the earth, Jesus does a recreation for this man, making him eyes from the earth. Either way, when the religious leaders find out that He "made" mud to put on this man's eyes on the Sabbath, they deem this as work and as a violation of the Sabbath. Then Jesus tells the man to wash in the pool of Siloam, not only to physically wash off the dirt but to represent purification.

While Jesus has been publicly on trial through His numerous debates with the Jews, a literal trial takes place over this healed blind man. The Pharisees ask this man how he was able to gain his sight, and he tells them what Jesus had done. So they gather together and put this man on trial to figure out exactly what happened. When they find out that this healing took place on the Sabbath, they use this as evidence to "prove" that Jesus is not from God because He is violating the Sabbath in their eyes. However, it is impossible to ignore the evidence of this incredible healing, so the religious leaders attempt to disprove what had happened. Assuming that this man must be lying, they call in his parents to ask if he was indeed born blind. The parents confirm that he was born blind but refuse to speak out more about Jesus because the religious leaders had threatened any who place faith in Jesus that they would be kicked out of the synagogue.

The religious leaders still refuse to believe this man's testimony about Jesus, so they ask him once again exactly what had happened. Confused why these leaders are asking him the same questions over again, he asks the religious leaders if they too want to become Jesus' disciples. Just as the previous crowd held to their lineage to Abraham as their hope of salvation, the Pharisees look to their allegiance to Moses as their salvation. Now we do not know how good of a speaker this blind man is, but we can learn something from his testimony. Our own story is one of the most powerful tools we can use when testifying about Jesus. We do not have to be Bible scholars or be prepared for every argument against Jesus. Like the blind man, you can simply say, "I was blind, but now I see"; or you can say, "I was lost and clueless, but now I can see the truth."

After the religious leaders dismiss the man, Jesus seeks out the man and reveals to him that He is the One who healed him. Jesus asks him if he believes in the Son of God. Then when Jesus identifies Himself as the Son of God, the man confesses that He truly believes in Jesus. Rather than questioning and fighting Jesus as the previous crowd did, this man worships Jesus, the response of true faith. This man is a great example of genuine faith. Unlike the crowds who believed that their lineage from Abraham saved them and who did not recognize their own bondage to sin—or the religious leaders who believed that their faith in Moses and the Law would save them—this man acknowledges that he was blind and needed Jesus to see. When Jesus heals this man's physical blindness, He also heals his spiritual blindness. At the end of this story, it is the blind man who can see the truth, whereas the Pharisees are deemed the blind ones. Because the Pharisees rely on their own self-righteousness rather than humbly coming to Jesus for salvation, they are the ones to end up blind. Yet the blind man who humbly came to Jesus asking for help is the one who is truly saved.

Thought Questions:

1. Think back to the day of your conversion. What was it that motivated you to believe in Jesus?

2. Do you identify more with the blind man or the Pharisees in this story? Why?

The Good Shepherd and Lazarus: John 10–11

Lesson 72

Throughout the gospel of John, Jesus reveals Himself in many different ways to different people. To Nicodemus, Jesus reveals Himself as the wise Teacher who offers new life. To the Samaritan woman, Jesus reveals Himself as the Water of Life who will permanently satisfy our souls. He is the Bread of Life who will feed our souls and the Light of the World who gives us truth and direction. In John 10, Jesus reveals two more of His famous "I am" statements. Jesus identifies Himself as the Door for the Sheep and as the Good Shepherd.

The metaphor that runs throughout chapter 10 is the shepherding metaphor. There is a lot that we learn about Jesus from this metaphor. To begin with, we learn that there are enemies of the sheep who long to attack and kill the sheep. These enemies seek to break into the pen and do not use the door. The sheep flee from these thieves and robbers but follow their shepherd, who comes in through the door. In fact, the sheep have such an intimate relationship with the shepherd that they will only follow his voice and run from others. Therefore, Jesus identifies Himself in two ways. *First*, Jesus identifies Himself as the Door for the Sheep. He provides the only legitimate means into and out of the sheep pen. Practically speaking, Jesus is making it clear here that He is the only legitimate means of salvation and that every other person or means for salvation is a fraud.

Second, Jesus identifies Himself as the Shepherd. One of the responsibilities of the shepherd is to guide the sheep to where they can find pasture to graze; like a shepherd, Jesus guides us to true rest in heaven and sustenance on earth. Also, Jesus is not a stingy Shepherd; in verse 10 we see that He came to give us life more abundantly. The thief, Satan, does not care about people and seeks to destroy, but Jesus truly cares about His sheep and longs to give them abundance. Not only does Jesus provide for His sheep, He loves them enough that He will give His life for them. The hired man has no relationship with the sheep; and when danger comes, he runs away, but a good shepherd will fight for his sheep to protect them. Unlike the other metaphors that Jesus has used in the gospel of John, this metaphor speaks to the intimate relationship Jesus has with His sheep. The sheep hear Jesus' voice and respond to only Him. This helps to explain the various responses that people have given to Jesus throughout the gospel of John. Only the true sheep, whom God the Father has given to Jesus, will respond when He calls to them. Much of John's gospel focuses on the distinction between the true sheep who respond with faith to Jesus and the false sheep who ultimately reject Him. One of the other elements of Jesus as Shepherd that Jesus highlights in this teaching is that He has the power to choose when He will lay down His life. It is possible for a thief or a robber to overpower a shepherd, but no one will overpower Jesus. When Jesus dies, it is because He lays down His life, not because someone takes it from Him.

As we have seen a number of times already in the gospel of John, there is a mixed reaction by the crowds to this teaching. Some accuse Him of being demon-possessed or crazy, yet others believe in Him. So, finally, the Jews ask Jesus directly if He is the Christ. To answer, Jesus directs them to His works and tells them that His actions have made it abundantly clear that He is the Christ. Yet Jesus' answer goes further. Jesus tells them that the reason they cannot see the abundant evidence is that they are not His sheep. The Father has given certain people into His hands, and Jesus will give His sheep eternal life and protect them. In fact, for those who are Jesus' sheep, nobody will be able to take them away from Jesus. Yet the fact that the crowds refuse to believe in Jesus shows that they are not His sheep.

Once again, Jesus speaks of His deity and the unity between Himself and the Father in verse 30 when He says that they are one. The crowd picks up on this; and once again, the people pick up stones to throw at Him. When Jesus asks them why they are getting ready to throw stones at Him, they say it is because He claims to be God. Interestingly, Jesus responds by quoting Psalm 82, where people are called "gods" (verse 6). This does not mean that there are multiple gods. Rather, Jesus is wittily responding to them by referencing this Psalm where rulers are called "gods." If rulers are sarcastically called "gods" in Scripture, how much more appropriate is the One who was sent from God and who does the works of God to be called God? But the people refuse to believe and seek to seize Him. Yet Jesus escapes and goes down to the Jordan River, where John the Baptist had ministered; and many believe in Him there.

As the time draws closer to the Holy Week when Jesus will be crucified, He receives a note about a friend of His who has grown sick. Lazarus, the brother of Mary and Martha from the town of Bethany, is dying. However, rather than coming right away, or even healing His friend from a distance, Jesus waits for two days. Jesus is about to perform one of His greatest works. After two days, Jesus tells His disciples that He is going to go to the town of Bethany because Lazarus "sleeps." Of course, the disciples misunderstand Jesus and take Him literally rather than figuratively, so Jesus clarifies that Lazarus is dead. Because Bethany is so close to Jerusalem, the disciples know that Jesus is putting His life in danger by going there. Here Thomas speaks up for the first time and motivates the disciples to go with Jesus and die with Him. This is the same Thomas who will later be known as "doubting Thomas." Yet here we see that he trusts Jesus enough to die with Him.

When Jesus arrives in town, Martha comes out to confront Jesus. They had sent Jesus notice about Lazarus before he died, and Jesus could have prevented his death. Nevertheless, even though Martha is upset, she has incredible faith. She knows that Jesus can have whatever He asks. Jesus tells her that Lazarus will rise again. Jesus knows that He is going to resurrect Lazarus, but Martha assumes He is speaking about the resurrection on Judgment Day. This leads to yet another one of Jesus' famous "I am" statements. Jesus is the Resurrection and the Life who offers eternal life. Not only is Jesus the Source of all life here on earth, but Jesus is the Source of eternal life. Unlike the crowds who refuse to put their faith fully in Jesus, when Jesus asks Martha if she believes Him, she acknowledges that He is the Christ. So Martha goes and tells Mary, and she too comes to Him.

When Mary arrives, she too wonders why Jesus had not come sooner. Thus, when Jesus sees the pain that Mary is in, He weeps. Even though Jesus knows what He is about to do, He cares about His friends and weeps with them. So Jesus has the people bring Him to the tomb, and there He calls out for Lazarus to leave the tomb. As one could imagine, the crowd that had gathered is absolutely amazed by this miracle. It is one thing to heal a sick person, but to give life to one who has been dead for four days is irrefutable evidence that Jesus is the Messiah. In fact, before Jesus raises Lazarus from the dead, He prays to the Father before the people so that they could see that this is a work of God.

As a result of this incredible miracle, many people believe in Jesus. When word of this miracle reaches the religious leaders in Jerusalem, they put together a council to decide what to do with Jesus. They have tried to keep Jesus quiet and under control for some time now, but there is no way they can stop Jesus now if word of this resurrection goes out. The religious leaders are afraid that the Romans will hear about this movement and take away their positions of power and even possibly take away Israel from the Jews. So Caiaphas the high priest suggests that Jesus be killed in order to save the people. This is ironic because that is exactly what would happen, but not in the way that he thinks. So the plan is made that when Jesus comes to the Passover Festival, He is to be arrested.

Thought Questions:

1. Many people have found great comfort in the words from John 10:28 when Jesus says, "neither shall anyone snatch them out of My hand." Why do you think this is? What does this verse say about the security of our salvation?

2. Even with the convincing force of the resurrection of Lazarus, many people still refuse to believe in Jesus. Why do you think this is? What implications does this have for when we share the gospel with others?

The Anointing and Triumphal Entry: John 12

Lesson 73

Following the incredible resurrection of Lazarus from the dead, sometime later he and his sisters, Mary and Martha, invite Jesus and His disciples over for dinner. While they are eating, Mary takes a very expensive jar of perfume and anoints Jesus with it and wipes His feet with her hair. This is not the first time that an event like this has happened; while Jesus was in the house of a Pharisee, another woman, labeled a "sinner," had previously anointed Jesus. Since we have already examined this anointing in previous lessons, we are not going to examine it in detail now. However, John does provide details that the other gospel writers do not. We learn here from John that Judas Iscariot is the disciple who speaks out against this anointing because he is in charge of the money and had been taking some money for himself all along. Judas not only betrays Jesus to the cross but also has been betraying Jesus all along.

The next day, following the anointing at Bethany, Jesus enters Jerusalem publicly in the event known as the Triumphal Entry or Palm Sunday. As with the anointing, we have already covered this event in previous lessons. As with the anointing, however, John provides information that the other gospel writers do not include. We learn from John that a large portion of the crowd that comes with Jesus and praises Him are the people who had gathered to see Lazarus after the resurrection. The reason so large a crowd follows Jesus is that they had already assembled in Bethany to see Lazarus.

After the Triumphal Entry, the other gospel writers mention the cleansing of the temple. Yet John has already mentioned this cleansing at the beginning of his gospel. Instead, as John has been doing all along, he focuses on the various responses of the Jews to Jesus and His response to the people. This section of Jesus' words is given as a response to the request of some Greeks to see Jesus. Philip and Andrew, two of Jesus' disciples, are excited about this meeting, as they may see it as the beginning of the Messianic Kingdom that they had expected. If the Greeks begin to follow Jesus, perhaps the worldwide kingdom will follow. However, Jesus makes it clear to the disciples that the only way He will receive glory is if He dies. He is not going to receive glory by the crowds and Greeks following Him; His glory will be from the Father after He finishes His works. When Jesus speaks of a grain of wheat falling on the ground and becoming more grain, He is metaphorically explaining that He must die in order for the kingdom to grow. In fact, Jesus uses this fact as a teaching tool to tell those who are listening that they too must be willing to die in order to gain eternal life. Jesus is setting an example for us to follow. We must be willing to lay down our lives for Christ and His kingdom. Moreover, rather than praying for God to take away His upcoming pain, Jesus simply asks that God's name would be glorified (verse 28). This is very similar to His words at Gethsemane when Jesus says, "not My will, but Yours, be done" (Luke 22:42).

As with the baptism and the Transfiguration, God audibly responds to Jesus' prayer, and the crowds hear Him speak. God confirms that He will honor Jesus' prayer to glorify Himself. Jesus now speaks, however cryptically, of His coming death and resurrection. Throughout the gospel of John, Jesus has been saying that His hour has not come. Yet here He says that "now" is the time when judgment will come upon the world and the ruler of this world, Satan, will be cast out. There is much debate as to what precisely Jesus means when He says that Satan will be cast out. Most scholars believe that Satan had been kicked out of heaven long before this day. Most likely, Jesus is speaking about Satan's defeat on the cross as he loses authority and power over the lost. Satan has been able to keep people slaves in darkness, but now that the light has come and Jesus reveals salvation, Satan's real power is gone.

Sadly, in verse 37, we learn that the crowds still refuse to believe in Jesus, even after all of His signs. However, here John gives the explanation as to why the crowds have rejected Jesus. Just as Jesus had previously said that the sheep that God had prepared beforehand would receive His message and follow Him, and those who are not His sheep would reject Him, here we learn that the people are unable to hear because God has hardened their hearts. This is a doctrinal view that many people have had a tough time understanding and accepting throughout the years, yet it is in Scripture. While we may not know why, we see from the gospel of John that God does harden some people so that no matter how much evidence may be laid before them for the gospel, they will not receive the message. God's ways are greater than our ways, and we will not understand much of what He does; however, we can pray that God would open the eyes of the lost so that they can see and respond to the gospel.

Even though many from the crowds reject Jesus, some powerful and prominent "rulers" of the people do believe in Jesus. Sadly, because of the threat of persecution by the religious leaders, these rulers refuse to publicly make known their support and belief in Jesus. John identifies that the reason these men refuse to publicly acknowledge Jesus is because they are more concerned about the praises of men than the praise from God. It is worthwhile to examine ourselves to see if we too are more concerned with how others think of us than how God thinks of us.

Jesus once again draws attention to the Father. From the beginning, Jesus' goal was not simply to have people come to Him and follow Him, but that through faith in Him people would be restored to the Father. As we have seen in John 3, Jesus' mission on earth is not to bring judgment or destruction, but to bring salvation. However, when people reject that salvation, the very words and actions that Jesus has performed are already judgment on the people. Jesus does not have to judge others; their actions judge them.

Thought questions:

1. Why do you think that God hardens some people's hearts as He does the crowds here?

2. What are some ways that Christians sometimes seek out the praise of man rather than the praise from God? Is there a time that you can remember when you have done this?

The Last Supper: John 13–14

Lesson 74

When it comes to the Last Supper, the synoptic gospels focus on the significance of the meal and how Jesus transforms the symbolism of the Passover meal. John's gospel is different and offers us more insight into some of the final teachings and words that Jesus offers His disciples.

Jesus has been trying to teach His disciples for over three years that greatness in His kingdom comes through service. In the world, greatness is determined how many servants people have, yet in Christ's kingdom greatness is determined by how well we serve others. As Jesus and His disciples prepare to eat the Passover feast, Jesus does something incredible; He begins to wash His disciples' feet. There are a number of things to point out from this event. *First*, we are told that Jesus does this "knowing that the Father had given all things into His hands, and that He had come from God and was going to God" (verse 3). Jesus knows that He is the greatest Person ever to live and that He deserves to worshiped and honored. Yet, as Philippians 2 says, He "did not consider it robbery to be equal with God, but made Himself of no reputation, taking the form of a bondservant" (verses 6 and 7). *Second*, this is a truly humble activity for Jesus to do. To wash someone's feet would be a fairly disgusting endeavor. People did not have shoes as we do now but most likely wore sandals. These feet would be quite dirty. *Third*, Jesus does this act of humility to teach us a lesson. He explicitly tells His disciples that they need to follow in His footsteps. If the God of this universe is willing to lower Himself and serve the humans that He has made, certainly there is not anything too low for us to do for one another.

As Peter does so often, he speaks before he thinks. The thought of the Messiah serving His disciples is unfathomable to Peter. It is they who ought to be serving Jesus. So when Jesus prepares to wash Peter's feet, Peter refuses. However, this is such an important lesson for Peter to learn that Jesus tells Peter that he can have no part with Him if he does not let Jesus wash His feet. Jesus knows that Peter is going to be the leader of the disciples and the Church when He leaves, and it is critical that Peter understands the importance of service.

Next, John draws his attention to the coming betrayal by Judas. According to John's gospel, Jesus plainly tells the disciples that one of them is going to betray Him. In fact, we learn uniquely from John's gospel that Jesus basically tells John that it is Judas Iscariot. John, who identifies Himself simply as the "disciple whom Jesus loved," asks Jesus privately who the betrayer will be. After Jesus tells John that it is the person with whom He will dip bread, He gives the next piece to Judas. We also learn from John's gospel that this betrayal is also a spiritual endeavor, as Satan enters Judas to lead him to betray Jesus. When Judas leaves, however, the disciples do not understand what he is doing but suppose that he is going to buy something for the feast or give a gift to the poor.

Jesus continues His final words to the disciples after Judas leaves. Knowing what is coming, Jesus no longer speaks of His glorification as a future event, as He has throughout John's gospel, but He says, "Now the Son of Man is glorified" (13:31). As Jesus has said to the crowds, Jesus tells His disciples that He is going away to a place that they cannot follow; and like the crowds, the disciples ask Him where He is going. Jesus is speaking about His upcoming death and ascension into heaven; so when Peter asks where He is going, He says that Peter cannot follow now, but some day he will follow Jesus (through death). Peter boldly says that he is even willing to die for Jesus, but Jesus predicts that Peter will deny Jesus three times before the rooster crows. At the end of chapter 13, Jesus gives a critical commandment to the disciples; with Jesus gone, the disciples are to love one another. For the work that they have to do, they have to stick together and love one another. This is a major theme in John's writing.

In chapter 14, Jesus continues this dialogue with the disciples. The disciples are troubled by the news that Jesus is going away, and they long to figure out where He is going. While Jesus does not tell them explicitly where He is going, He tells them that He is going to His Father's house (heaven) to prepare a place for them. Yet, without Jesus, the disciples still will not know what to do or where to go, so Thomas asks Jesus how they can know what way to go. This leads to yet another of Jesus' famous "I am" statements. Jesus says, "I am the way, the truth, and the life. No one comes to the Father except through Me" (verse 6). In other words, they do not need to know specifics about what to do or where to go; but if they remain in Jesus' teachings, they will get to where they need to go.

Even after three and a half years, the disciples still have so much to learn. Philip knows that when Jesus speaks of His Father, He is speaking of God; and Philip asks Jesus to show them the Father. He does not realize that this is precisely what Jesus has been doing all along. He is God in the flesh. Jesus tells the disciples that by knowing Him, they have already seen the Father. At this critical hour, before Jesus is betrayed and taken away from His disciples, He pleads with His disciples to believe in Him. He draws their attention to all of the works (miracles) that He had done and says to believe in Him through those works.

From here, Jesus focuses on what is to come next for the disciples. If the disciples exercise true faith and hold to their belief in Jesus, they too will be able to perform the same works and miracles that He had performed. They have already received a taste of this when Jesus sent them out to do ministry. Just as Jesus had cast out demons, so also did the disciples. Jesus tells them that, with Him gone, they are to pray to the Father through His name; and the Father will answer and provide for them on His behalf. When Jesus says that the Father will give them whatever they ask for if they ask in Jesus' name, this does not mean that we automatically get whatever we want as long as we end our prayers with "in Jesus' name." What Jesus is saying is that with Him gone, the Father will honor their prayers and provide for the disciples. Yet, more than simply answering prayers, God is going to give the disciples power through the Holy Spirit, called the Helper here.

Even though Jesus is leaving, He is not abandoning them. They will not be like orphans, but will have the presence of God Himself with them through the Holy Spirit. Jesus will be with them and in them, even though physically He will not be there anymore. However, now that Jesus is going away, the disciples are to focus on obeying the commandments and the teachings that they had received from Jesus. Jesus has prepared them for this time and has taught them all that they need to know. They need to focus on obedience. In fact, just in case they are afraid that they will forget what Jesus has taught them, when the Holy Spirit is given to them, He will remind them of Jesus' teachings. While it is sad that Jesus has to leave, Jesus offers them peace and suggests that it is better for everyone if He returns to the Father because the Father is greater than all. Satan will have his day, but he has no power over Jesus and he will be defeated.

Thought Question:

What are some examples of "washing someone's feet" in today's world? What are some ways you can better serve the people around you?

The Vine and the Branches: John 15

Lesson 75

After leaving the upper room with the disciples, Jesus continues to give His final words to His disciples. We are given yet another one of Jesus' famous "I am" statements in chapter 15. Jesus tells us here that He is the true Vine and the Father is the Vinedresser. This is the predominant metaphor that runs through chapter 15. The key idea with this metaphor is that the disciples are to abide, or remain, in the Vine (Christ) when He leaves. Even though Jesus has to die, rise from the dead, and go to the Father, the disciples need to continue to believe in and follow Jesus while He is gone.

There are a number of lessons that Jesus teaches from this metaphor. *First*, our focus as the branches needs to be to abide with Christ. Everything else that Jesus commands here requires that we receive the nourishment that comes from being connected with Jesus. Just as a branch receives its nourishment from the vine so that it can bear fruit, we need to stay connected with Jesus so that we can bear fruit. If a branch is cut off from a vine, it will wither and die. If we try living the Christian life without being connected to Jesus, we will spiritually wither and die. So what does it mean to "abide" in Christ? We must first hold to and obey His teachings. Yet this is not enough in itself. We must regularly spend time with Jesus. Even though Jesus is currently in heaven, seated at the right hand of God, the Holy Spirit is the presence of God here on earth. When we pray, or gather together with other believers, we are coming into the presence of Christ to find nourishment so that we can bear fruit. It is easy to tell if a Christian has been neglecting his relationship with Jesus; he will spiritually wither and bear no fruit.

Second, this leads to the next lesson from this metaphor. As branches, we have the responsibility to bear fruit. Throughout the Bible, God refers to His people as a vine that is supposed to bear fruit. Sadly, most of the times that this metaphor has been used, it is because the branches are not bearing any fruit. So what does it mean to bear fruit? There are a few definitions of fruit in the Bible. To bear fruit means to perform good deeds. To bear fruit means to share the gospel so that more people come to faith in Christ. To bear fruit means to develop those virtues mentioned in Galatians 5 as the fruit of the Spirit. We bear fruit when we continue to exhibit the behavior and values of the kingdom of God and when we do our part to share the message of that kingdom with others.

Third, there are consequences if we do not bear fruit. Jesus warns us that every branch that does not bear fruit "He takes away" (verse 2). This could be a reference to death and hell. However, another translation of "takes away" could be "lifts up." Because vines often grow close to the ground, sometimes the branches are on the ground and trampled by people. By lifting up these branches, the vinedresser protects the branches so that they can bear fruit. Yet, even if we are bearing some fruit, Jesus tells us that the Father is also going to prune us. People who work with plants know that it is important to cut off the dead parts of plants so that it is easier for the live parts to get their nutrients. Like plants,

those parts of us that are not honoring to God and are not producing fruit will be cut off so that we can bear even more fruit. Doctrinally, this is called the process of **sanctification**. We must ask ourselves, are there parts of our lives that interfere with the fruits that we can bear for the kingdom? If so, expect the Father to cut those parts out of our lives.

It is critical to Jesus that we abide in Him by keeping His commandments. He explicitly says in verse 10, "If you keep My commandments, you will abide in My love." Also, the most important of these commandments is the commandment to love one another. This love is not just superficial; this love is sacrificial, as it even involves giving up our lives for one another. When we live lives of obedience to Jesus, He is not ashamed to call us friends. Even though Jesus is called "a Friend of sinners" throughout His ministry, Jesus tells us here that His friendship is conditional upon obedience. If a person refuses to obey Jesus, he or she is not considered His friend.

The doctrine of **predestination** shows up again in verse 16. Jesus makes it clear that they did not choose Jesus, but Jesus chose the disciples. However, Jesus did not just choose them so that they could enjoy eternal life; He has a job for them to do. They must bear fruit.

Jesus moves on and begins to speak of the persecutions that will inevitably come to the disciples as they abide in Jesus. If the world has such hostility and hatred toward Jesus, who is perfect, and who made the world, how much more will the people hate the disciples. If the disciples act like the world, the world will not hate them. Yet they have been called to act differently from the world. We should expect the same kind of results that Jesus received from His ministry. Those whom the Father has prepared beforehand will respond positively to us and to the gospel message. However, those who have not been chosen beforehand by God will respond negatively to us and to the gospel.

Now that Jesus has come and provided light to the world, there is no longer any excuse for people to walk in the darkness. Jesus says in verse 22, "If I had not come and spoken to them, they would have no sin, but now they have no excuse for their sin." In other words, they could have claimed ignorance before. Jesus, however, has made the choice abundantly clear for the world: continue in sin and reject Jesus, or repent and walk in the light. Those who cling to the darkness will hate us and Jesus. Those who love the light will receive our message and come to Jesus.

sanctification: "to make holy" or "to set apart"; to be holy as God is holy; a progressive work done by the Holy Spirit over the course of a believer's entire life

predestination: the doctrine that states that God is the One who chooses beforehand who will be saved; the focus of this doctrine is not on human choice, but on God's divine choice before the creation of the world.

Thought Questions:

1. What are some ways that you abide with Jesus? Do you feel that you regularly do a good job with this? What are some practical steps you can take to abide in Christ more?

2. What are some fruits that you bear right now for the kingdom of God?

Final Warnings: John 16

Lesson 76

As the time draws closer to the moment when Jesus will be separated from His disciples, He speaks more and more clearly to them. Bad things are about to take place, and Jesus knows that the faith of His disciples is about to be severely tested. So Jesus does everything in His power to prepare them for what is about to happen.

Jesus explains precisely what He means when He says that the world will hate the disciples. Not only will the people dislike the disciples because of their belief in Jesus, the disciples will be kicked out of the synagogues and shunned by their fellow Jews. Even worse, people will seek to take away their lives and will believe that they are serving God by doing so. This is seen most clearly through Saul. In the book of Acts, we will be introduced to a man named Saul who becomes one of the greatest persecutors of the Church. Saul persecutes Christians with so much passion because he believes he is serving and obeying God by doing so (Acts 22:3–5).

Jesus can see that all of these warnings are bothering the disciples. The disciples are filled with sorrow as they think about Jesus leaving and the persecutions that will follow. So Jesus clarifies that it is actually a really good thing that He go away. If Jesus remains with the disciples, the Holy Spirit will not come. However, when Jesus leaves and accomplishes the Father's plan, the disciples will have the Holy Spirit with them. The Holy Spirit will also accomplish what is necessary for the mission of the disciples to succeed. The Holy Spirit will bring conviction to the world so that the people

respond to the message of the gospel. Without the conviction of the Holy Spirit, the disciples will experience the same kind of overwhelming rejection that Jesus had experienced from the crowds. Moreover, even beyond convicting the world, the Holy Spirit will teach the disciples many of the things that Jesus cannot teach them yet. There is still much to learn, and the Holy Spirit will be the key to understanding these things.

Jesus then speaks cryptically again. He tells the disciples that He will only be with them a little while longer, and then they will not be able to see Him anymore. Yet a little while after that they will see Him again. We know, looking back, that Jesus is speaking about His coming death and resurrection. He will be gone for a short time (three days), but the disciples will see Him again. Of course, the disciples do not know about the resurrection (even though Jesus has told them about it), so the disciples are confused. Yet Jesus knows their hearts and minds and decides to speak plainly to them.

When Jesus leaves, the disciples will be filled with sorrow. Even worse, as they are weeping, the world will be rejoicing. They will have to watch as others find joy in the very thing that will cause them sorrow, the death of Jesus. Yet, just as a woman quickly forgets the pains of childbirth after the child has come, the sorrow of the disciples will go away when Jesus returns. Jesus tells them plainly that He is going to have to leave in order to return to the Father. With Him gone, the disciples should pray in His name. Just as they had seen the incredible power and effectiveness of Jesus' prayer life, they too will see the same results as they pray in His name. Once again, this does not mean that we simply need to add the words "in Jesus' name" to the end of our prayers; it means that we need to pray, knowing that Jesus is our Advocate who speaks to the Father on our behalf. Not only that, Jesus gives us direct access to the Father so that we can ask Him whatever we need.

Now that Jesus has spoken plainly and clearly to the disciples, they confess their faith in Him and that He has indeed come from God. No doubt the disciples are proud of this statement of faith. However, Jesus immediately tells them that their faith will be shortly tested and they will fail. They will be scattered and abandon Jesus in His time of need. Yet, even when everyone else abandons Him, Jesus finds comfort in the presence of the Father. Things are about to look really bad for the disciples, but Jesus encourages the disciples by telling them that He has overcome the world. The world will have its moment of "triumph" very soon, but Jesus is the true Conqueror.

Thought Question:

In what ways have you seen the Holy Spirit work in your life? From this passage, what are some things that we can expect the Holy Spirit to do?

Jesus' High Priestly Prayer: John 17

Lesson 77

When a person knows that he is going to die soon, his parting words usually reveal what is most important to him. Jesus knows that He is about to be betrayed and that these are some of the very last words He'll be able to say in the presence of His disciples. Perhaps even more significant, Jesus knows that He is about to go through the greatest trial of His life, and so He offers one of His final prayers in John 17. This prayer is often referred to as Jesus' high priestly prayer. The job of the high priest is to stand as a mediator between God and men and to make prayers on their behalf. This is precisely what Jesus does here in John 17.

The prayer in John 17 can be broken down into three sections: Jesus' prayer for Himself, Jesus' prayer for His disciples, and Jesus' prayer for us. Knowing that He is about to complete the work that God had sent Him to do, Jesus looks back on His ministry in this prayer. Jesus' first request from the Father is that the Father would glorify Him so that He could in turn glorify the Father. Jesus has been purposeful not to seek out the praise and glory that comes from man; rather, He depends on the Father to manifest His glory. Perhaps the greatest temptation that Jesus faces during His temptation in the wilderness is to have glory without the cross.

Even though this prayer is directed to God, we can learn from the prayer. Many of the themes in this prayer have been mentioned before in this gospel. First, the significance of God's sovereign choice in salvation is highlighted in verse 2 as Jesus gives eternal life to "as many as You have given Him." In other words, Jesus understands from the beginning that God has sovereignly directed the lives of those to whom Jesus has ministered, and only those whom God has given to Jesus would respond to the message. In this prayer, Jesus clarifies precisely what it is that brings eternal life: "that they may know You, the only true God, and Jesus Christ whom You have sent" (verse 3). Salvation and eternal life are based upon a relationship with God Himself. And so, now that Jesus is about to complete His mission, He prays that God would receive Him back into the glory that He had before He came to earth.

Jesus next prays for His disciples. Continuing the theme of God's sovereignty, Jesus recognizes that His disciples are not truly His but are first the Father's. God has given these friends and disciples to Jesus, and Jesus has been a faithful Steward of those whom God has entrusted to Him. Jesus has taught His disciples all that God had ordained for Jesus to teach, and the disciples have accepted His teaching and have believed in Him. Jesus has also protected the disciples, and now that He is going away, His prayer for the disciples is that God would keep (protect) them while He is gone. Jesus knows that the disciples will face many enemies while they are on the earth. If the world hated Jesus, it will certainly hate the disciples. Also, Satan himself will be against the disciples. Jesus does not ask for God to take the disciples away from danger, but that God will protect them in the midst of danger. Not only does Jesus ask God to protect them from physical danger, but also from corruption. Jesus asks that God would "Sanctify them by Your truth" (verse 17). Sanctification is the process of being made holy, and this involves the fight against sin.

In verse 20, Jesus begins to pray for us as believers. He prays, "for those who will believe in Me through their word." This speaks of all believers who have come to faith in Christ through the word of the disciples. Jesus' prayer for us is both telling and tragic. He prays that we would be unified as Christians so that through that unity the world will come to faith in Christ. Sadly, unity is very often lacking among Christians. Not only are there thousands of different denominations that fight and argue against one another, but even within our own small communities we fight and gossip and argue. Unity is something that requires hard work and sacrifice. Yet this is precisely what Jesus desires most from us. We need to sacrifice our own agendas and seek to place Christ and His kingdom first.

Finally, Jesus prays for us that we would be able to be with Him in heaven. Jesus wants us to see and behold His glory. Throughout Scripture, God has been revealing His glory, and now Jesus longs for the day when we can see Him in all of His glory. Someday we will be with Jesus, and we will have the honor of seeing Him as He is.

Thought Questions:

1. Have you ever experienced unity within community before? What kinds of things happened in that community that helped develop unity?

2. What are some practical things that you can do to help develop unity within the communities with which you are involved?

The Trial and Crucifixion of Jesus: John 18–19

Lesson 78

From the synoptic gospels we have already seen the basic events that take place between Jesus' arrest and crucifixion. While all four gospels follow the same basic timeline for these events, each one offers some unique details. John's gospel is no exception to this rule.

We learn from John's gospel that the soldiers who arrest Jesus fall back onto the ground when Jesus says, "I am He" (18:6). While "I am He" is a good translation, this could simply be translated as "I am." Jesus is granting us yet another hint of His deity, and the response of the soldiers adds power to this. We also learn from John's gospel that the name of the servant of the high priest whose ear Peter cuts off is Malchus. We also learn that John (called "another disciple") is the one who gets Peter into the courtyard of the high priest because John knows the high priest.

When Annas begins to question Jesus about who He is and about His disciples, rather than testifying about Himself, He says to "ask those who have heard Me what I said to them" (18:21). In other words, Jesus directs Annas to the testimony that others have about Him. Because Jesus does not answer directly, one of the officers nearby strikes Jesus. Yet Jesus has done nothing wrong and asks them what He has said that is wrong. They have no answer, so they send him to Caiaphas, the acting high priest at the time. John does not include any details about the trial before Caiaphas, but instead spends more time on the interactions with Pontius Pilate.

Pilate does not want to have to deal with this problem, so he asks the religious leaders what their accusation against Jesus is. We know from the synoptics that their accusation is that Jesus claims to be a king against Caesar. However, in John's gospel they simply tell him that Jesus is an evildoer and that they would not have brought Him to Pilate if He were a good man. Pilate tells them to judge Jesus; but because they cannot put someone to death, they insist that Pilate take this case.

The dialogue between Jesus and Pilate is very interesting. Pilate asks Jesus plainly, "Are You the King of the Jews?" (verse 33). Once again, Jesus does not directly answer the question but poses another question back at Pilate. Jesus makes this personal by asking Pilate if he thinks that Jesus is the King of the Jews or if he is just asking what others have intended. Pilate refuses to directly answer Jesus and says that this is not his problem, but rather a Jewish problem. He asks Jesus what He has done to merit this kind of response from the Jews. Jesus clarifies that His kingdom is not an earthly kingdom. Jesus is, in fact, a King, but not an earthly king. As Jesus has been doing all throughout the gospel of John, He speaks about Himself as the ultimate source of truth. Pilate, most likely influenced by Greek philosophy, questions the very nature of truth. Jesus is masterful at getting to the heart of the matter. Pilate realizes that Jesus does not deserve death, so he goes to the Jews and tells them that he finds no fault in Jesus. In an attempt to subvert this whole problem, Pilate has the people choose whom to set free, Jesus or a robber named Barabbas. The religious leaders, however, would rather have a robber set free than Jesus and get the crowd to choose Barabbas instead.

In chapter 19, presumably in order to appease the crowds, Pilate has Jesus scourged. Afterwards, the soldiers mock Him and give him a mock crown made of thorns and give Him a purple robe and strike Him. Then Pilate brings out Jesus wearing the robe and the crown of thorns, hoping that the people would accept this punishment and let Him go. Yet when the crowds see Jesus, they shout, "Crucify Him!" Pilate tries once again to set Jesus free, so he goes to speak to Jesus. When Pilate tells Jesus that he has the power to set Jesus free and the power to crucify Him, Jesus tells Pilate that the only reason he has that power is because God has allowed it. Even though Pilate is going to have Jesus killed, Jesus says that the ones who handed Him over are guilty of a much greater sin. Finally, when the religious leaders accuse Jesus of setting Himself up as King against Caesar, they back Pilate into a corner. If Pilate lets Jesus live, they claim, then Pilate is siding with a traitor to Rome. In a truly tragic scene, the chief priests claim that they have no king but Caesar. The entire hope for the Jewish nation was that someday the Messiah King would come and save them, but those who should cling to this hope the most, the religious leaders, completely abandon their hope because of their desire to see Jesus die. While they so desperately cling to the Scriptures, they abandon the very hope about which the Scriptures speak because of their hatred of Jesus.

So Pilate issues the judgment on Jesus and has Him led away and crucified. John emphasizes the fulfillment of Scripture that takes place during the crucifixion. From the dividing of Jesus' clothes to the sponge filled with wine to the unbroken bones of Jesus to the piercing of His side, this whole event is prophesied in the Old Testament. John also includes an interaction between Jesus and John that none of the other gospels include.

On the cross, Jesus still honors His mother Mary and provides for her by telling John to take care of her. The last words of Jesus recorded by John are, "It is finished!" (19:30). Jesus does not merely die; He gives up His spirit. Throughout John's gospel, Jesus has been saying that nobody has the power to take His life, but He has the ability to willingly lay it down. When Jesus dies, it is precisely because He allows it to happen.

When Jesus dies, Joseph of Arimathea requests His body and places it in a new tomb that he owned. Because the Sabbath was upon the people, Joseph of Arimathea hastens to get His body in a tomb before nightfall. Nicodemus, the Pharisee whom we encountered in chapter 3, provides the spices for Jesus' burial.

Throughout the entire book of John, the Jews have been on trial for their rejection of Jesus. Even though Jesus is officially on trial in these chapters, the ones who really are on trial are the people. Sadly, they show themselves to be quite guilty. Not only does Jesus' trial break the laws of what is an appropriate trial under the Law, but the Jewish people commit the very blasphemy of which they accuse Jesus when they claim that their only king is Caesar. Yet all of this is part of God's sovereign plan to bring salvation to the world. Earlier in John, we found that God does harden the hearts of people. Perhaps God has hardened the hearts of the people on this day so that He can show the depths of His love and save us from our sins.

The Resurrection: John 20

Lesson 79

As with the rest of his gospel, John provides us with unique material about the resurrection. From the other gospels we learn that Mary Magdalene and some other women arrive at the tomb as the sun is rising on Sunday. John reports that Mary Magdalene goes to the tomb while it is still dark, meaning that she left early in the morning. After Mary goes back and informs the disciples about the empty tomb, John adds that another disciple goes with Peter to investigate the tomb. Not only does this other disciple go with Peter, this other disciple actually outruns Peter and arrives first. This other disciple is John himself.

When they arrive, they find the tomb empty and John adds that the face cloth was in a separate place, folded, from the rest of the grave clothes. This provides additional proof that robbers had not come and taken the body of Jesus. If some people wanted to steal the body of Jesus, with Roman guards around they would not have folded the face cloth. When John (the other disciple) sees the empty tomb, he believes that Jesus is indeed resurrected and is the Messiah. For John, this is what initiates his true faith. Throughout John's gospel, Jesus has been seeking true believers, and it seems to take different things to bring about true belief for different people.

John also includes the encounter between Jesus and Mary after the disciples had returned home. As Mary remains at the tomb, weeping, she is met by two angels. She tells the angels that she is weeping because she does not know where Jesus is. Yet when she turns around she sees Jesus, though she assumes He is the gardener at first. It is when Jesus says her name that she recognizes that it is the resurrected Jesus. Mary probably grabs hold of Jesus because He tells her not to cling to Him. Jesus is not going to be around for very long. He is going to ascend to the Father, as He has been saying all along. Mary becomes the first eyewitness to the resurrection and goes back to the disciples and tells them what Jesus has said to her.

That same day, the disciples are gathered together in the upper room with the door locked because they are afraid that they will be arrested next. Jesus then appears to them in the midst of the locked room and greets them by saying, "Peace be with you" (verse 19). Jesus, now glorified in His resurrected body, could be terrifying, but He comes offering peace. In order to prove that He is in fact Jesus, He shows them the holes in His hands and His side. There is one theory of the resurrection that states that Simon of Cyrene died on the cross in Jesus' place. The holes in His hands and side provide proof against this argument. After revealing Himself to the disciples, Jesus immediately reminds the disciples of the mission. Just as the Father had sent Jesus into the world to accomplish His mission, so also Jesus now sends out His disciples for their mission. As part of that mission, Jesus equips them and gives them authority. He tells them to receive the Holy Spirit, who will give them the power to fulfill their mission. He also gives them the authority to forgive sins. There is some debate as to what precisely this means. The Roman Catholic Church believes that the church has the power to condemn a person or to offer forgiveness. Others believe that Jesus is giving power to the process of church discipline. At the very least, Jesus has been offering people forgiveness throughout His ministry; and the disciples, who are continuing Jesus' ministry, are given authority to continue Jesus' works.

When Jesus meets with the disciples the first time, Thomas is not with them. So when the disciples tell

Thomas about the resurrection appearance, Thomas refuses to believe. While we are not told specifically why Thomas has a hard time believing in the resurrection, perhaps it is because it sounds too good to be true. Thomas says that he will not believe unless he is able to put his finger into the mark of the nails and his hand into Jesus' side. For Thomas, this is what it will take to develop true belief. So, eight days later, Jesus appears to the disciples with Thomas there. After speaking peace to them once again, Jesus immediately tells Thomas to put his finger in his hands and his hand in Jesus' side. Now Thomas gets a bad reputation for his doubt here, yet his confession is one of the most profound in the gospel of John. He confesses not only that Jesus is his Lord, but also he goes much further and confesses that Jesus is God (verse 28). People have been struggling throughout Jesus' ministry to even see Him as a good Man, let alone the Christ; but Thomas sees that He is God. Still, Jesus uses this as an opportunity to teach us about true faith. Both John and Thomas have to see with their own eyes in order to believe in Jesus, but Jesus calls people blessed if they believe without seeing. This is a word to us; we have not seen Jesus, yet we choose to believe in Him. There is a special blessing for us when we choose to believe in Jesus by faith rather than by sight.

John finishes chapter 20 by telling us the purpose of this book. He acknowledges that there are far more stories to share about Jesus. Yet John shares these stories with us so that we "may believe that Jesus is the Christ, the Son of God, and that believing [we] may have life in His name" (verse 31). This gospel is evangelistic. John is not merely recording history. John desires that, through the story of Jesus, those who hear or read would be convicted and choose to believe in Jesus. There is a reason why many Christians throughout the centuries have directed people to read this gospel first when people seek to read Scripture. Naturally we must ask, what will it take for me to believe?

Thought Questions:

1. Think about the time that you started to believe in Jesus. What was it that led you to finally believe? If you do not believe in Jesus, what do you think it would take to believe in Him?

2. In the culture of Jesus' time, the testimony of a woman was deemed less authoritative than the testimony of a man. In light of this, why do you think Jesus first appears to Mary Magdalene?

Peter's Redemption: John 21
Lesson 80

Just about everybody loves a good redemption story. Somebody makes a mistake and hurts the team but in the end gets the final point to win the game. Or someone misses a golden opportunity that he or she has been waiting for his or her whole life, but another unexpected opportunity arises and he or she capitalizes on it. Perhaps the reason why so many of us love redemption stories is that we can all think of a time when we have made a mistake and have never been given the opportunity to make things right. The main story in chapter 21 is all about Peter's redemption.

For the disciples, the appearance of the resurrected Jesus brings great joy. Yet for Peter, the resurrected Jesus also reminds him of his own betrayal of Jesus. Peter has always been prone to speak first and think later, and he makes promises that he cannot keep. In Jesus' greatest moment of need, out of fear Peter denies Jesus three times. What is worse is that Jesus had predicted precisely that Peter would do this. How could Peter look Jesus in the eye after he had denied Jesus three times, especially after Jesus has told His disciples that He would deny anyone who denies Him before men (Matthew 10:33, Luke 12:9)?

So one morning Jesus appears to the disciples again. This time Peter and a few of the other disciples decide to go fishing (remember that this is what Peter does for a living). Similarly to when Peter first commits to following Jesus, they fish all night and catch nothing. Yet the next morning a stranger calls out to them from the land and tells them to cast out their nets again. This time, when they do, they have an incredible catch of fish. This is almost exactly what happens when Jesus first calls Peter to follow Him (Luke 5). Everyone immediately recognizes that this stranger is Jesus Himself. Peter immediately jumps in the water and swims to Jesus, whereas the other disciples bring the boats to shore. When they find Jesus, He is cooking up some fish; and He offers them some fish and bread, just like when He fed the 5,000 and the 4,000.

Jesus then talks to Peter individually. One could only imagine how Peter feels going into this conversation. He is probably prepared for a rebuke and the consequences from His betrayal. Yet Jesus asks Peter a question: "Simon, son of Jonah, do you love Me more than these?" (verse 15). Jesus asks Peter to confess his love for Jesus. Peter acknowledges that of course he loves Jesus. So Jesus commissions him and tells him to feed His lambs. In other words, Jesus tells Peter that he needs to provide for the rest of God's flock. Jesus repeats this two more times, asking Peter if he loves Jesus and then commissioning him to take care of God's flock. The third time Peter breaks down and is grieved. It is worth noting that the Greek word used for "love" is different the third time. The first word (*agapao*) is often associated with divine love, whereas the word that Jesus uses for love the third time refers to brotherly love (*phileo*). While there may be some significance to this word change, the more significant issue is that Jesus has just brought redemption to Peter. Just as Peter had denied Jesus three times during His trial, now Peter has been given the opportunity to confess his love for Jesus three times, and he gladly does it. However, Jesus does not just restore the relationship with Peter; He restores Peter's mission. While we may never know what would have happened if Jesus had not provided this redemption, perhaps Peter would not have had the confidence to become the leader of the Church that Jesus had predicted. Every time that Peter confesses his love, Jesus tells him to be the leader that Jesus had prepared him to be. Jesus completes this redemption by renewing the call that He had given to Peter from the beginning, "Follow me" (verse 19).

Before calling Peter to follow Him, Jesus offers a cryptic prophecy about Peter. He tells Peter that he is going to die someday by stretching out his hands and being led to a place that he does not want to go. John, who writes this after Peter's death, tells us that this is about Peter's death. This description is consistent with church tradition, which states that Peter dies by being crucified upside down. Also consistent with church tradition is what Jesus says about John. Jesus says, "If I will that he remain till I come, what is that to you?" (verse 22). John clarifies that Jesus is not actually saying that John will remain alive until the second coming; rather, He is saying that Peter does not need to know what He has in store for John. Nevertheless, it is worth noting that John lives the longest of all of the disciples and is an old man before he dies.

As we have seen throughout the gospel of John, Jesus has been constantly on trial by the Jews, whether literally before His crucifixion, or practically through the constant resistance by the Jews. Central to the trial of Jesus is the importance of testimony. The Jews rejected Jesus because He testified about Himself. Jesus says that the Father and His works also testify about Him. Yet at the end of his gospel, John adds his voice to the list of witnesses about Jesus. At the end of this book, John acknowledges that he was there to see all of these things and this book is his testimony on Jesus' behalf. John acknowledges that Jesus has done significantly more things than what John has testified about in this book; but if people were to try to record them all, there would not be enough books in the world.

As we come to the end of the gospels, hopefully we are more equipped to answer one of the most important questions in the universe, "Who is Jesus?" While Jesus is an incredibly wise and brilliant Teacher, He is so much more. Jesus is God Himself, come to earth to sacrifice Himself in order to save us. Jesus is the fullest Revelation of God; and He is the perfect Mediator, who came to redeem us and restore our relationship with the Father by destroying sin on the cross. However, it is not enough if we simply learn about Jesus. John demands that we respond to Jesus by placing our faith and trust in Him. Are we going to be like the religious leaders in Jesus' day who are blinded to the obvious truth, or are we going to respond with Thomas, "My Lord and my God!"

Thought Questions:

1. Looking back on all of the gospels, what are some things about Jesus that you have learned that you never noticed before?

2. What is your favorite story from the gospels? Why do you like this story so much?

3. If Jesus is to be an example to us, what is something from the life of Christ that you can apply to your life today?

UNIT 3: *Acts, Romans, and 1 & 2 Corinthians*

Introduction to Acts

Lesson 81

We have spent our time so far focusing on the life and ministry of Jesus. We have examined His birth, His ministry, His miracles, His interactions with others, His death, and finally His resurrection. Jesus accomplished the most incredible act in history by conquering death and providing salvation to humanity. Yet the story does not end with the resurrection. In fact, in many ways the death and resurrection of Jesus is simply the beginning of the story. Jesus has spent years training and equipping His disciples to build the Church, and there is still much work to do. The book of Acts, also known as "The Acts of the Apostles," describes the growth of the Church from just the disciples to a widespread movement that fills the Roman Empire.

The book of Acts is actually part of a two book series. In the prologue to the book of Acts, the author says that this is the second book that he has written to Theophilus. We know that the first book written to Theophilus in the Bible is the third gospel. In the introduction to Luke, we discussed the evidence that Luke is in fact the author. This book certainly carries on many of the themes that are present in the third gospel. We will go into more detail on these themes later. It is safe to assume that the care that Luke applies to the investigation for the third gospel also is applied to this historical book.

Because of the abrupt ending to the book of Acts, most scholars believe that this book was written in the early to mid-60s A.D. At the end of the book of Acts, Paul is awaiting trial in Rome. The best explanation for why this book ends on this note is that Luke had shared the events up until the time of the writing. In other words, when Acts was written, Paul was still awaiting trial in Rome.

Like the gospels, the book of Acts is a history book. Unlike the gospels, this book is written in chronological order rather than thematic order. There are four main characters in this book, though two are more obvious than the other two. The two most obvious people on which Acts focuses are Peter and Paul. Peter is the central figure in the evangelization of the Jews and the growth of the church in Jerusalem. Paul is the central figure in the evangelization of the Gentiles, and he plays a critical role in the spread of Christianity outside Israel. Yet even more significant than these two people

are the other two characters—the Holy Spirit and the Word of God. Before Jesus died and rose from the dead, He had told the disciples that they were going to receive the Holy Spirit, who will empower them to complete their mission. Throughout the book of Acts, the Holy Spirit is abundantly active in the events that take place. However, the Word of God is also mentioned on multiple occasions in this book as it spreads to different areas (Acts 6:7, 12:24, 13:49, 19:20).

There are many themes that run throughout this book. *First,* one of those themes is that the Church is the ongoing body of Christ. There are multiple situations in the book of Acts in which the Church does the very same things that Jesus did during His life on earth. For example, the final words of the first martyr, Stephen, are very similar to the final words of Jesus on the cross (Acts 7:59, 60; Luke 23:34, 46). Just as Jesus raised a girl from the dead by saying, *Talitha, cumi* (Mark 5:41), Peter raises a girl from the dead named Tabitha, possibly by saying, *Tabitha, cumi* (Acts 9:40). *Second,* another theme is the importance of the resurrection. There are many sermons recorded in this book, and all of them emphasize the significance of the resurrection. In fact, when deciding on a person to replace Judas as the twelfth apostle, one of the criteria is that the person must have been a witness of the resurrection (Acts 1:22). A *third* theme is the role of the Holy Spirit in the life of the Church. The Church does incredible things throughout this book, but it is the Holy Spirit who enables them to accomplish these things. *Fourth,* another theme is the continued rejection of the gospel by the Jews and the inclusion of the Gentiles into the Church. Just as the Jews rejected Jesus by and large, they also reject the message of the apostles. Yet, when the Jews reject the gospel, the gospel is brought to the Gentiles, who receive it joyfully.

When reading the book of Acts, one of the questions that we should ask is, "Why do we not see the same things happen very often today?" The same Spirit who enables the early Christians to do incredible things is also in us. The Church today has the same power and potential to be just as effective as the early Church. Perhaps the only reason we do not seem to have this power is because we do not ask.

The Ascension and the Replacement of Judas: Acts 1

Lesson 82

In the introduction to Acts, we learned that the book of Acts is the second part in a two-part series that begins with the gospel of Luke. Also, this book picks up right where the gospel of Luke finishes. As with the third gospel, this book is written to Theophilus. Because this name means "lover of God," it may have been a specific person or a generic name given to all Christians. In the prologue to this book (verses 1–5), Luke summarizes his gospel. Previously, he had written about the life of Jesus and the resurrection appearances. We learn in this prologue that Jesus made a number of appearances to various people over the course of forty days. We also learn that Jesus commanded the disciples to remain in Jerusalem until the day when they are baptized with the Holy Spirit.

During Jesus' ministry, the disciples consistently had one big misconception about the mission of Jesus. The Christ, they believed, was supposed to conquer Israel's enemies and establish a kingdom that will be the greatest on the earth. In the disciples' minds, the Christ is supposed to be a great warrior, not the Suffering Servant that Jesus was. Now that Jesus has accomplished His work of dying for the world and now that He has been glorified with a new body, surely it must now be time for Jesus to bring the kingdom to Israel! So the disciples ask Jesus plainly if the kingdom is about to come. Jesus tells the disciples that they should not worry about the kingdom and they will not know the time, but rather they should wait for the coming Holy Spirit so that they can fulfill the mission that Jesus has for them.

Once the disciples receive the Holy Spirit, they will be witnesses to Jesus "in Jerusalem, and in all Judea and Samaria, and to the end of the earth" (verse 8). And this is precisely what will happen. The Church will begin in Jerusalem (Acts 2–7), move to the surrounding regions of Judea and Samaria (Acts 8), and then spread throughout the world (Acts 9–28).

What happens next often does not get a lot of attention or celebration in churches today. Churches love to celebrate Jesus' birth during Christmas and His death and resurrection during Good Friday and Easter Sunday, but the ascension of Jesus is also incredibly significant. Right after Jesus commissions His disciples and gives them His parting orders, He is brought up to heaven in the clouds. This is the fulfillment of the prophecy in Daniel 7 about the Son of Man. In this prophecy, "One

like the Son of Man" (Daniel 7:13) comes before God ("the Ancient of Days") with the clouds of heaven and receives a kingdom. When Jesus ascends into heaven, He is ascending to the right hand of God, where He will reign over the earth until the time when He returns. The disciples had just inquired about the kingdom, and little do they know that Jesus is about to receive that kingdom; His throne will be in heaven, not earth. As the disciples are observing this, two angels appear and tell them that someday Jesus will return on the clouds of heaven, just as He has left. So the disciples return to the upper room, where they had been staying.

As the disciples wait for the promised Holy Spirit to come, there is one major issue that needs to be resolved. Jesus had chosen twelve disciples for a reason, and now there are only eleven. In the Old Testament, there were twelve tribes of Israel, and when Jesus chooses twelve disciples, He is creating a new symbolic Israel. Yet that symbolism is in danger of being lost because of Judas Iscariot, who had betrayed Jesus. The betrayal by Judas poses a problem for the disciples. Do they replace Judas or continue on with just the eleven? Sadly, there is no room for reconciliation for Judas because after he betrays Jesus he hangs himself and dies. Does this mean that Jesus has somehow failed by losing one of His disciples? Peter puts an end to that argument by pointing out that this betrayal had been prophesied beforehand in the Old Testament. In verse 20, Peter quotes two verses that speak about betrayal from the Psalms, one speaking about the death of the betrayer (Psalm 69:25) and the other speaking about the need for a replacement (Psalm 109:8).

So the disciples decide to find someone to replace Judas Iscariot as the twelfth apostle. There is some wisdom to be learned from the process that the disciples follow. The first thing that they figure out is what criteria must be met for a person to be considered an apostle. Since the primary job of the apostles is to serve as a witness to Jesus and His resurrection, the main criterion for Judas' replacement is that it must be someone who had been a disciple of Jesus from the time of John's baptism and who was an eyewitness of the resurrection. Out of the 120 disciples of Jesus who had gathered together in the upper room, only two people fit this criterion: Joseph called Barsabas and Matthias. So how are they to choose between these two equally qualified men? They pray and cast lots, and the lot falls upon Matthias; he is chosen as the twelfth apostle. In making decisions, we need to be wise and seek out God's direction. Since both of these men fit the criterion, the disciples leave the decision up to God. They use a lot, a device of chance similar to dice today. They trust that God will direct the lot to the person whom He wants (cf. Numbers 27:21).

There is an opinion that should be mentioned at this point. This will be the last time we hear anything about Matthias. After replacing Judas, he does not appear in the story anymore. Some people believe that this is a mistake because God had already ordained for Paul to be the twelfth apostle. Paul certainly plays a much more significant role in the development of the Church than Matthias does. There is nothing in the text itself, however, that suggests that what the disciples are doing is wrong.

Thought Questions:

1. Do you think that the disciples are right to choose Matthias as Judas' replacement?

2. The disciples still are seeking an earthly kingdom in Israel, yet Jesus' kingdom is in heaven. Do you think that there will be an earthly kingdom someday? Why or why not?

Pentecost: Acts 2

Lesson 83

During the last days of Jesus' life on earth, and even in His final moments before His ascension, Jesus prepared His disciples for the coming of the Holy Spirit. Even though the disciples will be grieved at Jesus' absence, Jesus tells them that they will be better off having the Holy Spirit inside them, instead. Throughout the Old Testament, the Holy Spirit had been given to select individuals (prophets, priests, kings, etc.) but had never been given to the common person. Through the power of the Holy Spirit, people were given great wisdom, incredible strength, and miracle-working powers. Now that power is about to be given to the whole Church.

The events in Acts 2 take place during one of the three great festivals in the Jewish calendar. This is incredibly significant for what is about to come. During these festivals, Jews from all over the Roman Empire would gather together to Jerusalem to celebrate the festivals in the temple. Many of these people came from very diverse cultures and native languages. This is an ideal time for such a public event that is about to come. Also significant is what this festival is designed to celebrate. The feast of Pentecost is also called the Feast of Weeks in the Old Testament and was instituted by God to celebrate the harvest. This particular Pentecost is going to celebrate an entirely different kind of harvest.

At the beginning of Acts 2, the disciples are all gathered together "with one accord" (verse 1). They all are united in purpose as they pray and await the promised Holy Spirit. Suddenly, they hear the sound of a mighty rushing wind and see what looks like divided tongues of fire coming down from heaven upon the disciples. This harkens back to the baptism of Jesus when the Holy Spirit descends upon Him like a dove (Luke 3:22). For Jesus, the dove represented peace and that His ministry would be a ministry of peace. However, even John the Baptist himself said that Jesus would baptize with fire (Luke 3:16). Now, when the disciples receive the Holy Spirit, the Spirit comes in the form of fire. Whereas Jesus' reception of the Holy Spirit marked peace, the disciples' reception of the Holy Spirit marks power, as fire represents power here.

The first sign of the Holy Spirit in the disciples is that they begin to speak in tongues. The other tongues that they speak are actual languages. People from all over the Roman Empire who are gathered in Jerusalem hear the disciples speaking in their own native languages, and the crowds are amazed. Yet, just as the crowds always seemed to have a mixed response to Jesus, this crowd is divided in their response to this event. Some people are amazed, but others accuse the disciples of being drunk. This provides an opportunity for Peter to address the crowd and give his first major sermon.

Peter begins by addressing the murmurings of the crowd about them being drunk. He clarifies that they are in no way drunk, considering that it is only the third hour of the day (9 a.m.). Rather, what the people are observing is the fulfillment of a prophecy from Joel 2:28–32. In this prophecy, Joel speaks about a powerful day when the Holy Spirit will be poured out on all flesh. The evidence of this will be incredible signs, including prophecies and visions. What is more, that day will also be a day of salvation for whoever calls upon the name of the Lord.

Moving on from his explanation of the events that the people are seeing that very moment, Peter immediately draws their attention to Jesus. Since Pentecost is only about a month and a half after the Passover Festival, the death and rumored resurrection of Jesus would still be fresh in the minds of the people. Peter reminds the crowds of all the miracles and wonders that Jesus had performed in their midst. He speaks of Jesus' death and points out two very important facts about His death. *First*, Peter reminds the people of their role in Jesus' death as the Jews unlawfully put Him to death. *Second*, even though the people played an active role in Jesus' death, this was all preordained in God's sovereign plan.

Peter uses two phrases to emphasize that this was God's plan, "determined purpose and foreknowledge of God" (verse 23). Jesus' death was not a mistake; it was all part of God's plan.

The rest of Peter's sermon focuses on the resurrection. Remember that the primary criterion for being an apostle was that the person would serve as a witness to the resurrection. Here, Peter not only stands as a witness to the resurrection, but he also explains to the crowds how the resurrection was always part of God's plan. First, he quotes Psalm 16 wherein David says, "You will not leave my soul in Hades [or Sheol], nor will You allow Your Holy One to see corruption" (verse 27, cf. Psalm 16:10). Since David did die and his body did decay, he must be speaking about someone else. Peter shows that the Person about which David was talking was the coming Messiah. In other words, the Messiah would be killed but not stay dead for long.

Peter wraps up his sermon by bearing witness to the ascension and by explaining that the outpouring of the Spirit is proof that Jesus is the Messiah. He explains the ascension by quoting Psalm 110, the most often quoted passage in the New Testament. In this Psalm, David says, "the LORD said to my Lord, 'Sit at My right hand, till I make Your enemies Your footstool'" (verse 1). There are two "Lords" here, but David is the king and has no authority over him other than God. The first "LORD" here is therefore God, and the second "Lord" is the coming Messiah. This passage serves as a prophecy concerning the ascension. Following the ascension, Jesus is now sitting at the right hand of God, just as David had said. Peter finishes his sermon by going straight to the point, "Therefore let all the house of Israel know assuredly that God has made this Jesus, whom you crucified, both Lord and Christ" (verse 36).

Confronted with the overwhelming evidence that Jesus is the Christ, the crowd says to Peter and the apostles, "Men and brethren, what shall we do?" (verse 37). Peter's response is not to have them simply say some prayer; Peter tells them that they need to repent and be baptized. Salvation begins with a deep felt conviction about our sin and then turning away from that sin. Baptism is the public act that marks identification with Christ. By telling the people to be baptized in the name of Jesus, he is telling them that they need to break from Judaism as their hope for salvation and publicly place their faith in Christ. Moreover, just as Peter had previously had two miraculous catches of fish when Jesus was around, here he has a miraculous catch of men when 3,000 people are baptized.

With such a large influx of believers all at once, one would expect chaos. Yet, rather than chaos, the early Christian community is marked by unity and generosity. The believers all gather together regularly and devote themselves to four things—the teaching of the apostles, fellowship with one another, breaking of bread, and prayer. With the Holy Spirit now guiding the Church, incredible miracles and signs are regularly being performed by the apostles. In addition, people are filled with a sense of generosity, and many people sell their property and give the proceeds to the Church to disperse to any who are in need. These people love each other and selflessly serve one another, and they love God. The effects of this community are felt even outside the Church, as we are told that Christians at this time have favor with all the people. In addition, as Jesus had prayed in John 17, when the Church is unified, the world sees and acknowledges that Jesus is the Messiah, for "the Lord added to the church daily those who were being saved" (verse 47).

Thought Questions:

1. What are some techniques that Peter uses to connect with his audience in this sermon?

2. What do you think it would take for the Church today to be as effective as the early Church?

The Gospel Spreads: Acts 3–4
Lesson 84

At the end of Acts 2, we are told that the apostles perform incredible miracles and signs among the people. In chapter 3, we see one of these miracles. During the hour of prayer, Peter and John go to the temple to pray with the rest of the Jews. However, while they are entering the temple, they encounter a man who had been lame since birth. Because this man cannot make a living, he is at the temple gates in order to beg for money. When he sees Peter and John, he begs them for some money. Yet, rather than giving him money, Peter looks straight at the man and heals him "in the name of Jesus Christ of Nazareth" (verse 6).

As one can imagine, this kind of public healing creates quite a stir among the Jews at the temple. Also, because this man had apparently been begging at the temple for quite some time, everyone recognizes him as the former lame man who can now walk. As more and more people hear about this and see this former lame man dancing and praising God, a large crowd gathers. Naturally, Peter takes advantage of this great opportunity and preaches to the crowd.

The sermon in Acts 3 is very similar to Peter's sermon from Acts 2. In Peter's Pentecost sermon, he begins by explaining the supernatural event of the outpouring of the Spirit that the people have seen, evidenced by speaking in tongues. Here, Peter begins by explaining how this man was healed. Peter is very quick to draw attention away from himself and John and to give Jesus the credit for what has just happened. Also, as in Peter's sermon from Acts 2, Peter is not afraid to remind the people about the part that they played in putting Jesus to death, although here Peter draws out even more the evil that the people showed in putting Jesus to death. He reminds the people that Pilate had intended to let Jesus go, but the people would rather have a murderer set free among them than to have Jesus set free. As with Peter's earlier sermon, Peter highlights that God raised Jesus from the dead and testifies as a firsthand witness.

Peter clarifies once again that it is their faith in the name of Jesus that has healed the lame man. Also like his former sermon, Peter calls for a response from the people. He concedes that the people were ignorant in their role of putting Jesus to death. Now, however, they must repent of their sins so that they can be forgiven. Also like his previous sermon, Peter quotes Scripture to show the people that what he is saying is what God Himself has foretold. *First*, he quotes Deuteronomy 18:18 in which Moses prophesies that someday God will send another Prophet like him who will lead the people. *Second*, Peter says that all the prophets have spoken about Jesus. *Third*, Peter quotes God's covenant with Abraham, a passage with which the Jews would be intimately familiar, to show that Jesus is the true Seed of Abraham through which all the nations will be blessed. As a result of this event and Peter's sermon, the number of Christians grows to about 5,000.

News of this healing makes its way to the religious leaders; and as can be predicted, Peter and John are taken into custody and are questioned by them. Because this miracle is undeniable, the religious leaders instead ask Peter and John where they got the power to do this and in whose name they are doing this. Peter's response must be particularly disheartening for the high priest and the religious leaders. They had gone to incredible lengths to silence Jesus by unlawfully putting Him to death; and now, just a short time later, His disciples are doing some of the same things, riling up the crowds with miracles and doing it in the name of Jesus. Peter does not hold back as he directly accuses them of crucifying Jesus. Once again, Peter testifies that God raised Jesus from the dead. Peter next quotes Psalm 118:22, which speaks of the people rejecting the Messiah and shows the religious leaders that their rejection of Jesus

fulfills Scripture. Finally, Peter finishes boldly by declaring that it is only through the name of Jesus that men can be saved.

The religious leaders are amazed to hear these two ordinary men speak with such boldness and confidence, so they confer among themselves to figure out what to do. They know that they cannot deny this event that has taken place, but if the apostles stop telling people about Jesus perhaps they can stop the movement. So they command Peter and John to stop speaking in the name of Jesus. Peter's response is very significant. He says, "Whether it is right in the sight of God to listen to you more than to God, you judge" (4:19). In other words, when those in authority tell us to do something that requires us to disobey God, we are called to disobey those authorities.

This is the first act of persecution that the Church has to endure. One might expect this to create fear in the believers. Yet the response is the exact opposite. The believers find incredible comfort in the sovereignty and provision of God. They know that God is in control and that nothing can happen unless God allows it to happen. Even more, they identify with Jesus' sufferings as the Messiah. In fact, they quote Psalm 2:1–2, which talks about the conspiracy and rebellion of the nations against God and against His Christ. The irony here is that the Jews are included among the nations who have rebelled against God, along with Herod and Pontius Pilate. Yet even this has been determined by the purpose and hand of God. The believers finish this prayer, not asking for protection or that the persecutions would stop, but rather that God would give them boldness to proclaim God's word and the power to perform miracles and signs. These believers are not interested in self-preservation, but rather the furthering of God's kingdom.

Just as at the end of chapter 2, chapter 4 ends with another description of the early Church community. The early Church is characterized by power, boldness, unity, and generosity. People are so generous, in fact, that people do not even consider their possessions to be their own, but everyone shares with anyone else in need. This is not socialism, however, as these people joyfully sacrifice their own belongings out of a love for everyone else. This chapter ends by mentioning one of these generous men in particular, a man named Barnabas. Barnabas sells some of his land and gives the money to the apostles. Barnabas will prove to be a very important person later in the story of the Church.

Thought Questions:

1. What are some similarities between this healing and Jesus' healings? What are some differences?

2. What might be some specific situations in which it might be appropriate to disobey authorities, based on this passage?

3. What lessons can we learn from the response of the believers to this persecution?

Discipline and Deacons: Acts 5–6

Lesson 85

As we have seen in the first chapters of the book of Acts, the early Church is characterized by unity, generosity, and power. Through the power of the Holy Spirit, the Church grows rapidly and incredible miracles are performed by the apostles. It would appear that the early Church is perfect. Yet the early Church is still made up of sinners, and still exists in a world where Satan has influence. Sadly, it is only a matter of time before someone succumbs to temptation on a larger scale.

In chapter five, we are introduced to a couple named Ananias and Sapphira. Like many people during this time, this couple sells their land and gives the money to the Church. However, rather than giving all the money to the Church, they hold back some of the money for themselves. So far, this is not a sin. Because it is their property, they can do whatever they want with the money they receive. Yet, when Peter asks Ananias if the money he has given is all of the money gained from the sale of his property, Ananias lies and says that it is. Peter, however, is filled with the Holy Spirit and is able to discern that Ananias is lying. When Peter confronts him with this lie, Ananias falls down dead on the ground. About three hours later, Sapphira comes to Peter, and she too lies to Peter about the sale of the property. When Peter confronts her, she too dies. Understandably, when news of this event spreads to the rest of the community, the people are filled with fear. Just as Nadab and Abihu were put to death for offering an unauthorized fire (Leviticus 10) and Achan was put to death for stealing some plunder from Jericho (Joshua 7) as the nation of Israel was being established, God disciplines and purifies the Church in its beginnings. God teaches the Church a lesson—you have been forgiven from all your sins, but you still need to live an obedient life. In spite of this event and, perhaps because of this event, the Church continues to multiply greatly.

As mentioned in the introduction, one of the themes of the book of Acts is that the Church is the ongoing body of Christ that continues Jesus' ministry in His absence. One of the ways that this is evident is by Luke's description of the power that Peter has. The Holy Spirit is so powerful in Peter that people are healed just by being in his shadow. This is very similar to the time when a woman is healed from bleeding just by touching Jesus' garment (Luke 8:44).

When the high priest hears about the growth of the Church and the miracles that the apostles are performing, he has the apostles put in prison. However, that night an angel opens the prison doors and tells the apostles to go back into the temple and share the gospel. The next day, when the high priest calls for the apostles to be brought out from the prison, it is discovered that the apostles are gone, even though the prison is still securely locked. Having heard that the apostles are back in the temple preaching, they bring the apostles before the Sanhedrin, or council. As with Jesus, the high priest is afraid of the crowds because of the popularity of the apostles, so they convene in a private meeting.

Remember that the high priest had previously forbidden the apostles to speak in the name of Jesus. So the high priest begins by reminding them of that command. He is also angry that the apostles are blaming the high priest and the council for the death of Jesus, even though they clearly are the ones who made sure that Jesus was put to death. However, Peter responds with basically the same response that he gave the first time he was commanded not to speak in the name of Jesus. He tells the high priest that he must obey God rather than man. Yet Peter goes further this time with his response as he makes sure to tell the council that Jesus is the Savior for Israel who came to bring them repentance and forgiveness.

As with Jesus, the Sanhedrin plots to put the apostles to death. Yet this time Gamaliel, a well-respected teacher of the Law, responds with wisdom. Jesus is not the first person to claim to be the Messiah and is not the first person to start a movement. With every previous Messianic movement, shortly after the leader died the movement came to an end. Gamaliel is willing to recognize that this movement may be from God and suggests that the council should let things progress naturally, for if it is from God they cannot stop it. So the apostles are beaten and commanded once again not to speak in the name of Jesus. Once again, the response of the believers to this is to rejoice that they were counted worthy to suffer for Jesus.

Due to the increasing number of believers, a logistical problem develops within the Church. Up until this point, the apostles had been distributing the money that people offered to those who are in need. However, a dispute develops between the **Hellenistic** Jews and the Hebraic Jews. The Hellenistic Jews are those who are culturally Greek but have converted to Judaism, and the Hebraic Jews are those who are culturally and ethnically Jewish. The Hellenistic Jews argue that their widows are being overlooked in the distribution of money and that the Hebraic widows are getting all the money. Realizing that this issue is taking up too much of the apostles' time and energy, the apostles commission the rest of the disciples to find men who could take care of the finances. These men become the first deacons. Wisely, in order to help settle the complaints of the Hellenistic Jews, the disciples choose seven Hellenistic men to be the first deacons.

Most notable among the deacons is a man named Stephen. Even though Stephen is given the specific task of overseeing the finances of the Church, he also performs miracles and signs; he also is a great preacher. While Stephen is performing these miracles and speaking to the people, some Hellenistic Jews come and begin to dispute with Stephen. However, Stephen's responses are so wise that these people resort to lies in order to get rid of Stephen. This is precisely what the religious leaders had to do in order to get rid of Jesus. In fact, the false accusations that arise against Stephen are the same two accusations made against Jesus, namely that he speaks against the Law and against the temple. Stephen is even accused of saying that Jesus would destroy the temple, the exact same accusation that resulted in Jesus' conviction (Matthew 26:61). Unlike Jesus, however, Stephen will not remain silent when accused; but that we will see in the next chapter.

Hellenistic: Greek or pertaining to Greek culture

Thought Questions:

1. Why do you think Ananias and Sapphira lie about the money?

2. Why do you think the Hellenistic widows might be overlooked in the distribution of money?

Stephen's Sermon: Acts 7

Lesson 86

In the previous lesson, we learned that one of the first deacons, Stephen, is brought to trial because of his witness concerning Jesus Christ. Following a public debate with some Hellenistic Jews, Stephen is brought before the Sanhedrin, where he stands trial. Once no legitimate accusations can be made against Stephen, some men falsely accuse Stephen of blaspheming Moses and the temple. This is the same accusation that was made against Jesus. In chapter seven, Stephen gives his response to these accusations.

Most of Stephen's response is a history lesson. Starting with Abraham, Stephen recalls the history of the Israelites. Rather than examining this history lesson in detail, we are going to highlight some of the points that Stephen makes through the history lesson. With Abraham, Stephen highlights the prophecy that Abraham receives telling him that his descendants will be persecuted but the nation that persecutes them will be judged. Stephen is communicating two things to the Sanhedrin with this: *first*, God's people have been persecuted from the very beginning, just as the Jews are now persecuting the Church; and *second*, God is going to judge the Jews for persecuting the Church. This theme of persecution is going to continue throughout Stephen's sermon. The next person whom Stephen highlights is Joseph, who is persecuted and oppressed by his brothers, just as the Jews are persecuting Christians in Stephen's day.

Particularly significant for Stephen's defense is his description of Moses' life. Remember that Stephen has been accused of blaspheming Moses. Stephen describes Moses as "well pleasing to God" (verse 20) and "learned in all the wisdom of the Egyptians, and was mighty in words and deeds" (verse 22). Stephen knows that the Jews venerate Moses as a great man, and he is more than willing to acknowledge the greatness of Moses. The first major act that Moses does is strike down an Egyptian who is oppressing an Israelite. Yet Stephen points out that, even in his own time, Moses was misunderstood by his own people. After killing the Egyptian in an attempt to save one of his people, when Moses tries to play mediator between two Israelites, they say, "Who made you a ruler and a judge over us?" (verse 27). In other words, the people in Moses' own day did not even accept him as their leader. Just as the people have rejected Jesus, the One who offers salvation to the Jews, they had previously rejected Moses, who offered salvation.

Moses also prophesies that another Prophet will come after him to whom the Israelites are supposed to listen. We know, of course, that the Prophet about whom Moses is speaking is Jesus, and Stephen is implying this here. Moses is given the Law, which Stephen highlights and adds, "Whom our fathers would not obey, but rejected" (verse 39). Even worse, while Moses is up on the mountain receiving the Law, the people say to Aaron, "Make us gods to go before us; as for this Moses who brought us out of the land of Egypt, we do not know what has become of him" (verse 40). Once again, the Israelites reject Moses and now directly rebel against the Law. Even worse, over the forty years that the Israelites wander in the wilderness, many of the Israelites turn to idolatry and worship a number of foreign gods.

Stephen finishes his history lesson by talking about the development of the temple. First, the place of worship was the tabernacle until the time of David. David desired to build a temple, but it was Solomon who eventually built the temple. However, Stephen quotes Isaiah 66:1–2, as he emphasizes that the temple could never contain God. The temple is merely a building that God has established as a place to worship God, not a place to worship in and of itself. Basically, Stephen answers the second accusation, that he had blasphemed the temple, by saying that they are idolizing the temple.

Stephen now says directly what he has been implying all along through this history lesson. The Israelites in this generation are acting just like the rebellious Israelites throughout their history. He calls the people "stiff-necked and uncircumcised in heart and ears" (verse 51). Stephen's defense is really no defense at all; it is an exhortation to the religious leaders to repent. Just as the Israelites have killed the prophets, who had come before, here they are again looking to kill a prophet shortly after killing the Prophet Jesus. In fact, he calls them "betrayers and murderers" (verse 52).

When the people hear this, they are infuriated. They are angry at the very core of their beings. Then Stephen says something that throws them over the edge. He is given a glimpse of heaven, and he tells the people, "Look! I see the heavens opened and the Son of Man standing at the right hand of God!" (verse 56). Jesus had regularly identified Himself as the Son of Man in His teachings, so the crowd understands that Stephen is talking about Jesus. It is interesting that Jesus is characterized as standing rather than sitting. Perhaps Jesus does this to honor Stephen for his faithfulness. Once the people hear this, they cover their ears and throw him out of the city and stone him. What happens next is yet another example of the Church being the ongoing body of Christ, who continues His mission. While Stephen is dying, he says two things that should sound very familiar: "Lord Jesus, receive my spirit," and "Lord, do not charge them with this sin" (verses 59–60). Both of these are statements that Jesus says on the cross. Jesus says, "Father, into Your hands I commit My spirit"

(Luke 23:46) and, "Father, forgive them for they know not what they do" (Luke 23:34). Also, as with Jesus, after saying these words, Stephen dies.

While the Church has been experiencing more and more persecution, Stephen is the first person who dies for his faith in Jesus. Sadly, Stephen will not be the last. For there is a young man at Stephen's execution named Saul who is going to be inspired by this event. However, we will learn more about this in future chapters.

To Judea and Samaria: Acts 8
Lesson 87

Tertullian, one of the early Church fathers, famously said, "The blood of the martyrs is the seed of the church" (*Apologeticum*, A.D. 197). It is in the context of extreme persecution and suffering that the Church has grown the most throughout the centuries, both in numbers and in maturity. Without conflict, there is rarely any growth. Starting with the death of Stephen, a wave of persecution afflicts the Church; and through this persecution, the Church will grow and mature.

The mention of Saul during the stoning of Stephen is not random. Starting with the stoning of Stephen, Saul makes it his personal mission to eradicate the followers of Jesus. He goes house to house and drags the believers away to prison. This persecution is so severe that the majority of believers are forced to flee from Jerusalem. Historically, this event is called the Christian **diaspora**, or dispersion of Christianity.

Earlier, when Jesus commissioned the apostles, He told them that they would be His witnesses in Jerusalem, Judea, Samaria, and to the ends of the earth. So far, the Church has only been in Jerusalem. Yet, as a result of this persecution, believers flee to the surrounding regions of Judea and Samaria and start to share the gospel there. It is another one of the deacons who plays a critical role in the evangelization of Samaria. The conversion of the Samaritans is very important for the spread of Christianity. Up until this time, the only believers are Jews. The Samaritans are only partly Jewish and culturally very different from the Jews. Christianity is no longer a Jewish sect, but a new religion that is available to all.

When Philip goes to Samaria, he is able to perform incredible miracles and cast out demons. There is a great reception of the gospel by the Samaritans, and large numbers come to faith in Jesus. One of the people who comes to believe in Jesus is a sorcerer named

Simon. Before Philip came to Samaria, Simon had the admiration of the crowds because of his sorceries. However, when Philip comes, the miracles that Philip performs are far more powerful and numerous so that even Simon believes in Jesus.

News of the Samaritan conversions makes its way to Jerusalem and to the apostles. So they decide to send Peter and John to Samaria to see what is happening. When they arrive in Samaria, they see the large number of believers but realize that they do not yet have the Holy Spirit. Even though many people had been baptized in the name of Jesus, God had not yet given them the Holy Spirit. So Peter and John lay hands on the people, and they receive the Holy Spirit. So why is there a delay in the giving of the Holy Spirit? Is it possible to have genuine faith in Jesus Christ but not have the Holy Spirit? The key to understanding these questions lies with Peter. Up until this point, Christianity has been entirely Jewish. How could the apostles be sure that God has accepted these non-Jewish Samaritans? By withholding the Holy Spirit from the Samaritans until Peter and John can arrive, God shows the apostles that He has accepted the Samaritans just as He had accepted them.

When Simon the sorcerer sees that the apostles have the ability to give the Holy Spirit to people, he offers them money to give him this power. Even though Simon is a believer, he still has his old sinful nature and longs to use his faith as a means for power and fame. Peter, however, sternly rebukes Simon and tells him to repent and pray for forgiveness for the wickedness in his heart. Centuries later, as more corruption enters the church, people are able to use money to buy powerful positions in the church. Because of the similarity to what Simon does here, the process of buying or selling church offices is later called **simony**.

The ministry of Philip is not yet over. God sends an angel to Philip to tell him to travel south along one of the desert roads, and he obeys. Along the way, he encounters a man who is sitting in his chariot. It turns out that this man is a very powerful man in Ethiopia. He is one of the personal servants of the queen, who has been put in charge of the treasury. He had gone up to Jerusalem to worship God and is now returning home. Because this man is a eunuch, it would be impossible to be circumcised, so he would be called a god-fearer rather than a proselyte. In the Roman Empire, there were a number of Gentiles who believed in God but did not go through the process of circumcision, so they were allowed to worship, but only from a distance.

When Philip finds this man, he is reading a scroll from Isaiah the prophet. It turns out that he is reading from the passage in Isaiah 52–53, which talks about the Suffering Servant who will die in order to save the people from their sins. Philip tells him that this Suffering Servant is none other than Jesus Christ. The Ethiopian eunuch believes in Jesus, and Philip baptizes him right there. Interestingly, there is some evidence to suggest that in the times of the Roman Empire, Ethiopia was considered to be the ends of the earth. If this is in fact true and well known, this conversion of a full Gentile is a direct fulfillment of the last stage of Jesus' commission when He tells the apostles that they will be His witnesses "to the end of the earth" (Acts 1:8).

After the Ethiopian eunuch is baptized, as soon as he comes up out of the water, Philip disappears miraculously. He reappears in a town called Azotus (Ashdod) and continues to preach the gospel as he travels. However, this Ethiopian eunuch is only the beginning of what God has in store for the Gentiles.

> **diaspora:** an event that forces a people group to flee and spread out

> **simony:** buying or selling positions of authority in the church

Thought Question:

1. Based on Peter's strong rebuke of Simon the sorcerer, do you think Simon is a true believer? Why or why not?

2. Some people use the story of the Samaritans as evidence to suggest that God may still delay the Holy Spirit today from believers. How would you respond to this idea?

The Conversion of Saul: Acts 9

Lesson 88

God seems to use the unlikeliest of people in order to accomplish His plan. The most successful prophet in the Old Testament, Jonah, did not even want to prophesy to Nineveh; yet Nineveh has the greatest repentance in the Old Testament. Peter was a common fisherman who always seemed to act before he thought, yet he would be the main leader among the apostles. Also, when we are introduced to Saul of Tarsus, he is viciously attacking the Church and throwing believers in prison. Yet God has great plans for Saul, which we see in Acts 9.

Because of Saul's initial persecutions of the Church, Christians had spread to the surrounding regions to find safety. When Saul hears that this movement has spread, he goes to the high priest in order to obtain permission to pursue Christians outside Jerusalem. He is granted permission and begins his journey to Damascus. As a side note, we see in verse 2 what the Church had originally been called. It was called "the Way." Perhaps this is because the early believers were so adamant that faith in Jesus is the only way for salvation.

On the road to Damascus, Saul has an encounter that will change his life forever. While he is riding, he sees a bright light that knocks him to the ground. Out of that bright light, Jesus speaks to Saul. Jesus begins by asking Saul why he is persecuting Him. This reveals something about the intimate connection between Jesus and His people. Saul was not directly persecuting Jesus; he was persecuting the Church. Yet Jesus identifies the suffering of the Church with His own sufferings, so to persecute the Church means to persecute Jesus. When Saul asks who is speaking, Jesus identifies Himself and then says, "It is hard for you to kick against the goads" (verse 5). A goad was used to prod oxen to keep moving, and often the oxen would kick against it. However, the more one resists the goad, the more it hurts. Jesus is basically telling Saul, "Why are you resisting Me? You are only going to hurt yourself." Jesus then tells Saul to go into the city and wait until he is told what to do. Consequently, Saul has been blinded by this event and has to be helped to the city.

In the meantime, Jesus tells one of the disciples in Damascus to go and speak to Saul. Ananias, the disciple, is told to go to Straight Street and seek out Saul of Tarsus. Now Saul had developed quite the reputation for persecuting the Church by this time; and Ananias knows about his reputation, so understandably he is hesitant to go and speak on behalf of Jesus. Yet Jesus insists and tells Ananias that He has chosen Saul to be the apostle to the Gentiles and that he will stand before kings and share the gospel. He also tells Ananias that Saul will have to suffer much for the sake of His name. For Saul, suffering is an essential element of his mission.

So Ananias goes to Saul and tells him that he had been sent by Jesus to heal him. Also, as Ananias prays for Saul, something like scales falls from Saul's eyes, and he is able to see. Saul is baptized and immediately begins to argue in the synagogues that Jesus is the Son of God. We will learn later that Saul is actually a Pharisee and, as such, would be incredibly well-versed in the Scriptures. So when he disputes with the other Jews, he is able to prove emphatically that Jesus is the Mes-

siah. The people are amazed at this change of heart by Saul, and many come to believe in Jesus through him. However, as will become a consistent pattern, the Jews do not want Saul around, and they begin to plot to kill him. Saul is forced to flee through a hole in the city wall in a large basket in order to be spared.

When Saul leaves Damascus, he goes to Jerusalem to meet the apostles. Understandably, the believers in Jerusalem are afraid to accept Saul into their group. Considering that Saul may have thrown some of their own friends and families in prison, this makes sense. Yet Barnabas, whom we had met earlier in Acts as the generous man who sold his property and gave it to the Church (Acts 4:36–37), stands up for Saul and brings him to the apostles. So in Jerusalem, Saul publicly debates with others and proves that Jesus is the Messiah; but once again there is a plot to kill him, and he is sent away to his hometown of Tarsus. With Saul's persecutions coming to an end, the Church enjoys a time of relative peace, and more and more people come to believe in Jesus.

With this newfound peace, Peter begins to travel outside Jerusalem. At the town of Lydda, Peter heals a man who had been paralyzed for eight years. Just as Jesus had told the paralytic to get up and walk, Peter tells this man to get up and make his bed. As news of this healing spreads, more and more people in Lydda come to believe. Meanwhile, in the nearby town of Joppa, a well-respected disciple named Tabitha gets sick and dies. Having heard about the miracles that Peter had just performed in Lydda, the people seek out Peter and have him come to Joppa. When Peter gets there, he goes to the upper room where Tabitha's body had been laid and he prays for her. When he says, "Tabitha, arise" (verse 40), she opens her eyes and sits up. Peter raises this girl from the dead. This event is especially interesting because of its connection with something that Jesus had done in His ministry. Jesus too raised a girl from the dead. When Jesus raised the girl from the dead, He said in Aramaic *Talitha, cumi*, which is translated "Little girl, arise" (Mark 5:41; Luke 8:54). Here, if we were to translate what Peter says into Aramaic, it would be *Tabitha, cumi*. Once again, this is evidence that the Church is the ongoing body of Jesus that continues His ministry.

Thought Questions:

1. Why do you think God chooses Saul of all people to be His witness to the Gentiles?

2. What do you think you would do if you were in Ananias' shoes and were asked to share the gospel

with someone who is persecuting Christians? Do you think you would do it?

Cornelius and the Gentile Church: Acts 10–11

Lesson 89

When Jesus commissions His apostles to share the gospel, He tells them that they will be His witnesses in Jerusalem, Judea, Samaria, and to the ends of the earth. So far we have seen the gospel spread throughout Jerusalem and into the regions of Judea and Samaria. We have been introduced to Saul, who will become the apostle to the Gentiles. Now, in chapter 10, we will see the beginning of the Gentile church.

In chapter 10, we are first introduced to a centurion by the name of Cornelius. As a centurion, he is a man with much authority in the Roman Empire. Even though he is a Gentile, he is a follower of Judaism. Like the Ethiopian eunuch, this man would be considered a god-fearer. He follows many of the customs of the Jews and follows the Scriptures, but he is still a Gentile and has not been circumcised. One day, while he is praying, he is visited by an angel. This angel tells him that he is to send to Joppa and find Peter. So Cornelius sends some of his servants to Joppa to search for Peter.

In the meantime, Peter is lodging at the house of Simon the tanner. As a tanner, Simon would prepare the hides of many dead animals, and as such would have them in his house. According to the Law, if a Jewish person touches something dead, he or she becomes unclean. This is significant for what is about to take place. While Peter is praying on the roof of the house, he falls into a trance. He sees a vision of a sheet descending from heaven, filled with all sorts of ceremonially unclean animals. He then hears a voice telling him to eat these animals. Peter refuses to eat because it would make him unclean. However, Peter is not consistent. Here he is not willing to eat these animals because they would make him unclean, yet he is residing in the presence of dead animals that would also make him unclean. God is revealing to Peter a cultural bias. God tells Peter to eat these animals because they are now clean.

So what is the purpose of this vision? Just as certain foods are considered unclean, Gentiles are considered unclean for Jews. However, as with the food, this is more than just a legal issue for Jews. There is a cultural bias and even a hatred of the Gentiles in the Jewish community. So when God tells Peter to eat foods that are unclean, He is actually telling Peter that He considers Gentiles as clean, that is, worthy of the gospel. This is significant because at the very moment that Peter is pondering this vision, the servants of Cornelius arrive. Normally, Peter would not have gone with these men, but because of this vision, Peter goes with them.

When Peter arrives at Caesarea, the town where Cornelius lives, Cornelius explains to Peter the interaction that he had with the angel. Cornelius had gathered his friends and family together to listen to what Peter has to say. Peter explains his vision and the lesson that he had learned from that vision, namely that God will accept people who fear Him from any nation. Peter recounts what Jesus had done during His life on earth, and he tells about Jesus' death and resurrection. As Peter speaks about the forgiveness that can be given to all through faith in Jesus' name, the Holy Spirit comes upon all in Cornelius' house, and they begin to speak in tongues. It is particularly significant that the Holy Spirit manifests Himself in this way among the Gentiles. Peter, and those who came with him, see that the Gentiles are manifesting the Holy Spirit in the exact same manner that Peter first manifested the Holy Spirit at Pentecost. This is tangible evidence that God has accepted the Gentiles and included them on an equal standing in the Church. So Peter has all who had gathered there baptized.

This event is incredibly important for the history of the Church. Up until this point, Christianity had been thoroughly Jewish and had belonged to the Jews. Now the gospel has been officially given to Gentiles, as well. At first, this will be a very difficult concept for the Jewish believers to accept. When Peter returns with the report of what had happened among the Gentiles, the brothers in Jerusalem do not believe it. However, when Peter and the other witnesses speak about how Cornelius and his friends and family received the Holy Spirit by speaking in tongues, they accept it.

This marks a new era in the history of the Church. Now that the Church officially recognizes and accepts Gentiles into it, the Church will look quite different. In fact, shortly after this event, a strong church develops in the thoroughly Gentile city of Antioch. Some of the brothers who had been scattered by the persecutions of Saul make their way out to Antioch and form a church there. The harvest is very ripe in Antioch, and a large number of people come to believe in Jesus there. So the church in Jerusalem sends Barnabas to Antioch to oversee that church. This is the same Barnabas who had stood up for Saul when he was converted. In fact, Barnabas goes to Tarsus to bring Saul to Antioch so that they can partner together in this ministry.

It is in Antioch that the word *Christian* is first used to describe the followers of Jesus. Up until this point, followers of Jesus are simply called "followers of the Way." Also, among the believers in Antioch, a prophet emerges who predicts that a great famine is going to come over the world in the coming years. So the church in Antioch decides to send financial relief to Jerusalem.

Thought Questions:

1. What kind of specific challenges might a Gentile church pose for Christianity?

2. Why do you think Peter is willing to reside with a tanner, yet he will not eat unclean foods?

The First Missionary Journey: Acts 12–14

Lesson 90

Even though great persecutions had swept over the church in Jerusalem during Saul's persecutions, for the most part, the twelve apostles were spared. Saul, however, is not the only one who persecutes the Church; we learn in chapter 12 that King Herod has begun to persecute the Church, as well. Herod has the apostle James, the brother of John, put to death by the sword. He then proceeds to have Peter put in prison so that he could put Peter to death, as well. However, the night before Peter is to be put to death, God sends an angel, who releases Peter from prison. At the time, Peter thinks that it is just a vision, but when he gets to the streets he realizes that it is real. So Peter goes to the believers who had been gathered together to pray for him. When he arrives at the house where they are gathered, a funny scene takes place. The servant girl, Rhoda, hears Peter at the gate and is so astonished that she leaves him there to go tell the other people. As the people are arguing with Rhoda, Peter continues to knock at the door. When the people hear Peter's story, they rejoice. Then Peter says something interesting. He says, "Go, tell these things to James and to the brethren" (verse 17). Either Peter does not know that James the apostle has been killed, or the James that he mentions is James the brother of Jesus. We will see in the next lesson that by this time James the brother of Jesus has grown quite powerful in the church in Jerusalem, and it is this James to whom Peter says to tell his story.

King Herod's story does not end here, however. Because of some political moves, when some of his subjects begin to worship him as a god, God kills King Herod. Earlier, when Cornelius had tried to worship Peter,

Peter immediately gave glory to God and told him not to worship him (Acts 10:25–26). However, King Herod enjoys this praise and does not stop the people. So God afflicts him, and he is eaten by worms and dies.

When Saul and Barnabas return from Jerusalem, having given the church the financial gift, they bring with them John Mark, the very person who will later write the gospel of Mark. Among the believers in Antioch, certain men arise as leaders among the people. As these men pray and seek out the will of the Lord, the Holy Spirit makes it clear that Saul and Barnabas are to be sent out as missionaries. So the church at Antioch commissions Saul and Barnabas, and they begin their first missionary journey along with John Mark.

The first place that they go is the island of Cyprus (Acts 4:36). This makes sense since Barnabas is from the island of Cyprus. While in Cyprus, Saul and Barnabas begin to share the word of the Lord with the people, and they gain the attention of a powerful man, the proconsul Sergius Paulus. Yet, as Saul and Barnabas begin to speak the gospel to this man, they are opposed by a sorcerer named Elymas, who also calls himself Bar-Jesus, which means "son of Jesus." This man had been an advisor to Sergius Paulus. However, when he opposes Saul and Barnabas, Saul looks right at him and rebukes him and blinds him. Then the proconsul believes in the gospel.

It is worth noting something about Saul's name. It is as Saul begins his first missionary journey that we see him start to go by the name of Paul. For the rest of the Bible, Saul will be called Paul. Many people believe that Saul's name is changed to Paul around this time, but that is not likely what is happening here. As a Jewish Roman citizen, Paul would have had both a Jewish and a Gentile name. The Jewish name is for when he is around the Jews, and the Gentile name for when he is around the Gentiles. Because Paul is beginning his official ministry among the Gentiles now, this is why he is called Paul.

Paul's mission is to plant churches among the Gentiles, so he often does not stay in one place very long. Consequently, Paul and Barnabas leave the island of Cyprus and travel north to the mainland, to the region of Galatia. When they leave Cyprus, however, John Mark leaves them and goes back to Jerusalem; this will be important later. When they arrive at a different Antioch, the Antioch in Pisidia, they begin their ministry by speaking in the synagogue on the Sabbath. This will be Paul's strategy throughout his missionary journeys. Even though Paul is sent to the Gentiles, he

Paul's First Missionary Journey (Acts 13:4–14:26)

C. A.D. 46–47

Barnabas and Paul first visited Barnabas's home region of Cyprus before sailing to the southern region of Asia Minor. When they reached Perga in Pamphylia, John Mark left the group and returned to Jerusalem. Making their way to Antioch (in Pisidia), Iconium, Lystra, and Derbe, Paul and Barnabas were driven out of each city by jealous Jewish religious leaders. Later they returned by the same route, strengthening the new churches as they went. From Attalia they set sail for their home in Antioch of Syria.

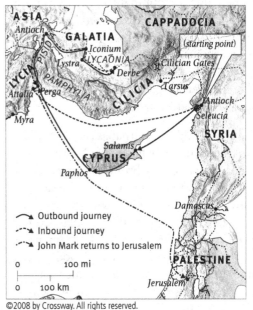

Itinerary of Paul's First Journey

City	Province/Region	Reference
Antioch	Syria	13:1–3
Seleucia	Syria	13:4
Salamis	Cyprus	13:5
Paphos	Cyprus	13:6–12
Perga	Lycia (region of Pamphylia)	13:13
Antioch	Galatia (region of Pisidia)	13:14–52
Iconium	Galatia	14:1–6
Lystra	Galatia (region of Lycaonia)	14:6, 8–19
Derbe	Galatia (region of Lycaonia)	14:6, 20–21
Lystra	Galatia (region of Lycaonia)	14:21–23
Iconium	Galatia	14:21–23
Antioch	Galatia (region of Pisidia)	14:24
Perga	Lycia (region of Pamphylia)	14:24–25
Attalia	Lycia	14:25
Antioch	Syria	14:26–28

routinely goes to the Jewish synagogue to preach there until the door opens for the Gentiles. He does this for practical reasons, as the synagogue provides a ready-made opportunity to preach the gospel.

Paul's approach to his sermon here is very similar to Stephen's approach. Paul provides a history lesson for the Jews. Rather than emphasizing Moses, Paul emphasizes David and uses David as a bridge for the gospel. Paul points out that the Old Testament Scriptures had predicted that the Messiah would come from the line of David. Jesus is in fact the Messiah that the Scriptures had predicted. Paul continues to talk about the witness of John the Baptist about Jesus. John was quite popular among the Jews, so his testimony would hold a lot of weight with them. As with all of the sermons so far, Paul goes on to speak about the death and resurrection of Jesus and the number of witnesses of His resurrection. Paul quotes a number of passages that speak about Jesus as the Messiah and the resurrection. Paul also quotes Habakkuk 1:5 as a warning to the people not to ignore the works of God in their midst.

Interestingly, it is the Gentiles who beg for Paul and Barnabas to speak the following Sabbath, and a large number of the people follow Paul and Barnabas to hear more. Paul and Barnabas grow so popular that almost the whole city gathers the following Sabbath to hear them. Out of jealousy, the Jews oppose Paul and his message. So Paul tells them that because they have rejected the gospel, it will be given to the Gentiles.

Naturally, the Gentiles there rejoice over this; but the Jews stir up a number of powerful people, and they are able to get Paul and Barnabas expelled from their city. This is going to be the pattern for most of the cities Paul visits. Paul will preach in the synagogues, many of the Gentiles will want to hear more; and then the Jews will stir up a crowd to persecute Paul and kick him out of the city.

This same pattern happens in Iconium, so Paul ministers there until they are kicked out. They then go to the cities of Lystra and Derbe. In Lystra, Paul and Barnabas heal a man who had been crippled from birth. However, when the people of the city find out about this miracle, they begin to worship Paul and Barnabas as gods. They call Barnabas "Zeus" and Paul "Hermes" because Paul is the primary speaker. When Paul and Barnabas hear about this, they tear their clothes and beg the people not to worship them and try to direct their worship towards God. Around the same time, some of the Jews from the previous cities that Paul and Barnabas had visited come to Lystra and stir up the crowds to stone Paul. This stoning should kill Paul, but when the crowds leave his body, Paul is able to get up and leave the city.

From there, Paul and Barnabas return to the cities in which they had previously planted churches. They strengthen the believers in those churches and eventually return to their home church in Antioch of Syria. After they give their report of the conversion of the Gentiles, they remain in Antioch for a long time.

Thought Questions:

1. What kind of practical lessons can we learn from Paul's strategy of evangelism during his first missionary journey?

2. Compare Paul's sermons to the Gentiles with the other sermons in Acts 2 ,3, and 7, which are given to the Jews. How are they different? How are they the same?

The Jerusalem Council: Acts 15:1–35

Lesson 91

In Jesus' high priestly prayer in John 17, His main prayer for the Church is that we would be characterized by unity. In the early chapters of Acts, we have seen that the early Church fits that characterization extremely well. Yet these early Christians have one major advantage when it comes to unity; they all have the same basic culture and background. The church in Jerusalem is originally composed of Jewish people and has a distinctive Jewish flavor. Now that the Church has spread to the Gentiles, however, that unity is at risk.

Even though Christianity springs from Judaism, Paul has been preaching to the Gentiles that they can maintain their own unique cultural identities while still finding forgiveness and salvation through Jesus Christ. In fact, if salvation is truly by faith in Jesus and not by works, observance and obedience to the Law of Moses cannot be a means of salvation. Yet the Law plays an incredibly important role in the culture of the Jewish Christians. A tension develops after the growth and development of the Gentile church, regarding whether or not Gentiles need to become Jewish in order to become Christians or if Christianity is a whole new movement.

This tension comes to a boiling point when some Jewish Christians come to the Gentile believers and tell them that they must be circumcised in order to be saved. Considering the intimate and painful nature of this procedure, it is understandable that the Gentiles would not want to have this procedure done. This would stand as a strong deterrent for many Gentiles to become Christians. Paul and Barnabas oppose these Jewish Christians, and a large dispute develops. In an effort to protect unity in the Church and in order to settle this dispute, the church in Antioch sends Paul and Barnabas to Jerusalem to seek out the apostles.

After Paul and Barnabas arrive in Jerusalem, they share the stories of what has happened among the Gentiles. Yet some of the Christians who are Pharisees oppose Paul and Barnabas and argue that it is necessary for the Gentiles to be circumcised and to follow the Law of Moses. So a council is set up to discuss the matter.

The first major person to speak up at this council is Peter. Peter recounts how he had seen Cornelius receive the Holy Spirit in the exact manner that he had received the Holy Spirit. We have already seen that God specifically withholds the Holy Spirit from the Samaritans so that Peter could see them receive the Holy Spirit in the same manner, as well. If God manifests the Holy Spirit in the same way to the Gentiles before they had been circumcised, this is proof that circumcision is not necessary for salvation. Moreover, Peter argues that it is inappropriate to require a person to follow the Law in order to be saved since no one has been able to completely obey the Law. Rather than the Law being a means of salvation, Peter argues that it is only by the grace of Jesus Christ that we can be saved.

After Peter says this, Paul and Barnabas recount all of the incredible things that they had seen God do among the Gentiles. Finally, James, the brother of Jesus, speaks to the council. The fact that James is given the last word shows just how much authority James has been given among the apostles. James argues that the plan from the beginning was for the Jews to bring salvation to the Gentiles. Also, since it has always been God's plan for the Gentiles to be saved, James determines that there should be no unnecessary barrier put in their way. James concludes that the Gentiles are not to be required to be circumcised, nor should they have to follow the Law of Moses. However, so that there can be no unnecessary cultural barriers between the Jewish Christians and Gentile Christians, four restrictions are suggested—do not eat things polluted by idols, stay away from sexual immorality, stay away from meat that had been strangled, and stay away from eating meat with blood still in it. Three of these restrictions have to do with dietary issues that would be incredibly offensive to Jewish people; and because of the rampant sexual perversion in the Roman Empire, sexual purity is highlighted as important.

The council agrees with James and puts together a letter to send to the Gentile churches so that they will be able to refute anyone else who demands circumcision. Paul and Barnabas are sent with this letter, as well as a few other believers, most notably Silas, who will later join Paul on his next missionary journey. So these men go back to Antioch and share the good news about the council's decision with the brothers there. Silas stays with Paul and Barnabas, and they remain in Antioch for some time.

Thought Questions:

1. What do you think would have been the result if the church in Jerusalem had decided to require circumcision?

2. There are thousands of church denominations that exist today that divide over a number of issues

MAP 13: PAUL'S FIRST AND SECOND MISSIONARY JOURNEYS

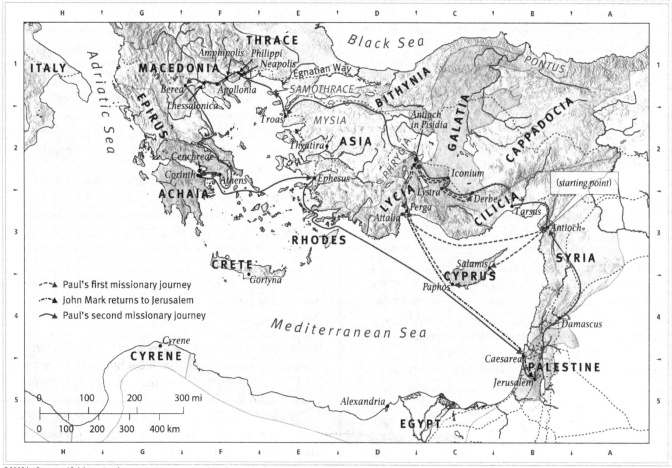

from doctrine to church practice. What do you think the people from the Jerusalem Council would say about these divisions today?

3. In many ways, the Gentile Christians are allowed to maintain their own cultural identities yet still be considered Christians. What might be some cultural issues today that we might need to part from as good Christians?

The Second Missionary Journey: Acts 15:36–18:22

Lesson 92

Now that Paul and Barnabas have been given the letter from the church in Jerusalem, declaring that Gentiles do not need to be circumcised, they decide to go and visit the churches that they had planted on their first missionary journey and give them the news. However, a dispute develops between Paul and Barnabas over John Mark. Barnabas wants to bring John Mark with them on the journey, but Paul does not trust him because he

had abandoned Paul and Barnabas on their previous missionary journey. This dispute is so strong that Paul and Barnabas decide to part ways. Paul takes Silas with him and goes to visit the churches that he had planted on the first missionary journey.

While in the city of Lystra, Paul is introduced to a young believer named Timothy. The people of that city speak highly of Timothy, so Paul brings him along on his journey. Interestingly, even though Paul is carrying a letter saying that Gentiles do not need to be circumcised to be saved, he has Timothy circumcised. Even though this circumcision is not necessary for salvation, it would stand as a barrier for evangelizing the Jews.

After visiting the churches in Galatia that Paul had planted previously, Paul desires to continue to a region called Asia to preach there. This is the western portion of what is now the modern state of Turkey—the region where the city of Ephesus is located. However, the Holy Spirit does not permit Paul to go to Ephesus; rather, while Paul is in the city of Troas, he receives a vision from God telling him to go to Macedonia (now the northern portion of Greece). Something happens grammatically at this point in the story. Up until this point, the author has spoken of all of the events in the third person, but suddenly the author includes himself in Paul's journey. Luke must have joined Paul's journey from Troas.

The first major city that Paul visits in Macedonia is Philippi. While in this city, Paul is bothered by a demon-possessed girl, who follows him around proclaiming that he is offering the way of salvation. While she is speaking the truth, not only is her constant shouting annoying and distracting, but a demon-possessed person is not exactly the best witness. So Paul casts the demon out of her. Because this girl had been able to make much money for her masters through her ability to predict the future, her owners grab Paul and Silas and have them beaten and thrown in prison. Yet, that night, while Paul and Silas are praising God in prison, God sends an earthquake and the doors to the cells open. Fearing that he will be put to death for the prisoners escaping, the jailer gets ready to kill himself. However, Paul assures him that nobody has left and then shares the gospel with the jailer. When the jailer asks what he must do to be saved, Paul says, "Believe on the Lord Jesus Christ, and you will be saved, you and your household" (16:31). Then the jailer and his whole household are baptized. As a side note, the fact that this offer of salvation is given to the jailer's entire family upon his belief has led some to suggest that the children of believers are saved. However, we are told in verse 34 that his whole household believes in the gospel. The jailer's family is not saved by his faith, but by their own faith.

The next day, the authorities send a messenger to tell Paul and Silas that they are free to go. However, Paul and Silas are both Roman citizens; and according to Roman law, they are to be given a fair trial before receiving a beating. So Paul insists that the leaders come personally to get them out, and the leaders oblige.

From Philippi, the next notable city that Paul visits is the city of Thessalonica. Paul uses his typical strategy of first going into the synagogues to preach the gospel. While some people do come to faith in Christ here, very quickly the Jews stir up a mob to get Paul kicked out of the city. In fact, when they cannot find Paul to have him punished, they punish a disciple named Jason instead. The two accusations that they make against Paul and the Christians are interesting. First, they have "turned the world upside down"; and second, that they are advocating another king other than Caesar (17:6–7). The first accusation shows the effect that the gospel is having in the Roman world already. The second accusation is the

same accusation that the high priest made before Pilate in order to get Jesus crucified (Luke 23:2). Paul, however, is spared, and he quickly leaves to go to the city of Berea. The Bereans are described as "more fair-minded" (verse 11) than the Thessalonians. Rather than immediately attacking Paul's teachings, they diligently study the Scriptures to see if what Paul is saying is indeed true. Many churches today encourage their communities to be like the Bereans and search the Scriptures. Sadly, the Jews from Thessalonica come down to Berea and stir up the crowds there, too, and Paul is forced to flee again.

Next, Paul goes to the city of Athens. Athens is a city rich with Greek history and is known for its philosophy and culture. Because the Romans are **polytheists**, there are altars scattered throughout the city to their various gods. As always, Paul goes to the synagogues to preach the gospel, but here in Athens he also goes to the marketplace to preach the gospel. Some of the philosophers in the area hear Paul and invite him to speak at the **Areopagus**.

Paul's sermon at the Areopagus is very different from most of the sermons we have encountered so far in the book of Acts. Because this audience is almost entirely Gentile, there is no reference to the Old Testament Scriptures. Instead, Paul finds connections within their own culture to talk about the gospel. *First*, he notices that there is an altar in the city "TO THE UNKNOWN GOD." Paul sees that the people are open to new ideas. Paul tells them that he is going to reveal to them the God that they do not know. *Second*, Paul speaks about the universal nature of God. God is the Creator, who is all-powerful and sovereign over everything. Rather than quoting the Bible, Paul quotes their own poets, which have spoken about the concept of an all-powerful God. *Third*, after establishing that there is a sovereign Creator God, Paul then talks about God's judgment. This God is going to hold people accountable for their actions, and we need to repent of our sins. As proof that this God exists and that He will judge the world, God raised Jesus from the dead. Even if a person does not have any understanding of the Old Testament, when someone rises from the dead it demands a response. While some mock at the idea of a resurrection, some who listen are persuaded and come to believe in Jesus.

In chapter 18, Paul moves on next to the city of Corinth. There he meets a couple named Aquila and Priscilla, and they become good friends. Like Paul, these people make a living by making and selling tents. God tells Paul to remain in Corinth for a long time because God has "many people in this city" (verse 10). In other words, God has prepared the hearts of many people to respond to the gospel in that city. So Paul stays there for a year and six months. Once again, the Jews of that city form a mob to try to get rid of Paul, but the proconsul of that region will not even hear the case. Nevertheless, as in Thessalonica, in their anger the people of that city decide to hurt another man instead, Sosthenes, the ruler of the synagogue.

Paul then leaves and, after a short stay in the city of Ephesus, makes his way back to the city of Antioch, thus finishing his second missionary journey.

> **polytheists:** those who believe in many gods

> **Areopagus:** translated "Ares Rock," located northwest of the Acropolis in Athens; the location of the supreme court of appeals; also the name of the judicial body that presided there

Thought Questions:

1. After being beaten and arrested, Paul and Silas spend the night in jail praising God. Why do you think they do this? What can you learn from this?

2. With today's technology, it is easy to gain access to a number of pastors and sermons. How can we be like the Bereans in today's world?

3. In what ways is Paul's sermon to the Areopagus different and unique from the other sermons in Acts? What elements of this sermon are the same as the other sermons in Acts?

The Third Missionary Journey: Acts 18:23–21:14

Lesson 93

After spending some time back at his home church in Antioch, Paul once again decides to visit the churches that he had planted in order to encourage them and strengthen them. As Paul is visiting the churches in Galatia, in the city of Ephesus a new leader is emerging. A man named Apollos, who is an eloquent speaker and who is well-versed in the Scriptures, comes to the city of Ephesus. In fact, even though he does not know much about Jesus, he had been instructed up until the point of John the Baptist and is able to teach accurately about the Messiah. When Paul's friends, Aquila and Priscilla, hear Apollos speaking, they take him aside and fill in the rest of the story about Jesus, and he believes in Jesus. Apollos becomes a powerful **apologist** for the gospel and is able to publicly refute those who oppose him. Apollos then crosses over to the region of Achaia, and more specifically the city of Corinth.

Shortly after Apollos leaves Ephesus, Paul arrives in Ephesus. Upon arriving there, Paul meets a group of disciples who believe in everything up until John's baptism. Most likely these people had been converted by Apollos before he had been instructed about Jesus. So even though they are believers, when Paul asks them if they have received the Holy Spirit, they have no idea what he is talking about. They had been baptized, but their baptism was John's baptism of repentance. So Paul baptizes them in the name of Jesus. When Paul lays hands on them, to confirm that they have indeed been given the Holy Spirit, they begin to speak in tongues and prophesy.

Paul then continues his typical pattern of going to the synagogues and preaching until he is forced out of the synagogues. When Paul is resisted in the synagogue, he preaches daily in the school of Tyrannus. Paul does this for two years and has an incredibly powerful ministry in Ephesus. Paul is able to perform incredible miracles so that even clothes that touch him are able to heal people. Paul becomes so popular that other people try to mimic his ministry. Paul casts out a number of demons, and some Jewish traveling exorcists try to cast out demons through Paul's authority. Yet, one day, as the seven sons of Sceva are trying to cast out a demon, the demon replies by saying that he knows Paul and Jesus, but he does not know them. Then the demon attacks them and overpowers them, and they are forced to flee naked.

As God had told Paul, he has an incredibly fruitful ministry in Ephesus, as many people repent of their sins. However, in the course of time, strong opposition arises against Paul. So many people repent of their sins and come to faith in Jesus that this tangibly harms the sale of idols in Ephesus. Ephesus was famous for having a great temple to the goddess Artemis (Diana). Because of this, the silversmiths in this city make a lot of money as they make idols. Paul is severely hurting their business, so they start a riot and accuse Paul of attacking Diana. This stirs up the whole city, and there is much confusion. Many of the people do not even know why they are there, but they join in with the crowds. Once again, because the crowds are unable to get Paul, they find someone else and try to have him punished. Eventually, the city clerk is able to quiet down the crowd and dismiss them.

So Paul leaves Ephesus and visits the churches in Macedonia and Achaia, strengthening and encouraging them. One night, while Paul is in Troas, he preaches so long that a man literally dies from his preaching. Paul preaches into the night, and a man named Eutychus,

MAP 14: PAUL'S THIRD MISSIONARY JOURNEY AND HIS VOYAGE TO ROME

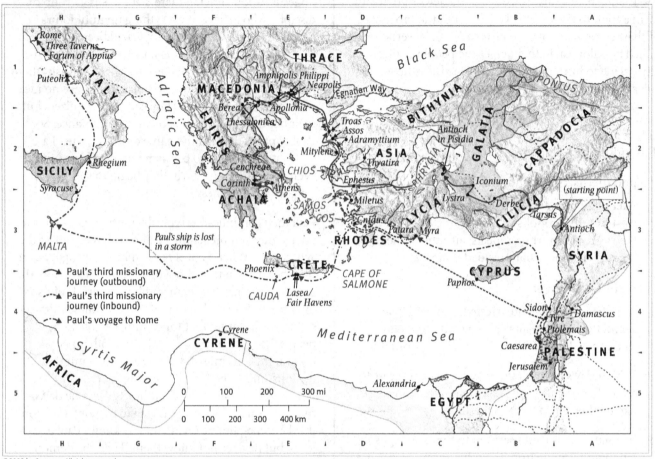

who is sitting in the window, falls asleep and falls out of the window and dies. However, Paul goes down and falls upon the man and raises the man from the dead. Subsequently, Paul wants to return to Jerusalem, so he continues his journey back there. He passes through a number of cities but does not stay long in any of them. Even though Paul avoids Ephesus because he does not want to spend much time there, he still wants to say goodbye to some of the people there, so he sends for them to meet him at Miletus.

It is clear from Paul's goodbye to the Ephesians that this church has a particular place in his heart. Paul recounts his ministry among the Ephesians and tells them that he is going to Jerusalem, where he expects to suffer. Because it is very likely that Paul will not be able to return from Jerusalem, he wants to prepare the Ephesian church for what may come in his absence. Paul exhorts the leaders of the Ephesian church to be the shepherds that God has made them over the flock. Paul warns them that false teachers will arise and lead people astray, so they must be ready. When Paul is done speaking, there are many tears shed between Paul and the Ephesians.

As Paul draws closer and closer to Jerusalem, more and more people warn Paul that Jerusalem is going to be a very dangerous place for him. At Tyre, some disciples tell Paul through the Holy Spirit not to go to Jerusalem. And at Caesarea, the prophet Agabus warns Paul that he will be bound up and delivered to the Gentiles. When the believers hear this prophecy, they beg him not to go to Jerusalem. However, Paul is ready to suffer and die for Jesus and continues to go to Jerusalem.

apologist: someone who is able to give a defense for his or her faith

Thought Question:

If God sends so many people to warn Paul about going to Jerusalem, do you think that he is disobedient to go anyway? Why or why not?

Paul in Jerusalem: Acts 21:15–23:22

Lesson 94

With all the warnings that Paul had received on his way to Jerusalem, we know that this trip is not going to be uneventful. Upon arriving in Jerusalem, Paul goes to meet with James and the leaders of the Jerusalem church. After Paul shares more stories about God's work among the Gentiles, James informs Paul that he has developed a bad reputation among the Jews. Paul's efforts to protect the Gentiles from circumcision have been twisted and misconstrued by the Jews. The rumor among the Jews in Jerusalem is that Paul had been telling the Jews that they do not need to obey the Law or practice circumcision. In order to try to pacify the Jews, James suggests that Paul should find four men who are making a vow and participate in that vow with them. Although we are not explicitly told what this vow is, it is most likely a Nazarite vow (Numbers 6).

For a short time, things go relatively smoothly while Paul is in Jerusalem. A problem, however, arises shortly before the vow would be completed. While Paul is in the temple, some Jews from Asia (where Ephesus is) recognize Paul and create quite a stir. These Jews had seen Paul traveling with Gentiles and assume that he had brought them with him into the temple. So they stir up the Jews, and a riot develops as they seize Paul and drag him out of the temple. The clamor from this event draws the attention of the commander of the Roman forces in the area. The commander has Paul placed in custody to protect him from the crowds.

When Paul asks for permission to speak to the crowds, the commander grants it. Paul speaks to the people in Hebrew, the sacred language of the Israelites. This is a very tactful decision by Paul, as he had developed a false reputation of being against the Jews and for the Gentiles. By speaking in Hebrew, he is showing them that he is a devout Jew. Paul then proceeds to recount his own conversion story. Rather than being against the Jews, Paul highlights that he was the epitome of the Jews. He was a Pharisee who was so zealous for the Law that he persecuted the Church. The people listen as Paul recounts the rest of his story up until the point when Jesus sends him to the Gentiles. The Jews cannot bear the thought of God sending someone to the Gentiles. As soon as Paul says this, the crowd goes into an uproar and cries out for Paul to die. What happens here is also very similar to what happens to Jesus. The crowds shout, "Away with such a fellow from the earth,

for he is not fit to live!" (22:22), just as the crowds had shouted, "Crucify Him! Crucify Him!" about Jesus. Also, as with Jesus, the Roman commander takes Paul back to have him whipped. However, unlike Jesus, Paul is a Roman citizen; and before he can be flogged, he informs the centurion nearby that he is a Roman citizen. According to Roman law, Roman citizens are to be given a fair trial before being punished. So Paul is spared from this flogging.

In order to get to the bottom of this whole ordeal, the Roman commander calls together the council of the Jews (Sanhedrin) and has Paul address the council. As Paul begins to speak, the high priest commands that those nearby strike him in the mouth. Paul responds by calling the high priest a whitewashed wall, very similar to Jesus' words to the religious leaders when He called them "whitewashed tombs" (Matthew 23:27). Yet Paul does not know that this was done by the order of the high priest and repents of his words, even though this was an unfair and unlawful command. Paul still respects the authority of the high priest, even if the high priest is corrupt. Paul is then able to address the council. Recognizing that half of the council is made up of Sadducees and half of Pharisees, Paul decides to set the council against itself. Having been a Pharisee himself, Paul knows the conflict that exists between these two groups. The Sadducees do not believe in the resurrection, whereas the Pharisees do. So rather than identifying himself simply as a Christian and thus unifying these two groups against him, Paul identifies himself as a Pharisee and uses the resurrection to divide the council. Paul says, "Concerning the hope and resurrection of the dead I am being judged!" (23:6).

As Paul is surely used to by now, the council comes to an uproar, and the commander is forced to take him away in order to save him once again. However, Jesus comes to Paul that night and encourages him, telling him that He has plans for Paul to bear witness concerning Jesus in Rome. It has always been Paul's ambition to spread the gospel in Rome. Shortly after this encouragement, a plot develops among the Jews to have Paul put to death. Forty Jews make a vow not to eat nor drink until they kill Paul. They are able to convince the chief priests and elders to request that Paul be brought to them so that they could ambush and kill Paul on the way. However, Paul's nephew hears of this plot and informs Paul and then the commander of the Roman army about the plot.

Thought Questions:

1. What can we learn about how to respond to authority based on Paul's response to the high priest?

2. Why do you think the Jews have such a problem with Paul being sent to the Gentiles?

Before Gentiles and Kings: Acts 23:23–26:32

Lesson 95

When Paul was commissioned by Jesus to be the apostle to the Gentiles, Jesus also told Ananias that Paul would be His witness before kings (Acts 9:13). So far we have seen Paul preach the gospel throughout the Gentile world, planting churches throughout the Roman Empire. He has stood before leaders and prominent people in various cities, but thus far he has not stood before kings. This is all about to change.

Because of the plot to kill Paul, which had been discovered by Paul's nephew, the commander of the Roman garrison decides to send Paul away from Jerusalem to the city of Caesarea on the coast. So the commander, Claudius Lysias, writes a letter to the governor of that region, Felix, explaining the situation concerning Paul.* Included in this letter is Claudius Lysias' assessment of the situation that Paul has not done anything deserving of death. Just as Pilate had concluded that Jesus had done nothing worthy of death, so also Claudius comes to the same conclusion concerning Paul.

Once Paul is transferred to Caesarea, Felix decides to hear Paul's case, but only once his accusers arrive to make their formal accusation. After five days, not only does the high priest come to Caesarea, but the Jews bring with them an "orator" to make their case. This would be roughly equivalent to a lawyer today. This shows how badly the high priest wants to get rid of Paul that he would bring along a specialist to make his case. They accuse Paul of being "a plague, a creator of dissension among all the Jews," and they accuse him of trying "to profane the temple" (24:5–6). Paul then is given the opportunity to make his defense. Paul argues that he had never done anything to incite the Jews; and in fact, he had gone quietly to Jerusalem to worship there according to the Law. While in the temple, Paul did not argue with anyone nor did he argue in the synagogues

in Jerusalem. Paul directly challenges their accusations, asserting that they have no proof for their accusations. Yet, even in his defense, Paul uses the opportunity to speak about the gospel. Paul argues that the only accusation that they can legitimately make against him is that he has publicly spoken about Jesus' resurrection.

Upon hearing both sides, Felix adjourns the proceedings and says that he will make his judgment when Lysias comes down. Until Felix makes his decision, he has Paul kept in custody, but with a considerable amount of freedom, including the freedom to have visitors. We are told that Felix has a "more accurate knowledge of the Way" (24:22), and so he comes to Paul with his wife Drusilla to hear more from him. However, even though Felix is the governor of that region and has a lot of authority, Paul understands that he is just a man and convicts him concerning "righteousness, self-control, and the judgment to come" (24:25). Paul does not water down the gospel, even before rulers. Yet this conviction scares Felix, so he sends Paul away until a more "convenient time." Even though Felix does not like this conviction, for over two years Felix continues to meet with Paul, hoping that Paul would try to bribe him for his freedom.

After two years, Porcius Festus succeeds Felix as the governor of that region. When Festus goes to Jerusalem, the high priest and the leaders of the Jews ask him to have Paul sent to Jerusalem so that the Jews could ambush and kill Paul. Once again, Festus orders that Paul stand trial before his accusers, and many of the Jews come to Caesarea to accuse Paul. Once again, Paul gives his same defense. Yet this time, Festus asks Paul if he would be willing to go to Jerusalem to face his accusers there. Paul is an intelligent man, however, and he knows what the Jews in Jerusalem have in mind. Paul knows that he would not have a fair trial among the Jews, so instead he appeals to Caesar to have his trial before the Romans. One of the privileges that Roman citizens have is that they have the right to have their case seen before Caesar himself. So rather than being sent to Jerusalem, Paul is sent to Rome.

Around the time of Paul's appeal to Caesar, King Herod Agrippa comes to Caesarea. This Herod is a descendant of the same Herod who had killed the Hebrew male babies at the time of Jesus' birth. Festus explains the whole situation with Paul to King Agrippa and asks him to hear his case. After hearing Paul's case, Festus has concluded that Paul is innocent; but because Paul had appealed to Caesar, he has a right to have his case heard before Caesar. Yet, because his case is such an easy case to judge, Festus is anxious about sending Paul

---

* The letter Claudius Lysias wrote is humorous. In 23:27, he says that he resuced Paul because Paul is a Roman citizen. In Actuality, he initially thought that Paul was an Egyptian (21:38).

to Caesar without a formal accusation. So an assembly is called together, and Paul is given an opportunity to speak to King Agrippa.

As Paul has now done on many occasions, he recalls his former manner of life before becoming a Christian and explains his conversion on the road to Damascus. Once again, Paul highlights the resurrection and asks, "Why should it be thought incredible by you that God raises the dead?" (26:8). Paul explains to the assembly that God had commissioned him to the Gentiles, "To open their eyes, in order to turn them from darkness to light, and from the power of Satan to God, that they may receive forgiveness of sins and an inheritance among those who are sanctified by faith in Me" (26:18). Also, as Paul has consistently done with his defense, he calls all who listen to repent of their sins and turn to God. As Paul directly shares the gospel with Agrippa and speaks about the resurrection of Jesus, Festus finally responds. He accuses Paul of being crazy because of his great learning. Just as Felix before, when Paul gets personal with the gospel and calls for a response, Festus tries to change the subject. Yet Paul responds by arguing that "I am not mad, most noble Festus, but speak the words of truth and reason" (26:25). Then Paul directly appeals to Agrippa and calls for him to believe. Agrippa is amazed that Paul is even trying to convert him so quickly. So Paul responds, telling him that he wishes that everyone could have what he has, with the exception of his chains. However, when he is confronted with the gospel, Agrippa and all those who are with him get up and leave, concluding that Paul has done nothing wrong. Ironically, Paul could have been set free if he had not appealed to Caesar, but he will get his trial. So it will be on to Rome for Paul.

Thought Question:

Think about how these people have responded to the gospel. What kinds of responses have you gotten when you share the gospel? Do you ever find that people get uncomfortable and make excuses when confronted with the gospel?

To Rome: Acts 27–28

Lesson 96

The book of Acts began with Jesus' commission to His disciples, telling them that they would be His witnesses in Jerusalem, Judea, Samaria, and the ends of the earth. We have seen the gospel spread throughout Jerusalem and into the surrounding regions of Judea and Samaria. Through Paul's ministry and the faithful witness of those who dispersed from Paul's original persecutions, we have seen the gospel spread throughout the Roman Empire. Yet Paul's ambition for quite some time has been to bring the gospel to the capital city itself and, if possible, to Caesar himself. In the final two chapters of Acts, Paul will get his opportunity to bring the gospel to Rome.

Because Paul had appealed to Caesar rather than facing an unfair trial before the Jews in Jerusalem, it is determined that he should travel to Rome. However, remember that the technology during Paul's day was not as advanced as our technology today. He could not just hop on a plane and arrive hundreds of miles away in mere hours. In Paul's day, there were two primary means of transportation—by land (on foot or donkey) or by boat. Even though the Romans had done a lot of work to make the roadways and seaways safe, there was always the danger of nature. It is determined that Paul's journey to Rome would be by boat rather than land, and so he begins what would be a perilous journey.

Luke's account of Paul's journey contains a number of locations and details that we are not going to go into detail about here. To see the path of Paul's journey, see the map on page 118. Because Paul is coming to Rome as a prisoner, he travels in a ship with other prisoners. This journey, under good conditions, would take months. Unlike ships today, with powerful engines, the ships in Paul's day move primarily by wind power. Sadly for Paul and the other passengers on this ship, the winds are not going to agree with them on this trip.

This journey is perilous practically from the very beginning. At some points along the journey, the winds beat against the ship, slowing them down drastically. At other points, the winds pick up and drag the ship way off course. In fact, early on in this journey, Paul warns the crew that he "perceive[s] that this voyage will end with disaster and much loss" (27:10). Nevertheless, the captain of the ship ignores Paul's warning and continues the journey. Another problem that this ship is about to face is that the winter is coming soon. They need to get to a suitable place to dock for the winter until the sea conditions allow for further travel. Yet the captain decides to push this journey on, even though winter is coming soon.

As this journey continues, a strong storm strikes the ship, known as a "Euroclydon" (27:14) or a *Gregale* (a Mediterranean, northeasterly wind). The powerful winds from this storm toss the ship to and fro. Even worse, this storm lasts two weeks. Because of the power of this storm, much of the cargo of the ship is thrown overboard; as a result, food has to be rationed by the crew and passengers. After about two weeks, Paul addresses the people and tells them that they should have listened to him when he warned them. However, God had sent an angel to him telling him that everyone's lives will be spared; only the ship will be lost. Finally, after two weeks, it becomes evident that the boat is about to make landfall. So Paul gets everyone to eat some food to prepare for coming on land. At first, the sailors let down a boat in order to row to land, but Paul warns the soldiers that the only way they will survive this ordeal is if the sailors stay on the boat, so the soldiers cut the ropes. At another point, the soldiers plot to kill the prisoners, lest they escape. Yet the centurion prevents them from doing this because he wants to save Paul. Finally, the ship strikes land and is destroyed, but all the passengers are able to make it to land safely.

The island into which the ship crashes is the island of Malta. The natives of that land show kindness to their new guests and provide for their needs. However, while Paul is warming himself by the fire, he is bitten on the hand by a viper. Normally, the poison from the viper would kill a person quickly or make him very sick. Yet Paul is able to shake the snake off his hand without any effect from the bite. If Jesus had in fact said the words in Mark 16:18 that believers would pick up snakes or drink poison without being harmed, this would be the fulfillment of these words. However, as a side note, there are some Christians that tempt God by playing with snakes, claiming this passage for their protection. This is not a call for foolishness; this is a miracle as God protects Paul. When the natives see that Paul is not harmed, they assume that he is a god.

While on this island, Paul heals many of the inhabitants, including the father of the leading citizen of that island, Publius (28:8). Paul and the rest of the passengers stay the winter on this island; and three months later, they set sail for Rome. They eventually do arrive in Rome, and while the other prisoners are taken to the captain of the guard, Paul is given his own place and is allowed to receive visitors. Upon arriving in Rome, Paul calls together the leaders of the Jews in order to let them know about his situation. Paul probably expects them to want to kill him, considering that the Jews everywhere else in the Roman Empire seem to want Paul dead. Paul also assumes that the Jews in Jerusalem had written to Rome about Paul. Yet no such correspondence had been received, and the Jews in Rome do not know much about Paul. These Jews had heard about the Christian movement and are interested to hear more. So Paul speaks to them on more occasions. However, once Paul quotes the passage in Isaiah 6:9–10 that speaks of the hardened hearts of the Jews and the

acceptance of Gentiles into the kingdom of God, the Jews leave him, disputing among themselves. Once again, the Jews cannot bear the thought of Gentiles being included as God's people.

Paul ends up spending at least two years under house arrest in Rome. However, just because Paul is under house arrest does not mean that his mission and ministry are over. Paul spends these two years sharing the gospel and encouraging the believers in the churches that he had planted. In fact, some of the very letters that we have in the New Testament are written while Paul is under house arrest in Rome. We will learn from the book of Philippians later that even members of Caesar's household become believers through Paul's preaching (Philippians 4:22). Jesus' promise has come to fruition; not only has Paul stood before kings and Gentiles, but the gospel has spread to the ends of the earth.

Thought Question:

Paul's journey to Rome is a perilous journey. What kind of encouragement or lessons can you learn about your future ministry from Paul's experience here?

Introduction to the Epistles
Lesson 97

One of the questions that we should always ask when seeking to interpret and understand a Bible passage is, "What kind of genre is this?" The genre determines how we should read a passage. For example, we would not read or interpret poetry in the same way that we would interpret narrative history. Thus far in our study of the New Testament, we have encountered two main types of genre—gospel and narrative. We have also encountered some small bits of prophecy and some sermons. To some degree, the rest of the New Testament is going to fit the category of epistle. Simply put, an **epistle** is another name for a letter. For the New Testament, these epistles are authoritative letters written from one of the apostles to an individual, a local church, or a group of churches.

Unlike our letters or e-mails today, these letters from the apostles were instantly understood as authoritative and were placed on par with the Scriptures. Remember that at the time of these letters, the New Testament had not been put together. Christians utilized the Old Testament and the words of the apostles in order to guide their lives and doctrine. The letters that comprise the New Testament are not just any letters from the

Book	Author	Date	Recipients	Place of Writing
James	James	40–45	Jewish Christians in or near Palestine	Jerusalem?
Galatians	Paul	48	South Galatian churches	Syrian Antioch
1 Thessalonians	Paul	49–51	Church in Thessalonica	Corinth
2 Thessalonians	Paul	49–51	Church in Thessalonica	Corinth
1 Corinthians	Paul	53–55	Church in Corinth	Ephesus
2 Corinthians	Paul	55–56	Church in Corinth	Macedonia
Romans	Paul	57	Church in Rome	Corinth
Philippians	Paul	62	Church in Philippi	Rome
Colossians	Paul	62	Church in Colossae	Rome
Philemon	Paul	62	Philemon	Rome
Ephesians	Paul	62	Churches in Asia Minor (circular letter?)	Rome
1 Timothy	Paul	62–64	Timothy	Macedonia?
Titus	Paul	62–64	Titus	Nicopolis
1 Peter	Peter	62–63	Churches in Roman provinces in Asia Minor	Rome
2 Peter	Peter	64–67	Churches in Roman provinces in Asia Minor?	Rome
2 Timothy	Paul	64–67	Timothy	Rome
Jude	Jude	Mid–60s	Jewish Christians in Egypt? Asia Minor? Antioch?	Unknown
Hebrews	Unknown	60–70	Jewish Christians in Rome or in or near Palestine	Unknown
1 John	John	85–95	Churches near Ephesus?	Ephesus
2 John	John	85–95	Church or churches near Ephesus	Ephesus
3 John	John	85–95	Gaius	Ephesus

apostles; there is an authority behind the words of these epistles as they give guidance to the churches.

As with all of the books of the Bible, it is important to do some background work as part of the study of the epistles. A majority of the epistles are written within a twenty-year span of time, with the possible exception of the book of Revelation (which many scholars believe was written about thirty years after the other epistles). The earliest epistles are written within fifteen years of Jesus' death and resurrection. Some of the major events that occur during the time of these epistles include: the Jerusalem Council from Acts 15, the expulsion of Jews from Rome under Claudius, and the persecutions of Christians under Emperor Nero.

There are a number of different authors for the epistles. A majority of the epistles are written by the apostle Paul. In fact, the New Testament is organized in such a way that all of Paul's epistles, also known as the **Pauline Epistles**, are lumped together first (Romans–Philemon). Following Paul's epistles, the remaining epistles are called the **General Epistles**. Unlike many of Paul's letters, these General Epistles are not written to specific churches but were intended to be spread throughout all the churches. However, this does not mean that Paul's letters were not spread; even though many of Paul's letters are very specific to a local church, there is evidence that these letters were also distributed among the churches. The other authors for the epistles are James (the half-brother of Jesus), Peter, John, and Jude (the half-brother of Jesus). Nobody knows for sure who the author of Hebrews is, and because the author of Hebrews is unknown, there was some dispute among the early churches as to whether or not it should be considered Scripture. Nevertheless, a basic reading of Hebrews makes it abundantly clear that this epistle belongs as part of Scripture.

There are three types of audiences for the epistles. As mentioned before, many of Paul's epistles are written to *specific churches* that meet in a particular town. Some examples of this kind of audience include: Romans, 1 and 2 Corinthians, 1 and 2 Thessalonians, Galatians,

Ephesians, Philippians, and Colossians. Some of Paul's letters are not written to specific churches but rather to *specific people*. These include 1 and 2 Timothy, Titus, and Philemon. The rest of the epistles are written to *general audiences* and include exhortations and encouragements that are far broader in scope.

When reading the epistles, one of the interpretive issues we face today is how to contextualize into today's world some of the specific commands given to first century churches. For example, in 1 Corinthians 11, Paul commands women to worship with their heads covered. This command is given because of some specific issues of disrespect and disorder within the church of Corinth. When applying this passage for today, we have to ask ourselves whether or not this command is to be applied directly into today's context or whether or not there is a broader principle that we are to apply for today. For those who say that women do not need to have their heads covered today, the principle from this passage that they apply is the broader concept of not worshiping in a way that is disruptive or disrespectful of others or of authority. While we believe that all Scripture is authoritative and "profitable for doctrine, for reproof, for correction, for instruction in righteousness …" (2 Timothy 3:16), we understand that we need the wisdom from the Holy Spirit to know how to apply these Scriptures for today.

> **epistle:** a letter from one of the apostles; epistles make up much of the New Testament
>
> **Pauline Epistles:** the epistles written by Paul
>
> **General Epistles:** all of the epistles from Hebrews-Revelation that are written to more general audiences

Introduction to Paul's Epistles

Lesson 98

Paul plays an interesting and unique role in the development of the Church. Unlike the twelve apostles, Paul was not one of Jesus' disciples when He lived on earth; the first resurrection appearance of Jesus that Paul witnesses is on the road to Damascus after Jesus had ascended into heaven. Paul is explicitly chosen to be the apostle to the Gentiles; and, as such, the Christianity that Paul helps develop looks very different from the Jewish Christianity of the other apostles. During his life, Paul is often in conflict, not only with those outside the Church, but also with those in the Church who have a difficult time with Gentile Christianity. It is no wonder, then, that Paul spends so much time

and space in his epistles defending his own authority. Moreover, this is the first of the common themes that run throughout many of Paul's epistles. There are large sections of 1 Corinthians, 2 Corinthians, and Galatians in which *Paul defends his own authority as an apostle.*

The most prominent theme that runs throughout Paul's letters is *the doctrine of* **justification by faith** *alone*. This doctrine has often been misunderstood by the Christian community throughout the centuries. Simply put, this doctrine states that the only way that we can be made right with God is through faith, or belief, in Jesus Christ. There is no amount of good deeds or works that we can do in order to be good enough to be saved. Yet, in order to fully understand this doctrine, it is critical that we remember the situation in which Paul finds himself as the apostle to the Gentiles. As the apostle to the Gentiles, Paul is often in conflict with the Jewish believers. Many of the Jewish believers argue that Gentiles need to be circumcised and obey the Law of Moses in order to be saved. From our study of Acts, we saw that the decision of the Jerusalem Council is that Gentiles do not need to become Jewish or follow the Law of Moses in order to be saved. When Paul argues that works cannot save us and that it is only by faith that we are saved, it is in response to the Jews who are arguing that it is necessary to observe the Jewish customs from the Law of Moses. This does not mean, as many have misinterpreted it as saying, that Christians do not have to do good works or obey God.

Another theme that appears throughout Paul's letters is what has become known as the **Pauline Triad**. There are a number of places where *the triad of virtues of faith, hope, and love* show up in Paul's letters. Perhaps most famous is in 1 Corinthians 13. After Paul's excursus on the nature of love, Paul concludes: "And now abide faith, hope, love, these three; but the greatest of these is love" (verse 13). *Faith*, to Paul, is an enduring trust and firm conviction that something is true; and this is the means by which we receive the free gift of salvation. *Hope* is more than a wish, as we would use the word today, but rather it is an assurance of something that has not come yet. *Love* is the key virtue that binds up all the other virtues together.

As a church planter, Paul is very interested in the development of godly leaders who can protect the church from false doctrine and from temptations. Three of Paul's letters are known as the **Pastoral Epistles**. These letters are not written to churches in general, but rather to specific leaders of churches whom Paul had been mentoring. In these letters, Paul exhorts the pastors of these churches to protect sound doctrine and to appoint godly men who can help lead these churches. The books of 1 Timothy, 2 Timothy, and Titus are known as the Pastoral Epistles.

Finally, because of the various attacks on Christianity and on the gospel, Paul puts a lot of effort in his letters *to clearly explain the gospel and to guard that gospel*. Even though the letter to the Romans is written to deal with a specific issue with the church in Rome, many people see the book of Romans as Paul's magnum opus on the gospel. Paul clearly explains, for eleven chapters, exactly what the gospel is and how we can be saved through it. The epistle to the Galatians is written by Paul to correct the false gospel that the believers in that region had begun to believe. Colossians is written by Paul to protect the church in Colossae from some of the false teachers who had been spreading a false gospel. Paul even exhorts Timothy to keep "That good thing which was committed to you" (2 Timothy 1:14). In other words, Timothy is to protect the gospel.

> **justification by faith:** the doctrine that states that the only way that we can be made right with God is through faith in Jesus, not by our own works

> **Pauline Triad:** faith, hope, and love

> **Pastoral Epistles:** 1 and 2 Timothy and Titus; called pastoral because they are letters to pastors of local churches and are written to help them lead their churches

Introduction to Romans: Romans 1

Lesson 99

As mentioned in the last lesson, the epistle to the Romans has developed the reputation of being Paul's magnum opus on the gospel. This masterful work clearly develops the gospel and its implications for everyday life. However, Paul does not write this letter simply to explain the gospel; he has another motive for this letter. It is pretty evident that Paul had not visited Rome yet by the time of this letter, and part of the purpose of this letter is to prepare the church in Rome for his coming visit. As we have seen in the book of Acts, one of the major issues that the early Church faced was the conflict and confusion between the Jewish Christians and Gentile Christians. Apparently, this conflict plagues the church in Rome, which contains both Gentile and Jewish Christians, who do not get along with each other. Paul writes this letter and expounds the gospel so that rather than division, there could be unity between the Jewish and Gentile believ-

ers in Rome. Because of this, much of the epistle to the Romans deals with the relationship between God's plan for Israel and God's plan for the Church.

Paul begins this epistle in the manner that he begins most of his epistles, with a customary greeting. He identifies himself as "a bondservant of Jesus Christ, called to be an apostle, separated to the gospel of God" (verse 1). Paul recognizes that he is bound to Jesus Christ. Paul also identifies himself as one who has been called to be an apostle. As mentioned in the last lesson, because Paul was not one of the twelve apostles, he needs to remind people that he had received a special calling to be an apostle by Jesus Himself. Paul next describes Jesus in a way that would connect with both the Jews and the Gentiles. To the Jews, Jesus is characterized as the Messianic seed of David; to the Gentiles, Jesus is described as the powerful Son of God. The evidence of both of these things is that Jesus has risen from the dead. Moreover, just as Jesus had called Paul to be an apostle, He calls all believers to Himself to be "saints" or holy ones. Everyone who is a believer in Jesus Christ is called a "saint," according to Paul. Paul then combines the customary Jewish and the customary Gentile greeting. When Jewish people would greet one another, they would say "Shalom," or "peace to you." When Gentiles would greet one another, they would say "grace to you" (verse 7). Both peace and grace are incredibly important theological terms, and Paul wishes both upon his hearers.

The fact that Paul has not yet visited Rome is evident in verses 8–15. Paul has been praying diligently for the believers in Rome for quite some time and has desired for a while to visit them. Paul's desire has been to strengthen the believers and to "impart to you some spiritual gift" (verse 11). On multiple occasions, Paul had made plans to come to Rome but had been hindered from doing so. Because Paul has been unable to strengthen this church in person, he writes this letter to them.

Verses 16 and 17 can be seen as the summary of the entire book of Romans, and they begin the content portion of this letter. Paul defines the gospel here as "the power of God to salvation for everyone who believes." Paul is so concerned with the gospel because it is only the message of the gospel wherein a person can receive salvation. However, this salvation is "for the Jew first and also for the Greek." This is not an issue of favoritism; but because the Jews were first God's people, they have been given the opportunity to receive the gospel first. Through their rejection of the gospel, the gospel has now come to the Gentiles. This fits with

Paul's plan of evangelism, as he consistently first went to the Jews until they rejected the gospel and then went to the Gentiles. In the gospel, a righteousness is revealed, but it is not our righteousness. Rather, in the gospel "the righteousness of God is revealed" (verse 17). This is such a critical idea for the gospel. Our own righteousness can never save us; only the righteousness of God can save us. And this righteousness is revealed "from faith to faith." The means of obtaining God's righteousness is through faith in Jesus Christ.

For the next eleven chapters, Paul expounds on the gospel. He begins explaining the gospel by revealing the universal condition of mankind. The good news of the gospel begins with the bad news—God is angry with our sin. God's wrath is revealed because of the unrighteousness of men. Yet what about those who claim ignorance, that they did not know any better because they had never heard about God? Paul argues that all men have an innate knowledge of God but suppress the truth because of their unrighteousness. In other words, everyone knows that there is a God, but because they want to continue to sin and pursue unrighteousness, they push that truth away.

However, if a person has never read the Bible, how can he be responsible to a God that he has never known? Paul answers that a person does not need to have the Bible to know that there is a God. The mere fact that there is a creation is enough evidence to show us that there is a Creator. Even though we cannot see God's "invisible attributes," we can see the visible creation; as a result, Paul says that "they are without excuse" (verse 20). Sadly, in humanity's effort to suppress their clear knowledge of God, their very way of thinking has become corrupted. By rejecting the truth, humans can no longer think correctly.

We often think about the punishments for sin. However, what Paul argues for the rest of chapter 1 is that sometimes the consequence of sin is more sin. In other words, when we are persistent in our sin, God will give us over to that sin so that we become enslaved to it. Looking at history, Paul argues that, rather than worshiping the God that was so clear to humans, they made their own idols to worship instead.

Because humanity chose to worship the creation rather than the Creator, God "gave them up to uncleanness, in the lusts of their hearts, to dishonor their bodies among themselves" (verse 24) and "God gave them up to vile passions"(verse 26). Paul goes on to describe that these "vile passions" are women exchanging what is natural for what is unnatural and men lusting after one

another. This is one of the clearest passages in the New Testament regarding the sinfulness of homosexuality. Paul very clearly says that these relationships are not part of God's design for humanity. However, homosexuality is not the only sin mentioned here as Paul gives a list of many kinds of sins that humanity commits. Interestingly, in the midst of such sins as "murder" and "haters of God," Paul places "disobedient to parents" (verse 30). While we may think of our disobedience to our parents as a small matter, to God it is a big deal. Sadly, even though humanity knows that they will have to give an account someday for their actions, they still practice these sins and approve of others who practice them. This is why God's wrath is being revealed against humanity.

Thought Questions:

1. In light of this passage, what do you think will happen to those people in remote parts of the world who have not yet heard the gospel?

2. Based on this passage, do you think it is possible for a person to be a genuine atheist? Why or why not?

3. If people suppress the knowledge of God because of their sin, how might this affect the way you speak to those who reject God?

Do Not Judge: Romans 2
Lesson 100

In chapter 1, Paul has established the concept of universal guilt. Whether a person has read the Scriptures or not, every human being has knowledge of God and is going to have to give an account to Him someday. In light of this, Paul begins chapter 2 by arguing that nobody has the right to pass judgment on someone else. In this case, to judge does not mean to make a judgment call, but to consider oneself higher or better than someone else. It is absurd for us to look down upon someone else when we do the exact same things. There is no reason to boast in our own deeds because all of us are sinners.

Our own tendency to judge is even more egregious in contrast to God's goodness, patience, and kindness toward us. If anyone has the right to judge correctly, it is God. Yet Paul reminds us that it is "the goodness of God" (verse 4) that leads us to repentance. So for those in the church in Rome who persist in their judgmental attitude toward others, they are the ones who are "treasuring up for yourself wrath in the day of wrath" (verse

5). In light of the argument that Paul will make later on in this chapter, it is probably the Jews in the church of Rome who are judging the Gentile Christians.

Once again, Paul puts both Jews and Gentiles on equal footing when he argues that anyone who seeks to do what is right will find eternal life, but those who are "self-seeking and do not obey the truth" will only find wrath (verse 8). This applies first to the Jew, because they have the Law and have more responsibility, and then to the Greek. Both Jew and Gentile will have to give an account of their deeds and will face judgment. The difference between the Jews and the Gentiles is that the Jews have been given the Law, wherein God has made clear what He expects. However, Paul puts both Jew and Gentile on equal footing once again by arguing that it is not a matter of having the Law that makes a person right, but it is a matter of doing what is right. Even though the Gentiles do not have the Law, they do have a conscience and can do the right thing. Even though the Jews have the Law, this does not mean that they will obey it. At the end of the day, what matters is whether or not we do the right thing.

Paul then directly addresses the Jews in the church in Rome. He points out the things about which they are prone to boast, that they "rest on the law," "make [their] boast in God," "know His will, and approve the things that are excellent," that they "are a guide to the blind, a light to those who are in darkness …" (verses 17–19). In other words, the Jews take pride in the fact that they have been given special revelation by God and that they know what God approves and what He rejects. Nevertheless, Paul argues that all this knowledge ought to result in a more righteous and obedient life; yet, even with all this knowledge, they continue to disobey and do the very things that they condemn. Paul then quotes Isaiah 52:5 to argue that these Jews who take pride in being God's people are causing the Gentiles to blaspheme God because of their hypocrisy (verse 24).

We have already seen the issue of circumcision and how it had the potential to divide the early Church. Paul argues that a person who is circumcised but disobeys the Law is worse off than the uncircumcised Gentile who is living a more righteous life. It is not the outward ritual of circumcision or the privilege of having the Law that is important, but the issues of the heart are what are important. The important circumcision is the circumcision of the heart, or a heart that is changed by the gospel and one that leads to an obedient life. Significantly, Paul also argues that it is not circumcision that makes a person a Jew, but it is a heart of obedience that makes a person a true Jew. What is important is the spirit of the Law, not the letter.

Thought Questions:

1. What are some practical things you can do to guard yourself from having a judgmental spirit?

2. If having the Law is not what is important, what would be the advantage of being Jewish then?

The Gospel: Romans 3
Lesson 101

Paul has just spent two chapters leveling the playing field between the Jews and the Gentiles. In chapter 1, Paul argues that nobody has an excuse for disobeying God. God is angry about our sin, and He is going to give all people what they deserve. Paul argues that it is mankind's own desire for sin that has led to their rejection of God, and it is their rejection of God that has led to even more sin in humans. In chapter 2, Paul argues that the Jew has no right to boast over the Gentile, even though the Jews have been given the Law. Having the Law and circumcision does not make anyone any more righteous or better than anyone else; rather, it is the obedience to the Law that is truly important.

However, if having the Law does not make the Jew better than the Gentile, what is the advantage of being a Jew? This is the precise question with which Paul begins chapter 3. Throughout the epistle to the Romans, one of the stylistic things that Paul does is to ask rhetorical questions and then to answer them. Here, Paul argues that, even though having the Law does not make a person more righteous, it is still an incredible privilege for God to have revealed Himself to the Jews. Sadly, though, most of the Jews have failed to live up to the Law that God has given. Does this mean that God's plan has somehow failed? Paul argues that the failure of the Jews reveals the righteousness of God, even more by contrast, so that God is still glorified. Yet, if God is glorified by disobedience, why does He still get angry when we are disobedient? Paul argues that this is an absurd argument that has an obvious answer. It is inherently better to do good than to do evil. Even though God receives glory through our disobedience, God still has the right to be angry when we violate His commands.

Verses 10–18 contain a series of quotes from throughout the Old Testament that have a common theme, the idea of **total depravity**. The doctrine of total depravity states that the whole person has been corrupted by the sinful nature, including the mind and the will of man. This does not mean that we are as sinful as we can possibly be; but it does mean that, apart from God's intervention, we are utterly lost in our own sinful state. Just as Paul had argued in chapter 1, he now quotes a number of verses that very clearly state that no one is righteous before God. Every single human being (with the exception of Jesus) is unrighteous because of sin. Moreover, not only is every single human being unrighteous; but also, on our own, no human being would even seek out God. This places every single human being, whether Jew or Gentile, in a position of guilt before God. Consequently, this puts every human in the condition where he or she needs to be saved.

If every single human being is totally corrupted by his or her own sinful nature, what is the point of having the Law? If no human being will meet the standards of the Law, why does God give the Law in the first place? Paul argues that one of the main purposes of the Law is not to make one righteous, but to make a person realize just how unrighteous he truly is.

The next paragraph in Romans 3 is probably the most theologically dense paragraph in all of Scripture. There are a number of significant theological words in this paragraph; and when we unpack this paragraph, we will have a much greater understanding of the gospel. Just as Paul had said earlier in chapter 1, God's righteousness has now been revealed. However, how has God's righteousness been revealed, and why has God now revealed it? Paul tells us that God's righteousness has been revealed apart from the Law. It is not through the Law, but rather through the completely obedient life of Jesus Christ that God's righteousness has been revealed. Moreover, God reveals that righteousness through Jesus so that we can receive that righteousness by faith in Jesus Christ. When we place our faith and trust in Jesus alone, we do not magically become righteous enough to get into heaven; rather, Jesus' righteousness is counted for us so that through His righteousness we can be saved.

Verse 23 is one of those verses that are particularly helpful to remember when sharing the gospel. What Paul has already been arguing, he now says clearly in this verse, namely that every single human being has sinned and has fallen short of God's standard. Unless a person first realizes that he has fallen short of God's standards, he or she will have no desire for Jesus. This is where the Law becomes extremely helpful. When we examine ourselves according to the standards of God's Law, we see just how far short of God's standards we fall. This is the bad news of the gospel.

Thankfully, however, the gospel does not end with the bad news. In verse 24, we learn that we are justified freely by His grace. There are two theologically significant words in this clause. The word **justify** means "to declare another person righteous." *Justification* is a legal term referring to the decision by the judge to declare a person innocent. The second significant theological word in this clause is the word **grace**. *Grace* simply means "unmerited favor or a free gift" and that we are receiving something good that we do not deserve. Putting these two words together, Paul argues that, even though we are all guilty, for those who place their faith in Jesus, God freely declares them righteous as they receive Jesus' righteousness. We receive this gift through the **redemption** that is in Christ Jesus. The term *redemption* is a term associated with slavery. If a person owed a large sum of money, he or she could sell himself or herself as a slave to pay off that debt. If a person redeems that slave, it means that this person pays off the remaining debt of that slave so that the slave could go free. Thus, God declares those who place their faith in Jesus to be righteous freely because Jesus has paid the price to set them free.

This all works legally, but there is another issue with which we have to deal. God is a holy God who hates sin; and when we sin, we build up wrath. The justice of God demands that a punishment be given for sins. This is where the word **propitiation** comes in. Paul tells us that God sent forth Jesus "as a propitiation by His blood" (verse 25). Jesus' obedient life would have been enough to reveal God's righteousness, but His death was necessary to appease God's wrath against sin. Jesus took upon Himself the full wrath of God, so that we who place our faith in Him would not have to face that wrath. For those who have not placed their faith in Jesus, that wrath still awaits them. Through this, God can be a righteous, good Judge who receives the payment of sin and also the One who makes us righteous through Jesus.

In light of all this, we see that the gospel is in no way about our goodness or righteousness, but entirely about the kindness and generosity of God and the faithfulness of Jesus. We have no room to boast. Moreover, this is what ultimately puts both the Jew and the Gentile on equal footing before God. Jesus did not only die for the Jew, but also for the Gentile, and both are saved in the exact same manner. It is not the Law that saves a person; rather, it is faith in Jesus Christ that saves a person. Does this mean that the Law is useless now that we are saved through faith in Jesus? Paul argues quite to the contrary. Now that we are saved by faith, we are more equipped to establish the Law in our lives.

total depravity: a doctrine that states that, because of sin, the whole person has been corrupted; and as a result, we are incapable of saving ourselves

justify: to declare another person to be righteous

grace: unmerited favor or a free gift

redemption: the payment that one person makes in order to buy back a slave and set him free

propitiation: the doctrine that states that Jesus took upon Himself the wrath of God in order to appease God's wrath and save us at the same time

Thought Questions:

1. If it is true that nobody seeks out God, then how can somebody choose to believe in Jesus?

2. How can it be considered just for God to condemn an innocent man (Jesus) while allowing guilty people (Christians) to be set free? (Hint: Jesus' willingness to die is significant.)

3. If we are saved by faith alone, is it important to still live a righteous life? Why or why not?

Abraham and Adam: Romans 4–5

Lesson 102

Even though there are many people in the Old Testament who are significant, two of the most significant people in the minds of most Jews in Paul's time were Abraham and Moses. We have already seen that the Jews revere Moses because he is the one who gave them the Law. However, Abraham was also revered because he was the father of the Jewish nation. Up until Abraham, God had worked with humanity as a whole; but starting with Abraham, God chose to work with one family that would eventually become the nation of Israel. A Jewish person would take great pride in being a descendant of Abraham; after all, God made some incredible promises to Abraham and his descendants. Also, Abraham is the one to whom God gave the covenant of circumcision, which we have already seen is extremely important for Jews.

In light of this, Paul argues in chapter 4 that even Abraham was a man who found salvation by faith. The key verse on which Paul focuses concerning Abraham in this chapter is verse 3, "Abraham believed God, and it was accounted to him for righteousness" (cf. Genesis 15:6). Abraham could not have been made righteous through

the Law because it had not been given. Yet, in this verse, we see that God declares Abraham righteous because he believed in the promises of God. In fact, Abraham's entire story is an illustration of his faith. By faith Abraham leaves the home of his family and goes to a place that God says would be his. By faith Abraham believes that God will give him a son, even though he was almost 100 years old. By faith Abraham also prepares to offer up his beloved son, trusting that God could even raise this son from the dead (Hebrews 11:8–19). Abraham is an amazing example of faith. Abraham is not declared righteous because he had done enough good deeds, but God credits Abraham with righteousness because of his faith.

Also significant for Paul's overall argument in Romans is that Abraham had already been declared righteous before he was circumcised. If it is necessary for a person to be circumcised in order to be righteous, as the Jews are claiming, then even Abraham could not be righteous. Paul argues that both the Jews and Gentiles can claim to have Abraham as their ancestor, for the uncircumcised Gentile can exercise the same faith that Abraham had exercised and, as such, would be a descendant of Abraham. In the same manner, Abraham is the ancestor of the circumcised Jews who also exercise his same faith. Once again, both Jews and Gentiles are placed on equal footing as both are saved by faith alone, not by works.

Having established that salvation is by grace alone, through faith alone, Paul begins to draw out some of the implications of that salvation in chapter 5. Once we have been declared righteous by faith in Jesus Christ, we now have "peace with God" (verse 1). Whereas God's wrath was upon us before we were justified, now we are at peace with God; our hostility and rebellion toward God has ceased. This is the relational benefit of the gospel. Along with that peace, we also have a sure hope. We know that we have eternal blessings awaiting us, even though we will face trials and tribulations in this life. Moreover, along with that hope, we know that God loves us as the Holy Spirit testifies in our hearts. Here we have all three of the Pauline Triad of virtues—faith, hope, and love.

What is extraordinary about this gospel is that God offers us salvation while we are still ungodly. God does not demand that we get our lives together before applying Christ's righteousness to us. Romans 5:8, another excellent verse to memorize for sharing the gospel, says this excellently, "But God demonstrates His own love toward us, in that while we were still sinners, Christ died for us." Even though we are saved while we are still ungodly, we can also rest assured that we no longer have to face the wrath of God. Through Jesus, we now have **reconciliation** with God. To be *reconciled* means to be brought back into a peaceful relationship after two sides are at odds with one another.

Another way to understand the gospel is through the concept of **headship**. For the rest of chapter 5, Paul makes a series of comparisons between the first man, Adam, and Jesus. Some people wonder how it can be fair for Jesus' righteousness to apply to us even though we are not righteous on our own. This is where the concept of headship comes in. Even though Adam sinned in the garden of Eden, every single human being who has ever lived has been forced to pay the consequences of that sin. Even before we commit our first sin, we are already born out of the paradise of Eden into a sinful, fallen world. Also, because of Adam's sin, we are born with a sinful nature and stand guilty before God. Adam represented all of the humanity to come while he was in the garden; and when he fell, we all fell with him.

However, the salvation given through Jesus works in the same manner. When we are saved, we become part of a new humanity with Jesus as the new head of this humanity. Also, just as the consequences of Adam's sin brought condemnation to all of humanity, the rewards of Jesus' righteousness bring salvation to all of this new humanity. Jesus is the representative Head of a new humanity. Yet the effect of Jesus' actions is far more glorious than what Adam had done, for it only took one sin to mess up humanity, but Jesus lived a fully righteous life so that the new humanity could become righteous.

Paul goes back to the Law at the end of chapter 5. Before the Law came, humanity was bound by the sinful nature that they had inherited from Adam. There was plenty of sin before the Law ever came into existence. However, the Law made it clear precisely how we are sinning against God. The Law amplifies those sins so that they could be seen as clearly sinful. Moreover, God allows this to happen so that the more evident our sin is, the more abundant His grace will be. If we do not understand how bad of sinners we are, we will not understand just how abundant God's grace is that He would still save us in spite of that great sin. As Jesus has said, paraphrasing, "He who has been forgiven much loves much, but he who has been forgiven little loves little" (Luke 7:47).

> **reconciliation:** the process of bringing two or more people who were previously at odds with one another back into a peaceful relationship

> **headship:** the teaching that the father is the one who represents his family; thus Adam is the "federal head" of the human race; "So Paul must be meaning that when Adam sinned, God considered true that all men sinned in Adam."*

Thought Questions:

1. In what ways would God be glorified through His wrath? In what ways would God be glorified through His grace?

2. Do you think it is fair that all of humanity would be condemned through Adam's one sin? Why or why not?

The Battle Against Sin: Romans 6–7

Lesson 103

In the gospel, we learn that through our sin we are storing up God's wrath. However, through the redemption that is found through Jesus on the cross, we have been forgiven of those sins so that, rather than wrath, we have salvation, peace, and grace from God. This is all wonderful news, but what happens after we receive the salvation that comes by faith? If we have been saved from sin and our sins have been forgiven, does this mean that we will automatically stop sinning? We all know that the answer to this is, "No!" We all still continue to sin. Yet, now that we have been forgiven of all our sins, what is to stop us from sinning freely, considering that we are no longer under God's wrath?

The issue of sin in the life of the redeemed believer is what chapters 6 and 7 address. Paul begins chapter 6 with another rhetorical question, "Shall we continue in sin that grace may abound?" (verse 1). Paul has just asserted that the more we have sinned, the more we will get to experience God's grace. So should we sin so that we could experience even more of God's grace as He forgives us and restores us? Paul argues that this is absurd. Jesus did not just die to set us free from the consequences of sin; He died to set us free from sin itself. Prior to receiving salvation through Jesus Christ, we were all enslaved by our sins; so why would we ever want to go back to slavery once we have been set free from sin?

This is where Paul brings in the idea of baptism. There are two symbolic elements to the act of baptism. When

---

* Grudem, Wayne. *Systematic Theology*, Zondervan Publishing House, Grand Rapids, Michigan, 494.

a person goes under the water in baptism, this symbolizes that that person has died along with Christ. When that person comes up out of the water, it symbolizes that that person has been raised from the dead with Christ. Even though Jesus died in our place, taking our punishment upon Himself, there is still a sense that we die with Him when we are saved. Even though there is nothing we can do to earn this gift of salvation, part of the reception of this gift is for us to die to our old self. Prior to salvation, we only had one nature, a sinful nature, which enslaved us. By accepting the free gift of salvation, we agree to put to death that old person and to become a new person in Jesus Christ. When we accept the gospel, we lay down the ownership of our own lives; so that like Jesus, the life we live, we live to God and not for ourselves.

So rather than using the gospel as an excuse to sin, we should use the gospel as the power to be set free from sin. Rather than using our bodies "as instruments of unrighteousness to sin," we should use our bodies as "instruments of righteousness to God" (verse 13). Prior to salvation, we had no choice but to be slaves to our own sinful passions and desires. Yet now, because God has given us a new nature through the Holy Spirit, we have a choice of which we will serve—sin or righteousness. Paul encourages us to examine the "fruit" of our old lives when we were enslaved to sin. There is nothing to be gained from this kind of life. Rather, now that we are slaves to righteousness, we bear the fruit of holiness and everlasting life. We only hurt ourselves when we sin, so why should we go back to it? This leads to another excellent verse worth memorizing for sharing the gospel, Romans 6:23: "For the wages of sin is death, but the gift of God is eternal life in Christ Jesus our Lord."

Paul goes on to show how the Law could never set a person free from sin as the gospel has just done. To illustrate Paul's argument, imagine that someone puts you in a room with a big red button that says, "Do not press this button!" Does the mere command create in you a desire not to press the button, or do you find yourself desiring even more to press that button? While commands and restrictions help us to see what is right and wrong, they do not change our desires so that we despise what is wrong and love what is right. So also, while the Law is good in that it reveals to us what is good and what is evil, it cannot change our hearts so that we pursue what is good and flee from what is evil. However, Paul's argument goes one step further. Not only is the Law powerless to change us so we pursue what is good and abhor what is evil, our own sinful nature feeds off the Law and actually leads us to sin more. Think about the red button illustra-

tion. Though we may want to press the button out of curiosity, the fact that we are explicitly told not to press the button will often make us want to press it more. We need something more than the Law to change us at the very core. We need a new nature that delights in doing what is right and hates doing what is wrong. Only the gospel, through the gift of the Holy Spirit, can change our hearts.

Nevertheless, while we are here on this earth, we are always going to live in a tension between our two natures. Even though our old self has been crucified with Christ, our sinful nature has not been taken away from us completely. God has given us a new nature that delights in obedience and despises sin. These two natures are at war within the believer. We genuinely want to do what is right and find pleasure in it, but we also desire the pleasures of sin. We want to do what is right, but we often do the very thing that we hate. In Scripture, this is known as the "Spirit-flesh struggle." Our flesh delights in sin and disobedience, but our spirit delights in righteousness and obedience. We have to choose which of our two natures we are going to feed and follow. The more we feed the flesh, the stronger that set of desires will be. However, the more we seek to listen to and obey the Holy Spirit, the stronger that set of desires will be.

Even the great apostle Paul struggles with sin, as he highlights in the latter portion of chapter 7. Just as it is frustrating for us, Paul also is frustrated with this battle between the two natures. Paul concludes, "O wretched man that I am! Who will deliver me from this body of death? I thank God—through Jesus Christ our Lord!" (verses 24–25). Paul longs for the day when he will be set free from his own sinful nature, and that day will only come through Jesus Christ.

Thought Questions:

1. Do you find that you genuinely delight in doing what is good and hating what is evil most of the time, or do you usually need to be persuaded to do what is good or to avoid evil?

2. What are some ways you can fight your sinful nature? What are some ways you can strengthen the new person that God created when you came to believe?

3. Have you ever met a person who claimed to be a Christian but who did not seem to care about doing what is right? What do you think Paul would say about such a person?

Slaves or Children?: Romans 8

Lesson 104

In chapter 8, Paul continues to draw out the implications of the gospel for everyday living. He begins with a wonderful promise that "There is therefore now no condemnation to those who are in Christ Jesus, who do not walk according to the flesh, but according to the Spirit" (verse 1). As Christians, we do not have to fear the future because we can have confidence that we will not be condemned, but rather that we will have eternal life. Because Jesus stood condemned, we do not have to face condemnation. Rather than us being condemned, it is sin itself that is condemned.

Paul continues to draw out the implications of the Spirit-flesh dichotomy. Because of the flesh, the Law would always be insufficient for creating righteousness in us. Yet, now that we have the Holy Spirit, we can finally fulfill the righteous requirements of the Law. When we set our minds on the Spirit, we will live according to the Spirit and we will have life and peace. But when we set our minds on the flesh, we will live according to the flesh and be at **enmity** with God, and we will have death. In fact, Paul says that those who are in the flesh cannot please God. Only those who have been saved through the gospel can live according to the Spirit rather than the flesh, so even the "good" deeds of nonbelievers are not pleasing to God. By definition, a person cannot be a Christian without having the Holy Spirit. Paul explicitly says that "if anyone does not have the Spirit of Christ, he is not His" (verse 9). Back in chapter 6, Paul asked the rhetorical question, "Should we go on sinning that grace may abound?" In verse 13 of chapter 8, Paul concludes his answer to this question by saying that we will die if we continue to live by the flesh but we will live if we put to death the flesh through the Holy Spirit.

One of the other benefits of the gospel is the security that comes with being adopted into God's family. For the past couple of chapters, Paul has talked about how we can either be slaves to sin or slaves to righteousness. To be a slave in God's kingdom would be an incredible privilege. However, God does something even more incredible for us! Instead of viewing us as slaves, God adopts us into His family so that we are His children. A servant or slave could be fired or kicked out of a family, but children will always be a part of the family. Moreover, even though children may be at odds with their parents at times, there is a great security that comes from being a member of the family. As such, we are able to call God "Abba," or "Father." This is a privileged term reserved for only those who are in the family.

It is common for people to wonder, "How do I know if I am saved?" Paul gives us the answer in verse 16. It is the Holy Spirit who testifies with our spirits that we are children of God. While the Bible does give many clear descriptions of what makes up a Christian, our assurance of salvation is an inward assurance through the Holy Spirit. So how do we know we are saved? The answer is that inwardly we just know because of the testimony of the Holy Spirit in our spirits.

So now that we have been saved from the wrath of God and given a new nature and adopted into God's family, life should be easy, right? Sadly, that is not the case. Even though we have all these things, we are still living in a fallen world that is filled with sin. We have enemies that hate us. We have a world that is hostile to us. We have our own sinful flesh that wages war against our spirits. Persecutions and sufferings are a guarantee. That is why Paul addresses the topic of suffering in the rest of this chapter.

Even though suffering is a certainty for Christians, in verse 18 Paul asserts that the sufferings that we endure now are nothing compared with the blessings that await us in the end. We have a sure hope that greater things are coming. We not only have this great hope, but creation itself is waiting for the day when everything will be made right. When Adam sinned, not only was humanity affected, but all of creation was made subject to decay. Creation itself waits for the day when there will be no more decay. There is a call to patiently persevere in our present sufferings as we cling to the hope of the eternal blessings that will come someday. This provides the context for yet another benefit to the gospel. We are not alone in our sufferings. We may not know what to ask or know what to do, but the Holy Spirit **intercedes** for us with groanings too deep for words (verse 26).

As part of our eternal security, we should find incredible comfort in God's sovereignty. Because God is sovereignly in control of all things, we can trust that He will work out all things together for our good. This does not mean that everything that happens to us will be pleasant, but rather that God can use even the sufferings in our lives to bring about our greater good. Though we may not be able to see the good in what we are going through, we have this promise in Romans 8:28 that somehow God will use it to bring about our greater good. Also, God, who began the salvation process in us even before we were born, will finish what He started.

Verses 29 and 30 tell us that our salvation had been determined by God well before we were even born. God knew us before we were born and chose us (predestined) for salvation and called us to receive the gospel, and through that gospel made us righteous, and someday He will finish the salvation process by glorifying us.

Since God did all of this for us, we can rest fully secure in our salvation. If God Himself has already declared us righteous and adopted us as His children, we are safely in His arms and no enemy can take us away from God. No matter how many accusations Satan may make against us, and no matter how hard he may try to condemn us, we do not have to fear. Not only is the Holy Spirit interceding with the Father on our behalf, but Jesus Christ Himself is defending us to the Father. If the Father loves us so much that He was willing to send His only Son to die for us, then we know how deeply God loves us. No matter how much we may have to suffer in this life, we can find peace and hope in God's love for us. Thus, Paul concludes this argument in chapter 8 by poetically saying that, once we are in Christ, there is absolutely nothing that can separate us from Him and from His love.

enmity: hostility between two people or groups

intercede: to pray on behalf of someone else

Thought Questions:

1. These last few chapters are filled with blessings that come with the gospel. What are some blessings for which you are particularly grateful?

2. Have you ever felt secure in your salvation? How do you feel about the security of your salvation after reading these chapters?

3. Why should we fight sin, based on the last three chapters?

4. If God predestined us for salvation, do we choose God, or does He choose us?

What about Israel?: Romans 9–11

Lesson 105

When many Christians think of the book of Romans, they think of the gospel. While the gospel is certainly central to Paul's argument in Romans, Paul's overall purpose for writing Romans is to show how both the Jews and the Gentiles are saved in the same manner. For eight chapters we have seen Paul expound on the

gospel and its implications for our lives. Paul has shown us that both Jew and Gentile are saved by faith in Jesus Christ alone. This is incredible news for both Jew and Gentile alike. In Paul's experience, the gospel has been received extremely well by the Gentiles. Unfortunately, the Jews do not receive the gospel with the same enthusiasm. In fact, in Paul's experience, the Jews have mostly rejected the gospel. This poses a theological problem for Paul. If the Jews have always been God's people, and the Jews have rejected the salvation that God has given them, what does this mean for the Jews? This is what Paul addresses in chapters 9 through 11.

Even though Paul had been chosen by Jesus to be an apostle to the Gentiles, he is still Jewish and loves the Jewish nation. This is why Paul is so bothered that the Jews are rejecting the gospel. Paul loves his own people so much that he would be willing to give up his own salvation if that meant that the Jews could be saved. In light of the fact that the Jews had been God's chosen nation and had such history with God, it is even sadder that they are rejecting God's salvation. Does the rejection by the Jews mean that all of God's work over the centuries has failed? This is what Paul will spend the next three chapters explaining.

The key to understanding Paul's argument is with the phrase "they are not all Israel who are of Israel" (9:6). Paul is going to argue that all of those who have rejected the gospel are not true Israelites. To make this argument, he goes back to the origin of the Israelite nation. Abraham is said to be the father of the Israelites, yet even in his own story there is a distinction between his children. Ishmael had been born before Isaac, and by birthright he should have been the one who received the blessing. Yet God chooses to give the blessing and the promise to Isaac. If physical ancestry is all that it takes to be a true Israelite, then Ishmael would have had a part in the blessing. Rather, it is the children of promise who are the true Israelites. By saying this, Paul is arguing that the Israelites who reject the gospel are not true Israelites at all and that the Israelites who accept the gospel are the true children of promise. The story of Jacob and Esau also illustrates that physical ancestry is not enough to be a true Israelite. While Rebecca was still pregnant with Jacob and Esau, she was told that the younger child will be the child of promise, not the expected older son. Once again, if physical ancestry makes a person a true Israelite, then Esau would also have received the blessing.

It is at this point that Paul begins to draw out the doctrine of **predestination**. God chooses Jacob over Esau before either person had done anything, either good or bad. Jacob is the child of promise, not because he had earned it through good deeds, but simply because God chooses him. As support for this, Paul quotes Malachi 1:2–3, which states that God loves Jacob but hates Esau. As a side note, in the context of Malachi, hatred is more associated with rejection. This does not mean that God literally hates Esau; in fact, in the story of Jacob and Esau, God provides for Esau as well as Jacob. Paul continues to draw out the doctrine of predestination by quoting Exodus 33:19. In this passage, God basically says that He gets to choose on whom He will show mercy or compassion. It is not our will that saves us, but it is God's choice to show us mercy that saves us. To illustrate that salvation is not about our decision to choose God but rather God's decision to choose us, Paul brings up the story of Pharaoh. On numerous occasions, we are told in the story of the Exodus that God hardens the heart of Pharaoh so that He could pour out all of the plagues upon Egypt. If God hardens Pharaoh's heart, He could certainly also harden the hearts of the Israelites. Thus Paul concludes in Romans 9:18, saying, "Therefore He has mercy on whom He wills, and whom He wills He hardens."

Yet, if God hardens people's hearts and opens people's hearts, is it unfair to condemn people? This is the rhetorical question that Paul asks in verse 19. Paul's answer may be difficult for some people to accept, yet it is completely true. Paul basically says that God is God, and we are not. God can do whatever He wants. However, Paul does offer one possible explanation for why God chooses some people and not others. He suggests that God may prepare some people for wrath and destruction in order to make His mercy that much more glorious to those whom He has chosen. This is admittedly difficult to accept when we think of this in terms of individual salvation, but it makes more sense when we remember the context of Israel's rejection of the gospel. Paul is suggesting that perhaps God has hardened the hearts of the Israelites so that the Gentiles could experience an even greater mercy. Very often when people look to Romans 9 for the doctrine of predestination, they do not look at the argument in its bigger context. This fits with the Scriptures that Paul quotes at the end of chapter 9. First, Paul quotes Hosea, which speaks of God calling the Gentiles His people who were formerly not His people. Then Paul quotes Isaiah, which speaks of Israel being cut short with only a remnant remaining (verse 27, cf. Isaiah 10:22, 23). This is precisely what has happened with the gospel; the Gentiles have been brought in, and only a small percentage of the Jews have been saved.

Paul suggests that the reason that the Jews have not found salvation is that they continue to seek it through the Law rather than through faith. In light of this, Paul now directly applies the principles of the gospel to the situation with the Jews. The Jews have been trying to establish their own righteousness rather than receiving the righteousness that God has revealed. To be saved, there are two things that we must do: (1) we must confess with our mouths our trust in Jesus and (2) believe in our hearts that God raised Him from the dead (10:9). This is the simple formula for salvation, and it applies to all people, whether Jew or Gentile. Moreover, this is why Paul suggests we preach the gospel, because faith can only come through hearing the gospel, and it can only be heard once someone preaches.

Chapter 10 finishes with a series of quotes from Scripture that represent the situation between the Jews and the Gentiles. Even though both have heard the word of the gospel, the Jews have been "disobedient and contrary" (verse 21); whereas the Gentiles are those by whom God was found, though they did not seek Him. Yet, through the acceptance of the Gentiles, Paul's hope is that the Jews would be jealous and someday repent.

Does this mean that the Jews are no longer God's people? Remember that Paul has told us that not all of the Israelites are true Israelites. Just as in Elijah's day, when most of Israel had turned away from God, a remnant remains who are faithful to God. While the nation of Israel has not obtained salvation, those whom God has chosen (the elect) have found that salvation. Paul even suggests that the Israelites who have rejected the gospel have done so because they are blinded and cannot see the gospel. Yet there is still hope for Israel because a remnant remains. In the meantime, the Jewish rejection of the gospel has opened the door for the Gentiles to be saved. Also, Paul's hope and expectation is that someday the Jews will repent.

Another way that Paul illustrates the relationship between the Jews and the Gentiles is with a tree. The tree represents God's people. Originally, Israel was that tree, but through their disobedience and rejection of the gospel, many of the Israelites have been cut off from the tree. Though the Gentiles were not originally part of the tree, God has grafted them in so that they are now part of the tree. As a result, God's people are now composed of those faithful Israelites who have accepted the gospel and those Gentiles who have believed in the gospel. However, there is a warning with this illustration: if God was willing to cut off the natural branches (Israel) for their lack of faith, He will do the same with the unnatural branches (the Gentiles) if they do not persist in faith (11:17–21). So Paul concludes that God has currently blinded the hearts of the Israelites "until the fullness of the Gentiles has come in" (verse 25). Moreover, through the fullness of the Gentiles and the later repentant Israelites, finally "all Israel will be saved" (verse 26).

After eleven chapters of intense theology and expounding the incredible blessings that God has given us through the gospel, Paul ends this section on a **doxology**. In light of everything, the only appropriate response is to praise God and glorify Him. Paul praises God for His incredible wisdom and knowledge. God's plan is so much more glorious than anything we can devise. Even if we have known the gospel for a long time, when we meditate on the gospel it should motivate us to praise and worship God.

> **predestination:** God, according to His sovereign purpose and knowledge, determined beforehand whom He will save and bring with Him to heaven (Romans 9); "a broader term [that] includes the two aspects of election (for believers) and reprobation (for unbelievers)"*
>
> **doxology:** δοξα meaing "glory" and –λογια meaning "word"; thus, a word of praise

Thought Question:

> How do you feel about the doctrine of predestination? Do you find it difficult to accept? Why or why not?

How Then Shall We Live?: Romans 12

Lesson 106

For eleven chapters, Paul has systematically explained the gospel and its implications in the life of the believer. We have learned that we are all sinners and deserve death and separation from God. We have learned that through our sins we are destined for God's wrath. However, we have also learned that God sent Jesus to take care of all of that for us who believe. Jesus was the perfect sacrifice who died in our place, appeasing the wrath of God and purchasing salvation for us. We also have learned that the means of obtaining that salvation is purely by faith, both for the Jews and the Gentiles. If God has done all this for us, how ought we to respond? The biblical authors never give theology just so that we could feel smarter and use bigger words. The end

goal of every theological idea is practical application and a transformed life. In the final chapters of the book of Romans, starting with chapter 12, Paul is going to expound on how we ought to live in light of the gospel.

Because Jesus was the perfect sacrifice, we no longer need to keep making animal sacrifices to deal with our sin. So Paul beseeches us to offer ourselves as living sacrifices to God. Whether we are Jew or Gentile, the kind of sacrifice that God seeks from us is a life of sacrifice. This does not mean that we are all supposed to die for our faith in Jesus; rather, as living sacrifices, we are supposed to live our lives for Jesus. The word "reasonable" in verse 1 could also be translated as "logical" or "rational." The logical or rational response to the gospel is to live our lives for Jesus.

When it comes to actually living an obedient and righteous life, there are two overarching things that Paul argues we must do. First, we need to be diligent to not allow ourselves to conform to this world. In other words, we have to be careful that our values and desires are not influenced by the values and desires of this world. Also, since we are immersed in the world through media and personal interactions, we have to constantly keep on guard. This is a lifelong process that requires consistently being aware and critical of the messages around us. The second overarching thing that we must do is related to the first: we must be transformed by the renewing of our minds. The most practical way to do this is to consistently put ourselves in environments where we are exposed to the truths of Scripture. This involves prayer, reading our Bibles regularly, spending Christ-centered time with other believers through Bible study, and so forth. The more we are able to stay focused on the truths of Scripture, the more we will be able to expose the lies of the world and avoid conforming to the world.

Because the gospel puts all of us on equal footing (we are all saved by grace through faith), this should lead to unity among Christians. One of the biggest sins that destroys unity in the Church is pride. When we think that we are better than other people or think that they are "below" us, we put a barrier in between us and those persons. So Paul exhorts us to not think of ourselves more highly than we ought, but rather we are to think of ourselves with sober judgment. In other words, we need to be humble. Related to this, we need to recognize that God has made people and designed them to be different. Like different parts of a body, which have different functions yet work together, Christians are unique and function differently but must work together to make the body of Christ work.

---

* Grudem, Wayne. *Systematic Theology*, Zondervan Publishing House, Grand Rapids, Michigan, 670.

Rather than thinking of our gifts and abilities as better or more valuable for the Church, we need to appreciate and value the role that each person plays in the Church. This is radically different from the way that the world thinks. The world says that the most gifted or the most talented person is the most valuable; but it ought not to be this way in the Church. In light of this, Paul gives a series of examples of the types of gifts that people may have in the Church and the role that they ought to play. Some of these gifts are more visible to many people such as prophecy, teaching, or exhortation; but other gifts are more private and individual such as giving, ministering, and mercy. Yet all of these are valuable gifts and necessary if a church is to run well.

Starting in verse 9, Paul gives a series of commands that all have to do with community life. We are not going to highlight every one of these commands in this lesson, but we will highlight some of them. Paul begins this section by saying that love must be "without hypocrisy." Another way to word this is to say that the love that we have for one another must be genuine. We need to actually care for one another; we should not just put on a smile and act like the other people are important to us. This is a heart issue and must be done through the Holy Spirit. Similarly, we need to "abhor what is evil" and "cling to what is good." These are also issues of the heart. It is one thing to think of a particular sin as "bad," but it is another thing altogether to consider it "disgusting." When we are repulsed by sin, we will be far more likely to overcome the temptation for that sin; but when we simply think of it as "bad," it may actually make us want to do it more. Similarly, we need to go beyond simply thinking that something is "good"; we need to delight in things that are good.

We are also supposed to honor others above ourselves. Rather than focusing on building ourselves up, as the world encourages us to do, we are to encourage and build up others. This does not mean that we are supposed to tear ourselves down, but rather build up others. We also need to fight **apathy**. If a person is apathetic toward something, it means that he or she simply does not care and does not have any passion about that thing. Sadly, far too many people today are apathetic. Rather than apathy, we are commanded not to lack in diligence and to be "fervent" in spirit. We are also commanded to provide for the needs of others. We are to distribute to the needs of the saints and to show hospitality. To show hospitality involves inviting people into our homes and providing for their needs. This does not mean that we should be foolish and invite strangers or dangerous people into our homes, but we should be generous and take care of others.

In verses 14–21, Paul repeats some of the commands that he has just given. However, one of the ideas that runs throughout this paragraph is how we ought to treat those who treat us poorly. Paul says that rather than retaliating or getting revenge on others, we are to bless those who persecute us. These are the same words that Jesus had said in the Sermon on the Mount (Matthew 5:44). This is essential if there is to be unity in a community of believers. It is inevitable that people are going to hurt each other. Yet, if we retaliate or get revenge, this simply perpetuates that pain and leads to others getting hurt. If we respond by blessing the other person and treating him or her well, there can be healing and restoration. This is all only possible, however, if we recognize and trust that God is sovereign and He will bring about justice. If we truly believe that God is going to wisely bring about punishment or justice on the other person, we can learn to forgive and let things go and respond with love.

apathy: an attitude of not caring about something

Thought Questions:

1. What kinds of gifts do you think you have? In light of this, what might be a role you can play in your local church?

2. Have you ever felt apathetic toward something? What are some things you can do to fight apathy?

3. What are some good rules you can follow while taking in media (such as TV, music, video games, internet, etc.) to prevent yourself from conforming to the world?

Government and Conscience: Romans 13–14

Lesson 107

The key to forgiving those who hurt us and blessing those who persecute us is to trust that God knows what He is doing and that He will bring about perfect justice someday. The idea that began at the end of chapter 12 picks up in chapter 13. At the end of chapter 12, we learn that vengeance is the Lord's and that He will repay when someone sins. We know that there is a judgment day that we will all face when all our deeds will be exposed and justice will be given. However, God also brings about justice on earth. Also, one of the means that God uses to bring about justice is the government.

While many people may not like the government, we are told in chapter 13 that the government is an institution that gets its authority from God Himself. All authority ultimately comes from God as He chooses to distribute it. Therefore, Paul argues, to resist the government is tantamount to resisting God Himself. Paul even calls the authorities "ministers" of God to bring about justice (13:4). One of the big responsibilities of rulers is to execute God's wrath on those who do evil and to reward and protect those who do what is good. In light of this, Paul commands us to pay taxes and respect to the government.

This argument, however, demands that we address the question of governmental corruption. Not all governments punish evil and protect the good. Many leaders and rulers are self-serving and do not care about justice. Are we called to obey such a government? Are we supposed to pay taxes if that money from the government is spent on abortion clinics or some other form of evil? It would be ignorant to think that the government in Paul's day was free from corruption, and Paul would have known this; yet he still commands us to respect that government and pay taxes. We must understand that, since God is the One who gives the government its authority, it is God who will punish those in the government who fail at the job that God had given them to do, not us. Yet we have already seen some examples of what Christians are supposed to do when the government stands opposed to God. When Peter and John are commanded not to preach in the name of Jesus, they refuse to obey this command because they are accountable to God first. If the government commands us to do something that goes against what God has commanded us to do, then we have the responsibility to disobey that government. Otherwise, we need to be respectful and work within the government for change.

After many chapters of discussing the Law given to Moses and its role in the life of the Christian, Paul summarizes the Law here. The entire Law can be summarized with a single command: love. If we love God and love others, we will have obeyed the entire Law. So whether a person is a Jew and has studied the Law his or her entire life, or whether a person is a Gentile who has never studied the Law, if he or she focuses on loving one another, the Law will be fulfilled in him or her.

Having established in chapters 6 through 8 that we have no more reason to sin, Paul addresses sin once again at the end of chapter 13. Paul uses the metaphor of light versus darkness to address the issue of sin here. Now that we have been brought into the light of forgiveness and truth, why would we ever live like we are in darkness? When we are in the darkness, we hide because we do not want to be exposed. However, all our sins have been exposed and forgiven, so we should not live in such a manner that we would have to hide. Life in the light is freedom, and it is better, so we need to fight against the darkness.

With love being the fulfillment of the Law, Paul expands on one application of the law of love in chapter 14. Unity is not going to be easy between Jewish Christians and Gentile Christians. There are many things within the Gentile culture that the Jewish culture would find repulsive, and vice versa. One of these divisive problems is the issue of food sacrificed to idols. Idolatry is so repulsive in the Jewish culture that Jews would avoid anything even remotely associated with idolatry. This poses a problem when it comes to buying food in the marketplace in the Roman world. Much of the meat that is sold in the marketplace comes from the leftover sacrifices from the temples of the Roman gods. In order to avoid participating in idolatry, many Jews would avoid eating meat found in the marketplace altogether. Yet the Gentiles do not see this as participation in idolatry but simply as a meat market. As a result, not only are the Jewish Christians refusing to eat with their Gentile Christian brothers, but they are condemning these Gentile Christians for eating that meat. Another divisive issue is the celebration of holy days. In the Law, Jews are commanded to celebrate a number of holy days throughout the year. The Gentile Christians, however, are not celebrating those days. Once again, the Jews are taking great offense at this.

So how could people with such diverse convictions within the same Christian community find unity? The key is to put love above these convictions. If both sides do what it takes to truly love the other, then unity could be achieved. Paul identifies the one without the freedom to eat meat as a person with a "weak" conscience. Paul exhorts the person with the weak conscience not to despise or judge the person who has freedom. Conversely, Paul exhorts the person who has freedom to be willing to lay down that freedom when he or she is around someone with a weak conscience. In other words, our love for that person should be more important to us than the freedoms that we have. Paul summarizes this idea when he says, "Therefore let us pursue the things which make for peace and the things by which one may edify another" (verse 19).

It is important to clarify that the issues of the weak brother and the strong brother have to do with gray areas in Scripture. There are a number of things about which Scripture is abundantly clear. For example, Paul does not say that it is okay to bow down to an idol if your conscience allows you to do so. Scripture is abundantly clear that idolatry is a sin. Yet Scripture does not speak dogmatically about the issue of food that had been sacrificed to an idol. Some people have tried to apply this principle to issues that the Scriptures make very clear. There is a movement within some Christian circles to include homosexuality as one of these gray areas. However, Scripture is very clear that homosexuality is a sin. This is not an issue of conscience, but an issue of God's explicit commands. Gray areas, however, can become sin according to verse 23; Paul says that "whatever is not from faith is sin." If our conscience convicts us not to do something in one of these gray areas and we do it anyway, we are sinning against our conscience.

Thought Questions:

1. If the government has been given its authority from God, is it ever okay to overthrow a government? Why or why not?

2. What might be some gray areas in today's world?

Concluding Words: Romans 15–16

Lesson 108

One of the incredible effects of the gospel is that it can bring unity to people who would in no other way be unified. Paul does not just push for unity as a theoretically good idea; he knows that the gospel has the power to unify radically different people in spirit and purpose. Paul appeals once again in chapter 15 for the believers in Rome to strive for unity together.

To be unified, we need to put the interests and well-being of others ahead of our own self-interests. Just as those who have a weak conscience need to not judge those with a strong conscience, those with a strong conscience need to be understanding of those who have a weak conscience and bear with their scruples. Jesus Himself put the interests of others ahead of His own, and we should follow in His footsteps. In verses 5–6, Paul offers a benediction, a prayer asking God to help the Roman believers to be united.

Paul goes on to explain a little further how Jesus fits in for God's plan for both the Jews and the Gentiles. To the Jews (called the "circumcision" here), Jesus came as a Jew in order to fulfill the promises made in the Old Testament. Yet there are also promises made concerning the Gentiles that through the Jews the Gentiles would come to praise God too. We now see these promises fulfilled

as the Gentiles have come to believe. Paul offers another benediction in verse 13 as he prays that the believers in Rome would be filled with joy, peace, and hope.

Now we must remember that Paul has never met these believers from Rome in person. However, in this letter Paul speaks with boldness and authority. Paul gives these believers a number of commands throughout this letter. So in verses 15–33, Paul reminds the Romans of the authority that he has received from Jesus. Because he has been appointed by Jesus to be the apostle to the Gentiles, he has a vested interest in them. It is his responsibility to guard and protect the gospel for the Gentiles. Paul reminds them of the mighty signs and wonders that the Holy Spirit had performed through him among the Gentiles. Paul also explains why he had not yet come to Rome, because Paul's desire is to first bring the gospel where it has not been heard. Yet, now that the gospel has spread in the regions around Paul, Paul is planning to visit Rome. First, however, Paul is going to make a trip to Jerusalem to give them some money that he had collected from the Gentile churches.* Then, if possible, Paul plans on making a trip to Spain while stopping in Rome along the way. Paul, however, asks for prayer that he might be delivered from unbelievers in Judea.

Just as Paul begins his letter with a customary greeting, he ends with a customary salutation. There are a number of people whom Paul commends to the church in Rome. While we will not get into detail about every one of these people, a few of them merit mention here. First, Paul commends Phoebe, whom he calls a "servant" of the church in Cenchrea (16:1). The word "servant" could also be translated "deacon" (διαχονος). If Paul is using this word in its technical sense, then we have an example of a woman in the office of deacon. Yet the word can simply mean servant as well, without referring to the office of deacon. It is interesting when Paul mentions Priscilla and Aquila that he puts the wife's name first. Some have argued that she may have been the predominant speaker between the two. We have previously encountered these two in the book of Acts in Ephesus (Acts 18). Altogether, Paul exhorts the church in Rome to greet one another with a "holy kiss" (verse 16). It was customary in Paul's day for people to greet one another with a kiss, just as a handshake would be more customary today.

Paul cannot help but to give more direction to the church in Rome. So Paul urges the brothers in the church in Rome to stay away from divisive people. These

---

* This also explains Paul's determination to go to Jerusalem despite the warnings that he was receiving in Acts 21. He was fulfilling his responsibility to deliver the offering.

people are deceivers and have led astray some simple people. Paul is encouraged by the report of the goodness of the Romans, but he still wants them to be wise when it comes to good and evil. Also, as they continue to remain faithful, Paul says that "the God of peace will crush Satan under your feet shortly" (verse 20). This is a reference to Genesis 3:15 where God prophesies that the Seed of the woman will crush the head of Satan. While Jesus ultimately crushed Satan on the cross, we continue to crush Satan through our faithfulness.

Paul then sends greetings from a number of people with whom he was close. Even though Paul is the author of this epistle, he is not the one who actually writes the epistle. Paul dictates this epistle, and a man named Tertius is the scribe who writes this epistle down. Moreover, just as Paul begins this letter calling for grace on this church, he calls for grace once again in verse 24. Finally, Paul finishes with another doxology in verses 25–27, praising God, who is able to establish the Romans in the gospel.

Thought Question:

How easy do you find it to be like-minded and unified with other believers? Are there any people in particular with whom you find this difficult to achieve? Why?

Introduction to 1 Corinthians: 1 Corinthians 1–2

Lesson 109

Contrary to its name, the letter of 1 Corinthians is not Paul's first letter to the church in Corinth. In 1 Corinthians 5:9, Paul makes reference to a previous letter that he had sent the church in Corinth, which they had misunderstood. The Corinthians had sent Paul a letter responding to his first letter and asking for clarification on some issues, and 1 Corinthians is Paul's response.

The mention of Apollos tells us that Paul must have written this epistle some time after his third missionary journey began, most likely while he was still in Ephesus for his two year stay (Acts 19). Because of this, and because Paul does not mention imprisonment, it is likely that he wrote this in the mid-50s A.D.

The city of Corinth lies in southern Greece on the Peloponnesian peninsula. During the Roman Empire, it was an important port city in the region of Achaia. Even though the ancient city of Corinth had been destroyed a century before Christ, shortly before Jesus was born

the city was rebuilt. As a port city, Corinth was wealthy; but with that wealth also came a lot of immorality, particularly sexual immorality. In addition, idolatry was quite common in Corinth, as many temples to different gods were in that city.

Sadly, the church in Corinth is influenced by the culture around it. Sexual immorality had made its way into the church of Corinth, and the leaders of that church ask Paul what should be done about it. In general, Christians in the church of Corinth were largely out of control. Rather than unity, there was division and disorder in this church. Yet, in spite all of this, the church of Corinth was very spiritually gifted. The overarching purpose of 1 Corinthians is to give order and direction to the church in Corinth.

As with all of Paul's letters, Paul begins with his customary greeting. As with Romans, Paul reminds the believers in Corinth that he had been called by God to be an apostle. He characterizes the church in Corinth as "those who are sanctified in Christ Jesus, called to be saints" (verse 2). This will be very important for later in this epistle. Both "sanctified" and "saints" come from the root word "holy." To be holy involves living a righteous life. Sadly, due to the immorality in this church, they have not been living up to their calling to be sanctified. As with Romans, Paul also greets the church in Corinth with "grace" and "peace" (verse 3). Paul is grateful that the believers in Corinth have been enriched in their knowledge of Jesus and that they are not lacking in any spiritual gift. Paul is also grateful that God will help them to stay blameless until the day Jesus returns.

After his greeting, Paul moves on to his primary petition for the church in Corinth. Paul pleads with the church of Corinth not to be divided. It had been reported to Paul that believers in the church of Corinth have been fighting among themselves over which person they follow. Paul had originally planted the church in Corinth (Acts 18:1–17); but some time later, Apollos had come to Corinth and had become a leader in the church (Acts 18:27–19:1). Apparently, people had begun to argue over who is a better leader, whether it be Paul, Apollos, Cephas (Peter), or even Jesus. Paul puts an end to this and argues that the only person whom Christians should boast about following is Jesus Christ Himself.

One of the reasons so many people in the church of Corinth are priding themselves for following Apollos is because he is a very gifted speaker. This is why Paul speaks about the simplicity of the gospel. The power of the gospel is not based on the giftedness of the speaker, but in the power of the message. It is not the speaker who saves people; it is the sacrifice of Christ on the cross that saves us. To the Jews, the concept of a suffering Messiah is a stumbling block that many cannot seem to get past; to the Gentiles, the simplicity of the message is seen as foolishness. Remember that philosophy and rational thought are very important to the Greeks. There is nothing extremely profound or complicated about the gospel; it is simple but powerful. Since it is not extremely profound, the Gentiles consider it foolish. However, God seems to take a particular joy in using "foolish" things or humble things to shame the prideful (verse 27).

This is why Paul had chosen not to come "with excellence of speech or of wisdom," but rather he "determined not to know anything among you except Jesus Christ and Him crucified" (2:1–2). We know that Paul is very well educated and very intelligent, but he chooses not to depend on that intellect but on the power of the gospel itself. This should be encouraging for us today. It is not our power of speech or ability to be persuasive that saves people; it is the gospel. To the average person, this message would be seen as foolishness, but to the person who has the Spirit of God it is seen as God's wisdom. Only God's Spirit can reveal to us the thoughts and wisdom of God.

Paul argues all of this to show the people in Corinth that it is not the speaker of the gospel who is important, but it is the gospel itself that should matter. The difference in the effectiveness of the gospel is not the person sharing the message, but the presence of the Holy Spirit in the one who receives the message. Therefore, it is absurd to fight over who the better leader is. The only person who is important to follow is Jesus Christ, and the only power to change people is the gospel itself.

Thought Question:

Have you ever met any Christians who argue over who has a better pastor? What does 1 Corinthians have to say about this?

Spiritual Architects and Being a Good Father: 1 Corinthians 3–4

Lesson 110

The argument that Paul began in the first two chapters is continued in the next two chapters. Paul will not tolerate this competition and division within the church of Corinth over who is a better leader. In chapter 3, Paul begins by rebuking the Corinthians for their "carnal" way of thinking. The word *carnal* means "fleshly,"

and from Romans we learned that there is a struggle between the flesh and the Spirit. To be fleshly, therefore, means to not be thinking in line with the Holy Spirit. Also, this kind of dispute is childish. Like babies, the Corinthians cannot be fed with solid food but only with milk. In this context, milk is a metaphor for basic doctrines and ideas, whereas solid food is a metaphor for deeper theology.

Paul uses a couple of simple metaphors to describe his and Apollos' roles in the church of Corinth. The first metaphor that Paul uses is a farming metaphor. Paul was the first to bring the gospel to Corinth, and as such he planted the church there. Apollos came later and strengthened the church, and as such he watered the plant of the church there. However, neither the planter nor the waterer are what brings the growth and produces fruit. God is the One who makes the church grow, and as such only God is truly important. The other metaphor that Paul uses is an architectural metaphor. Like a builder, Paul laid down the foundation, and Apollos built upon that foundation. Yet Paul and Apollos are not that foundation; that foundation is Jesus Christ, and it is upon Him alone that any church will stand. Paul is so concerned for the Corinthians because, as an architect, he bears responsibility for the building's ability to stand. If the architect uses strong and wise materials (such as gold, silver, or precious stones), the building will stand when fire (adversity) comes; but if the architect is cheap and uses weak materials (such as wood, hay, or straw), the building will be destroyed by the fire. Paul does not want the church in Corinth to be destroyed.

Paul takes this architectural metaphor one step further. The church of Corinth is not just any "building"; it is the very "temple of God." In the Old Testament, God's house was the temple, and His presence was uniquely there. Now, however, through the gospel and the work of Jesus Christ, God dwells with believers as a spiritual temple; and since we are God's new temple, we are very precious to God and it is crucial that we protect and preserve the Church.

Therefore, the Corinthian believers need to stop tearing down God's temple by fighting among themselves. In their efforts to be "wise," they have become divisive. Rather, they should humble themselves and become like fools so that they would rely on God rather than their own intellect. This does not mean, however, that we should do foolish things. Paul has already declared that the gospel is "foolishness" because of its simplicity. To be "foolish" here means to focus on the simplicity of the gospel.

It would appear based on Paul's response in chapter 4 that the Corinthians have been saying some hurtful things about Paul. Those who have been following Apollos or other teachers have been putting down Paul and declaring him to be a lesser leader. Yet Paul makes it clear in chapter 4 that at the end of the day, the only opinion that matters to him is God's opinion. They can judge him all they want, but he is only a servant to God and Jesus Christ, and it is their judgment that matters. Nevertheless, because Paul is a spiritual father to so many of them, he still cares about them and wants them to grow and become more mature.

Paul refuses to boast in his intellect or his learning, but he will boast in his weaknesses and hardships. He reminds the Corinthians that he has been willing to endure much so that they can experience blessings. Paul has suffered much for them, and they should be willing to do the same for others. As a good father, Paul wants them to imitate his way of life so that they can also be mature. For this reason, Paul informs the Corinthians that he is sending Timothy, who is like a son to Paul, in order to remind them about how Paul lives and how they should live. Not only will Paul send Timothy, but also Paul himself plans on visiting them shortly if God allows. In some sense, this is like a father who calls his children who have been disobeying their mother, warning them that he is coming home soon, so they better get their act together. So Paul finishes this chapter with a warning and a choice: either they repent of their divisiveness, or Paul will come with the rod of discipline.

Thought Question:

Paul wants the Corinthian believers to imitate his way of life. Who are some godly people in your life whom you should imitate? What is it about them that you would like to imitate?

Sexual Immorality and Marriage: 1 Corinthians 5–7

Lesson 111

We live in a culture that is increasingly tolerant of many forms of sin. One of the most prominent issues of tolerance in our society today has to do with sexual sins. As long as a person is happy and is not hurting another person, he or she can do whatever he or she wants, according to our culture. Regrettably, this mentality has also made its way into many churches today. There are many Christians today that boast in their tolerance of sins.

Divisiveness is not the only issue that plagues the church in Corinth. Like our society, the church in Corinth has to deal with sexual sins. From the introduction to 1 Corinthians, we learned that, because Corinth is a port city and is fairly wealthy, sexual immorality is a big issue there. This cultural problem also affects the church. From the letter that the Corinthians had sent Paul, he has learned that there is a man in that church who had had sex with his stepmother. Rather than disciplining this man, the church in Corinth boasted in their tolerance of this sin! Paul says that they are to discipline such a man, saying, "Deliver such a one to Satan for the destruction of the flesh, that his spirit may be saved in the day of the Lord Jesus" (5:5). Now there is some debate as to what precisely this means. Some suggest that this means that the Christians at Corinth are to disassociate with this man with the hope that this loss would lead him to repent. Others suggest that this means that this man is to be cut off from taking Communion but would still be able to attend church services, but as an outsider. Based on the command in verse 11 not to keep company with a sexually immoral brother, it would appear that this person is to be kicked out of the church until he repents of this sin.

Paul uses the metaphor of leaven to address this issue of sin. Just as a little leaven (yeast) works its way throughout an entire loaf of bread, a little tolerated sin left unchecked could destroy the purity of a group of believers. This is why Paul commands the church in Corinth to stay away from believers who are known to be "sexually immoral, or covetous, or an idolater, or a reviler, or a drunkard, or an extortioner" (verse 11). Yet Paul also makes it clear that we are only supposed to avoid these people if they call themselves Christians. We are only to judge those within the church; God is the One who will judge those outside the Church. When it comes to nonbelievers, we need to be careful about holding them to standards with which they do not agree. Our responsibility with nonbelievers is not to judge them but to share the gospel with them.

Another problem in the church of Corinth is that of lawsuits among believers. Not only are the believers in Corinth fighting and quarreling among themselves, but they are also suing one another and bringing their cases before unbelievers. By doing this, they are taking the division within that church and making it public. Paul says that it would be better to simply suffer the wrong than to take the other believers to court. Why not just appoint someone within the church to settle these disputes? When one believer takes another believer to court, even if he or she wins the case it is a loss for the kingdom of God.

Once again, Paul rebukes the church of Corinth by reminding them that they are not living the way that God has made them to live. Paul reminds them that the unrighteous will not inherit the kingdom of God. Among the list that Paul gives are "fornicators," "adulterers," "homosexuals," and "sodomites." Sexual immorality is a big deal to God. However, Paul reminds them that all these things are who the believers in Corinth used to be. When they came to faith in Christ, He washed them and cleansed them from their previous life. Even though there is incredible freedom through the gospel, we should not use that freedom to go back to the old life that we had before Christ. Paul's argument in 1 Corinthians 6:11–14 is similar to his argument in Romans 6. While Christ forgives us of all our sins, He also saves us from sin itself so that we should no longer pursue sin.

In light of this, Paul returns to his warnings against sexual sins, but this time he focuses on prostitution. There is a spiritual union that happens when two people have sex. As Scripture says, in sex "the two … shall become one flesh" (verse 16). However, if our bodies now belongs to the Lord and we are united with Him through the gospel, it is entirely inappropriate to develop this spiritual connection with a prostitute. God intended this spiritual union to take place within the established covenant of marriage. Because we are now the temple of God, we defile that temple by being united with someone who is not a part of that temple. Jesus died and paid the ultimate price for us; as a result, our bodies no longer belong to us but to God. In light of this, we do not get to do whatever we want with our bodies; we need to honor God with our bodies.

In chapter 7, Paul begins to address some specific questions that the Corinthians had asked him in the letter that they had sent him. Apparently, the Corinthians had questions about marriage and how to handle singleness. Paul begins by arguing that it is a blessing to be single and that, if a person can handle it, he or she should remain single. Nevertheless, Paul knows the power of sexual attraction and admits that marriage is the appropriate context in which to express those passions. In light of this, Paul orders both husbands and wives to give sex to their spouses. Since marriage is the God-given institution to express sexual desire, it is wrong for a husband or a wife to deny that for his or her spouse. The only concession that Paul gives for withholding sex is if the husband and wife agree to refrain for a time for the purpose of fasting.

Moving on from the topic of sex, but still in the topic of marriage, Paul reiterates that married couples should not get divorced. When Paul says "not I but the Lord" (verse 10), he is reminding them that it is Jesus Himself who had forbidden divorce. Paul also suggests that married couples should not separate, but if they do, they should remain unmarried or be reconciled. What should happen, however, if a Christian is married to a non-Christian? Should they get divorced? While Jesus had only given one concession for divorce (sexual infidelity; Matthew 5:32), Paul gives a second concession here. If a nonbelieving spouse wants to leave the believer, then the believer can get a divorce. However, if the nonbeliever wants to stay, the believer should stay in the marriage. When Paul says that the unbelieving spouse is sanctified by his believing wife, this does not mean that the unbeliever is saved, but that God's presence is there in the household because of the believer. This also applies to children.

Paul goes on to suggest that people should stay in the situation they were in when they were saved. If a person was a slave, his priority should not be to gain his freedom but to live as a free man in the Lord. Yet, if a person can gain his or her freedom, he or she should. This applies to marriage and singleness. Now what Paul suggests here is unclear. He says that, because of "the present distress" (verse 26), Christians should not focus on marriage if they can avoid it. It is not clear what precisely this "present distress" might be. Paul could be referring to the entire time before Christ returns, or there might be an issue of persecution that is causing distress. Whatever that distress might be, Paul is not forbidding marriage but suggesting that there are more important issues to attend to than marriage. The married person is divided in his or her priorities. The unmarried person has the freedom to focus entirely on his relationship with Christ and the work that he is called to do for the kingdom. The married person, however, has the responsibility to provide for and take care of his or her spouse.

So Paul concludes that "he who gives her in marriage does well, but he who does not give her in marriage does better" (verse 38). The single life is far more simple than the married life; and if a person can control himself or herself, it is better to remain single.

Thought Questions:

1. If you have any Christian friends who are involved in unrepentant sexual immorality, what should you do based on this passage?

2. Do you think it is wrong to sue other Christians after reading 1 Corinthians 6? Why or why not?

3. How do Paul's thoughts on marriage and single-ness compare to the messages of our culture today? Is singleness valued in our culture?

4. In light of Paul's arguments, what advice could you give a person who is single but is not content with his or her singleness?

Idolatry, Hair, and the Lord's Supper: 1 Corinthians 8–11

Lesson 112

Another issue that the church of Corinth had asked Paul about in their letter is the issue of food sacrificed to idols. We have already run into this issue in Romans 14. Because food from the temples was sold in the marketplace, many people refused to eat any meat from the marketplace. However, meat in the marketplace came from other sources, as well; it was not a guarantee that all the meat came from idolatry. So some people in Corinth would eat meat from the marketplace without hesitation, while others refrained.

Paul begins by speaking about the prideful nature of knowledge. Those who are more knowledgeable about things are often "puffed up" or prideful about the things that they know. Knowledge may puff up a person, but love "edifies" or builds up others. Regarding idolatry, those who are knowledgeable know that there is only one God and that idols are nothing at all. Through that knowledge, these people recognize their freedom to eat that meat since it is meat that had been sacrificed to nothing. Yet there are others who cannot eat that meat with a clean conscience, and they are con-flicted by seeing other Christians eating that meat. As Paul had commanded in Romans 14, the person who has the freedom should avoid using that freedom when it hurts a fellow believer. So Paul concludes, "if food makes my brother stumble, I will never again eat meat, lest I make my brother stumble"(8:13).

In the midst of his argument about food sacrificed to idols, Paul takes a detour to defend some of the deci-sions that he had made as an apostle. Paul could have had the right to demand money from the Corinthians for the ministry that he had done among them. Since he had given them spiritual blessings, it would be appropriate for them to give him material blessings. Yet, for the sake of the gospel, Paul willingly gave up his rights as an apostle so that he could offer the gospel free of charge. We know that Paul had skills as a tentmaker, and it appears that he worked building tents so that he would not have to take any money from the Corinthi-

ans. Paul is willing to make sacrifices and do whatever it takes to get the gospel out to people. As Paul says, "I have become all things to all men, that I might by all means save some" (9:22b). In order to be as effective as possible with the gospel, Paul works hard to discipline his own body. If Paul is willing to work so hard for the sake of the gospel and is willing to give up so much, so also should the Corinthians be willing to sacrifice their own freedoms and rights for the sake of the gospel.

Chapter 10 continues the argument that Paul has been making. Paul has just said that he works hard to disci-pline himself so that he will not be disqualified from the prize of eternal life. So also should the Corinthian believers work hard to fight against immorality, lest they be disqualified. He reminds them of the first genera-tion of Israelites who came out of Egypt. Interestingly, even though Jesus had not yet come, Paul argues that Christ was with them spiritually. Even though they had the spiritual blessings of Christ, that generation also engaged in idolatry and sexual immorality. In addition, we know that there were terrible consequences for that generation as a result of their sins. There is a very real warning in this passage, "Therefore let him who thinks he stands take heed lest he fall" (verse 12). It is in light of this that Paul gives an encouraging promise: "God is faithful, who will not allow you to be tempted beyond what you are able, but with the temptation will also make the way of escape, that you may be able to bear it" (verse 13). We will never be put in a situation in which we will be trapped by sin; either God will give us the power to overcome that sin, or God will give us a way out of the situation.

Paul then returns to his argument about idolatry. He begins by making a comparison to eating food sac-rificed to idols with partaking of the Lord's Supper. By partaking of the Lord's Supper, we understand as Christians that in some way we are united with Christ and communing with Him through the process. If we feel this way about the Lord's Supper, would not eating food sacrificed to idols be a form of union and partici-pation with idols? Although the idols are not gods, Paul suggests that the idols are in fact demons. Therefore, Paul suggests, we ought to avoid anything that we know has been associated with demons. Nevertheless, because it is not known for sure that food from the market-place had been sacrificed to demons, it is not inher-ently wrong to eat food from the marketplace. So Paul concludes that it is okay to eat that food, as long as you or the person with whom you are eating does not know that that food had been sacrificed to an idol. However, the overall principle that should govern this entire discussion is a desire to glorify God in everything and a desire to bring no unnecessary offense to people.

In chapter 11, Paul moves on to discuss some of the traditions that he had passed down to them. The first of these traditions has to do with head coverings. According to the traditions of the day, women were supposed to worship with their heads covered, while men were supposed to worship with their heads uncovered. Apparently, some people from the church of Corinth were fighting against this tradition. Paul's argument is that head coverings are symbolic of authority. When a woman covers her head, she is honoring her husband, who is the authoritative "head" of the relationship. This does not mean that women are to be abused by their husbands, but there is an authoritative difference between husbands and wives. Paul says that a woman ought to shave her head if she does not cover it. The exact nature of this tradition is not known, but some scholars have suggested that a woman who lets down her hair and has it uncovered in that society would be declaring that she was single and available. If this is the case, it would be very disrespectful to her husband if the wife does this. Paul's argument for head coverings is two-fold, an argument from nature and an argument from practice. From nature, Paul argues that long hair is a natural form of head covering that God has given to women. Women's hair typically grows much faster than men's hair. From practice, Paul argues that it is the tradition of all the churches for women to worship with their heads covered.

So why do many churches not require women to keep their heads covered today? Part of the reason is that the symbolism is lost in our culture. In our culture, we do not associate long hair or head coverings with submission to authorities; but also, Paul appeals to the practices of the churches in his day as evidence for head coverings. If this same appeal were made today, the more common practice is for women to have their heads uncovered in worship. This is another gray area of the faith where we ought to follow our consciences but also respect the traditions and convictions of those around us.

The second tradition that Paul addresses in chapter 11 is the Lord's Supper. Apparently, as with just about everything in the church of Corinth, the Lord's Supper had become a point of division. Unlike many churches today, when the early church took the Lord's Supper it was an entire meal. Yet, for the church in Corinth, this meal became a time of division rather than unity. Some people would arrive early at the meal and eat and drink everything so that those who arrived late would not have anything left to eat or drink. Most likely, it is the wealthier people who had arrived first and eaten everything so that those who had to work would be left with nothing. Paul argues that the Lord's Supper is not about a feast, but rather it is about proclaiming the death of Christ. This tradition is so important to God that some people in Corinth had actually died because of the way that they had taken the Lord's Supper. Paul exhorts them to take the Lord's Supper in a worthy manner while examining themselves and remembering what this event is all about.

Thought Questions:

1. Have you ever felt like a temptation is too strong for you? What can you learn from 1 Corinthians 10:13 regarding that temptation?

2. Do you think that women should worship with their heads covered today? Why or why not? If not, what principles can we apply from the passage on head coverings for today?

3. What has been your personal approach to taking the Lord's Supper? In light of what Paul says in 1 Corinthians 11, what might you do differently the next time you take the Lord's Supper?

4. Some suggest that the Lord's Supper should be withheld from children because they do not understand what it means. Do you agree with this? Why or why not?

Spiritual Gifts and Love: 1 Corinthians 12–14
Lesson 113

It only makes sense that a church that is divided over who is a more gifted leader would have issues among themselves over spiritual gifts. In chapters 12 through 14, Paul addresses the topic of spiritual gifts and how we ought to view these gifts. It would appear that certain gifts are valued more highly than others in the church of Corinth. Of particular interest to the believers in Corinth is the gift of tongues. Paul is going to argue in these chapters that the values of the believers in Corinth are not in line with what is important to God.

One of the key things that unites believers is the presence of the Holy Spirit in each of us. While we may be radically diverse in our personalities and cultures, all believers have the same Spirit inside them. In fact, Paul argues that it is impossible for a person to declare Jesus as his or her Lord if he or she does not have the

Spiritual Gifts in Paul's Letters

Romans 12:6–8	1 Corinthians 12:7–10	1 Corinthians 12:28	Ephesians 4:11
Having gifts that differ according to the grace given to us	*To each is given the manifestation of the Spirit for the common good*	*God has appointed in the church*	*And he gave*
		apostles	the apostles
prophecy	prophecy	prophets	the prophets
			the evangelists
	ability to distinguish between spirits		
	utterance of wisdom		
teaching	utterance of knowledge	teachers	the shepherds and teachers
exhorting			
	working of miracles	miracles	
	gifts of healing	gifts of healing	
service		helping	
leading		administrating	
	various kinds of tongues	various kinds of tongues	
	interpretation of tongues		
giving			
	faith		
mercy			

Holy Spirit. That same Spirit equips believers for their roles in the church. We learn in verse 7 that each person is given "the manifestation of the Spirit ... for the profit of all." This means that every believer has been given some gift by the Holy Spirit and that this gift is to be used to benefit others in the church. The Spirit does not give us these gifts so that we can compete with one another about who is better or more valuable, but rather so that we can work together for the benefit of everyone.

As Paul did in Romans 12, he compares the church to a body here, though Paul expands the analogy much more in 1 Corinthians. Like a body, the church is composed of many diverse members that all have different roles. While some parts of the body play a more critical role, such as the heart or the brain, every part of the body plays an important part in the overall function of the body. Something as small as a single toe would radically hurt a person if it were lost. So also, there are some people who play a more critical role in the church, such as an elder or a pastor, but for a church to run well all the members need to use their gifts for the sake of the church. In fact, Paul argues that we need to give special honor to those parts that are not as popular. God does not desire that every person have the same role in the church; rather than seeking gifts that God does not intend for us to have, we ought to seek to use the unique gifts that God has given us to build up the church.

This means that not every person is designed to be a pastor, nor is being a pastor the ultimate form of obedience for believers. Many believers today feel that being a pastor is the greatest thing that they can do for the kingdom, when actually God may have a much different role for that person. We also need to learn to value the unique giftedness of each person in the body and stop trying to make people become something that God has not meant for them. Once again, as with Romans 12, Paul gives a list of various gifts that God has given and the roles that these people play in the church. At the end of this list, Paul tells them to "earnestly desire the best gifts" (verse 31), which he will define in chapter 14.

There is something that is far more significant than giftedness for the sake of the kingdom—love. Chapter 13 is often known as the "love chapter" in the Bible because in this chapter Paul gives one of the most detailed descriptions of love in the entire Bible. Without love, it does not matter how gifted or generous or knowledgeable a person might be. Love ought to be what motivates us and drives us to use our gifts; we should not use them for selfish gain or to be seen as greater by others.

Paul then gives a detailed description of love. To love someone means "to suffer long" (that is, to be patient) with that person. When we love people, we will not generally be harsh with them, but rather kind. We will find joy with their joys rather than envying them. When we love others, we will not be interested in building ourselves up but in building up others. Love leads us to be considerate of others and to think about their feelings. When we love others, we assume the best about others and give them the benefit of the doubt rather than being frustrated with them. If we love others, we will not find joy in their sins but will speak the truth to them. Love leads us to continue to hope and endure with people even when they fail again and again.

While gifts are valuable for the body of Christ, they have an expiration date. God gives us gifts as a means to an end. However, love is something that we will always be required to give, and as such it will never fail. It is at this point that we need to discuss **cessationism**. According to cessationism, certain gifts, such as tongues, prophecy, and knowledge, have ceased to exist since the time of the early church. This argument comes out from 1 Corinthians 13:8 where Paul says, "But whether there are prophecies, they will fail; whether there are tongues, they will cease; whether there is knowledge, it will vanish away." It is clear from this verse that these gifts will cease, but the question is: "When will they cease?" Paul gives us that answer in verse 10: "But when that which is perfect has come, then that which is in part will be done away." So what is "that which is perfect"? There are three predominant views on this. The *first view* is that the perfect is referring to Christ and His second coming. Since Christ has not come back yet, these gifts would still be alive. The *second view* is that the perfect refers to the inclusion of Gentiles into the Church. Since Gentiles have already been brought into the Church, these gifts would have ceased. The *final view* is that the perfect refers to God's revelation of Himself. With the completion of the Bible, it is argued that these gifts have now ceased. It is up to the individual believer to figure out which argument seems stronger.

Having established all these principles, Paul gets very practical in chapter 14. The gift over which the church in Corinth appears to be fighting is the gift of tongues. Those who have this gift appear to be bragging and placing this gift above the other gifts. Yet Paul argues that there are far better gifts for the church than tongues. The tongues about which Paul speaks in this chapter are different from the tongues mentioned in Acts 2. In Acts 2, when the disciples speak in tongues, they speak in actual, recognizable languages. In this chapter, however, tongues have become a type of prayer language that is not discernible to others. Unlike the other spiritual gifts, which are said to be given for the benefit of the Church, tongues only seem to benefit the one who speaks in tongues. Rather than being selfish and pursuing the gift that only benefits you, Paul argues that we ought to pursue gifts that build up others.

Prophecy is a much better gift to pursue, according to Paul. When a person prophesies, those who are around will understand and be convicted. Tongues are a sign gift, designed to show that God has accepted that person; but if a nonbeliever hears a person speaking in tongues, he or she will be confused and will not benefit from it. However, if someone prophesies in the church and a nonbeliever is present, he or she might be convicted because he or she will understand the message. In fact, Paul forbids speaking in tongues during worship services if there is no one there to interpret the tongues so that others can benefit from the message.

The goal of this command is order in the church. Unlike our services today, where a set worship leader and team do most of the talking and singing, the early church was much more interactive. Anyone who had a word of prophecy or tongues or a song could share it during the church meetings. Yet, in this divisive church, rather than working together, people are speaking over one another and chaos ensues. So Paul lays down a series of commands designed to bring order. If someone speaks in a tongue or prophesies, only one should speak at a time with an interpreter. If someone else has a message, the first person needs to be silent and sit down. Women are to be silent in the churches and ask their husbands at home if they want to learn something. Now this concept is extremely offensive in our culture that encourages equality between men and women. This also connects to the idea of headship in marriage. The husband ought to be able to represent his wife fairly. It is likely that men and women would have sat in different sections of the house or church during worship meetings at this time. Apparently, during the service, the women were talking over the men asking their husbands to explain what people were saying. As one can imagine, this would be highly distracting. Paul suggests that there is a proper place for this, and that the place for this should be at home where it will not distract others.

Paul concludes his argument about gifts by encouraging the believers in Corinth to pursue prophecy, but not to forbid speaking in tongues.

> **cessationism:** the belief that certain gifts, particularly tongues, prophecy, and apostleship have ceased to exist since the first century church

Thought Questions:

1. Do you find that there are some gifts or roles in the church that you value more than others? What might these gifts be, and why?

2. What might be some aspects of love on which you might need to work?

3. Do you believe that the gift of tongues exists today? Why or why not?

4. Compare Paul's description of a church service in chapter 14 with your own church services. How are they different? How are they the same?

The Resurrection and Final Greetings: 1 Corinthians 15–16

Lesson 114

Perhaps the most significant issue with the church in Corinth is that some people from that church have begun to argue that there is no resurrection from the dead. Paul will by no means allow this false doctrine to take hold in the church of Corinth, so he writes an entire chapter arguing for the resurrection.

Chapter 15 begins with a concise definition of the gospel. The simple message of the gospel is that Jesus died for our sins, He was buried, He rose from the dead on the third day, and He made a number of post-resurrection appearances (verses 4–8). These are the facts with which a person has to wrestle as he or she comes to believe in Jesus Christ. We learn here that Jesus had appeared to many more people than the gospels or the book of Acts mention. Not only had Jesus appeared to the disciples and Paul, but He had also appeared to James and more than 500 people at one time! For those who argue that the disciples hallucinated when they saw the resurrected Jesus, it is impossible for 500 people to have the same hallucination.

For some reason, people in the church of Corinth have begun to doubt the resurrection of the dead. It is hard to imagine the Christian message without the hope of resurrection, but perhaps these believers thought that the resurrection was metaphorical. Paul makes it abundantly clear that the resurrection is essential for believers. If the resurrection does not happen, then even Jesus had not been raised from the dead and we would not be forgiven of our sins. There is no Christianity without the resurrection. Not only this, but if the resurrection has not occurred, then Christians are false witnesses of God and will be under judgment.

As with the epistle to the Romans, Paul compares Jesus to Adam here. Just as Adam was the first human who, in essence, brought death to all of humanity through his sin, Jesus as the new Adam brings resurrection to the new humanity. As humans, we can all be said to be "in Adam," just as all believers in Christ can be said to be "in Christ" (verses 45–49). The resurrection is also essential for the hope of the end times. Jesus' resurrection is the first step in the ultimate completion of God's plan when Jesus will hand over the kingdom, which is currently being built, to the Father.

There is one strange practice that Paul references in verse 29. Here he speaks of those who had been "baptized for the dead." It is not entirely clear what this practice had been. Because many of these people were first generation Christians, perhaps they had been baptized on behalf of their dead loved ones who had not heard the gospel before they died. There is not much explanation, but Paul argues that this practice would be useless if the resurrection does not occur. The question follows as to what kind of resurrection will take place. Will this resurrection be a spiritual resurrection or a physical resurrection? Paul argues that the answer is both. We will have physical bodies after the resurrection, but they will be of an entirely different nature than our current physical bodies. These bodies will be spiritual bodies and will be incorruptible. In fact, Paul argues "that flesh and blood cannot inherit the kingdom" (verse 50); only a transformed body has a place in God's kingdom. Yet what about those who are still alive when Christ returns? Paul argues that, when Christ comes with trumpet sound, in that very instant those who are alive will be transformed into their spiritual bodies. This is why death has lost its power. Death itself cannot hold us as we are raised from the dead. In light of this, Paul exhorts the believers in Corinth to "be steadfast, immovable, always abounding in the work of the Lord, knowing that your labor is not in vain in the Lord" (verse 58).

Paul finishes this letter by preparing the believers in Corinth for his coming visit. The first issue that Paul addresses related to this is a one-time gift that he wants to collect for the church in Jerusalem. Paul knows that there is going to be a famine in the land, and he has been collecting money from the churches to give to those in Jerusalem. He asks them to set aside a certain amount of money regularly for this gift so that it will not be a great burden all at once. Paul expects to remain in Ephesus for some time still, but he does plan on coming to visit them to receive this gift for Jerusalem. In the meantime, Paul prepares them to receive Timothy if he passes through that city on his way to visit Paul.

In light of everything in this letter, Paul exhorts the believers to "Watch, stand fast in the faith, be brave, be strong" (verse 13). Along with this, Paul exhorts them to "let all that you do be done with love" (verse 14). As with Romans, Paul sends greetings from a number of Christians and encourages the believers in Corinth to greet one another with a holy kiss. The fact that Paul explicitly says that he writes a salutation with his own hand tells us that the rest of the letter had been dictated by Paul but written down by someone else.

Finally, Paul calls down damnation upon anyone who does not love Christ. When Paul says "let him be accursed" (verse 22), this is a condemnation to hell. At the same time, Paul longs for the return of Christ and prays, "O Lord, come," which in Aramaic is the word *maranatha*. As with Romans, Paul finishes this letter as he begins it, with a call for the grace of Jesus to be with them. After his letter, which has been bold at times and defensive at times, Paul also reminds the believers in Corinth that he loves them. Paul has done all of this because he loves these people and cares about what is best for them.

Thought Question:

If our resurrected body is supposed to be like Jesus' resurrected body, based on what you remember from the gospels, what will our body be like?

Introduction to 2 Corinthians: 2 Corinthians 1–2

Lesson 115

Just as the name 1 Corinthians is a bit of a misnomer (because it is actually Paul's second letter to the Corinthians), 2 Corinthians is also a bit of a misnomer. In-between 1 and 2 Corinthians, Paul had written a third letter which he calls the "harsh letter." Second Corinthians, therefore, is actually Paul's fourth letter to the church in Corinth. Whereas Paul writes 1 Corinthians near the beginning of his third missionary journey while in Ephesus, Paul has since left Ephesus and writes 2 Corinthians while in Macedonia. Some scholars believe that 2 Corinthians is actually a combination of two letters by Paul based on the radical change in tone in chapter 10. While this is a possibility, it is more likely that Paul had received some news about the church of Corinth after writing 2 Corinthians 1–9, and he responds to that new news with the final chapters.

One of the elements of Scripture that is important to understand is the **tone** of a passage. The tone of a passage is the emotion with which that passage is written. The tone of 2 Corinthians is very different from 1 Corinthians, at least for the first nine chapters. First Corinthians is more of a rebuke, and at places Paul is fairly harsh with this church. The tone of 2 Corinthians is more of encouragement and comfort, though he returns to more of a defensive tone in the final chapters.

That comfort is the tone of 2 Corinthians is evident from the first chapter of this letter. After his customary greeting, the operative words in the next paragraph are "comfort" and "consolation," which is just another form of "comfort." Paul speaks about the comfort he has received from God as God had protected him from what appeared to be certain death in Ephesus. Most likely, Paul is referring to the mob that had formed because of the silversmiths who tried to have Paul killed (Acts 19). Yet Paul had been able to escape. Paul tells us that the comfort that we have received equips us so that we can comfort others who are suffering. This is relevant for the Corinthians because, as he had been harsh in his previous letters, he is now ready to comfort them.

One of the purposes of this letter is for Paul to explain to the Corinthians why he has not yet visited them. Paul had told them on a couple of occasions that he wanted to visit them soon. However, Paul had not yet come, and it might appear that Paul was a liar. So Paul makes it clear that when he says "Yes" he means it, and when he says "No" he means it. Yet Paul seems to turn everything back to God and to the gospel and asserts that in Christ, all of God's promises are a "Yes" (verse 20). Paul then explains that the reason that Paul had not yet visited was because he did not want that visit to be a painful or sorrowful visit. The last few letters that Paul wrote to the Corinthians were difficult and harsh, and Paul did not want to have to be that way in person. Paul held back from coming to Corinth so that they could have more time to repent and get things in order so that Paul's visit could be a pleasant visit.

Part of what has made Paul's letters so harsh is the discipline that he has required to be done to someone from that church. Paul does not give any specifics about who this person is or what he has done. It is possible that this person is the man from 1 Corinthians 5 who had been having sex with his stepmother, but this may be another person altogether. The church does enact discipline upon this man, and it appears that this man had repented. So Paul tells them in 2 Corinthians to receive back this person so that he would not be "swallowed up with too much sorrow" (2:7). Now that this person has repented, the church should take him back and forgive, comfort, and love this person. If the church in Corinth forgives this man, Paul also will forgive this man. Paul knows that Satan could take this act of discipline and use it to destroy the man who had repented, so Paul wants to make sure they receive him back.

Paul continues sharing the story of his journeys in 2 Corinthians 2:12. After leaving Ephesus, Paul had gone to Troas, which is the ancient city of Troy. While in Troas, the door for the gospel was opened; but Paul's friend Titus was not there, so he went to Macedonia to look for him. Nevertheless, Paul is still grateful for the openness to the gospel in Troas, and it leads Paul to praise God for the victory that we have through Him. This leads Paul to speak about the effect that the gospel has on the people whom Paul encounters. Some people are excited about the gospel and receive it with open arms, while others reject the message and Paul. For those who have been transformed by the gospel and by Christ, it is as though the smell of Christ is on us and follows us wherever we go. For those who are destined to perish, this is a foul stench, like the smell of death; and these people are repulsed by Christians. However, to those who are being saved, this is the aroma of life and they cling to Christians. In Troas, most of the people had responded so favorably to the gospel that Paul was the aroma of life to them. And Paul finishes the second chapter by reaffirming the sincerity of his ministry, that he is not doing it for personal gain, but because he has been entrusted with this responsibility by God.

tone: the emotion of a passage

Thought Questions:

1. Do you find it comforting to know that other people have gone through the same things that you are?

2. Have you ever been able to comfort someone else because you had been through the same situation? What happened, and how did you help him or her?

The New Covenant and Paul's Ministry: 2 Corinthians 3–4

Lesson 116

As we have seen in the book of Acts, throughout Paul's ministry he is regularly opposed by the Jews in the various cities in the Roman Empire. Not only would they regularly kick Paul out of their own cities, but they would follow after Paul into the surrounding cities and challenge the doctrines of the churches that Paul had planted. When Paul is not in those cities to oppose these people face to face, he writes to the churches and encourages them to stand up for the gospel. We saw in 1 Corinthians that the believers in Corinth had begun to doubt Paul's leadership because he was not as eloquent or as gifted as a speaker as Apollos was. Now it appears that the church in Corinth had been infiltrated by Jewish members of the circumcision party who had been influencing the believers there to follow Judaism.

Paul continues his defense of his own ministry in chapters 3 and 4. Rather than giving more credentials for his authority as an apostle, Paul speaks about his deep love for the believers in Corinth. They are like an epistle

written on Paul's heart, and everyone else can see how much Paul loves and cares for them.

For the rest of chapter 3, Paul compares the glory of the New Covenant with the Old Covenant. At first glance, this appears to be a random set of thoughts by Paul. He goes from defending his ministry to speaking about the gospel and comparing the covenants. However, if the church in Corinth had been infiltrated by the circumcision party, this comparison would make sense. The church in Corinth has had many issues to fix, and Paul wants to make sure that their doctrine is not corrupted, as well.

There are a number of ways that Paul argues that the New Covenant is better than the Old Covenant. The Old Covenant was based around the letter of the Law, whereas the Spirit is given in the New Covenant. The letter of the Law brings condemnation and death, but the Spirit brings life. The glory of the New Covenant is much greater than the glory of the Old Covenant, as well. The Old Covenant was indeed glorious. Whenever Moses had gone into the presence of God, his face was radiant. In fact, his face was so radiant that the people of Israel could not bear to look upon it (Exodus 34:33–35). Paul uses this story as a metaphor for those who insist on following the Old Covenant. In order to protect the people from the glory that they could not handle, Moses had put a veil over his face whenever he came from the presence of God. That veil, Paul argues, is now over the hearts of those who still depend on the Old Covenant. "Nevertheless when one turns to the Lord, the veil is taken away" (verse 16). Unlike the Jews in the Old Covenant who could not handle the glory, those who are in Christ can not only behold a greater glory, but we ourselves are becoming more glorious.

Paul returns in chapter 4 to his defense of his ministry, but ties it in with the glory of the New Covenant of which God has made him a minister. Paul does not have to try to manipulate people in order to get them to believe in the gospel; rather, Paul simply speaks the truth and allows the gospel to change people. Paul also understands that not everyone will be able to behold the gospel. Like the veil, which Moses put on to hide the glory so that the people could not see it, there is a veil over the hearts of those who are perishing. This also speaks to God's sovereignty and to the doctrine of predestination. Those who are perishing are unable to receive the gospel because "the god of this age" has blinded them and put a veil over their hearts (verse 4). People are unable to remove the veil themselves. It is only once God removes that veil that a person can and will receive the gospel. In light of this, Paul does not need to deceive people to get them to believe in the gospel. He simply speaks the truth of the gospel, and those from whom God has removed the veil will gladly receive the message.

When Paul received his commission from Jesus, he was told that suffering was an essential part of his calling and ministry (Acts 9:16). For the rest of chapter 4, Paul speaks about his sufferings. Even though the gospel is powerful and glorious, and Paul has the incredible privilege of being a minister of the gospel, Paul himself faces weakness. God has allowed Paul to suffer much and to face weakness so that people would not be drawn to him but to the gospel message. Paul is always facing death and sufferings of various kinds for the sake of the gospel. He is able to endure these things by faith because of the hope of greater eternal things to come.

Thought Question:

If the gospel is veiled to those who are perishing, what does this say about our will to choose God and the gospel?

Paul's Ministry Résumé: 2 Corinthians 5–6

Lesson 117

Typically, when a person applies for a job today, he is first required to submit a résumé. For many businesses, this résumé is the only opportunity a person has to make himself or herself known to the employer. In that one or two page sheet of paper, a person is supposed to prove why he or she would be a great employee for that company. In that résumé, a person is supposed to sell himself or herself to that company and write down all the positive qualities that he or she has, related to what that job requires. Most commonly, people focus on skills, education, and previous experience on their résumés. In the book of 2 Corinthians, Paul provides the church in Corinth with a résumé of sorts, but we will see that his résumé looks quite different from what would be acceptable in businesses today.

In the world, the ideal leader is someone who is strong, talented, and charismatic. Paul, however, had gone through incredible sufferings and, as a result, was weak. Unlike other speakers, such as Apollos, Paul did not present himself as a gifted speaker. Paul simply spoke the truth to whoever would listen. Yet, in chapters 5 and 6, Paul shows the Corinthians why he is a fit leader and why they need to listen to him.

Rather than strength and great physical stature being Paul's boast, Paul continues to speak of his physical weaknesses as his boast. Paul's basic argument is that his sufferings prove his sincerity and that he has been obedient to Christ. If Jesus Himself had suffered for obedience, Paul's sufferings are evidence that he is following in Jesus' footsteps. In the beginning of chapter 5, Paul expresses this through metaphor. In this section, Paul refers to his body as an "earthly house," or a "tent." Paul longs to be free from the limitations of this earthly body and looks forward to his new heavenly body, which will not be weak. Paul also is confident that he will receive this new body because of the abundant evidence of the Holy Spirit in his life. Paul identifies the Holy Spirit as his "guarantee" that he will someday receive that new body (verse 5). Paul would rather have that new body right now so that he could enjoy being in the presence of the Lord, but he also finds joy in pleasing the Lord while he is still here.

Paul's résumé begins, therefore, with the purity of his intentions. He can be trusted as an apostle and a good leader because of *his genuineness in his ministry*. Paul does not do his ministry in order to please himself but rather to please God. His second motivation for his ministry is *his fear or terror of the Lord*. There will be a day in which all people will stand before the judgment seat of Christ and will have to give an account for how they have lived their lives. Because Paul will have to ultimately answer to Jesus for how faithful he has been with his ministry, he can be trusted. And Paul's third motivation for his ministry is *the love of Christ*. This phrase can and should be taken two ways. When Paul says "love of Christ," this means both the love that Christ has and shows and Paul's love for Christ. Paul is motivated to be faithful in his ministry because of the experience that he has had of the love that Jesus showed him by dying for him. Yet he is also motivated to do ministry because he loves Jesus and wants to please Him.

Next, Paul follows with a theologically rich description of what his ministry is. Paul begins by expressing how he views people now. Before he was saved by Jesus, Paul regarded people "according to the flesh" (verse 16). What this means is that Paul saw people in a worldly way, valuing and evaluating people by the standards of the world. However, now that Paul has been saved, he sees Christians as brand new creations. The idea of us being new creations is incredibly significant for the gospel. Many people believe that they are broken vessels that need to be fixed by God. While it is true that we are all broken vessels, the problem is that these vessels cannot be fixed. Rather than "fixing" us, Jesus re-creates us when we are saved so that we become brand new creations. Also tied into this idea is the hope for future glory. We await a day when all of creation is made new, but that process begins with us the moment we receive the Holy Spirit at salvation.

Paul describes his ministry as "the ministry of reconciliation" (verse 18). At the core, as Christians our mission is to reconcile people with God. As we learned in Romans, reconciliation is the process wherein two or more people solve their differences so that they can have a healthy relationship again. Without Christ, all people are enemies of God, and there is a deep hostility between the two. Yet, through the gospel, God provides a way for that relationship breach to be filled. As Christians, it is our role to appeal and plead with people to take that step of reconciliation and return to God. In light of this, Paul speaks of himself and us as "ambassadors for Christ" (verse 20). An ambassador is someone whom a country sends to other countries in order to represent the interests of the country that sent him or her. We have been sent by God to represent Him to the world and to help reconcile the world back to God.

The final verse in chapter 5 describes the great exchange that takes place in salvation. This verse effectively summarizes the work of Christ in the gospel. God made Jesus, who had never sinned, to become sin for us. In other words, even though Jesus had never sinned, He took upon Himself all our sins and paid the penalty for all our sins on the cross. Conversely, upon taking our sins upon Himself, Jesus gives us His own perfect righteousness when we place our faith in Him. In this exchange, Jesus receives our sins and we receive His righteousness.

In light of the ministry responsibilities that Paul has received and his faithfulness as a minister of the gospel, Paul appeals to the Corinthians to guard and protect that gospel that he gave them. In the first verse from chapter 6, Paul pleads with the Corinthians not to receive "the grace of God in vain." Paul is concerned that the Corinthians have been and will be deceived by false teachers who are trying to lead them away from the message of the gospel. Paul reminds them of the kinds of things he has been willing to endure to protect that gospel. Paul has gone through incredible physical pain and discomfort, he has worked hard to keep his own life pure, and he has worked incredibly hard to defend the truth of the gospel. More often than not, the price of faithfulness for Paul is rejection and pain. Yet the gospel is so important to Paul, and his responsibility to protect it is so important to Paul that he willingly takes on those struggles. So if Paul has been willing to go through so much for the gospel, which he had gra-ciously given to the Corinthians, they ought to protect themselves and the gospel.

In light of this, Paul commands the Corinthians to "not be unequally yoked together with unbelievers" (verse 14). A yoke is a device that farmers would place between two oxen, connecting them so that as they walk they would plow the ground behind them. If the oxen are not close in size and weight, one will end up dragging the other behind and both will be injured. In this context, Paul is warning the Corinthians not to get too close with unbelievers, lest they be pulled down in the process. It would appear that the Corinthian believers had allowed unbelievers to be in positions of influence within the church of Corinth. Paul wants them to guard themselves from such people, lest they become corrupted in the process. As a side note, this verse is often used by people in the context of marriage and relationships. To be unequally yoked in a relationship involves dating or marrying someone who is not a strong believer. This is certainly an appropriate interpretation of this passage, but the application of this passage is far broader. We must guard ourselves from becoming too close to anyone who would hinder us in our faith. This does not mean that we must completely avoid nonbelievers, otherwise Jesus would have sinned in this area; but it does mean that we must be careful and protect ourselves from allowing such people to strongly influence us.

Thought Questions:

1. What would you say is your main motivation for serving God?

2. What do you think it means to regard someone from a fleshly point of view? How might you look at someone differently if you regard him or her as a new creation?

3. What might be some dangers of dating nonbelievers?

Godly Sorrow and Generous Giving: 2 Corinthians 7–8
Lesson 118

One of the ways that the Holy Spirit helps us live out our Christian lives is that He convicts us of our sins so that we are more motivated to repent. However, we also have a crafty enemy that can counterfeit that conviction. Rather than fighting the conviction of the Holy Spirit, the enemy amplifies that conviction and turns it into discouragement and condemnation. It requires wisdom to be able to distinguish between the two forms of "conviction." Paul is going to speak to this in 2 Corinthians 7.

Because the gospel is so precious and we need to guard it, we also need to guard ourselves lest we walk away from the gospel. Paul had finished the sixth chapter by warning the Corinthians not to get too close to non-believers so that they would not be led astray by them. Paul concludes that argument in the first verse of chapter 7 when he exhorts the Corinthian believers to cleanse themselves "from all filthiness of the flesh and spirit, perfecting holiness in the fear of God." Because we have been given such a great salvation, we are to work hard to stay pure and to protect ourselves from corruption.

As Paul has been doing throughout this letter, he returns to his own personal story about his interaction with the Corinthians. We learned in chapter 2 that Paul had visited Macedonia on his way to visit the Corinthians, but because he did not want to have another painful visit, he had delayed coming to Corinth. In chapter 7, we learn that Paul's experience in Macedonia was filled with trouble and tribulation. However, in the midst of this difficult time, Paul had been encouraged by the coming of Titus. Titus had given him a favorable report about the Corinthians, which had given Paul great comfort. In Paul's previous letter, he had been quite harsh and had demanded repentance of the Corinthians. Titus reported to Paul that the Corinthians had indeed repented and had expressed a great desire to prove that repentance to Paul.

It is in this context that Paul gives us wisdom between "godly sorrow" and "the sorrow of the world" (verse 10). Godly sorrow is another name for the grief that comes from the conviction of the Holy Spirit. When the Holy Spirit convicts us, we feel really bad about the sins that we have committed. This godly sorrow is a good and productive sorrow that leads us to repent of our sins and experience the joy of obedience. The sorrow of the world, however, produces death according to Paul. One major difference between the two is that godly sorrow does not lead to regret, whereas worldly sorrow discourages us through regrets. The best way to distinguish between the conviction of the Holy Spirit and worldly sorrow is by examining the effects of that sorrow. Godly sorrow equips and motivates us to repent of that sin, whereas worldly sorrow condemns and discourages us so that we are less equipped to turn from that sin. In addition, godly sorrow finds its completion upon repentance so that afterwards there is no reason to feel bad or regret anything. Worldly sorrow continues to condemn

even after repentance so that we do not feel the joy of obedience. Paul's previous letter had resulted in godly sorrow for the Corinthians, as they had experienced the fruit of repentance, and for this Paul has no regrets.

Even though it appears that the Corinthian church had repented of many of their previous sins, there is still another matter about which Paul feels the need to exhort them. Because of a great famine that was coming upon the land, Paul had begun to go to the churches that he had planted in order to ask them for money to send to Jerusalem. About a year before this letter, the Corinthians had agreed to set aside a certain amount of money for this gift. Now Paul exhorts them to be faithful to collect this money. As a means of motivating the Corinthians to go through with this gift, Paul informs them of the incredible generosity of the churches in Macedonia. He also reminds them of the incredible generosity of Jesus that He was willing to become poor in order to make us rich. Paul does not intend for this command to be a burden, but simply a fulfillment of a promise to which they had agreed a year before. Thus, Paul informs the Corinthians that he is sending a number of reliable and responsible men with this letter to collect that money. Paul even uses perhaps a little bit of guilt by asking the Corinthians to prove to be faithful in this so that his boasting about them would not prove to be in vain. In other words, Paul informs them that he has been boasting to others about their agreement to give this gift; if they do not give it, this would make them and Paul look bad.

Thought Questions:

1. Can you think of a time when you experienced godly sorrow? How about worldly sorrow? What is the difference between these two experiences?

2. Based on what Paul has said about godly sorrow and worldly sorrow, is it ever okay to do something that causes another person to be filled with sorrow? If yes, what might be an example?

Cheerful Giving and Paul's Further Defense: 2 Corinthians 9–10

Lesson 119

Paul completes in chapter 9 the exhortation that he had begun in chapter 8 concerning the gift for Jerusalem. The churches in Macedonia had been so incredibly generous in their gift, and Paul had boasted so much about the Corinthians, that he does not want the Corinthians to be ashamed when men from Macedonia hear about their gift. Once again, this gift should be something that they joyfully offer; it should not be a "grudging obligation" (verse 5). This is the interesting thing about money. When it comes to giving money, God wants us to give cheerfully, not merely out of obligation. When we give money merely out of obligation, we will begin to hold a grudge against God, and we will be robbed of the joy that we should have when we give. Paul also reminds the Corinthians that God is involved in the giving process. As with a farmer who sows his seed, when we are generous with our money, we will have a better return from God. Paul reminds the Corinthians of a number of promises that God had previously made that He will provide for all their needs. Giving is a matter of faith; do we truly believe that God will provide for us? Besides the benefits that this act of giving will give to the Corinthians, it will also provide for the needs of fellow brothers, and it has resulted in thanksgiving by all who hear about this gift. This gift also provides proof to the other churches of the genuineness of their confession to the gospel of Christ.

As a side note, it is worthwhile to mention the idea of tithing at this point. Many people point to this passage and argue that tithing is not necessary, but rather, we should simply give cheerfully. The **tithe** simply refers to giving ten percent of our income to God. The tithe found its origin in the life of Abraham when he gave ten percent of his plunder from war to Melchizedek, the priest of Salem. Throughout the Old Testament, the Israelites were required to give ten percent regularly. While this is an area in which each individual must develop his or her own convictions, this is mentioned here because the gift described in 2 Corinthians 8–9 is not a tithe, but rather a one-time gift. This gift would have been given in addition to the regular tithe that people would have given.

As mentioned in the introduction to 2 Corinthians, the tone of this letter appears to change in chapter 10. Throughout this letter, Paul has spoken multiple times about his deep affections for the believers in Corinth. As recently as chapter 8, Paul has spoken about the great comfort he had received from Titus about the genuineness of their repentance based on Paul's last letter. In chapter 10, however, Paul returns to a tone of self-defense. While this tone change seems to be quite abrupt, the content is consistent with Paul's earlier forms of self-defense.

The very first words of chapter 10 inform us about why Paul has spent so much time defending his sufferings and weaknesses. Apparently, some people in Corinth had been slandering Paul, claiming that he is all talk and no action. Paul has been quite bold in his letters, yet in person he has been quite humble and weak. Paul has been purposefully meek and gentle, however, because Jesus Himself had been that way toward His people. Jumping ahead in chapter 10, Paul warns them that when he comes, he is going to be as bold as he has been in his letters. It is not Paul's desire to be harsh or bold with them; he would rather enjoy being in their presence, but if they insist, he will come with boldness.

Paul also defends once again his own weakness. If Paul were waging war the way the world wages war, his physical weakness would be a problem indeed. Yet we are engaged in a spiritual war and "the weapons of our warfare are not carnal but mighty in God for pulling down strongholds" (verse 4). Our battle is a battle of the mind and spirit; this is why for Paul it has been a battle of words. Paul has spoken boldly because he is "casting down arguments and every high thing that exalts itself against the knowledge of God, bringing every thought into captivity to the obedience of Christ" (verse 5).

Once again, Paul reminds the Corinthians that they should not be examining people from a worldly or fleshly point of view. The value of a person is not based on his or her physical stature or power of speech, but rather through the work of Christ in that person. However, because the Corinthians have been viewing Paul in a worldly manner, when he comes to them he will have to come with boldness. Paul does have authority among the Corinthians because he was the one who brought the gospel to them. He has no interest in taking credit for the work that others have done, but his ambition has always been to bring the gospel where it has not previously been. However, even though Paul is going to give more evidence of his authority and reliability as a minister of the gospel, as Paul has told them before, the only approval that Paul needs is from God.

> **tithe:** an offering of ten percent of our income to God

Thought Question:

> Do you often give your money to God? If so, how do you feel about giving this money to God? Do you find that you do it out of obligation or out of joy? Why do you think this is?

Strength in Weakness: 2 Corinthians 11–13

Lesson 120

Paul continues his defense of his authority in the final three chapters of 2 Corinthians. Because the Corinthians have continued to slander Paul and question his authority as an apostle, Paul finally allows himself to boast, though Paul has no desire to do so. The "folly" about which Paul speaks in the beginning of chapter 11 is the boast that he is about to do. The Corinthians had begun to follow some false teachers who were more charismatic than Paul but who preached a false gospel. Paul, however, came to them with meekness and generosity. Rather than collecting money from the Corinthians to provide for his needs, Paul chose to use the money provided from other churches and money from his own earnings to provide for his needs. Sarcastically, Paul suggests that he should have charged them for his services so that they would see him as strong.

Even though these false teachers come across as charismatic speakers and great leaders, they are deceiving the Corinthians. This is what is particularly dangerous. From outward appearance, these false teachers are extremely appealing. However, even Satan himself appears not as a beast to people but as an angel of light. Even worse, these crafty false teachers are taking money from the people for their services! While Paul does not want to have to compare himself with these false teachers, he reminds them that Paul has a great pedigree, as well. If these false teachers could claim that they are true Israelites, Paul has just as much of a claim as an Israelite. Yet, unlike these deceitful leaders, Paul has gone through considerably more for Christ. In fact, Paul gives a list of the incredible sufferings and persecutions that he has had to endure for the gospel. Not only has Paul faced incredible opposition from those outside the Church, but he also faces daily the burden of his deep concern for the churches. Paul does boast, but not in the things that make for good outward appearance, but rather those sufferings that prove his genuineness.

Next, Paul moves on to a strange boast. He speaks about a person whom he once knew who had had a vision of heaven. As he continues this story, it becomes clear that he is speaking about himself. Yet along with this vision of heaven also comes what Paul calls his "thorn in the flesh" (12:7). It is unclear what precisely this thorn in the flesh might be. Some have suggested that it might be terrible eyesight, considering how Paul had been blinded before conversion. However, he identifies this thorn in the flesh as a messenger of Satan to torment him. Paul believes that God has sovereignly allowed Satan to torment him so that he would remain humble in spite of the incredible vision he had just received. When Paul prays for God to take away that thorn in the flesh, God responds: "My grace is sufficient for you, for My strength is made perfect in weakness" (verse 9). Unlike the false teachers, who strive to appear strong, Paul has learned from this experience that his weakness is actually what God wants to use. For when Paul is weak, then he will need to rely on God and His strength. Therefore, the very weakness that the believers in Corinth are using against Paul is the very weakness that God has intended for Paul in order for God's strength to be made more manifest. Paul also reminds them of the incredible signs and miracles that he had performed among them. The miracles in themselves should prove to the Corinthians that he is an apostle just like the other apostles.

Now that Paul has made his defense for his apostleship, he tells the Corinthians that he is going to visit them for the third time. Paul does not want this visit to be burdensome, and he is not going to request that they provide for his material needs while he is there. Paul, however, is concerned that when he comes to Corinth, he will find that they have not repented. Rather, Paul suspects that the church in Corinth will be filled with quarreling and backbiting. Even though earlier Paul had encouraged the church to restore the person who had previously engaged in sexual immorality because he had repented, Paul expresses concern that when he arrives in Corinth he will find that this person had not repented. This is what leads some scholars to believe that Paul had received a new report about the church in Corinth some time after he began to write this epistle and before he started writing chapter 10. Paul does not want to come as a disciplinarian, but he is afraid that he will have to be precisely that. Because the Corinthians have claimed that Paul is weak and that Paul does not back up his words with actions, when he comes he will be strict and harsh. After all the trouble that this church has caused Paul, he exhorts the believers in Corinth to examine themselves to see if they are truly saved. Jesus Christ should be evident within them.

Finally, Paul finishes this letter with a few exhortations and a salutation. He tells them to "become complete" (verse 11). In light of their immaturity and childish behavior, Paul exhorts them to basically grow up. He exhorts them to be comforted and to be united in mind and to live at peace. All of these are characteristics in which this chaotic church is weak. As we have already seen before, Paul exhorts the believers to greet one another with a holy kiss. Paul also sends greetings as with his previous letters, but here he does not name anyone in particular. Lastly, Paul finishes this letter with a Trinitarian formula. He calls for the grace of Jesus, the love of the Father, and the communion of the Holy Spirit to be with the believers in Corinth.

Thought Questions:

1. Practically, how might our weaknesses make God's strength perfect in us?

2. Looking back on this letter and Paul's defense of his own ministry, what characteristics should we look for in our spiritual leaders?

UNIT 4: *The Epistles and Revelation*

Introduction to Galatians: Galatians 1–2

Lesson 121

As with Romans and 1 and 2 Corinthians, the apostle Paul is the author of the epistle to the Galatians. Unlike Romans and the two epistles to the Corinthians, this letter is not written to one particular church, but rather to the churches in a particular region within the Roman Empire. Paul had founded these churches in the region of Galatia during his first missionary journey. There is some dispute as to when this letter was written. The key to dating this letter is its timing in relation to the Jerusalem Council described in Acts 15. Paul's main message in this letter is that Gentiles do not need to be circumcised or become Jewish in order to be saved. If this letter had been written after the Jerusalem Council, one would expect Paul to make mention of the decision of the Jerusalem Council in this letter, but he does not. If this letter was indeed written before the Jerusalem Council, then it is one of the earliest books of the New Testament.

As we have seen in the book of Acts and in 2 Corinthians, false teachers had infiltrated the churches that Paul had planted after he had left them. This is precisely the situation with the churches in Galatia. After Paul had planted these churches and moved on, Jewish leaders had moved in and begun to preach that Gentiles need to become Jewish and follow the Law of Moses if they want to be saved. Upon hearing about this, Paul writes this letter to sternly warn the Galatians not to fall into the trap of these false teachings.

The tone of this letter is much sterner than even 1 or 2 Corinthians. This is evident almost right from the very beginning of this letter. As with many of his other letters, Paul introduces himself by referencing his divine calling to be the apostle to the Gentiles. With the strong words that he is about to write to these Galatians, he needs them to remember that he has the authority to say the things that he is about to say. Also, like Paul's other letters, he greets them with the phrase "grace and peace," but here Paul adds the description of Jesus Christ as the One "who gave Himself for our sins" (1:4). Unlike his other letters, however, Paul does not have anything good to say about these churches at the beginning of his letter. All of Paul's letters that we have encountered contain a section where Paul mentions his prayers of gratitude for

the churches; but here, Paul immediately rebukes the Galatians after his introduction.

Paul addresses the big problem with the Galatians right away in this letter. Because of the influence of these false Jewish teachers, many of the believers in Galatia had abandoned the gospel and had fallen into Judaism. Paul does not hold back his words as he condemns these false teachers to hell. When Paul says for the false teachers to be "accursed," he is literally condemning them to hell. Paul, however, makes it clear that the issue is not that they are opposing him but that they are opposing the gospel. If even Paul were to preach a different gospel, he would curse himself. Paul reminds them that the gospel he received had not been taught to him by another man but had been revealed to him by Jesus Himself.

As evidence that Paul's gospel is genuine and is not something he had received by another man, Paul reminds them of his own history. Paul had previously been the model Jew who had persecuted the Church. Yet God had called Paul from his previous life and declared to him that he should preach the gospel to the Gentiles. Upon receiving that calling, Paul did not rely on others for his authority, but rather he avoided the region of Judea for some time. He did eventually go to Jerusalem and meet with the apostles, but years later. It was only after fourteen years that Paul had gone to Jerusalem with Barnabas and Titus in order to receive commendation by the apostles for their ministry. Moreover, the only reason Paul had done this in the first place was because some false teachers had begun to dispute with Paul and teach the very things that the Galatians had begun to believe. When Paul met with the apostles, they commended him to speak to the Gentiles just as they commended Peter to speak to the Jews.

Paul had even rebuked Peter for his hypocrisy in this matter. From the moment that Peter had received the vision from God of the sheet with animals that God had declared clean (Acts 10), he had begun to eat and fellowship with Gentiles. Yet, because Peter was afraid of what the Jews would think, when some Jewish people had come to Antioch who were sent by James, Peter stopped eating with Gentiles. Paul would have none of that, however, and he rebuked Peter in front of everyone for his hypocrisy. Paul's argument against Peter is that it is hypocritical for Peter to live like a Gentile and yet require the Gentiles to live like Jews. For even Peter had come to know that it is not the Law of Moses that saves people but that it is faith in Jesus Christ that saves people. Moreover, even if we are found sinning after being justified through faith in Jesus, this does not reflect poorly on Christ but on us. That justification does not give us a license to sin freely. Rather, when we receive the gospel, it is not only Christ who was crucified, but we are also crucified with Christ so that our lives are no longer our own. Our motivation for fighting sin is not so that we could be justified before God, but rather that, through the justification that we already have, we fight sin because our lives are no longer our own.

Thought Question:

We have already seen Paul sternly warn people not to follow any false teachers. Do you know of any popular false teachers today? What do they teach that is false and dangerous?

Faith vs. Works: Galatians 3–4
Lesson 122

Many of the arguments that Paul makes in Galatians 3 and 4 are arguments that we have already encountered in the epistle to the Romans. Because of the circumcision party that had begun to demand that Gentiles receive circumcision and follow the Law of Moses, Paul emphasizes a **dichotomy** between law and faith. We did not receive the Holy Spirit by observing or obeying the Law of Moses, but rather by faith. Also, through that Holy Spirit, many works and miracles had been performed; but once again these miracles were not through the Law of Moses but by faith.

As with Romans, Paul turns to Abraham as his great example of salvation by faith. Before the Law of Moses had ever been given, Abraham, the father of the Jewish nation, had been declared righteous because of his faith. Moreover, as Paul had argued in Romans, it is not the natural sons of Abraham who are his true sons, but those who exercise the same faith as Abraham are his true sons (Romans 4:11). From the beginning, God had declared to Abraham that through him all of the nations would be blessed. From the very beginning, it was the mission of the Israelites to bring the gospel to the Gentiles, not to force them to become Jews.

Rather than giving the blessing that the descendants of Abraham are supposed to give to the Gentiles, they are actually giving a curse by requiring obedience to the Law of Moses. Within the Law of Moses, it is said that the person who does not obey the entire Law will be cursed; and since nobody will obey the entire Law all the time, to subject people to the Law will neces-

sarily result in a curse for them. Rather than the Law of Moses bringing justification to anyone, Paul quotes the prophet Habakkuk to argue that the only means of justification is faith, for "the just shall live by faith" (3:11; cf. Habakkuk 2:4). Also, because the Law of Moses brings about a curse, Jesus took that curse upon Himself by hanging on the tree so that there would no longer be that curse for us. So to require a person to once again be bound by the Law of Moses is to render useless the curse that Jesus took upon Himself on the cross for us.

Because Jesus took the curse of the Law of Moses upon Himself, He fulfilled the mission given to Abraham that salvation would come to the Gentiles. Paul then does some interesting interpretive work. When God had made His promise to Abraham, that promise was given not only to Abraham, but also to his "Seed." Because the word *seed* is singular rather than plural, Paul argues that it is not intended for the entire Jewish race, but instead to Jesus Christ as the Seed. And since the Law of Moses came over 400 years after the promise to Abraham, the Law of Moses cannot nullify that promise.

If the promise is more important than the Law of Moses and is the only means of salvation, what is the purpose then of the Law of Moses? Paul argues that the purpose of the Law of Moses was to serve as a tutor until the Christ would come. Through the Law of Moses, we become aware of our sin and even more aware of our need for a Savior. However, once we come to receive that salvation by the Savior, the Law no longer binds us because it has fulfilled its function. Therefore, everyone is now put on an equal footing before God, whether Jew or Greek, slave or free, male or female; everyone is saved through the same means—faith in Christ.

Through that same faith, we not only receive salvation from our sins, but we receive a secure place in God's family as those who have been adopted by God. We have also seen this argument before in the book of Romans; as sons and daughters of God, we also have God's Spirit within us, who cries out, "Abba, Father!" (Romans 8:15). So after receiving all these benefits from the gospel, Paul argues, why would you want to go back to the life that you had before salvation?

As we have seen Paul do before, he gets very personal in Galatians 4:11–20. He reminds them of how he had first come to them because of a physical infirmity. When Paul had first come to them, they received him with open arms and cared deeply for Paul. As Paul says, "you would have plucked out your own eyes and given them to me" (verse 15). This is another clue that Paul may have been suffering some permanent effects from that original blindness on the road to Damascus. His physical infirmity very well could have been a limitation on his eyesight. Paul reminds them of how they met Paul because now they have begun to follow other people and have forgotten that love that they first had for Paul. Paul also cares for them and compares his concern for their growth and maturity to a woman in labor, longing for her child to be born.

As another illustration of Paul's point that salvation is by faith rather than by the Law of Moses, Paul concludes chapter four with an **allegory**. An allegory is a story in which each element of the story represents something else. In Paul's allegory in chapter 4, he makes a series of comparisons. The first comparison is between Abraham's first son through the servant Hagar and Abraham's son of promise through Sarah. These two children represent the Old Covenant and the New Covenant. Like Hagar's son Ishmael, the Old Covenant is a covenant of slavery to the Law of Moses. However, like Sarah's son Isaac, the New Covenant is a covenant of freedom and promise. Hagar and her son represent Mount Sinai (the place where the Law of Moses was given) and the present Jerusalem that is in bondage to the Law of Moses. Sarah and her son represent the heavenly Jerusalem that is free. Moreover, just as the child of slavery, Ishmael, persecuted the child of promise, Isaac, when they were children, the Israelites are presently persecuting the new children of promise, the Christians. Therefore, Paul argues, why submit yourself again to slavery to the Law of Moses since we are children of the free woman?

> **dichotomy:** a division or contrast between two opposite things

> **allegory:** a story in which each element of the story represents something else

Thought Question:

Paul speaks of the primary purpose of the Law of Moses as being a tutor to bring us to Christ. Do you think there is any other purpose of the Law of Moses for us as Christians?

Freedom in the Spirit: Galatians 5–6

Lesson 123

Theology is never intended to be merely an intellectual exercise. For every theological idea, there is a practical response that should lead to a transformed and obedient life to Christ. Paul has spent four chapters arguing that the gospel has set us free from the requirements of the Law of Moses; so how should this practically impact our lives? For Paul, this breaks down into one word—*liberty*. Because Jesus died to set us free from the curse of the Law of Moses, we now have freedom. So for the final two chapters, Paul is going to expound on the implications of the liberty that we now have in Christ.

The *first implication* that this liberty in Christ has is that we must guard ourselves from surrendering that freedom to unnecessary bondage. For the Galatians, this means that they should not be circumcised or bind themselves again to the Law of Moses. If people choose to bind themselves to the Law of Moses, they will fall from grace, since it is no longer grace that they are relying upon for salvation, but works. Under Christ, it is no longer circumcision or uncircumcision that matters, but rather love that results from faith. In light of this, Paul exhorts these believers to get rid of those people who are preaching bondage to the Law of Moses. Paul even gets a little crass in verse 12 when he suggests that those who are so concerned with circumcising the flesh should just go all the way and emasculate themselves.

The *second implication* that this liberty in Christ has is that we should not abuse this freedom and use it as "an opportunity for the flesh" (5:13). This is similar to Paul's argument in Romans 6 when he argues that Jesus came to not only set us free from the consequences of sin, but from sin itself. While we have freedom in Christ, when we choose to use that freedom to indulge in sin, we are in fact submitting ourselves to just another form of slavery. Rather, now that we have this new freedom, we need to use it to love one another. In fact, the entire Law is fulfilled in the commandment to love one another.

In light of this, we have a choice—we can either choose to live by the Spirit or live by the flesh. As Christians, we now have two natures: the flesh and the Spirit. The Spirit motivates us and equips us to walk in obedience and love, but the flesh motivates us to sin. These two natures are constantly at war with one another. Now, however, that we have the Holy Spirit within us, guiding and directing our consciences, we no longer need the Law because the Law is within us.

Yet, just in case the Galatians cannot distinguish between the two natures of flesh and Spirit, Paul gives two lists of actions and affections that are consistent with the flesh and Spirit. When we submit to the flesh and follow its desires, we will engage in sexual immorality, idolatry, quarreling and fighting with others, selfishness, false doctrines, and destructive behaviors. When we submit to the Spirit and follow His desires, however, we will experience love, joy, peace, longsuffering, kindness, goodness, faithfulness, gentleness, and self-control. It is actually quite easy to determine which of the two natures we are following to at any given time.

Right doctrine not only results in a better way of living for us, but it also results in proper treatment of others. As those who are submissive to the Spirit of God, we will not envy or provoke one another, but humbly we will look out for the best interests of others. As part of this, we will be patient with one another when our brother or sister falls into sin. In chapter 6, Paul exhorts the one who is "spiritual" to gently restore the brother caught in sin. The "spiritual" person here is the person who walks by the Spirit and exhibits the fruits of the Spirit mentioned in Galatians 5:22–23. We do have a responsibility for one another as brothers and sisters in Christ. If we recognize that a fellow believer is overtaken by some sin, we have the responsibility to help that person be restored to repentance. Yet we should not do this in a harsh or judgmental manner, but rather we should do this gently. We also need to be careful to guard ourselves from the same temptations. Part of restoring a fallen brother or sister may involve looking deep into the sins that he or she is committing, and this may afford the enemy an opportunity to tempt us to fall. We must be wise and careful when restoring a brother or sister caught in sin.

Just as Paul had previously summarized the Law of Moses in the command to love one another, here he summarizes the Law of Moses by commanding us to bear one another's burdens. Unlike this world, which says that we need to leave others alone, as Christians we should care for the burdens of those around us. This needs to be balanced with Galatians 6:5, however, which says that each person shall bear his own load. While we are called to help bear the burdens of one another, those burdens are still ultimately the other person's to bear; we are just called to help.

Returning to the dichotomy between flesh and Spirit, Paul gives us a little more help for understanding how to walk in the Spirit. Paul uses the metaphor of sowing and reaping to explain the struggle between flesh and Spirit. If a farmer wants to have a good harvest, he must be diligent to sow abundantly. Typically, the more a farmer sows, the more a farmer will harvest. If we invest or sow into the flesh, we will reap greater sin and corruption; but if we sow to the Spirit, we will reap everlasting life. These two natures have been compared to two beasts. Whichever beast we feed more will grow

stronger, and the one that we feed less will grow weaker as we starve it. So also, the more we engage in activities that connect us with the Spirit of God and align our passions and desires with His, the more the Holy Spirit will play a more prominent role in our lives. Yet the more time we spend indulging in our own pleasures and desires of the flesh, the more those desires will grow and become stronger. In light of all this, Paul exhorts us to sow good deeds so that we will reap benefits later. Also, we should be particularly purposeful in doing good deeds for other Christians.

Those who are trying to get the Galatians to submit to circumcision do not really care about the Galatians, but rather their own agendas. Many of these people push for circumcision because they are afraid of the rejection and persecution they might receive from the Jews if they do not push for this. Rather than boasting in these rituals, Paul says that the only thing that he will boast in is the work of Jesus on the cross. It is no longer about who is circumcised and who is not circumcised; the only thing that is important is who is a new creation in Christ and who is not a new creation in Christ.

For those who have come to understand and submit to the gospel that Paul has just proclaimed, he leaves them with grace and mercy. Paul then says something theologically significant at the end of verse 16. As he calls upon God to grant grace and mercy to those who follow the gospel, he also wishes for this "upon the Israel of God." In light of Paul's argument and the context, Paul is identifying the Church as the "Israel of God." This is consistent with Paul's argument in Romans 11 that not all of Israel is Israel, but rather all who are of faith in Jesus are the true Israel of God. In verse 17, Paul speaks of the marks of the Lord Jesus that he bears in his body. This could merely be a reference to the scars that he has from all the sufferings that he has gone through with Christ. However, this also could be another reference to an ongoing sight problem from his conversion. Finally, Paul leaves them once again with the grace of Jesus Christ.

Thought Questions:

1. What does it look like practically to "walk in the Spirit"? How do you walk in the Spirit?

2. What might be some ways you can guard yourself when you are restoring a brother or sister who is caught in sin so that you do not fall into that temptation yourself?

Introduction to Ephesians: Ephesians 1–2

Lesson 124

The epistle to the Ephesians is one of Paul's epistles that he wrote while he was in prison in Rome around A.D. 62. We know from the end of the book of Acts that Paul spent at least a couple years in Rome under house arrest and had considerable freedom in spite of that arrest. It is believed that Paul wrote the epistles to the Ephesians, Philippians, Colossians, and Philemon all while in prison in Rome. Unlike many of Paul's other epistles, this epistle is far more general and broad in its scope and contains very little that is specific to the church in Ephesus. In addition, as more early manuscripts have been discovered, the words "in Ephesus" are absent from the earliest and best manuscripts. This has led many scholars to believe that this letter was intended to be more of a "circular letter" to be distributed to many churches rather than to just one. Yet, even if these words were not originally included in this epistle, church tradition states that this letter was indeed originally intended for the church in Ephesus.

Paul has a very rich history with the church in Ephesus. Because God had opened up a huge door for the gospel in Ephesus, Paul had remained there longer than at any other city, for three years (Acts 19). When Paul finally made his visit to Jerusalem, he had a very tearful goodbye with the leaders of the church of Ephesus (Acts 20). This is a church that is very dear to Paul's heart.

This epistle is extremely theologically and practically rich. As with most of Paul's letters, he begins this letter by identifying himself and calling for grace and peace upon this church. The operative word that seems to describe chapter 1 is the word *rich*. Paul immediately begins to unpack the rich blessings that believers have when they receive the gospel. *First*, through the gospel, we are given every spiritual blessing in the heavenly places in Christ. *Second*, through God's sovereign choice, we have been made holy and blameless through the gospel. The idea of God's sovereignty and His predestination is a prominent theme in the letter to the Ephesians. Because of God's great love, God has sovereignly chosen to bless us through the gospel before we or creation ever even came into existence. Moreover, God made that choice according to the good pleasure of His will. *Third*, through the gospel, we receive adoption as sons and daughters into God's family. *Fourth*, through Christ and the gospel, we are now accepted by God. *Fifth*, through Christ and the gospel, we have been redeemed from sin and the consequences of sin. *Sixth*, we get to receive the abundant riches of God's grace through the gospel. *Seventh*, God has blessed us by giving us revelation of the mystery of His will. *Eighth*, and once again according to God's predestination, we will receive a heavenly inheritance. Finally, *ninth*, as a seal or guarantee of that inheritance, we have received the promised Holy Spirit.

What is clear throughout all these blessings is that all of them find their origin in the grace and generosity of God. Again and again throughout this paragraph, Paul highlights that God does all these things for us because of His own gracious will. These things are not only given to us for our own benefit, but also so that the result would be praise and glory for God. Also clear in this paragraph is the centrality of Christ for all these blessings. While salvation is by God's grace, it is through the work of Christ that we can receive this grace.

It is only after this long, theologically rich, introduction that Paul mentions his prayer for the Ephesians. Yet even this prayer is incredibly theologically rich. Paul prays that God would give the Ephesians a spirit of wisdom and revelation through their knowledge of Jesus. Paul's desire for the Ephesians is that they would have an even greater understanding of God and the blessings that they have in Him. There are three things in particular about which Paul prays that they would have greater knowledge and understanding. *First*, he prays that they would know the hope of God's calling for them. This calling is salvation itself, and Paul wants them to have an even richer understanding of the blessings of that calling. The *second* thing that Paul prays for them to understand is the riches of the glory of their inheritance to come. Paul wants them to understand what is waiting for them when they die. *Third*, Paul prays that they would have a greater understanding of the power that they have through the Holy Spirit. This is the same power that raised Jesus from the dead and brought Him to the right hand of God.

All these incredible blessings are even more glorious when we think about what we were before that salvation. We were once dead in our sins and trespasses. We were controlled by the lusts of our flesh and our sinful nature. Because of that very nature and our evil actions, we also were under the wrath of God. Yet the very power that raised Christ from the dead has also raised us from the dead and saved us from our sins. God did this for us because He is very rich in mercy and love toward us. He did not wait until we could pull ourselves out of the pit of our sins, but even while we were still dead in our sins He made us alive through the free gift of His grace. Paul makes it clear that salvation is entirely the work of God by His grace and not by our works. We receive that grace through faith in Jesus Christ. However, even though it is not by our works, we were created for good works, which God has prepared for us to do. The works of the Christian life are the result of salvation, not the cause of salvation.

As Gentiles, this salvation should bring a unique appreciation to those who have received it. The Jews have had a long history with God and have been included in a covenant with God. Yet, for centuries, the Gentiles were excluded from the benefits of being in covenant with God. Prior to the gospel of Christ coming into their lives, there was no sure hope of salvation. Through Jesus Christ, however, both Jew and Gentile have been brought together into one people of God. The Gentiles now get to experience the blessings of the people of God. Previously, the Law of Moses made it very difficult for Gentiles to be included among God's people, but through Christ that wall of separation has been abolished and there is now peace between the two.

There is now one people of God, and both Jew and Gentile have access to God through the same Holy Spirit. The foundation for this new people is not the Law of Moses, but rather the ministry of the apostles and prophets with Jesus Christ being the ultimate foundation. As Paul had said in 1 Corinthians 3:16–17, we as believers are now the true temple of God. God does not dwell in a physical building, but rather He dwells within all believers through the Holy Spirit.

Thought Question:

Based on Paul's argument in Romans, Galatians, and Ephesians 2, if good works are not necessary for salvation, why should we do them?

The Mystery of the Gospel and the Body of Christ: Ephesians 3–4

Lesson 125

One of the concepts that appears multiple times in Paul's letters is the idea of the mystery of the gospel. When we think of a mystery, we think of something that we cannot understand. To Paul, a mystery is something that was previously hidden but has now been revealed. Also, the great mystery of the gospel is that now, through Christ, the Gentiles are full and complete members of God's people. Even though the promise of this unity between Jew and Gentile is certainly pres-

ent in the Old Testament, for most Jews in Paul's day it had been hidden. Paul has also been the one appointed by Jesus Christ Himself to reveal this mystery to the Gentiles. Paul's mission, though he deems himself unworthy of such a mission, is to unpack all the blessings of salvation to the Gentiles so that they could experience all the blessings of Christ. Also, through the unity of Jew and Gentile in the Church, the wisdom of God will be revealed to everyone, both angels in heaven and people on earth. In light of this incredible calling that Paul had received, he tells the Ephesians not to be discouraged by the trials and sufferings that Paul had to endure, for through those sufferings the glory of salvation has been brought to the Gentiles.

Paul includes yet another prayer for the Ephesians near the end of chapter 3. In this prayer, Paul describes God as the Father through whom every family in heaven and earth is named. Both Jew and Gentile can be said to be in God's family through the gospel. This prayer for the Ephesians is fourfold. *First*, Paul prays that God would strengthen them at their core, through His riches and the Holy Spirit. *Second*, Paul prays that Christ would dwell in their hearts; in other words, that Jesus would reign at the center of their lives. *Third*, Paul prays, because the love of God is their foundation, that they would be able to further grasp the incredible bounds of Christ's love for them. *Fourth*, as a result of these other three prayers, Paul prays that they would be filled with the fullness of God. Paul wants the believers in Ephesus to grow in their experience and knowledge of the incredible richness of their salvation.

After meditating for some time on the grace and mercy and power and kindness of God and on the incredible riches of salvation, Paul finishes chapter 3 with a doxology. In light of everything that God has done for us, and because God is able to do considerably more than we can even imagine, God deserves all the glory from the Church. Our reaction to all of this should certainly be to bow before God and give Him all the glory.

Paul picks up in chapter 4 what he had begun to say at the beginning of chapter 3 before he sidetracked himself with even more theology. Chapter 4 begins the exhortation section of this letter as Paul draws out the implications of this theology for everyday life. In general, because we have been given so great a salvation, we should strive to live lives that are worthy of that calling. We ought to be humble and gentle and patient with one another, and we should bear with one another in love. We should also work hard to keep unity through the Spirit in the bond of peace. Even though there is some incredible diversity within the body of Christ and from church to church, we all are part of one body and have one Spirit, one hope, one Lord, one faith, one baptism, and one God.

As part of that unity which we should seek, we must recognize that God has equipped different people for different roles within the Church so that we can all be more effective. God has gifted all of us in some way and has set aside some people to be apostles, some to be prophets, some to be evangelists, and some to be pastor-teachers. The goal of those who are in these four offices is to equip the other believers for the work of ministry. This is sadly one of the ways that many believers and churches today get things wrong. It has been said that 20% of the people in church do 80% of the work, and 80% of the people do 20% of the work. Many people believe that ministry should be left to the professional pastors; but in reality, most of ministry should be done by the lay people. The job of the pastors and elders is primarily to equip others in the church to do the work of ministry.

Another responsibility that pastors and elders have for the church is to edify the believers in that church. This involves teaching and encouraging and building up those in their churches. The goal for this is that those in the church would be unified in their faith and knowledge of Jesus, that people would become perfect (or mature), and that people would come closer to experiencing the fullness of Christ in them. When this happens, believers will no longer be like children who will believe everything and be tossed back and forth by any new idea that comes forth. A mature believer will be able to test new ideas and teachings and will have the wisdom to recognize and reject falsehoods in these teachings. Sadly, far too many Christians today will believe anyone if he calls himself a pastor or wears a suit and says big words. Also, through this maturity, with Christ at the center of the Church, the result will be unity, with each part doing its share and with every person building up one another rather than tearing each other down.

Because we have been saved from a lifestyle of sin and slavery to that sin, we need to no longer live the way that the rest of the world lives. Without Christ, those in the rest of the world have their understanding darkened and cannot perceive the world and think correctly. Because even their hearts have become blind, they have also given themselves over to inappropriate passions and actions. We were once described this way, but now through Christ we have put on the new person who lives in truth and righteousness.

Since we have been made a new creation in Christ, we ought to live as new creations. We need to stop lying to one another since our connection with other believers means that we are ultimately hurting ourselves through that lying. While it is okay to be angry, we need to not allow that anger to result in sin. More often than not, our selfish anger will result in a lack of control and will lead us to hurt others. There is a righteous anger that should lead us to righteous actions. When we are angry, we should not hold onto that anger for long, but rather we should not let it last until the morning lest Satan could use that anger to corrupt us. Rather than stealing, we should each contribute to the needs of others. We need to protect our speech so that the things that come out of our mouths will not tear down others, but rather build them up. In general, we should not do anything that will grieve the Holy Spirit. We also must get rid of those feelings and words that lead us to destroy one another or to attack one another. Instead, we need to be kind, compassionate, and forgiving toward one another.

Thought Questions:

1. Who do you think does most of the work in your church, the pastors and elders or the regular people in the church? What can you do to help change that?

2. What can you do to prevent yourself from being tossed back and forth by false doctrines and teachings?

3. Think about the kinds of jokes that you usually give or enjoy. Do they typically build up others or tear them down? If they tear others down, why do you think you find them so funny?

Christian Living and Spiritual Warfare: Ephesians 5–6
Lesson 126

We have already established that the gospel always has implications for everyday living. Paul had begun to unpack some of the implications of the gospel in chapter 4, and he continues the implications of the gospel in chapters 5 and 6. Since our entire salvation is based upon the work of God through Christ, we also ought to imitate God. We are to love one another because Christ first loved us enough to die for us.

If Christ-like love is appropriate for us as believers, sexual immorality and impurity are not appropriate for us as believers. God has reserved sex for the context of marriage and, because God is faithful to us, we need to be faithful in our relationships. However, we need to not only guard against impurity in actions, but also with our words. It is also inappropriate to engage in crude humor or foolish talking or course jesting. Rather, the words that we speak should build others up and should be filled with thanksgiving. In light of the purity and beauty of the gospel, we should not joke about things that dishonor and disobey God. Also, because Christ has redeemed us from a life of sin, we should not excuse sin or tolerate sin, but rather we should confront and expose it. This requires a lot of wisdom in our day with all the access we have to technology. Far too often we find ourselves entertained by sin and desensitized to that sin when we should confront it and think about those things that are pleasing to God. Unlike the world, which often gets drunk with wine, we need to be filled with the Holy Spirit.

Since we are not supposed to talk about or joke about those things that are sinful or not pleasing to God, about what are we supposed to talk? Paul suggests that we should fill our words with songs and hymns and spiritual songs and that we should sing and make melody in our hearts to God. We should consistently fill our speech with words of gratitude to God for what He has done for us.

Paul then moves on to what has become known as the household code. Here he gives a series of commands to different types of people. He begins with the general command to submit to one another in the fear of God. He then lays out how different people are supposed to submit to one another, with Christ serving as the motivation for each one of them. *First*, Paul gives commands to wives. Just as Christ is the Head of the Church and the Church is to submit to Christ, wives are to respect and submit to their husbands. This does not mean that all women are supposed to submit to all men, but specifically to their husbands. This also does not mean that women are supposed to sit back and simply take abuse from their husbands. Submission is a willful decision to place oneself under the authority of another person and to support him or her as that authority. *Second*, Paul gives commands to husbands. It is interesting that Paul writes a lot more about the responsibilities of a husband. Just as Christ sacrificially loves His bride, the Church, husbands are to sacrificially love their wives. Husbands are to take care of their wives and provide for them, just as Christ does the Church. And when a husband loves his wife the way that Paul commands here, it will not be difficult for his wife to submit to him because he has been putting her needs above his own all along.

Third, children are to obey their parents. Out of the Ten Commandments, the only command that carries a promise is the command to obey and honor your parents. *Fourth*, parents are not to provoke their children but to train them in the Lord. When parents are too harsh with their children, their children will be discouraged and filled with anger. However, rather than being too harsh, parents are to patiently train their children to follow the Lord. *Fifth*, slaves or servants are to be obedient to their masters because they are ultimately serving Christ. Rather than just doing what they are supposed to do when their masters can see them, they are to be faithful always because God always sees them. Even though this command is specifically given to slaves, it also applies to employees today. Even when our bosses are not around, we need to be faithful because God is our ultimate Boss. *Sixth*, masters are to be fair to their servants because they too have a Master in heaven.

The last major exhortation in this letter is a call to "be strong in the Lord and in the power of His might" (verse 10). Specifically, Paul mentions this with reference to spiritual warfare. The way in which we stand firm and stay strong in the power of God's might is to put on the whole armor of God. It is important to recognize that the purpose of the armor of God is to be able to stand our ground when we are attacked by Satan and his demons. Of course, since this is a spiritual war, this armor is not physical, but rather spiritual armor. The *first piece of armor* is truth. Since Satan is the father of lies, we need to be purposeful to hold on to the truth when he attacks us. The *second piece of armor* is righteousness. Satan is also known as the tempter, so when he attacks us we have to be purposeful about doing what is right. In addition, because we have been made righteous through what Christ has done, we can stand firm when Satan accuses us because we know that we are righteous before God. The *third piece of armor* is readiness to share the gospel. When we are under attack, we may lose heart and stop with the ministries that God has given us. We need to be aware and continue to share the gospel when given the opportunity. The *fourth piece of armor* is faith. It is our faith and trust in God that will enable us to overcome the attacks of Satan. The *fifth piece of armor* is salvation. Similarly to righteousness, there is a boldness that comes with knowing that we are saved. Satan wants to cast doubt on our salvation. Finally, the *last piece of armor* is the only offensive piece in the entire set, the sword of the Spirit, the Word of God. This is precisely what Jesus used against Satan when He was tempted in the wilderness. Jesus responded to Satan by quoting Scripture, and Satan had to flee. The more we know the

Word of God, the more equipped we will be to stand our ground and fight back when Satan attacks.

In addition to the armor of God, we need to be faithful and watchful in prayer. If we stay in communication with God, we will be more equipped to resist Satan when he attacks. In addition to watchful prayer, Paul requests that the Ephesians pray for him that he would be given the ability to boldly proclaim the gospel.

Finally, Paul informs the Ephesians that he is sending this letter with Tychicus. He is sending Tychicus to inform them about how Paul is doing. Paul finishes this letter by calling for peace, love, faith, and grace to be upon the Ephesians.

Thought Questions:

1. Why do you think Paul's primary command for men is to love their wives and his primary command for wives is to respect their husbands?

2. Some have suggested that we should constantly put on the armor of God, and others have suggested that we should only put on this armor when we are under attack. Which of these two options do you think we should do? Why?

3. In what ways do you think Satan or his demons might attack us?

Introduction to Philippians: Philippians 1–2

Lesson 127

The epistle to the Philippians is the second of Paul's prison letters that we will examine in this class. The city of Philippi was located in the northern portion of the region of Macedonia, and the church in Philippi was founded by Paul during his second missionary journey. In fact, God had specifically called Paul to go to Macedonia during this missionary journey by sending him a dream telling him to go to Macedonia (Acts 16:9). Even though Paul experienced much persecution and suffering in Philippi, by the tone of this letter it is apparent that Paul had a great relationship with the church in this city.

The occasion that spurs Paul on to write this letter is to inform the church in Philippi that one of their members whom they had sent to take care of Paul was returning to them. This man, Epaphroditus, had grown quite ill and almost died. Yet God saw fit to allow him to live and heal, so Paul sends him back with this letter

to comfort the Philippians, for they had heard that he was sick. The key word that keeps appearing in this letter is the word "joy" or "rejoice." Unlike the epistle to the Galatians, which was basically a rebuke, or Romans, which was basically a treatise on the gospel, this letter is filled with affection and joy.

Paul begins this letter with his typical greeting, though he does include Timothy as one of the authors of this letter. As is Paul's custom in his letters, he begins this letter with grace and peace upon this church. After his initial greeting, Paul expresses to the Philippians the things for which he gives thanks to God on account of them. Paul is grateful for their willing partnership in the work of the gospel, and he is confident that the work that they had begun to do will be brought through to completion until Christ returns. Paul then expresses his love and affection for the church in Philippi because of how willing and ready they have been to support him in the ministry of the gospel.

Paul then offers his prayer for the Philippians. He prays that their love would abound more and more through their knowledge and discernment. We have seen before in 1 Corinthians 8 that sometimes knowledge leads to pride rather than love. However, the more that we know about Christ and the gospel and God, the more we will have opportunity to love God and others. The more knowledge and discernment we have, the more we will also be able to recognize and approve of things that are excellent. In addition, the more we will be able to recognize and approve of things that are excellent, the more genuine and blameless we will be until the day that Christ returns. Thus, in the meantime, we will bear the fruit of righteousness through Jesus, resulting in praise and glory for God.

Next, Paul informs the Philippians of his own condition. Even though he has had a rough journey, Paul's own sufferings and imprisonment have resulted in good things for the kingdom. Through Paul's imprisonment, he has been able to preach the gospel to the whole palace guard, and others have been encouraged to be bolder with the gospel because of Paul. Paul admits that not everyone's motives are pure in their efforts to spread the gospel, but as long as they are sharing the true gospel, Paul does not care about their motives. Paul also does not expect that this current imprisonment will result in death, but that he will be delivered. In light of this, it is Paul's desire to live in such a way, whether in prison or free, that he will have nothing to be ashamed about and that Christ will be shown through his life to others. This is where Paul gives his famous phrase, "For to me, to live is Christ, and to die is gain" (1:21). If Paul lives, he can use that life to honor Christ and to do the work that Christ has him do. If Paul dies, however, he gets to be with Jesus, which is better by far. Yet Paul is pretty confident that God still has more work for him to do, so he is pretty sure he is not going to die any time soon.

Paul then challenges the Philippians to act in a manner worthy of the gospel of Christ. Paul plans on visiting the Philippians; and when he gets there, he wants to see them united in their faith and in their mission to share and protect the gospel. In addition, Paul wants them to be bold and fearless in the presence of those who would oppose them so that through their confidence it would be evident to their enemies that they are perishing and that the Philippians are saved. They should expect people to oppose them and persecute them, for suffering should be expected for those who have believed in the gospel.

Following this, Paul exhorts the Philippians to be united through humility. If these believers have experienced the blessings that come from the gospel, they ought to strive to be united in purpose and in mind. Moreover, the key to being unified is to put the needs of others before our own needs. If we are each busy pursuing our own selfish ambitions and pride, we will never work together for the gospel. We need to be willing to humble ourselves and consider other people to be more important than ourselves. Our motivation for this comes from the ultimate example of humility and self-sacrifice, Jesus Christ.

Many scholars believe that Paul is quoting an established hymn in Philippians 2:6–11. This section is written poetically and may have been an early hymn that had circulated among the churches. In this section, Paul highlights the incredible humility that Jesus expressed in His life and death. Even though Jesus is God Himself, He chose to empty Himself of the privileges that come from being God and took on the limitations of being a man. Also, Jesus did not come to earth as a powerful and rich king, but rather as a poor person. Even more incredibly, He was willing to take on the humiliation of death on a cross for our sake. Yet the story does not end there for Jesus, for through that very humiliation God then exalted Him and gave Him the highest honor possible so that someday every person who has ever lived will bow down before Him and confess that He is Lord.

In light of what Christ has done, we should be all the more eager to work out our salvation with fear and trembling. This does not mean that we should work to earn salvation, but rather through that salvation we should be all the more eager to do the works that are consistent with that salvation. Yet even the very works that we do are the result of God working in us, equipping us not only to do those works but also to desire to do those works in the first place.

In addition, we need to be careful not to complain or to be quarrelsome. If we are to shine in this wicked world as we hold out the gospel to others, complaining and quarreling are inconsistent with that witness. Who would want to pursue the beliefs of a person who is complaining all the time? As the Philippians continue to share the gospel with the world, they also need to hold strongly to the word of salvation that they had received, lest Paul's work in them would be in vain.

Paul then returns to personal matters and explains why he has written this letter. Paul intends to send Timothy shortly to the church at Philippi so that he can hear how they are doing and so that they can hear how he is doing. Paul then commends Timothy, calling him like-minded and one who cares about the needs of others above his own needs. In fact, Paul considers Timothy to be like a son to him. Paul also plans on coming to Philippi shortly. However, with this letter Paul has sent Epaphroditus. The church in Philippi had sent this man previously to Paul to provide for his needs, both financially and as a friend. However, this man had grown quite sick and almost died. Yet, since he had recovered, Paul sees fit to send him back in order to encourage the Philippians and to save them the sorrow of worrying for him. Paul exhorts the Philippians to receive this man back and to honor him and men like him who are willing to sacrifice themselves for the sake of the gospel.

Thought Questions:

1. Have you found that the more you have learned about God and the gospel the more you are prone to love God and others? Why or why not?

2. Is there a difference between complaining and disagreeing with something? If so, how can we express disagreement without complaining?

Joy, Peace, and Contentment in Christ: Philippians 3–4
Lesson 128

There are some who would make a distinction between happiness and joy. Happiness, they say, is contingent upon one's circumstances, whereas joy comes regardless of circumstances. Whether or not it is appropriate to make a distinction between these words, it is true that joy is something that we are supposed to have regardless of our circumstances. One of the major themes that runs throughout the epistle to the Philippians is the concept of joy. Paul is able to rejoice in spite of the fact that he has gone through incredible suffering and is currently in prison. Even if our circumstances are poor and life is difficult for us, we can have joy because of the work that Christ has done for us and because of the presence of God with us.

After speaking of his own joy in the midst of his sufferings, Paul exhorts the Philippians in the beginning of chapter 3 to rejoice in the Lord. Note that Paul does not tell them to rejoice in their positive circumstances or blessings, but rather in the Lord. Paul immediately follows this exhortation with a warning. There are those who would seek to steal our joy in Christ. Paul warns the Philippians about the circumcision party, which we have already encountered multiple times. These people had followed Paul and had begun to deceive the believers in the churches that Paul had planted by requiring the Gentiles to be circumcised and by requiring them to follow the Law of Moses. Instead of calling them the circumcision party, Paul calls them the "mutilation" since they are so concerned with the cutting off of flesh. Paul argues, however, that believers are the true circumcision because we worship God in the right way, in the Spirit and because we rejoice in Jesus Christ rather than our own flesh.

Paul uses his own example in order to argue against the message of the circumcision party. The goal of the circumcision party is to make it so that the Gentiles become Jews. Yet Paul had been the ideal Jewish man. From the day Paul was born, he was a follower of the Law of Moses. He had been circumcised on the eighth day according to the Law. He was born as an Israelite in the tribe of Benjamin, the very tribe from which Israel's first king, Saul, had come. Both of Paul's parents were Hebrews (Jews). Regarding Paul's life before becoming a Christian, he was a Pharisee. As we have seen, there is no one who values and obeys the Law of Moses more than the Pharisees. Yet Paul was not just any Pharisee; he was incredibly zealous for God to the point where he had persecuted the Church. If anyone were to try to find a fault in Paul with regards to the Law of Moses, Paul was blameless.

Yet, even though Paul was the perfect Jewish man, he considers all these qualifications as useless compared to knowing Jesus. Paul would gladly give all this up in order to have Jesus. In fact, Paul considers these things about which he once boasted to be rubbish compared

to what he has now in Jesus. After all, what good is our own righteousness when we could have the righteousness of Jesus Christ Himself given to us? Consequently, rather than striving to meet the standards of the Law of Moses, Paul strives to know Christ more and to share in the power of His resurrection. However, Paul understands that along with the power of the resurrection also comes a sharing in the sufferings of Christ. Therefore, Paul does not look to the past in order to find his confidence, but rather he looks forward and presses forward toward the prize to come if he faithfully lives for Christ.

Paul says that this is the mentality that all mature believers should have. We should not seek to find our confidence and hope in our accomplishments, but rather we should focus on the joy we have in Christ and the prize that is to come. In fact, we should not only seek to have this same mentality, but we should seek out and take note of other people who have this same mentality. There are others, particularly those of the circumcision party, who would try to persuade them to find their confidence in their flesh. Yet these men are enemies of the cross of Christ and will be destroyed someday, whereas we are destined for heaven and a new glorious body that will never be destroyed.

Chapter 4 begins with some more exhortations. *First*, after once again expressing his deep affection for the Philippians, Paul exhorts them to stand fast in the Lord. They should not allow anyone to move them from the confidence and hope they have in Jesus Christ. *Second*, Paul exhorts some women who had been quarreling to come to peace and agreement with one another. As part of this, Paul asks for other members of the church in Philippi to help these women out. *Third*, Paul exhorts the believers in Philippi not to be anxious about anything. Rather than worrying, Paul suggests that we should focus on prayer with thanksgiving. If we were to develop the discipline of turning our worries into prayers, we would experience the peace of God that surpasses all understanding. This is why many Christians are able to remain calm and peaceful in the midst of terrible circumstances. The *fourth* exhortation that Paul gives is to meditate on things that are pleasing to God. Paul gives a list of the kinds of things we should regularly be thinking about, things that are true, noble, just, pure, lovely, of good report, virtuous, and praiseworthy.

Paul then finishes this letter on a personal note. Paul thanks the church in Philippi (by rejoicing in the Lord) for their generosity and financial gifts that they had given him. He reminds them that, even though he greatly appreciates those gifts, he would have been fine without them. He knows what it is like to live with plenty and to live in want, and yet he has found contentment in either circumstance. So what is the secret to Paul's contentment? He understands that his entire life is lived through the power of Christ; so whether he has a lot of money or no money, he trusts by faith that Christ will provide. However, even though Paul knows that Jesus would provide for him with or without the Philippians' aid, Paul is very grateful. He is grateful because he knows that they will bear fruit through the gifts that they had given to him. The very gift that they had given to Paul is "a sweet-smelling aroma, an acceptable sacrifice, well pleasing to God" (verse 18).

As with many of Paul's letters, he finishes this one with a small doxology and a salutation. Simply put, Paul prays for God to be glorified forever. He commands the Philippians to greet every saint (believer) in Christ Jesus. Conversely, Paul sends greetings from all the saints, but especially from those in Caesar's household, to whom Paul has had the pleasure of preaching the gospel. Also, as Paul often does, he finishes with a call for grace upon the Philippians.

Thought Questions:

1. Have you ever been anxious and found peace through prayer and thanksgiving? Would you say that prayer is one of your first responses to anxiety?

2. Examine the list of things that we should focus on in Philippians 4:8. Can you think of any television shows, movies, or songs that have all these characteristics? What implications does this verse have for the kinds of media that we consume regularly?

3. Would you consider yourself a content person? If so, why do you think that is? If not, what principles can you use from Philippians to find contentment?

4. Based on this letter, what do you think it takes for a person to regularly rejoice in the Lord?

Introduction to Colossians, Supremacy of Christ: Colossians 1–2

Lesson 129

The last two prison epistles are Colossians and Philemon. We will examine these epistles together because Philemon was a member of the church at Colossae. Colossae was an important city in the region of Phrygia in Asia Minor. This city lay northwest of the region of Galatia and east of the city of Ephesus. This city was also very close to the city of Laodicea, which would later be the recipient of one of the letters to the churches in the book of Revelation (Revelation 3:14–22). In fact, at the end of this letter, Paul makes reference to a lost letter that he had written to the Laodiceans and encourages the believers in Colossae to read that letter and pass this letter on to them (4:16).

As with the epistle to the Romans, Paul writes this to a church that he had never visited. Paul had not planted this church, but rather a man named Epaphras (possibly the same Epaphroditus from Philippians 2:25) had planted that church. However, even though Paul does not know these people personally, he feels a burden to make sure that they are walking strongly in their faith. He writes this letter in order to preserve the gospel with them and to counter some false teachings that had infiltrated that church. As with just about every church that Paul had planted, Jewish people had infiltrated this church and had argued that the Gentiles need to be circumcised and follow the Law of Moses. This church, however, faces another unique form of false teaching. Apparently, people in this church are being influenced by Greek philosophy, possibly an early form of **Gnosticism**. Gnosticism is a religion that teaches that everything that is physical is evil and that only the spirit is good. Through a special knowledge, which the Gnostics claim only they have, a person can be set free from the physical and find salvation. In light of both of these forms of false teaching, the main message in Colossians is that Jesus Christ is sufficient and supreme for everything we need.

Paul addresses this letter from himself and from Timothy. Like the majority of his letters, he greets this church with grace and peace. Also, like many of his letters, he begins by thanking God for the work that He has done in this church. Because Paul does not know these believers in person, he is responding to the report that he had received by Epaphras, the founder of this church. The Pauline Triad of faith, hope, and love shows up in verses 4 and 5. Paul is grateful because of the report of their faith in Christ, their love for all believers, and the hope that they have in the gospel. Paul is also grateful for the growth and maturity that has been occurring in Colossae as the gospel has been bearing fruit in them.

Paul's prayer for the Colossians is similar to his prayer for the Philippians and Ephesians, that they would be filled with the knowledge of God's will through all wisdom and spiritual understanding. If these believers are to be able to stand firm in their faith and grow, they need to have greater knowledge of God and His will for them. As they grow in this spiritual wisdom and knowledge, the result will be that their lives will be worthy of the Lord and pleasing to Him. There are four natural consequences of this spiritual wisdom and knowledge that are pleasing to God. *First*, through that spiritual wisdom and knowledge, they will bear the fruit of good deeds. *Second*, they will grow in their knowledge of God Himself. *Third*, they will be strengthened with God's power so that they can stand firm in their sufferings. *Fourth*, they will abound in gratitude to the Father for the incredible salvation that He has given them. In that salvation, we have been delivered from the power of darkness and have been given an inheritance in the kingdom of Jesus. Moreover, through Jesus, we have been redeemed and forgiven of our sins.

Next, Paul gives what is perhaps the richest description of Jesus in all of Paul's writings. In fact, the poetic nature of verses 15 through 20 has led many scholars to believe that Paul is quoting another hymn that may have been circulating among the churches at this time. It is clear from Paul's description of Jesus that He was not just some good teacher or a martyr, but God Himself in the flesh. *First*, Paul describes Jesus as "the image of the invisible God, the firstborn over all creation" (verse 15). Jesus is the firstborn, not as one who did not exist and came to exist, but in the sense that the firstborn is the most significant child for the inheritance. God, who cannot be seen by human eyes, has also made Himself seen through Jesus Christ. *Second*, Jesus is God's Agent of creation. Jesus is the One who created everything, and everything was created for Him. *Third*, He existed before anything in creation itself, and He is the One who sustains the universe and holds it together. *Fourth*, Jesus is the Head, or Leader, and Sustainer of the Church. *Fifth*, Jesus is the first to rise from the dead. *Sixth*, as Paul had begun this section saying, all of God's fullness dwells in Jesus. *Seventh*, Jesus is the One who reconciles people to the Father through the blood of His cross.

Before we came to know Jesus, we were separated from God and enemies of God. We were hostile toward God and dead in our sins. Yet Jesus reconciled us to God through His own death so that we would be seen as holy, blameless, and above reproach by the Father. However, all these blessings are contingent upon our continuance in our faith in Jesus Christ for salvation. Verse 23 makes it clear that these blessings come, "if indeed you continue in the faith … not moved away from the hope of the gospel." Even though Jesus has done all the work for us on the cross, our role is to persevere by continuing to cling to Him as our only means of salvation.

In verse 24, Paul makes a statement that could sound like heresy if we do not look carefully at what he says. Paul says that he rejoices in his sufferings because he is filling up in his own flesh "what is lacking in the afflictions of Christ." At first glance, it would appear that Paul is saying that there is something lacking with Jesus' death on our behalf. However, the word "afflictions" is never used with reference to the crucifixion. In fact, this word consistently refers to the ongoing sufferings of God's people. So what does Paul mean by this statement? Paul understands that through his own sufferings, the message of the cross is able to go forth; and as such, Paul is helping to complete the work that Jesus began with the cross. If people never heard of Jesus' sacrifice for them, they would never be saved.

Paul continues this section by telling the Colossians about the nature of his personal ministry. He had been appointed by God to reveal the mystery of Christ, that the Gentiles are now included as God's people. Paul's greatest desire in his ministry is to present every person mature or "perfect" in Christ Jesus. All of Paul's labors and energy are spent toward this purpose, and this is why he has written this very letter. Even though Paul has not met these believers in person, his desire is that they would be encouraged, united in love, and that they would have full understanding of the gospel.

This is where Paul addresses the potential problem with the church in Colossae. He does not want them to be deceived by false teachers who come with persuasive words. He wants them to remain rooted and grounded in Jesus Christ and the gospel, and to continue to live their lives "in Him." Paul warns them to be aware of those who would use philosophy or empty deceit that would pull them away from Christ. This does not mean that Christians should not study philosophy, but we should beware of any ideas that would pull us away from the sufficiency of Christ for our salvation.

The sufficiency of Christ is highlighted through a number of "in Him" statements by Paul. *In Him*, all the fullness of God dwells bodily. *In Him*, we are complete, lacking nothing. *In Him*, our hearts were circumcised as our old sinful nature was put away. *In Him*, we were buried and raised from the dead into a brand new life. He did all this through the cross, where he "wiped out the handwriting of requirements that was against us" (2:14); in other words, the cross wiped out our violations of the Law of Moses. Through the cross, Jesus also conquered His spiritual enemies and disarmed them and humiliated them.

In light of this, Paul warns the Colossians about the restrictions of the circumcision party. If we have truly been set free from the burden of the Law of Moses through the cross, we should not let anyone bind us once again to that burden. The festivals, new moons, and Sabbaths in Colossians 2:16 all refer to the ritual requirements of the Law of Moses for the Jews. While these things once had value, their value was to point to Christ; but now that they have Christ, they do not need these rituals anymore. Beyond this, the false teachers who had influenced this church had begun to preach that they need to practice asceticism and angel worship. In **asceticism**, it is believed that through harsh treatment of the body a person could overcome sin and temptation. Yet all of these efforts are attempts to find salvation without Christ. Now that we have Christ, we are not bound by these strict restrictions. In fact, it may seem religious and pleasing to God to neglect our bodies and practice asceticism, but these things "are of no value against the indulgence of the flesh" (verse 23). This is a very important concept to understand. When we simply focus on rules and on all the things that we cannot do or have, we fail to deal with the core problem of our fleshly nature. Simply saying "No" will not result in a godly life; the key to this will come in the next chapter.

> **Gnosticism:** a religion that teaches that the physical is evil and the spiritual is good; salvation is achieved through a special knowledge that members of this group claim to exclusively hold
>
> **asceticism:** harsh treatment of the body in order to fight against sin and pleasure

Thought Questions:

1. Based on what you have read so far in Colossians, what would you say to the person who sees Jesus as simply a good teacher?

2. If we cannot overcome our fleshly nature and temptation just by saying "No" to things, what do you think it takes to overcome that nature and temptation?

The New Life and Freedom: Colossians 3–4 & Philemon

Lesson 130

One of the most common ways that we try to fight temptation is with willpower. We know that something is a sin, so we focus hard on not doing that particular thing. This does work sometimes, but often our very effort to say "No" to a particular temptation seems to make that temptation even stronger. Part of the reason for this is that, in our efforts to fight that temptation, we find ourselves dwelling on that temptation. In Colossians 2, Paul argued that rules and regulations and severe treatments of our bodies may look very religious, but they are of no value in helping us overcome the flesh. So what does Paul recommend instead?

Rather than setting our minds against the temptations that are before us, Paul suggests that we set our minds on heavenly things. When we meditate on the things that are above—such as the blessings we have in Christ, the eternal salvation that awaits us, the relationship with God that we have now, and the very person of God Himself—the temptations of our flesh become far less powerful. Why would we want a small piece of candy (sin), when a huge dessert (heavenly blessings) is available to us? We also must remember that the sinful nature that once drove and controlled us is part of the old person that we were. However, we have become a brand new person in Christ.

Since we are a brand new person in Christ, we need to wage war against the person that we used to be. Paul says that we should actively "put to death your members which are on the earth" (verse 3:5). He then gives a list of some of the strongest desires of our flesh: fornication (sexual immorality), uncleanness (improper thoughts and actions), passion (lust), evil desires (our longing for those things that are against God), and covetousness (longing for things that are not ours). Paul gives another list that has to do with how we think about and treat others: anger, wrath, malice (intent to harm others), blasphemy (speaking ill of something that is sacred), filthy language (crude humor or words that tear others down), and lying. Paul points out that these characteristics and actions used to define us before Christ, but they are not consistent with the new life we have in Christ.

Conversely to the things that we are to put to death, Paul gives a list of characteristics that we are to put on. All these actions and characteristics have to do with the relationships we have with others. We are to be compassionate toward others, kind toward others, humble and meek toward one another, patient with one another; we should bear with one another and forgive one another when they sin against us. Yet the key to all these things is love, which Paul calls "the bond of perfection" (verse 14). In addition, through all that Christ has done, we should let the peace of God rule in our hearts. Once again, Paul reminds us that we are to be thankful. Moreover, we are to let the word of Christ dwell in us as we teach one another and rebuke one another, even through our worship songs and hymns. To summarize all this, Paul says that everything we do should be done in the name of Jesus and filled with thankfulness.

As with Ephesians 5:22–6:9, Paul gives another description of the household code here in Colossians. Wives are to submit to their husbands, and husbands are to love their wives and be patient with them, not allowing any bitterness to arise toward them. Children are to obey their parents, and parents are to be careful not to be too harsh with their children, so that they will not be discouraged. Servants or workers are to work hard for the Lord, whether their masters are watching them or not because, whether their masters reward them or not, God will reward them. Finally, masters are to be fair with their servants because they have a Master in heaven.

Paul's final commands all have to do with the spreading of the gospel. He commands the Colossians to be faithful in prayer, once again with thanksgiving. Specifically, Paul asks that they would pray for Paul to have an open door for the gospel and for Paul to be able to speak the gospel when that door opens. As the Colossians interact with outsiders, Paul also commands them to be wise and to take advantage of the opportunities that God gives them to share the gospel. When they do speak with outsiders, their speech is to be "seasoned with salt" (4:6); in other words, they are to speak to outsiders in a way that is appealing to them. This does not mean that we put on a show for the gospel, but merely that we are thoughtful and purposeful about our words.

Paul finishes the epistle to the Colossians with a set of greetings. Paul is sending two men, Tychicus and Onesimus, with this letter in order to inform them about how Paul is doing. Paul also sends greetings from some Christians from the circumcision party who had actually been a blessing to Paul. In addition, Paul sends greetings from Epaphras, who had founded the church at Colossae and who had reported to Paul their condition, along with Luke (who wrote Luke and Acts), and Demas. After sending greetings, Paul tells the Colossians to seek out his letter to the Laodiceans and read it and also send this letter on to them.

As has already been mentioned, the book of Philemon is included with the book of Colossians here because Philemon is from the church of Colossae. The issue that leads to this letter is that Paul is sending back Onesimus to Philemon. This is the same Onesimus that Paul mentions at the end of Colossians. This would not normally merit an entire letter, but Onesimus is Philemon's runaway slave. Apparently, since running away,

Onesimus has met Paul and has received the gospel. So Paul exhorts Philemon to receive back Onesimus, not as a slave, but as a fellow brother in Christ.

One of the downsides of having these letters but not being able to hear how Paul intended them to be read is that we cannot always tell the tone of these letters. It would appear that Paul uses a lot of sarcasm in this letter, though he may be serious. For example, Paul offers to pay back any debt that Onesimus owes, but he immediately follows this by mentioning that Philemon owes Paul his very life. How could Philemon demand money after a statement like that? Another example in this letter is that Paul says that he could command Philemon to take back Onesimus, but he would rather just appeal to Philemon to do so. And after Paul makes all these appeals for Onesimus, Paul mentions for Philemon to prepare a place for Paul since he plans to visit him. After all this, how could Philemon not take back Onesimus?

Over the years, Christians have looked to this letter as progressive on its views of slavery. Paul does not view Onesimus as less of a person because he is a slave, but he sees him as an equal because he is a Christian. In addition, Paul encourages the slave owner, Philemon, to set his slave free and to view him as a brother in Christ. As Paul has said elsewhere, in Christ there is neither slave nor free (Colossians 3:11).

Thought Question:

1. Do you find that when you spend time with your friends you are all purposeful to teach and rebuke one another so that the Word of God dwells in you more richly? What would it look like practically to do this?

2. Have you ever met someone who consistently conducts himself or herself wisely toward outsiders and who seasons his or her own speech "with salt"? What can you learn from this person?

Holy Living and Christ's Return: 1 Thessalonians 1–5

Lesson 131

Paul had founded the church in Thessalonica during his second missionary journey (Acts 17). Even though quite a few people responded positively to the gospel, the Jews in the city of Thessalonica were vicious and kicked Paul out of the city. As a result, Paul did not get to spend much time with the Thessalonians. Most scholars believe that Paul writes this letter during that same second missionary journey while in Corinth, not too long after he had planted this church. If this is true, this is one of Paul's earliest letters.

The main theme that stands out in this epistle is the second coming of Jesus. In every chapter, Paul makes at least one reference to the second coming. Because Paul was unable to spend much time in Thessalonica, the believers there still had some doctrinal questions for Paul, particularly regarding the end times, or eschatology. Specifically, the Thessalonians were concerned for those who had died as to whether or not they would miss the second coming of Jesus. It is possible that all this emphasis on the end times has led the Thessalonians to neglect their own holy living. This may explain the second big theme in this letter, that of the need to work on personal holiness. If a person expects Jesus to come back at any time, it could be tempting to not worry about trying to be more righteous since it will all end soon anyway. Yet Paul exhorts the Thessalonians that holy living should be far more important to them than worrying about the second coming of Jesus.

This letter follows Paul's basic pattern with his epistles. He introduces himself, along with Timothy and Silas (Silvanus), and greets them with grace and peace. Paul commends the Thessalonians for their works that come from faith, their labors of love, and their patient hope in Jesus Christ. Once again the Pauline Triad shows up. Paul's commendation of the Thessalonians continues as he recalls his history with them and the reports that he has heard about them. Though the environment in Thessalonica was hostile toward believers, the Thessalonians had received the gospel joyfully. Moreover, upon their faith in Christ, these believers had turned away from idols and turned to God.

As Paul often does, he reminds them of his conduct among them. When Paul came to them, not only had he just left an environment filled with suffering, but he even suffered in their city. Yet Paul was faithful to preach the gospel, and he did so honestly, not deceitfully. Unlike so many of the popular teachers who opposed Paul, Paul did not seek to use flattery in order to win people over. Paul was not concerned with people praising him or giving him glory, but he was concerned that people would receive the gospel. However, rather than manipulating the Thessalonians, Paul genuinely loved them. Paul was gentle among them like a mother; and he exhorted, comforted, and charged them like a father to walk worthy of the calling that they had received.

Unlike the Corinthians or the Galatians, it appears that the believers in Thessalonica received Paul and the gospel without much quarreling. Rather than fighting against the gospel, they embraced it wholeheartedly; and for this Paul is incredibly grateful. Perhaps the reason for this is that the gospel was very costly for the Thessalonians. Like Paul, they too faced strong adversity in their city. Because the gospel is so costly to the Thessalonians, they treasure it.

Paul writes this letter to the Thessalonians because he has not yet been able to visit them in person. Paul may have been concerned that the Thessalonians were offended that he had not come back to them. So in his place, Paul sends Timothy to help them grow more established in their faith. Considering the hostile environment toward the gospel in Thessalonica, Paul was worried that the believers there had shrunk back from the gospel. However, when Timothy came back to Paul and reported the faith of the Thessalonian believers, Paul was greatly encouraged. Still, though, Paul wants to visit the Thessalonians; and he informs them that he has been praying constantly for an opportunity to come to them. Paul also prays that God will increase their love for one another and that they will be found blameless and holy when Jesus returns.

After dealing with these personal matters between Paul and the believers in Thessalonica, Paul offers them some exhortations. For those who constantly are seeking the will of God, Paul makes the will of God known in chapter 4. God's will for us is our sanctification, that we will live holy and pure and obedient lives. Rather than burning with lust and engaging in sexual immorality, we need to control ourselves with sanctification and honor. Though there is much for which Paul commends the Thessalonians, he does not commend them in this area. Paul does, however, commend the Thessalonians for their love for one another. Rather than being quarrelsome, Paul urges the Thessalonians to lead quiet lives, to take care of their own business rather than dabbling in other people's problems, and to be diligent workers.

Paul then addresses the Thessalonians' questions about the second coming. Those who have died in Christ will not in fact miss out on Jesus' return. They will actually be the first people to join Jesus as He returns on the clouds of heaven. Those who are still alive when Jesus returns will then be transformed and meet Jesus in the air. Yet when that day will come, nobody knows. Rather than worrying about when that day will come, we need to live the kind of lives that will not bring shame when He does come. We need to live soberly and righteously, rather than hiding in the darkness; for when Jesus returns everything will be exposed. Since we do not know when Jesus will return, we need to comfort one another and build each other up while we are still here. Paul also exhorts the Thessalonians to honor their spiritual leaders. It is possible that Paul gives this command because they are looking to him to be their leader and not submitting to their own leaders.

There are a series of exhortations to finish this letter. In 1 Thessalonians 5:14, Paul says to "warn those who are unruly, comfort the fainthearted, uphold the weak, be patient with all." Those who insist on being disobedient, we are to patiently warn; those who have lost hope, we are to comfort; those who are struggling, we are to help. In 1 Thessalonians 5:16–18 we are once again given God's will: "Rejoice always, pray without ceasing, in everything give thanks; for this is the will of God in Christ Jesus for you." Similarly to Paul's commands in Romans 12, Paul says that we are to "hold fast what is good" and "Abstain from every form of evil" (verses 21 and 22). Paul's benediction for these believers is that God would sanctify them through and through so that, when Jesus does return, they will be blameless. As Paul commonly does, he also gives his typical salutation of grace.

Thought Question:

How much would you say your life is affected by the knowledge that Jesus will return someday? How might you live your life differently knowing that He would return at any time?

Clarification about Jesus' Return: 2 Thessalonians 1–3

Lesson 132

Paul's second letter to the Thessalonians was written not too long after his first letter to this church. Some time after Paul had written 1 Thessalonians, he received a report that there was more confusion by the Thessalonians concerning Christ's second coming. There may have been a false letter that they had received, claiming to be from Paul, telling them that the Day of the Lord had already come and they missed it. For whatever reason, the Thessalonians had begun to believe that they had missed Christ's second coming, and Paul writes this letter to clear up this confusion. In addition, as in 1 Thessalonians, Paul uses this letter to once again exhort these believers to pursue holiness.

As with his first letter to these believers, Paul commends them for their great faith and love for one another,

especially in the midst of the consistent persecutions that they had faced. It makes sense in light of their sufferings that they would take so much comfort and interest in the return of Christ. For as Paul says in verses 6 and 7: "it is a righteous thing with God to repay with tribulation those who trouble you, and to give you who are troubled rest with us when the Lord Jesus is revealed from heaven…." When Jesus returns, the Thessalonians will finally have justice upon those who are persecuting them. Those who have opposed the gospel of Christ will receive everlasting destruction away from the presence of the Lord. In light of this justice to be revealed, Paul's prayer for the Thessalonians is that God would count them worthy of the calling of salvation. He prays also that Jesus would be glorified in the Thessalonians and that they would be glorified in Him.

In chapter 2, Paul brings clarification about the second coming of Christ. It would appear that someone had suggested to the Thessalonians that Jesus had already returned and they missed it. To argue against this ridiculous notion, Paul reminds them of the things that have not yet taken place but must before Jesus returns. Simply put, before Christ returns the Antichrist must first show up. Here Paul refers to the Antichrist as "the man of sin" or "the son of perdition" (verse 3). When this man comes, there will be a great rebellion against God and this man will sit in the temple, claiming himself to be God. Through Satan, this Antichrist will perform many false signs and wonders, which he will use to deceive those who perish. In fact, because of people's love of unrighteousness and because people do not love the truth, God gives them over to a strong delusion so that they will be deceived by this man. However, God is restraining this man of lawlessness until the appropriate time.

Yet, unlike those who are perishing, the Thessalonians do love the truth. Because of this, Paul gives thanks to God. Moreover, because they love the truth, Paul exhorts them to stand fast and hold onto the traditions and teachings that they had received from Paul. In light of this, Paul gives a benediction for the Thessalonians, that God will comfort them and establish them in their good works. He also asks for prayer that God will deliver him from those who oppose the gospel. Paul is also confident that they will obey the things that he has commanded and hold onto the teachings that he has given them.

There are some matters that Paul does need to address with the community in Thessalonica. After praying that God will direct their hearts to His love and the patience of Christ, he tells the Thessalonians to withdraw from anyone who "walks disorderly and not according to the tradition which he received from us" (3:6). What Paul means by this is that there are some people in the church of Thessalonica who have chosen not to work but to depend on the generosity of the wealthier members of the church. Rather than working, these people fill their time with gossip and meddling in others' affairs. So Paul commands that those people who are not willing to work should not be given food. Each person should work in quietness and eat the bread that he has earned. In addition, if a person refuses to obey Paul's command here, Paul encourages the believers in Thessalonica not to keep company with that person. This does not mean that they should treat him harshly as an enemy, but that when they see him they should admonish or rebuke him. The goal of this is that from the loss of fellowship, this person would feel ashamed and repent.

For this church that has consistently faced suffering and persecution, Paul's final benediction for them is that God would grant them peace in all situations. The fact that Paul gives a salutation in his own hand and explicitly mentions that he does this in all of his letters provides more evidence that a false letter had been sent to the Thessalonians. Paul does not want them to be led astray again.

Thought Questions:

1. If the Antichrist is supposed to go into the temple and declare himself as God, what should we make of the fact that there is no temple in Jerusalem today for the Antichrist to enter?

2. If Paul says that those who do not work should not be given food, is it wrong to provide food for the poor? Why or why not?

Right Doctrine and Right Leaders: 1 Timothy 1–3

Lesson 133

The epistles of 1 Timothy, 2 Timothy, and Titus are traditionally known as the Pastoral Epistles. These letters are called this because Paul writes these to individual leaders of local churches and gives them advice as to how to lead those churches well. Both Timothy and Titus were trusted friends of Paul and had ministered alongside Paul for quite some time. Paul and Timothy had a very close mentoring relationship, and Paul viewed Timothy as a son. By the time Paul writes his letters to Timothy, Timothy was an established leader in

the Christian community. We learn from 1 Timothy 1:3 that Paul had left Timothy in Ephesus in order to help establish that church further. Practically speaking, Timothy plays the role of the head pastor over this church. Many of the exhortations in this book have to do with establishing an orderly structure of leadership in this church. Paul also encourages Timothy to establish this church with correct doctrine and to protect this church from false teachers.

Based upon the nature of 2 Timothy, it is believed that these two letters are written shortly before Paul was put to death. Paul is in prison as stated in these letters, but the way that Paul speaks of this imprisonment is different from the way he speaks of his initial imprisonment in Rome. Scholars believe that Paul had eventually been set free from his first imprisonment in Rome, but some time later under the persecutions of Nero, Paul was arrested again and then put to death. It is most likely under this second imprisonment that Paul writes these letters.

The introduction to this letter is very similar to Paul's other letters. Paul identifies himself as an apostle of Jesus Christ and identifies Timothy as the recipient of this letter. Interestingly, in his greeting he also includes mercy along with the typical grace and peace that Paul writes in all his letters. Immediately, Paul exhorts Timothy to protect this church from false teachers. It would appear that some people had infiltrated this church and had engaged in a lot of argumentation over peripheral issues to the faith. These people seem to be more concerned with arguing than with holiness or godliness. In order to build themselves up and make a name for themselves, these people debate about unimportant things such as genealogies. While it is a good thing to wrestle through what Scripture actually says in order to have correct doctrine, we must remember that the goal of all doctrine is a transformed, sanctified life. Some people are so concerned with being right that they forget that they need to have a right relationship with God and others. The people in Ephesus have an unhealthy obsession with the Law of Moses, and Paul reminds them that the Law of Moses was not made for the righteous, but for sinners that they could see their need for a Savior. As those who are now righteous, we need to have a healthy perspective on the Law of Moses, which these false teachers do not have.

Paul next reminds Timothy of Paul's own testimony. Even though Paul had formerly been a persecutor of the Church, Jesus called Paul and gave him the privilege of his ministry. If God had saved and commissioned a great sinner like Paul, He will use anyone. This is why

Qualifications for Elders in 1 Timothy and Titus

	1 Timothy
3:2	above reproach
3:2	husband of one wife
3:2	sober-minded
3:2	self-controlled
3:2	respectable
3:2	hospitable
3:2	able to teach
3:3	not a drunkard
3:3	not violent but gentle
3:3	not quarrelsome
3:3	not a lover of money
3:4–5	manage his own household well, care for God's church
3:4	keeping his children submissive
3:6	not a recent convert
3:7	well thought of by outsiders
	—

	Titus
1:6, 7	above reproach
1:6	husband of one wife
1:8	disciplined
1:8	self-controlled
	—
1:8	hospitable
1:9	able to give instruction
1:7	not . . . a drunkard
1:7	not . . . violent
1:7	not be arrogant or quick-tempered
1:7	not . . . greedy for gain
1:7	God's steward
1:6	children are believers (or "faithful"), not insubordinate
	—
	—
1:8	a lover of good; upright, holy

Paul encourages Timothy and all who read this letter to hold on to the saying: "Christ Jesus came into the world to save sinners, of whom I am chief"(verse 15). If we all truly believe this saying and apply it to ourselves, we will be far more humble and merciful and patient with others. Yet when we consider ourselves to be better or more righteous than others, pride will come and lead to division with others. In light of the incredible mercy in spite of our sin, Paul gives a doxology in verse 17.

After Paul reminds Timothy to take heed of two men who have abandoned the faith, Hymenaeus and Alexander, Paul moves on to his next set of exhortations for Timothy. Paul wants Timothy and the believers in Ephesus to be faithful to pray for all those in authority. The goal of this prayer is that we may lead quiet and peaceable lives in all godliness and reverence. The goal of authorities, especially government authorities, is to protect us so that we may live out our lives peaceably. Our desire should be to have a government that interferes with our lives as little as possible.

If the government steps out of the way and allows us to live out our lives peaceably, we will have more freedom to fulfill our ministries and to bring the gospel to the world. We know in some sense that God "desires all men to be saved and to come to the knowledge of the truth" (2:4). This does not mean that every person will be saved, as Scripture makes clear. This shows that there are some things that God desires that sadly will not come to pass. Paul summarizes the gospel and his ministry once again in 1 Timothy 2:5–7.

Paul finishes chapter 2 with a miniature form of the household code. Here Paul gives commandments for both men and women. For the men, Paul's desire is that they would be faithful in prayer without fighting or doubting. For the women, Paul's desire is that they would focus on modesty and godliness. Rather than focusing on wearing expensive clothing or jewelry, Paul wants women to focus on building their character and godliness. Paul's next command for women is very controversial today. Paul says that women should learn in quietness and submission and that women cannot teach or have authority over men. This certainly is not a popular idea in our society, which preaches equality between men and women. In fact, this idea is not even popular in many churches today that employ women pastors. These people would argue that this idea is antiquated and no longer applies in our society because women are more educated and capable today. Interestingly though, Paul does not speak about ability as being what limits women from this role, but he goes back to creation and Genesis. Paul seems to suggest that Eve's deception and the curse that comes from that deception is what precludes women from these leadership roles. Paul suggests that women should focus on faith, love, holiness, and self-control rather than having authority over men.

After speaking about the limitations of women in ministry, Paul moves on to give requirements of what makes an acceptable leader in the church. The first office that Paul addresses is that of bishop or elder. In general, elders are men who should have self-control, respect from everyone, good control of their homes; they should have the ability to teach, and they should not be new believers. Deacons have very similar requirements, though because deacons deal with matters of money and the practical running of the church, they do not have to have the ability to teach. Both elders and deacons must be the husband of only one wife. There are two possible meanings for this command. This could mean that they should not have multiple wives, which was still possible back then, or it could mean that he should not be divorced and remarried. Because deacons have to be incredibly trustworthy since they deal with money, even their wives need to be found faithful.

Paul once again summarizes the gospel at the end of chapter 3, calling it "the mystery of godliness"(verse 16). Remember that for Paul the great mystery of the gospel is that the Gentiles are now included among God's people. Timothy's most significant responsibility is to protect and preserve that gospel.

Thought Question:

Do you believe that it is okay for women to be pastors today? If not pastors, what kinds of roles do you think are appropriate for women, based on Paul's restrictions in 1 Timothy 2?

Godliness with Contentment: 1 Timothy 4–6

Lesson 134

In the final three chapters of this epistle, Paul continues his basic exhortations to Timothy to protect true doctrine and to give practical direction to the church in Ephesus. God has made it clear that, as we draw near to the final days, more and more people will depart from the faith and follow deceptive doctrines taught by false teachers. Paul gives some examples of this that had been occurring in Ephesus. As with the Colossians, some false teachers had begun to teach that believers cannot enjoy pleasures here on earth, specifically the pleasures of

certain foods or marriage. Yet Jesus had already declared all foods clean (Mark 7:19*), and if we receive them with thankfulness, those foods are sanctified. Refraining from pleasure is not what God desires from us, but rather active, godly lives are what God desires. It is valuable to discipline our bodies and to learn to say no to some pleasures, but godliness is far more valuable since it has implications for eternity. This is the second saying that Paul recommends that we hold onto, that godliness is more valuable than bodily exercise.

In 1 Timothy 4:10, Paul calls God the Savior of all men, especially of those who believe; does this mean that all men are saved? Paul cannot mean that all men are saved, considering he has explicitly talked about those who are not saved on multiple occasions. What this means is that, as a whole, God saved humanity through Jesus; this does not mean that every single human being is saved, just the entity that is humanity. Paul next exhorts Timothy not to be discouraged or to let anyone despise him because of his youth. Even though Timothy is still relatively young (though he is likely in his thirties or forties by now), he can still set an example for others through his life. Timothy also needs to work hard to study the Scriptures in order to protect his own doctrine, for as a leader of others, what he believes and teaches will impact many people.

Paul continues with an altered form of the household code in chapter 5. Here Paul exhorts Timothy how to respond to different people groups. Because older men are worthy of respect simply by virtue of their age, when confronting an older man on an issue of sin, we must not rebuke him as we would a friend, but exhort him in a respectful manner, as we would our own father. In fact, we should treat all people in the church with the same kind of respect we would show our own family. There is one people group in the church for which Paul offers extensive advice, the widows. It would appear that there were some problems with the widows in the church in Ephesus. The church was generous and had been providing financially for many of the widows. However, Paul suggests that there needs to be some discretion when handing out money to the widows. If a widow has a family, it is their responsibility to provide for her, not the responsibility of the church. In fact, if a person does not provide for his own family, he is considered by Paul to be worse than an unbeliever. If a woman is still young and is a widow, Paul sug-

---

* Note that the parenthetical note ("Thus he declared all foods clean." [ESV, NASB; cf. NIV]) is an editorial comment by Mark and is not considered part of Jesus' quotation. The KJV and NKJV do not contain this note, although this note is found in the original Greek manuscripts.

gests that she should get married again. When a young woman is placed as a widow, there are two potential dangers. First, she may burn with passion to get married. Second, she will have a lot of free time since she has nobody to take care of, and she will be tempted to gossip and meddle in others' affairs. Paul suggests that a widow should be at least sixty in order to be put on the register of widows.

Going back to the topic of elders, Paul commands that the elders that rule well should be especially honored in the churches. Not only that, but the teaching elders (what we would call pastors today), should be able to receive their income from the church. If God had explicitly commanded in the Law of Moses that oxen should be free to eat as they are working, so much more should ministers of the gospel make a living from the gospel. In addition, as part of the honor that elders should receive, believers should be very careful about making accusations against elders. If an elder has done something that does merit a rebuke, because his ministry is such a public ministry, he should be rebuked in the presence of all so that the others in the congregation could learn from it.

Paul returns to personal exhortations for Timothy at the end of chapter 5. Timothy had apparently developed a stomach ailment, so Paul encourages him to take a little bit of wine in order to make his stomach feel better. He also exhorts Timothy to be careful when laying hands on people. Laying hands on people does not mean to hit or hurt that person, but to impart authority upon that person. Timothy should be patient and wise, considering to whom he gives public approval and authority.

Returning once again to the household code in chapter 6, Paul has some commands for servants or slaves. Rather than despising or being rude to their masters, servants are to give special honor to their masters. Similarly, those servants who have masters that are believers should honor the masters even more. It can be tempting to take advantage of a person because he is a fellow-believer; but Paul suggests that servants should not use that as an excuse to respond poorly to their masters.

Paul also returns to another argument that he has made earlier in this letter, his warning against false teachers. Once again in chapter 6 Paul gives a harsh description of these false teachers, they are "proud, knowing nothing, but … obsessed with disputes and arguments over words." The results of these disputes are not godliness or peace, but rather "envy, strife, reviling, evil suspicions" and "useless wranglings" (6:4–5). Remember that the goal of doctrine should always be a more

sanctified and godly life, but these men are using these arguments for personal and financial gain.

Where these false believers seek to exploit doctrine for financial gain, the faithful leader should strive to be content and live a godly life. As Paul says "godliness with contentment is great gain" (verse 6). There are many dangers and snares that come from the pursuit of money, whereas peace comes with contentment. In fact, Paul identifies "the love of money" as "a root of all kinds of evil" (verse 10). This does not mean that money is an evil in itself; after all, God often blesses faithful people with financial gain. Rather, it is the love and pursuit of money that often leads to a wide variety of sins, including thievery, envy, and quarreling. Instead of pursuing money, Paul says that we should pursue "righteousness, godliness, faith, love, patience, [and] gentleness" (verse 11). Later on in this chapter, Paul tells Timothy to command those who are rich not to be prideful in their riches, but to be generous with others and rich in good works.

In verse 12, Paul exhorts Timothy to "Fight the good fight of faith, lay hold on eternal life." Even though our salvation only comes through the work of Jesus Christ, we must strive to remain faithful until the day when we stand before the Judgment Seat of Christ, or the day when Jesus returns. Paul then offers a doxology about Jesus, calling Him the "King of kings and Lord of lords," and the One who dwells in "unapproachable light" (verses 15 and 16). All that we do is so that Jesus would be given honor.

Before concluding this letter, Paul warns Timothy once again to guard the gospel and to avoid those who would get caught up in "idle babblings" (verse 20). Rather than resulting in godliness and salvation, these arguments have led some to stray from their faith. Paul then finishes this letter by calling for grace to be upon Timothy.

Thought Question:

> How can you keep a healthy perspective on money so that you do not fall into the traps of loving money too much?

Preserve the Gospel: 2 Timothy 1–2
Lesson 135

The epistle of 2 Timothy is Paul's last letter that we have recorded in the New Testament. It is pretty clear from the way that Paul writes this letter that he anticipates his own death coming soon. As such, Paul believes that these words may be the final words that he gets to share with Timothy. The tone of this letter is very affectionate, like the words that a dying father would impart to his children. In this letter, Paul gives Timothy guidance and direction and encourages him to remain strong in the faith.

After Paul's customary greeting, which like the first epistle also includes mercy along with grace and peace, Paul gets personal with Timothy. Paul reminds Timothy of his prayers for him that he would be able to see Timothy soon. Paul also is very grateful for Timothy's genuine faith, which is so evident. That faith had originated in Timothy's grandmother and had been passed down to his mother, who had also passed that down to Timothy. When Paul met Timothy, he too passed on the faith to Timothy and, through the Holy Spirit, had imparted spiritual gifts to Timothy by laying hands on him. In light of this, Paul encourages Timothy to "stir up" (verse 6) or strengthen the gift that God had given him, reminding him that the Spirit of God in us does not fill us with fear, but with power and love and a sound mind.

Because the Spirit of God in us does not fill us with fear, but with power, Paul exhorts Timothy to stand firm for the gospel. It can be tempting in the face of persecution to shrink back and be ashamed of our faith, but Paul exhorts Timothy not to be ashamed of the gospel or of Paul. Instead, Paul encourages Timothy to be willing to suffer with him for the sake of the gospel. Always seeming to take advantage of any opportunity to share the gospel, Paul once again summarizes the gospel and his ministry for the gospel in verses 9–11. Paul himself is not ashamed of the gospel, and he is willing to endure sufferings for the gospel because he trusts that God will preserve the gospel even if he were to die.

In light of Paul's confidence that God will preserve the gospel, he exhorts Timothy to hold fast to the teachings that he had received from Paul. Timothy needs to fight for the gospel, to preserve its purity and to prevent it from being perverted. Sadly for Paul, at the current moment he has been abandoned by most of his friends, either by their abandonment of the faith or because of their own ministry responsibilities. Paul does not want Timothy to abandon the faith, as well.

Like a runner passing the baton to the next person on the team, Paul encourages Timothy to take the message that Paul had given him and to pass it down to other faithful men who can do the same. Throughout Paul's entire Christian life, he has fought to protect and preserve the gospel against all kinds of enemies. Yet, when Paul is gone, someone else will have to pick up that fight to protect and preserve the gospel. This is the responsibility of each generation of Christians. The attacks upon the purity of the gospel may be different in every generation, but the need to preserve the gospel is the same in every generation. As faithful believers in the gospel, we need to be aware of false teachings and we need to be faithful to teach the next generation so that they can pick up the baton as we did from those who passed the faith down to us.

There are three metaphors that Paul uses to describe the life of the minister of the gospel. *First*, Paul exhorts Timothy to endure hardship as a good soldier of Jesus Christ. So long as we are on this earth, with enemies all around, we need to recognize that we are at war. We need to discipline ourselves and be prepared for attacks and scars that come from this spiritual war. The soldier at war must always be aware of the dangers that surround him or her, but the civilian is able to enjoy peace. We are to live like the soldier, not like the civilians in this spiritual war. *Second*, Paul uses the metaphor of an athlete. The best athletes have to spend much time disciplining their bodies and learning the rules of the game in order to perfect that game. We must do the same for the faith. *Third*, Paul compares the life of the minister of the gospel to a hardworking farmer. Farmers have very tedious and difficult jobs. They have to get up before sunrise and often work until after sundown in order to reap a bountiful harvest. We must also work hard while on this earth, trusting that we will get to enjoy the harvest of salvation when it comes.

However, in order to receive the prize or the harvest, we have to be found to be faithful and we have to live our lives in the correct manner. Paul has endured an incredible amount of suffering and is currently in prison because he has striven hard to be faithful to the gospel. As Paul had done on multiple occasions in his first letter to Timothy, he gives another trustworthy saying to Timothy to hold onto: "For if we died with Him, we shall also live with Him. If we endure, we shall also reign with Him. If we deny Him, He will also deny us. If we are faithless, He remains faithful; He cannot deny Himself" (2:11–13). In other words, we have two options: deny Jesus and be denied by Him, or endure faithfully and reign with Christ.

As Paul had spoken about in his first letter to Timothy, he exhorts Timothy once again not to get caught up in useless quarrels with false teachers. These arguments are idle babblings that result in more ungodliness. Paul compares these arguments to cancer, which when tolerated within a church will kill many of the members. As with cancer, these teachings and people who offer them need to be cut away. This is illustrated through an architecture metaphor. There are a number of materials that an architect can use to build a house. Those strong materials will endure when the winds come. These false teachers and teachings are like the wood and clay, which will not endure and must be removed so that the stronger materials could endure.

Rather than engaging in quarrels or useless arguments, Paul encourages Timothy to "avoid foolish and ignorant disputes, knowing that they generate strife" (verse 23). When Timothy does have to dispute something with others, he needs to be gentle and patient. This is the key for understanding how to argue with others. We must not let the goal of our argument simply be to win the argument, for in doing so we may destroy the person with whom we are arguing. When we turn an argument into a battle, the other person will be put on the defensive and will not be likely to listen to what we have to say. However, if we are gentle and patient with the other person, we can persuade him or her and build that relationship at the same time. When disputing with people over issues of sin, the goal of that argument should be to get them to repent and to help them discover the truth.

Thought Questions:

1. Who passed your faith down to you? Who might be someone to whom you can pass it on?

2. Have you ever won an argument but hurt the relationship with that person? How could you have handled that argument differently so that you could preserve that relationship in the process?

3. How do you distinguish between a useless argument (such that Paul warns about here), and something that is really worth arguing about?

Final Words: 2 Timothy 3–4

Lesson 136

One of the affections that will be evident in the life of a mature believer in Jesus Christ is a love for the truth. It would seem to make sense that everyone should love the truth rather than embracing lies. Yet we live in a fallen world that has been corrupted by sin. It is sadly far more common for a person to love his own sin and live in a delusion rather than embracing the truth. This is the situation that Paul addresses as he finishes this letter. Rather than pursuing truth, people would rather

find people who will tell them what they want to hear so that they can continue in their sinful lives.

There is an eschatological element in Paul's teachings here. Remember that eschatology deals with the issues surrounding the end times. In chapter 3, Paul informs us that "in the last days perilous times will come" (3:1). Rather than this world always getting better, as we get closer to the end people will get more and more out of control. Paul gives a long list of the types of characteristics that will be more and more prevalent as we get closer to the end. What is particularly dangerous is that these characteristics will exist in people who call themselves believers. In verse 5, Paul says that they have a form of godliness but deny its power. These people appear to be believers on the outside, but their lives are filled with sin. It is sad to think how many people in our churches today fit this description. And Paul encourages us to turn away from such people.

These are the same kinds of people who are leading people astray in Timothy's church. On the outside they look like great teachers, but their lives and their doctrines are false. However, those who are weakened by their own guilty consciences are vulnerable to such men and are being deceived by them. Even today this sort of thing is taking place. Many people today feel guilty and have many regrets, so they turn to Internet preachers in order to try to feel better. This does not mean that Internet preachers are evil, but there are plenty of false teachers that are deceiving people to be found on the Internet. Paul compares all of these deceptive false teachers to Jannes and Jambres,* the magicians of Pharaoh who had resisted Moses at first but were proven to be false in due time.

While these false teachers are currently being praised by people, faithful ministers of the gospel are enduring suffering right now. Paul reminds Timothy of the various sufferings that he had endured as a minister of the gospel. In fact, Paul argues, "all who desire to live godly in Christ Jesus will suffer persecution" (3:12). It should make us wonder just how godly we truly are if we never suffer persecution. While this might mean that God is currently protecting us from persecution, it might mean that we are not living obedient enough lives to merit persecution from outsiders. While evil men continue to grow more and more corrupt, faithful men endure sufferings and strive to hold on to the faith that they have received.

---

* The names Jannes and Jambres are found in early Jewish writings to the Egyptian magicians who opposed Moses in Exodus 7:8–13. In these writings, Jannes and Jambres became symbols of opposition to God's truth. Even though their names do not appear in the Old Testament, they would be familiar to the Jewish people.

Instead of being deceived by these false teachers, Paul exhorts us to diligently study the Scriptures. One of the most glorious statements on the power and value of the Scriptures comes in these final verses in chapter 3. We learn in verse 15 that the Scriptures are able to make us wise for salvation through faith in Jesus. In the Bible, we learn everything we need to know about how to obtain salvation. We also learn the origin and power of the Scriptures in verses 16 and 17. All Scripture ultimately is inspired, or breathed out, by God Himself to the authors. This does not mean that each of the biblical authors heard an audible voice from heaven as he wrote down his book(s). However, it does mean that God was intimately involved in the process of each book, filling up the authors with the Holy Spirit and sovereignly directing their hearts as they wrote these books. Also, all of Scripture is "profitable for doctrine, for reproof, for correction, for instruction in righteousness." Everything that we ultimately need for living Christian lives can be found in the Bible. All of Scripture is valuable for us, even the seemingly endless chapters of genealogies in 1 Chronicles!

Since we are equipped with the Word of God, and since people are susceptible to deception, we need to be all the more diligent to preach the word whenever we are given opportunity. While it is true that Paul writes this to Timothy, an overseer in the church in Ephesus, it applies to us, as well, if we know the Scriptures. If we know the truth, we have been given the responsibility to defend that truth in the presence of falsehood and deception. As we learned earlier, many people would rather hear something that sounds good to them rather than listening to the truth. This is an especially big problem today with access to the Internet. With just a few clicks of a mouse, we can find plenty of false teachers who will tell us what we want to hear, rather than the truth that we need to hear.

Paul finishes this epistle on a very personal note. In Philippians 1, when Paul spoke of his first imprisonment in Rome, he was confident that he would be set free. Yet the tone of this letter is quite different. Paul speaks of himself as a drink offering and says, "the time my departure is at hand" (4:6). Paul expects to die this time. Rather than speaking of the race of life as a present or future reality, Paul says that his race is already finished. Because Paul has been faithful, in spite of incredible sufferings, he also knows that his reward is coming soon.

Once again, Paul expresses his desire for Timothy to come and visit him. The only person who had stuck with Paul was Luke. Paul also asks for Timothy to find Mark and bring him with him when he comes to visit Paul, for "he is useful to me for ministry" (verse 11). This is the same Mark over whom Paul had broken fellowship with Barnabas because Mark had previously abandoned Paul. It is clear from this request that Mark and Paul had been reconciled by this time. Even though Paul expects to die soon, he does not know when, so he asks Timothy to bring his cloak and parchments with him when he comes. With his end coming soon, Paul is confident that God will deliver him from evil and preserve him for the kingdom.

Paul concludes this letter with a series of greetings and requests that Timothy come before winter. As always, he leaves Timothy with God's grace.

Thought Question:

How can you guard yourself from the temptation to find people who will tell you what you want to hear rather than what you need to hear?

Order and Good Works: Titus 1–3
Lesson 137

The last of the Pastoral Epistles is the epistle to Titus. The style and content of this epistle is very similar to 1 Timothy. Titus is one of Paul's traveling companions whom Paul had left on the island of Crete to help lead and organize the church there. The island of Crete lies southeast of Greece. Based on Paul's description of Crete in Titus 1:12, there is a lot of immorality on this island at the time that Paul writes this letter. He characterizes the people as "liars, evil beasts, lazy gluttons." It is difficult to pinpoint the exact date of this letter. The mention of Apollos tells us that this letter could not have been written before Paul's third missionary journey. The fact that Paul does not seem to be in prison gives us two possible ranges of dates for the writing of this letter. Paul could have written this before his first imprisonment in Rome near the end of his third missionary journey, or he could have written this after he had been set free from his first imprisonment in Rome before his second imprisonment.

As in many of Paul's letters, he begins with a description of his calling as the apostle to the Gentiles. In Paul's general description of the gospel in verse 1, Paul connects the importance of faith, truth, and godliness. We must not only pursue the truth, but we should strive to add to that truth a life of godliness. As with

Paul's two epistles to Timothy, Paul adds mercy to his typical greeting of grace and peace.

From the beginning, Paul reminds Titus of the mission that Paul had commissioned him to do. After Paul had planted the church on the island of Crete, he had given Titus the responsibility of setting up a church structure in that area. The most critical component for establishing healthy churches is establishing godly, able leaders over the people. As Paul had done for Timothy, he gives Titus a list of the qualities that must be present in a man in order to be worthy to be an elder or overseer of a church. In general, this person has to be blameless, has to have a healthy, obedient family, has to have self-control, and has to be well-versed in Scripture and established in his doctrine so that he can defend the church from false teaching and exhort the believers to obey Christ.

Paul explicitly warns Titus about the circumcision party, which has been a thorn in Paul's side from the very beginning. These men have been not only teaching false doctrines, but consuming the people with useless arguments that do not result in greater godliness. For those who are struggling with sin, Paul usually advocates a more gentle approach, but for those who are spreading false doctrines, Paul says to "rebuke them sharply" (verse 13). God is far more critical of leaders who are in positions of influence than of the average people in the church; this is why He will say later in the book of James that not many should strive to be overseers. While false teachers often appear to be strong Christians, without a regenerate heart through the Holy Spirit, everything they do is corrupted and will be revealed as corrupt in due time.

Next, Paul gives Titus a form of the household code by giving him instructions for the different people groups in the churches in Crete. Older men are to be "sober, reverent, temperate, sound in faith, in love, in patience"(2:2). In other words, older men should strive to be the self-controlled, wise people that the younger people in the church should be able to turn to as a great example of what it looks like to be a Christian. Older women are also to be self-controlled and respectable, not given to slandering others. And as those who have gone through life, they are to teach the younger women to be hardworking wives and mothers. Younger men are to be sober-minded, not controlled by their passions that often burn within them. They are to strive to do good works and to have solid, sound doctrine. Young men are to maintain purity and integrity when it comes to their understanding of Scripture, and they should be able to communicate the Scriptures in such a way that those who would argue against them would be ashamed. Finally, servants or slaves are to respectfully obey their masters and exercise faithfulness in the work that they have been assigned to do.

The motivation for all these commands to the different people groups is the gospel. Not only does the grace of God bring us salvation, but it is also through God's grace that we are equipped to say no to ungodliness and worldly lusts. We often assume that our struggle against sin is simply a matter of our own strength or willpower, but God works in us to overcome sins and temptations. Rather than giving in to our sinful desires, we all should live self-controlled, righteous, and godly lives. We do this because we also look forward to our blessed hope of Christ's return. Jesus came in the first place to set us free from lawlessness and sin so that we would be a new, purified people, passionate to do what is right.

As with Timothy, Paul reminds Titus of the authority and responsibility that he has to communicate the Word of God to the people. Paul then continues to tell Titus the things about which the Cretans need to be exhorted. They need to respect and submit to the rulers and authorities rather than rebelling against them. Rather than slandering or speaking evil of others, they need to be peaceable and gentle, showing humility in all situations. Slandering and rebellion are things that they used to do before they found Christ, but the gospel changed all of that. In Titus 3:4–7, Paul summarizes the gospel, as he has done many times throughout his letters. Because of God's mercy and kindness, not because of our righteousness, He washed us and renewed us through the Holy Spirit so that we could obtain eternal life. Therefore, we should devote ourselves to good works that profit others.

It is precisely in comparison to this last point about doing good works that profit others that Paul warns Titus to get rid of these false teachers. Their endless arguments and quarrels about meaningless issues of the Law of Moses do not benefit anybody. So Paul tells Titus to warn these people to stop their quarreling two times; then, if they still insist on being divisive, Paul tells Titus and the church in Crete to reject those divisive men.

Paul finishes this letter with personal issues. He is going to send Artemas or Tychicus to relieve Titus for a time so that he will be freed up to come and visit Paul. He also encourages the people in Crete to help out Zenas and Apollos on a journey that they are taking so that they can get to their destination fast. Paul concludes this letter by repeating the main message for the people of Crete: they should be faithful to do good works and to provide for one another. As always, Paul leaves this church with the grace of God.

Thought Question:

Into which of the people groups in Paul's household code in this book do you fit? In which people group will you fit next? What are some things that you should work on in light of this?

Jesus Is Better Than the Prophets: Hebrews 1–2

Lesson 138

By far, the most disputed book in the New Testament is the book of Hebrews. For the first few centuries of the Church, there was much debate as to whether or not this book should be included as Scripture. The most important criterion for inclusion in Scripture for the early Church was the connection of that book with an apostle. The book of Hebrews, however, does not identify its author. Nobody knows for sure who the author of Hebrews is, though many suggestions have been offered for who the author might be. The most commonly suggested author is Paul (Hebrews 13:23). The mention of Timothy at the end of this epistle provides some evidence to suggest it is Paul. However, the style of writing in this book is very different from any of Paul's letters. In addition, the author of Hebrews speaks of the gospel as something that had been handed down to him, yet Paul is always very careful in his letters to argue that he did not get the gospel from any man but from Jesus Himself. Other commonly suggested authors are Apollos, Barnabas, Priscilla, Clement of Rome, or Luke.

In spite of the uncertainty of the author, the content of Hebrews speaks a lot for itself. This is by far the most masterful work in the New Testament for explaining how Jesus fulfills the Old Testament. It is the power of the content of this letter that led many early churches to fight for the inclusion of this epistle in the Scriptures, so that eventually all churches agreed to its inclusion in Scripture.

Just as the author is uncertain, the audience is also uncertain. Based on the main message of this book, it would appear that the recipients of this letter are Jewish believers who are beginning to return to Judaism because of the persecutions they are suffering from their fellow Jews. The general nature of this letter may be evidence that it is intended to be a circular letter to be distributed among all the churches. Yet the fact that the author is sending Timothy to the recipients of this letter suggests that it was at least originally intended to a specific audience.

The purpose of this letter is to persuade these Jewish believers not to fall back into Judaism. There are numerous warnings throughout this book against falling away. Throughout this entire letter, the author systematically shows how Jesus and the New Covenant are far superior to everything in the Old Testament. Because this audience is in danger of rejecting Christianity in order to revert back to Judaism, the author argues that Judaism is inferior to Christianity and that the fulfillment of Judaism is Christianity.

The author begins this letter by showing that Jesus is far greater than the prophets. The job of the prophets is to reveal the Word of God to the people. In the past, God used various prophets and communicated to them and through them in various different ways. He spoke to prophets through visions, audible words, dreams, impressions on their hearts, and even through a donkey! Now, however, God has given us the best revelation of Himself through Jesus Christ. What better revelation of God can we receive than God Himself becoming a human! God no longer needs to use a variety of prophets in order to reveal Himself to humanity because He has done it perfectly through His Son. We also see the majesty of Jesus in that He is characterized as the Creator and Sustainer of the universe.

There was a belief among the Jews during this time that all the Old Testament Scriptures were ultimately communicated through angels. This is why the author of Hebrews moves on to show that Jesus is far superior to all the angels. The author shows this by quoting a number of Old Testament passages about angels and Old Testament passages concerning God's Son. Angels are characterized as servants, but Jesus is called the Son of God. Also, Jesus is even called God Himself in Psalm 45:6–7, which is quoted in Hebrews 1:8. Not only that, the Scriptures speak of Jesus as the Creator, and it is said that all enemies will be made a footstool under His feet. Jesus is far superior to the angels!

The first warning from Hebrews comes at the beginning of chapter 2. If Jesus is far greater than the prophets and even angels, we need to hold onto the message that we have heard so that we do not fall away. For if there was judgment for those who disobeyed the Word of God given by angels and prophets, how much more severe will be the judgment if we abandon the great salvation given by the very Son of God. Moreover, the author reminds the audience that they had seen the message of Jesus confirmed by the apostles with miracles and gifts of the Holy Spirit.

In Hebrews 2:6–8, the author quotes another passage that connects the discussion of Jesus' superiority to the angels with the necessity of Jesus' sufferings. In Psalm 8:4–6, David is amazed that God pays attention to humanity, considering that He had made us lower than the angels. Yet the language that David uses here is prophetic; for he speaks of the "son of man" as lower than the angels. We know from the gospels that the phrase "Son of Man" is the most common phrase that Jesus uses to refer to Himself. In addition, at the end of this passage, it speaks of everything being put under the feet of this Son of Man. We have already seen at the end of the first chapter of Hebrews that Jesus is the One who will have all His enemies placed under His feet. Jesus is the One who, though being God Himself, was made lower than the angels when He took on flesh and became a human. However, His humiliation went much further than just becoming a human, for He was humbled to the point of suffering death.

Here we have the gospel once again. Jesus was humbled to the point of facing death, and through that death He endured the death that should be ours. In verse 10, the author makes an interesting statement: "For it was fitting for Him … to make the captain of their salvation perfect through sufferings." This does not mean that Jesus was sinful and imperfect. Rather, this means that through the cross, Jesus perfected His obedience to the Father by obeying to the point of death. Also, now that we know that death has been conquered, Jesus is able to set us free from the fear of death. While the idea of dying may still be scary, we know as Christians that something far greater awaits us afterward, so we need not fear as much.

Because Jesus took the humiliation of humanity and died in our place, we also can be said to be His brothers. By taking on the limitations of humanity, Jesus became the only perfect High Priest. Under the Law of Moses, the job of the high priest was to stand as a mediator between God and man. The high priest would represent God to the people by teaching God's Word to the people. The high priest would represent the people to God by making prayers and appeasing His wrath through appropriate sacrifices. Jesus, however, is the perfect High Priest. He is God and perfectly reveals God to us. As a human, He also understands our weaknesses and temptations fully. As the perfect High Priest, Jesus offered Himself as the sacrifice to permanently appease God's wrath for us. Yet we will see far more on this in the later chapters of Hebrews.

Thought Question:

We see that, because Jesus was tempted, He is able to aid those who are tempted. How might the fact that Jesus was tempted help you when you are tempted?

Heavenly Rest: Hebrews 3–4
Lesson 139

We have already seen that Jesus is greater than all of the prophets because He revealed to us the fullness of God, and Jesus is greater than the angels because He is the Son of God. The author of Hebrews begins chapter 3 telling us that Jesus is also greater than Moses. This is a dangerous statement to make in a Jewish context. One of the accusations that set the Jews against Jesus is that He had spoken against Moses, and even the first Christian martyr Stephen was put to death because he was falsely accused of speaking against Moses. To be fair, the author of Hebrews does not speak evil of Moses. He does, however, show that Jesus is greater than Moses.

To compare Jesus to Moses, the author of Hebrews compares the builder of a house to the servants within the house. In this case, the house has a double meaning. First, the house is a reference to the tabernacle, in which Moses served. Yet the house also is a reference to the people that comprised the nation of Israel. Moses did not build Israel; God did. Moreover, we have seen that Jesus is the Agent of creation and the Sustainer of the universe. Certainly, Jesus is greater than Moses as the very builder of God's house. Just as Israel was originally God's house, we as Christians are now the house of God. The author gives a second warning against falling away from the faith here in verse 6. We are only part of God's house "if we hold fast the confidence and the rejoicing of the hope firm to the end."

The rest of chapters 3 and 4 are a commentary on Psalm 95:7–11. In this Psalm, the psalmist speaks about the judgment that came upon Moses' generation in the wilderness and uses it as motivation to respond favorably to God in our time. In order to understand what the author of Hebrews does with this passage, we need to know our biblical history. Moses had the privilege of miraculously leading the Israelites out of Egypt. It would appear that the Israelites had been saved. Yet their salvation would not be complete until their journey came to an end in the Promised Land. Also, it is the gap between coming out of Egypt and coming into the Promised Land that the author of Hebrews uses to warn the recipients of this letter. Sadly, even though Moses' generation had seen God's incredible deliverance from the Egyptians, that generation would never get to finish the journey because of their lack of faith. While that first generation was in the wilderness, they grumbled, complained, and rebelled against Moses and God. So God swore an oath that they would never be able to enter into the rest that would come in the Promised Land (Numbers 14:20–25).

The author of Hebrews breaks down this Scripture, piece by piece. This part of Psalm 95 begins with a warning, "Today, if you will hear His voice, Do not harden your hearts as in the rebellion." The author of Hebrews exhorts the believers, as long as it is called "today" that they would exhort one another so that no one would depart from God through their unbelief. Once again, the author emphasizes the need to persevere in faith in verse 14 when he says that we only become "partakers of Christ if we hold the beginning of our confidence steadfast to the end." He reminds the recipients of this letter that the very people who were disqualified from the Promised Land were the disobedient people who had experienced the salvation out of Egypt.

For the generation that died in the wilderness, they had begun the journey of salvation but did not have the faith to finish it. This is the main warning to the Hebrews. They had begun their journey by placing faith in Jesus, but if they do not finish that journey by holding fast to Jesus, they too will not enter the Promised Land of heaven. This concept is illustrated through the idea of rest in chapter 4. In Scripture, we see that the concept of rest goes back all the way to creation itself. Even though God does not tire as man does, on the seventh day of creation God rests. When the Israelites are tormented in Egypt, they call out to God for some rest. The Promised Land was to be the place where the Israelites would finally find rest. Even though they had left Egypt, they had not yet achieved that rest while in the wilderness. Also, because of their unbelief and rebellion, that generation never gets to experience rest. As Christians, we also are awaiting our day of rest, when we get to enjoy God for all eternity with our heavenly rest. So also the author of Hebrews exhorts them to "be diligent to enter that rest, lest anyone fall according to the same example of disobedience"(verse 11).

Sadly, this understanding of salvation is often not communicated in Christian circles. Far too often it is preached that we simply need to make a prayer and then our job is done and we are saved. It is true that, upon the profession of true faith in the works of Christ and the repentance of our sins, we are saved to some extent. When we first place faith in God, we are given the Holy Spirit as a deposit to give us the sure hope that salvation is coming. Yet, in Scripture, salvation is more than just a one-time event; it is an ongoing process. We are not saved by our works, but we are saved through a faith that perseveres. If a person says the sinner's prayer and then walks away from Jesus and abandons his or her faith, never to return, then he or she is not saved.

Having just spent two chapters interpreting a particular section of Psalm 95, the author of Hebrews speaks about the power of the Word of God to convict us and transform us. From simply five verses in the Bible, the author has been able to exhort the Hebrews and us not to fall away from Jesus. This is the power of the Word of God. The author of Hebrews compares the Word of God to a sharp, two-edged sword, capable of piercing to our souls. A truly sharp sword or knife can cut through many things. When we read Scripture, the Holy Spirit uses that Scripture to cut through to our hearts and convict and encourage us. The Word of God is truly powerful! This is one of the many reasons we regularly need to be meditating on Scripture. God will transform us through His Word.

The author returns to an argument that he had begun in chapter 2, that Jesus is the perfect High Priest. Unlike earthly high priests, who can relate to humanity but not necessarily to God, Jesus is a great High Priest who has passed through the heavens. Jesus also understands the trials and temptations that we are going through because He too had to endure them. In the face of suffering and persecution, it can be tempting to take the easy way out and abandon our faith; but if Jesus Himself endured that suffering, so also can we. For those who argue that Jesus was not really tempted because He is God, the power of Jesus as our High Priest is lessened. He faced the desires that we face, but He never once gave in. He has shown us that it is possible to face temptation and still say, "No."

In order to understand the privilege that we have in the last verse from chapter 4, there is something else we need to know about high priests. According to the Old Testament, nobody could enter the Most Holy Place in the tabernacle or temple except for the high priest, and that only one day a year on the Day of Atonement (Leviticus 16). The Most Holy Place was built as the throne room of God, and the ark of the covenant with the cherub angels above it formed God's throne. If anyone entered that Most Holy Place who was not supposed to be there or who did it in an inappropriate manner, he would be instantly killed. As one could imagine, this resulted in incredible fear from the people. Yet now, because Jesus died as our perfect High Priest, we have access to the throne of God and we can enter with boldness rather than just fear. Jesus gives us far greater access to God so that we can find mercy and grace to help us in our time of need.

Thought Question:

If our salvation requires us to be persistent with our faith, does this mean that we are in some way saved by our own works? Why or why not?

Jesus, the Great High Priest: Hebrews 5–6

Lesson 140

As we continue our journey detailing the supremacy of Christ over everything in the Old Testament, the author of Hebrews expands in chapter 5 on the supremacy of Jesus over the Old Testament high priests. The high priest is appointed by God to offer gifts to God and sacrifices for the sins of the people. The high priest, however, is also supposed to help out the people and have compassion on them since he knows what they are going through since he too has to deal with weaknesses. In addition, because every high priest is a sinner himself, he not only has to make sacrifices on behalf of other people, but he has to make sacrifices for his own sins.

Because the high priest represents the people before God, he cannot choose this honor for himself, but has to be appointed to his position by God. Hence, Jesus did not choose for Himself to be the High Priest, but He was appointed to that position by God Himself. There is one big problem with Jesus as a high priest, though. According to the Old Testament, priests must come from the tribe of Levi, but Jesus was from the tribe of Judah. This is where Psalm 110, the most oft-quoted passage from the Old Testament, comes in. In this psalm, which we have already seen as a prophetic psalm about the Christ, we learn that the Christ will be a priest in the order of Melchizedek (Genesis 14:18–20). Therefore, like a good high priest, Jesus offered up prayers and supplications for the people while He was on the earth.

The author of Hebrews puts the discussion on Jesus as the High Priest on hold in order to address directly a major issue with the Hebrews. He wants to go into far more detail on these things, but he is afraid that these Hebrews are not ready for advanced theology. He rebukes the Hebrews, saying that "by this time you ought to be teachers," but instead "you need someone to teach you again the first principles of the oracles of God" (verse 12). These Hebrews have been believers for long enough that they should be leaders and teachers, but sadly they have not continued to mature in their faith over time. They are not ready for the solid food of advanced doctrine; they are only ready for the milk of the basics. The mature person is the person who, through training and studying the Word of God, can discern between good and evil. In the beginning of chapter 6, the author also gives a list of basic doctrines—"repentance from dead works," "faith toward God," "baptisms," "laying on of hands," "resurrection of the dead," and "eternal judgment." These are the basic doctrines of the gospel of which the Hebrews should have a solid grasp, and they should be ready to deal with more advanced ideas; but sadly, they are not.

The evidence of the Hebrews lack of maturity is that they are falling away from Jesus, trying to find salvation through the Old Testament. This leads the author to make a statement in Hebrews 6:4–6 that is very difficult to interpret. In these verses, the author argues that it is impossible for certain people to be brought back to repentance if they fall away from the faith. There are a couple difficulties with this idea. *First*, do these verses imply that genuine believers can fall away from the faith and lose their salvation? *Second*, if it is impossible to be brought back to repentance after falling away, what about those people who have walked away from the faith and returned? To the first question, there is reason to believe that the people the author is talking about are not genuine believers. He refers to these people as "once enlightened," "tasted the heavenly gift," "partakers of the Holy Spirit," and those who "have tasted the good word of God." All these descriptions could be speaking of people who get to experience the blessings of Christianity because they are in the Christian community, but they may not be saved. These people have "tasted" Christianity, but they have not taken it in. To the second question, it is important to remember to what these people are returning. These are Jewish believers who are looking to return to Judaism for salvation. Now that Jesus has come, however, there is no longer any means of salvation or repentance through Judaism. This does not mean that people cannot turn away from their sins if they backslide; it means that if they abandon Jesus they cannot find salvation in anything else.

In spite of these warnings, the author of Hebrews is confident that these believers are not going to fall away. The works that they did at first when they came to believe in Jesus provide hope and evidence that they are truly saved. Yet they have to be diligent to hold on to that hope that they had at first until the end. Even though they have been discouraged by the persecutions and trials that they have had to endure, they need to fight against getting sluggish. In order to motivate them to endure, the author of Hebrews brings up the example of Abraham.

Abraham is one of the best examples of someone who remained faithful, even though he did not receive what he was promised for a very long time. Abraham had to wait twenty-five years from the time that God made a promise to give him a child until the time when that promise was fulfilled. All that Abraham had over that time was God's promise. The amazing thing is that God was willing to put His own reputation on the line in order to help Abraham to trust that promise. God made an oath by His own name, putting His own reputation on the line (Genesis 22:16–18), and Abraham believed Him and patiently endured until God fulfilled His promise. So also, we have many precious promises from God for which we must patiently wait until we receive the fulfillment of them. Like Abraham, we too can and must endure in order to receive the promises.

Having addressed directly the issue facing these Hebrews, the author finishes chapter 6 by returning to his argument about Jesus as the High Priest in the order of Melchizedek. We will examine this more in the next chapters.

Thought Question:

Do you believe that a person can lose his or her salvation after becoming a Christian? What evidence would you give for this belief?

A New Priest, a New Covenant, and a New Law: Hebrews 7–9

Lesson 141

In chapter 7, the author of Hebrews picks up where he had left off in chapter 5 and the end of chapter 6. After establishing that Jesus is a new High Priest in the order of Melchizedek, in chapter 7 we see the significance of this. Yet, in order to understand how Jesus is in the order of Melchizedek, we must first examine Melchizedek himself. Melchizedek appears almost out of nowhere in the story of Abraham (Genesis 14). After Lot and his family are taken captive by some kings, Abraham raises an army to fight those kings, and he is victorious. As he passes by the city of Salem on his way home from this battle, Melchizedek meets Abraham. Melchizedek is known as a priest of God Most High, even before the Levitical priesthood had been established. This same

Melchizedek is also the king of Salem. Melchizedek brings out bread and wine, and Melchizedek blesses Abraham. Abraham also gives Melchizedek ten percent of the plunder from this victory, thus establishing the foundation of the tithe for Israel centuries later.

There are a number of elements of the story of Melchizedek that are prophetic of Jesus Christ. First, this is the only time we see a priest who also happens to be a king. Because the Israelite kings must come from the tribe of Judah and the Israelite priests come from the tribe of Levi, this never happens for Israel. In addition, the name *Melchizedek* means "king of righteousness." The word *Salem* means "peace"; and because Melchizedek is the king of this city, this also makes him the king of peace. These are both terms that are applied to Jesus Christ elsewhere.

The author of Hebrews shows that the priesthood of Melchizedek is greater than the Levitical priesthood. The fact that Melchizedek blesses Abraham shows that Melchizedek is greater than Abraham. Since Levi is a descendant of Abraham, this implies that Melchizedek is greater than Levi and the Levitical priesthood, as well. Also, since Abraham paid the tithe to Melchizedek and Levi is one of Abraham's descendants, it is as though Levi paid the tithe to Melchizedek. In addition, to become a priest in the order of Levi, one simply needs to be born as a Levite. Yet the priesthood of Melchizedek comes with an oath, which the author of Hebrews argues is more meaningful and powerful than just birth. Also, the fact that Psalm 110 speaks of another priesthood in the order of Melchizedek argues that the Levitical priesthood was never intended to be permanent but would be replaced someday.

There are still other ways that Jesus is a greater priest than the Levitical priests. Unlike the Levitical priests, Jesus is an eternal Priest. Under the Levitical priesthood, each priest was limited by his own death and another priest would have to arise to take his place. Jesus, however, is able to intercede or pray for the people to whom He ministers forever. Because Jesus was sinless, He also does not have to make sacrifices for His own sins, whereas the Levitical priests have to make regular sacrifices for their own sins. Even though Jesus can sympathize with our weaknesses, He has been perfected forever, whereas the Levitical priests only have their weaknesses. Not only is Jesus a greater priest than the Levitical priests, He serves at a far greater tabernacle (temple). The earthly tabernacle and temple were built according to the pattern of the heavenly tabernacle. Now that Jesus is at the right hand of God in heaven, He regularly serves at the heavenly tabernacle.

Because there is a bond between the Law of Moses and the Levitical priests, the author of Hebrews argues that this new priesthood in the order of Melchizedek also brings a new law. In fact, because of the weakness of the Law of Moses in that it could not make anyone perfect, the author of Hebrews suggests that the Law of Moses has been annulled. This directly ties in to the New Covenant. The Law of Moses was the cornerstone of the Mosaic covenant. However, if there is a New Covenant, that covenant will have its own terms, or laws. Once again, if the Mosaic covenant were sufficient, there would be no need for a New Covenant. Yet the author of Hebrews quotes Jeremiah 31, which speaks in detail of a New Covenant to come that will accomplish things that the Mosaic covenant could not.

There are three primary differences between the New Covenant and the Mosaic covenant. The *first difference* is that the law in the Mosaic covenant was written on tablets of stone. In the New Covenant, however, the law is written on people's hearts and minds. In other words, in the New Covenant, people will delight in the law and want to obey it. The *second difference* is that in the New Covenant everyone will know the Lord. It was possible to be born into the Mosaic covenant and not know the Lord, but you cannot be in the New Covenant and not know the Lord. The *third difference* is that there is complete forgiveness of sins under the New Covenant. The author of Hebrews also argues in Hebrews 8:13 that the old covenant is made obsolete by the New Covenant; and because of this, the old covenant is ready to vanish.

The author of Hebrews goes on in chapter 9 to discuss the tabernacle and the sacrificial system. In the first five verses, the author describes the furniture in the tabernacle; and if he had more time, he would explain the significance of each of the pieces of furniture. He does, however, talk about the significance of the two rooms. Regular priests could enter into the first room, known as the Holy Place; but the second room was separated from the first, and only the high priest could enter into that room—and that only one time a year with the blood of sacrifices to atone for the sins of the people. In between these two rooms was a curtain that separated them; and the author of Hebrews points out that the way into the "Holiest of All," or the Most Holy Place, had not yet been made.

The ultimate function of the sacrifices under the old covenant was symbolism. The sacrifices under the old covenant could not truly bring forgiveness or cleanse a guilty conscience. The purpose of these sacrifices was to point the way to the true sacrifice, Jesus Christ. Jesus did not offer animal sacrifices because the blood of bulls and goats could never bring forgiveness; rather, He offered the only truly acceptable sacrifice, Himself. Also, through Christ's sacrifice, our consciences can be cleansed. So, as Moses was the mediator of the Mosaic covenant, Jesus came as the Mediator of the New Covenant. Moreover, just as a will does not go into effect until the death of the owner of the will, the New Covenant required the death of Jesus in order to be brought into effect. God has established that the shedding of blood is necessary to ratify a covenant. When the Israelites ratified the Mosaic covenant, Moses sprinkled blood on the people; so also does Jesus' blood ratify the New Covenant.

Also, unlike the old sacrificial system, which required daily sacrifices that would never end, Jesus died once and for all. There is no longer any need for daily sacrifices now that the ultimate sacrifice has been made. When Jesus died, He also bore the sins of many so that those who eagerly wait for Him until He returns will be given salvation.

Thought Questions:

1. After reading these chapters, summarize in your own words the purpose of the sacrifices in the Old Testament.

2. If you were given an opportunity to talk religion with a Jewish person, what arguments from Hebrews 1–9 do you think you would bring up to him or her? Why?

Endurance and Faith: Hebrews 10–11

Lesson 142

By now, it should be clear to the readers of Hebrews that there would be no value in falling back into Judaism. Not only is Jesus far superior to any hero from the Old Testament, and the salvation that He offers greater than anything from the Old Testament, but Jesus has also nullified the Mosaic covenant by bringing the New Covenant. Because the main purpose of Judaism was to pave the way for Jesus, Judaism no longer has any value if a person does not have Jesus. The author of Hebrews completes this argument in chapter 10.

The author of Hebrews speaks of the Law of Moses as merely a "shadow" of the good things to come. As Paul had said earlier, the purpose of the Law of Moses is to be a tutor, written in order to prepare for the New Covenant that Jesus would bring (Galatians 3:24). Also, just as the purpose of the Law of Moses was to prepare for the New Covenant, the purpose of the sacrifices was to prepare for the ultimate sacrifice, Jesus Christ. The mere fact that sacrifices have to be continuously offered is proof that they are unable to make people perfect or atone for all of their sins. Rather, these sacrifices serve as "a reminder of sins every year" (verse 3). To prove that sacrifices are insufficient to please God, the author quotes Psalm 40:6–8, which argues that God would rather have obedience than sacrifices and offerings. Under the Mosaic covenant, priests are required to make sacrifices and offerings every day, but after Jesus made His one sacrifice, He is resting at the right hand of the Father until all His enemies are made a footstool under His feet. As Jeremiah had prophesied, there will also be a New Covenant, and in that New Covenant sins will finally be forgiven. So if God has provided the final forgiveness of sins through Jesus Christ, there is absolutely no value in going back to a system that is dependent upon daily sacrifices.

In light of everything that the author has argued so far, he now turns to exhortation to argue how we ought to respond to this information. *First,* because we have access to the Most Holy Place through our great High Priest Jesus, we need to draw near to God with a clean conscience. All our sins have been forgiven so that we can approach God with confidence rather than just fear. *Second,* we need to hold firmly to the gospel, which we first believed. *Third,* we need to help out one another so that we can all endure until the end. We need to "consider one another in order to stir up love and good works" (verse 24). We need to not only seek to help out our fellow believers in need, but we need to be purposeful to think about how we can help each other out. Related to this, the author of Hebrews exhorts the Hebrews to continue to gather together so that they can help each other out. Practically speaking for today, we need to consistently gather together with other believers so that we can be encouraged and so that we can encourage others. We were never meant to live out our Christian lives by ourselves, but rather in community with others.

It is extremely important that we help one another endure in our Christian lives because the consequences of falling away are dire. In verses 26–31, the author of Hebrews issues a warning for those who do fall away from Jesus. If we reject the work of Jesus on our behalf, there is no other means by which our sins can be forgiven. Therefore, if we go on sinning after rejecting Jesus, the only thing we can expect to receive is judgment. Also, if there were serious consequences to breaking the Law of Moses, how much more severe will be the consequences of rejecting the very Son of God. God has promised that He will judge His people. So the author summarizes this warning in verse 31: "It is a fearful thing to fall into the hands of the living God."

Suffering and persecution are not new for these Hebrews. When they first believed in the gospel, they experienced intense persecution to the point where their belongings were taken away by others. They not only endured these sufferings, but they once did so joyfully, knowing that they have a great reward awaiting them. Yet over time it appears that they have lost that joy and have begun to fall away under the weight of these persecutions. The author of Hebrews exhorts them to keep their confidence that they once had and to endure so that they can receive the reward of their faithfulness. Though things are now difficult, they must hold onto their faith that greater things are awaiting them. As the author had said after his warning in chapter 6, he is also confident that these Hebrews will be able to endure.

Since the key to enduring suffering and persecution is faith, the author devotes an entire chapter to the issue of faith in chapter 11. The author defines faith as "the substance of things hoped for, the evidence of things not seen" (verse 1). Faith is the confidence that we have that the things that God promises, He will do; and faith is also the conviction we have that God exists, even though we do not see Him. In fact, it is impossible to please God without faith since we must first believe in Him and believe that He will reward people who seek Him.

The rest of chapter 11 has been called "the Hall of Faith" by some. Here the author of Hebrews examines the lives of many of the Old Testament heroes and shows that each one of them was able to accomplish so much because he or she had faith. Not only did these great men and women have faith, most did not receive what they were expecting for until after they had acted in obedience to God. Noah spent 100 years building a boat, even though there had never been a flood before, and possibly no rain either, because he had faith in God's promises. Abraham left his home and started walking by faith, even though he did not know where he was going, because he trusted God by faith when God told him that He would bless him. Abraham trusted God by faith when God told him to sacrifice Isaac, his only true son of promise. Abraham's faith was so great in the promises of God that he reasoned that God would simply raise Isaac from the dead, even though he had never seen a resurrection before.

It is likely that some of the Hebrews addressed in this epistle had lost their homes due to persecution. This ties in to another common theme of these people who walked by faith, namely that they lived their lives as strangers and aliens as they awaited their permanent home. Abraham lived in the land of Canaan, even though it would be 400 years before his descendants would possess the land. Moses chose to abandon his home in Egypt and suffer with the Hebrews because he had faith in God and in His promises. All these people also waited for the day when the Savior would be revealed. Most of these great heroes of the faith had to endure incredible sufferings, but they endured because they had faith that the Savior would come. Now we have the fulfillment of everything for which they had waited by faith because Jesus has come. Certainly, we too can endure as these great heroes endured.

Thought Questions:

1. Based on the exhortations given in Hebrews 10, what would you say to the person who rejects church but instead listens to sermons online or watches preaching on TV?

2. In Hebrews 10:14, the author says that God has perfected forever those who are being sanctified. If we are still in the process of being sanctified, how can we already be perfect?

Finish the Race: Hebrews 12–13

Lesson 143

For those who have ever competed in a marathon, it is quite the challenge to endure. First, in order to prepare for this great race, the athletes have to train for months, building up endurance. Good racers are also very particular about the foods that they eat the night before and the day of the race so that they will have maximum energy and strength. They also pay attention to their clothes and shoes, seeking to have as little extra weight on them as possible so as not to slow them down. One of the techniques that runners often use when running a marathon is to fix their eyes on the feet of the person ahead of them so as to take their minds off the pain that they are enduring. Very rarely can a person run this race without much training and preparation.

In chapter 12, the author of Hebrews compares the struggles that the Hebrews are enduring to two things—a race and the discipline of a father. In a race, there are often spectators who cheer on the runners. The author of Hebrews speaks about the Old Testament heroes of the faith as the spectators who are cheering us on as we run the marathon of the Christian

life. Like good racers, we need to get rid of all the extra weights, but in this case that extra weight is sin. Practically speaking, sin messes things up and slows us down as we run the Christian life. For example, if we tell a lie, we might have to keep on making up lies to defend that lie, and our focus will be on self-preservation rather than on pleasing God. Also, as a runner often finds a fixed point on which to focus as he endures the race, we are to keep our eyes fixed on Jesus in order to endure the marathon of the Christian life. Jesus Himself masterfully ran this race, enduring suffering but remaining faithful. He is the perfect example for us to follow. When we get discouraged or lose hope in the midst of sufferings, perhaps the best thing to do is meditate on Jesus and what He endured. Not only that, during a race, there comes a time when a runner metaphorically hits a wall. His mind and body want nothing more than to just shut down and rest. Experienced runners, however, know that they are able to push their bodies even further and go through that wall. When we are exhausted with life, we can find motivation and encouragement by the endurance of Jesus, who resisted sin even to the point of shedding blood.

The second comparison that the author of Hebrews makes for the sufferings in the Christian life is that of the discipline of a father. A good father cares about the development and maturity of his son or daughter and disciplines him or her when he or she needs it. When a parent refuses to discipline his or her child, it is actually a form of neglect. When a good father disciplines his son or daughter, it shows just how much he loves that child. Of course, discipline is never enjoyable, but the maturity that it helps to develop is well worth it. Discipline is much more than mere punishment, however. An athlete disciplines his or her own body not as a form of punishment, but as a means of strengthening that body. The author of Hebrews tells the Hebrews to view their current sufferings as a type of discipline from the Lord. This does not necessarily mean that their sufferings are punishments for doing something wrong, but they are designed to help them grow and mature. As discipline proves that a father loves his child, this period of suffering actually proves that God loves the Hebrews enough to help them mature. Also, as with all discipline, the ultimate goal of that suffering is to produce great fruit at the end of the process. For believers, our suffering can produce "the peaceable fruit of righteousness to those who have been trained by it" (12:11).

In light of all this, the author quotes Isaiah 35:3, which exhorts us to strengthen our weak hands and feeble knees so that we can be healed. When people suffer, they are more prone to do and say things that hurt other people, so the author exhorts the Hebrews to pursue peace with all people. Also, when we suffer, we are more susceptible to temptations and sins, so the author of Hebrews exhorts the Hebrews to pursue holiness and to fight bitterness and to avoid sexual immorality and improper speech. Bitterness is a particularly dangerous consequence of suffering that can really damage the person who is bitter, as well as those around him or her. Bitterness kills the joy that we can have as Christians and puts up barriers between us and the people around us.

As the author of Hebrews has been masterfully doing throughout this entire epistle, he uses Old Testament examples to provide encouragement. The first illustration that the author uses is a warning from the life of Esau. Esau was the brother of Jacob who sold his entire inheritance to Jacob for a single meal (Genesis 25:29–34). Later, when he wanted to repent of that decision, it was too late because the deal had been made. We must not make foolish and hasty decisions to abandon Christ because of a temporary trial, lest we not be given the opportunity to repent later on. The next illustration that the author of Hebrews uses is the terror associated with Mount Sinai. When God gave the Law of Moses at Mount Sinai, the Israelites were not able to even touch the mountain, lest they die (Exodus 19–20). Mount Sinai, which represents the Mosaic covenant and the Law of Moses, shows that in that old system there is separation from God and fear. However, we do not come to Mount Sinai; rather, we come to the heavenly Jerusalem and to the new people of God who now have access to the Father through the sacrifice of our new Mediator and High Priest, Jesus Christ. The last illustration that the author of Hebrews uses is Abel, the first righteous man after Adam. Because Abel had made an acceptable sacrifice and his brother Cain's sacrifice was not accepted by God, Cain killed Abel out of jealousy. Yet God says that Abel's blood cried out to Him from the ground (Genesis 4:10). If Abel's blood is that powerful and he was still a sinner, how much more powerful is the blood of Jesus Christ? Therefore, we must not turn away from this great salvation, but instead we must "serve God acceptably with reverence and godly fear" (verse 28).

Chapter 13 is filled with practical exhortations for how we ought to live as Christians. We need to be diligent to continue to love one another. We must show hospitality and provide for others in need, for by doing so we may be entertaining angels, just as Abraham had done when God and two of His angels had visited him (Genesis 18). We must also remember those who are suffering or who have been imprisoned for their faith.

We must also honor marriage and strive to remain pure until marriage. This is a command that is particularly relevant for our society today. It is rare for a person to remain pure until his or her wedding day, sadly even in the Christian community. Sex is seen as a pleasure to be freely enjoyed, rather than something that is to be reserved for marriage. When it is done right, marriage is an incredibly beautiful institution, and we as Christians need to honor it. We must also avoid covetousness or envy, but rather seek to be content with what we have, for God has promised us all throughout the Scriptures that He will provide for us. We also must remember those whom God has placed over us as our spiritual leaders and pay attention to their lives that we may learn from them.

The next command not to be "carried about with various and strange doctrines" (verse 9) is a warning against the Judaizers or the circumcision party. It is not the rituals of the Jewish laws that will heal and establish our hearts, but rather grace. Once again, the author shows how Christianity offers far greater blessings than Judaism. Just as the sacrifices had to be made outside the Israelite camp, and Jesus died outside the Israelite camp, so also we are to approach God outside the Israelite camp. Unlike Israel, which was bound to the city of Jerusalem, there is no central earthly city to which we are bound. Rather, like the heroes of the faith that came before us, we are waiting for the city to come. Moreover, rather than making animal sacrifices, which have no more value and cannot bring forgiveness, we are to bring the sacrifice of praise to God. God is also pleased when we do good to others and when we are generous with others. Finally, we are to be obedient to those whom God has placed over us as leaders. They bear the great responsibility for our souls and will have to give an account to God someday. So rather than making their lives more difficult by resisting them and fighting against them, we need to be submissive to make their work easier.

The author of Hebrews finishes this epistle on a personal note. He asks for the Hebrews to pray for him because he wants to come and visit them as soon as possible. His prayer of benediction for the Hebrews is that "the God of peace" would "make you complete in every good work to do His will ..." (verses 20–21). Because some of the exhortations in this letter may be a little bold, the author asks the Hebrews to bear with these exhortations. Timothy, who apparently had been arrested, has been set free and is planning on visiting these people. Just as the author has commanded these believers twice to remember and submit to their leaders, he now also exhorts them to greet those who rule over them. Whoever the author is, he is probably in

Italy at the time that he writes this, for he sends greetings from those in Italy. In conclusion, as Paul had done with his letters, the author of Hebrews finishes with a call for grace upon the Hebrews.

Thought Questions:

1. What are some practical ways that you can fix your eyes on Jesus daily?

2. Can you think of a time that God might have disciplined you? What kind of fruit did you bear as a result of this discipline?

3. Do you find that marriage is held in honor among your friends? If not, why do you think that this is? What can you do to honor marriage in your heart?

The Proverbs of the New Testament: James 1–2

Lesson 144

The epistle of James was written by James, the brother of Jesus (Matthew 13:55). As we saw with the Jerusalem Council in Acts 15, this James had become a leader in the church of Jerusalem. We know that this letter could not have been written by James the apostle because that James had been beheaded very early on in the history of the Church (Acts 12:2). The epistle of James is known as one of the general epistles because there is no specific audience that has been named in this letter. However, we can surmise from this letter that the audience of this epistle was comprised mainly of Jewish believers. As with many of the General Epistles, these believers had been undergoing suffering through persecution, and one of the purposes of this letter is to encourage these believers to remain faithful in the midst of suffering. Because the situation of the audience is unclear, it is difficult to pinpoint an exact date for the writing of this letter. Church tradition tells us that James died in the year A.D. 62., so this must have been written before that date. Because this letter deals with the issues of faith and works, as Paul's letter to the Galatians does, some suggest that this letter must have been written before the Jerusalem Council; otherwise, James would have mentioned the verdict of that council in this letter. It is likely that Paul's teaching on faith and works was familiar to the audience of this epistle, and James corrects their misunderstandings in this letter. If this is the case, this letter would have been written some time after Paul's views had become well known to all the churches.

Echoes of Jesus' Sermon on the Mount in James

James	Teaching	Matthew
1:2	joy amid trials	5:10–12
1:4	exhortation to be perfect	5:48
1:5	asking God for good things	7:7–11
1:17	God the giver of good	7:11
1:20	against anger	5:22
1:22	hearers and doers of the word	7:24–27
2:5	poor inherit the kingdom	5:3, 5
2:10	keeping the whole law	5:19
2:13	merciful receive mercy	5:7
3:12	know them by their fruits	7:16
3:18	blessings of peacemakers	5:9
4:2–3	ask and you will receive	7:7–8
4:4	serving God vs. friendship with the world	6:24
4:9–10	consolation for mourners	5:4
4:11–12	against judging others	7:1–5
4:13–14	living for today	6:34
5:2–5	moth and rust spoiling earthly treasures	6:19
5:10	prophets as examples and patterns	5:12
5:12	against oaths	5:33–37

This letter has developed the reputation of being the Proverbs of the New Testament because of how very practical everything is in this book. Structurally, it also plays out like a wisdom book, full of pithy sayings to use in life. Much of the material in this book has been directly influenced by the teachings of Jesus, particularly the Sermon on the Mount. In this letter, there also are a number of themes to which James returns multiple times. Some of these themes include the relationship between faith and works, the need to control our tongues, the way we treat the rich and poor, and how to handle suffering.

The very first verse in this letter suggests that James is writing to a Jewish audience. He writes this "to the twelve tribes which are scattered abroad." Some have suggested that he is speaking about the Church in a metaphorical way by calling us the true Israel. However, since James' ministry was to the Jews in Jerusalem, it is likely that this is written to a Jewish audience. The first exhortation in this letter is an encouragement regarding how to deal with suffering and persecution. When facing trials of many kinds, we are exhorted to count it all joy because through those trials we become more mature. Suffering develops patience, and patience helps us to become mature. If we learn to find joy in maturity rather than circumstantial pleasure, we can then find joy even in trials.

The next exhortation in this letter is to ask God for wisdom when we need it. This command comes with a promise, for if we ask God He is generous and will give it to us. However, James warns us that we must ask in faith, believing that God will give it to us; otherwise, we will not receive anything. Following this exhortation, James moves on to deal with the issue of favoritism toward the rich. James says that the poor person has reason to rejoice, for he will be exalted by God. Yet the rich person has to work hard to remain humble, because riches are a snare and can be taken away in an instant. This teaching on rich and poor was probably inspired by Jesus' very teachings on the subject. Jesus had said that it is easier for a camel to fit through the eye of a needle than for a rich man to enter heaven (Matthew 19:24). With riches often come self-sufficiency and pride. The rich person can often put more faith in his or her own wealth than in Jesus Christ. It may actually be easier to live a poor life than a rich life.

Even though the believers to which James is writing are facing the trial of external persecutions, the internal trials of temptation are equally as powerful. While we should never strive to put ourselves in a position of temptation, James says that the person who endures through temptation is blessed because he or she will have a great reward. Even though God sovereignly allows trials in our lives, God never tempts us to sin. It would go against God's very nature to sin, and it would be against His character to tempt us to sin. Rather, James suggests, sin originates within us, with our own desires. There is a process to sin. James compares sin to childbirth. In childbirth, there is conception, then the embryo grows into a child over time, and finally that child is born. Sin begins with conception; then as temptation develops over time it eventually gives birth to sin. If sin is allowed to grow and develop, it will also lead to death. However, if there is no original desire, then temptation has no power. For a person who hates chocolate, it will not be tempting to steal a chocolate bar. God does not implant the desire to sin into us; rather, God gives us good and perfect gifts.

Continuing with his practical exhortations, James commands us in verse 19 to be "swift to hear, slow to speak, slow to wrath." Sadly, most of us are far swifter to speak than to listen. If we could simply get into the habit of listening carefully before we speak, we would spare ourselves a lot of trouble. We also need to be "slow to wrath," or slow to anger. This does not mean that we should never be angry, but it does mean that it should take a lot to get us angry. We should not have a short fuse, but we should be patient. There is such a thing as a godly anger, such that Jesus exhibited when He cleansed the temple; godly anger always produces righteousness, but man's anger does not.

We need to put away our sinful desires and instead humbly focus on the Word of God. When we meditate on Scripture and apply it, we will be able to put away our own sinful desires and pursue righteousness. Yet we must be purposeful to do more than simply read the Bible; we must seek to apply the things that we read. Otherwise, we are wasting our time. James compares the person who reads the Word but does not do it to a person who sees his own reflection in a mirror but immediately forgets what he looks like. Another modern example is the person who looks at his watch only to realize a second later that he does not know what time it is.

The next commandment, which will be expanded upon in greater detail in the third chapter, is to control our tongues. James tells us that, if we think we are religious but do not control our tongues, our religion is useless. The kind of religion that pleases God is to provide for the poor and the widows and to protect ourselves from being polluted by the world. Also, the main way that we can prevent ourselves from being polluted by the world is by meditating on and applying Scripture regularly.

James returns to his discussion on the rich and poor in chapter 2. Here he warns us not to show partiality toward those who are rich. It can be tempting to treat rich people better than poor people because we have more to gain materially from the rich. If we treat a rich person well and honor him, perhaps he will return the favor. Yet, if we treat a poor person well, he has nothing materially to offer us. James argues that this is not the way we ought to treat people. We are called to fulfill the "royal law" (2:8), to love our neighbors as ourselves. Jesus has told us that this law, along with the law to love God, summarizes all of the Law (Matthew 22:37–40).

James then goes on to a discussion on the Law. We have already seen that the Law of Moses is incredibly important to Jewish people. However, for the person who depends on obedience to the Law of Moses as the means of becoming righteous, his or her must then obey the entire Law of Moses. Anyone who obeys even the smallest commandment in the Law becomes a transgressor and becomes guilty of disobeying all of them. If a person is bound by a strict adherence to the Law, he will miss out on mercy. There is no room for mercy in the Law, but for the one who gives mercy, he will receive mercy from God. Even though the Law of Moses is valuable, mercy triumphs over the law and judgment.

James finishes chapter 2 with a lengthy discussion about the relationship between faith and works. We have already seen Paul's views on this subject throughout his letters. Paul makes it very clear that works never save us, but only faith. Yet this can lead to a misunderstanding on the necessity of works, and this is what James clarifies in chapter 2. James tells us that faith and works are connected by necessity. It is impossible to have faith if it does not manifest itself through works. In fact, James clearly says that faith without works is dead. Even faith in God Himself is not sufficient without works. The demons have faith that God exists, but they do not combine that faith with obedience to God. Even Abraham, whom Paul uses as his primary example of salvation by faith alone, combined that faith with works. Abraham not only left his family to go into the Promised Land, but he also took his son Isaac up onto the mountain to sacrifice him before God prevented him from doing so. If Abraham simply said that he believed God but did not manifest that belief through actions, that faith would be useless. James even uses Rahab the prostitute as an example of faith and works. During the days of Joshua, he had sent out spies to Jericho to check out the city. When Rahab saw these spies, she protected them because she believed that God was with them (Joshua 2). If Rahab had simply believed that God was with the spies but did nothing for the spies, she would never have been spared when that city was destroyed.

Thought Questions:

1. If God cannot be tempted by evil and Jesus is God, how could Jesus be tempted while He was on the earth?

2. If sin begins with our desires, how can we make sure that our desires stay good rather than evil?

3. If disobeying one commandment in the Law means that we have disobeyed all of them, does this mean that all sins are the same in the eyes of God?

4. How would you reconcile James' teaching on faith and works with Paul's teachings on the subject? Do they contradict each other, or are their views compatible?

The Tongue, Heavenly Wisdom, and Prayer: James 3–5

Lesson 145

As sinners, every one of us could look back on our lives and find a myriad of mistakes and sins that we have committed. There are all kinds of sins that we all commit—sins of the mind, sins of rebellion, sins of pride and lust and other desires that run contrary to God's desires for us. Yet, for the vast majority of us, the area where we have sinned and continue to sin the most is with our mouths. We talk when we should not talk, and the things that we say bring great harm to ourselves and others. Even the most righteous person today would be able to look back and find a number of sins of the tongue. It is the topic of the tongue that constitutes most of chapter 3.

James begins his discussion of the tongue by first warning about becoming teachers. Because of the authority and influence that teachers have, they will be judged more strictly for the words that they say. In the Sermon on the Mount, Jesus warned against those teachers who teach others not to obey the Law, saying that they would be least in the kingdom of heaven (Matthew 5:19). So also those who have been given positions of influence and authority need to always be on guard to protect the words that come out of their mouths. James makes it clear that this is an issue that every one of us needs to work on. In fact, James argues that there is no one today who can claim to have complete control over his or her tongue. Because this is the easiest type of sin to fall into, James suggests that if a person could control his or her tongue, he or she could control the entire body. Moreover, the words that we speak have the power to do incredible damage. The old phrase "sticks and stones may break my bones, but words will never hurt me" is not true. Sticks and stones may give bruises that heal relatively quickly, but the harsh words that we say can scar a person for life. We need to be diligent to think before we speak and say words that build up others rather than tearing them down.

James also expands on the topic of wisdom that he mentioned early in chapter 1. In that chapter, James encouraged the readers to pray for wisdom. Here, however, James clarifies what true wisdom looks like. The wisdom of this world teaches us that we need to be ambitious and that we need to be better than the person next to us. The world tells us that we need to compete against others and make a name for ourselves. Yet God's wisdom is radically different. The "wisdom that is from above is first pure, then peaceable, gentle, willing to yield, full of mercy and good fruits, without partiality and without hypocrisy" (3:17). Rather than seeking to tear others down in order to build ourselves up, we must be merciful and willing to yield to others. We must be genuine with others and treat everyone fairly, whether they are "better" than us or not.

The tone of this letter changes in chapter 4. Up until this point, James has spoken more like a teacher who is imparting wisdom. In chapter 4, however, the tone changes more to that of a rebuke. Apparently, the readers of this letter were not living righteous lives. Perhaps they took Paul's teachings about salvation by faith rather than works too far and began to indulge in sinful behaviors. James warns them that they have to learn to control their desires, for it is their very desires that are causing so much pain and division. They are coveting and envying one another rather than asking God to provide. When they do pray and ask God to provide, they also ask for things to fulfill their ungodly desires. These believers are being influenced by the world, and it appears that they want to obtain a good standing with the people of the world. Yet James argues that friendship with the world means becoming an enemy of God. They must not try to please the people of this world, but rather God. The world values pride and self-reliance, but God opposes the proud. They must humble themselves so that someday God will exalt them. If they continue in pride, God will oppose them.

James basically tells the readers of this letter to humble themselves and repent. They think that they have their lives all together, but James argues that they need to repent of all their sins. They need to weep and wail and mourn over their sin so that they can be free from it. They need to both draw near to God and resist the devil because apparently they have not been resisting Satan. Rather than fighting with one another and building themselves up, James tells them not to speak evil of a brother or judge him.

One of the areas in which the readers of this letter have pride is their business skills. These businessmen boast about their ability to make a profit. They say that they will be able to go into any city and make a profit. Yet James reminds these big-shot businessmen that they do not control what happens tomorrow; God does. Rather than boasting in their own skills, they should humble themselves and say, "If the Lord wills, we shall live and do this or that" (4:15). These people also already know all of this. So James tells them that, if they know what they are supposed to do but do not do it, they are sinning. This broadens for us the scope of what can be

considered sin. There are plenty of things about which Scripture does not directly speak, yet we know what we are supposed to do. When we do not do these things, we also sin against God.

Even though James has been practically speaking to the rich people in the audience for a while now, he directly addresses them in chapter 5. Just as the whole audience needs to repent of their sin and humble themselves, he tells the rich to weep and howl for what is coming upon them. These rich people have made their money by robbing and cheating others, and James warns them that the time is coming when their great wealth will fade away. God has heard the cries of those whom the rich people have cheated, and judgment is coming.

For those who have been cheated by the rich and who are suffering persecution, James encourages them to be patient until Jesus returns. Just as a farmer must wait to reap the reward of the harvest, those who suffer now must wait until their reward comes. As they wait upon the Lord, they need to stop grumbling and fighting with one another because judgment is coming soon. As motivation for patient endurance, James reminds them of the prophets, who had to endure much suffering, and Job, who patiently and faithfully obeyed God in spite of losing everything.

James makes a direct reference to the Sermon on the Mount in verse 5:12. Here he tells the people not to make any oaths, but to let their "yes" be "yes" and their "no" be "no." In other words, we must be honest; and when we say we will do something, we should do it. We should not have to promise or make an oath in order for a person to take us seriously.

There are different ways that we are to respond to God based on our situation in life. When we are suffering, we should pray; when we are cheerful, we should sing psalms or praise God; and when we are sick, we should call for the elders of the church to pray over us. The prayers of some people are more powerful than others. The prayers of an elder, after he anoints the sick, have a special blessing from God. In fact, the prayers of any righteous person are especially effective. Also, there is a connection between sufferings and sin. James tells the readers of this letter to confess their sins to one another and pray so that they would be healed. When we do suffer, even though it does not necessarily mean that we have sinned to cause that suffering, it is worthwhile to examine ourselves for any unconfessed sin. Even though only God can forgive our sins, we are also commanded to confess our sins to one another so that we can receive prayer from others. As evidence that the prayers of a righteous man are effective, James mentions Elijah. Elijah prayed for rain to stop, and for three and a half years it did not rain (1 Kings 17:1). If Elijah could accomplish that, a righteous person's prayers for a sick person can certainly be effective.

After all this, James ends this letter by encouraging the readers of this letter to seek to bring back those who have wandered from the truth. For anyone who turns a sinner from his way plays a role in saving that person from death and covering over his sins.

Thought Questions:

1. What are some practical ways that you can learn to control your tongue?

2. Do you think that James' exhortation applies to all rich people? Why or why not?

3. Would you say that you regularly confess your sins to other people? Why or why not? To what kind of people do you think it would be safe to confess your sins?

Graceful Suffering: 1 Peter 1–2

Lesson 146

As the name suggests, the epistle of 1 Peter is written by the apostle Peter. This Peter is the same Peter who emerged as a leader of the disciples and of the early Church. Even though Peter primarily ministered to the Jews, this letter is written to a largely Gentile audience. In the introduction to this letter, he addresses this letter to the "pilgrims of the Dispersion in Pontus, Galatia, Cappadocia, Asia, and Bithynia." While there were Jewish believers in all these regions, the churches in these areas were composed mainly of Gentiles.

The main theme that runs through this letter, as with many of the General Epistles, is that of suffering. Throughout this entire letter, Peter offers multiple perspectives that we ought to have when dealing with suffering. In light of this, it is safe to assume that the believers to which Peter writes are going through a season of heavy persecution. The reference to "Babylon" at the end of this letter (5:13) is actually a reference to Rome, where Peter likely is when he writes this letter. Because Emperor Nero began heavy persecutions in the year A.D. 63, Peter would not have remained in Rome at that time. Therefore, he probably writes this shortly before A.D. 63.

In the greeting of this epistle, Peter identifies the audience as "pilgrims." This word refers to a refugee or a sojourner, someone who has no permanent home but is just passing through. This is an important idea to grasp for someone who is suffering. If this world is meant to be temporary, we know that we have a permanent home that awaits us in heaven. Peter also identifies the audience as "elect" or chosen by God. This election is a process in which each member of the Trinity is involved, as the Father foreknew and foreordained our election, the Spirit brings this about through sanctification, and that sanctification results in obedience to Christ, and all of it is because of the blood of Christ, which was sprinkled for us.

Peter begins immediately to offer perspective on suffering. He praises God because of His great mercy on us and because of the hope that we can have through the resurrection of Jesus Christ. If God raised Jesus from the dead, we can expect that we too will be raised from the dead. Also, unlike the things of this earth, which can be corrupted and can break and fade away, the hope that we have is incorruptible and cannot fade away. Even though persecutors can take away our property and even our lives, they cannot take away our hope. Also, God is protecting us for the salvation that we will receive at the last time. No matter what happens here on earth, this hope is a great reason to rejoice. The trials that we endure as we wait for the fulfillment of our hope also have a purpose, as well. Like fire, which purifies gold or silver, our trials help to purify us and prove that we are truly saved. As the author of Hebrews had said, our trials serve as discipline, helping us to become more mature (Hebrews 12). Even though we cannot now see Jesus Christ, we also love Him and, because we believe in Him, we can have inexpressible joy as we wait for the fulfillment of our salvation.

Even though our salvation is often the cause of persecution by the people around us, that salvation is an incredible privilege. For centuries, the prophets longed for the day when Jesus would be revealed and salvation would be offered. They searched carefully to find out the day when that salvation would be revealed. Even the angels longed to see the salvation that would come through Jesus. Now we have this salvation.

Because we have been given such a great salvation, we need to stay sharp and stay focused. When Peter says to "gird up the loins of your mind" (verse 13), he is referring to what people would have to do to prepare to run. Many of the garments that people wore back in Peter's time would go all the way to the ground; girding up the loins means picking up the bottom of the garment so that you do not trip on it. To gird up the loins of your mind means to prepare yourself and get ready for action. There are two things we need to do as those who have prepared our minds for action—we need to set our hope fully on the grace to be revealed when Jesus returns, and we need to live holy lives as we wait for that day. We should not revert to the behaviors and habits that we had before we met Christ, but we should work hard to make sure that our conduct is holy.

Though many things are not guaranteed or protected here on this earth, our salvation is. We were not purchased from our bondage to sin with gold or silver, but with something far more precious, the blood of Christ. Once again, God had set into motion the plan of salvation through Jesus Christ before the foundation of the world, and now we get to see the fulfillment of history through Jesus. Because we have been born again through the work of Christ and of the Holy Spirit, we need to love one another fervently and sincerely. Since we have been born again, we ought to put away those evil actions and thoughts that accompanied our lives before Jesus. Instead, we need to crave and meditate on the Word of God. For the Word of God is incorruptible and will not fail us.

And now, as those who have been saved by Jesus and redeemed by Him, we are part of the new temple of God. Like the Levites of the Old Testament, we are all now holy priests of God who can offer spiritual sacrifices that God accepts. In this new people of God, the new temple, Jesus is also the chief cornerstone. For those who are obedient to God, Jesus is very precious, but those who are disobedient will stumble. In 1 Peter 2:9, Peter quotes a number of Old Testament statements and promises concerning Israel and argues that they are now fulfilled in us. We are now "a chosen generation, a royal priesthood, a holy nation, His own special people."

Because we belong to God and yet still remain on this earth as sojourners and pilgrims, we need to live obedient and honorable lives among the Gentiles. This is the message that will run for the rest of chapter 2 and into chapter 3. Rather than giving in to our sinful desires, we must work hard to live blameless lives so that even if unbelievers hate or persecute us, they will see our good works and someday glorify God. One of the ways that we are to live blameless lives among unbelievers is to submit to those authorities that have been placed over us. Even though we have ultimate freedom in Christ, we should never use that freedom as an excuse to sin. We should live such honorable lives that those on the outside would be ashamed if they said anything bad against us.

Peter's exhortations to servants apply more broadly to all of us. He exhorts servants to be submissive to their masters, not just the good and gentle masters but even the harsh ones. If we rebel against the authorities and are punished for it, we gain nothing. However, if we remain obedient and submissive, and still these harsh masters punish us, we will receive a great reward from the Lord. As our great motivation, Peter reminds us of the behavior of Jesus Christ Himself. If anybody suffered unjustly and unfairly, it was Jesus Christ. Rather than fighting back or retaliating, Jesus entrusted Himself to the just Judge, God. We will all face situations in which we will suffer unjustly at the hands of evil people. Rather than rebelling against these people, we need to remain obedient and entrust ourselves to God, knowing that He will bring about true justice someday.

Marriage, Witness, and Warfare: 1 Peter 3–5
Lesson 147

Because we live in a fallen world that is corrupted by sin, we will often find ourselves in situations that may not be fair. We will have bosses or parents that are harsh and unfair with us. We have already seen in chapter 2 that we are to remain faithful and submissive, even to those authorities that are not fair to us or cause us to suffer. Chapter 3 begins with another unfair situation, that between a believing wife and an unbelieving husband.

Peter's exhortation to wives is consistent with the rest of Scripture. Women are to be submissive to their husbands and to devote themselves to character development rather than physical appearance. Peter, however, adds another element to this command. Specifically, Peter mentions how women with unbelieving husbands are to treat their husbands. It could be confusing for a believing wife to submit to her unbelieving husband, especially if he does not share her same values. Peter suggests, however, that it is through the wife's submission to her husband that she may win him over. The hope is that, as he sees her character and submissiveness, he will want to know where it comes from.

Husbands are not off the hook, however. Peter commands husbands to live with their wives in an understanding and honorable manner. The reason for this command is that wives are the "weaker vessel" (3:7). What does it mean for women to be weaker vessels? It is possible that Peter has physical stature in mind for this statement, but more likely he is referring to her position of weakness that a wife has as the submissive partner. How a man treats his wife has an effect on his prayer life. If a man is not considerate and understanding toward his wife, his prayers will be hindered according to verse 7.

Just as husbands are to be considerate and understanding toward their wives, everyone is to be loving and compassionate toward one another. In verse 8, we are all commanded to "be of one mind, having compassion for one another; love as brothers, be tenderhearted, be courteous." Rather than responding to evil with more evil, we are to bless those who persecute us. The phrase "hurting people hurt people" is particularly relevant here. When we go through pain, we are far more likely to respond to others by hurting them. But we are exhorted in verse eleven to "turn away from evil and do good" and we should "seek peace and pursue it." God sees all that we do, and we have no excuse to ever do evil to another person, even when they cause us to suffer. In fact, as Peter argued in chapter 2, if we suffer for doing good, we are blessed.

Our actions with outsiders should be done in such a way as to win them over. Throughout this letter, Peter has suggested that when we do good to those who are harsh or unfair with us, we are serving as a faithful witness of Jesus Christ. So Peter commands us in verse 15 to "always be ready to give a defense to everyone who asks you a reason for the hope that is in you, with meekness and fear." When we bless those who persecute us or treat us poorly, they will be more prone to ask why we are treating them this way. Peter tells us that we need to have already thought through our response for when they ask us why we believe in Jesus. Once again, Peter reminds us that it is a good thing to suffer for doing what is right because this is what Jesus Himself endured.

In verses 19 and 20, Peter makes a reference to something that is highly debated. He speaks of Jesus, after His death, preaching to the spirits in prison during the days of Noah. There are a number of questions that this reference creates. Is this referring to the time between Jesus' death and resurrection? Are these spirits those people who were in hell or some holding place? If this is in hell, how can God be in hell? What is Jesus preaching to these spirits? If He is preaching the gospel, is this a one-time opportunity for those spirits to be saved? Are these spirits people or demons? And what does Noah's generation have to do with all this? It is difficult to conclude that Jesus went to hell to preach the gospel because Jesus told the thief on the cross that he would be with Jesus that very day in Paradise (Luke 23:43). This would seem to imply that Jesus was in heaven, rather than in hell, after His death. Also, the word for

"preach" here is not the word that is commonly used in Scripture to refer to preaching the gospel, but rather means "to proclaim victory." It is possible that Jesus went on a victory lap following the cross proclaiming His victory over Satan. Because Peter mentions Noah, and there is a lot of Jewish literature and myths concerning Noah and Enoch, it is likely that Peter is making a reference to a story that the audience would have understood but is lost to us. There also may have been a special holding place for the disobedient people from the days of Noah, and Jesus speaks specifically to them. It is also possible that Jesus may have proclaimed victory during the days of Noah before He ever came to earth. This may just be a mystery that we will not be able to solve.

Even though Peter's reference is difficult to understand, there is something we can learn from the story of Noah. Just as the ark was able to save Noah and his family from the destructions of the waters, Peter tells us that baptism now saves us. It is not the physical action of baptism that saves people, but the spiritual reality of a clean conscience that has been forgiven that saves us.

Once again, Peter turns to Jesus as our example and motivation in chapter 4. One of the odd blessings of physical suffering is that it helps us to fight against the desires of our flesh. Suffering reminds us that our bodies are not to be used selfishly for our own pleasures, but to do the will of God. Our sinful practices and habits should be a thing of the past. In fact, this is another thing that we can do to be a good witness to others. Though nonbelievers may think it strange and may attack us for it, when we stop doing the sinful activities that we used to do with nonbelievers, we are being a witness to them of the power of Jesus and the gospel.

In verse 6, Peter makes another reference to Jesus preaching to the dead and argues that His preaching to them was an act of judgment. Also, because there is a judgment day that is coming, we need to "be serious and watchful in your prayers" (4:7). This world is temporary, and the end can come at any time, so we need to live faithfully and be aware of the times. We must also help one another out so that we can all endure these trials until Christ returns. We are to passionately love one another and do so in a manner without grumbling. We are to use the gifts that God has given us to minister faithfully to one another.

Peter argues that it is to be expected that we would go through fiery trials and persecutions. If Jesus Himself has suffered for righteousness' sake, we should expect to endure the same things. It is also a great honor to suffer along with Jesus. However, if we react poorly to these sufferings and respond by abandoning good deeds and righteousness, we will be judged. In fact, judgment begins with the people of God.

Next, Peter encourages and exhorts the leaders or elders of the people to remain faithful in their ministries. God compares the Church to a flock of sheep and argues that elders are to be faithful shepherds over God's flock.* The office of elder, however, is something that should be taken voluntarily, not under compulsion. It also should not be a position that a person takes in order to make money from the church. Moreover, leadership in the church should not be authoritarian, but rather servant leadership. An elder should not demand allegiance and obedience, but should earn it by being a great example to the people.

Even though the leaders in the church should not demand allegiance or obedience from their people, the younger people in the congregation do have a responsibility to submit themselves to their elders. As Paul had said in Ephesians 5, there is an extent that we all should be submissive to one another in the body of Christ. We must humble ourselves and consider others to be better than ourselves because God opposes the proud but gives grace to the humble. Because God is the ultimate Shepherd over us, we can cast all our cares upon Him because He cares about us.

As we draw near to God and cast our cares upon Him, we must also be vigilant and aware of our enemy, Satan. Peter describes the devil as a roaring lion, searching for some prey to destroy. If we are not aware or careful, we will be attacked by that lion. Remember that our primary command in regard to Satan is to resist him and to stay strong in the faith. We can also find comfort in the fact that we are not alone in our sufferings; there are other Christians around the world who are going through the same things we are.

As with many of Paul's letters, Peter ends this letter with a benediction and greetings. He prays that God would strengthen, perfect, establish, and settle us after we endure our sufferings. He sends greetings from Silvanus, who is also known as Silas, one of Paul's traveling companions. The mention of Babylon cannot be a reference to the literal Babylon because that had been destroyed; metaphorically, Babylon refers to Rome. This is why many scholars believe Peter writes this from Rome. Mark is also the same Mark who traveled with Paul and wrote the second gospel. As with Paul, Peter encourages his audience to greet one another with a

---

* This is the same imagery that Jesus used with Peter in John 21.

kiss. Yet, unlike Paul, Peter does not finish his letter with grace, but rather peace.

Thought Questions:

1. If a Christian woman is married to a non-Christian man and he tells her that he does not want her to go to church, should she submit to him? Why or why not?

2. Have you ever had a time when you responded with kindness to someone who treated you poorly? If so, how did he or she respond to your kind treatment?

3. What would be your response if someone asks you why you believe in Jesus?

False Teachers in the Last Days: 2 Peter 1–3 & Jude
Lesson 148

There is some considerable debate by scholars as to the authorship of 2 Peter. Even though the author identifies himself as Simon Peter and speaks of his experience on the Mount of Transfiguration, the style of this letter is radically different from 1 Peter. The writing in 2 Peter is far less sophisticated than 1 Peter, so some scholars conclude that it was a different author. However, there is a much simpler explanation for this: Peter probably used a scribe to write down 1 Peter, but writes 2 Peter himself. The audience for this letter is unclear. Most likely, it was intended to be a circular letter to be distributed to all the churches. Based on the content and Peter's reference to an earlier letter, we can conclude that this letter was written after 1 Peter in the mid-60s A.D.

The content of 2 Peter and Jude is very similar, so similar in fact, that one probably had access to the other. Both letters deal with issues of the end times, false teachers, and angels; and both make references to the same Old Testament allusions. For this reason, we are going to examine both of these letters together.

There are three ideas that permeate this letter that work together. *First*, Peter reminds the readers of this letter about the gospel and the precious promises that we have in the gospel. *Second*, Peter exhorts the readers of this letter to strive to live righteous lives in light of the gospel. *Third*, Peter warns the readers of this letter about false teachers and their need to avoid such people.

Peter addresses this letter in verse 1 to "those who have obtained like precious faith with us by the righteousness of our God and Savior Jesus Christ." There are two important ideas that Peter conveys through this introduction. First, the faith that we have received is very precious. Second, we receive this faith through the righteousness of Christ. Peter describes Jesus as "our God and Savior," yet another reference in Scripture to the deity of Christ. As with the letters we have already studied, Peter calls for grace and peace to be upon the recipients of this letter.

In the gospel, we receive a myriad of blessings. We see in verse 3 that God's divine power has given us everything that we need for life and godliness. Through the great and precious promises, we also have become partakers of the divine nature and have escaped the corruption through lust. The reference to the divine nature is a reference to the Holy Spirit, whom we receive upon salvation, who works in us to desire and to act according to what pleases God. With the Holy Spirit, we are now able to put to death the desires of the flesh, which wage war against the Spirit, so that we can escape the corruption of the flesh.

Because we have all these blessings through the gospel, we need to respond by living virtuous and faithful lives. Peter gives a list of character traits that we need to strive to increase, including virtue, knowledge, self-control, perseverance, godliness, brotherly kindness, and love. If we do not grow in these character traits, we will become near-sighted and lose a healthy perspective on life. Over time, it can be easy to forget what it was like when we first received forgiveness of our sins and the motivation this gave us to live virtuous lives. When we continue to strive to be more virtuous, we will be reminded about what it was like to be forgiven. In fact, Peter argues that increasing in these virtues is one of the ways that we can know that we are saved. In verse 10, Peter says, "Therefore, brethren, be even more diligent to make your call and election sure, for if you do these things you will never stumble." We can make our salvation sure when we grow in these virtues.

Peter then gets personal and explains why he is writing this letter. The things that Peter has said in this letter are not new, but mere reminders of the things that the readers of this letter would already know. This letter is probably written near the end of Peter's life, as he speaks of shortly putting off the "tent" of his body. Because Peter suspects he is going to die soon, he takes this last opportunity to build up and encourage the churches. Unlike the false teachers who had been infiltrating the church and deceiving people with new ideas, Peter was an eyewitness to the life of Jesus and received the gospel from Jesus Himself. When Peter speaks of

being an eyewitness to Jesus' majesty on the mountain, He is referring to the Mount of Transfiguration where Jesus was glorified before Peter, James, and John. With Jesus, all the prophecies of the Old Testament have found their fulfillment, and Peter himself was a witness to that fulfillment. This provides the context for Peter to make a statement on the nature of Scripture that the Scriptures did not come about because of individual interpretations, but rather through the inspiration of the Holy Spirit.

However, just as there were false prophets in the Old Testament, there are false teachers and prophets now. Peter has a number of very harsh things to say about these false teachers, which turns into a stern warning for the recipients of this letter. These false teachings are described as "destructive heresies" that will bring destruction upon the one who teaches them and upon the ones who believe them. Sadly, many people will be prone to be deceived by false teachers; and as a result, Christianity will get a bad name. This is very true for today, as many people preach ideas and doctrines that are against the Bible and give Christianity a bad name.

Peter gives a number of Old Testament examples of the destruction that comes upon those who are disobedient to the word. First, he mentions the angels who were cast out of heaven when they rebelled and are reserved for judgment. He also mentions the destruction that came upon the earth with the flood and how only Noah and his family were spared. Finally, he brings up the story of Sodom and Gomorrah and the destruction that came upon that city but the salvation that came upon Lot. Peter does offer more insight into the story of Lot, however. From the Genesis 19 account, Lot does not look very righteous in the story of the destruction of Sodom and Gomorrah. Yet Peter informs us that Lot was tormented by the wickedness of the people around him. These examples show us that God will punish the ungodly while sparing and saving the righteous.

The description of these false teachers continues through the rest of chapter 2. These false teachers have no sense of honor, as they blaspheme those in authority. They are only concerned with their own agenda, and they are covetous of other people. They lead others astray by their teachings, while they themselves indulge in their own sinful desires. Peter compares them to Balaam, a prophet who used his gift for his own personal monetary gain. In the Old Testament, Balaam was hired by a foreign king to curse the Israelites; however, every time he attempted to do so, he ended up blessing them instead (Numbers 22–24). However, these false teachers in Peter's day are not bringing any blessing; instead, they are using their position of influence to make money. Moreover, they deceive people with teachings that sound good but are full of emptiness. These people who are deceived are those who had experienced the freedom of salvation but are once again brought back into slavery through the teachings of these false teachers. Sadly, these people who had experienced freedom and lost it through this deception are worse off than if they had never believed in the first place. It is likely that these false teachers about which Peter is talking are those of the circumcision party, who demand that people obey the Law of Moses, but they themselves are filled with wickedness.

Once again, Peter is not teaching the readers anything new, but he writes this to remind them to be on guard against false teachers when he is gone. Peter is concerned that when he leaves the churches will be corrupted by these false teachers, so he reminds them of what they already know. One of the arguments that these false teachers are using to discredit the teachings of the apostles is that Jesus has not yet returned. There is certainly a sense of immediate expectancy in the early Church concerning Christ's return. By the time that Peter writes this, Jesus had been gone for over thirty years. Peter reminds the readers of this letter that destruction came with the flood when people were not expecting it. As it is, though God promised never to destroy the earth with a flood again, the current world is reserved to be destroyed with fire. Also, God does not work on our time frame. We might consider Jesus' delay to be a really long time, but to God a thousand years is like a day. God is not a liar or lazy to fulfill His promises. The reason God has delayed the return of Christ is so that more people would have a chance to repent and be saved. God desires that all people would come to repentance, though sadly this is not the reality.

Jesus is going to return; and when He comes, it will be sudden, like a thief in the night. When that day comes, there will be swift and complete destruction as the very creation itself will be destroyed by fire. If these things can come any time, Peter asks, "What manner of persons ought you to be in holy conduct and godliness?" (3:11). If you really expected Jesus to return at any moment, how would that change the way that you live? Yet, for those who are in Christ, when He returns, it will not mean destruction but will mean a new heaven and a new earth to which they look forward. Rather than seeing Christ's delay as a bad thing, Peter tells us to "consider that the longsuffering of our Lord is salvation" (verse 15).

Peter equates Paul's writings with Scripture in verses 15–16. He reminds the hearers that Paul had also given them this same message and that some have distorted and perverted that message, as they do the other Scriptures. Also, just as people have distorted Paul's writings, people are prone to misunderstand and distort the gospel. Peter warns these readers that they need to be on guard, lest they be led away into the errors of the wicked. Rather, they need to continue to grow in the grace and knowledge of Jesus.

The epistle of Jude is written by Jude, the brother of James and half-brother of Jesus (Matthew 13:55). As with 1 and 2 Peter, this epistle is written to a general audience and intended to be distributed among all the churches. The content of this letter is very similar to 2 Peter. Like 2 Peter, the main message of this letter is that we need to guard ourselves against false teachers. Also like 2 Peter, Jude uses Old Testament examples to represent these false teachers and those who are deceived by them. First, he reminds the readers of the generation of Israelites who left Egypt but died in the wilderness because of their unbelief. In addition, he mentions the punishments of the fallen angels and Sodom and Gomorrah. Also, these false teachers blaspheme and disrespect authorities. Jude contrasts the blasphemy of these false teachers with the reverence of the archangel Michael. The story that Jude shares here is not in the Scriptures but was probably a part of Jewish lore. Apparently, after Moses died, there was a dispute between Satan and Michael over who would have the body of Moses. Yet Michael showed respect, even to Satan, and said, "The Lord rebuke you!" Jude also uses the stories of Cain, Balaam, and Korah as evidence that judgment is coming upon these false teachers. Even Enoch prophesied about the judgment coming on such false teachers.

Jude then reminds the readers of the warnings given by the apostles, that in the last time people will be mockers and will follow their ungodly lusts. He exhorts the readers to build themselves up in the faith, to pray in the Holy Spirit, to keep themselves in the love of God, and to look for the mercy of Jesus in eternal life. Now when it comes to false teachers, some teach falsehood out of ignorance, but others do so out of evil intentions. For those who are ignorant, we are to show compassion and patience as we correct their false doctrine. For those who teach false doctrine out of evil intentions, we need to be stern, motivating them by fear.

Finally, Jude finishes this epistle with a doxology, praising God because He is able to keep us from stumbling and to present us as faultless before God. Of course, God is the One who gets all the glory.

Thought Question:

How confident would you say you are that you are saved? From 2 Peter, how can you be more confident of your salvation?

A Beautiful Symphony: 1 John 1–3

Lesson 149

The author of 1 John does not directly identify himself in this epistle. Yet church tradition and a basic reading of this letter make it very clear that the writer of this epistle is the same author as the fourth gospel, which is attributed to John. In addition, the author of this epistle speaks about events in the life of Christ that he had seen firsthand, so he must have been one of the disciples. In light of this, we can surmise that the author of 1 John is John, the son of Zebedee, who was one of the inner three from among the disciples. This is the same disciple who identifies himself as "the disciple whom Jesus loved" in the fourth gospel.

The audience of this letter is not identified. As such, it is reasonable to assume that this letter was intended to be distributed as a circular letter to all the churches. Unlike the other epistles that we have encountered so far, this epistle lacks a greeting and a customary salutation. Because John lived the longest of all the disciples by about thirty years, many scholars date this letter close to the end of the first century A.D., though it is possible he wrote this as early as the late 60s A.D.

The style of this letter is also unique. Rather than developing a single linear thought throughout the letter, John interacts with many themes multiple times throughout the letter. The style of this letter can be compared to a musical symphony. In a symphony, themes are developed early on. Then, as the symphony continues, the composer comes back to those themes but brings them with variations. John does this same thing; he comes back to the same themes over and over again, but each time he adds something.

Overall, the main purpose of this letter is to prepare Christians for how to identify false teachers. In the process, John gives a number of characteristics that need to be present in a Christian if he or she is truly a Christian. As the reader goes through this epistle, it is worthwhile for the reader to examine himself or herself to see if John is describing him or her.

Back in the first chapter of Acts, we learned that one of the most important criteria for being an apostle is that the man must be a witness to the life, death, and resurrection of Jesus Christ. John begins this letter by identifying himself as a witness to the life, death, and resurrection of Jesus and offers his testimony on Jesus' behalf. John had personally seen Jesus and heard Him speak and had touched Jesus. This is very important, considering one of the heresies that appears to be spreading at this time, which John will address later in this letter. By the time John writes this letter, some people have begun to argue that Jesus was never a human but was merely a spirit. John testifies from the beginning that Jesus was a real human. Here John also identifies Jesus as "eternal life" in verse 2. John tells us why he testifies concerning these things. John wants the readers to be filled with more joy, and he wants to be able to share fellowship with these believers.

The *first theme* that John addresses in this epistle is the metaphor of light and darkness. In John's gospel, he developed this same theme masterfully. Here light is associated with truth and righteousness, and darkness is associated with hiding from the truth and sin. A true Christian cannot live a hidden life because God is light, so to come into God's presence requires that we are open and honest and exposed to God. To be in the light does not mean that we never sin, however. John makes it clear that anyone who claims to be without sin is a liar and should not be trusted. We are all sinners, but the one who brings that sin into the light by confessing that sin is a true believer and will experience forgiveness or cleansing from that sin. So the *first mark* of a Christian according to John is that the believer is willing to humble himself or herself and confess his or her sins to God, not hiding anything.

The *second theme* that John addresses is the necessity of obedience in the life of a Christian. Just because we are forgiven and have Jesus as our Advocate before the Father does not mean that we can openly and freely sin. Jesus came to take the wrath of God for our sin as our **propitiation**; we should not then take that as an excuse to sin. When John says that Jesus is the propitiation for the whole world, this does not mean that everyone is saved but that Jesus died for people from everywhere in the world. In 1 John 2:3, John gives the *second mark* of a true Christian: "Now by this we know that we know Him, if we keep His commandments." John puts it bluntly in verse 4 when he says that the person who claims to know God but does not obey God is a liar. In fact, God's love is perfected in us through our obedience. It only makes sense that a person who claims to have Jesus in him or her would act the way that Jesus did.

The *third theme* that John addresses is the importance of love. The commandment of which John speaks that is not new is the commandment to love one another, even though he does not identify it as such yet. John speaks of love in the opposite way by telling us that a true believer does not hate his or her brother or sister in Christ. Hate should never be what characterizes us as Christians; thus, the *third mark* of a believer should be love for one another, which characterizes us instead. John combines themes by arguing that hatred is connected with darkness and we should be in the light.

John then directly addresses little children, young men, and fathers and gives them each encouragements. While it is possible that John is speaking specifically to people of different ages here, it is likely that he is addressing people in different stages of their faith journeys. The little children are new believers, the young men are those who have been believers for a while, and the fathers here are those who have been believers for a long time and are now leaders in the church. John reminds the new believers that their sins are forgiven and that they know the Father. He reminds those who have been believers for a while that they have overcome Satan and that they are strong and have the Word of God in them. He reminds the older believers that they know Jesus, who was from the beginning.

The *fourth mark* of a true believer is that he or she does not love the world. Because the values of this world are often the opposite of what God desires for us, we cannot love both God and the world. The world advocates feeding and fulfilling the desires or lusts of the flesh, whereas God says to follow the Spirit. The world says to pursue more and more wealth, but God says to learn to be content and grateful for what you have. The world says to boast and have pride, but God tells us to be humble.

In 1 John 2:18–29, John addresses the crisis that these believers are facing. Once again, false teachers had been infiltrating the churches and deceiving the believers, leading some to abandon their faith. Unlike the false teachers whom Paul encounters, these false teachers do not appear to be trying to get Christians to become Jewish. These false teachers deny that Jesus is the Christ. John calls such false teachers "antichrists" and argues that there are many of them. John encourages his readers and builds them up, telling them that he is confident that they know the truth and that they will abide in the truth. John acknowledges that Jesus is going to

return, and so we need to abide in Christ now so that when He does return we will not be ashamed.

In chapter 3, John readdresses the themes that he introduced in the first two chapters. We have already learned that true believers will live in obedience to God. John now repeats this by saying it the other way around, that true believers will not continue to sin. This does not mean that we will never sin, but that sin should not be a pattern in our lives. When confronted with sin, true believers will repent rather than hold on to that sin and continue in it. John puts it plainly; sin is of the devil but obedience is from God. When we sin we are following what Satan desires, but when we obey we do what God desires. Related to this, when we love one another, we are walking in obedience to what God desires. Likewise, when we hate one another, we do what the devil desires. As an example, John brings up Cain and Abel. Cain was evil and hated his brother, killing him because Abel was righteous and Cain was not. So also, the world will hate us if we are righteous.

Yet what does it mean to love one another? John tells us that loving others is something that is costly. The best example of love is Jesus, who laid down His life for us. So also, we ought to lay down our lives for others. If we see someone in need, we should be willing to sacrificially give for them. However, if we see people in need and shut off our hearts toward them, we are not manifesting the love of God. Therefore, John says in 1 John 3:18, "let us not love in word or in tongue, but in deed and in truth."

If we exhibit all these characteristics, we should have confidence in our hearts that we are in Him and that we are truly saved. Yet, even if our hearts condemn us, God knows us better than we know ourselves, and He is the Judge. If our heart does not condemn us, we can live our lives with confidence, knowing that we are saved. Also, if we know that we are with God, we can pray with confidence before Him, knowing that He will answer our prayers. When John says that we will receive whatever we ask, this does not mean that God will give us everything for which we pray, but simply that God will answer our prayers, so we should pray confidently. Finally, John ends chapter 3 with the *fifth mark* of a true Christian. The true Christian knows that he or she is saved because the Holy Spirit confirms it in us.

> **propitiation:** the turning away of wrath by an offering; appeasing or satisfying the wrath of God by the atoning sacrifice of Christ

Thought Questions:

1. After reading these three chapters, do you find yourself more confident or less confident that you are saved? Why?

2. How can you determine if you love the world or not?

Marks of a True Christian: 1 John 4–5

Lesson 150

In the very last words of the third chapter, John tells us that one of the ways that we know that we abide in Christ is through the inner testimony of the Holy Spirit. Yet how do we know if we are really hearing the Holy Spirit or not? John begins chapter 4 by addressing this question. There are other forces than the Holy Spirit that vie for our attention. We need to learn to test any teacher that claims to speak truth about Jesus. John clarifies that any prophet or spirit that claims that Jesus was never a human is not speaking from the Holy Spirit. As time progressed and fewer and fewer people were alive who had seen Jesus in the flesh, one of the heresies that developed was the belief that Jesus was just a spirit. John makes it abundantly clear that Jesus was indeed a human and not just a spirit in the last two chapters.

John returns to the theme of war with the world in chapter 4. We have already been warned by John that we cannot love both the world and God. John has also told us that the world will hate us because we are different from the world, though to be fair, this idea originated from Jesus Himself rather than John (John 17:14). Even though we will be hated and persecuted by the world, we can also have confidence that "He who is in you is greater than he who is in the world" (4:4).

Some of the Bible's most famous teachings on love comes in chapter 4 of this letter. We are commanded to love one another because God is love. If we are truly followers of God and have His Spirit in us, love ought to be what governs everything we do. Plainly put, if we do not love one another, John tells us that we do not know God. The greatest act of love in history was the sacrifice that the Father and Jesus made when Jesus died for our sins. Certainly, we should follow this up by loving one another. This is also our primary motivation for why we love God. Our love is always a responsive love, as we respond to God's love for us. When we learn to love the way that God loved us, His love is perfected and we can have confidence on the day of judgment

that we are saved. In fact, John argues that "perfect love casts out fear" in verse 18. For those who have not received nor understood the love of God, when God judges them there is only fear. However, those who know that they are loved by God and have seen that love transform the way that they love others will not need to fear on the day of judgment.

As we have already seen in this letter, all of the themes of this letter are connected. In chapter 5 we see this again. Those who believe that Jesus is the Messiah are born again and will love God. Whoever loves God and keeps His commandments will also love other people. Whoever is born of God will also overcome the world through his faith. Also, the one who overcomes the world is the one who believes that Jesus is the Son of God. Our beliefs will by necessity affect the way that we live. If we truly have good doctrine, we will follow that doctrine up with a godly life.

John has already made it clear that anyone who does not acknowledge that Jesus came in the flesh is a liar and a false teacher and an antichrist. In chapter 5, John expands on this idea. John speaks of Jesus being born of both water and blood. This could be a reference to the cross, where the Romans pierced Jesus' side and water and blood came out. It could also just be a reference to the physical nature of His body. As John continues his argument in verse 7, there is a discrepancy between the King James Version (or New King James Version) and most modern translations of the Bible. In the manuscript that the King James Version used, there is a reference to the Trinity: "The Father, the Word, and the Holy Spirit; and these three are one." The problem with this reference is that none of the earliest manuscripts have this part of the verse; yet, it would make sense for believers to add this in later as evidence for the Trinity. Nevertheless, there is good reason to believe that verse 7 should only read, "For there are three that bear witness." Even so, John certainly points to the Holy Spirit, the water, and the blood as evidence that Jesus did indeed come in the flesh. The Holy Spirit testifies to us in the inner man, and the water and blood are physical evidence.

Reminiscent of John 3:16, John tells us in verses 11 through 14 that through Jesus Christ we have eternal life. Just as John told us that the purpose of his gospel was to get us to believe in Jesus (John 20:31), the purpose of this letter is also to help us to know that we have eternal life through Jesus Christ and to help us to continue in our belief in Jesus Christ. Once again, as those who know that we have eternal life, this also means that we can pray with boldness.

The next thing that John writes requires some discussion. John tells us that we should pray for a brother or sister who is sinning, that God would give that person life. Yet John makes a strange distinction here between sins that lead to death and sins that do not lead to death. John tells us not to pray for people who commit sins leading to death, only for those sins that do not lead to death. However, we have already seen in Scripture that the wages of any sin is eternal death (Romans 6:23). So what is the death about which John is speaking? It is likely that John is talking about those sins that lead to physical death. Perhaps he is talking about capital punishment and those crimes that result in death. Regrettably, John does not give us any specific examples, so all we can do is speculate.

John leaves us with a series of facts. Those who are truly saved do not continue in their sin, but are protected from the evil one. Those who are truly saved know that they are of God and that the whole world is deceived by the evil one. Also, those who are truly saved know that Jesus is the Son of God and that He has given us understanding about Himself. Through that understanding, we know the One who is truth itself and we know that we are in Him. Because of all this, we can know that we have eternal life. Finally, John finishes with an exhortation that almost seems out of place. He tells the readers to stay away from idols. Even so, an idol is anything that rivals God, and the Jesus that these false teachers have been advocating is nothing but an idol. We do not follow man-made idols or religions, but the very real person of Jesus Christ.

Thought Question:

If perfect love drives out fear, and the fear of the Lord is the beginning of wisdom, what role should the fear of God play in the life of the Christian?

Wise Hospitality: 2 John & 3 John
Lesson 151

The author of both 2 and 3 John identifies himself simply as "the elder." So why is it that we attribute these epistles to the apostle John? There are two main reasons why scholars believe that the apostle John wrote these epistles. *First*, church tradition had attributed these letters to the apostle John within a century of his death. *Second*, the language and content of these letters are very similar to the gospel of John and the epistle of 1 John.

John writes this second letter to "the elect lady and her children." It is certainly possible that this is written to a specific woman, considering that many women hosted churches in their homes at this time. If this is written in the 90s A.D., Christians were undergoing some serious persecution by the Roman Empire; this could explain why John does not mention this woman by name, in order to protect her from persecution. The other option for the audience of this letter is that the elect lady is a reference to the Church, thus making this a circular letter to be sent among all the churches. The Church has been called the Bride of Christ multiple times throughout Scripture, so it is consistent to refer to the Church as a woman. Third John is written to a specific man named Gaius. Though there have been a few people already mentioned in the New Testament named Gaius, it is unclear who precisely this is. Church tradition states that John had moved to Ephesus near the end of his life, so it is possible that this Gaius is a wealthy member of the church at Ephesus.

The main point of both of these letters is to warn the readers of these letters not to show hospitality to false teachers and to show love and hospitality to faithful preachers. Hospitality is a virtue that was highly valued in biblical times. Many wandering preachers would go from city to city and depend on the hospitality and generosity of individuals within that city to provide them with shelter and food. John writes these letters to make sure that Christians are not contributing to the spread of false doctrine by showing hospitality to these false teachers.

There are two themes that permeate 2 John—love and truth. In order for us to be faithful as Christians, we need to fight for both of these ideas. If a person values and fights for truth but does not have love, that truth can be used to hurt people rather than help them. Conversely, if a person exhibits love but does not protect the truth, he or she will only help to perpetuate a lie. For example, if a person is an alcoholic but his friend ignores this and continues to bail this friend out of trouble, this does not help the alcoholic. The most helpful thing that friend can do is speak the truth to the alcoholic, but in a caring and loving way. In the case of 2 John, the specific for which that John wants us to fight is the truth of the gospel. Practically from the beginning of the Church, the Church had been infiltrated by false teachers who deceived people and led them away from the truth of the gospel. John rejoices that some of the believers had indeed continued to walk in the truth in spite of the false teaching going around. In addition, John reiterates the importance of loving one another. Not only should we love one another, but we should love God by obeying His commandments. These are the same commands that John had given in 1 John. Finally, John exhorts the reader of this letter in verse 10 to refuse hospitality to anyone who "does not bring this doctrine." This letter is so short because John plans to come and visit the recipient of this letter shortly. Thus, he finishes this letter with greetings from another unnamed "sister."

John writes his third epistle to encourage and exhort a man named Gaius. John rejoices because he had received a report from some of the brothers that Gaius had received them into his home and provided for them. In the report, John learned that Gaius had been faithful to hold to the truth of the gospel and had not wavered from it. Because Gaius had remained faithful and had held onto the truth of the gospel, John warns him about a man named Diotrephes. This man had apparently grown in power and influence in the local church. Diotrephes had slandered John and had forbidden people from the local church to show hospitality to the wandering preachers. John warns Gaius not to follow the example of this man or others who are doing what is evil. Rather, John commends Demetrius, who had remained faithful to the truth, as an example to follow. As with his second letter, this letter is short because John intends to visit Gaius shortly. For both of these letters, it makes sense that they are so short considering the incredible danger they would be in if the Romans received information on their whereabouts. John is very careful in these letters not to write too much information that could get people in trouble. Finally, John finishes this letter by calling for peace upon Gaius and by sending greetings.

Introduction to Revelation

Lesson 152

Perhaps the most often debated book in the entire Bible is the book of Revelation. This book has scared, baffled, and fascinated Christians for millennia. This book is filled with incredibly rich scenes of devastation, worship, and victory. Sadly, because of misunderstandings of this book and because of all the debate that surrounds this book, many Christians avoid this book altogether. Yet this book should be a source of great hope and encouragement for all of us.

The author of this book is the apostle John. Many of the themes that permeate this book are present in all of John's writings. For example, the most well-developed statements on the deity of Christ are found in John's writings, and the book of Revelation highlights the deity of Christ. Because of the persecutions going on in the Roman Empire at this time, John is exiled to the island of Patmos. While on this island, John receives the visions that will make up this book. Most scholars believe this was written shortly before the end of the first century, in the late 90s A.D. Some scholars argue that this was written in the late 60s A.D. before the destruction of the temple. Both of these dates would be consistent with the kind of persecution that is described in this book, with the persecutions under Nero in the 60s and the persecutions under Domitian in the 90s.

The audience of this book is the churches in the cities in Asia Minor, modern day Turkey. We have already encountered two of these churches before, Ephesus and Laodicea. This book was intended to be distributed to all of the seven churches mentioned in chapters 1–3. However, even though it was originally intended to be distributed to these seven specific churches, it was quickly recognized as authoritative and spread to all the churches in the Roman world.

In order to understand the book of Revelation, it is critical that the reader have an understanding of the genre in which Revelation is written. There are actually multiple genres contained in this book. This book contains many of the same features of an epistle, including a greeting and a salutation. The first three chapters in particular follow the structure of an epistle. Yet the vast majority of this book is **apocalyptic**. There are not many apocalyptic writings in the New Testament, though there are plenty in the Old Testament. Much of Daniel and parts of Isaiah, Ezekiel, and Zechariah are apocalyptic in the Old Testament. Apart from Revelation, the Olivet Discourse in Matthew 24 and the parallel passages in the other gospels are the main apocalyptic passages in the New Testament, though 1 and 2 Thessalonians speak about the end times, as well.

So what is it that makes something apocalyptic? The apocalyptic genre is a subcategory of the genre of prophecy. Apocalyptic writings show up in the context of suffering and strong persecution. In these writings, the author is given incredible visions of heaven and of angels. While everything on earth is chaotic and it appears that God's people are being defeated by their enemies and the forces of evil, the pictures of heaven show that God is completely in control. The reader of these writings is supposed to find great comfort that God is working behind the scenes and that He knows exactly what He is doing. The hope that comes from apocalyptic writings is that God sees all the sufferings that His people are enduring and that someday God is going to come back and bring about justice on His enemies. Believers are encouraged to remain faithful in the midst of sufferings and to hold by faith to the hope that God will bring about justice. Another element of the apocalyptic genre is that the visions are highly symbolic. For example, the number seven appears multiple times in the book of Revelation. Seven is an important number in Scripture, going back to creation itself, and symbolizes completion or perfection. Twelve is another important number in Revelation and represents the twelve tribes of Israel and twelve apostles in the New Testament. Another example is the phrase "King of kings and Lord of lords," which is used to describe Jesus. The reader of this letter would have immediately recognized this phrase since there were banners throughout the Roman Empire with this phrase referring to the emperor. By using these words for Jesus, John shows that Jesus is the true Emperor.

In order to fully grasp all of the references in the book of Revelation, it is necessary that the reader have a good grasp of the Old Testament. Almost everything in this letter is a reference to something from the Old Testament. For example, the two witnesses in Revelation are called the "two olive trees and the two lampstands standing before the God of the earth" (Revelation 11:4); this is a direct reference to a prophecy in Zechariah 4 about olive trees and lampstands. Even the judgments of seals, bowls, and trumpets are very similar to the plagues poured out upon Egypt during the Exodus. As we study this book, we will examine not only Revelation itself, but we will explore the Old Testament passages that Revelation either quotes directly or alludes to indirectly.

There is a humility and sense of wonder that a person ought to have when reading and examining the book of Revelation. Many people speak with incredible assurance that their interpretation of Revelation is correct while forgetting that the Jews in Jesus' day could not read the Old Testament prophecies concerning Christ correctly. Even though we have the Holy Spirit, we must recognize that prophecy is not always an exact science, and we must study with an open heart and an open mind. With this in mind, we will examine three common lenses through which people view Revelation, though it is up to the reader to wrestle with Revelation to determine which lens, if any, he or she wants to use for this book.

The *first lens* through which people view Revelation is called the futurist lens, or **premillennialism**. With all of the views that we are going to examine, the key event on which we will focus is the **Millennial Kingdom**. In Revelation 20, John speaks of a thousand year reign of Jesus known as the Millennial Kingdom. Those who hold to the futurist view, or premillennialism, believe that all of the events in Revelation, including the Millennial Kingdom, will be fulfilled in the future. There are a number of events that will take place in the future according to this view. First, there is going to be a seven year period of great persecution known as the **Great Tribulation**. During this time of suffering and persecution, the Antichrist will arise and come to power and many people will be deceived. In addition, God will pour out His wrath on the earth as described with the judgments of the seals, trumpets, and bowls. Following the seven year tribulation, Jesus will return with His second coming and He will destroy all of His enemies. He will then bind Satan in the abyss and establish a kingdom on earth for 1,000 years. This will be a time of great peace and prosperity on earth. Following the Millennial Kingdom,

Classical Premillennialism
(Christ comes before the millennium but *after* the tribulation; the chair, in this and following illustrations, represents the judgment seat of Christ)

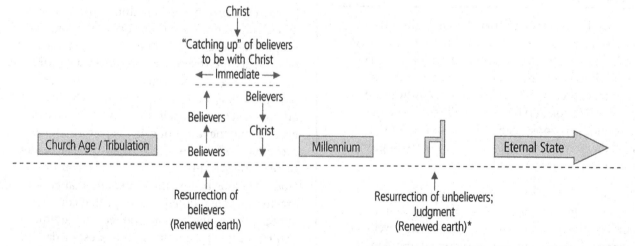

*Classical Premillennialists differ over whether the renewed earth will begin in the millennium or the eternal state.

Pretribulational Premillennialism
(Christ comes before the millennium and *before* the tribulation)

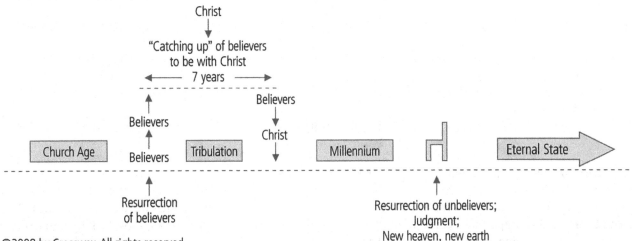

Satan will be released and there will be a final battle that Jesus wins. At this point, all of the dead will be raised to life and will appear before the Judgment Seat of Christ. This event is called the **Great White Throne Judgment** by scholars. During this judgment, the books of all our deeds will be open and we will be judged for our actions. Following this judgment, everyone will enter into the **Eternal State.** Those whose names are written in the Book of Life will spend eternity on the new earth, but to those whose names are not written in the Book of Life will spend eternity in the lake of fire.

Within premillennialism, there is another concept that merits discussion called the **rapture.** The doctrine of the rapture states that during the Great Tribulation, Jesus will return on the clouds of heaven to take away all the Christians in order to spare them from the suffering. Some people believe that this will happen before the Great Tribulation; this view is called pretribulationism. Others believe that Jesus will come in the middle of the tribulation, after three and a half years, in order to spare Christians from the wrath of God, which He will pour out at the end of the Great Tribulation. This

view is called midtribulationism. The final view is not really a rapture at all but the idea that Jesus will return after the Great Tribulation with His second coming. This view is called posttribulationism.

The *second lens* through which people view Revelation is preterism or **postmillennialism.** This view sees many of the events in Revelation as already fulfilled. According to this view, the seven year Great Tribulation was fulfilled in the years A.D. 63–70 with the persecutions under Emperor Nero. These persecutions were indeed severe, as Nero burned Christians to light up his own garden. The culmination of this seven year persecution came when Emperor Titus besieged and destroyed Jerusalem in the year A.D. 70. Proponents of this view understand Nero to be the Antichrist, and they see many of the visions of destruction in Revelation as a reference to the destruction of Jerusalem. As evidence for this view, in Revelation 13:18 we are told to calculate the number of the beast, for it is the number of a man, and that number is 666. In the study of numerology, where number values are associated with letters of the alphabet, Caesar Nero equals 666. In addition,

Postmillennialism
(Christ comes after the millennium)

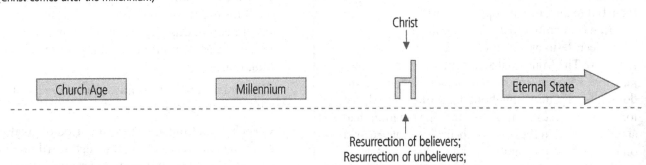

Amillennialism
(No future millennium)

Christ

Church Age

Eternal State

Revelation 20:1–6
is now

©2008 by Crossway. All rights reserved.

Resurrection of believers;
Resurrection of unbelievers;
Judgment;
New heaven, new earth

in Revelation 16:21, it speaks of hailstones the size of a cubit coming down upon the people. In Josephus' account of the besieging of Jerusalem, he speaks of the Romans using white stones, the size of a cubit, in their catapults. With Jerusalem destroyed and the Jewish age at an end, the proponents of postmillennialism argue that we are currently building the Millennial Kingdom as Christians spread the gospel and Christian ethics around the world. Only once the world becomes Christian will Jesus return to bring about Judgment Day. Historically, postmillennialism lost much of its popularity in the twentieth century with World War I, World War II, and the Vietnam War. To many, it appears that this world is not getting better, but worse. However, postmillennialists would argue that the world is still getting better; it just took a few steps back.

The *third and final lens* through which people view Revelation is **amillennialism**. This view is radically different from the first two. According to this view, because Revelation is apocalyptic and so much in this book is symbolic, there is no reason to believe that this book should be taken literally. Rather than referring to specific historical events, amillennialists believe that Revelation is describing the general situation of Christians throughout history. The seven year tribulation, therefore, is not a description of a specific seven year persecution, but rather the persecutions and sufferings that Christians over all time have endured. The Antichrist in Revelation need not be a reference to a specific man, but to anyone who opposes Christians and right doctrine (remember that John identifies any person who rejects Jesus as an antichrist in his letters; cf. 1 John 4:3). The Millennial Kingdom is not an earthly kingdom with physical boundaries, but rather the kingdom of Christians throughout the world. As evidence for this view, Jesus Himself said that the kingdom had already arrived in the hearts of believers while He was on the earth. In the parable of the mustard seed, Jesus speaks about the kingdom starting small but gradually growing until it becomes huge (Matthew 13:31–32). This would imply a process for the kingdom to develop, not a sudden kingdom brought about by the second coming of Jesus. Regarding the binding of Satan, amillennialists point out Jesus' response to the Pharisees when they accuse Him of being demon-possessed. Jesus argues that the fact that He is casting out demons is evidence that He had already bound Satan. In Matthew 12:29, Jesus says, "how can one enter a strong man's house and plunder his goods, unless he first binds the strong man?" There is still an expectation of Christ's return under amillennialism, but it will be to destroy His enemies and bring about Judgment Day.

As the student reads through this book, he or she should seek to determine for himself or herself which lens makes the most sense of this book. Yet no matter how one interprets the specifics of this book, the message of this book is clear. God is victorious and will bring about justice and judgment upon His enemies. We will suffer while we are on this earth, but if we overcome by holding on to our testimony of Jesus and remaining obedient to Christ, we will be richly rewarded someday. Jesus is going to return as the Conquering King and anyone who opposes Him will be destroyed.

apocalyptic: describing or prophesying the complete destruction of the world, involving terrible violence, suffering, and persecution

premillennialism: the view of Revelation that sees all of the events in this book as having a future fulfillment; in this view, Jesus will come back before the Millennium to establish an earthly kingdom

Millennial Kingdom: a thousand year reign of Christ on the earth

Great Tribulation: a seven year period of great suffering and persecution; during this tribulation, the Antichrist will appear and deceive many

Great White Throne Judgment: the final judgment of all humanity; for those whose names are written in the Book of Life, this will result in salvation, but for everyone else this will result in damnation

eternal state: the final situation of all people, whether it be on the new earth or in the lake of fire

rapture: a time in the future when Jesus will come on the clouds and take all believers to be with Him in heaven

postmillennialism: the view of Revelation that sees most of the events in Revelation as occurring in the years A.D. 63–70; under this view, we are currently building the Millennial Kingdom and Christ will return when the kingdom is finished

amillennialism: the view of Revelation that sees most of Revelation as symbolic rather than literal; this view does not see the Millennial Kingdom as an actual earthly kingdom, but as the reign of Christ in the Church

The Glorious Son of Man and the Seven Churches: Revelation 1–3

Lesson 153

As we saw in the introduction to Revelation, even though this book is filled with prophecy, it still has the structure of a letter. As with most epistles, John identifies himself and calls for grace and peace upon the recipients of this letter. However, we also learn much about this letter from the introduction. First, we see that the events that John mentions in this book must take place soon. We also learn that the messages that John will share in this letter were given to him by angels. Finally, we learn that there is a blessing that comes from reading and obeying this letter.

The first chapter of this letter is filled with powerful descriptions of Jesus. He is identified as the One "who is and who was and who is to come" (verse 4). He is also characterized in verse 5 as "the faithful witness, the firstborn from the dead, and the ruler over the kings of the earth." Each of these descriptions is relevant in this letter. Just as Jesus is the faithful Witness, we are going to be encouraged to be faithful witnesses of Jesus. Just as Jesus rose from the dead, we have hope that we too will be raised from the dead. Also, because Jesus is the Ruler over the kings of the earth, we need not fear these rulers who are oppressing and persecuting us. John

then offers a doxology to Jesus as the One who washed us with His blood and made us as a kingdom of priests. We learn after the doxology that Jesus is going to return on the clouds of heaven and everyone will see Him. We have already seen throughout the New Testament that Jesus would return to earth in the same way that He had left, on the clouds of heaven. The mention of the "tribes of the earth" and "they who pierced Him" brings about a sense of vindication, for those people who killed Him will see His glorious and victorious return. Jesus also identifies Himself in verse 8 as the "Alpha and the Omega." Alpha is the first letter of the Greek alphabet, and Omega is the last. Jesus was before creation, and He will remain until the end. Later, at the end of Revelation, the Father will describe Himself with these same words (Revelation 21:6), thus proving that Jesus is God.

John next explains what happened that led to him writing this letter. He had been exiled to the island of Patmos and was praying when Jesus appeared to him. Jesus identifies Himself as the Alpha and the Omega and then commands John to write down all that he is about to see and to send this letter to the seven churches in Asia Minor. As John looks at Jesus, he gives us the description of how Jesus appears to him. The description of Jesus as the Son of Man, combined with white hair and fire is an allusion to Daniel 7, which speaks of one like a Son of Man coming to the Ancient of Days in order to receive a kingdom. Interestingly, in Daniel's vision, it is the Father (the Ancient of Days) who is characterized with white hair and with a throne of flames. This is another subtle statement on the deity of Christ; He looks just like God Himself. The reference to a golden band around His chest represents how precious and pure Jesus is, and the reference to feet of brass symbolizes His purity and strength. In His right hand, the hand of strength, are seven stars, which we will see symbolize the seven churches. The imagery of Jesus holding onto the churches in His right hand shows that He will guard and protect His people. Out of His mouth comes a sharp, two-edged sword. This sword is the same sword of the Spirit from the armor of God, the Word of God (Ephesians 6:17; Hebrews 4:12). Jesus wages war with His Word, Scripture.

We are given a further description of Jesus at the end of chapter 1. We learn that Jesus is the One who lives, was dead, and is alive forever. This is very similar to the earlier statement that Jesus was, and is, and is to come. Moreover, Jesus also has the keys to Hades and Death. When Jesus died on the cross and was raised from the dead, He gained control over death itself. Therefore, we need not fear death. For churches facing

Christ's Edict-letters to His Seven Churches

Church	Reference	Description of Christ	Commendation	Rebuke	Solution	Consequence of Disobedience	Promise for Conquerors
Ephesus	2:1–7	holds the seven stars in his right hand; walks among the seven golden lampstands	doctrinal vigilance and endurance	loss of first love	remember, repent, and do the works done at first	removal of their lampstand	will be given the tree of life in paradise to eat
Smyrna	2:8–11	the first and the last, who died and came to life	spiritually rich, enduring persecution	—	be faithful unto death	—	will be given the crown of life and will not be hurt by the second death
Pergamum	2:12–17	has the sharp two-edged sword	holding fast Christ's name, not denying their faith	false teaching	repent	war against them with the sword of Christ's mouth	will be given hidden manna and a white stone with a new name on it
Thyatira	2:18–29	has eyes like a flame of fire, feet like burnished bronze	growing love, evidenced in deeds of service	lack of discernment; toleration of heresy	hold fast and keep Christ's works till the end	each given as their works deserve	will be given the morning star and authority over the nations
Sardis	3:1–6	has the seven spirits of God and the seven stars	a few remain pure and loyal	dead works	keep the Word and repent	Christ will come like a thief	will be clothed in white garments; name never blotted out of the book of life; name confessed before God and angels
Philadelphia	3:7–13	the holy one, the true one, who has the keys of David	patiently enduring, keeping God's word and not denying his name	—	hold fast what you have	—	will be made a pillar in the temple of God, inscribed with the names of God, the new Jerusalem, and Christ
Laodicea	3:14–22	the Amen, the faithful and true witness, the beginning of God's creation	—	spiritually blind, bankrupt, naked, lukewarm	buy gold, white garments, and salve from Christ; be zealous and repent	will be spit out of Christ's mouth	will dine with Christ; will be granted to sit with Christ on his throne

strong persecution, this is a great comfort. Finally, at the end of chapter 1, we learn that the seven stars are seven angels and that the seven lampstands are the seven churches. The churches are symbolized by lampstands because we as Christians provide light in a dark world (Matthew 5:14–15). The reference to the seven angels has a couple of possible interpretations. These could be seven literal angels who oversee the works of the seven churches, or they could be a reference to the earthly leaders of these churches.

Chapters 2 and 3 are filled with messages to each of the seven churches. The structure of these messages is very similar to some of the imperial decrees given by the Roman emperors. Because the Roman Empire was so large, one of the ways that the emperor would keep tabs on the regions of his empire was to send out decrees to the leaders of each region. In these decrees, the emperor would point out the areas where

that region was strong and the areas that they need to work on. The emperor would then give consequences for those regions if they did not fix the things that need work. In general, the seven messages to the seven churches follow this same pattern, with statements of good things that they are doing and warnings about the areas where they are weak.

The *first church* that Jesus addresses is the church at Ephesus. Each message begins with a description of Jesus from chapter 1 that is particularly relevant to the situation of that church. In this case, Jesus is identified as the One who walks among the lampstands. Jesus is observing the actions of each church and watching to make sure they remain faithful. Jesus commends the church in Ephesus because they had worked hard for the gospel and to protect right doctrine. They have tested false teachers and have proven that they are false. They also had opposed a group of heretics known as the Nicolaitans. Yet Jesus warns them that they have lost the love that they had at first. This church had become so focused on protecting doctrine that they forgot to live out that doctrine through love. Jesus warns them to repent or else He will remove them as a church. Perhaps the reason some churches fail today is because they have not remained faithful and Jesus removes them. This message finishes the way that all the messages finish, with a call to overcome. The reward for this is that they will get to eat from the Tree of Life, which is in Paradise.

The *second church* that Jesus addresses is the church at Smyrna. Jesus is described here as the First and the Last and as the One who was dead and came to life. The death and resurrection is particularly relevant because this is a church where many have died and will die for their witness of Jesus. Since Jesus conquered death, they too will conquer death. While Jesus commended the Ephesians for their work on the gospel and their defense of the gospel, He commends the people of Smyrna for their suffering. This church has experienced great persecution by the Jews in that city (called the synagogue of Satan here). Unlike Ephesus, Jesus does not have anything negative to say about this church. However, He does warn them that persecution is coming and encourages them to remain faithful. The reward for this church for overcoming is that they will not have to experience the second death. Though they may die once for their faith, they will then live forever.

The *third church* that Jesus addresses is the church at Pergamos, or Pergamum. Jesus is characterized here as the One with the sharp, two-edged sword, which we know is the Word of God. This is relevant because the people in this church will be rebuked for allowing false teaching to be tolerated among them. Jesus commends this church for holding to their faith in Jesus even when people had been killed for their faith. Twice Jesus mentions that Satan dwells in this city. Historically, this city is the location of the temple to Zeus, the head of the Greek gods. Jesus is calling Zeus Satan here. While the people in this church held to their faith in Christ, Jesus rebukes them for following in the footsteps of Balaam and for tolerating the Nicolaitans. Balaam was a prophet who compromised his message by selling his skills to the highest bidder and who recommended that Balak tempt the Israelites by sending foreign women among them (Numbers 31:16). The leaders of this church are tolerating false teachers who are leading the believers astray into sin and false doctrine. As with Ephesus, this church is called to repent or else Jesus will use that sword that comes out of His mouth for judgment. The reward for overcoming is hidden manna and

a white stone with a unique name known only to him who receives it. The reference to manna is reminiscent of the time of Balaam when God provided manna to the Israelites. The reference to the new name is also consistent with how God changes people's names when they encounter Him throughout Scripture.

The *fourth church* that Jesus addresses is the church at Thyatira. Jesus is identified to this church in Revelation 2:18 as "the Son of God, who has eyes like a flame of fire, and His feet like fine brass." All of these descriptions depict Jesus as the King who sees everything in His kingdom. Regrettably for the church at Thyatira, Jesus sees some things that He will not tolerate. Yet, before Jesus rebukes this church, He commends them for their love, service, faith, and patience. However, the believers at Thyatira had tolerated someone whom Jesus calls Jezebel. Jezebel is the most wicked woman in the Bible (1 Kings 16–22). She stood opposed to God and made it her goal to rid Israel of the worship of God. Whoever this person is at the church of Thyatira, this person has led many people astray into sexual immorality and idolatry. It is possible that this sexual immorality is a spiritual adultery by worshipping other gods. Apparently, Jesus had been patient with this person, but because this person refused to repent, Jesus is going to bring judgment. Jesus warns the people of Thyatira to repent, or they too will be affected by that judgment. To the person who overcomes at this church, Jesus will allow him to rule with Him. The reference to ruling with a rod of iron and dashing the enemies of God to pieces is a quote from Psalm 2, a Messianic Psalm that speaks about the victory of the Messiah over His enemies. The reference to the morning star is probably a reference to Jesus Himself, who is later identified as the Bright and Morning Star (Revelation 22:16).

The *fifth church* is the church in Sardis. Jesus is identified to this church as having the seven spirits of God and the seven stars, which we have already seen is a reference to the seven churches. Jesus has nothing good to say about this church. This church feels that they are healthy and strong, yet Jesus tells them that they are dead. This is a spiritually dead church that is in danger of disappearing. They may have done some work for Jesus, but they are so spiritually dead that these deeds are tainted. They must repent and be aware, because if they do not Jesus will come as a thief and destroy them. Yet, in the midst of this dead church, there is some life, some believers who are strong in their faith. The reference to white garments is a symbol of purity used throughout Scripture. Moreover, for this church, the person who overcomes will be given a white garment and will not be blotted out of the Book of Life.

The *sixth church* is the church in Philadelphia. Jesus' message to this church is the opposite of the church at Sardis. Whereas Jesus has nothing positive to say about the church at Sardis, He has nothing negative to say about the church at Philadelphia. Here Jesus is described as holy and true and as having the key of David, with which He can open or shut doors. This church has endured much persecution and suffering. Yet they have held fast to the Word of Christ and have not denied Jesus. They had apparently been persecuted heavily by their Jewish neighbors, but Jesus tells them that He will make their oppressors fall down at their feet. Their reward for their faithfulness is that Jesus will protect them from the hour of trial that will come upon the whole world. If this letter was written before the destruction of the temple in A.D. 70, this can be a reference to that event. Otherwise, this can be a reference to the Great Tribulation, or some other wave of persecution. The person who overcomes at this church will become a pillar in the spiritual temple of Christ, and he will be given the name of the new Jerusalem and Jesus' new name. To receive a special name is to receive a special relationship with that person.

Finally, the *seventh church* that Jesus addresses is the church at Laodicea. Here Jesus is identified as the Faithful and True Witness. Sadly, the church in Laodicea had not remained faithful and true. Once again, Jesus does not have anything positive to say about this church. Rather, He rebukes them for being lukewarm. This is a phrase that would make unique sense to the people of Laodicea. Laodicea was uniquely positioned in between a hot spring, which was useful for taking baths, and a cold spring, which was great for drinking. The problem for the Laodiceans is that in their city the water is neither cold nor hot and useful for nothing. When Jesus says that He wishes that they would be either cold or hot, He is not saying that He would like for them to be cold toward Him or on fire for Him, but rather He wants them to be useful for Him. In addition, the people of Laodicea had become rich through some of the products that they had shipped out to the Roman world. However, the believers in Laodicea had trusted in their own riches rather than Christ. So Jesus reminds them that they need to find their satisfaction in Him and not their money. Judgment is coming if they do not repent, and they will be exposed. So they need to wake up and be zealous and repent. It is both sad and encouraging that Jesus is knocking at the door. It is sad because Jesus is not in their midst, but on the outside. It is encouraging because He is patient with them and is still pursuing them. The person who overcomes at this church, he will be given the privilege of sitting on Jesus' throne with Him.

Thought Questions:

1. Which of the churches do you think yours resembles the most? Why?

2. What do you think it means to forsake your first love today?

3. What do you think it means to be lukewarm today?

Heavenly Worship: Revelation 4–5

Lesson 154

One of the more glorious passages on worship in the entire Bible is found in chapters 4 and 5 of Revelation. These two chapters have inspired a number of powerful worship songs throughout the history of the Church. In these two chapters, not only do we get to see how the angels in heaven praise God regularly, but we get a glimpse of the kind of praise of which we will be a part for all of eternity. When reading this, we should allow ourselves to be captivated by the greatness and majesty of God.

After John receives the specific messages for the seven churches, he is brought in a vision to heaven itself. He is brought into the throne room of God, and he sees God on His glorious throne. This is not the first time in the Bible that God's throne is described. In the tabernacle and then the temple, the Most Holy Place represents God's throne room with the ark of the Covenant and the cherub angels making up His throne. Yet, more relevant to this passage is Ezekiel's vision of the glory of the Lord in chapter 1 of Ezekiel. Here the throne of God is characterized as a glorious chariot, and there are living creatures around the throne. The expanse above this throne is compared to precious stones. In John's vision of God's heavenly throne, we see these same elements. God is described in terms of precious stones, and there are living creatures around the throne. In addition to these living creatures, there are twenty-four elders, perhaps symbolizing the union of the twelve tribes of Israel with the twelve apostles of the Church. These elders are pure, as they are described with white robes; and they are royalty as shown by their crowns of gold. This throne is majestic as lightning, and thunder and voices proceed from the throne. Also, there are seven lamps that burn before the throne, which represent the seven spirits of God. We have already seen that these seven lampstands represent the seven churches. With these lamps being before the throne, it shows that God has been sovereignly watching over these churches.

John's description of these angels is a combination of the description of the angels in Ezekiel's vision in chapter 1 and the description of the angels in Isaiah's vision in chapter 6. In Ezekiel's vision, the faces of the angels are almost the same as these living creatures, with one face being human, one a lion, one an eagle, and one an ox. The lion, the human, and the eagle faces are exactly the same, with only the calf replacing the ox from Ezekiel's vision. The reference to the six wings and the praise by these angels are the same as in Isaiah's vision in chapter 6. The very first time we encounter the phrase "holy, holy, holy" comes in the sixth chapter of Isaiah. Now here we see these creatures proclaim in verse 8, "Holy, holy, holy, Lord God Almighty, Who was and is and is to come!" The reference to "was and is and is to come" was used concerning Jesus in chapter 1. Here is yet another reference to the deity of Christ.

However, it is not only the living creatures that praise God and give Him glory; whenever they give glory to God, the elders also fall down before God and cast down their crowns and praise God. They declare that God is worthy to receive "glory and honor and power" (verse 11). They also praise God because He created everything. Notice that they praise God not only with their voices, but with their bodies (falling down) and with their possessions (laying down crowns). When we are truly captivated by the majesty of God, we will give Him everything that we have.

After John observes the praise and worship of God in this heavenly vision, he notices that God has something in His hand. In His right hand, God has a scroll that has seven seals on it. John weeps because he discovers that there is nobody on earth or in heaven who is found worthy to open this scroll. This scroll is going to be the focus of the next section of Revelation. The judgments of the seals, trumpets, and bowls are all revealed as this scroll is eventually opened. As with most of Revelation, there is a lot of speculation and debate as to what exactly is written on this scroll. Some see this scroll as the title deed to the world. Yet there is another scroll in the Bible that had previously been sealed until the end. At the end of the book of Daniel, God gives Daniel some revelation of what is supposed to happen at the end of time; but in Daniel 12:9, God tells Daniel "the words are closed up and sealed till the time of the end." If the scroll in the book of Revelation is this same scroll that had been shut up, this scroll is the revelation of what will happen at the end of time.

John weeps because nobody is found worthy to open this scroll; but then he is told by the angel that there is indeed someone who is found worthy to open the scroll, Jesus Christ. Jesus is characterized as the Lion of the tribe of Judah, the Root of David. The reference to the lion of Judah goes back to Genesis 49 in which Jacob blesses his sons. Even though Judah was the fourth-born son of Jacob, Jacob predicts that Judah will be a lion who will be the ruler over his brothers. Jesus is the ultimate fulfillment of this. In addition, the reference to the Root of David is a reference to the fact that the Christ, or Messiah, would come from the line of David. John then sees Jesus, but He is not a powerful lion but rather a Lamb that looks like it had been slain. This is an allusion to the Passover lamb whose blood saved the Israelites from the angel of death. Jesus was the ultimate Passover sacrifice whose blood saves us from death. This Lamb has seven horns and seven eyes, which John interprets as the seven Spirts of God sent into all the earth. In apocalyptic literature, horns represent kings or rulers, so this may be a reference to Jesus as the Ruler over the seven churches in Revelation. Yet the seven spirits of God are those who oversee the seven churches, so this shows that Jesus is watching over the churches and that He has them safely in His hand.

In this powerful and majestic moment, for the first time in all of history someone is found worthy to take and open the scroll. Imagine the anticipation that you have when you have been waiting for something for a long time. Nobody had been found worthy to open this scroll from the beginning of time until Jesus takes it here. These angels are filled with joy and excitement. So when Jesus takes the scroll, the four living creatures and the twenty-four elders sing a new song to Jesus. They have in their hands two things—a harp and golden bowls full of incense. The harps are there practically so that they can play the song. Yet we are told that the incense in these golden bowls is the prayers of the saints. When we pray to God, it is like a sweet-smelling incense, and we get to participate in heavenly worship.

In this new song, the living creatures and the elders praise Jesus because He is worthy to open the scroll. They also praise Him for the work accomplished on the cross as He redeemed people from the whole world with His blood. Now people from all over the world have been made kings and priests in Jesus' kingdom and will reign with Him on the earth. This is a reference to the Millennial Kingdom, which we will examine further in chapter 20.

Following this new song, these living creatures and twenty-four elders are joined with thousands upon thousands of angels declaring worth and praise to Jesus. Just as the living creatures and elders declared how worthy God is to receive glory, honor, and power, here these angels declare that Jesus is worthy to receive power, riches, wisdom, strength, honor, glory, and blessing. This uproar of praise gets even vaster as every living creature in heaven and on earth joins in. Now both the Father and the Son are praised together as everyone declares that they are worthy to receive blessing and honor and glory and power forever. Finally, this scene of praise ends with the living creatures declaring "Amen" and the elders bowing down and worshiping.

Thought Questions:

1. What is the most glorious time of praise that you have ever been able to observe? Did you find yourself more motivated to worship God at that time?

2. For what kinds of things do you normally praise God? How does that compare to the things for which God and Jesus are praised in these two chapters?

The Seals Are Opened: Revelation 6–7

Lesson 155

Even though Revelation has the reputation of being a difficult book to interpret, up until this point the book has been pretty straightforward. Starting in chapter 6, this is where most of the debates about interpretation take place. Although it is impossible to explain this book without some degree of interpretation, it is the goal of this class to encourage the student to wrestle with the text and interpret it for himself or herself. In light of this, there will be less of a focus on when or how these prophecies will be fulfilled, but rather there will be more of a focus on what these prophecies mean in context.

Now that Jesus has the scroll and has been found worthy to open the scroll, He begins to break the seven seals on this scroll. Because the content of this scroll is so incredibly important, the opening of these seals is accompanied by major cataclysmic events on the earth. With the *first four seals*, the four horsemen of the apocalypse are revealed. This is not the first place where different colored horses show up in the Bible. In the sixth chapter of Zechariah, he sees a vision of different colored horses that were sent to scout out the earth. The job of the horses in Revelation 6 is different, however. The rider of the first horse, *the white horse*, is given

a crown and a bow, and he comes to conquer. Some have suggested that this rider is Jesus Christ Himself and that He conquers through the spread of the gospel. Yet this interpretation would render the first horse unique from the other three horses. Interestingly, at the time that Revelation is written, the Parthians posed the biggest threat to the Romans, and they were known for riding on horses and using bows and arrows. Another interpretation of this first horse is that it is a nation that is bent on conquering other nations. The rider of the second horse, *the fiery red horse*, is given the power to take away peace and to cause people to kill each other through war. The rider of the third horse, *the black horse*, brings economic ruin and famine to the earth. The reference to wheat and barley selling for a denarius communicates that food is really expensive; this is a sign of a deteriorating economy due to a famine. The rider of the fourth horse, *the pale horse*, is identified as "Death" or "Hades," and he is given the authority to kill a fourth of those who live on the earth. This angel kills with the sword, with hunger, and with the beasts of the field. So far, these "plagues" or judgments are all devastations that humans can inflict on one another.

Following these judgments, the breaking of the *fifth seal* brings John back to a vision of heaven. Here the martyrs who had died for their faithful witness of Jesus Christ are vindicated. They cry out, asking God how long it will be until God brings about justice upon those who had killed them. God gives them white robes, which represents purity, and tells them to wait a little longer until they are joined by all those destined to die for their faith.

These martyred saints receive part of their vindication with the *sixth seal*. Whereas the first four seals represented the devastation caused by humans, the sixth seal reveals cataclysmic natural disasters that torment the people. Earthquakes are a common form of divine judgment, and there are multiple prophecies in the Old Testament that speak of earthquakes coming at the end, including the second chapter of Haggai. The reference to the sun turning black and the moon becoming like blood and the stars falling to the earth all have many previous references, including Isaiah 13 and Matthew 24; but this language is taken directly from Isaiah 34, which depicts God's judgments on the nations with these cataclysmic events. Finally, this judgment results in the displacement of mountains and islands, which fits the effects of a powerful earthquake. While the exact fulfillment of this seal is open to interpretation, in the context, the significance of these events is seen with the effects on the people. The people of the earth, both great and small, hide from these cataclysmic events, recognizing that these plagues are God's wrath poured out on them. Even though the martyrs from the fifth seal are told to wait a little longer until the full number of martyrs joins them, they get a picture of vindication when God afflicts their oppressors with these natural disasters on the earth. Even though these kings and rulers have the power and authority to persecute and kill Christians on earth, even they are subject to the forces of nature, which God controls.

Chapter 7 plays out as an interruption in the revelation of the seven seals, but an important interruption. John next sees four angels, who are holding back the winds from the four corners of the earth. This is both a good and a bad thing, as winds can be both destructive and helpful. Winds can bring relief from scorching heat, and they provide the force for ships to move; but they also bring about devastation. The second thing that John sees in this chapter is an angel carrying the seal of God. In the ancient world, a king would have a special signet ring with a specific design, which he would use to seal a document. That seal would show that the document was indeed issued by the king. We are not told exactly what this seal is, but simply that it would be put on the foreheads of Christians. As with just about everything in Revelation, this has an Old Testament precedent. The prophet Ezekiel sees a vision of an angel putting a mark on the foreheads of those in Israel who had not engaged in idolatry (Ezekiel 9:14). So also, this seal in Revelation is to be put on the foreheads of the servants of God. Some people suggest that this seal is the Holy Spirit, who is compared to a seal elsewhere in Scripture (Ephesians 1:13). Others suggest that this seal is baptism, which is the symbolic action that identifies us as Christians. While we are not told precisely what this seal is, we learn that this seal will protect those who have it from the wrath of God.

John also discovers that the recipients of this seal are 144,000 from the tribes of the children of Israel. Of course, there is much debate as to who precisely these 144,000 people are. There are two predominant theories about the 144,000 within Christian scholarship. In regard to the *first main interpretation*, some believe that the 144,000 are the faithful believers from among the Jews who will later get to enjoy life in the Millennial Kingdom. This follows the more literal interpretation of this passage. However, there are some difficulties with this interpretation. First, throughout the book of Revelation, there is no other place where Israel is singled out and given blessings; everything in this book is directed to the Church. Second, if this is taken literally to be the descendants of Abraham, there are two tribes missing from this

list, Dan and Ephraim. The *second main interpretation* of this list is that it is symbolic and refers to all believers as the new Israel. The omission of Dan and Ephraim has symbolic significance. The tribe of Dan was famous among the tribes of Israel for idolatry (Judges 18). The tribe of Ephraim grew to represent the Northern Kingdom when Israel was divided, and the Northern Kingdom proved time and time again to be idolaters and rebels against God. By excluding these tribes in this vision, God is providing a warning against idolatry and rebellion. The number 144,000 is 12 x 12 x 1,000 and can represent the united body of Christ including Israel (represented by twelve tribes) and the Church (represented by the twelve apostles). If this is a reference to the Church, this would provide hope to those reading that God will protect Christians from His wrath.

Following this vision of the 144,000, John sees another scene of praise. In this case, a great multitude from all the nations gathers together before the throne and before the Lamb to praise Him. Some Christians believe that this great multitude is another reference to the 144,000, which had received the seal of God on their foreheads. However, we know the number of those sealed to be 144,000, whereas this second group is too large to be numbered. As is a common theme in the book of Revelation, this great multitude is given white robes to represent purity and righteousness. These people are also given palm branches as part of their praise of God. This is an allusion to the Triumphal Entry, during which Jesus was accompanied into Jerusalem with shouts of praise and palm branches. During the Triumphal Entry, Jesus rebuked the resentful Pharisees saying, "I tell you, if these [disciples] were silent, the very stones would cry out" (Luke 19:40, ESV).

Just as in chapters 4 and 5, the angels and the living creatures and the elders join in this chorus of praise to God and to Jesus as the Lamb. Here they praise God and Jesus because of the salvation that They purchased for us. As with the earlier pictures of praise, these beings all ascribe great things to God: "Blessing and glory and wisdom, thanksgiving and honor and power and might" (7:12). Then one of the elders identifies who makes up this great multitude. These people are those Christians who remain faithful during the tribulation and who are killed for their faith. Their reward is that they get to be priests in heaven and get to serve before the heavenly temple and throne. Their suffering has come to an end, and they will no longer hunger or thirst or feel pain. Jesus, the Good Shepherd, will shepherd them and give them eternal satisfaction through living fountains of waters. Jesus Himself had earlier offered living water to the Samaritan woman at the well in John 4. Now we see this fulfilled for those who remain faithful to Jesus.

Thought Question:

Why do you think that God accompanies the breaking of the seals with these cataclysmic events?

The Trumpet Judgments: Revelation 8–11

Lesson 156

As we draw closer and closer to the revelation of the sealed scroll, chapter 8 begins with the opening of the *seventh and final seal.* We are left with a feeling of expectation as silence fills heaven for a half an hour. Yet, rather than the scroll being revealed, instead there are seven angels that are given seven trumpets to sound. The purpose of trumpets in Scripture is always to warn or prepare the people. There is even an entire feast devoted to the blowing of trumpets in order to warn the people about the Day of Atonement (Leviticus 23:24). So now that the seals are opened, God prepares trumpets to mark the revelation of this scroll.

Before the angels can blow their trumpets, however, John sees a vision of the temple in heaven. Like a priest, one of the angels carries a censer full of incense before the altar in heaven. Once again there is a connection between our prayers on earth and worship in heaven. Connected with the incense is the prayers of all the saints. The purpose of incense in the sacrificial system was to create a pleasant aroma before the Lord; by connecting our prayers with that heavenly incense, God is communicating that our prayers are like a pleasant aroma to the Lord. The angel then fills his censer with fire and throws it upon the earth, and the skies and the land rumble.

The trumpet judgments follow the same basic pattern that the judgments of the seals had followed. The first four trumpets are all associated with judgment upon the earth. With all of these judgments, there is a reversal of creation itself. Just as God created the light, the seas, the land, and the sun, moon, and stars on the first four days of creation, all of these are affected by the first four trumpets. Also, there is a symbolic connection between these trumpet judgments and the plagues poured out on Egypt during the Exodus. However, the symbolic connection extends beyond the escape from Egypt and includes some imagery from the time of Israel's wandering in the wilderness after leaving Egypt. With

the *first trumpet,* hail and fire, along with blood, are thrown upon the earth and a third of the earth's vegetation is destroyed. This is similar to the seventh plague on Egypt (hail) that destroys the crops, though here it is fire that destroys rather than the hail. With the *second trumpet,* something like a flaming mountain is thrown into the seas; and a third of the sea becomes like blood, destroying a third of the sea animals and ships. This is similar to the first plague on Egypt when the waters of Egypt turn to blood. With the *third trumpet,* a meteor falls upon the earth, named Wormwood; and a third of the waters become so bitter that many men die. This also is similar to the first plague on Egypt with the waters being affected, but this is more closely a reverse of what happens to the Israelites at Marah. When the Israelites entered the wilderness after leaving Egypt, they complained at Marah that the waters were too bitter to drink. God graciously cleanses the waters at Marah, making them drinkable (Exodus 15:23–25). Yet with this trumpet the opposite happens on the earth. With the *fourth trumpet,* a third of the heavenly lights (sun, moon, and stars) are darkened so that there is darkness for a third of the day. This is similar to the ninth plague on Egypt, though that darkness was for the entire day.

With the final three trumpet judgments, these are each preceded by a "woe" upon the inhabitants of the earth for what is about to be revealed. With the *fifth trumpet,* we are introduced to the bottomless pit, or the abyss, which will show up again later in Revelation. In this vision, John sees a star fallen from heaven that is given the keys to the bottomless pit. This fallen star is an angel, which we will see again in chapter 20. When this angel opens up the bottomless pit, an army of demons comes out of the pit to bring devastation on the earth. These creatures are characterized as an army of locusts with the power to sting like scorpions. Similarly to the angels before the throne of God, these angels appear as a combination between humans and animals. One would expect this army of demons to come and attack Christians, but they are explicitly forbidden to attack people with the mark of God on their foreheads. So rather than attacking God's people, they attack their own. These locusts torment the unbelievers on the earth for five months, yet the people are not able to escape this torment through death. We learn that the leader of this vast army is named Abaddon (which means "destroyer") or Apollyon (which also means "destroyer"). Interestingly, the locust was one of the symbols for the Greek god Apollo. The Roman emperor Domitian believed that he was Apollo incarnate. If this book is written in the late 90s, this could be a subtle attack on the emperor. This angel could be the angel of death, but the angel of death appears to be a servant of God rather than Satan. Others have suggested that this king of the locusts is Satan himself.

With the *sixth trumpet*, the angel that blows the trumpet is told to release the four angels who had been prepared for that very moment. These four angels lead another army, most likely a demonic army, and they kill a third of humanity. While the first demonic army was characterized as locusts, this army is characterized as horses. These horses are able to kill with their mouths and with their tails. Out of their mouths come fire, smoke, and brimstone. This is a reference to Sodom and Gomorrah, which are destroyed by fire and brimstone. Just as the locusts had tails like scorpions, these horses have tails like serpents. After all these judgments, one would expect people to repent of their sins and turn to God, but the response of the people is a stubborn refusal to repent. The reference to their idolatry and sexual immorality stands as a warning to the churches at the beginning of this letter who had been warned not to commit idolatry or sexual immorality.

As with the opening of the seals, there is an interlude between the sixth judgment and the seventh judgment. For the first time in Revelation, John himself becomes a part of the vision. Here a mighty angel appears with a little scroll in his hand. As this angel speaks, the thunders themselves speak, but John is told not to repeat what they say but to seal their message, just as God had Daniel do centuries before (Daniel 12:4). This angel makes a strong declaration that there would be no more delay on the sounding of the *seventh trumpet* and the revelation of the now unsealed scroll. This revelation is the completion of the mystery of God, namely His plan for the end of the world. The angel then tells John to eat the little scroll, and it takes sweet at first but becomes bitter. This is not the first time that we see someone told to eat a scroll. God earlier had Ezekiel eat a scroll, which represents God's words being a part of his very self (Ezekiel 3:1). Thus when God has John eat these words, God is commissioning John as a prophet to communicate His words of this revelation to the people. The fact that it is sweet first and then bitter says that the message that John is going to share has both pleasant and horrible implications for the people.

John is active in this vision a second time in chapter 11. In this chapter, an angel tells John to measure the temple of God, the altar, and those who worship there. There is much debate as to what precisely this temple is. If this book was written before the destruction of the temple in A.D. 70, then this can be a reference to Herod's temple,

which was there during Jesus' life on earth. If it is a reference to Herod's temple, this is a prophecy of judgment on that temple. Some suggest that the temple here symbolically represents the Church, which has regularly been called the temple of God throughout the New Testament. This vision could then be a reference to protecting the Church. The final option for this temple is that it is a future temple or a reference to Ezekiel's temple. In chapters 40–48 of Ezekiel, he receives a vision of a new temple and is told to measure it. There has never been a temple built with the dimensions of Ezekiel's temple, so some see this as a future temple to be built.

Perhaps the most hotly debated topic in the book of Revelation is who precisely the two witnesses are that are mentioned in chapter 11. These two witnesses are described in many ways—they are called the two olive trees and two lampstands, fire proceeds from their mouths and kills their enemies, and they have the power to perform great signs such as causing a drought and sending down plagues. The reference to the two olive trees and two lampstands is a direct allusion to Zechariah's prophecy. In Zechariah 4, the two olive trees and two lampstands refer to Joshua (the high priest) and Zerubbabel (the king). Whoever these two witnesses are in Revelation, they may carry on the offices of priest and king. There are a number of suggestions as to who these two witnesses might be. First, it could be Enoch and Elijah, who were prophets but had never died; perhaps this is when they return to the earth. It could also be Moses and Elijah, who had met with Jesus on the Mount of Transfiguration. Others have suggested that it is Peter and Paul, or any other number of important people in Christian history. If we do not take these witnesses to be referring to two individuals, it could be a reference to the Church as a whole as the new kings and priests in God's kingdom. Also, some have suggested that these two witnesses represent Jesus Himself as the true High Priest and King. Regrettably, these two witnesses are not identified specifically, so all we can do is speculate.

What is clear about these witnesses is that their ministry is a prophetic ministry. Their job is to serve as witnesses of Christ and to call the people to repent. For the first time in Revelation, we are introduced to the three-and-a-half-year theme. These witnesses will perform their ministry freely for three and a half years. This same time frame of three and a half years will appear again in Revelation and has its Old Testament backing from Daniel's prophecy. In Daniel chapter 9, in the midst of the final "week" (seven years), we learn that for half of this time (three and a half years) sacrifice will be cut off from the temple. In Revelation, this fits with the seven-year tribulation that John describes in these chapters. For half of the tribulation, these witnesses will be protected and will call the people to repent.

At the end of their ministry, the beast that comes up from the abyss will make war against these witnesses and kill them. This beast will be described in far greater detail in the following chapters. The bodies of these witnesses will lie in the street of the great city that is called Sodom and Egypt. We know that Sodom is famous for its gross immorality, and Egypt was famous for oppressing and killing God's people. We learn, however, from the next description that this city of Sodom and Egypt is Jerusalem itself, as it was the place where Jesus was crucified. This is another theme that will show up in the book of Revelation. On multiple occasions, the corruption of Jerusalem will be highlighted as it is compared to famous wicked cities.

The two witnesses remain dead in the streets and are refused burial for three and a half days. Because the people hate the light and do not want to hear the truth that they need to repent, they rejoice and even give gifts to each other to commemorate the deaths of these two witnesses. Yet the two witnesses do not remain dead. The breath of life enters them, and they ascend to heaven in a cloud before the sight of their enemies. There are elements of this description that would fit Jesus Himself as the witnesses, for He was raised from the dead and ascended into heaven. However, these two witnesses are not buried, while Jesus was; and they are dead for three and a half days, whereas Jesus rose at the beginning of the third day. Nevertheless, the description of the resurrection and ascension shows that these two witnesses are ministering in the same manner that Jesus had previously done. In addition, these events are accompanied by a great earthquake. For the first time in the book of Revelation, some of the people seem to respond positively to this event as they give glory to God. This does not mean, however, that the people repent. It merely means that they recognize God's greatness and are afraid of Him.

Finally, the seventh trumpet sounds and there is yet another scene of heavenly praise. There is some question as to what precisely makes up the third woe that has been forewarned. Some suggest that the third woe is actually the bowl judgments later in Revelation. Yet considering the pattern so far, it would appear that this seventh trumpet is the revelation of that third woe. Though we do not see the description of what happens from that woe, the proclamation of Christ's kingdom would be a great woe upon those who reject Christ. The worst thing that could happen to a person is to see

his enemy glorified and given all power. The heavenly chorus proclaims that Jesus now has all the kingdoms of this world, and He will reign forever and ever. This is incredibly important for the original readers of Revelation to understand. Many of the original readers have been greatly oppressed and overpowered by the great might of the Roman Empire, but here we see that Jesus is the One with complete authority.

The twenty-four elders offer more words of praise here. They praise God for His power and rule and that He has defeated His enemies. The reference to the anger of the nations is probably an allusion to Psalm 2, in which the nations gather together to throw off the reign of God. In Psalm 2, however, God laughs at the nations and terrifies them and rules them with a rod of iron. God's wrath will come against all the nations that do not bow before Him, and God's kingdom is the only one that will last forever. The elders also praise God because perfect judgment is coming soon, when the faithful will be rewarded and the enemies of God will be destroyed.

Finally, to commemorate this great event, God allows John to see the temple of God opened in heaven and to see the ark of the covenant. The ark of the Covenant was the most significant piece of furniture in the temple, and it represented the very presence of God Himself. The ark, along with the cherub angels above it, formed a throne for God's throne room in the Most Holy Place. The ark had previously disappeared by the time Israel was conquered by Babylon centuries before this. By revealing the ark of the covenant, God is showing John that His presence is now accessible. Previously only the high priest could see the ark of the covenant; now John and we are able to see the ark of the covenant. As is often the case when God appears in the Bible, this is accompanied by a powerful storm.

Thought Questions:

1. Why do you think the locusts attack their own people?

2. From your readings of these judgments, do you think that these are actual events that will happen at some time in the future or that they are just symbolic visions? Why?

3. Whom do you think the two witnesses are in chapter 11?

The Unholy Trinity: Revelation 12–14

Lesson 157

With the final trumpet blown, God's great mystery has been revealed as the kingdoms of this world have become the kingdom of the Christ. Chapter 11 ends the section that begins in chapter 4, and it culminates with a declaration of the victory of Christ over all the world kingdoms. However, chapter 12 begins another unit in the book of Revelation that looks at the same events from a different perspective. Even though John sees these visions one after another, it does not mean that the events in these visions follow one after another. In fact, some of the events mentioned in chapter twelve likely go back before the fall of man in Genesis 3. So far we have seen the wrath of God poured out on mankind for their rejection of the gospel; in these chapters we will see the wrath of man and Satan poured out on Christians. We have seen the glory of the Trinity revealed in powerful praise, and now we will see the counterfeit unholy trinity of the dragon, the beast, and the false prophet.

In the beginning of chapter 12, John sees the vision of a woman in heaven who is characterized as "clothed with the sun, with the moon under her feet, and on her head a garland of twelve stars." The imagery of the sun, moon, and twelve stars is borrowed from Joseph's visions in Genesis 37, in which Jacob and Rachel are symbolized as the sun and the moon, and the eleven stars are Joseph's brothers. With this imagery as the background, the woman here represents Israel, which gave birth to Jesus. However, based on what happens to this woman later on, this woman symbolizes not just Israel but God's people in general.

Along with the vision of this woman, John also sees a vision of a great battle in heaven. Satan and his

army wage war against the archangel Michael and the army of angels. Here Satan is symbolized by a fiery red dragon having seven heads and ten horns. The reference to seven heads symbolizes the scope of the dragon's authority, and the ten horns harken back to the seven horns that Jesus is characterized as having in chapter 5. In apocalyptic literature, horns symbolize military power and often represent kings. In Daniel 7:7, the fourth great beast, identified as the Roman Empire, has ten horns, which represent ten kings. There is a connection, therefore, between Satan and the Roman Empire. Also, with this vision we see the beginnings of what will be the counterfeit unholy trinity.

Satan and his demonic angels lose this battle against Michael and the angels, and he and his army are kicked out of heaven. We see that Satan sweeps a third of the angels out of heaven with him. This tells us that there are twice as many angels out there than there are demons. There is some question as to when exactly this battle takes place, but most scholars believe that this battle takes place after creation but before the fall of man in Genesis 3. In verse 6, we see another reference to the three and a half years, but this is the period of time that the woman is protected from the dragon.

With Satan and his demonic angels defeated, there is a proclamation similar to the proclamation at the end of chapter 11. Once again, the kingdom of Christ and His salvation is proclaimed. However, there is a new element that will be critical for the message of this book and for the upcoming chapters. Even though Jesus is victorious and His kingdom has come, there are still going to be casualties in this war. We are now engaged in a war with Satan on earth, and we do not conquer by killing Satan but by remaining faithful even unto death. Satan is filled with wrath and seeks to attack us who remain on the earth, but his time is short. The connection with Satan as the dragon and as a serpent goes back to Genesis chapter 3 where Satan tempts Adam and Eve through a serpent. Now that Satan knows that he is defeated, he wants to do as much damage as he can to us.

In the beginning of chapter 13, we are introduced to a second creature, a great beast that comes up from out of the sea. As with the dragon, this beast has seven heads and ten horns. This also is an attempt to counterfeit the Trinity. Just as Jesus is the exact image of the Father, this beast is very similar to the dragon. Many scholars believe that this beast is a kingdom or a government. Already we have seen in Daniel's visions that beasts represent empires. Daniel sees four beasts, and they represent the Babylonian, Persian, Greek, and Roman Empires; and

Satanic Imitations of God's Reality

God's Reality		Satanic Imitation	
the real Trinity (Father, Son [Lamb], Spirit)	1:4–5	the false trinity (dragon, beast, false prophet)	16:13; 20:10
Lamb standing, as though it had been slain	5:6	many-headed beast with mortal wound healed	13:3
sealing of the saints	7:2–3	mark of the beast	13:16–18
Bride in white	19:7–8	prostitute in purple and scarlet	17:1–6

the final beast has ten horns like the beast in Revelation 13. Many conclude from this that this beast symbolizes Rome. One of the heads of this beast had been mortally wounded, but that wound was healed. This is a mockery of Jesus and His resurrection, and continues the counterfeit unholy trinity theme. There are a number of theories as to what precisely this healed mortal wound might symbolize. This head could be Nero, who killed himself in A.D. 68, which resulted in turmoil for the Roman throne, but the throne was "revived" with the next emperor who took over. There was also a legend that another leader would return in the spirit of Nero. In addition, one of the Roman emperors, Caligula, had come down with a serious illness but had recovered, so this may be a reference to him.

This beast is given power and authority from the dragon and continues to wage the war that the dragon had begun against Christians. Just as Jesus has ultimate authority over every tribe, tongue, and nation, Satan gives this beast authority over those who are not saved from every tribe, tongue, and nation. We also see that all of those whose names are not written in the Book of Life will worship this beast. If this beast is indeed Rome, this is a reference to the imperial cult. By the time that John writes this letter, it was common and expected that the people of Rome worship the emperor as a god. Much of the persecution of Christians that happened at this time resulted from their refusal to worship the emperor. As this beast wages war on Christians, we are called to have patience.

A second beast comes up out of the earth, and he has two horns like a lamb and is given the authority of the first beast. Most scholars believe this beast to be a reference to the Antichrist. The reference to the lamb is once again a mockery of Jesus, who has been characterized consistently as the Lamb of God who receives His authority from the Father. This second beast, also known as the false prophet, is given the power to perform great signs in order to deceive the people. His mission is to get the people to worship the first beast. Like the mark that God earlier gave believers to protect them from His wrath, this beast requires people to receive his mark on their right hands or on their foreheads. Without the mark of the beast, nobody will be able to buy or sell anything. There is a lot of speculation as to how this prophecy will be fulfilled, but it appears clear that nobody will receive this mark by accident; they will know what they are receiving. Chapter 13 ends with a call to calculate the number of the beast, which is 666. There are a number of things that could be said about this number. First of all, it is the number six hundred and sixty-six, not just three

sixes in a row. Some people have a problem if a number just happens to have three sixes in a row in the midst of it, but that is not the number of the beast. Also, if seven is the number of completion or perfection, many suggest that the number six represents falling just short of perfection. Finally, it is worth noting that we are encouraged to "calculate" the number of the beast. The art of assigning a number value to letters and names was quite common at the time that this was written. The readers would probably have understood this to be a challenge to calculate names to equal six hundred and sixty-six. Finally, though it is not an exact science, it has been shown that one could manipulate the name of Caesar Nero to equal six hundred and sixty-six. This would fit with the Nero imagery throughout this book.

Now that we have seen what the unholy trinity is up to, we are brought back into the presence of Jesus in chapter 14. While Satan and his associates, the beast and the false prophet, are waging war against Christians, we see that those who have remained faithful are with Jesus. Here Jesus, as the true Lamb, is standing on Mount Zion along with the 144,000 that we encountered earlier in Revelation. These faithful Christians are given the privilege of hearing a new song of praise to the Lamb. The 144,000 are characterized as virgins who speak the truth and have no deceit. Nowhere else in Scripture do we see that celibacy is more righteous than marriage, so it is likely that these people being virgins is more of a spiritual reference than a physical reference. The idea here is that these people have kept themselves pure by not giving in to sexual immorality or idolatry, two of the main sins decried in this book.

For the first time in this book, we see a focused attempt to share the gospel. Here it is an angel who proclaims the "everlasting gospel" to people from every nation, tribe, tongue, and people. This message is a message of repentance, calling the people to fear God and give Him glory because judgment is coming soon. A second message is sent out alongside the gospel, a proclamation that Babylon has fallen. There will be much more on this message in the future chapters, but for now Babylon represents the enemies of God's people. Babylon was the country that demolished the temple in the Old Testament, but since Babylon was no longer a nation, this must be a symbolic reference. The message of the third angel is a warning not to give in to the beast or to receive his mark. For even though anyone who does not receive that mark will face the wrath of man by not being allowed to do commerce, those who do receive the mark will face the wrath of God. This outpouring of wrath is spoken of in terms of drinking the wine of the wrath of God. Throughout the Bible,

God often expresses judgment in terms of drinking the cup of God's wrath. Even Jesus speaks of this cup when He asks the Father to take it away from Him.

The messages of these angels are clear for the churches who receive this letter—remain faithful and do not give in to the enemy, for the temporary relief on earth is not worth it compared to the wrath of God to come. So for a second time there is a call for patience by the saints, who keep the commandments of God and have faith in Jesus. This patience may result in death by persecution, but God declares the person blessed who dies in the Lord from now on. Those who die in Christ may suffer on earth, but they will finally be able to rest.

Chapter 14 ends with two "harvests." The first harvest appears to be that of the righteous, with Jesus Himself (identified as the Son of Man and as the One who rides on the clouds), using the sickle to harvest the earth. While we are not told explicitly that this harvest is for the righteous, the idea of a two-fold harvest has been mentioned before. Jesus often speaks of a future separation between the righteous and the wicked. In the parable of the wheat and the tares, we learn that both will grow together until the end, and then they will be harvested and separated (Matthew 13). With this harvest coming first, it is possible that this is a reference to the rapture or the second coming of Jesus. This may also be a description of the end of the world before the Great White Throne Judgment. There is a second harvest, and this one is clearly for the wicked. This judgment is depicted as grapes that are harvested and thrown into the winepress to be crushed. Yet here it is the people who will be crushed by God for rejecting the gospel and for receiving the mark of the beast.

Thought Questions:

1. Some people have spoken about putting chips under the skin of people in order to buy things; do you think we should have a problem with this as Christians, based on the discussion of the number of the beast? Why or why not?

2. What do you think is the Babylon that is said to fall here?

3. Why do you think Satan, the beast, and the false prophet are characterized so similarly to Jesus, the Father, and the Spirit in this book?

4. If it is clear that Satan has already lost, why do you think he continues to wage war on us?

The Bowl Judgments: Revelation 15–16

Lesson 158

With the seals opened and the trumpets sounded to warn of the revelation of the end, it is now time for God to reveal what will happen at the end. In chapter 14, we have just seen God speak about His wrath against those who receive the mark of the beast; now we see that wrath poured out upon the earth. However, in chapter 15, we have another interlude, another picture of praise in heaven, in order to prepare for the coming judgments.

When the seven angels with the seven last plagues are revealed, John also sees a multitude of people before the presence of God. These people, who have remained faithful and have achieved victory over the beast by holding to their testimony of Jesus, are given harps to play as they stand on something like a sea of glass and fire. These faithful martyrs are rewarded with the opportunity to praise God before His throne, and they sing the Song of Moses. There are actually two songs in the Bible that are called the Song of Moses—one in Exodus 15 after the Israelites escape Egypt and one at the end of Moses' life in Deuteronomy 31. There are themes from both of these songs here, so it is probably a combination of both that they sing here. These faithful witnesses praise God because of His great works and because He is true, just, and holy. All of the nations will come and worship God after His judgments are revealed.

As we have seen before in Revelation, this next judgment will come from out of the heavenly temple. It is out of the temple that the seven angels come with the last seven plagues. One of the living creatures gives these angels seven bowls that are filled with the wrath of God. Then, because of the presence of God and His glory, the temple is filled with smoke so that no one could enter the temple until the plagues are completed. This is not the first time that the temple must be evacuated because of God's glory being there. When both the tabernacle and temple are dedicated, the glory of the Lord fills them with smoke from His glory so that people have to leave (Exodus 40:35; 2 Chronicles 7:2).

If the first two sets of judgments derive their imagery from the plagues poured out on Egypt during the Exodus, this last set of judgments does so even more. These judgments of the bowls follow the same basic pattern as the other two judgments, with the first four being similar, then the next two working together with a separated seventh seal. However, unlike the first two sets of judgments, there are no interludes in these judgments; they are swift. The bowl judgments are very similar to the trumpet judgments, but these last judgments are more complete as they destroy everything rather than just a third of everything.

The *first bowl* results in painful sores inflicted upon all those who had received the mark of the beast. This is the same as the sixth plague on Egypt as the Egyptians are inflicted with boils. As with the trumpet judgments, the second and third bowls result in the waters turning to blood and the sea animals dying. The *second bowl* affects the seas, and the *third bowl* affects the fresh water. This is the same as the first plague on Egypt when the Nile and the waters of Egypt are turned to blood. After the third bowl judgment, there is a very brief interlude of praise as the angel over the waters praises God for the justice of these judgments. It is only appropriate that those who shed the blood of God's people would be forced to consume blood. The *fourth bowl* affects the sun and allows it to scorch the people of the earth. While there is no plague on Egypt that allows the sun to scorch the people, there is a plague that affects the sun by causing it to go dark, the ninth plague. But rather than repenting to be spared from this plague, the people blaspheme God and refuse to repent. This tells us the tragic nature of the stubborn, wicked hearts of men. People would rather suffer immensely and hold on to their pride than humble themselves and worship God.

The *fifth bowl* of judgment is poured out directly on the throne of the beast. This is the only place where the throne of the beast is mentioned; and this is to be contrasted with the throne of God, out of which the word comes for these judgments. The only throne that will ever endure is the throne of God. The fifth bowl brings about complete darkness on the people. Like the ninth plague on Egypt, which is said to be so dark that the people can feel it, this plague causes the people to gnaw their tongues because of the pain. It is likely not the darkness itself that causes this pain, but the reality that it represents God's coming judgment. Once again, rather than repenting, the people in the kingdom of the beast blaspheme God because of their pains and their sores. The reference of blaspheming God associated with sores harkens back to the situation with Job. In spite of Job's great losses and the festering sores on his body, he refuses to curse God (Job 2:10). These people, however, openly curse God, even though repentance would give them relief from their suffering.

The *sixth bowl* results in the drying of the Euphrates River so that the way of the kings of the east might be prepared. The drying of the Euphrates River alludes to the drying of the Red Sea for Israel to cross during the Exodus and the drying of the Jordan River for Israel to cross as they entered the Promised Land. Yet this drying allows the kings of the east to come and gather together for a great battle. The Parthians were the feared enemies of the Roman Empire at this time, and they lived just east of the Euphrates River. If this river were to dry up, it would allow an invasion into Rome. However, based on what happens next in the vision, it would appear that the kings that come from the east are going to gather together against God's people rather than against Rome. It appears that this bowl is designed to remove physical barriers so that this final battle can occur.

After the Euphrates River is dried up, the dragon, the beast, and the false prophet send out demons to gather together the armies of the earth against God's people. The reference to frogs alludes to the second plague on Egypt, in which frogs are sent upon the land of Egypt. However, this is not as much a reference to the plague that Moses poured out; rather, it is a reference to the frogs that Pharaoh's magicians were able to create as a response to the second plague. The sorceries of Pharaoh's magicians were ultimately the acts of demons, just as the frogs that come out here are clearly identified as demons. The intention of this gathering is to destroy the people of God. Before we learn more about this battle, however, Jesus arrives on the scene and warns us that He is coming as a thief. We must remain faithful, or else when He comes we may be ashamed.

The name of the place where the armies gather together is called Armageddon. This is a reference to Mount Megiddo in Israel. In Hebrew, the word for *mountain* is "har," so literally Mount Megiddo would be called "Har Megiddo" or "Armageddon." Megiddo is an ideal place for a war to take place, as it is a wide open plain where massive armies could gather together for war. Rather than hearing about the outcome of this war, we are instead given the description of the *seventh bowl*. This bowl is poured into the air, and the voice from God's throne declares, "It is done!" (16:17). This is similar to the words of Jesus on the cross, as He proclaimed, "It is finished!" (John 19:30). Following these words, there is a powerful storm (an image that has already appeared multiple times in Revelation) that culminates in an immense earthquake. This earthquake is so powerful that it divides the "great Babylon" into three parts. The two most common views for Babylon are either that it is Rome or Jerusalem. In the next chapters, there are descriptions of "Babylon" that fit both Rome and Jerusalem, so this could be either. Not only is this city affected by this earthquake, but also every city is affected, and even the islands and mountains are lost.

Along with this great earthquake, God sends down massive hailstones to afflict and kill the people. This is similar to the seventh Egyptian plague, though that plague affected mainly the livestock. This also alludes to the battle for Southern Canaan in the book of Joshua in which God kills Israel's enemies more by hail than by the sword (Joshua 10:11). As mentioned in the introduction to Revelation, it is worth noting that the Romans initially used white stones the size of one cubit when they laid siege to Jerusalem in A.D. 70. Nevertheless, once again the people stubbornly refuse to repent but respond by blaspheming God.

Thought Questions:

1. What can we learn about people from the stubborn refusal of the people here to repent even in the midst of great suffering? How might this affect how you share the gospel with others?

2. Why do you think that this last set of judgments comes so quickly without the long interludes of the previous two sets of judgments?

The Fall of Babylon and the Great Feasts: Revelation 17–19

Lesson 159

In chapter 16, one of the angels proclaimed that Babylon had fallen. This foreshadowed the primary imagery in chapters 17 and 18. The person who is judged in the beginning of chapter 17 is the "great harlot." The description of this person as a great harlot will stand in contrast to the pure Bride of Christ, which will appear in chapter 19. Already on multiple occasions in this book, there has been a warning against adultery and fornication, both sexually and spiritually through idolatry. It should be no surprise that there is much debate as to who this woman might be. It is worth noting that there was a coin produced around this time with a picture of the goddess Roma seated on top of Rome's seven hills. However, it is not the specific person to whom this refers that is important; rather, it is the image itself that is significant.

This woman is arrayed in purple and scarlet, colors that are both associated with royalty and associated with sin. Unlike God, who had poured out the cup of His wrath upon the world, this woman has a cup full of fornication and abominations. She also has a

title on her forehead, identifying her as Babylon itself, "THE MOTHER OF HARLOTS" (17:5). This woman is also drunk with the blood of the saints and martyrs of Jesus. This could be a reference to Jerusalem, which was famous as the place where prophets are killed. However, under the persecutions of Nero and other emperors, such a large number of Christians were killed by the Roman Empire that this is the more likely reference. Tradition tells us that both Peter and Paul were martyred while in Rome. The beast that this harlot rides on is the same beast from Revelation 13, with seven heads and ten horns.

Chapter 17 is not as much interested in the judgment upon this woman and Babylon but in describing what these images mean. As is common in apocalyptic literature, the angel that oversees the vision explains what the vision means to John. We have already examined the description of the beast as the false Jesus, who "was, and is not, and yet is" (verse 8). The seven heads on this beast represent two things, seven mountains and seven kings. This is very likely a reference to Rome, which was known as the city on seven hills with seven mountains in the city. There is an incredible amount of debate as to who precisely the seven kings are in this vision. We learn that five kings have already fallen, one still is, and one has not yet come. If we understand these to be Roman emperors starting with Julius Caesar, the sixth emperor would be Nero. This would add some evidence to suggest that this is written during the reign of Nero. Yet there are other ways of viewing these emperors. Some would not include Julius Caesar in this list because it is with Augustus that they are first seen as emperors. Others believe that the reference to kings "falling" means that it only refers to five emperors that have fallen violently. The fifth emperor to die violently was Titus, thus leaving Domitian upon the throne, which would fit with a later date for Revelation. The beast in Revelation 13 is an eighth king like the other seven and likely refers to the Antichrist, who will exercise dominion like the emperors of Rome.

The reference to the ten kings is also open to much interpretation. These ten kings are only given power and authority for a short time, and they work together to wage war against God's people. If this is linked with the call of the dragon, the beast, and the false prophet to gather together kings from all the nations, then it is possible that these ten kings are the leaders of ten nations that join with Satan to wage war on the saints. However, these ten kings could also refer to the heads of the ten provinces in the Roman Empire. In verse 14, Jesus is characterized as "the Lord of lords and King of kings." As we saw earlier in Revelation, this is a phrase designated for the emperor during the Roman Empire. This is a subtle attack on the emperor, reminding everyone that Jesus is the true King. We also learn that the waters under the harlot represent the peoples and nations that commit adultery with Babylon. The ten kings, which had previously gathered together to wage war on the saints, are actually led by God Himself to give their authority to the beast. When the time comes, these ten kings will turn on the beast and kill it. With such a vast empire, this is one of the common fears that the emperors had, namely that people would turn on the empire.

In chapter 18, the focus returns once again to the downfall of Babylon. Here a powerful and glorious angel proclaims that Babylon has fallen. Because of the material wealth of this Babylon, the merchants and kings of the earth loved Babylon. Yet these nations also participate in the fornication or idolatry of this Babylon, as well. There is a warning given to the people of God here. The angel warns the people of God to get away from Babylon because of the plagues that are coming upon her. God does not want His people to fall into the same idolatry and immorality that the other nations had. This command to leave her has both literal and figurative meaning. Just as God warned Lot to get out of Sodom and Gomorrah before He destroyed those cities, He wants to spare His people from the destruction of this city. Moreover, to get out of Babylon is a call to stay away from the immoral things that she is doing.

The destruction of Babylon comes as an act of justice. Everything that comes upon her is a reaction to the luxury and pride with which she lived. As God has said numerous times throughout the Bible, He opposes the proud but gives grace to the humble. The destruction of Babylon will come quickly and completely, all in one day. And all of the kings and people who had previously benefited from the wealth and prosperity of this city will mourn as they see her burn. These would be the same people who had received the mark of the beast and were able to engage in business while God's people could not. Now the tides have turned as the source of their wealth is gone. The lamentation over the loss of material blessings from Babylon has an Old Testament precedent with the lament over Tyre in Ezekiel 27. At that time, Tyre was a merchant city that was quite wealthy and made other cities wealthy through her trade. When Babylon conquered Tyre, it cut off the wealth of those who traded with her, and there was mourning. So here there is a great lament as people stand far off watching this city burn.

Yet, contrasted to the lamentation of the nations, there is a call to God's people to rejoice, for finally they have been avenged. Remember that earlier we had encountered the souls of those who had been killed for their testimony of Jesus. These souls cried out to God, asking how long it would be until they were avenged (6:10). With this vision, these people are finally avenged. All of the signs of merriment and joy that once filled this city of Babylon are gone. Also, the motivation for this great destruction is revealed in the last verse of chapter 18, because many of God's saints and prophets were killed in that city. God will bring about justice and avenge the deaths of His people.

Following the vision of the destruction of Babylon, there is another interlude of praise. The multitude in heaven praises God for His salvation and for His justice. He has finally avenged the blood of the martyrs, and there is much rejoicing. The elders and the living creatures also join in this praise. Even the voice from the throne calls for the people to praise God. So this chorus of praise grows even more intense as they praise God with the alleluia chorus.

Chapter 19 finishes with a reference to two meals that are in contrast to one another. The first great meal is the Marriage Supper of the Lamb. Jesus regularly had referred to Himself as the Bridegroom and the Church was His Bride. However, when Jesus ascended into heaven, the Bride had to wait for the Bridegroom to return so that the marriage could be completed. The Marriage Supper is the celebration of the union of the Bridegroom with His Bride. Following the destruction of Babylon, the Church is now joined with Christ and is able to celebrate that union with this meal. During a wedding ceremony, the woman usually wears a white dress to symbolize that she has kept herself pure for her husband, and here the Bride of Christ is given clean garments made of fine linen. These clothes symbolize the righteous acts of the saints. When John sees all this, he falls down to worship the angel that tells him about this, but the angel does not allow him to, reserving worship to God alone.

The next meal is the meal for the carnivorous birds on earth. With Babylon fallen, it is time for Jesus to finish this war. So we see Jesus appear in heaven, riding on a white horse. There are a number of descriptions given about this Rider on the horse. This Rider is called Faithful and True, and He judges and makes war in righteousness. He has eyes like flames of fire and has many crowns on His head. He also has a name written that only He knows. Moreover, He wears a robe dipped in blood and is called the Word of God. All these descriptions are descriptions given about Jesus Christ in the book of Revelation. He also wages war with a sharp sword that comes out of His mouth, symbolizing the power of the Word of God. In addition, unlike the first time that Jesus came as the Suffering Servant, He comes here as the Conquering King, ready to execute God's wrath on the inhabitants of the earth. Along with Jesus comes an army of angels, ready to make war.

Before this battle, an angel calls to the birds of the air to gather together to feast on the remains of Satan's army. This is a direct reference to Ezekiel 39, which speaks of a very similar battle with all the nations gathered together against God. In Ezekiel, the leader of this army is a man named Gog, of the land of Magog. Gog and Magog will be mentioned in the very next chapter. As the birds are gathered together, so also the armies of Satan gather together to wage war against Jesus and His army.

While we have a build up for what looks like will be a massive battle, there is no mention of the battle itself. Jesus simply conquers and captures the beast and the false prophet and throws them into the lake of fire. The rest of the army that had gathered is killed by the sword that comes out of Jesus' mouth. The reason for the lack of the mention of the battle is that there is no real fight here. All of the power and glory of man and Satan are nothing compared to the power and glory and might of Jesus Christ. It is absurd to wage war against Jesus, and this easy victory is proof of this. With these armies killed, the birds get their meal. So the question that the reader is left with at the end of this chapter is: "Are you going to remain faithful so that you get to enjoy the Marriage Supper of the Lamb, or are you going to be faithless and be the meal for the carnivorous birds?"

Thought Question:

> With all the imagery of Rome in these chapters, do you see these events as fulfilled in the past or a reference to a new empire in the future? Why?

The End of the Story: Revelation 20–22

Lesson 160

With the final chapters of Revelation, we come to the end of the biblical story. Chapter 19 finished with the destruction of the forces of Satan as the beast and the false prophet are captured and thrown into the lake of fire. However, there is something missing from the story of this great victory. If the beast and the false

prophet have been captured, what happened to the dragon, Satan? We learn immediately in chapter 20 what happens to the dragon.

John sees a vision in chapter 20 of another angel that holds the key to the bottomless pit. This is the same pit that the locust demons had previously ascended from in chapter 9. It is likely that the angel that appears here is the same angel who was given the key to the bottomless pit in order to unlock it in chapter 9. However, rather than opening the bottomless pit, in chapter 20 this angel is going to use that key to lock the bottomless pit. This angel is given power and authority to take the dragon, Satan, and throw him into the bottomless pit and lock it so that he could not deceive the nations any longer. We have seen throughout this book that the primary weapon of Satan has been deception; and through that deception, he was able to gather the armies of the earth together against God's people. Now Satan is taken out of the picture so that he cannot influence nor deceive people for a thousand years, the time of the Millennial Kingdom. There are two simple possibilities as to when this binding of Satan takes place; either it has already happened or this is a future event. According to the futurist, or premillennial interpretation of Revelation, this is a future event that will mark the beginning of the Millennial Kingdom. However, according to amillennialists and some postmillennialists, this binding may have been done with Christ's first coming. In the introduction to Revelation, we learned that Jesus had earlier spoken of Satan being bound as evidenced by Him casting out demons. To those who hold that this binding is yet in the future, they would argue that the binding in Revelation 20 is different from what Jesus had earlier spoken about, as Satan still appears to be deceiving the nations right now.

Throughout this book, we have encountered a number of thrones. Most significant is the throne of God and the throne of the Lamb. Yet there is a throne for Satan in this book, as well. After Satan is bound, John sees another set of thrones, but these thrones are reserved for those who had been martyred during the Great Tribulation for remaining faithful to Jesus. As Jesus has promised many times in this book, these people are given the authority and power to reign with Christ for a thousand years. Even though these people have died, like Jesus Himself they are raised from the dead to reign with Him. These resurrected martyrs will not only be kings with Christ, but they will also be priests in this Millennial Kingdom.

As we have seen, it is the nature of this Millennial Kingdom that is at the center of most debates on Revelation and the end times. Futurists (premillennialists) see this Millennial Kingdom as a future event that will follow Christ's second coming. According to this view, this will be a literal earthly kingdom wherein the resurrected martyrs will rule with Jesus on the earth. Preterists (postmillennialists) believe that this Millennial Kingdom may be right now or in the future, and it will come only after the world is transformed by the power of the gospel. In addition, amillennialists believe that this Millennial Kingdom is not a physical kingdom at all, but is a reference to the kingdom of the Church. It is interesting to note that the descriptions of this Millennial Kingdom are consistent with the descriptions of the Church. Those who get to enjoy this Millennial Kingdom are the ones who have been resurrected. Throughout the New Testament, the Bible uses resurrection language to refer to salvation as we go from dead in sin to being alive in Christ. These same people are called blessed because they will not experience the second death. The second death is a reference to the lake of fire, from which all Christians will be spared. Also in this Millennial Kingdom, those who enjoy it will be priests and kings, which all believers are called in 1 Peter 2:9. However, there are two difficulties with this interpretation. It is explicitly the dead martyrs who are resurrected here, and the most natural reading would imply a physical rather than a spiritual resurrection. Also, the second resurrection is certainly a physical resurrection, so this would require two different kinds of resurrections. Interestingly, considering all of the debate about this Millennial Kingdom, there is no description given here of what this kingdom will be like.

At the end of the thousand years, Satan will be released and will once again deceive the nations in order to amass yet another army. It is possible that this battle in chapter 20 is merely another description of the battle from chapter 19. Or, this could be a second army that Satan gathers together. The mention of Gog and Magog comes from Ezekiel 38 and 39. In Ezekiel 37, God has Ezekiel prophesy to an army of dry bones, and he watches as these dry bones are resurrected and form a massive army. In the context of Ezekiel, these dry bones represent the nation of Israel that had been devastated by Babylon and was practically dead. After this army is resurrected, the nations will gather together under Gog, the king of the land of Magog, in order to fight against Israel. In Ezekiel, these nations are utterly defeated, and their bodies become food for the birds of the air and beasts of the field. We have already encountered a reference to these chapters of Ezekiel in chapter 19 of Revelation, following the first great battle. These same elements are present here in chapter 20. After a resur-

rection scene, Gog and Magog gather together a massive army in order to destroy God's people. However, this massive army is destroyed without even a battle, by fire that comes from heaven. Everyone is devoured, and Satan is thrown into the same lake of fire as the beast and the false prophet.

There is a difficulty with this final rebellion that merits some discussion here. If the only people who are allowed to experience this Millennial Kingdom are Christians who have been resurrected, who is it that Satan is able to deceive in order to fight against the Christians? There are a few solutions to this problem. First, since it is specifically the army that is destroyed in chapter 19, the other people may still be alive during the Millennial Kingdom. Those who had been allowed to live would then make up this new army at the end of the Millennial Kingdom. Another solution is that this army could be an army of demons. A third option is that this rebellious army comes from the children of believers that were born during the Millennial Kingdom. This poses a difficulty, since it appears that marriage is not something people will get to experience with resurrected bodies. The fourth option is that, at the end of the Millennium, the rest of the dead are raised from the dead for this battle. One final option is that this battle in Revelation 20 is simply another description of the battle from chapter 19.

Following the destruction of this final army, the ultimate day of justice occurs. John sees a vision of a great white throne with God Himself sitting on it. It is at this point that the current heavens and earth disappear and only this throne remains. All of the dead who had ever lived now stand judgment before God. All of the books of each person's deeds are opened, and everyone is exposed. Nothing is hidden, and perfect justice finally happens to all of the people. Everyone whose name is not written in the Book of Life will be thrown into the lake of fire where the dragon, the beast, and the false prophet are thrown. Even Hades or hell itself is thrown into the lake of fire. Contrary to popular opinion, nobody will spend eternity in hell, but rather the lake of fire.

With judgment and punishment poured out on the enemies of God, the ultimate reward is given to those who believe in Jesus. Now that the first heaven and earth are destroyed, God makes a new heaven and a new earth. Even this mention of a new heavens and a new earth has an Old Testament background from Isaiah 65. In this new earth, there is no more sea. Throughout Scripture the sea is a symbol of chaos, and the abyss was located in the midst of the seas. Now there is no more chaos and no more abyss. The rest of the description of the new earth is a combination of two things—the great city of Jerusalem and the garden of Eden.

John sees Jerusalem come down from heaven prepared as a bride. In many ways, this city is symbolic of the Church itself. In Galatians 4, Paul calls the Church the heavenly Jerusalem. Jerusalem was such a special city throughout the Bible because that was where God's special presence had been located. Now God is present through the Church, so it is only appropriate to connect the two ideas. In this new Jerusalem, there will no longer be any pain or tears or sorrow. There is a purpose to the revelation of this vision, however. Remember that this entire book is written in order to encourage and motivate Christians to remain faithful and pure, even unto death. So God speaks from heaven, identifying Himself as Jesus had done in chapter 1 as the Alpha and Omega. He tells us that He will give the fountain of the water of life, a reference to Ezekiel 47 where living water comes out from the temple to nourish the nations. This serves as a warning, however, because only he who overcomes will be able to experience these blessings. Those who give in to the wickedness of the world will instead be thrown into the lake of fire.

John is given a further description of this new Jerusalem by one of the angels, who had one of the seven bowls of judgment. Once again the city of Jerusalem is called the Bride of the Lamb, which we know to be the Church. It is possible that all of these descriptions are actually intended to be symbolic of the Church, rather than an actual city. Or, this city itself is built in such a way to represent the Church. As this city descends, it emits a glorious light like the light that reflects from a precious stone. The twelve gates of this city are named after the twelve tribes of Israel. Also, the foundations of the walls are named after the twelve apostles. This city represents a union between Israel and the Church. The descriptions of this city are similar to the descriptions of Jerusalem in the final chapters of Ezekiel, though this city is significantly larger and more glorious. Interestingly, the narrative of Ezekiel's visions goes from resurrection, to a massive battle, to the description of a new city of Jerusalem and a new temple. The last chapters of Revelation follow this same basic narrative flow with the resurrection of the martyrs followed by a massive battle followed now by this new, glorious Jerusalem. Like the city in Ezekiel's vision, this city is square; but John is also given the height of this city, actually making it a cube. Ezekiel's city about 850 feet by 850 feet, whereas this new Jerusalem is about 1,500 miles by 1,500 miles.

The foundations of the wall of the city, which we have already seen were named after the apostles, are made from precious stones. It is hard to pinpoint exactly what these specific precious stones represent, if anything. It is possible that the mention of the precious stones is simply designed to show the glory and beauty of this city. However, according to the Law of Moses, there were to be twelve precious stones in the breastplate of the high priest (Exodus 34:10–13). Eight of these twelve stones are the same here, so it is possible that this is a priestly reference. In addition to these precious stones, the gates of the city are made from twelve pearls, and the street of the city is made from pure gold. Whatever these precious materials may represent individually, collectively they show that this is an incredibly glorious city.

Unlike Ezekiel's city of Jerusalem, this city does not have a temple in it. There is no longer a need for a temple building, for there is no longer a reason to separate God from us. Jesus is the very presence of God among us, so He is in essence the temple. In addition, unlike the original creation that needed the sun, the moon, and the stars for light, God Himself is the light for this city. This is just like in the first day of creation when God Himself had provided the light for the world before He entrusted that responsibility to the sun, moon, and stars. Unlike the city of Jerusalem and the temple that had to be shut to protect it from enemies, the gates of this city will be constantly open so that the nations could bring their wealth into this city. The idea of the nations bringing their wealth into Jerusalem is found throughout the prophets, though it is a major theme in Isaiah's oracles against the nations. In some capacity, this has already been fulfilled by people from every tribe, tongue, and nation worshiping God now. However, in Revelation this is on a much larger scale, as all the nations bring their wealth into the city as a form of sacrifice of praise. Once again, John warns the readers that anything that causes abominations or lies will not be able to enter this city, only those whose names are written in the Book of Life.

The imagery of the city of Jerusalem shifts in chapter 22 to the imagery of the garden of Eden. As a masterful way of wrapping up the Bible, God restores the garden of Eden on this new earth. In some manner, the very scope of human history has been marked by a desire to regain the paradise of the garden that had been lost by sin. People have come up with millions of ways to try to recreate that garden, but all efforts have fallen woefully short. Now to those who have remained faithful to Christ and are allowed to be on the new earth will get to experience that garden once again. The background for the images in chapter 22 is not only the garden of Eden, but also Ezekiel 47. The central focus of this image is the river of the water of life that flows out from the throne of God. In Ezekiel 47, living water flows from out of the temple. This water flows into the streets of the city and provides nourishment for the Tree of Life, which is on both sides of the river. This is the same Tree of Life that had been in the garden of Eden, but God had kicked out humanity from the garden so that they could not eat from the tree of life. Now, in the new garden in Jerusalem, we are given the tree of life to eat from freely. This tree also brings healing to the nations, which is a direct quote from Ezekiel 47:12. With our new glorified bodies, we will be able to see God face-to-face, something that would destroy us in our current estate. Also, on our foreheads will be the name of God. Earlier there had been a seal placed on the foreheads of believers (Revelation 7); perhaps this is what was on the seal, the name of God. Also, as we have already been told, in this new garden city, there will be no need for light because God Himself will provide light; and we will reign with Christ forever.

This epistle comes to a completion with a series of warnings and encouragements. As with the beginning of this epistle, we are told once again that these events will happen shortly. Jesus Himself speaks, telling us that He is coming quickly, so we are to be diligent to obey the words of this book. Once again, John turns to worship the angel, who is communicating much of this to him; but the angel refuses and tells him to worship God alone. Unlike Daniel, who had been told to seal up the message that God had given him, John is explicitly told not to seal up the words of this book because the time has come for these things to take place. Jesus warns the people that He is coming quickly, and He will give to each person what he or she deserves. He will reward those who are faithful; but those who insist on doing evil will be left out of the city. Jesus once again identifies Himself as the Alpha and the Omega, and He also identifies Himself as the Root of David and the Bright and Morning Star. Both the reference to the Root of David and the Morning Star are passages about the Messiah who will be the star that comes out of Jacob (Numbers 24:17) and the descendant of David (Psalm 2).

After all these things have been revealed, there is a response by the Holy Spirit and by the Church (the Bride) calling for Jesus to come quickly. Also, we who hear the words of this prophecy are told to call for Jesus to come quickly, as well. Though there are some scary things in this book, Jesus is gracious and freely offers to us to drink from the water of life. It is not difficult to find salvation, but we must cling to that salvation. There is a stern warning given, however, to the person who attempts to change the words of this prophecy. If anyone adds anything to this prophecy, God will send the plagues of this book upon him. Moreover, if anyone takes away anything from this prophecy, his name will be taken away from the Book of Life and from the blessings in this book. Finally, Jesus testifies once again, telling us that He is coming quickly. Therefore, with John, we reply, "Amen. Even so, come, Lord Jesus!"

Thought Questions:

1. There is a lot of talk in this book about these events happening shortly, but it has been about 2,000 years since this has been written; how do you reconcile these two things?

2. After examining Revelation, do you lean more towards the futurist (premillennial), the preterist (postmillennial) or the amillennialist interpretation of Revelation?

3. After examining the glorious scenes of worship through this book, how has this impacted your own view of God and of worship?

4. How often do you pray for Jesus to return quickly? Do you think this would change if you were going through a period of suffering? Why or why not?

Index

Numbers

144,000 from the tribes of Israel 215, 220
666 207, 220

A

Aaron 108
Abaddon (or Apollyon) 216
Abba, Father 158
Abel 1, 190, 202
Abihu 106
abomination of desolation 27, 47, 48, 69
abortion 137
Abraham 1, 7, 8, 25, 45, 55, 65, 76, 85, 86,
        105, 107, 129, 133, 153, 158, 159,
        186, 188, 190, 193, 215
Abram 1, 76
Achaia 117, 139
Acts
    Acts 12:12 32
    Acts 13:13 32
    Acts 15:37-39 32
    Acts 19 73
    Acts 20:5 ff 53
    Acts 22:3–5 93
    Acts 28:3 33
    book of 53, 62, 72, 73, 93, 101–122, 125, 138,
        147, 149, 157, 161, 201
Adam 1, 10, 21, 53, 55, 130, 147, 190, 219
adoption 161
adultery 42, 211, 223
Agabus, the prophet 118
Agrippa 120, 121
Ahab 2
Alexander 175
Alexander the Great 3, 5
allegory 159
Alpha and Omega 209, 227, 228
ambassadors for Christ 151
amillennialism 208, 225–226
Ananias and Sapphira 106, 110
Ancient of Days 102, 209
Andrew 10, 14, 33, 56, 76, 89
angels 25, 27, 28, 45, 80, 106, 111, 112, 182,
        190, 200, 205, 210, 212, 213, 215, 223
    angel holds key to bottomless pit 225
    angel of death 2, 69, 213, 217
    angel proclaims the "everlasting gospel" to
        people 220
    ark of the Covenant and cherub 218
    at the tomb 72
    four angels lead a demonic army 217
    guardian 20
    Jesus comes with an army of 225
    legions of 29
    messages of (for the churches) 221
    messages of John given by 209
    mighty angel with a little scroll 217
    Satan and his demonic 219
    the archangel Michael 200, 219
    thousands upon thousands of 213
Anna 54
Annas, the high priest 95
Antichrist 27, 47, 173, 206, 220, 223
    Nero as the 207
Antioch (on the Orontes River) 111, 112,
        113, 114, 117, 157
Antioch in Pisidia 112
Antiochus IV Epiphanes 3

apocalyptic literature 205, 208, 213, 219,
        223
Apollo (Greek god) 216
Apollos 117, 139, 140, 141, 149, 150, 180,
        181, 182
Apologeticum 108
apologist 117
apostles 106, 109, 120, 122, 139, 143, 154,
        157, 163, 174, 180, 182, 183, 191,
        195, 200, 201, 204–205, 205, 206,
        227
    commission of 111
    criteria for being an apostle 102
    twelve 112
Aquila and Priscilla 116, 117, 138, 182
Areopagus 116
ark of the covenant 2, 212, 218
Armageddon 222
armor of God 10, 164
Artemas (Paul's associate) 181
Artemis (Diana) 4, 117
ascension 73, 84, 91, 102, 103
asceticism 170
Asia 115, 195
    Minor 168, 205, 209
Assyrians 2
Athens 116
authority
    head coverings symbolic of 144
    laying on hands imparts 177
    of God 137
    of Jesus 36, 39
    of Paul 117, 124, 138, 154
    of teachers 193
    of the husband 175
    of Titus 181
Azotus (Ashdod) 109

B

Baal, prophet 199
Babylon 2, 8, 218
    as a metaphor of Jerusalem 222
    as a metaphor of Rome 195, 198, 222
    destruction of 27, 220, 223–224
Babylonian Empire 219
backbiting 154
backsliding 185
Balaam, the prophet 200, 211
Balak (king of Moab) 211
baptism 31, 163, 197, 215
    mark of a Christian 104
    of 3,000 people 104
    of Ethiopian eunuch 109
    of Jesus 18, 22, 76, 89
    of John 24, 33, 44
    of repentance 9
    of repentance (John's) 117
    of Saul 110
    symbolism of 130
Barabbas 30, 50, 71, 95
Barnabas 32, 105, 110, 111, 112, 113, 114,
        115, 157, 182
Bartholomew 14
Bartimaeus 43
Bathsheba 8
bearing fruit 92, 168, 169
beast 160, 218, 223, 225
    Daniel sees four beasts 219
    from the sea 219

    in Daniel 219
    mark of the 220, 221
    number of the (666) 207
    of the earth 220
    Satan gives beast authority 220
    symbolizes Rome 220
beatitudes 10, 57
Beelzebub. *See* Satan
benediction 138, 173, 190, 198
Benedictus 54
Benjamin, tribe of 167
Berea 116
Bethany 28, 43, 48, 89
Bethlehem 8, 54, 84
bishop. *See* elders
Bithynia 195
bitterness 171, 190
blasphemy 12, 170
    against the Holy Spirit 15, 35
    Jesus accused of 49
    of these false teachers 200
blindness
    for the glory of God 86
    of Paul 159
    of the heart 163
body of Christ 101, 135, 146
Book of Life 207, 211, 220, 227, 228
bottomless pit 216, 225
bowls
    bowl judgments 218, 221–222
    full of incense 213
    judgment of seven 206
bread and wine
    in the Lord's Supper 186
Bread of Life 81–82, 87
Bride of Christ 204, 223, 224, 228

C

Caesar 25, 45, 68, 95, 116, 121, 207
    Augustus 54
    believers in household of 122
    Caligula 220
    Domitian 205, 216, 223
    household of 168
    Julius 223
    Nero 32, 123, 174, 195, 205, 207, 220, 223
    Paul's appeal to 120
    Titus 47, 207, 223
Caesarea 111, 118, 120
Caiaphas 29, 30, 88, 95
Cain 1, 190, 200, 202
Caligula 220
Calvary 71
Cana 80
Canaan 1, 2, 189, 223
Canaanite woman 17
Capernaum 19, 56, 81
Cappadocia 195
Cenchrea
    church in 138
centurion 12, 72
    Cornelius 111
Cephas. *See* Peter
cessationism 146
cheerful giving 152
chief priests 31, 44, 45
childbirth
    sin compared to 192

children
  do not despise the little 20
  should not hinder the little 21, 41
Christian
  characteristics of a 201
  keeps His commandments 201
  marks of a true 201–203
Christ's Edict Letters
  to the Seven Churches (chart) 210
circular letter 161, 182, 201, 204
circumcision 109, 114, 115, 119, 127, 138,
    159, 160
  party 149, 158, 167, 170, 171, 181, 190, 200
Claudius 123
Claudius Lysias 120
Clement of Rome 182
Colossae 125
  church in 168, 169, 171
Colossians
  book of 125, 161, 168–171
confession
  of Peter 18
  of sin to God 201
conscience 137, 138, 159
  clean 143, 188
conviction
  about giving 153
  of the Holy Spirit 152
  that God exists 188
  two forms of 152
Corban 39
Corinth 116, 117, 124, 139, 140, 141, 148,
    149, 152, 172
  church in 142, 144, 147, 151, 154, 155
1 Corinthians
  book of 139–149, 157
2 Corinthians
  book of 148–155, 157
Cornelius 111–112, 114
cornerstone
  Jesus as the chief 196
  stone the builders rejected 68
Court of the Gentiles 24, 44
covenant
  God's (with the Jews) 162
  New Covenant. *See* New Covenant
  of freedom and promise 159
  of slavery 159
covetousness 62, 170, 190
creation 175, 206
  Jesus is God's agent of 169
  seventh day of (rest) 184
  six days of 1
Creator 116, 182
Crete 180, 181
  church in 181
cross 140, 158, 166, 169, 170, 203, 209
  not humiliation, but exaltation 78
crucifixion 17, 28, 30, 50, 70, 82, 95, 98, 169
cult of the emperor 4, 220
Cyprus 112
Cyrus the Great 2

D

Damascus 110, 121, 124, 159
damnation 15, 148
Dan
  tribe of 215
Daniel 27, 217, 228
  book of 205, 213, 219
  Daniel 7 18, 209
  Daniel 7:13-14 29, 102

Daniel 7:13–14 70
  Daniel 12:11 69
  prophecy of 29, 217
darkness
  hiding from the truth and sin as 201
David 2, 7, 8, 35, 45, 55, 68, 104, 108, 113,
    125, 183, 228
  having the key of (Philadelphia) 212
  Messiah is descendant of 25
  Root of 213, 228
Day of Atonement 184, 216
Day of the Lord 173
day of wrath 126
deacons 107, 108, 138, 176
Dead Sea Scrolls 4
death
  angel of 2, 69, 217
  for anyone who causes a little child to sin 19
  for women caught in adultery 85
  Jesus has power over 37, 49
  life after 25
  of Alexander the Great 3
  of Jesus 5, 15, 18–19, 22, 24, 29, 30, 31, 34, 35,
    37, 40, 41, 42, 43, 48, 49, 53, 54, 60, 66, 71,
    72, 75, 78, 80, 83, 84, 88, 89, 91, 93, 95,
    102, 103, 105, 106, 111, 113, 123
  of John the Baptist 16, 38, 60, 73, 81
  of king's servants 25
  of Peter 98
  of the disciples 26
  of the firstborns in Egypt 29, 69
  second (in lake of fire) 86, 211, 226
Decapolis 39
deity of Christ 36, 74, 88, 95, 199, 205
Demas 171
Demetrius 205
demigod 74
demon-possessed 12, 15, 33, 35, 36, 37, 56,
    59, 60, 62, 88, 116, 208
demons 14, 33, 34, 35, 41, 45, 49, 51, 108,
    116, 117, 164, 193, 208, 222, 225
  food sacrificed to 143
  sent into pigs 12, 36, 59
  son afflicted by 19
Derbe 113
destruction 9, 12, 26, 90
  of Jerusalem 27
  of the flesh 141
  of the temple 205
Deuteronomy
  Deuteronomy 6:13 55
  Deuteronomy 6:16 55
  Deuteronomy 8:3 55
  Deuteronomy 16:16 22, 43, 69
  Deuteronomy 18:15–19 76
  Deuteronomy 18:19 105
  Deuteronomy 19:15 5, 85
  Deuteronomy 31 221
Diana (Artemis) 117
diaspora 108
dichotomy between law and faith 158
Diotrephes 205
disciples 65, 69, 70, 72, 82, 86, 89, 90, 91, 93,
    94, 101, 102, 103, 124, 147
  seventy-two sent out 61
discipleship
  cost of 61, 64
  failure of 50
discipline
  Church 18
  discipline of a father 189–190
disobedient to parents 126
Dispersion 84

Divided Kingdom 1
division 175
  within the church 140, 141, 144
divorce 20, 142
Domitian 205, 216, 223
doxology 135, 139, 162, 168, 175, 177, 200,
    209
dreams
  God spoke to prophets through 182
  Joseph and Mary warned in a dream 8
  Joseph had (Jacob's son) 8, 27
  Paul's dream (to go to Macedonia) 165
  wise men warned in dream 8
drink offering
  Paul as a 180
Drusilla 120

E

earthquakes 26, 47, 69, 116, 214, 218, 222,
    223
Echoes of Jesus' Sermon on the Mount
  in James (chart) 191
Edomites 4
Egypt 1, 8, 29, 80, 108, 143, 183, 200, 206,
    218, 221, 222
Egyptians 1, 2, 69, 107
elders
  as faithful shepherds 198
  qualifications for 176, 177, 181
    chart of qualifications 174
  to pray over sick 194
elect 134, 195
  lady and her children 204
Elijah 2, 8, 9, 14, 18, 38, 40, 54, 55, 58, 60, 61,
    76, 195, 217
Elisha 55, 58
Elizabeth 53, 54
Elymas the sorcerer 112
Emmaus 51, 72
emperors of Rome 210–211, 220, 223
end times. *See* eschatology
endurance
  in the race of life 189
  motivation for patient 194
enemies
  call down fire from heaven on 61
  enemy plants weeds in a field 15
  Jesus says to love our 11, 57
  of God 169, 194, 206, 211, 218, 226
  of God's people 87, 132–133, 166, 178, 205,
    220, 223
  of Jesus 49, 66, 167, 169, 183, 188, 206, 208
    made His footstool 104, 182, 188
  of the disciples 69, 94
  of the Israelites 2, 65, 102, 223, 227
  of two witnesses in Revelation 217–218
  Parthians (of Roman Empire) 222
  Satan as an enemy 1, 151, 160, 198, 221
Enoch 197, 217
Epaphras 168, 171
Epaphroditus 165, 166, 168
Ephesians
  book of 161–165
Ephesus 4, 73, 115, 117, 118, 138, 139, 147,
    148, 168, 174, 175, 176
  church in 161, 180, 204, 205, 210
  Jesus' letter to the church in 210
  problem with the widows 176
Ephraim 2
  tribe of 215
Epicureanism 5

epistles
  customary greetings 125, 138, 148
  Epistles Chart 123
  General Epistles 123, 191, 195
  introduction to Paul's epistles 124–125
  introduction to the 122–124
  Pastoral Epistles 124–125, 174, 180
  Pauline Epistles 123
  prison 161, 165, 167, 168, 174
Esau 1, 133, 190
eschatology 179
Essenes 4
eternal life 21, 42, 66, 74, 78, 81, 82, 83, 88,
      89, 92, 94, 127, 131, 201, 203
Eternal State 207
Ethiopian eunuch 109, 111
Euphrates River 222
Euroclydon (northeasterly wind) 121
Eutychus 117
evangelists 163
Eve 10, 21, 175, 219
exhortations 154, 162, 164, 167, 173, 174,
      175, 177, 188, 190, 192, 196, 204
  Paul's (to Timothy) 176
Exodus 8, 45, 134, 206
  Exodus 15 221
  Exodus 33:19 134
exorcism 35, 56
eye of a needle 42
Ezekiel
  book of 205
  eats a scroll 217
  Ezekiel 27 224
  Ezekiel 37-39 226
  Ezekiel 39 225
  Ezekiel 40-48 217
  Ezekiel 47 228
  temple of 217
  vision of 213, 227

F

faith 26, 124, 129, 158, 163, 168, 169, 176,
      180, 192, 200, 206
  and works are connected 193
  defined (Hebrews 11:1) 188
  fourth piece of armor 164
  genuine 74
  good fight of 177
  grace received through 162
  imprisoned for 190
  in Christ 211
  journeys 202
  need to persevere in 184
  of church in Thyatira 211
  the just shall live by 158
  works that come from 172
faithfulness 160, 181, 188
  of the believers in Philadelphia 212
fall
  asleep (disciples) 49
  back into Judaism 157, 182, 187
  from grace 159
  into idolatry 2
  into sin 65, 128, 143, 160, 193
  into temptation 49
  of Babylon 220, 223, 224
  of man in Genesis 3 219
fallen
  angels 200
  world 130, 132, 179, 196
falling
  away from faith 15, 35, 59, 82, 182, 183, 184,
      185, 188

down before God 213
  of kings (emperors of Rome) 223
  of the stars 27, 48
false prophets 69, 219
false teachers 154, 157, 168, 170, 174, 176,
      177, 179, 180, 181, 199, 200, 204
  called antichrists (1 John) 202
  how to identify (1 John) 201
false witnesses 29
famines 26, 47, 214
fasting
  ritual of 34
Father God 133, 162
fear
  fearful thing to fall into the hands of the living
      God 188
  motivating false teachers out of 200
  of God 62, 86, 106, 150, 152, 164, 184, 190, 203,
      220
  perfect love casts out 203
  ready to give a defense in 197
  work out our salvation with 166
Feast of Tabernacles 5, 83–84
Feast of Unleavened Bread 22, 43, 69
Feast of Weeks. *See* Pentecost
feeding of the 4,000 17, 39
feeding of the 5,000 16, 38, 39, 60, 73, 81, 82
Felix 120, 121
fellowship
  loss of 174
  with one another 104, 201
Festival of Lights 3
Festus 120, 121
fig tree
  budding of (summer coming) 69
  Jesus curses 24, 43
fire
  burn the chaff with 9
  destruction of the world through 200
  disciples want to call down 61
  divided tongues of 103
  first trumpet, hail and 216
  Jesus' eyes like flames of 211, 224
  Jesus with white hair and 209
  lake of 86, 207, 225, 226, 227
  massive army destroyed by 226
  Messiah will baptize with 9, 54, 103
  offering an unauthorized 106
  pillar of 8
  sea of glass and 221
  sixth trumpet, horses breathe 217
  Sodom and Gomorrah destroyed by 217
flesh
  and blood cannot inherit the kingdom 147
  bread represents Jesus' 82
  carnal refers to the 140
  cleansing from all filthiness of the 152
  destruction of the (by Satan) 141
  Holy Spirit poured out on all 103
  Jesus is God in the 91
  Jesus put on 75, 203
  Jesus' teaching about eating His 73
  lusts of the 161, 202
  opportunity for the 159
  Paul's thorn in the 154
  people according to the 150
  power of the 49
  Spirit-flesh struggle 131–132, 140, 159–160
  two shall become one 142
flood
  destruction of the world through the 200
  during the days of Noah 1
food sacrificed to idols 138, 143
foreknowledge of God 104

forgiveness 20, 29, 34, 64, 65, 85, 96, 106,
      109, 114, 121, 190, 201
fornication 223
freedom
  as a free man in the Lord 142
  but not make your brother stumble 143
  in Christ 159, 196
  in the Spirit 159
  life in the light is 137
  New Covenant is a covenant of 159
  of salvation 200
  of unmarried person 142
  should not be abused 159
  through the gospel 142
  to those who are enslaved 55
fulfillment of the Law 10–11
fullness
  of Christ 163
  of God 169, 183
  of the Gentiles 135

G

Gabriel 8, 53, 54
Gaius 204, 205
Galatia 112, 115, 195
  churches in 117, 157
  region of 157, 168
Galatians 125
  book of 157–160, 165, 191
  Galatians 4 227
Galilee 8, 31, 34, 39, 50, 55, 56, 73, 76, 79,
      80, 83, 84
Gamaliel 106
garden
  of Eden 1, 10, 130, 227
  of Gethsemane 14, 29, 70
genealogies 174, 180
genealogy of Jesus
  in Luke 53, 55
  in Matthew 7, 8
General Epistles 123, 191, 195
generosity 104, 105, 204
  of God 161
  of Jesus 152
  of the Philippians 167
Genesis
  book of 175
  Genesis 3 219
  Genesis 3:15 139
  Genesis 37 219
Gentiles 5, 8, 21, 24, 25, 32, 39, 56, 69, 70,
      101, 109, 110, 111, 112, 113, 114,
      118, 119, 120, 121, 122, 124, 125,
      133, 134, 137, 138, 140, 157, 158,
      162, 167, 168, 176, 180, 195, 196
Gethsemane 14, 29, 70, 89
gift for Jerusalem church 147, 152
Gnosticism 4, 168
god-fearer
  Cornelius 111
  Ethiopian eunuch 109
godliness 174, 175, 176, 177, 180, 200
  a form of (but no power) 179
  the mystery of (the gospel) 176
"god of this age" 149
Gog and Magog 225, 226
Golden Rule 12, 57, 192
Golgotha 30
Gomorrah 200, 217, 224
Good Friday 102
Good Shepherd 73, 87, 215
good works

of the Thessalonians 173
  rich in 177
  stir up love and 188
Goshen 1
gospels 5, 6
gossip 94, 174, 177
government
  authorities protect us 175
  commanded to pay taxes and respect the 137
  gets its authority from God 137
  Jesus affirms the validity of 25
  officials
    disciples brought before 47
    get authority from God 50
  or kingdom as the beast in Revelation 219
  to bring about justice God uses 136
grace 128, 130, 139, 151, 157, 159, 161, 162,
    165, 172, 174, 177, 180, 181, 182,
    191, 198, 200, 209
  and truth 75
  free gift of God's 162
  of God is sufficient 154
  of Jesus 155
Great Commission 32, 33, 51
greatest commandment. *See* Shema
Great Tribulation 27, 47, 206, 207, 212, 225
Great White Throne Judgment 207, 221
Greece 3, 115, 139, 180
Greek Empire 3, 5, 219
Greeks 5, 84, 89, 140
greeting
  author of Hebrews sends 191, 205
  author of Revelation sends 205
  customary (Jewish and Gentile) 125
  customary kiss of 58
  from an unnamed sister 205
  John greets fellow believers 205
  1 John lacks a 201
  John sends (from a saint) 205
  Paul greets fellow believers 139, 147, 155, 171,
    180
  Paul's customary 125, 138, 139, 165, 174, 178,
    181
  Paul sends (from saints) 168, 171
  Peter greets fellow believers 198, 205
  Peter sends (from saints) 198, 205
  Peter's (to "pilgrims") 195
Gregale. *See* Euroclydon

H

Habakkuk 113, 158
Hades 65, 104, 209, 214, 226
Hagar 159
Haggai
  book of 214
  the prophet 2
Hall of Faith 188
hand washing ritual 39
Hanukkah 3
harlots 24
  Mother of Harlots 223–224
Harmony of the Events of Holy Week chart
    22
harvest, two-fold 221
Hasmonean Dynasty 3, 4
head coverings 144
headship
  Adam represents all of humanity 130
  in marriage 144, 146
  Jesus represents new humanity 130
healing
  called "signs" by John 73
  from sins 80

lame man from birth 104
  ministry of Jesus 12
  miracles of Elijah and Elisha 58
  of a bleeding woman 13, 59, 106
  of a blind man at Bethsaida 40
  of a centurion's servant 12, 58
  of a deaf man with a speech impediment 39
  of a demon-possessed man 37
  of a leper 34, 56
  of a paralytic 12, 34, 56, 110
  of blind Bartimaeus 43
  of lame man from birth 105
  of man crippled from birth 113
  of the crippled man at pool 80
  of the man born blind 86
  of the sick 10
  of the Syro-Phoenician woman's daughter 39
  of two blind men 22
  on the Sabbath 57, 63, 83
heaven
  angels in (praise God regularly) 212
  believers destined for 167
  blessings in 57, 170
  bread from 82
  Daniel sees a vision of 70
  disciples want to call down fire from 61
  Elijah was taken into 54
  God makes a new 226
  God's voice from (affirms Jesus as Son) 9, 40, 55
  God's wisdom revealed to angels in 162
  hard for a rich man to enter 192
  Jesus appears in (on white horse) 224
  Jesus ascends to 14, 51, 67, 73, 84, 91, 102, 124,
    218, 224
  Jesus' authority is from 44
  Jesus given all authority in 31
  Jesus prays for us to be in 94
  Jesus seated at the right hand of God 92, 186
  John's baptism was from 24, 44
  John's vision in 212–227
  John testifies that Jesus is from 78
  kingdom of 6–7, 10–11, 12, 14, 15, 21, 32, 36,
    45, 68, 193
    Peter given keys to the 18
    who is the greatest in the 19
  masters have a Master in 164, 171
  more joy in (over repentant sinner) 64
  names are written in 61
  no marriage in 45, 68
  on the clouds of
    Jesus goes to the Father 49
    Jesus' return 27, 29, 102, 172, 207, 209
  parable of the rich man and Lazarus 65
  pattern of the tabernacle in 186
  Paul's vision of 154
  permanent home awaits us in 195
  Promised Land of 184
  rebellious angels were cast out of 199, 219
  religious leaders ask for a sign from 17
  Satan kicked out of 89, 219
  stars falling from 48, 216
  Stephen given a glimpse of 108
  store up treasures in 11, 62
  tongues of fire coming down from 103
  true rest in 87, 184
  vision of a sheet descending from 111
  vision of a woman in 219
  visions of (and of angels) 205
Hebrews
  book of 123, 182–191
  Paul's parents were 167
Heli (father of Joseph) 55
hell
  condemnation to (by Paul) 148
  false teachers condemned to 157

fire (to burn chaff) 9
  Hades or 226
  Jesus descended into 71
  Jesus preaching to the spirits in 197
  reference to death and ("He takes away") 92
  remove body parts instead of sin dooming to 41
Hellenistic Jews 107
Hellenization 3, 5
Hermes 113
Herod I (Herod the Great) 8, 16, 25, 38, 46,
    60, 63, 71, 105, 112, 217
Herod Agrippa. *See* Agrippa
Herodian Dynasty 4
Herodians 4, 25, 45
Herodias 38
high priest 49, 70, 88, 95, 105, 106, 110, 119
  breastplate of the 227
  Jesus only perfect High Priest 183
high priestly prayer of Jesus 114
holiness 152, 174, 176, 190
  believers to pursue 173
  personal 172
Holy Place 30, 50, 187
Holy Spirit 6, 8, 9, 14, 22, 35, 47, 53, 54, 55,
    62, 69, 76, 78, 79, 84, 91, 92, 93, 96,
    101, 103, 104, 106, 109, 111, 112,
    114, 115, 117, 118, 124, 129, 131,
    132, 133, 136, 138, 140, 144, 145,
    149, 150, 151, 155, 158, 159, 160,
    162, 163, 164, 178, 180, 181, 184,
    195, 196, 202, 206, 215, 228
  baptism of the 102
  conviction of the 152
  gifts of 183
  grieve the 163
  power of 161
  pray in the 200
Holy Week 22, 26, 28, 69, 88
homosexuality 126, 138
hope 124, 168, 206
  fulfillment of our 195
  of God's calling 161
  patient 172
  Revelation as a source of great 205
horsemen of the apocalypse 214
hospitality 38, 136, 204
household
  code 164, 171, 175, 177, 181
  of Caesar 122, 168
  of the jailer 116
  of unbelieving spouse 142
house of prayer 24
humiliation of Christ 166, 183
humility 20, 32, 38, 41, 57, 66, 90, 166, 206
  of a true believer 201, 202
  of Christ 54
husband
  a believing wife and an unbelieving 196–197
  allowed to divorce wife 42
  and wife eat of the tree 1
  and wife in marriage relationship 142
  a wife is to submit to her 164, 171, 196–197
  bride wears white to show purity 224
  is to love his wife 171, 196
  of only one wife (elders and deacons) 176
  Samaritan woman has five 79
  to represent his wife fairly 146
  to sacrificially love his wife 164
  wife ask her (not in church) 146
  wife honors her 144
  woman marries seven brothers 68
Hymenaeus 175
hymns 164, 166, 171

hypocrisy 17, 25, 39, 62, 63, 127, 136, 157

I

"I am" statements 73, 82, 85, 87, 88, 91
  chart 82
Iconium 113
idolatry 2, 108, 114, 117, 137, 138, 139, 143,
      159, 204, 211, 215, 217, 220, 223, 224
incarnation 74, 75
India 14
inheritance 121, 161, 169
  of son of vineyard owner 24, 67
  of the prodigal son 64
  of twelve tribes of Israel 2
  of two brothers 62
Isaac 1, 25, 45, 133, 159, 193
Isaiah 122
  book of 67, 205
  commission of 36
  Isaiah 5 67
  Isaiah 13 27, 214
  Isaiah 34 214
  Isaiah 35:3 189
  Isaiah 40 54
  Isaiah 40:3 76
  Isaiah 52-53 109
  Isaiah 61:1-3 55
  Isaiah 65 226
  Isaiah 66:1-2 108
  prophecy of 33, 76
  vision of 213
Ishmael 133, 159
Israel 1, 3, 48, 67, 76, 134, 135, 149, 196, 211,
      215, 218, 219, 222, 223
  believers as the new 215
  cities of 14, 37, 41
  deliverance from Egypt of 70
  fig tree, illustration for 44
  lost sheep of 39
  nation of 129, 167, 183, 226
  of God (the Church) 160
  true 133, 191
  twelve tribes of 206, 212, 227
Israelites 1, 2, 29, 38, 39, 82, 107, 108, 119,
      133, 134, 135, 143, 167, 183, 190,
      199, 200, 211, 213, 221

J

Jacob 25, 45, 55, 76, 133, 190, 219, 228
jailer (Philippian) 116
Jairus (ruler of the synagogue) 37, 59
Jambres 179
James
  book of 181, 191–195
    as Proverbs of the New Testament 191
  half-brother of Jesus 123, 157, 191
  son of Alphaeus 14
  son of Zebedee 10, 14, 18, 19, 21, 29, 33, 37, 40,
    49, 56, 59, 60, 73, 112, 119
Jannes 179
Jason 116
Jeremiah 18, 26
  Jeremiah 31 187
Jericho 66, 106
Jerusalem 2, 3, 18, 20, 21, 23, 24, 26, 27, 28,
      30, 31, 35, 40, 42, 43, 46, 48, 54, 61,
      62, 66, 67, 68, 69, 80, 83, 102, 108,
      109, 110, 111, 112, 114, 118, 119,
      120, 121, 138, 147, 152, 157, 159,
      190, 191, 212, 215, 218, 227
  church in 191
  destruction of 63, 67, 69, 71, 207

Jesus sets His face toward 43
  siege of (a.d. 70) 223
Jerusalem Council 114–115, 123, 124, 157,
    191
Jesus
  anointed by woman 58
  anointing of (by Mary) 89
  ascension of 73, 218
  as Judge 81
  as King of the Jews 30, 50, 71, 95
  as our Advocate 201
  as the Agent of creation 74–75, 169, 183
  as the Alpha and Omega 209, 227, 228
  as the Bread of Life 81–82, 87
  as the Bridegroom 224
  as the Bright and Morning Star 211, 228
  as the chief cornerstone 67, 196
  as the Conquering King 225
  as the Creator 182
  as the Door for the Sheep 73, 87
  as the Faithful and True 212, 224
  as the fullest revelation of God 98
  as the Good Shepherd 73, 87, 215
  as the Head of the Church 169
  as the High Priest 186, 188, 190
  as the Lamb 215
  as the Light of the World 30, 71, 73, 78, 85, 86,
    87
  as the Lion of Judah 213
  as the new Moses 7
  as the perfect sacrifice 135
  as the Resurrection and the Life 88
  as the Root of David 228
  as the Son of David 7
  as the Suffering Servant 18, 40, 102, 109, 225
  as the true Emperor 206
  as the true High Priest and King 217
  as the true King 224
  as the true Vine 91
  as the Water of Life 79, 87
  as the Word of God 74
  baptism of 18, 54, 76
  birth and childhood of 8
  burial of 96
  calms the storm 36
  death of 15, 22, 29, 31, 187, 201
  deity of 36, 74, 88, 95, 97, 199, 205
  far greater than the prophets 182
  far superior to all the angels 182–183
  glorification of 91
  greater than Moses 183
  greater than the Levitical priests 186
  high priestly prayer of 94
  humanity of 201
  "I am" statements of (chart) 82
  Jesus Is God chart 74
  last journey to Jerusalem of 53, 60
  Mediator of the New Covenant 187, 190
  Paul compares (to Adam) 147
  powerful descriptions of 209
  rebukes storm 12–14, 59
  resurrection of 15, 17, 22, 28, 31, 201
  second coming of 172, 221
  suffering of 30, 183
  teaching of (as light) 59
  temptation of 9, 10, 18, 55
  ultimate Passover Lamb 29
  universal mission of 53
  warned teachers 193
  washes disciples' feet 90
Jews
  Hebraic 107
  Hellenistic 107
Jezebel 2
  evil woman in Thyatira 211
Joanna (wife of Chuza) 59, 72

Job 194, 222
Joel 2:28-32 103
John 96, 97, 109, 112, 123
  book of 73–87
  commissioned as a prophet 217
  disciple whom Jesus loved 73, 90, 201
  eats the little scroll 217
  John 2:19 29
  John 3:16 77, 78
  John 12:4–6 48
  John 17 114
  John 18:10 49
  John 19:30 222
  son of Zebedee 6, 10, 14, 18, 19, 21, 29, 33, 37,
    40, 49, 56, 59, 60, 73, 201
1 John
  book of 201–204
2 John
  book of 204–205
3 John
  book of 204–205
John Mark 112, 115. *See* Mark
John the Baptist 8, 9, 10, 14, 16, 18, 19, 24,
    33, 38, 40, 42, 44, 53, 54, 58, 60, 67,
    73, 75, 76, 77, 81, 103, 113, 117
Jonah 109
  sign of 17, 62
Joppa 110, 111
Jordan River 9, 16, 42, 54, 79, 222
Joseph
  called Barsabbas 102
  dreams of 27
  earthly father of Jesus 8, 54, 55
  of Arimathea 31, 50, 72, 96
  son of Jacob 1, 55, 107, 219
Josephus 208
Joshua 2, 217
  book of 223
  days of 193
joy 165, 166–167, 192, 195, 201
Judah 2, 73
  tribe of 213
Judaism 104, 107, 111, 114, 149, 157, 182,
    185, 187
Judaizers 190
Judas Iscariot 14, 48, 49, 89, 90, 101
Judas Maccabeus 3
Jude
  book of 200–201
  half-brother of Jesus 123, 200
Judea 20, 42, 66, 79, 102, 108, 111, 121, 138
  region of 157
  wilderness of 54
judgment 9, 15, 63, 65, 90, 126, 127, 136,
    182, 193, 197, 208, 211, 214, 220, 226
  bowl judgments 222
  coming upon the Jews 25
  in terms of drinking the cup of God's wrath 221
  Judgment Day 86, 88, 208
  Judgment Seat of Christ 150, 177, 207
  Moses' generation (in wilderness) 183
  of false teachers 200
  of Pilate on Jesus 95
  of religious leaders 45, 64
  of the rich 194
  of the seals, trumpets, and bowls 206, 213
  of the sheep and the goats 28
Julius Caesar 223
justice 26, 137, 196, 205, 208, 224
  of God 128
justification by faith 124, 128

K

kindness 126, 160, 162, 181
kingdom of God 6, 10, 13, 15, 21, 22, 24, 32, 36, 42, 45, 57, 62, 64, 65, 66, 68, 69, 77, 92, 122, 142, 147, 180, 217, 218
kingdom of heaven 6, 7, 10, 12, 15, 68, 193
kingdom of Herod 8
kingdom of Jesus 10, 11, 14, 15, 18, 19, 20, 22, 25, 29, 41, 42, 45, 48, 49, 57, 58, 60, 63, 64, 66, 67, 70, 71, 73, 89, 90, 94, 95, 102, 165, 169, 213, 218, 219
1 Kings
   1 Kings 17 38, 55, 58
2 Kings
   2 Kings 1 61
   2 Kings 5 55
knowledge
   gift of 146
   leads to pride 165
   of God 135
   of God's will 168
   of Jesus 161, 163, 200
   spiritual 169
Korah 200

L

Lamb of God 69, 220
   Marriage Supper of the 224, 225
   throne of the 225
lampstands 206, 210, 213, 217
Laodicea
   church in 205
   city of 168
   Jesus' letter to the church in 212
   letter to church in 171
Last Supper 90–91
lawlessness, man of 173
Law of Moses 3, 22, 34, 37, 43, 54, 81, 107, 114, 119, 124, 137, 157, 158, 159, 160, 162, 167, 168, 169, 170, 174, 177, 183, 187, 190, 192, 200, 227
Lazarus 62, 65, 88, 89
leadership
   orderly structure of 174
   requirements of (in the church) 176
Lebbaeus (Judas Thaddaeus) 14
leper 56, 65
   healing of 34
Levi. *See* Matthew
   tribe of 186
Leviticus
   Leviticus 20:10 85
   Leviticus 23 83
   Leviticus 24:16 86
Light of the World 30, 73, 78, 85, 86, 87
light versus darkness 74, 137
Lion of the tribe of Judah 213
living creatures 213, 215, 221
locusts, army of 216–217, 225
logos 74, 75
Lord's Prayer 62
Lord's Supper 29, 70, 143, 144
Lot 27, 186, 224
love 124, 133, 165, 168, 176, 177, 188, 204
   as gift of the Spirit 145
   as the bond of perfection 170
   Christ-like 163
   labors of 172
   of church in Thyatira 211
   of God 161, 202–203
   of Jesus 162, 203
   of money 62, 177
   of the Father 155

one another (commanded) 202–203
   Paul's (for Christ) 150
   summary of the Law 137, 160
   that results from faith 160
Luke 5, 6, 101, 171, 180, 182
   book of 32, 33, 53–72, 102
   Luke 5 97
   Luke 9:31 18
   Luke 12:9 97
   Luke 23:34 108
   Luke 23:46 108
   Luke 24 51
lukewarm
   church in Laodicea as 212
lust 193, 200, 202
Lydda 110
Lystra 113, 115

M

Macedonia 115, 116, 148, 152
   churches in 117, 152
   region of 165
magicians of Pharaoh 179, 222
Magnificat 54
Magog. *See* Gog and Magog
Malachi 14, 19
   Malachi 1:2-3 134
   prophecy of 33, 76
Malchus (servant of the high priest) 95
Malta 122
manna 38, 211
map
   Paul's first and second missionary journeys 115
   Paul's third and fourth missionary journeys 118
   Setting of Matthew 7
Mark 5, 6, 180, 198
   book of 32–51, 112
   Mark 14:51-52 32
   Mark 16:18 122
marks
   mark of the beast 220–222, 224
   of a Christian 201–203
   of God on His servants' foreheads 215–216, 220, 228
   on the body of Jesus 97, 160
marriage 21, 151, 164, 190
   covenant of 142
   God-given institution 142
   Marriage Supper of the Lamb 224, 225
   only for this life 25
Martha 62, 88, 89
martyrs 101, 108, 169, 183, 214, 215, 221, 223, 224, 225, 226, 227
Mary
   Magdalene 50, 51, 72, 96
   mother of James and Joses 50, 72
   mother of Jesus 8, 53, 54, 55, 76, 96
   sister of Martha 62, 88, 89
Mattathias ben Johanan 3
Matthew 4, 5, 9, 14, 23, 34
   book of 6–32, 38
   genealogy of 7, 8
   Matthew 10:33 97
   Matthew 24 214
   tax collector 6, 14, 34, 57
Matthias 102, 103
mediator
   between God and man 183
   Jesus as 94, 98
meekness
   ready to give a defense in 197
Melchizedek
   Abraham gave tithe to 153

order of (Jesus as High Priest) 186
   priest of God Most High 186
mercy 26, 134, 174, 175, 181, 193, 195
   of God 161, 162
Messiah 2, 9, 14, 18, 22, 26, 40, 43, 53, 55, 60, 65, 67, 70, 71, 73, 74, 75, 76, 80, 81, 83, 90, 96, 104, 106, 110, 113, 117, 140, 203, 213
   as chief cornerstone 45
   as Suffering Servant 18
   manifestation of the 54
   mythological view of 84
Messianic Kingdom 7, 89
Messianic Psalms
   Psalm 2 105, 211, 218, 228
metaphor
   architectural (of church growth) 140
   farming (of church growth) 140
   fig tree serves as a (of Israel) 24
   Jesus speaks in 18, 77
   light of the world 10
   of a good soldier 178
   of a grain of wheat falling on the ground 89
   of a hard-working farmer 178
   of an athlete 178
   of an earthly house or tent (i.e., the body) 150
   of being born again 79
   of eating Jesus' flesh and drinking His blood 82
   of eternal bread 82
   of leaven (representing sin) 141
   of light and darkness 137, 201
   of living water 79
   of Paul planting and Apollos watering 140
   of shepherding 87
   of sowing and reaping 160
   of the milk and solid food 140
   of the salt of the earth 10
   of the veil for old covenant followers 149
   of the vine and the branches 91–92
   the resurrection not as 147
Michael, archangel 200, 219
Miletus 118
Millennial Kingdom 206, 208, 213, 215, 225
ministry
   done by the lay people 163
   limitations of women in 176
   of James 191
   of the apostles and prophets 162
   Paul's personal 169
   prophetic ministry of two witnesses 217–218
miracles 12–13, 14, 16, 17, 33, 37, 55, 56, 58, 65, 73, 74, 81, 82, 88, 91, 103, 104, 106, 107, 108, 109, 110, 117, 154, 158, 183
missionary journey
   Paul's first 112, 157
   Paul's second 115–116, 165, 172
   Paul's third 139, 180–181
money
   believers in Laodicea had 212
   false teachers swindle 200
   love of 62, 177
money changers 24, 44
Mosaic covenant 187, 188, 190
Moses 1, 2, 7, 18, 40, 42, 60, 78, 81, 82, 86, 105, 107, 108, 113, 129, 149, 179, 183, 189, 217, 222
   allows for divorce in the law 21
   body of 200
   first five books of 25, 45
   mediator of the Mosaic covenant 187
   Song of 221
   the generation of (in wilderness) 183
   veil over his face 149

Most Holy Place 30, 50, 187, 188, 212, 218
Mount Megiddo 222
Mount of Olives 26, 29, 46
Mount of Transfiguration 17–18, 40, 60, 73, 75, 89, 198, 199, 217
Mount Sinai 159, 190
Mount Zion 220
mystery
 cults 4
 of Christ 169
 of God 217, 219
 of the gospel 162

N

Naaman the Syrian 55
Nadab 106
Nathanael 76
Nazareth 8, 55, 56, 76, 84, 104
Nazarite vow 119
Nehemiah 2
nephew of Paul 119
Nero 32, 123, 174, 195, 205, 207, 220, 223
new
 creations 150–151, 163
 garden in Jerusalem 228
 heavens and earth 226, 227
 moons 170
 temple 227
New Covenant 149, 159, 187
 far more superior 182
 glory of the 149
New Testament 122, 126, 157, 177, 182, 204, 206, 209, 217, 226
 Proverbs of the (James) 191
Nicodemus 77, 78, 79, 82, 84, 96
Nicolaitans 211
Nile River 222
Nineveh 62
Noah 1, 27, 65, 188, 197
Northern Kingdom 2, 79, 215
Numbers
 Numbers 21 78
 Numbers 24:17 228
numerology 207
Nunc dimitis
 prayer of thanksgiving 54

O

Old Covenant 149, 159, 187
Old Testament 72, 76, 95, 102, 109, 113, 116, 122, 127, 129, 138, 140, 162, 182, 187, 189, 196, 199, 200, 205, 206, 214, 215, 217, 220, 224, 226
Olivet Discourse 26, 46, 68, 69, 71, 205
Onesimus 171
overseers. *See* elders

P

Palestine 3, 79
palm branches 22, 43, 215
Palm Sunday. *See* Triumphal Entry
parable
 defined 35
 of a great wedding feast 25
 of a rich farmer 62
 of forgiveness of debts 58
 of persistent widow 66
 of prayers of tax collector and Pharisee 66
 of servants 63
 of the good Samaritan 61

 of the leaven 63
 of the lost coin 64
 of the lost sheep 20, 64
 of the mustard seed 16, 63
 of the net 16
 of the pearl of great price 16
 of the prodigal son 64
 of the rich man and Lazarus 65
 of the sower 15, 35, 59
 of the talents 28
 of the tenants of a vineyard 24, 67
 of the ten virgins 28
 of the treasure in a field 16
 of the vineyard 44
 of the weeds 15
 of the wheat and the tares 221
 of the yeast 16
 of two sons of a vineyard owner 24
Paradise 71, 197, 211
paralytic 12–14, 34, 56
Parthians 214, 222
Passover 2, 5, 22, 29, 30, 43, 48, 69, 70, 73, 89, 90, 213
Pastoral Epistles 124, 125, 174, 180
pastor-teachers 163
patience 126, 145, 177, 192, 211
Patmos 205, 209
Paul 5, 32, 191, 217, 223
 anticipates his own death 177
 apostle to the Gentiles 120, 124
 as a church planter 124
 as a prisoner in Rome 121
 deals with circumcision 114
 defends his ministry 141, 149
 dispute with Barnabas 115
 founded church in Thessalonica 171
 Gentiles beg (to preach) 113
 his first imprisonment in Rome 180
 in Jerusalem 119
 in the book of Acts 101
 Jesus appeared to 147
 magnum opus of 125
 ministry of 150–151
 on baptism 131
 plan of evangelism 126
 planted church in Corinth 139
 possible author of Hebrews 182
 raises Eutychus from the dead 118
 receives commendation by the apostles 157
 rejoices in his sufferings 169
 salvation by faith alone 193, 194
 shipwrecked on Malta 122
 stays in Corinth a long time 117
 sufferings of 150, 153, 154, 159, 162, 172, 179
 summary of the ministry of 175
 teaching on women by 175
 testimony of 121, 174
 thorn in the flesh 154
 under house arrest in Rome 161
 visits Philippi 116
 writings of (as Scripture) 200
Pauline Epistles 123
 introduction to 124–125
Pauline Triad 124, 129, 168, 172
Pax Romana 3
peace 160, 161, 165, 172, 174, 177, 190, 198, 209
Peloponnesian peninsula 139
Pentecost 5, 16, 84, 103–104
Pergamos
 Jesus' letter to the church in 211
Pergamum. *See* Pergamos
persecutions 42, 69, 92, 105, 108, 112, 154, 173, 174, 178, 179, 184, 188, 191,

 192, 194, 195, 197, 204, 205, 206, 207, 210, 211, 212, 220, 221, 223
 of Nero 174
 of the Church by Saul 110, 121
Persian Empire 2, 3, 8, 219
personal holiness 172
Peter 6, 10, 13, 17, 19, 29, 32, 37, 49, 53, 59, 60, 66, 72, 73, 76, 83, 95, 96, 101, 102, 103, 104, 109, 111, 112, 123, 195, 198, 217, 223
 confession of 18, 40
 denies knowing Jesus 30, 49, 70, 91, 97
 mother-in-law of 12, 33, 56
1 Peter
 1 Peter 2:9 226
 1 Peter 5:13 32
 book of 195–198
2 Peter
 book of 198–201
Pharaoh 4, 134, 222
Pharisees 3, 9, 13, 15, 20, 25, 31, 34, 35, 39, 40, 42, 45, 56, 58, 63, 64, 65, 66, 67, 77, 79, 85, 89, 96, 119, 167, 208
 Saul as one of the 110
Philadelphia
 Jesus' letter to the church in 212
Philemon
 book of 161, 168, 171
Philip 76, 89, 91, 108, 109
 of Macedon 3
Philippi 116
 church in 165, 166, 167
Philippians 122
 book of 161, 165–168, 180
Phoebe 138
Phrygia 168
plagues 1, 206, 222–223, 228
 death of the firstborn 69
 of the two witnesses 217
 seven last (Revelation) 221
polytheism 4, 116
Pompey 3
Pontius Pilate 30, 49, 71, 95, 105, 116, 120
Pontus 195
Porcius Festus. *See* Festus
postmillennialism 207, 226
potter's field 30
prayer 104, 171
 faithful in 165, 175
 for the Ephesians 162
 God answers 202
 life affected by how a man treats wife 197
 of righteous person is effective 194
 watchful in 165, 197
 without ceasing 173
predestination 92, 133, 161
premillennialism 206–207, 225–226
pride 175, 192, 193, 194, 202
priesthood
 Levitical 186–187
 of Melchizedek 186–187
 royal 196
priests 35, 196, 209
Priscilla. *See* Aquila and Priscilla
Promised Land 2, 83, 183, 193, 222
prophecies 2, 26, 27, 31, 33, 40, 46, 47, 48, 54, 80, 81, 98, 103, 104, 107, 118, 122, 136, 146, 199, 206, 214, 217, 220, 228
 apocalyptic genre is a subcategory of 205
 gift of 146
 in Daniel 18, 29, 102, 217

in Isaiah 33
in Joel 103
in Malachi 19, 33, 76
in Zechariah 22–23, 43, 48, 67, 206, 217
Jesus called a Nazarene 8
Jesus fulfills Old Testament 7
prophets 18, 60, 61, 65, 74, 103, 105, 182,
    194, 195, 203, 223, 224, 227
  Agabus (warns Paul) 118
  Balaam 199, 211
  Daniel 18, 27, 29, 69, 70, 102, 205, 209, 213, 217,
    219, 228
  David 183
  Elijah 2, 8, 14, 18, 58, 60, 76, 217
  Elisha 58
  Enoch 217
  Ezekiel 215
  false 199
  false messiahs as 69
  false prophet in Revelation 219–220, 222–226,
    225
  false teachers as 12, 199
  Habakkuk 113, 158
  in the Church 163
  Isaiah 109, 122
  Israelites killed the 108
  Israel's leaders killed the 26
  Jeremiah 26
  Jesus as the Prophet 26, 58, 79, 81, 84, 107, 108
  Jesus is better than the 182–183
  John as a prophet 217
  John the Baptist as a prophet 16, 54, 67, 76
  Jonah 109
  ministry of the apostles and 162
  Moses 105, 107
  not accepted in own country 55
  prophet from Antioch 112
  Samuel as a prophet 2
  two witnesses as 217
  written by the (fulfilled) 7
propitiation 128, 201
Proverbs
  Proverbs 9:10 86
Psalms
  Psalm 2 211, 218, 228
  Psalm 2:1-2 105
  Psalm 8:4-6 183
  Psalm 16:10 104
  Psalm 22 30, 50
  Psalm 40:6-8 188
  Psalm 45:6-7 182
  Psalm 69:25 102
  Psalm 91:13 9
  Psalm 95:7-11 183
  Psalm 109:8 102
  Psalm 110 25, 45, 68, 104, 186
  Psalm 118 26, 43, 45, 67
  Psalm 118:22 105
  Psalm 118:26 23
Ptolemaic Empire 3

Q

Q Theory 6
quarreling 159, 166, 167, 172, 177, 179, 181
  in the Corinthian church 154

R

Rachel 219
Rahab 8, 193
rapture 27, 66, 207, 221
readiness to share the gospel
  third piece of armor 164
Rebecca 133
rebellion 129, 181, 184, 193, 215

against God 173
  of the nations 105
reconciliation 65, 71, 130
  ministry of 151
redaction criticism 6
redemption 69, 79, 128, 161
  of Peter 97
Red Sea 2, 222
remarriage of widows 177
repentance 78, 106, 117, 160, 184, 185, 200,
  220
  baptism of 78
  of the Corinthians 153
resurrection
  appearances of Jesus after 102
  from the dead 147
  Jesus as the Resurrection and the Life 88
  life after death 25
  of Jesus 5, 15, 22, 31, 34, 40, 41, 42, 50, 53, 60, 70,
    71, 89, 93, 96–97, 101, 102, 104, 111, 113,
    120, 123, 147, 167, 195, 201, 218, 220
  of Lazarus 88
  Sadducees deny the 119
Revelation
  book of 27, 123, 168, 205–228
Rhoda 112
rich young man 21, 42
rich young ruler 66
righteousness 163, 165, 177, 181, 192, 197
  of God 126, 127, 128
  of Jesus 128, 129, 167
  peaceable fruit of 189
  second piece of armor 164
  slaves to 131
riot
  before Jesus' crucifixion 30, 71
  in Ephesus (Paul) 117
  In Jerusalem (Paul) 119
Roma (goddess) 223
Roman Catholic Church 18, 96
Roman Empire 2, 3, 4, 5, 84, 101, 103, 109,
  111, 114, 120, 121, 122, 139, 149,
  157, 204, 205, 206, 210, 218, 219,
  223, 224
Roman law 116
Romans
  book of 125–139, 140, 158, 165, 168
  Messiah to destroy the 67
Rome 4, 14, 32, 101, 119, 120, 121, 122, 123,
  125, 161, 222
  Babylon as a metaphor of 195, 198
  bishop of 18
  church in 127, 138
  Paul's imprisonment in 174, 180
  seven hills of 223
royal law 192. *See also* Golden Rule
Ruth 8

S

Sabbath 5, 14, 34, 35, 63, 72, 80, 81, 83, 96,
  112, 113, 170
  desecration of the 57
Sadducees 4, 9, 25, 45, 68, 77, 119
Salem 186
  priest of (Melchizedek) 153
salt and light 10–12
salutation 147, 154, 168, 174, 201, 205
salvation 4, 7, 8, 9, 10, 14, 17, 19, 26, 39, 54,
  61, 64, 71, 77, 78, 79, 80, 82, 84, 85,
  86, 87, 89, 90, 94, 96, 104, 107, 110,
  114, 115, 116, 124, 125, 129, 130,
  131, 133, 134, 135, 151, 152, 158,

  159, 161, 162, 170, 177, 181, 185,
  187, 190, 195, 215, 224, 228
  by faith alone 193, 194
  fifth piece of armor 164
  freedom of 200
  fulfillment of our 195
  harvest of 178
  Jesus, Captain of 183
  out of Egypt 184
  the blessing of 162
  work of God through Christ 163
  work out our 166
  worthy of the calling of 173
Samaria 79, 102, 108, 109, 111, 121
Samaritans 14, 61, 65, 80, 108, 109, 114
Samaritan woman 79, 80, 81, 82, 216
Samuel 2
sanctification 92, 94, 172, 195
Sanhedrin 4, 25, 68, 70, 106, 107, 119
Sapphira. *See* Ananias and Sapphira
Sarah 159
Sardis
  Jesus' letter to the church in 211
Satan 9, 10, 18, 31, 35, 55, 59, 71, 86, 89, 94,
  106, 121, 133, 139, 141, 148, 154,
  163, 164, 173, 194, 198, 200, 202,
  207, 219, 223, 225
  as a dragon 1, 219, 222
  as king of the locusts 217
  as the father of lies 164
  Beelzebub 15
  destruction of the forces of 225
  gives beast authority 220
  messenger of (torments Paul) 154
  Satanic Imitations of God's Reality chart 219
  synagogue of 211
  tempts Adam and Eve through a serpent 219
  the binding of 208
Saul 2, 108
  conversion of 109–110
  named change to Paul 112
  persecutes the Church 93
Sceva, sons of 117
scribes 34, 35, 39, 44, 45, 64, 85, 139
Scripture
  inspired, or breathed out, by God 180
  Paul's writings as 200
scroll 216
  Dead Sea Scrolls 4
  eaten by Ezekiel 217
  eaten by John 217
  in God's right hand 213–214
  little (in angel's hand) 217
seals
  first four (four horsemen) 214
  fifth seal (martyrs vindicated) 214
  sixth seal (cataclysmic natural disasters)
    214–215
  seventh seal 216
  seal of God 215
Sea of Galilee 17, 33
second coming of Christ 171–173, 200, 206,
  208, 221, 226
Seed of the woman 1, 9
  crushes Satan's head 31
Seleucid Empire 3
self-control 160, 176, 181
Sergius Paulus 112
Sermon on the Mount 7, 10–12, 20, 42,
  46–48, 57, 58, 136, 191, 193, 194
Sermon on the Plain 57–58
sermons
  Paul's sermon 113, 116
  Peter's Pentecost sermon 105

recorded in the book of Acts 101
Stephen's sermon 107
serpent 1, 9, 219
bronze (Moses) 78
seed of the 31
servant-leadership 22
seven
angels 216, 221
bowls 221
churches in Asia Minor (Revelation) 209–214
last plagues 221
seals 206, 213, 215
spirits of God 211, 212
stars 211
trumpets 216
years (Daniel 9) 217
sexual immorality 20, 79, 114, 139, 141, 143,
154, 159, 163, 170, 172, 190, 211,
217, 220, 223, 224
Shalom 125
Shema 25, 45
Sheol. *See* Hades
Sidon 17, 39
signs 103, 104, 107, 154. *See also* miracles
Silas (Silvanus) 114, 116, 172, 198
Simon
of Cyrene 30, 71, 96
Peter 33
the Canaanite 14
the leper 48
the sorcerer 109
the tanner 111
the Zealot 4, 14
simony 109
sinful nature 128, 161, 169
sinners 25, 34, 53, 63, 64, 85, 92, 126, 129,
135, 174, 193, 201
slavery 128, 163, 177
brought back into spiritual 200
covenant of 159
Smyrna
Jesus' letter to the church in 211
social outcasts
afflicted woman for twelve years 37
Jesus' ministry to 8, 53, 59
shepherds as 54
Sodom 27, 65, 200, 217, 218, 224
Solomon 2, 46, 55
Song of Moses 221
Son of God 9, 19, 31, 36, 72, 73, 97, 110, 125,
182, 188, 203, 204, 211
Son of Man 18, 48, 69, 70, 91, 102, 108, 183,
209, 221
Sons of Thunder
James and John 61
Sosthenes
the ruler of the synagogue 117
Southern Kingdom 2
sovereignty of God 82, 94, 96, 103, 105, 132,
149, 161
Spain 138
Spirit-flesh struggle 131, 132, 140, 159, 160
spiritual
adultery and fornication 223
gifts 144–145, 183
songs 164
understanding 168
warfare 153, 164, 178
Stephen 101, 107, 108, 183
Stoicism 5
stoning
of Paul 113
of Stephen 108

submission 164, 175, 196
of wife of unbelieving husband 196
suffering 66, 132, 140, 184, 188, 191, 194,
195, 197, 198, 205, 206, 215, 221
develops patience 192
of God's people 169
of Jesus 167, 183
of Paul 150, 153, 154, 159, 162, 172, 179
of the Church 110
of the church of Philadelphia 212
of the Philippians 166
of the saints 189, 190
of the Thessalonians 174
Paul rejoices in his 169
stand firm in 169
Suffering Servant 18, 40, 109, 225
sword
a sharp, two-edged (Word of God) 209, 211
of the Spirit 10
sixth piece of armor 164
symbolic
144,000 (of all believers in new Israel) 215
beast (of Rome) 220
book of Revelation highly (amillennialism) 208
Bride of the Lamb (of the Church) 227
darkening of the sun, moon, and stars 27, 48
elements of the Passover meal 29, 48, 90
fallen Babylon (of Rome) 220
feet of brass (of Jesus' purity and strength) 209
fiery red dragon (of Satan) 219
function of the sacrifices 187
head coverings (of authority) 144
healed mortal wound (of Nero or Caligula) 220
horns (of military power) 219
Jerusalem (of the Church) 227
lampstands (of seven churches) 210
locust (of Greek god Apollo) 216
of Israel (invalid of 38 years) 80
omission of Dan and Ephraim
(warning against idolatry and rebellion) 215
seal of God (of baptism) 215
sea (of chaos and the abyss) 226
seven (of completion or perfection) 206
seven stars (of seven churches) 209
sharp sword (of Word of God) 225
sun, moon, and twelve stars
(of Joseph's dream) 219
temple (of the Church) 217
Tower of Babel 1
trumpet judgments (of plagues on Egypt) 216
twelve apostles (of twelve tribes) 206
twelve disciples (of new Israel) 102
twenty-four elders
(of twelve tribes and apostles) 212
two elements to the act of baptism 130
two swords (peace is over) 70
visions are highly (Revelation) 206
white garments (of purity) 211, 224
wine represents Jesus' blood 70
woman (of Israel and God's people) 219
synagogues 5, 15, 16, 17, 33, 34, 37, 39, 55,
56, 59, 93, 110, 112, 113, 116, 117,
120
synagogue of Satan 211
synoptic gospels 5, 32
Syria 113
Syro-Phoenician woman's daughter 39

T

tabernacle 75, 108, 183, 212
heavenly 186
Tabitha 101, 110
Talitha, cumi 37, 101, 110
Tamar 8

Tarsus 109, 110, 111
tax collectors 13, 20, 24, 57, 64, 66
taxes
Paul commands us to pay 137
temple 19
to Caesar 25, 45, 68
technology
desensitizes us to sin 164
temple 2, 3, 20, 24, 56, 61, 67, 75, 80, 85, 104,
107, 108, 119, 120, 140, 142, 186,
192, 196, 212
and the seven last plagues 221
apostles preaching in 106
cleansing of the 77, 89
Jesus' 43–44
destruction of the 26, 27, 46, 68, 73, 205, 212
heavenly 215
of God 162, 217, 218
tax 19
to Zeus 211
veil of the 50
temptations 136, 170, 181, 183, 184, 190,
192
of believers 160
of Jesus 9, 18, 94
Ten Commandments 10, 21, 42, 57, 164
tentmaker 143
Tertius 139
Tertullian (early Church father) 108
thanksgiving 164, 171
Theophilus 53, 101, 102
Theos ("God")
applied to Jesus (chart) 74
1 Thessalonians
book of 171–172, 205
2 Thessalonians
book of 173–174, 205
Thessalonica 116, 117
church in 171, 173
thirty pieces of silver 29, 30
Thomas 14, 88, 91, 96, 97
confession of 98
thorn in Paul's flesh 154
throne of God 221, 225
as a glorious chariot (Revelation) 212–213
in the Most Holy Place 218
Thyatira
Jesus' letter to the church in 211
Timothy 115, 141, 147, 165, 166, 168, 172,
174, 176, 177, 180, 181, 182, 190
1 Timothy
book of 125, 174–178, 180
2 Timothy
2 Timothy 4:11 32
book of 125, 174, 177–179
tithe 153, 186
Titus 125, 148, 152, 153, 157, 174, 181, 223
book of 180–182
Emperor 47, 207, 223
tomb 72, 96
tone of a passage 148
tongue, control of the 192, 193–194
tongues
as a type of prayer language 146
of fire 103
speak in 51, 103, 117, 146
total depravity 127–128
Tower of Babel 1
tradition of the elders 3, 14, 34, 39
Transfiguration 18, 40, 60, 73, 75, 89, 198,
199, 217
Tree of Life 211, 228

Tree of the Knowledge of Good and Evil 1
trial of Jesus 49, 70, 71
tribulation 207–208
   Great Tribulation 27–28, 47, 206, 207, 212, 225
   seven-year 218–219
Trinity 31, 74
   counterfeit unholy trinity 219–220, 222, 223, 226
   glory of the 219
   in process of election 195
   Trinitarian formula 155
Triumphal Entry 22, 48, 67, 77, 89, 215
Troas 115, 117, 148
Troy 148
trumpets 206, 219
   trumpet judgments 216, 222
truth 127, 149, 163, 180, 204
   first piece of armor 164
   knowledge of the 175
   love for the 179
   of the gospel 204
   versus falsehood 74
Turkey 115, 205
twelve
   apostles 112, 124, 125, 206, 212, 215
   disciples 13–14, 16, 35, 59, 60, 73, 102
   precious stones 227
   stars 219
   tribes 1, 2, 21, 27, 102, 206, 212, 215
   Twelve Apostles chart 13
twenty-four elders 212, 213, 218
Tychicus 165, 171, 181
Tyrannus, school of 117
Tyre 17, 39, 118, 224

U

unclean animals 111
unequally yoked 151
unforgivable sin 15
unity 114, 137, 138, 144, 154
   among Christians 94
   between Jew and Gentile 162
   in faith and mission 166
   in the Church 163
   through the Spirit 162
upper room 48, 73, 91, 48, 48

V

Vietnam War 208
vineyard
   parables of the. *See* parable
visions
   Ezekiel's vision of God's glory 212, 215
   God spoke to prophets through 182
   Isaiah's vision 213
   of heaven and of angels (Revelation) 205
   of the prophecy of Joel 103
   Paul's vision of heaven 154
   Peter's vision of the unclean 111, 157
   vision of a woman in heaven 219
   vision of heaven 214
vows
   Nazarite 119

W

wall of separation
   between Jews and Gentiles 162
warnings 185, 228
   about becoming a teacher 193
   against sexual sins 142
   blowing of trumpets 216

from the life of Esau 190
given by the apostles 200
to the churches 217
warning in Psalm 95 184
water
   living water 79, 81, 84, 216, 227, 228
   of life 227, 228
   referring to natural birth 77
   sign of purification 77
   Water of Life 79, 87
wedding
   at Cana 76
   of Christ and the Church 224
white garments
   symbolic of purity 211, 212, 214, 224
white stones 223
whitewashed tombs
   Jewish religious leaders as 119
widow
   forced to pay religious leaders 68
   gave two mites 68
   in Zarephath 55
   Paul's advice for widows 176
   persistent (parable) 66
   religion that provides for the 192
   son of a (healed) 58
wilderness 2, 9, 38, 55, 82, 184
   Israelites died in the 200
   Jesus tempted in the 164
wineskins
   new and old 57
winnowing fork 9
wisdom 164, 168
   book 191
   of God 135, 162
   of the Holy Spirit 124
   pray for 193
   spirit of 161
   spiritual 169
   the beginning of 86
witnesses
   believers die for their witness (Smyrna) 211
   complaining and quarreling are poor (for gospel) 166
   demon-possessed person as poor witness 116
   disciples are (to Jesus) 69, 72, 102, 121
   faithful witnesses praise God 221
   false 29–30, 49, 147
   Jehovah's Witnesses 74
   Jesus as the Faithful (and True) Witness 209, 212
   Jesus calls forth three 81
   John bears witness for Jesus 98
   John the Baptist bears witness for Jesus 75, 113
   martyrs vindicated for their faithful witness 214
   Mary is first eyewitness to the resurrection 96
   Paul bears witness for Jesus 119, 120–121
   Peter as an eyewitness to the life of Jesus 199
   Peter bears witness to the ascension 104–105
   primary job of the apostles (to Jesus) 102, 108
   see where Jesus was laid 72
   serving as faithful (for Jesus) 197, 209
   shepherds first (of Jesus) 54
   Stephen bears witness to Jesus 107
   testimony of two or more 5, 20, 54, 85
   the Father Himself bears witness for Jesus 85
   three that bear witness
      Holy Spirit, the water, and the blood 203
   to historical reliability of Jesus' life 5, 74
   to the end of the earth (apostles) 109, 111
   two (in Revelation) 206, 217–218
   witness of the resurrection (primary criteria of an apostle) 101, 102, 104, 201
Word of God 10, 15, 36, 74, 75–76, 76, 101, 164, 165, 180, 181, 182, 185, 192, 196, 202, 211

as a sharp, two-edged sword 184, 211, 225
Jesus as the 74, 224–225
man shall live by every word of God 55
sword of the Spirit as the 209
worship
   all nations will worship God 221
   Antiochus IV Epiphanes attacks Jewish 3
   believers of the true circumcision 167
   blind man worships Jesus 87
   disciples (Jesus) 17, 31
   Ethiopian went up to Jerusalem to 109
   every tribe, tongue, and nation to 227
   false teachers urged asceticism and angel 170
   glorious passage on 212–214
   God establishes the tabernacle and 2
   humanity chose to worship the creation 126
   in heaven (connected to prayers on earth) 216
   Israelites (foreign gods) 108
   Jesus deserves 90
   Jesus refuses to (Satan) 10, 55
   Jews say that one must (in Jerusalem) 61, 80
   John tries to worship angel 224, 228
   Levites as worship leaders 2
   motivation to worship God 135
   of God almost disappears in Israel 2, 211
   of God is restored in Israel 3
   of the beast 220
   Paul and Barnabas refused (of people) 113
   Paul forbids speaking in tongues during 146
   Paul went to Jerusalem to 120
   Peter refused (from people) 112
   Revelation is filled with 205
   Romans worship emperors as gods 4, 220
   songs and hymns 171, 212
   subjects begin to worship Herod as a god 112
   temple and the sacrificial system central to Jewish 5
   temple as as place to (God) 108
   those who worship in John's vision 217
   women cover their heads to 124, 144
   worshiping in spirit and truth 80
wrath of God 29, 30, 78, 126, 128, 129, 130, 132, 134, 135, 137, 161, 183, 201, 206, 215, 218, 219, 220, 221, 223, 225

Y

Yahweh 86

Z

Zacchaeus 66
Zacharias 53, 54
Zarephath 55
Zealots 4, 14
Zebedee
   father of James and John 73
Zechariah 2, 26
   book of 205
   prophecy of 43, 48, 67, 206, 217
   vision in 214
   Zechariah 4 217
   Zechariah 9:9 22, 43, 67
   Zechariah 11:12-13 30
   Zechariah 13:9 48
Zenas 181
Zerubbabel 217
Zeus 3, 113
   Satan called (by Jesus) 211